JAPANESE FINANCIAL MARKET RESEARCH

CONTRIBUTIONS
TO
ECONOMIC ANALYSIS

205

NORTH-HOLLAND
AMSTERDAM • LONDON • NEW YORK • TOKYO

JAPANESE FINANCIAL MARKET RESEARCH

Edited by

William T. ZIEMBA
Faculty of Commerce
University of British Columbia
Vancouver, B.C., Canada

Warren BAILEY
Johnson Graduate School of Management
Cornell University
Ithaca, N.Y., U.S.A.

Yasushi HAMAO
Graduate School of Business
Columbia University
New York, N.Y., U.S.A.

N·H

1991

NORTH-HOLLAND
AMSTERDAM • LONDON • NEW YORK • TOKYO

ELSEVIER SCIENCE PUBLISHERS B.V.
Sara Burgerhartstraat 25
P.O. Box 211, 1000 AE Amsterdam, The Netherlands

Distributors for the United States and Canada:

ELSEVIER SCIENCE PUBLISHING COMPANY INC.
655 Avenue of the Americas
New York, N.Y. 10010, U.S.A.

Library of Congress Cataloging-in-Publication Data

Japanese financial market research : edited by William T. Ziemba, Warren Bailey, Yasushi Hamao.
p. cm. -- (Contributions to economic analysis ; 205)
Includes bibliographical references.
ISBN 0-444-88851-9
1. Financial institutions--Japan. 2. Stock-exchange--Japan. I. Ziemba, W. T. II. Bailey, Warren R. III. Hamao, Yasushi. IV. Series.
HG187.J3J355 1991
332.64'252--dc20 91-33849
CIP

ISBN: 0 444 88851 9

PRINTED IN THE NETHERLANDS

INTRODUCTION TO THE SERIES

This series consists of a number of hitherto unpublished studies, which are introduced by the editors in the belief that they represent fresh contributions to economic science.

The term "economic analysis" as used in the title of the series has been adopted because it covers both the activities of the theoretical economist and the research worker.

Although the analytical methods used by the various contributors are not the same, they are nevertheless conditioned by the common origin of their studies, namely theoretical problems encountered in practical research. Since for this reason, business cycle research and national accounting, research work on behalf of economic policy, and problems of planning are the main sources of the subjects dealt with, they necessarily determine the manner of approach adopted by the authors. Their methods tend to be "practical" in the sense of not being too far remote from application to actual economic conditions. In additon they are quantitative.

It is the hope of the editors that the publication of these studies will help to stimulate the exchange of scientific information and to reinforce international cooperation in the field of economics.

The Editors

ACKNOWLEDGEMENTS

We thank the following publishers for allowing us to reproduce the articles listed below:

pages 145-166: **Academic Press, Inc.**
Stock Market Rationality and Price Volatility: Tests Using Japanese Data
by T. Hoshi
Previously published in the Journal of the Japanese and International Economies **1**, pp. 441-462 (1987)
(Copyright 1987)

pages 251-264: **The Institute of Management Sciences**
Weekly Patterns in Japanese Stock Returns
by K. Kato
Previously published in Management Science, Vol. 36, No. 9, pp. 1031-1044 (1990)
(Copyright 1990)

pages 367-380: **John Wiley & Sons, Inc.**
The Market for Japanese Stock Index Futures: Some Preliminary Evidence
by W. Bailey
Previously published in The Journal of Futures Markets, Vol. 9, No. 4, pp. 283-295 (1989)
(Copyright 1989)

pages 439-450: **Association for Investment Management and Research**
Arbitrage Opportunities in the Japanese Stock and Futures Markets
by M. Brenner, M.G. Subrahmanyam and J. Uno
Previously published in the Financial Analysts Journal, March-April 1990, pp. 14-24
(Copyright 1990)

pages 503-524: **The Review of Financial Studies**
Private Information, Trading Volume, and Stock-Return Variances
by M.J. Barclay, R.H. Litzenberger and J.B. Warner
Previously published in The Review of Financial Studies, Vol. 3, No. 2, pp. 233-253 (1990)
(Copyright 1990)

pages 527-556: **The Bank of Japan - Institute for Monetary and Economic Studies**
Interpreting Changes in the Volatility of Yields on Japanese Long-term Bonds
by K.J. Singleton
Previously published in the BOJ Monetary and Economic Studies, Vol. 8, No. 1, pp. 49-78 (1990)
(Copyright 1990)

Contents

List of Contributors

Yakov Amihud, Leonard N. Stern Graduate School of Business, New York University, New York, NY 10006 and Faculty of Management, Tel Aviv University, Tel Aviv, Israel

Warren Bailey, Johnson Graduate School of Management, Cornell University, Ithaca, NY 14853-4201

Michael J. Barclay, Simon School of Management, University of Rochester, Rochester, NY 14627

Menachem Brenner, School of Business, Hebrew University, Jerusalem, Israel and Leonard N. Stern Graduate School of Business, New York University, New York, NY 10006

Peter Carr, Johnson Graduate School of Business, Cornell University, Ithaca, NY 14853-4201

K. C. Chan, Academic Faculty of Finance, The Ohio State University, 1775 College Road, Columbus, OH 43210

Masako N. Darrough, Graduate School of Business, Uris Hall, Columbia University, New York, NY 10027

Yasushi Hamao, Graduate School of Business, Uris Hall, Columbia University, New York, NY 10027

Trevor S. Harris, Graduate School of Business, Uris Hall, Columbia University, New York, NY 10027

Gabriel A. Hawawini, Associate Dean, INSEAD and Director of the Euro-Asia Centre, Boulevard de Constance, 77309 Fontainebleau, France

James E. Hodder, Department of Industrial Engineering and Engineering Management, Stanford University, Stanford, CA 94305

Takeo Hoshi, Graduate School of International Relations and Pacific Studies, University of California, San Diego, La Jolla, CA 92093-0519

Takatoshi Ito, Department of Economics, University of Minnesota, Minneapolis, MN 55455, and Institute of Economic Research, Hitotsubashi University, Kunitachi-shi, Tokyo 186, Japan

G. Andrew Karolyi, Academic Faculty of Finance, The Ohio State University, 1775 College Road, Columbus, OH 43210

Kiyoshi Kato, Center for Management Studies, Nanzan University, 18 Yamazato-cho, Showa-ku, Nagoya 466, Japan

Kwok-Wai Leung, Academic Faculty of Finance, The Ohio State University, 1775 College Road, Columbus, OH 43210

Robert H. Litzenberger, The Wharton School of the University of Pennsylvania, Department of Finance, 3620 Locust Walk, Philadelphia, PA, 19104-6367

James R. Lothian, Graduate School of Business, Fordham University, 113 West 60th Street, New York, NY 10023

Ronald W. Masulis, Owen Graduate School of Management, Vanderbilt University, Nashville, TN 37203

Haim Mendelson, Graduate School of Business, Stanford University, Stanford, CA 94305.

Victor Ng, School of Business Administration, University of Michigan, Ann Arbor, MI 48109-1234

Richard H. Pettway, College of Business Administration, University of Missouri, 329 Middlebush Hall, Columbia, MO 65211

V. Vance Rolley, Department of Economics, University of Washington, Seattle, WA 98195

Anthony Sanders, Academic Faculty of Finance, Ohio State University, Columbus, OH 43210

Ulrike Schaede, Japan-Zentrum der Universit, Japan-Zentrum der Universität Marburg, Wilhelm-Röpke-Str. 6E, Marburg 3550, Germany

Sandra L. Schwartz, Department of Administrative Studies, Simon Fraser University, P.O. Box 35007, Station E, Vancouver, B.C. V6M 4G1, Canada

Kenneth J. Singleton, Graduate School of Business, Stanford University, Stanford, CA 94305

Marti Subrahmanyam, Leonard N. Stern School of Business, New York University, 90 Trinity Place, New York, NY 10006

Y. K. Tse, Department of Economics and Statistics, National University of Singapore, 10 Kent Ridge Crescent, Singapore 0511

Haluk Unal, College of Business and Management, University of Maryland, University Park, MD 20742

Jun Uno, Nihon Quick Corporation Inc, 33 Whitehall Street, 2nd floor, New York NY 10004

Jerold B. Warner, Simon School of Management, University of Rochester, Rochester, NY 14627

William T. Ziemba, Faculty of Commerce, University of British Columbia, Vancouver, BC V6T 1Y8, Canada

Preface

Japanese financial markets have grown tremendously in size and in their interaction with the West in the 1980s. The stock markets have reached a level of trading volume and value that is similar to that in the United States and well above London or any other market. The land markets have exploded in value so that Japanese land in early 1991 was valued at some $17 trillion, about four times that of the Japanese or U.S. stock markets or U.S. land. Japanese land was then around a fifth of all the world's assets. The late 1980s have seen a tremendous opening up of Japanese financial markets. There are Japanese stock index futures, options and long dated warrants trading in Tokyo and Osaka but also in London, New York, Chicago, Singapore, Toronto, Sidney and other locales. Japanese currency, bond, interest rate and other instruments are also widely traded around the globe. Economic integration has increased to such an extent that one can make good predictions of the next day's market directions in Tokyo based on derivative security trading elsewhere.

This volume is a compilation of recent research on various aspects of Japanese financial markets. The papers discuss the economy, land and stock markets, the behavior of stock prices, exchange rates and hedging, derivative security markets, integration of capital markets, bond and fixed income markets, and the financing of Japanese corporations in the seven sections of the volume. The contributions cover both new theory and empirical studies in these general areas. They also provide much institutional detail and recent and historical data on these markets.

The research papers are a blend of new articles produced for this volume and reprinted articles recently published from a wide variety of sources. The volume grew out of the sessions on Japanese financial market research that William Ziemba organized for the Osaka International TIMS meeting in July 1989. Several of the papers presented there appear in this volume. These papers are supplemented with research from around the globe. In addition to authors from Japan and the U.S., there are papers from researchers in Canada, Singapore, Israel, France and Germany. All of the researchers have had considerable experience with and, in many cases, extensive research in Japan. William Ziemba and Yasushi Hamao have benefitted extensively from their involvements with two of Japan's big four brokerage firms, Yamaichi and Daiwa, respectively. These firms have been very generous in their support of their research including making available extensive data and materials. Other authors have benefitted greatly from their involvements with such agencies as Nihon Keizai Shimbun, the producers of the Nikkei financial newspaper and many other financial publications, the SIMEX, the Bank of Japan and Yamaichi Securities.

Part I. The Economy, Land and Stock Markets

Yasushi Hamao begins the volume by discussing institutional characteristics of the Japanese financial markets and historical data through 1990 on stocks, bonds, short-term interest rates, and inflation. The treatment starts in 1952 for Tokyo Stock Exchange Section I stocks and in 1971 for other assets. The article also provides some historical highlights of asset returns and compares them with the U.S. counterparts.

Sandra Schwartz and William Ziemba discuss the historical record of the Japanese stock market from the post war resumption of trading in May 1949 to the end of February 1991. From 1949 to the end of 1989 the Nikkei stock average increased over 220 times in yen and over 550 times in dollars. While the rise has been spectacular there have been twenty two decline of ten percent more along the way. These include two steep corrections coinciding with a steep rise in nominal and real interest rates in late 1989 and 1990. Simple interest rate models seem to explain well the under and over pricedness of the general market level.

Land prices in Japan have reached truly astronomical levels. There were sharp rises in the 1950s and 1960s and indeed most of the relative value of land versus other assets was established then. Historically land prices have been very steady with consistent yearly increases except for the first oil crisis in 1973/74. There were very sharp increases in land prices and stock prices particularly relative to earnings in 1986. William Ziemba studies the relationship between land and stock prices in Japan by focusing on the relationship between the relative levels of these two financial assets. Despite the fact that stock prices have had twenty-two declines of ten percent or more and land prices only one of 5-8 percent, the two assets have price levels that have historically moved in tandem. Stock price increases seem to lead land price increases rather than the reverse. Commercial land in the six largest cities is very closely related to stock values, and much more so than other types of land. Indeed stock market price levels seem to be almost perfectly matched with commercial land prices six months later. In early 1991 after a steep stock market fall, there is a gap in this relationship. The historical record would indicate a softening of real estate price increases and possibly a decline until the stock market begins rising again. Land prices in 1990 showed their historical resilience by not falling much, if at all, in the face of extremely sharp increases in borrowing costs. However, speculative land purchases in condos and golf course memberships have had a steep decline since March 1990.

The tremendous development of the Japanese economy over the past forty years has made it the world's largest creditor nation. Sandra Schwartz investigates how Japan attained its position and how it is currently using its new wealth. Being the dominant creditor provides a major challenge especially in making the transition to a more balanced role. Great Britain and the United States have previously been dominate creditors and did not handle the transition from debtor to creditor nation well. Will Japan do better? The dilemma and challenges facing Japan are explored and observations are made concerning the future.

Part II. The Behavior of Stock Prices

The relationship between price and volume on the Tokyo stock exchange is studied by Y. K. Tse. He used daily, weekly and monthly data on the Topix, the value weighted average of all TSE-I stocks, and the NSA 225 and 500, the price weighted average of 225 and 500 large capitalized stocks, respectively, from August 1983 to February 1989. During this time period, returns were statistically lower on Mondays and equal on the other days. Returns over daily, weekly and monthly intervals are negatively skewed and leptokurtic. While daily returns are slightly positively autocorrelated, the autocorrelations for weekly and monthly returns are statistically insignificant. There is evidence against the stable Paretian hypothesis for market returns. The results support market returns following a low order normal distribution mixture. Trading volume is highly positively autocorrelated and hence it is not a good proxy for information. The price-volume relationship is positive but it is weak and ambiguous.

K. C. Chan and G. Andrew Karolyi study the evolution of Japanese stock market volatility from 1977 to 1990. They document several stylized facts of the pattern of changes in the Nikkei Stock Average return volatility over this period. They propose and implement a generalized autoregressive conditionally heteroscedastic (GARCH) model to the returns series and, in the residual diagnostics, show that this model describes the empirical returns generating process well. They test whether the October, 1987, market crash and the introduction of NSA index futures and options trading influenced the pattern of volatility described by these models They find evidence consistent with the first hypothesis but not the second.

Takeo Hoshi tests the stock market rationality hypothesis which implies that a stock price is determined as the discounted sum of optimally forecasted future dividends. Mankiw-Romer-Shapiro volatility tests and new volatility tests which do not use the unobservable *ex post rational price* are applied to the data from a stock market in Japan. A Hausman type specification test of the market rationality hypothesis is also developed and applied to the data which consists of monthly observations from January 1952 to December 1981. The results suggest that one cannot reject the hypothesis that the Japanese stock market is rational.

Some variance inequalities are violated by the data but the violation does not seem to be significant.

Yakov Amihud and Haim Mendelson compare the price discovery processes at the opening and closing transactions for the fifty largest stocks trading on the TSE. Open-to-open returns have a greater volatility and a more negative autocorrelation pattern than close-to-close returns, similar to the pattern they found on the NYSE. The results are consistent with pricing over-reaction at the opening and partial price-adjustment at the close. These patterns persist over time and prevail when estimated for returns conditional on the contemporaneous market effect. Their analysis of daytime and overnight returns suggests that pricing errors at the opening are corrected over the trading day. They present a new measure of volatility - the relative dispersion of stock returns around the market return - and find that it is greater at the opening, consistent with a more noisy price discovery process.

Japanese companies must provide management forecasts of earnings simultaneously with their announcement of annual earnings. The announcements are made separately for a parent and for total consolidated earnings. Masako Darrough and Trevor Harris test whether the management forecasts have incremental information content in the announcement period. They conclude that (i) *analysts* forecasts provide the most accurate measure of expected parent-only earnings, (ii) investors react to unexpected parent-only earnings, (iii) investors also react to the management forecasts of next period's parent-only earnings, (iv) investors' reaction to unexpected consolidated earnings occurs but is not monotonic, and (v) investors react to the management forecasts of consolidated earnings. These results suggest that investors in Japanese stocks should pay attention to management's forecasts of both parent and consolidated earnings, and those interested in understanding the relatively high Japanese price/earnings ratios should consider the management forecasts. As Japanese influence on international capital markets grows, there may be pressure on non-Japanese managers to provide management forecasts.

Gabriel Hawawini studies the relationship between the mean return and the risk of a sample of common stocks traded on the TSE using data from 1955 to 1985. He investigates whether or not the capital asset pricing model is a valid predictor of common stock returns on the TSE given that this market exhibits two well-known anomalies, namely the size effect and monthly seasonality. He finds a strong January pricing effect for the CAPM but systematic risk is not priced in the rest of the year. Small stocks are also priced in June. The size effect is significant in January, June and July. This is consistent with findings for U.S. markets. In particular, these studies have shown that risk is priced during periods with high seasonally anomalous returns and not at other times. During January, Hawawini finds that returns increase sharply with increasing beta as they do in the U.S.

Kiyoshi Kato studies the day of the week effects in Japanese stocks using data from April 1978 to December 1987. Except for the largest capitalized firms all the gains are at night. Indeed the close to close returns from other quintiles is less than the close to open returns. He found significantly low returns on Tuesdays and high returns on Wednesdays. The weekly pattern is more pronounced for the returns of smaller firms. A reverse size effect is observed during the trading period. However, the returns on Mondays and Tuesdays are greatly affected by whether or not the previous week had Saturday trading. Weeks with Saturday trading tend to yield declines on Tuesday whereas with Saturday closed, the fall is, on average, on Monday.

Part III. Exchange Rates and Hedging

James Lothian reviews the history and traces the evolution of yen exchange rates against the U.S. dollar and British sterling from 1874 to the present. He also compares the behavior of these rates with that of the dollar/sterling rate. The yen has floated more frequently than either sterling or the dollar. It has also been more variable. These three nominal rates are related to indexes of purchasing power parity and the links among exchange-rate regimes, the exchange rates themselves and other macroeconomic variables. Relative purchasing power parity holds quite well for the yen over the long term. The variability of real yen exchange rates under the current float, moreover, does not differ greatly from the movements observed historically. Also uncovered is a close positive association between the variability in real yen exchange rates and Japanese inflation.

Takatoshi Ito and Vance Rolley investigate the daily yen/dollar exchange rates in four separate non-overlapping segments from January 1980 to September 1985. The dollar tended to appreciate in New York, fall in Europe, and be largely unchanged in Tokyo. The volatility of the exchange rate also differed across markets and in different time segments. However, volatility in Japan was dramatically decreasing throughout these five years. News from the U.S. on monetary matters and industrial production tended to offset the exchange rate much more consistently than Japanese monetary announcements.

William Ziemba studies currency hedging strategies for investment in non-cash instruments to and from Japan in the U.S. and Japan. The traditional approach is to fully eliminate the currency risk using forward or futures contracts to offset the long exposure to the foreign currency. If there is a substantial difference in interest rates, one can lock in guaranteed hedged returns by investing from the high interest rate country into the low interest rate country. During the late 1980s this was the case for U.S. investment in Japan where the rates were 1-4% lower. For Canadians investing in Japan or in the U.S., the mid 1990 rate differences were nearly 5% per year. Although improvements adding risk are possible, this approach is a very satisfactory resolution of this problem for these investors. The situation has been much more difficult and complicated for Japanese investment in the U.S. The forward/futures hedge eliminated the currency risk but at a cost of 1-4% per year until 1990. Strategies that do not lose this interest rate differential and in fact collect positive premiums are available by selling and buying yen put and call options. Simulations using an investment in three year Treasury bonds investigate this using recent currency movements and Black-Scholes estimated prices for plausible future scenarios to evaluate the risk-reward tradeoffs and the worst possible outcome using the various strategies. The added risk seems well worth taking for many investors to achieve substantial expected gains.

Part IV. Derivative Security Markets

Derivative security markets are not recent innovations. The Dojima rice market of 1730 is the oldest futures market in the world with detailed information. This market predates by more than a century the futures markets in Europe and Chicago. Ulrike Schaede studies this market. Futures were traded on standardized rice bills and the system also provided for daily mark-to-market and clearing houses. This market did not build on prior economic insight of the authorities, but materialized according to the traders' needs. Therefore, differences in trading practices, the most important of which is the *multiple clearing system* in Osaka, hint at alternative ways of futures market microstructure.

Index futures on the Nikkei 225 began trading in Singapore on the Simex in September 1986. In June 1987 the Kabusaki 50 began trading in Osaka. September 1988 saw the start of futures trading on the Topix on the TSE and NSA 225 in Osaka. NSA 225 and Japan 210 index futures and options began trading in Chicago and New York in late 1990. Warren Bailey discusses the early history of trading on the Simex and Osaka stock exchanges. He investigates the relationship between changes in the stock averages and futures trading volume. He found no evidence of correlation between price changes and futures volume. However, there is a strong relation between the absolute value of price changes and volume. Futures volume seems to increase as speculators and hedgers react to the arrival of new information and price changes. Bailey found that there were only small differences between the cost of carry theoretical prices and the actual market prices. The differences can be explained by observation errors, trading costs, short sale constraints, different borrowing and leading rates and other market imperfections. A complex stochastic interest rate model provides little improvement over the simple model

William Ziemba investigates seasonal regularities in the security price returns on the first section of the Tokyo Stock Exchange. The research uses data from the futures markets in Singapore for the Nikkei 225 stock average and in Osaka for the Kabusaki 50 index from September 1986 to September 1988. The questions of main concern are whether or not the seasonal anomalies observed in the spot markets are maintained, are they anticipated in the futures markets, and do the futures market anticipations alter the character of the seasonal regularity. Results are presented concerning day of the week, monthly, holiday, turn of the month and year and first half of the month effects. Although there is some anticipation and alteration, the basic seasonal anomalies were very strong is these two years.

Menachem Brenner, Marti Subrahmanyam, and Jun Uno examine the relationship between the prices of Japanese stocks and the prices of Japanese futures contracts using data from June 1987 to June 1988.. An important variable affecting this relationship is the size of the transactions costs, that are high relative to American markets. These costs establish a wide band and reduce the incentive to engage in spot-future arbitrage between the Simex NSA 225 and the Kabusaki 50. Cross-spreading strategies involving futures-futures trading are less expensive and, therefore, more attractive to many investors. They study two different approaches to the spreading strategy and find substantial profit opportunities in both cases. They also analyze another strategy involving switching from spot to futures markets with no additional risk, which allows a well-diversified investor such as a mutual fund, to earn extra profits from mispriced futures contracts.

In their follow up paper Brenner, Subrahmanyam, and Uno update their arbitrage research up to September 1989. This includes the possibility of arbitrage among the four futures contracts plus the cash markets in Tokyo and Osaka. The introduction of the new contracts in Japan in September 1988 led to the virtual elimination of volume in the Osaka 50. Hence the Simex NSA, the Osaka NSA and the Tokyo Topix were the futures contracts of interest in this period. Deviations from fair value became less and less over time. Past deviations can be explained by relatively high transactions costs and by trading restrictions such as on short selling and arbitrage actively by Japanese security firms. Relaxation of these restrictions has led to increased market efficiency. The deviations at the end of 1989 were generally within the transaction cost bands. Hence arbitrage was less frequently profitable.

Warren Bailey and William Ziemba briefly describe the index options and warrants traded on the Tokyo, Osaka, Nagoya and foreign stock exchanges and over the counter markets particularly in Toronto, on the American Stock Exchange and the Chicago Mercantile Exchange and their early trading history. They use a simple option pricing model to estimate Japanese index option prices. They also discuss a number of factors with may necessitate the use of more complex option pricing models to value Japanese index option products and to design risk management strategies which employ them.

Peter Carr presents analytical valuation formulas for bonds with detachable warrants such as the Japanese bonds sold in Europe. The bonds bear default risk on both coupons and principal. The warrants are American with a positive early exercise premium due to the existence of stock dividends. He provides formulas for valuing and hedging such bonds.

Part V. Integration of Capital Markets

Yasushi Hamao, Victor Ng, and Ronald Masulis analyze daily open-to-close returns from three major stock markets from 1985 to 1990, a period that includes the October 1987 stock market crash. The international transmission of volatility does not occur evenly around the world. The volatility spillover effects from Japan to the U.K. and U.S. markets have been strengthening over time, and these changes appear to occur following the 1987 crash. A possible explanation is that domestic investors become more aware of the growing international financial linkages and its importance after such major events as the 1987 crash which thereafter heightened their sensitivity to foreign market developments.

Michael Barclay, Robert Litzenberger and Jerold Warner note that institutional features of the TSE allow tests that provide new insights into the determinants of stock return variances. When the exchange is open on Saturday, the weekend variance is roughly sixty percent higher than when it is closed. However, weekly variances are not increased by Saturday trading. The increase in weekend volume and variance caused by Saturday trading is offset by lower volume and variance on surrounding days. These results are consistent with the view that Saturday trading changes the timing of trades, and that variance is caused by private information revealed through trading. U.S. stocks traded on Tokyo or Japanese stocks traded on the NYSE have increased trading hours, but trading of stock on the foreign exchange is typically light relative to domestic volume. The increased trading hours are not associated with an increase in stock return variance. This suggests that substantial volume is required for private information to be incorporated into stock prices and that there is no causal relation between trading hours and stock return variance.

Part VI. Bond and Fixed Income Markets

Kenneth Singleton investigates empirically the relations between changes in volatilities of holding period returns on long term Japanese government bonds and changes in U.S. interest rates and the yen/dollar exchange rate. Weekly and quarterly holding period returns are constructed for the period March 1986 through May 1988. Quadratic and Fourier series approximations to the conditional variances of these yields are estimated. Significant variation in the conditional variances of holding period returns is documented. These results are interpreted in the light of the changing patterns of trading volumes and capital flows between the U.S. and Japan in 1980s.

Kwok-Wai Leung, Anthony Sanders and Haluk Unal examine the variation in the time series behavior of the three month Gensaki rate, a principal indicator of the time value of money in Japan using data from 1980 to 1989. They find significant variation in the degree to which the Gensaki rate tends to revert to its long-run mean. Shifts in estimated mean reversion and volatility appear to be related to principal events in the liberalization of Japan's capital markets.

Part VII. Financing of Japanese Corporations

James Hodder examines the debate regarding cost of capital differences between the U.S. and Japan. It is argued that the *Pecking Order Theory* of capital structure implies a firm's cost of capital depends on its investment budget, which can vary across time. From this perspective, cost of capital estimates which average across firms and time can be very misleading. Hodder argues that lender monitoring in Japan may have flattened the cost of capital function faced by industrial firms. While this effect may not be advantageous for all firms, it does appear beneficial for rapidly growing firms.

Richard H. Pettway's summary of research on the nature and composition of mergers in Japan has found them to have characteristics which are in some respects different from mergers in the U.S. After a discussion of the nature of corporate mergers in Japan, Japanese merger research is summarized. These results are extended to suggest the potential characteristics of Japanese acquisitions of U.S. firms. Finally these suggestions are compared to the recent levels of Japanese direct investment in the U.S.

Acknowledgements

Continuing involvement by William Ziemba with research activities related to Japanese financial markets with the Frank Russell Company, Edward O. Thorp and Associates and the Gordon Capital Corporation has been very beneficial to this book. The chapters he has written have also benefitted from seminar and conference presentations at Dartmouth College, New York University, the Vancouver ORSA/TIMS, the Osaka International TIMS, the Athens IFORS, the DAIS Group client conference, the Frank Russell client conference, the Operations Research Society of Japan, Tokyo and Nagoya branches, the Berkeley program in finance in Asia and the U.S. and the Pacific Basin Finance conferences organized by the University of Rhode Island and the Taipex Foundation. Partial support of research activities on Japanese financial markets by the Social Sciences and Humanities Research Council of Canada and the Centre for International Business Research at the University of British Columbia is also gratefully acknowledged.

William Ziemba also wishes to thank Yukio Okada, formerly the vice chairman of the Yamaichi Research Institute and Professor Rinya Shibakawa of the University of Tsukuba for extensive and generous help during his stay in Japan during 1988-89 as the Yamaichi Visiting Professor of Finance at the University of Tsukuba. He would also like to thank other YRI colleagues particularly Shigeru Ishii, Asaji Komatsu, Hitoshi Shintani, and Hirokazu Yuihama for their generous help on many points concerning the Japanese financial system. Discussions with Professors Kiyoshi Kato, Hitoshi Konno, Kazuo Kishimoto and Katsushige Sawaki have also been helpful. Jun Uno of the Nihon Keizai Simbun, Inc., provided much valuable data and helpful information and comments. Special thanks also go to David Myers, Julian Shaw, Douglas Stone Edward O. Thorp, Andy Turner, and Peter Williamson for helpful discussions and comments on Japanese economic and financial research and to Sandra Schwartz for help in manuscript preparation and editorial assistance.

Warren Bailey would like to thank the SIMEX, JETRO and the Yamaichi Research Institute for providing him with helpful data.

Yasushi Hamao would like to thank the following individuals and institutions for their help: John Campbell, Teruyoshi Gotoh, Hiroshi Hori, Takeo Hoshi, Masahiro Hotchi, Roger Ibbotson, Jonathan Ingersoll, Osamu Kamijo, Fumiko Kon-ya, Josef Lakonishok, Junko Maru, David Musto, Takayuki Nakajima, Naohiko Nishibayashi, Richard Roll, Stephen Ross, Koichi Watanabe, Bing Yeh, Daiwa Securities, Japan Securities Research Institute, Nihon Keizai Shimbun and the Tokyo stock exchange. He would also like to thank seminar participants at Columbia University, Duke University, INSEAD, New York University, University of California, Berkeley, Los Angeles, and San Diego, the Berkeley Program in Finance, the Institute for Quantitative Research in Finance (The Q Group), and the Wharton Conference on Investment Management.

William T. Ziemba, Vancouver
Warren Bailey, Ithaca
Yasushi Hamao, New York
June 1991

PART I:
THE ECONOMY, LAND AND STOCK MARKETS

Japanese Financial Market Research
W.T. Ziemba, W. Bailey and Y. Hamao (Editors)

Japanese Financial Markets: An Overview[1]

Yasushi Hamao, Columbia University

ABSTRACT

This paper characterizes Japanese financial markets by presenting historical data in aggregate series and in summary statistics. The database, which is calculated from newly compiled raw data on individual security returns, is consistent with the CRSP/Ibbotson-Sinquefield methodology for the U.S. Thus, it allows direct comparison with U.S. financial markets.

I. Introduction

In their 1976 article, "Stocks, Bonds, Bills, and Inflation: Year-by-Year Historical Returns," Roger G. Ibbotson and Rex A. Sinquefield presented a comprehensive database for U.S. financial markets. This work, which is updated every year as Ibbotson Associates (1991), became the ultimate data source for studies in finance. It benefits numerous economists in their research and many practitioners in their decision making.

The present paper offers carefully compiled post-1971 Japanese financial data. (For the stock index, the data go back to 1952.) It serves as a description and analysis of the database on Japanese financial markets that the author has established. This database is compatible in its methodology with U.S. data.[2]

The emerging importance of Japanese capital markets has brought much attention to Japanese finance among researchers and investment professionals alike. Hardly a single week passes without one reading articles about Japanese markets and Japanese investors in the popular press. Despite this increasing popularity, it has been very difficult to get access to a high quality database on Japanese financial markets because of the lack of a standard database, such as Ibbotson-Sinquefield and CRSP (Center for Research in Security Prices at the University of Chicago) in the U.S. In extending the Arbitrage Pricing Theory to the Japanese economy in Hamao

---

[1] This is a revised and updated version of Hamao (1991).

[2] The raw data on individual securities were provided by Daiwa Securities Co., Ltd., Tokyo. They were computed and compiled according to the author's specifications. The author would like to thank Daiwa for their cooperation.

(1988), I found it necessary to create a database that serves as a basis for empirical studies on Japanese financial markets.

The series I present here are (1) Common Stocks (Tokyo Stock Exchange Section I and II Indices), (2) Long-term Corporate Bonds, (3) Long-term Government Bonds, (4) Short-term Interest Rates, and (5) Inflation. These returns are shown in Japanese yen terms and U.S. Dollar terms. In addition to these basic series, I present component returns. They are real (net of inflation) returns and excess returns above short-term interest rates. I take the Ibbotson-Sinquefield database as a model for the presentation of Japanese data here. By doing so, it becomes possible to compare the two systems.

The paper is presented in the form of summary statistics and yearly returns. The paper is divided into five sections. Following Section I, the Introduction, Section II describes notations and definitions of basic series of various financial assets. I also present some institutional aspects of Japanese financial markets. Section III derives and describes component returns, Section IV gives highlights of the data, and Section V concludes the paper. In addition, the Appendix provides yearly returns for the basic series in yen and dollar terms.

II. Basic Series

1. Notations and Definitions

Annual returns, R, are compounded from monthly returns, r, *i.e.*,

$$R = \prod_{t=Jan}^{Dec} [1 + r(t)] - 1 \ .$$

The wealth index V(T) is the value of wealth at month T of initial investment (100 yen) at the beginning of the period. Except for the Tokyo Stock Exchange Section One index, this is initialized at December 1970, *i.e.*,

$$V(T) = 100 \prod_{t=1/71}^{T} [1 + r(t)] \ .$$

Tables 1-1 and 1-2 show wealth indices for the series I describe below. Figure 1 depicts these index values in logarithmic scale.

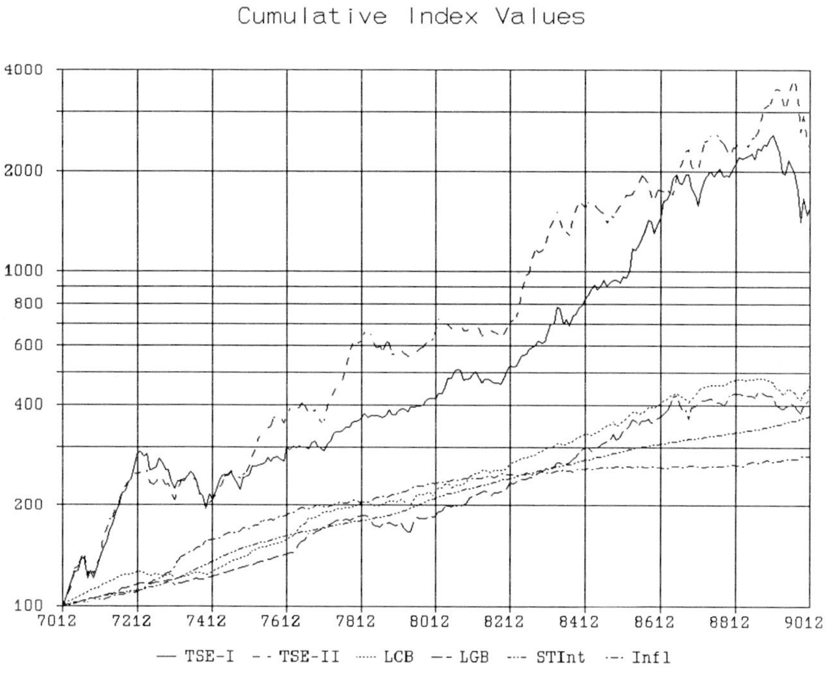

Figure 1

The arithmetic mean returns for the holding period are computed as

$$r_A(T_1, T_2) = \sum_{t=T_1}^{T_2} \frac{r(t)}{T_2 - T_1 + 1} \quad .$$

On the other hand, the geometric mean returns for the holding period are formed by

$$r_G(T_1, T_2) = \left[\prod_{t=T_1}^{T_2} [1 + r(t)] \right]^{1/(T_2-T_1+1)} - 1 \quad .$$

Notations for financial assets are as follows:

TSE-I: value-weighted Tokyo Stock Exchange Section One index (large, mature firms);

TSE-II:	value-weighted Tokyo Stock Exchange Section Two index (small, young, or troubled firms);
LCB:	long-term corporate bond index;
LGB:	long-term government bond index;
STInt:	short-term interest rate; and
Infl:	inflation rate.

Notations for derived series are given in Section III.

2. Common Stocks

Eight stock exchanges exist in Japan — Tokyo, Osaka, Nagoya, Kyoto, Hiroshima, Fukuoka, Niigata, and Sapporo. The Tokyo Stock exchange has more than 95% of the whole market value and is divided into two sections according to a standard set by the Exchange. The standard stipulates the minimum number of outstanding shares, trading volumes and frequencies, and the minimum dividend payment of the listed companies. It is customary for new companies to be listed in TSE-II first, before they satisfy the standard for TSE-I listing and are transferred to TSE-I.

At the end of 1990, the first section of the Tokyo Stock Exchange had 1191 companies and 357 trillion yen (2.6 trillion U.S. dollars) of market capitalization. It is larger than the New York Stock Exchange, which had 2.5 trillion dollars (1755 companies) of market capitalization. The second section had 425 companies and 14 trillion yen (103 billion U.S. dollars) of market value. This is comparable to AMEX which had 101 billion dollars (888 companies).

One caveat in discussing capitalization is that there are substantial cross-holdings among related ("keiretsu") corporations, and the outstanding volume does not necessarily represent the amount of liquid shares. Although it is difficult to obtain an accurate percentage of stocks cross-held for long-term purposes, it is estimated that approximately 20% was reciprocally held by the six largest keiretsu in 1986.[3]

There are daily upper- and lower-price limits for quoting prices at the Tokyo Stock Exchange. The limits vary according to the price of each stock, from ¥30 for stocks less than ¥100, to ¥10,000 for stock more than ¥100,000. The base price is the closing price of the previous day. The market is open from 9:00 am to 11:00 am and from 1:00 pm to 3:00 pm. The market was open in the morning on Saturday every week until December 1972, three Saturdays a month until July 1986, and two Saturdays a month until January 1989. Since February 1989, the market has been closed on all Saturdays. Except for the most actively traded 150 stocks in the first section, all stocks are traded through a computerized trade matching system. Unlike the specialist system of the New York Stock Exchange, the matching is done through clerks who do not take an inventory position.[4]

---

[3] See Kigyo Keiretsu Soran, Tokyo: Toyo Keizai Shimpo Sha, 1988.

The market indices I present first are value-weighted indices of Tokyo Stock Exchange Section One (TSE-I) and Section Two (TSE-II). From 1952 to 1970, I use the series provided by the Japan Securities Research Institute. The series after 1971 are constructed by the author. I consider dividends paid to be reinvested in these indices for the purposes of calculating returns. The universe I compute the index from includes delisted companies, thus the series (from 1971) is free from survivorship bias. I also divide total returns into their components, income and capital appreciation. These indices are different from the Tokyo Stock Price Index (TOPIX) published by the Tokyo Stock Exchange and the Nikkei 225 Index published by the Nikkei Newspaper Company. TOPIX is a value-weighted index of the first section, but does not include dividends. Nikkei 225 is similar to the Dow-Jones index and is a share-price average of only 225 prespecified companies. I also present the income (dividend) portion of the total return. Dividends are less significant in Japan than in the U.S. Out of the average monthly total return of 1.15% of the TSE-I index (Table 1), income accounts for 0.14%, whereas S&P income return is 0.35% out of an 0.88% total return.

It would be useful to briefly explain the Japanese tax system. From 1953 to 1989, capital gains were, in principle, not taxed for individuals. Since February 1989, an amendment of tax laws is in effect and capital gains for individuals are now taxed. The new law regards 5% of the sales proceeds of financial assets as capital gains and taxes it at 20%. Corporations are taxed on capital gains at the same rate as they are taxed for ordinary income. Dividend income is not taxed for corporations. For individuals, dividend income is taxed as ordinary income if it exceeds ¥500,000 ($4,000) and below that, taxation at source is applicable and lower tax rates are in effect.

Interest income for a corporation is added to other ordinary income, and individuals have a choice between ordinary taxation and a flat 35% tax at the source.

For reference, the effective tax rate for corporations with more than ¥8,000,000 ($64,000) of taxable income is 52.92% (1986) as compared to 51.18% (for corporations with more than $100,000 of taxable income) in the U.S. Marginal income tax rates for individuals start at 10.5% (income below $12,000) and go up to 60% (income above $400,000).

3. *Bonds*

The bond market in Japan, which is now the second largest in the world in outstanding volume (U.S.$2 trillion in 1989, U.S. market has $5 trillion), did not develop until the late 1970's. The first issue of long-term government bonds after World War II occurred in 1966, upon the amendment of the fiscal law that had prohibited the government from issuing debt. The

---

[4] For details of the trading system, see Japan Securities Research Institute (1988) and Amihud and Mendelson (1989).

government bonds were underwritten by syndicates of financial institutions and were later purchased by the Bank of Japan through open market operation. The underwriting was mandatory for the financial institutions, even at a low yield. The financial authorities were afraid of a drop in the price of bonds and therefore the financial institutions were not allowed to sell government bonds in the secondary market.

For corporate bonds, the government's policy of maintaining artificially low interest rates kept investors away from the bond markets, forcing corporations to depend mostly on bank loans. In this situation, the primary market remained inactive, and there was virtually no secondary market before 1975.

Massive offerings of government bonds started in 1975 when the oil crisis caused a serious recession. In 1977, facing the rapidly increased balance of government bonds, the Bank of Japan became unable to purchase them from the syndicates. Because of this, the financial institutions were finally allowed to sell bonds in the secondary market. This marked the beginning of the development of an active secondary market. In April 1981 and June 1985, secondary sales of bonds were further deregulated by reducing the required holding period after subscription. Bank dealing of government bonds was authorized in part in June 1984, and then completely liberalized in June 1985. The futures market for government bonds was established in October 1985. Reflecting these deregulations, the trading volume in 1988 became ¥2,905 trillion, which is ten times the 1977 level. As in the U.S., the majority of the trading of government bonds takes place in the over-the-counter market, which accounts for 97% of the trading.

The corporate bond market is still relatively small. Rigid conditions are set by the authorities on eligibility for issuing corporate bonds, and unsecured (hence rated) bond issues are still limited.

Because of the above-mentioned situation, the bond data before the starting date of this article is almost meaningless because of the lack of a liquid market.

3.1 Long-Term Corporate Bonds

It is difficult to obtain corporate bond returns for the entire period, but the long-term bonds issued by nine electricity companies offer the most consistently available data. These bonds have a ten year maturity (twelve years after March 1981) and the coupons are paid semi-annually. The series presented here are returns on value-weighted portfolios containing electricity company bonds and other small numbers of corporate bonds with nine to ten years to maturity. The electricity bonds represent about 75% of the portfolio contents.

3.2 Long-Term Government Bonds

The "Long-Term Government Bonds" in Japan include six, ten, fifteen and twenty year maturity bonds. In this database, I take ten year maturity straight bonds with semi-annual coupons, since these constitute the majority of government bonds and provide the most consistent series. I compute returns on value-weighted portfolios of bond using prices including the accrued interest. The portfolios are for bonds with nine to ten years to maturity. Since 1983, there has been a phenomenon known as the benchmark effect. Typically, a newly issued ten year bond with a large outstanding volume is chosen to be a benchmark and retains this status for a period of six months to a year. The benchmark issues are strongly preferred by bond market participants, and trading is heavily concentrated on these issues, causing a fairly large liquidity premium. The portfolio includes the benchmark issues most of the time.

4. *Short-Term Interest Rates*

Although there are short-term government bills in Japan, the interest rate on these bills is determined at an artificially low level, and hence the market has been insignificant. Instead, call money rate has often been used as the short-term interest rate in empirical studies of the Japanese economy. Since only the financial institutions participate in the call money market, it is often argued that the call money rate is a poor proxy for the riskless rate seen by investors. I therefore present another short-term interest rate, the Gensaki rate, after it became available.

Although the Gensaki market has existed since early 1960's, it grew substantially in volume in the late 1970's. The Gensaki rate is the interest rate applied to bond repurchase agreements which, as in the U.S., are essentially collateralized loans.[5] The agreement period varies from one month to three months, and unlike the call money rate, participants are not limited to only financial institutions, but also include corporations, government pension funds and non-residents. The Gensaki transaction is classified as bond trading by the Ministry of Finance and accounted for 20% of the entire trading volume of bonds in 1986.

In this study, the daily average (during a month) of overnight call money rates is used through November 1980 and is replaced by the one-month Gensaki rate prevailing around the 25th of each month after December 1980.

5. *Inflation*

To measure inflation, I use the consumer price index (general, not seasonally adjusted) taken from the Bank of Japan Monthly Statistics. The inflation rate is the first log relative of the monthly CPI. It must be noted that this data is not contemporaneous with other asset returns since the prices for the index are taken during the month, whereas other asset returns are measured at the end of the month.

---

[5] See Stigum (1983) for a description of the U.S. repurchase agreement (repo for short). The name "Gensaki" stands for "spot-and-forward."

6. Dollar-Translated Returns

In order to facilitate international comparison with U.S. data, I will transform the above asset returns into dollar terms. The month-end spot exchange rates are used to compute the dollar-translated returns, $r_\$(t)$ as follows:

$$r_\$(t) = \frac{S(t-1)}{S(t)} [1 + r(t)] - 1 ,$$

where $S(t) \equiv$ spot exchange rate (yen/dollar, telegraphic transfer mid rate) at the end of month t. Translation using spot rate creates an easily attainable strategy for U.S. investors. Because of the depreciation of the dollar over the entire period, especially after 1984, the dollar-translated Japanese returns are uniformly higher than their yen-term returns.

Figure 2 shows cumulative wealth index values in dollar terms for stocks.

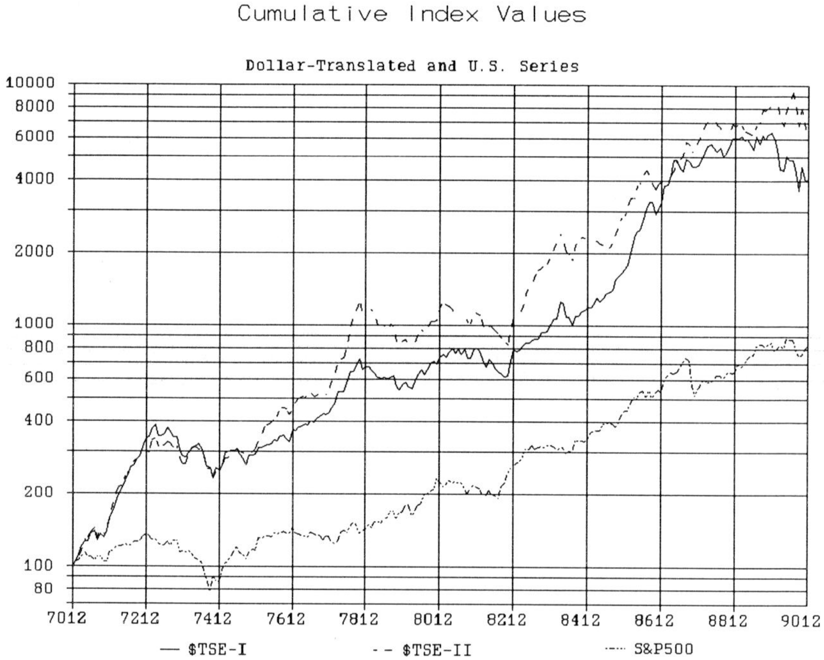

Figure 2

7. Summary Statistics

Summary statistics for monthly returns and for the U.S. data for the same period are shown in Table 2. Correlation matrices and autocorrelations with one lag for monthly returns are shown in Tables 3-1 and 3-2. The U.S. data are taken from Ibbotson Associates (1991).

III. Component Returns

Having described basic return series of financial assets, I can derive separate components of the returns, following the procedure established by Ibbotson and Sinquefield for the U.S. data.

I compute the nominal returns (net of inflation) and risk premia observed in the financial market in the following manner:

Equity premium = TSE-I return − Short term interest rate
Bond default premium = LCB return − LGB return
Bond maturity premium = LGB return − Short term interest rate
Inflation-adjusted returns = Returns − Inflation.

Note that the actual computation of these component returns is done using geometric differences, not arithmetic differences, *i.e.*, they are computed as

$$C = (1 + A)/(1 + B) - 1 \quad ,$$

where A and B are basic series and C is a component series.

Tables 4 and 5 present summary statistics. The U.S. data are taken from Ibbotson Associates (1991).

IV. Historical Highlights of Returns

1. Common Stocks

In the period of 1971 - 1990, both common stock indices outperformed other assets (Figure 1 and Table 1-1). The TSE-I and TSE-II achieved the highest cumulative index values of 2559.09 and 3380.53 respectively at the end of 1989. In dollar terms, the contrast with the U.S. indices is quite dramatic: for example, the TSE-I cumulative index value was more than seven times that of the S&P 500 at the end of 1989 (Table 1-2). In 1990, Japanese stock market experienced a stunning loss of 39 percent. Not only was this the largest drop in 39 years, but also it was the first year with a negative return in 13 years. This "crash" brought the wealth level of the TSE-I down to that of 1987.

The TSE-I averaged 1.27% monthly return, which is 0.28 percentage points higher than the U.S. S&P 500 index in the same period (Table 2). The volatility of the TSE-I index is slightly higher than the U.S. figure for this period. The dollar-translated TSE-I and TSE-II index returns are more volatile than the yen returns, but are higher in means as well.

The autocorrelation of the TSE-I returns is quite low (Table 3-1). We cannot reject the hypothesis that the true autocorrelations are zero with 95% confidence level. This suggests that the TSE-I index returns can be characterized as a random walk.

1976, 1978, 1983 and 1989 were very "good" years for small stocks: the TSE-II index had compounded returns of more than 40% in one year (Appendix). In addition to higher returns, the TSE-II stock returns displayed higher volatility as well (Table 2). The TSE-I and II indices are moderately correlated with each other, but the autocorrelation of the TSE-II index is quite high (Table 3-1). This is not surprising, given the inactive trading for smaller companies. Both stock indices have negative correlations with inflation.

Dollar-translated stock returns show low correlation coefficients with corresponding U.S. returns, suggesting that investment in Japanese equities can provide good diversification for U.S. investors (Table 2).

Equity risk premium, which is often used in the context of the Capital Asset Pricing Model, has monthly figures of 0.60% geometric mean and 0.72% arithmetic mean (Table 4), which is much higher than the U.S. data.

2. Bonds

100 yen invested at the end of 1970 would have become 421 yen for the long-term government bond and 459 yen for the long-term corporate bond (Table 1-1). Both bonds had less volatile returns compared to common stocks, but the long-term government bond returns have slightly higher volatility than the long-term corporate bonds (Table 2).

Both return series display significantly positive serial correlation (Table 3-1). If the inflation is largely unanticipated, negative correlation coefficients of LCB and LGB with inflation seem plausible since bonds are fixed income securities.

Compared with the U.S. data in the same period, both bonds had similar returns and much lower standard deviations (Table 2). Translating bond returns into dollar terms increases the mean return as well as the volatility. Although dollar-translated LCB's and dollar-translated LGB's, U.S. Corporate Bonds and U.S. Government Bonds show high correlation pairwise, dollar-translated bond returns and U.S. bond returns have low correlations (Table 3-2).

3. Short Term Interest Rates and Inflation

The index values for the short-term interest rates and cumulative inflation grew to 372.10 and 282.07, respectively (Table 1-1). The short-term interest rates and U.S. T-bill returns have similar summary statistics, except that the autocorrelation of Japanese rates is close to one, suggesting step-wise movements (Tables 2 and 3-1). The inflation rate is slightly lower in Japan than in the U.S., but it has more variability. Japan had high inflation in 1973 and 1974, but the inflation rate has since come down to a lower level.

V. Conclusion

This paper presented and characterized Japanese financial data for the period 1971-1990 in annual returns and summary statistics. Japanese data were also transformed into dollar terms to provide a comparison with the U.S. data over the same period from the perspective of U.S. investors.

Common stocks follow a random walk and have higher returns than other assets. Small stocks, above all, have even higher returns but also have higher volatility. Bond returns show moderate autocorrelations and less volatility than stocks. Compared with the U.S. series, Japanese common stocks are higher in means and similar in standard deviation. Bonds and short-term interest rates are comparable to the U.S. in both mean returns and standard deviation. Translation to dollar-terms adds more returns as well as more risk. The data show that investment in Japanese securities can provide good diversification for the U.S. investor.

References

Amihud, Yakov and Haim Mendelson, 1989, "Market Microstructure and Price Discovery on the Tokyo Stock Exchange," *Japan and the World Economy*, 1:341-370, reprinted in this volume.

Hamao, Yasushi, 1988, "An Empirical Examination of the Arbitrage Pricing Theory: Using Japanese Data," *Japan and the World Economy*, 1:45-61.

Hamao, Yasushi, 1991, "A Standard Data Base for the Analysis of Japanese Security Markets," *Journal of Business*, 64:87-102.

Ibbotson, Roger G. and Sinquefield, Rex A, 1976, "Stocks, Bonds, Bills, and Inflation: Year-by-Year Historical Returns (1926 - 1974)," *Journal of Business*, 49:11-47.

Ibbotson Associates, 1991, *SBBI Yearbook*, Chicago, IL.

Japan Securities Research Institute, 1988, *Securities Market in Japan*, Tokyo.

Stigum, Marcia, 1983, *The Money Market*, Homewood, IL.: Dow Jones-Irwin.

Toyo Keizai Shimpo Sha, 1988, *Kigyo Keiretsu Soran*, Tokyo.

Table 1-1

Cumulative Index Values

Basic Series

	TSE-I	TSE-I	TSE-II	LCB	LGB	STInt	Infl
1951	100.00						
1952	221.08						
1953	231.81						
1954	228.08						
1955	314.21						
1956	441.05						
1957	397.83						
1958	586.16						
1959	810.68						
1960	1190.87						
1961	1147.43						
1962	1195.10						
1963	1168.51						
1964	1225.66						
1965	1518.26						
1966	1683.78						
1967	1604.70						
1968	2194.44						
1969	3130.01						
1970	2697.86	100.00	100.00	100.00	100.00	100.00	100.00
1971	3759.70	139.36	138.77	114.27	106.76	106.61	104.67
1972	7766.64	287.88	249.07	126.16	116.11	111.76	110.68
1973	6044.82	224.06	207.16	120.41	115.89	120.03	130.66
1974	5641.86	209.12	206.83	126.33	122.44	135.97	157.79
1975	6704.76	248.52	262.88	142.57	132.23	151.21	169.97
1976	8131.15	301.39	373.11	158.50	142.97	162.11	188.07
1977	7877.11	291.98	360.71	191.35	173.91	171.74	197.38
1978	9907.92	367.25	621.97	202.97	186.71	180.23	204.88
1979	10340.53	383.29	577.93	205.79	175.57	190.10	216.53
1980	11315.23	419.42	668.01	219.96	187.21	210.51	231.28
1981	13324.81	493.90	686.96	247.63	213.27	226.38	241.90
1982	14144.38	524.28	707.24	269.85	235.09	241.95	246.79
1983	17740.62	657.58	1275.10	299.83	261.41	257.85	250.91
1984	22443.79	831.91	1555.33	328.04	298.11	274.27	257.61
1985	26106.98	967.69	1611.40	359.77	335.40	292.23	261.22
1986	39052.60	1447.54	1757.23	404.63	370.17	307.41	260.43
1987	42578.94	1578.25	2015.09	440.00	404.00	319.48	262.49
1988	56949.33	2110.84	2355.33	475.36	431.91	332.18	264.81
1989	69045.37	2559.09	3380.53	467.65	423.85	347.75	271.74
1990	41882.97	1552.35	2353.04	458.89	421.29	372.10	282.07

Table 1-2

Cumulative Index Values

Dollar-Translated and U.S. Series

	TSE-I	TSE-II	LCB	LGB	STInt	Infl	S&P500	USLCB	USLGB	USTBill	USInfl
1970	100.00	100.00	100.00	100.00	100.00	100.00	100.00	100.00	100.00	100.00	100.00
1971	158.01	157.34	129.57	121.05	120.88	118.68	114.31	111.01	113.23	104.39	103.36
1972	340.65	294.73	149.29	137.40	132.25	130.97	136.00	119.07	119.66	108.39	106.89
1973	286.44	264.83	153.94	148.16	153.44	167.04	116.06	120.43	118.33	115.91	116.29
1974	249.02	246.29	150.43	145.80	161.92	187.89	85.34	116.74	123.48	125.18	130.48
1975	291.52	308.37	167.24	155.11	177.38	199.38	117.10	133.84	134.84	132.45	139.63
1976	369.02	456.83	194.06	175.05	198.48	230.27	145.02	158.79	157.43	139.18	146.35
1977	435.38	537.88	285.33	259.33	256.09	294.32	134.60	161.51	156.37	146.31	156.26
1978	676.22	1145.23	373.73	343.80	331.86	377.25	143.43	161.40	154.56	156.81	170.36
1979	571.66	861.95	306.93	261.86	283.53	322.94	169.87	154.65	152.68	173.08	193.03
1980	718.67	1144.63	376.89	320.79	360.72	396.31	224.95	150.60	146.64	192.53	216.96
1981	803.24	1117.20	402.73	346.84	368.16	393.40	213.90	149.15	149.35	220.85	236.36
1982	796.04	1073.83	409.73	356.96	367.36	374.71	259.70	214.46	209.61	244.13	245.51
1983	1012.61	1963.53	461.71	402.55	397.07	386.37	318.17	224.54	211.03	265.61	254.83
1984	1186.15	2217.61	467.73	425.05	391.06	367.30	338.11	261.34	243.60	291.77	264.90
1985	1728.90	2878.96	642.78	599.22	522.10	466.71	446.83	342.11	319.03	314.31	274.89
1986	3254.01	3950.18	901.84	825.05	691.04	585.44	529.37	410.01	396.99	333.68	278.00
1987	4664.97	5956.18	1300.55	1194.14	944.31	775.85	557.06	408.91	386.28	351.91	290.93
1988	6040.28	6739.98	1360.28	1235.93	950.56	757.76	650.69	452.68	423.90	374.25	303.08
1989	6367.01	8410.75	1163.50	1054.54	865.19	676.09	855.60	526.16	500.68	405.58	317.17
1990	4088.36	6197.09	1208.55	1109.53	979.98	745.91	828.46	561.84	531.64	437.27	336.54

Table 2

Summary Statistics, Basic Series (1971-1990). Monthly (%).

Variable	Arithmetic Mean	Geometric Mean	Standard Deviation
TSE-I Index (Total Return)	1.27	1.15	4.92
$-Translated TSE-I Index (Total Return)	1.75	1.56	6.28
S & P 500 Index (Total Return)	0.99	0.88	4.66
TSE-I Index (Income)	0.14	0.14	0.27
S & P 500 Index (Income)	0.35	0.35	0.23
TSE-I Index (Capital Appreciation)	1.13	1.01	4.90
S & P 500 Index (Capital Appreciation)	0.64	0.53	4.65
TSE-II Index (Total Return)	1.46	1.32	5.10
$-Translated TSE-II Index (Total Return)	1.93	1.73	6.28
TSE-II Index (Income)	0.11	0.11	0.20
TSE-II Index (Capital Appreciation)	1.34	1.21	5.10
Long-Term Corporate Bonds	0.65	0.64	1.28
$-Translated LCB	1.12	1.04	3.96
U.S. Long-Term Corporate Bonds	0.77	0.72	3.11
Long-Term Government Bonds	0.62	0.60	1.74
$-Translated LGB	1.11	1.01	4.38
U.S. Long-Term Government Bonds	0.75	0.70	3.30
Short-Term Interest Rate	0.55	0.55	0.20
$-Translated STInt	1.01	0.96	3.36
U.S. Treasury Bills	0.62	0.62	0.22
Inflation	0.44	0.43	0.80
U.S. Inflation	0.51	0.51	0.35
TSE-I Index (Total Return), 1952-1990	1.43	1.30	5.17

Table 3-1

Correlation Matrix and Autocorrelations

1971 - 1990 (Monthly)

Basic Series

	TSE-I	TSE-II	LCB	LGB	STInt	Infl
TSE-I	1.000					
TSE-II	0.626	1.000				
LCB	0.349	0.163	1.000			
LGB	0.310	0.055	0.810	1.000		
STInt	-0.114	-0.073	0.030	0.025	1.000	
Infl	-0.087	-0.077	-0.118	-0.085	0.349	1.000
Autocorr	0.041	0.228*	0.281*	0.156*	0.974*	0.278*

(Asterisks indicate significance at 5% level)

TSE-I (1952-1990)	
Autocorr	0.042

Table 3-2

Correlation Matrix and Autocorrelations

1971 - 1990 (Monthly)

Dollar-Translated Series and U.S. Series

	$TSE-I	$TSE-II	$LCB	$LGB	$STInt	S&P	USLCB	USLGB	USTBill	USInfl
$TSE-I	1.000									
$TSE-II	0.759	1.000								
$LCB	0.666	0.587	1.000							
$LGB	0.657	0.546	0.974	1.000						
$STInt	0.610	0.573	0.950	0.928	1.000					
S&P	0.270	0.223	0.042	0.019	-0.015	1.000				
USLCB	0.099	0.065	0.198	0.214	0.136	0.372	1.000			
USLGB	0.131	0.071	0.201	0.226	0.122	0.349	0.929	1.000		
USTBill	-0.175	-0.188	-0.142	-0.109	-0.117	-0.084	0.056	0.077	1.000	
USInfl	-0.229	-0.183	-0.192	-0.180	-0.094	-0.205	-0.187	-0.202	0.359	1.000
Autocorr	0.064	0.219*	0.105	0.106	0.046	0.020	0.116	0.060	0.914	0.632*

(Asterisks indicate significance at 5% level)

Table 4

Summary Statistics, Risk Premia (1971-1990). Monthly (%).

Numbers in parentheses are U.S. data for 1971-1990.

Variable	Arithmetic Mean	Geometric Mean	Standard Deviation
Equity Risk Premium	0.72 (0.38	0.60 0.27	4.92 4.65)
Bond Default Premium	0.04 (0.03	0.04 0.02	1.02 1.21)
Bond Maturity Premium	0.07 (0.13	0.05 0.08	1.74 3.27)

Glossary:

Equity Risk Premium = (1 + Tokyo Stock Exchange Section I Index Return)/(1 + Short-Term Interest Rate) − 1

Bond Default Premium = (1 + Long-Term Corporate Bonds Return)/(1 + Long-Term Government Bonds Return) − 1

Bond Maturity Premium = (1 + Long-Term Government Bonds Return)/(1 + Short-Term Interest Rate) − 1

Table 5

Summary Statistics, Inflation-Adjusted Series (1971-1990). Monthly (%).

Variable	Arithmetic Mean	Geometric Mean	Standard Deviation
TSE-I Index	0.82	0.69	5.03
S & P 500 Index	0.49	0.38	4.71
TSE-II Index	1.05	0.91	5.19
Long-Term Corporate Bonds	0.20	0.19	1.56
U.S. Long-Term Corporate Bonds	0.26	0.21	3.18
Long-Term Government Bonds	0.18	0.16	1.96
U.S. Long-Term Government Bonds	0.25	0.19	3.38
Short-Term Interest Rate	0.11	0.11	0.75
U.S. Treasury Bills	0.11	0.11	0.34

Inflation-adjusted Series are defined as (1 + Total Return)/(1 + Inflation) − 1 for each series.

Appendix

Annual Percentage Returns[1]

	TSE-I Total Ret	TSE-II TR	LCB TR	LGB TR	STInt TR	Infl	$TSE-I TR	$TSE-II TR	$LCB TR	$LGB TR	$STInt TR	$Infl
1952	121.08											
1953	4.85											
1954	-1.61											
1955	37.76											
1956	40.37											
1957	-9.80											
1958	47.34											
1959	38.30											
1960	46.90											
1961	-3.65											
1962	4.15											
1963	-2.22											
1964	4.89											
1965	23.87											
1966	10.90											
1967	-4.70											
1968	36.75											
1969	42.63											
1970	-13.81											
1971	39.36	38.77	14.27	6.76	6.61	4.67	58.01	57.34	29.57	21.05	20.88	18.68
1972	106.58	79.48	10.40	8.76	4.83	5.74	115.59	87.31	15.22	13.50	9.40	10.36
1973	22.17	-16.83	-4.56	-0.19	7.40	18.05	-15.92	-10.15	3.11	7.83	16.03	27.54
1974	-6.67	-0.16	4.91	5.65	13.28	20.76	-13.06	-7.00	-2.28	-1.59	5.52	12.49
1975	18.84	27.10	12.85	7.99	11.21	7.72	17.07	25.21	11.17	6.38	9.55	6.11
1976	21.27	41.93	11.17	8.12	7.20	10.65	26.58	48.14	16.04	12.86	11.90	15.49
1977	-3.12	-3.32	20.73	21.64	5.94	4.95	17.98	17.74	47.03	48.14	29.03	27.81
1978	25.78	72.43	6.07	7.36	4.94	3.80	55.32	112.92	30.98	32.57	29.58	28.18
1979	4.37	-7.08	1.39	-5.97	5.48	5.68	-15.46	-24.74	-17.87	-23.83	-14.56	-14.40
1980	9.43	15.59	6.88	6.63	10.74	6.82	25.72	32.79	22.79	22.50	27.22	22.72
1981	17.76	2.84	12.58	13.92	7.54	4.59	11.77	-2.40	6.85	8.12	2.06	-0.73
1982	6.15	2.95	8.97	10.23	6.88	2.02	-0.90	-3.88	1.74	2.92	-0.22	-4.75
1983	25.43	80.29	11.11	11.19	6.57	1.67	27.21	82.85	12.69	12.77	8.09	3.11
1984	26.51	21.98	9.41	14.04	6.37	2.67	17.14	12.94	1.30	5.59	-1.51	-4.94
1985	16.32	3.60	9.67	12.51	6.55	1.40	45.76	29.82	37.43	40.98	33.51	27.06
1986	49.59	9.05	12.47	10.37	5.19	-0.30	86.61	36.04	40.30	37.69	31.23	24.37
1987	9.03	14.67	8.74	9.14	3.93	0.79	42.30	49.67	41.93	42.44	35.64	31.55
1988	33.75	16.88	8.04	6.91	3.98	0.88	29.48	13.16	4.59	3.50	0.66	-2.33
1989	21.24	43.53	-1.62	-1.87	4.68	0.26	5.41	24.79	-14.47	-14.68	-8.98	-2.33
1990	-39.34	-30.39	-1.87	-0.60	7.00	3.80	-35.79	-26.32	3.87	5.22	13.27	6.11

---

1 TSE-I: value-weighted Tokyo Stock Exchange Section One index;
TSE-II: value-weighted Tokyo Stock Exchange Section Two index;
LCB: long-term corporate bond index;
LGB: long-term government bond index;
STInt: short-term interest rate; and
Infl: inflation rate.
"$" denotes dollar-translated series.

Japanese Financial Market Research
W.T. Ziemba, W. Bailey and Y. Hamao (Editors)

The Japanese Stock Market: 1949-1991*

Sandra L. Schwartz
Faculty of Business Administration, Simon Fraser University, Burnaby, B.C.

William T. Ziemba
Faculty of Commerce, University of British Columbia, Vancouver, B.C. V6T 1Y8

Abstract
This paper discusses the historical record of the Japanese stock market from its postwar restart in 1949 to February 1991 measured by the Nikkei 225 Stock Average and the Topix. The various declines of 10% or more are studied. Simple interest rate models are briefly considered as valuation measures.

Introduction

Since 1980 the transfer of relative wealth to Japan from the U.S and other countries has been very large. This can be seen by comparing the world stock market capitalizations in October 1980 and September 1988. Europe's share of the world's stock markets stayed about constant (21% in 1988 versus 20% in 1980), the U.S. share dropped from 53% to 31% and the rest of the world's fell to 6% compared to 12% in 1980. Meanwhile, Japan's share increased from 15% to 42%. When adjusted for cross holdings, these values are 22.2% for Europe, 32.6% for the U.S., 39.0% for Japan and 6.2% for the rest of the world as of the end of 1988, see McDonald (1989). Net assets of Japan were $11.5 billion at the end of 1980 and those of the U.S. were $106.3 billion. By 1987 Japan's net assets grew over 20 fold to $240.7 billion. Meanwhile U.S. private and public assets fell by a negative $368.2 billion. There is much talk in the press about the U.S. trade and budget deficits. Indeed, the public deficit was $148.9 billion at the end of 1987. But the private sector of the U.S. was also $219.3 billion in the red.

The Nikkei stock average (NSA) is a price-weighted index, similar to the Dow Jones industrial average. The NSA is computed by adding the prices of 225 stocks traded on the first section of the Tokyo stock exchange (TSE) and dividing by a

---

* This research was partially supported by the Social and Humanities Research Council and the Center for International Business Studies at the University of British Columbia.

divisor that changes over time due to stock splits, rights issues, etc. At the end of December 1989, the divisor was 10.198. Table 1 gives the relative growth in value of the NSA since 1949 in yen and in U.S. dollars starting from 1¥ in 1949. The first section of the TSE amounts to about 86% of the trading value and volume on the eight stock exchanges in Japan. The index is tilted toward heavy industrials consisting of chemical, steel, and textile stocks, which have traditionally been the mainstay of the Japanese economy. Electronics and other recently developing industries are underweighted relative to their current capitalization and importance in the economy valuation measures.

The market value of the 225 Nikkei stocks amounts to about 50% of the market value of all stocks in the first section. These stocks account for about 75% of the trading volume on the first section of the TSE.

At the end of December 1989, the NSA was ¥38,915.87. The meaning of ¥38,915.87 is as follows. Suppose one had bought one share of each of the 225 component stocks listed on the Tokyo Stock Exchange at the time of the post-war inauguration of the exchange (May 16, 1949), then held them until the end of December 1989 without putting additional funds into new shares issued through rights offerings to shareholders. Instead one had reinvested the value of every right evenly in all of the component stocks. The average price would then have increased from ¥176.21 on the date of the original investment to ¥38,915.87 or 220.84 times, not counting dividends nor taxes. Total returns including dividends are discussed later in this paper. In U.S. dollar terms, the average increased a remarkable 553.04 times. Even after the steep decline in 1990, the value of each $1 invested in the NSA in 1949 was worth $405 at the end of February 1991.

The NSA suffers from the same criticisms as the Dow Jones industrial average. It is not a true representation of the real market because it only has a small percentage of all the stocks on the TSE, and, in addition, the price weighting scheme is not as representative a measure as value-weighting. Topix is the value-weighted average of the prices of all 1229 stocks (autumn 1990 count) on the first section of the TSE. The larger capitalized stocks tend to have higher prices. At the end of October 1989 the Topix average was 2693 compared to an equally weighted average of about 1796. See the last column in table 2. Compensation is made via an adjustment to the base value for any corporate activities that affect the current market value other than price changes, such as new listings, assignment of stocks from the second section to first section and vice versa, delisting, rights offering, public offerings, private placements, mergers, exercises of stock, subscription warrants, or conversion of convertible bonds or preferred stock into common stock.

Table 1
Yearly Yen Closing Prices of the NSA and Yen/Dollar Exchange Rates, 1949-91 (Feb)

			Current Value of	
End of Year	NSA	Yen/$	1¥ invested in 1949 in ¥	1$ invested in 1949 in$
1949	109.9	360.00	0.62	0.62
1950	101.9	360.00	0.58	0.58
1951	166.1	360.00	0.94	0.94
1952	362.6	360.00	2.06	2.06
1953	377.9	360.00	2.14	2.14
1954	356.1	360.00	2.02	2.02
1955	425.7	360.00	2.42	2.42
1956	549.1	360.00	3.12	3.12
1957	474.5	360.00	2.69	2.69
1958	666.5	360.00	3.78	3.78
1959	874.9	360.00	4.97	4.97
1960	1356.7	360.00	7.70	7.70
1961	1432.6	360.00	8.13	8.13
1962	1420.4	360.00	8.06	8.06
1963	1225.1	360.00	6.95	6.95
1964	1216.5	360.00	6.90	6.90
1965	1417.8	360.00	8.05	8.05
1966	1452.1	360.00	8.24	8.24
1967	1283.5	360.00	7.28	7.28
1968	1714.9	360.00	9.73	9.73
1969	2359.0	360.00	13.39	13.39
1970	1987.1	360.00	11.28	11.28
1971	2713.7	314.80	15.40	17.61
1972	5207.9	302.00	29.56	35.23
1973	4306.8	280.00	24.44	31.42
1974	3817.2	300.95	21.66	25.91
1975	4358.6	305.15	24.74	29.18
1976	4990.8	292.80	28.32	34.82
1977	4865.6	240.00	27.61	41.42
1978	6001.8	194.60	34.06	63.01
1979	6569.5	239.70	37.28	55.99
1980	7116.4	203.00	40.39	71.62
1981	7681.8	219.90	43.59	71.37
1982	8016.7	235.00	45.50	69.69
1983	9893.8	232.20	56.15	87.05
1984	11542.6	251.10	65.50	93.91
1985	13113.3	200.50	74.42	133.62
1986	18701.3	160.05	106.13	238.72
1987	21564.0	123.00	122.38	358.18
1988	30159.0	125.85	171.15	489.59
1989	38915.9	143.76	220.84	553.04
1990	23848.7	135.40	135.34	359.83
1991 (Feb)	26409.2	133.17	149.87	405.15

Source: Tokyo Stock Exchange

Table 2
Tokyo Stock Price Index (TOPIX) 1949-1991

	Year-End	High Index	High Date	Low Index	Low Date	Arithmetic Average all TSE-I Stocks for year*
1949	12.85	22.06	May 16	11.95	Dec 14	
1950	11.57	13.24	Aug 21	9.59	July 3	
1951	16.94	17.11	Oct 20	11.58	Jan 4	
1952	33.35	33.55	Nov 22	17.07	Jan 8	
1953	33.30	42.18	Feb 4	28.46	Apr 1	
1954	30.27	33.22	Jan 11	26.79	Nov 13	
1955	39.06	39.06	Dec 28	30.00	Mar 28	
1956	51.21	52.95	Dec 6	38.81	Jan 25	
1957	43.40	54.82	Jan 21	43.18	Dec 27	
1958	60.95	60.95	Dec 27	43.48	Jan 4	
1959	80.00	90.14	Nov 30	61.11	Jan 9	
1960	109.18	112.53	Nov 15	79.46	Jan 4	
1961	101.66	126.59	July 14	90.86	Dec 19	
1962	99.67	111.45	Feb 14	83.39	Oct 30	
1963	92.87	122.96	May 10	91.21	Dec 18	
1964	90.68	103.77	July 3	87.94	Nov 11	
1965	105.68	105.68	Dec 28	81.29	July 15	
1966	111.41	114.51	Mar 24	105.21	Jan 19	
1967	100.89	117.60	May 31	99.17	Dec 11	
1968	131.31	142.95	Oct 2	100.00	Jan 4	125.81
1969	179.30	179.30	Dec 27	132.62	Jan 4	171.65
1970	148.35	185.70	Apr 8	147.08	Dec 9	181.58
1971	199.45	209.00	Aug 14	148.05	Jan 6	184.70
1972	401.70	401.70	Dec 28	199.93	Jan 4	270.98
1973	306.44	422.48	Jan 24	284.69	Dec 18	309.10
1974	278.34	342.47	June 5	251.96	Oct 9	267.56
1975	323.43	333.11	July 2	268.24	Jan 10	268.95
1976	383.88	383.88	Dec.28	326.28	Jan 5	307.48
1977	364.08	390.93	Sept 29	350.49	Nov 24	320.77
1978	449.55	452.60	Dec13	364.04	Jan 4	365.68
1979	459.61	465.24	Sept 29	435.13	July 13	383.93
1980	494.10	497.96	Oct.20	449.01	Mar 10	382.92
1981	570.31	603.92	Aug.17	495.79	Jan 5	406.35
1982	593.72	593.72	Dec.28	511.52	Aug 17	381.98
1983	731.82	731.82	Dec 28	574.51	Jan. 25	463.29
1984	913.37	913.37	Dec.28	735.45	Jan 4	603.29
1985	1049.40	1058.35	July 27	916.93	Jan 4	682.47
1986	1556.37	1583.35	Aug 20	1025.85	Jan 21	866.18
1987	1725.83	2258.56	June 11	1557.46	Jan 13	1103.85
1988	2357.03	2357.03	Dec 28	1690.44	Jan 4	1294.17
1989	2867.97	2867.97	Dec 28	2364.33	Mar 27	1785.48
1990	1733.83	2867.70	Jan 4	1523.43	Oct 1	na
1991 (to Feb 27)	1935.37	1935.37	Feb 27	1647.56	Jan 16	na

*not available before 1968
Source: Tokyo Stock Exchange

Table 3
Number of companies, market value, PERs and yields by sector in the Topix, January 17, 1989

Sector	Number of Companies	Market Value (¥ bil)	Prospective Average PER	Weighted Average Yield
Fishery	6	738	132.9	0.44
Mining	7	1,024	86.0	0.45
Construction	91	16,541	54.9	0.62
Foods	55	12,485	58.6	0.52
Textiles	43	8,219	58.4	0.61
Pulp & paper	19	4,401	46.5	0.51
Chemicals	122	32,822	49.9	0.49
Oil & coal products	9	4,928	60.1	0.63
Rubber products	9	2,145	37.5	0.72
Class & ceramics	31	7,425	51.5	0.48
Iron & steel	36	21,526	58.4	0.54
Non-ferrous metals	24	6,764	73.2	0.48
Metal products	22	2,599	40.8	0.41
Machinery	86	12,417	60.6	0.59
Electrical machinery	106	45,325	47.6	0.59
Transportation equip	50	28,364	47.3	0.59
Precision instruments	18	4,231	47.8	0.70
Othermanufacturing	28	6,429	46.5	0.47
Commerce	125	29,999	58.1	0.55
Financial	128	149,964	51.1	0.32
Real estate	18	8,105	73.8	0.36
Land transportation	25	15,910	178.6	0.32
Shipping	14	3,287	-	0.15
Airlines	4	5,430	177.4	0.23
Warehousing	10	1,138	76.6	0.53
Communications	5	12,176	102.9	0.27
Electric power & gas	14	32,758	60.2	0.85
Services	25	3,909	86.1	0.34
Total (First Section)	1,130	481,057	55.8	0.48

Source: Tokyo Stock Exchange

In contrast to the actions above, a corporate decision that entails no change in the market value of shares of the company does not change the basic market value adjustment. Stock splits, capitalization issues (bonus issues), and stock dividends[1] are thus eliminated from the adjustment, as the new stock price multiplied by the increased (or decreased) number of shares is theoretically the same as the old stock price multiplied by the old number of shares. The formula for the adjustment is

[1]Hayashi and Jagannathan (1990) have shown that stock prices for the period 1983 to 1987 did indeed drop by essentially the full amount of the dividend.

$$\text{new base market value} = \text{old base} \times \frac{\text{new market value}}{\text{old market value}} \; .$$

The Topix is a better measure of overall market movements than the S&P 500 in the U.S. The corresponding index measure in the U.S. is the NYFE index which is the value weighted average of all NYSE securities. The Wilshire 5000, which is also value weighted, is broader than the Topix.

In addition to Topix, which covers all common stocks listed on the first section, the TSE computes and publishes the Topix sub-indices for each of 28 industry groups. Table 3 shows the number of companies, their market value, PER and yields by sector as of January 17, 1989.

Topix's initial value was set at 100 on July 4, 1968, and its value at the end of December 1989 was 2867.97, a record close. Before 1968, the Topix traded below 100; it was around 10 near the start of the new phase of the TSE in 1949.

Tables 4A and 5 show the first and second section market rates of return by month from 1952 to 1987 and 1974 to 1987 plus the percent of the return from dividends, which averaged 12.2% and 10.0%, respectively. Table 4B has the first section rates of return by holding period for 1952 to 1987. Table 6 has the mean daily return, standard deviation and percent positive returns by month for the NSA225 from 1949 to 1988.

Table 4A
First Section Market Rate Return of Month, 1952-1987

	Jan	Feb	Mar	Apr	May	Jun	Jul	Aug	Sep	Oct	Nov	Dec	VWI	EWI	Size	% from Div
1952	13.2	-3.9	1.5	12.9	11.2	9.2	3.8	2.1	8.1	12.3	12.2	1.3	-	-	-	-
1953	21.9	-11.0	-17.0	5.8	-4.5	4.2	9.4	4.9	12.0	-4.3	-2.2	-8.1	56.7	51.1	-5.6	17.4
1954	-6.3	-0.4	-5.6	5.5	-6.2	7.1	-4.7	4.2	2.2	-6.0	1.0	9.3	-6.9	-15.4	-8.5	-111.7
1955	3.2	1.6	-1.3	-0.9	1.9	1.4	5.2	6.6	2.7	6.7	-2.9	9.1	24.4	22.7	1.7	36.5
1956	0.2	3.6	5.7	3.8	4.7	2.4	0.8	-1.1	1.3	3.8	10.7	-0.9	47.8	52.1	4.3	17.3
1957	3.8	0.0	3.3	0.7	-10.8	0.0	-6.4	7.6	2.0	-3.7	-3.1	-2.5	16.2	18.0	1.8	42.7
1958	9.4	0.6	1.9	4.3	1.5	4.0	-2.4	4.3	0.9	4.8	3.7	6.7	15.8	8.5	-7.3	43.7
1959	4.6	3.2	9.1	-2.8	9.1	0.8	4.4	2.6	6.7	4.8	3.5	-11.4	57.0	53.8	-3.2	11.2
1960	6.9	3.7	8.5	4.5	-10.7	10.9	0.8	6.3	5.7	-0.1	1.2	3.1	39.0	43.1	4.0	12.6
1961	6.4	0.4	3.5	0.9	-0.7	4.7	-1.4	-8.6	-3.2	-12.6	0.6	8.2	25.7	60.7	35.0	17.7
1962	5.3	-2.3	-3.0	-3.4	-0.6	5.6	-1.3	0.7	-7.9	-3.4	17.2	-0.8	-4.8	-4.8	0.0	-93.6
1963	4.4	3.5	12.9	1.3	-1.5	0.0	-11.8	-0.4	-2.9	1.7	-5.1	2.5	19.1	10.5	-8.6	29.2
1964	8.3	-4.5	-1.0	-0.2	8.2	3.2	-2.3	-2.5	-2.6	3.1	0.0	2.3	-3.9	-13.0	-9.1	-133.7
1965	4.5	-0.5	-4.7	3.0	-5.3	-1.3	3.7	11.9	-1.6	0.8	7.3	5.3	5.7	-2.8	-8.5	102.2
1966	2.4	1.9	5.0	-0.7	-2.1	-0.4	2.5	-0.2	0.7	-0.4	-2.0	4.9	28.3	28.4	0.1	19.8
1967	2.0	1.4	-0.7	-0.1	5.2	-0.7	-0.6	-8.1	-0.3	3.7	-5.7	0.0	6.1	7.0	0.9	81.3
1968	2.7	1.9	2.8	4.6	1.8	4.8	5.4	6.0	9.8	-5.7	-1.0	-0.4	16.1	17.9	1.8	32.3
1969	5.7	-2.0	7.2	2.3	8.0	-2.7	-5.0	2.7	7.8	2.2	4.8	6.2	37.3	30.0	-7.3	13.2
1970	-1.9	1.5	5.5	-13.0	-2.5	1.6	1.6	-1.8	-2.1	2.3	-4.2	-0.3	12.3	17.4	5.1	33.2
1971	5.0	6.1	8.1	5.4	0.3	7.8	2.2	-13.0	5.1	-5.2	6.4	8.2	19.8	14.9	-4.9	22.1
1972	5.8	6.3	7.2	5.1	8.6	4.2	8.5	2.1	6.0	2.0	11.7	7.5	72.1	69.6	-2.5	5.0
1973	0.7	-3.3	2.1	-10.5	0.7	1.4	5.8	-3.1	-4.9	0.7	-7.6	-5.5	30.3	25.7	-4.6	7.8
1974	5.5	0.6	-0.6	3.3	3.6	-2.3	-3.9	-8.1	-2.5	-8.0	10.0	-3.0	-11.4	-1.4	10.0	-18.3
1975	3.8	8.6	4.6	0.2	-0.4	2.7	-4.2	-3.7	-3.9	8.9	0.4	1.8	5.9	5.1	-0.8	40.9
1976	6.0	-0.5	0.8	0.5	1.3	3.3	-2.7	2.8	0.7	-1.6	-1.6	11.2	16.1	20.4	4.3	14.8
1977	-2.3	2.0	-1.0	1.4	-0.6	-0.2	-1.4	4.8	1.1	-3.6	-2.1	-1.0	11.7	11.2	-0.5	18.4
1978	5.0	2.5	5.1	0.5	0.1	1.8	1.5	0.2	3.1	0.8	0.9	1.8	15.0	22.5	7.5	14.4
1979	3.0	-3.0	1.0	0.5	-0.5	-0.4	-0.5	2.1	3.0	-3.4	0.4	2.2	10.8	12.1	1.3	18.2
1980	1.8	0.1	-2.1	3.0	0.0	1.1	-0.4	1.8	2.7	1.6	-0.5	0.3	8.5	6.1	-2.4	21.8
1981	3.2	-0.4	5.4	5.9	-0.1	4.7	1.1	-0.4	-6.1	0.5	0.4	2.9	21.0	6.3	-14.7	9.2
1982	2.2	-1.8	-3.0	2.4	0.1	-1.3	-1.5	-0.1	-0.6	3.6	6.6	2.7	2.1	-1.1	-3.2	85.9
1983	-0.9	0.7	5.0	2.4	0.8	3.1	1.5	2.0	2.4	-0.8	0.4	6.5	23.0	22.7	-0.3	7.8
1984	6.2	-0.1	12.8	-1.0	-10.0	2.6	-4.0	7.0	1.2	4.6	1.8	4.3	29.4	26.4	-3.0	5.2
1985	2.0	5.0	2.7	3.2	3.1	3.2	-3.4	2.4	1.3	0.0	-1.7	4.1	27.0	27.3	0.3	4.7
1986	-0.7	4.8	16.5	-1.1	4.0	4.4	5.2	8.2	-1.6	-7.2	7.1	3.3	40.1	37.2	-2.9	2.7
1987	13.0	1.3	4.6	11.1	3.3	-5.0	-1.2	6.9	-0.6	-10.3	-3.5	-6.5	46.1	33.2	-12.9	1.7
Mean	4.3	0.8	2.9	1.7	0.6	2.4	0.1	1.4	1.3	-0.2	1.8	2.1	21.7	20.7	-0.9	12.4

Source: Japan Securities Research Institute (1988)

Table 4B: First Section Market Rate of Return by Simple Buy and Hold StrategyYearly Holding Periods,

Year Bought \ Sold	1953	1954	1955	1956	1957	1958	1959	1960	1961	1962	1963	1964	1965	1966	1967	1968	1969	1970
1952	57.1.	14.9	17.7	24.7	23.2	21.3	25.8	28.9	31.5	28.3	25.5	21.5	19.7	20.5	19.5	19.7	20.5	20.1
1953	-	-15.4	2.5	16.9	17.1	15.6	21.5	25.3	28.7	25.2	22.4	18.4	16.6	17.6	16.7	16.9	17.9	17.7
1954	-	-	22.7	38.0	31.4	25.1	30.9	34.1	37.2	31.6	27.5	22.3	19.8	20.7	19.6	19.6	20.6	120.1
1955	-	-	-	52.1	35.0	25.4	32.8	36.8	40.4	33.5	28.5	22.6	19.7	20.5	19.4	19.5	20.5	19.8
1956	-	-	-	-	18.0	13.8	26.7	32.9	38.0	30.8	25.6	19.4	16.7	17.9	16.8	17.1	18.4	17.9
1957	-	-	-	-	-	8.5	30.7	37.8	43.0	33.2	26.8	19.6	16.6	18.0	16.7	17.0	18.3	17.8
1958	-	-	-	-	-	-	53.8	52.2	55.1	38.4	29.7	20.7	16.9	18.3	16.9	17.2	18.6	18.1
1959	-	-	-	-	-	-	-	43.1	53.3	32.6	23.8	14.7	11.8	13.7	12.8	13.3	14.9	14.9
1960	-	-	-	-	-	-	-	-	60.7	25.9	18.0	9.0	7.0	9.8	9.2	9.9	11.8	12.2
1961	-	-	-	-	-	-	-	-	-	-4.8	1.7	-2.9	-2.1	3.1	3.6	5.2	8.2	9.1
1962	-	-	-	-	-	-	-	-	-	-	10.5	-0.7	-0.7	5.6	5.7	7.0	9.9	10.7
1963	-	-	-	-	-	-	-	-	-	-	-	-13.0	-7.4	3.5	3.9	6.2	9.9	10.7
1964	-	-	-	-	-	-	-	-	-	-	-	-	-2.8	12.4	9.9	11.7	15.7	5.7
1965	-	-	-	-	-	-	-	-	-	-	-	-	-	28.4	16.9	17.3	21.5	20.4
1966	-	-	-	-	-	-	-	-	-	-	-	-	-	-	7.0	12.6	19.7	18.9
1967	-	-	-	-	-	-	-	-	-	-	-	-	-	-	-	17.9	26.8	22.9
1968	-	-	-	-	-	-	-	-	-	-	-	-	-	-	-	-	30.0	23.6
1969	-	-	-	-	-	-	-	-	-	-	-	-	-	-	-	-	-	17.4
1970	-	-	-	-	-	-	-	-	-	-	-	-	-	-	-	-	-	-
1971	-	-	-	-	-	-	-	-	-	-	-	-	-	-	-	-	-	-
1972	-	-	-	-	-	-	-	-	-	-	-	-	-	-	-	-	-	-
1973	-	-	-	-	-	-	-	-	-	-	-	-	-	-	-	-	-	-
1974	-	-	-	-	-	-	-	-	-	-	-	-	-	-	-	-	-	-
1975	-	-	-	-	-	-	-	-	-	-	-	-	-	-	-	-	-	-
1976	-	-	-	-	-	-	-	-	-	-	-	-	-	-	-	-	-	-
1977	-	-	-	-	-	-	-	-	-	-	-	-	-	-	-	-	-	-
1978	-	-	-	-	-	-	-	-	-	-	-	-	-	-	-	-	-	-
1979	-	-	-	-	-	-	-	-	-	-	-	-	-	-	-	-	-	-
1980	-	-	-	-	-	-	-	-	-	-	-	-	-	-	-	-	-	-
1981	-	-	-	-	-	-	-	-	-	-	-	-	-	-	-	-	-	-
1982	-	-	-	-	-	-	-	-	-	-	-	-	-	-	-	-	-	-
1983	-	-	-	-	-	-	-	-	-	-	-	-	-	-	-	-	-	-
1984	-	-	-	-	-	-	-	-	-	-	-	-	-	-	-	-	-	-
1985	-	-	-	-	-	-	-	-	-	-	-	-	-	-	-	-	-	-
1986	-	-	-	-	-	-	-	-	-	-	-	-	-	-	-	-	-	-

Table 4B: (Concluded) 1971-1986

Year Bought \ Sold	1971	1972	1973	1974	1975	1976	1977	1978	1979	1980	1981	1982	1983	1984	1985	1986	1987
1952	19.9	21.6	21.0	19.4	18.8	18.6	18.4	18.4	18.0	17.5	17.4	16.9	17.1	17.3	17.5	17.9	18.5
1953	17.5	19.3	19.1	17.7	17.1	17.0	16.8	16.9	16.6	16.2	16.0	15.5	15.7	15.9	16.2	16.7	17.3
1954	19.6	21.4	21.3	19.6	18.9	18.7	18.4	18.4	18.1	17.6	17.4	16.8	16.9	17.2	17.4	17.8	18.3
1955	19.3	21.3	21.3	19.5	18.7	18.6	18.3	18.3	17.9	17.5	17.3	16.6	16.7	17.0	17.2	17.7	18.2
1956	17.5	19.7	19.7	18.0	17.3	17.2	17.0	17.0	16.7	16.3	16.1	15.5	15.7	16.0	16.3	16.9	17.5
1957	17.5	20.0	20.0	18.2	17.4	17.2	17.0	17.0	16.7	16.3	16.1	15.4	15.7	16.0	16.4	16.9	17.6
1958	17.8	20.6	20.8	18.7	17.7	17.5	17.2	17.2	16.9	16.4	16.2	15.4	15.7	16.1	16.4	17.0	17.7
1959	15.1	18.5	18.9	16.9	15.8	15.6	15.4	15.4	15.2	14.8	14.5	13.9	14.2	14.7	15.3	16.0	16.8
1960	12.9	17.0	17.6	15.6	14.4	14.1	14.0	14.1	14.0	13.7	13.4	12.9	13.1	13.8	14.5	15.3	16.2
1961	10.2	15.0	16.0	13.9	12.7	12.6	12.5	12.6	12.6	12.4	12.2	11.7	12.0	12.7	13.6	14.3	15.4
1962	11.7	17.1	18.3	15.8	14.3	14.0	13.7	13.8	13.8	13.6	13.2	12.5	12.8	13.5	14.3	15.0	16.0
1963	11.6	17.1	18.2	15.7	14.2	14.0	13.7	13.8	13.8	13.5	13.1	12.4	12.7	13.4	14.1	14.8	15.8
1964	15.8	21.3	21.8	18.7	16.8	16.5	16.0	16.1	15.8	15.4	14.8	14.0	14.2	14.8	15.5	16.2	17.1
1965	19.0	24.9	25.1	21.3	19.0	18.5	17.8	17.8	17.4	16.8	16.1	15.1	15.3	15.9	16.5	17.1	18.0
1966	17.3	24.5	25.0	20.8	18.2	17.6	16.9	17.2	16.7	16.1	15.4	14.1	14.7	15.5	16.1	16.8	17.8
1967	20.5	28.5	28.1	22.8	19.8	19.0	18.1	18.1	17.5	16.8	15.9	14.8	15.2	15.9	16.5	17.3	18.3
1968	20.7	31.6	30.8	24.1	20.2	19.3	18.2	18.2	17.6	16.9	15.8	14.5	14.9	15.7	16.4	17.3	18.4
1969	17.0	33.7	32.9	24.4	19.6	18.6	17.6	17.7	17.2	16.4	15.0	13.7	14.1	15.0	15.7	16.8	17.8
1970	14.9	40.9	36.8	25.2	19.6	18.8	17.6	17.8	17.1	16.1	14.9	13.4	14.1	15.1	15.7	16.8	17.8
1971	-	69.6	48.6	29.2	20.8	20.0	18.3	18.5	17.7	16.6	15.2	13.6	14.5	15.6	16.0	16.9	17.8
1972	-	-	25.7	11.5	7.9	10.5	10.7	12.4	12.2	11.6	10.9	9.6	11.1	12.5	12.9	14.1	15.1
1973	-	-		-1.4	1.4	7.5	8.6	11.2	10.8	10.1	9.7	8.4	10.2	11.8	12.3	13.7	14.8
1974	-	-	-	-	5.1	13.2	12.8	15.0	13.5	12.2	11.5	9.8	11.6	13.2	13.6	15.2	16.3
1975	-	-	-	-	-	20.4	16.2	18.2	16.1	14.1	12.7	10.6	12.5	14.4	14.9	16.3	17.6
1976	-	-	-	-	-	-	11.2	17.0	15.0	12.9	11.0	9.0	11.1	13.3	14.3	16.0	17.6
1977	-	-	-	-	-	-	-	22.5	17.2	13.8	11.2	8.7	11.2	13.7	14.7	16.5	18.2
1978	-	-	-	-	-	-	-	-	12.1	9.8	8.0	5.6	9.1	12.3	13.7	15.9	17.9
1979	-	-	-	-	-	-	-	-	-	6.1	5.9	3.5	8.3	12.2	13.9	16.7	18.9
1980	-	-	-	-	-	-	-	-	-	-	6.3	2.6	9.3	13.9	15.8	19.0	21.3
1981	-	-	-	-	-	-	-	-	-	-	-	-1.1	10.3	16.1	18.4	21.9	24.3
1982	-	-	-	-	-	-	-	-	-	-	-	-	22.7	25.5	25.4	28.2	29.8
1983	-	-	-	-	-	-	-	-	-	-	-	-	-	26.5	27.2	30.9	32.6
1984	-	-	-	-	-	-	-	-	-	-	-	-	-	-	-27.3	33.6	35.0
1985	-	-	-	-	-	-	-	-	-	-	-	-	-	-	-	37.2	36.7
1986	-	-	-	-	-	-	-	-	-	-	-	-	-	-	-	-	33.2

Source: Japan Securities Research Institute (1988)

Table 5
Second Section Market Rate of Return by Month, 1974-1987

	J	F	M	A	M	J	J	A	S	O	N	D	VWI	EWI	Size Effect	%Ret onDiv
1974	-	-	-	-	-	-	-	-	-	-7.8	3.0	1.3	-	-	-	-
1975	2.3	3.8	2.3	4.3	2.4	1.8	-2.7	-2.2	-2.3	2.8	1.8	3.9	--	-		--
1976	7.4	6.3	7.2	0.5	2.7	2.2	1.0	5.1	-1.1	1.7	-4.5	4.0	41.0	37.8	-3.2	5.3
1977	5.9	0.2	0.0	-0.5	3.3	-2.2	-4.0	0.5	-0.2	-4.9	-3.2	2.2	12.0	17.4	5.4	14.3
1978	9.2	5.3	4.6	2.5	1.9	4.6	8.7	10.6	5.9	1.5	-0.4	1.1	37.9	36.5	-1.4	6.6
1979	5.7	-1.2	0.0	-6.1	-3.0	1.0	-2.9	6.6	-0.7	-7.4	0.3	1.9	19.4	21.7	2.3	96.9
1980	1.1	-2.0	-2.3	0.8	1.2	1.6	1.8	1.1	2.2	0.2	2.7	5.3	1.3	-4.6	-5.9	6.4
1981	7.2	-1.5	-0.9	-1.6	-2.6	5.2	-0.2	-0.9	-5.8	-0.8	1.4	1.4	20.0	1.3	-18.7	33.7
1982	3.2	-4.3	-5.4	1.6	2.5	0.0	-1.5	-1.6	0.6	-1.1	4.8	4.0	-3.6	-1.0	2.6	2.3
1983	1.3	2.4	7.7	12.1	8.9	1.1	10.4	6.3	-1.7	0.6	2.8	7.2	53.4	31.5	-21.9	2.0
1984	7.6	5.0	4.6	-5.7	-7.3	-0.4	-1.5	13.5	5.1	43.1	-0.8	-2.3	43.2	40.9	-2.3	8.8
1985	3.7	2.0	-3.2	-2.8	-2.4	-0.5	-6.5	4.4	-0.2	3.9	3.3	2.0	8.2	24.0	15.8	3.5
1986	4.9	0.6	0.8	5.0	4.0	4.5	-2.0	-3.7	-8.5	-01.5	6.2	0.0	19.6	28.4	8.8	3.2
1987	-0.5	1.4	-2.5	-1.1	12.8	5.2	5.0	7.5	0.7	-10.8	-1.6	-0.8	17.6	22.0	4.4	3.2
Arithmetic Averages: by Month																
	4.5	1.4	1.0	0.7	1.9	1.9	0.4	3.6	-0.5	-1.4	1.1	2.2	22.5	21.3	-1.2	10.0

Source: Japan Securities Research Institute (1988)

Table 6
Mean Daily Return, Standard Deviation, and Percent Positive Returns by Month of the NSA, 1949-1988

Month	Sample Size	Mean Return %	Standard Deviation of Return %	t-Statistic	p-Statistic	% Positive Returns
All Days	11529	.0482***	.0933	5.56	.0001	54.3
January	885	.1816***	.0926	5.80	.0001	60.7
February	905	.0549	.0886	1.87	.0622	56.7
March	986	.0457	.0955	1.50	.1335	55.0
April	947	.0623*	.0913	2.10	.0359	54.2
May	956	.0074	.0835	0.27	.7843	53.1
June	1011	.0641*	.0852	2.39	.0169	56.8
July	1043	.0083	.1012	0.27	.7904	52.3
August	1038	.0790*	.0859	2.96	.0032	55.2
September	931	.0059	.0820	-0.22	.8252	51.6
October	998	.0088	.1150	0.24	.8089	50.9
November	910	.0371	.0879	1.27	.2031	52.4
December	919	.0470	.1038	1.37	.1706	53.8

*and *** represent statistical difference from zero at the 5% and 10% levels, respectively
Source: Yamaichi Research Institute

Declines

There have been twenty-two declines of ten percent or more of the Nikkei 225 stock average from 1949 to June 1991. These are listed in Table 7. Of the twenty-two declines, twelve have been for more than twenty percent, five more than thirty percent and one more than fifty percent. The average decline was 23.4% and the peak to the valley occurred in 6.2 months.

The 21st decline began on the first day of trading in 1990 and ended on April 2 for a fall of 28% from 38,916 to 28,002. The market then recovered 15.9% to 33,293 on July 17, 1990. The market then started to fall prior to the August 2 Iraq invasion of Kuwait and the decline accelerated climaxing on October 1 at 20,222 down fully 39.3% in the 22nd decline and 48.0% from the December 1989 high. Table 8 gives details on these declines in 1990. The 1990 declines are very large in comparison with the past declines. The 22nd decline itself was larger than any previous fall since the 51.8% fall in 1949/50.

Table 7
The Twenty-two Declines of 10% or More on the NSA from 1949 to 1990

Correction Number	Value at Peak	Value in Valley	Dates	% Decline	Duration (months)
1	176.89	85.25	9/1/49-7/6/50	-51.8	11
2	474.43	295.18	3/4-4/1/53	-37.8	2
3	366.69	321.79	5/6-6/3/53	-12.2	1
4	595.46	471.53	5/4-12.27/57	-20.8	8
5	1,829.74	1,258.00	7/18-12/19/61	-31.2	5
6	1,589.76	1,216.04	2/14-10/29/62	-23.5	9
7	1,634.37	1,200.64	4/5-12/18/63	-26.5	9
8	1,369.00	1,020.49	7/3/64-7/12/65	-25.5	13
9	1,588.73	1,364.34	4/1-12/15/66	-14.1	8
10	1,506.27	1,250.14	3/1-12/11/76	-17.0	9
11	2,534.45	1,929.64	4/6-5/27/70	-23.9	2
12	2,740.98	2,227.25	8/14-10/20/71	-18.7	3
13	5,359.74	3,355.13	1/24/73-10/9/74	-37.4	21
14	4,564.52	3,814.02	5/12-9/29/75	-16.4	5
15	5,287.65	4,597.26	9/5-11/24/77	-13.1	3
16	8,019.14	6,849.78	8/17/81-10/1/82	-14.6	14
17	11,190.17	9,703.35	5/4-7/23/84	-13.3	3
18	18,936.24	15,819.58	8/20-10/22/86	-16.5	2
19	25,929.42	22,702.74	6/17-7/22/87	-12.4	1
20	26,646.43	21,036.76	10/14-11/11/87	-21.1	1
21	38,916	28,002	12/29/89-4/2/90	-28.0	3
22	33,293	20,222	7/17-10/1/90	-39.3	2.5
Average				-23.4%	6.2

Table 8: Comparing the 21st and 22nd Declines

	high	low	change
21st Decline	38,916 Dec 28, 1989	28,002 April 2, 1990	-28.0%
Recovery	28,002	33293 July 17, 1990	+15.9%
22nd Decline	33293	20,222 Oct 1, 1990	-39.3%
Total Fall	38,916	20,222	-48.0%

Figures 1 and 2 show the day by day movement of the NSA from December 1989 to February 1991. The 1989 close was 38,916 and the 1990 low was 20,222 on October 1. The record increase on October 2 of 2677.55 or 13.24% to 22,896.41 reversed the oversold condition and ended the 22nd decline.

Figure 1: The NSA, Day by Day, December 1, 1989 to February 28, 1991

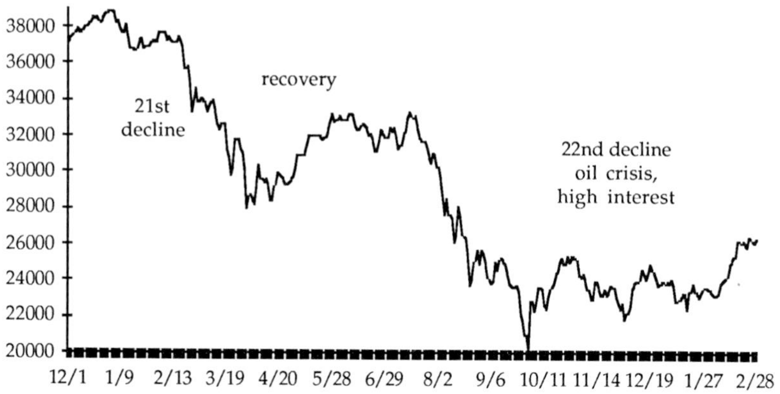

Source: Reuters Historical Information

Table 9 shows the ten largest increases and decreases of the NSA 225 index in percentage and absolute terms until the end of 1989. Tables 10 and 11 show the largest increases and decreases in 1990 and the number of large increases and decreases by month.

Figure 2: Daily Changes inthe NSA, December 1, 1989 to February 28, 1991

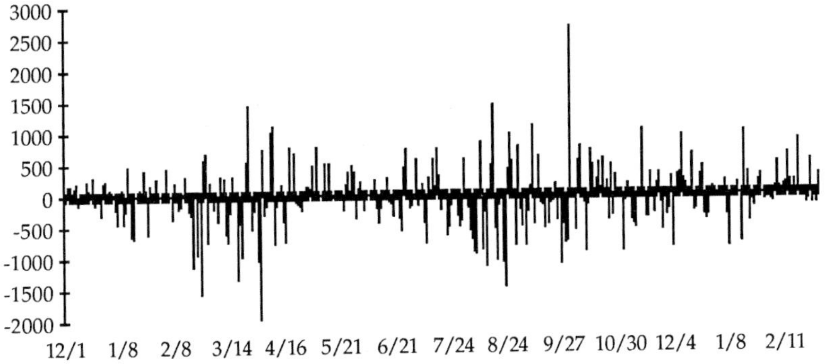

Source: Reuters Historical Information

Table 9: The Ten Largest Increases and Decreases in the NSA Index in Percentage and Absolute Terms to December 31, 1989

	Increases by % rate:		Increases by points:	
	% Increase	Date	Point Increase	Date
1	11.29	Dec 15 1949	2,037.32	Oct 21, 1987
2	9.30	Oct 21 1987	1,215.22	Jun 1, 1988
3	6.41	Apr 16 1953	906.42	Jul 2, 1987
4	6.31	Mar 6 1953	901.75	Nov 18, 1987
5	5.63	Jan 6, 1988	793.96	Mar 28,1989
6	5.51	Jul 15, 1950	731.15	Oct 10, 1987
7	5.39	Feb 13, 1950	632.40	Oct 27, 1987
8	5.32	Jun 26, 1972	604.54	Apr 14 1987
9	5.32	Jul 17, 1950	563.87	Oct 3, 1987
10	4.94	Feb 5, 1973	527.39	Oct 17, 1989

	Decreases by % rate:		Decreases by points:	
	% Decrease	Date	Point Decrease	Date
1	14.90	Oct 20, 1987	3,836.48	Oct 20, 1987
2	10.00	Mar 5, 1953	1,203.23	Oct 23, 1987
3	8.69	Apr 30, 1970	1161.19	Feb 21, 1989
4	7.68	Aug 16, 1971	1,096.22	Oct 26, 1987
5	6.97	Dec 14, 1949	935.87	Feb 23, 1989
6	6.73	Mar 30, 1953	831.32	Apr 27, 1987
7	6.61	Jun 24, 1972	731.91	Nov 10, 1987
8	5.93	Aug 19, 1971	666.41	Jan 15, 1989
9	5.41	Oct 9, 1974	658.28	May 20, 1987
10	5.03	Aug 23, 1971	653.36	Jan 12, 1989

Source: TSE

Table 10
The Ten Largest increases and decreases in the NSA index in absolute and percentage terms in 1990

	% Increase	Date	Point Increase	Date
1	13.23%	Oct 2	2,675	Oct 2
2	5.39%	Aug 15	1,458	Mar 26
3	4.80%	Mar 26	1,439	Aug 15
4	4.67%	Sep 10	1,119	Apr 9
5	4.54%	Nov 13	1,119	Sep 10
6	4.30%	Dec 5	1,042	Nov 13
7	4.04%	Aug 27	1,029	Apr 6
8	3.82%	Apr 9	976	Aug 27
9	3.64%	Apr 6	969	Dec 5
10	3.51%	Oct 8	856	Aug 8

	% Decrease	Date	Point Decrease	Date
1	-6.60%	Apr 2	-1,978	Apr 2
2	-5.84%	Aug 23	-1,569	Feb 26
3	-4.74%	Sep 26	-1,473	Aug 23
4	-4.50%	Feb 26	-1,353	Mar 19
5	-4.22%	Aug 13	-1,161	Feb 21
6	-4.15%	Mar 19	-1,153	Aug 13
7	-4.13%	Aug 22	-1,108	Sep 26
8	-3.87%	Oct 11	-1,087	Aug 22
9	-3.84%	Aug 20	-1,059	Aug 20
10	-3.80%	Dec 2	-1,046	Mar 30

Source: TSE

Table 11
The Number of large increases and decreases in the NSA index in absolute (500 and 350 points or greater) January 1990 to February 1991

Month	≥500	≤-500	≥350	≤-350
January 1990	0	3	2	5
February	2	3	3	4
March	2	7	2	9
April	5	3	5	4
May	3	0	7	1
June	1	1	2	4
July	4	4	4	6
August	5	11	7	11
September	2	5	2	9
October	6	3	8	4
November	1	3	2	7
December	2	2	4	3
January 1991	1	2	2	3
February	3	0	3	0

Valuation

The process of portfolio management involves individual security selection, market timing and other considerations. Many valuation methods can be used to evaluate specific securities and the general market. Table 12 gives yield, price earnings ratios and price to book value ratios at ten peaks and ten valleys of the NSA225 from 1957 to 1987.

There are monotonic decreases in yield, and monotonic increases in price-earnings and price to book ratios throughout this period. Hence it seems unlikely that these values by themselves will provide meaningful under or over valuation signals.

Table 12: Comparison of Fundamentals at Stock Peaks and Valleys for the NSA Index of 225 Stocks)

Date	NSA	Yield	PER	PBR
At Peak of Stock Prices				
May 4, 1957	595.46	5.06	8.77	0.90
Jul 18, 1961	1,829.74	2.92	20.06	2.23
Apr 5, 1963	1,634.37	3.50	19.54	1.73
Apr 1, 1956	1,588.73	3.68	16.37	1.62
Apr 6, 1970	2,534.45	3.17	12.76	1.98
Jan 24, 1973	5,359.74	1.57	25.10	3.07
Aug 17, 1981	8,019.14	1.35	24.18	2.38
May 4, 1984	11,190.17	1.06	28.77	2.80
Aug 20, 1986	18,936.24	0.64	59.55	4.31
Oct 14, 1987	26,646.43	0.45	72.99	6.33
At Bottom of Stock Prices				
Dec 27, 1957	471.53	6.77	7.06	0.71
Oct 29, 1962	1,216.04	4.80	14.65	1.25
Jul 12, 1965	1,020.49	5.85	10.34	1.06
Dec 11, 1967	1,250.14	5.11	9.10	1.19
Dec 8, 1970	1,963.40	4.35	9.22	1.39
Oct 9, 1974.	3,355.13	3.00	13.87	1.57
Oct 11, 1982	6,849.78	1.64	20.94	1.88
Jul 23, 1984	9,703.35	1.23	23.47	2.28
Oct 22, 1986	15,819.55	0.76	51.41	3.66
Nov 11, 1987	21,036.76	0.57	56.98	5.12

Source: Yamaichi Research Institute.

There are many models that may be used to evaluate relative overpriced or underpriced markets, that is risk relative to market fundamentals. Two very simple interest rate models are recorded here that have had considerable success.

Since 1981 Paul Aron of Daiwa Securities has been adjusting Japanese and U.S. price earnings ratios to make them comparable, see e.g. Aron (1989ab, 1990). See French and Poterba (1990) and Ziemba and Schwartz (1991) for more on these adjustments.

In August 1989 the average PER was 49.6% and the NSA was 34,808.43. The PER adjustments bring this PER down to 28.73. The calculation begins with ¥2.02 of stated earnings per ¥100 of stock held for the 49.6 PER. The adjustments for timing of earnings, differences between the Morgan Stanley Capital Investment Perspective (MSCIP) calculations and Japanese practice, reserves, consolidation of earnings and accounting and depreciation changes give an adjusted earnings of ¥3.48:

2.02 ↓	stated earnings per ¥100 of equity	$\frac{100}{2.02} = 49.6$	raw PER
+0.04 ↓	timing of earnings		
+0.15 ↓	differences with MSCIP		
+0.12 ↓	reserves		
+0.16 ↓	consolidation		
+1.10 ↓	accounting and depreciation		
= 3.48	adjusted earnings per ¥100 of equity	$\frac{100}{3.48} = 28.73$	adjusted PER

A final adjustment is then made for the difference in capitalization rates between Japan and the U.S. In August 1989, these rates were 5.0% and 8.2%, respectively. So the adjustment factor was 8.2/5 or 1.64. This gave a final adjusted PER value for Japan of 28.73/1.64 = 17.52. Table 13 shows the adjustments for various periods from 1981 to early 1991. It shows adjusted PERs for Japan and compares them with those in the U.S. for April 26, 1981, to February 28, 1991. The □'s indicate very overvalued periods and the 0's undervalued periods. By overvalued and undervalued we mean of high or low risk relative to price earnings fundamentals. The signals have been quite good. As U.S. stock market guru Martin Zweig has said "to keep one mostly out of market sbefore declines and mostly in markets before increases."

Table 13
Adjusted PERs for Japan Compared with those in the U.S.

Date	U.S. PER	Japan, adj PER	NSA
Apr 26, 1981	9.1	(4.0)	7548
Oct 19, 1984	10.0	(11.5)	10929
Apr 17, 1986	13.7	(13.5)	15827
May 26, 1987	17.4	[17.4]	24533
Sept 11, 1987	[20.3]	[18.1]	24829
Dec 31, 1987	14.4	14.5	21533
May 31, 1988	13.1	15.4	26963
Aug 30, 1988	11.3	15.5	27679
Aug 31, 1989	13.5	[17.5]	34808
Dec 31, 1989	13.5	[23.9]	38915
Mar 30, 1990	15.5	[19.7]	29980
Jun 29, 1990	[17.0]	[19.8]	31940
Sept 30, 1990	13.6	15.2	20983
Oct 1, 1990	14.3	(13.5)	20022
Oct 2, 1990	14.3	15.4	22896
Dec 31, 1990	13.6	14.8	23849
Feb 28, 1991	16.2	15.2	26409

The □s indicate very overvalued periods and the Os undervalued periods. December 31, 1989 was signalled as very overpriced and a strong sell period. October 1, 1990, was signalled as a major low and was a strong buy signal.

The values since August 31, 1989, use the following assumptions.

	Interest		Earnings Gain
	U.S	Japan	over Aug 89
Dec 1989	8.2	6.4	5%
Mar 1990	8.4	7.4	10%
June 1990	8.2	7.0	12%
Sept 1990	8.2	7.75	8%
Oct 1, 1990	8.1	7.5	7.5%
Oct 2, 1990	8.1	7.5	8%
Dec 30, 1990	7.6	6.5	8%
Feb 28, 1991	7.6	6.0	8%

A measure of the overpricedness or risk relative to fundamentals of the stock market is the reciprocal of the PE ratio, which is like a yield if all earnings were paid out, subtracted from the long term bond yield. This measures the *bond minus stock earnings yield*. Let us illustrate this in the context of over valuation of the S&P500 index prior to the October 1987 crash. Table 14 lists the S&P500 index values and the corresponding price earnings ratios along with the interest rates on 30 year government bonds for 1986 to August 1988. From January 1962 to August 1988 this measure averaged -0.36% with a standard deviation of 2.00.

From January 1973 to August 1988, it averaged -0.12% with a standard deviation of 2.46%. Finally during the 1980s it averaged 1.53% with a standard deviation of 1.62%. This premium was less than 2% from February 1986 to March of 1987. It then increased to above 2.5% from April to September and it was 4.14% at the end of September 1987.

After the October 1987 crash the premium fell to less than 2% where it has stayed because of the drop in interest rates and the increase in stock price earnings yield due to the lower stock prices and increasing earnings. Even the increase in interest yields to the 9.3% level in August 1988 did not move the premium above 2% because of the lower PE ratios.

Using the historical values yields a premium of -0.36% with a 2.00% standard deviation and a rule to *sell* when the premium gets above 1.65 standard deviations - corresponding to 95% confidence of being overvalued with a one tail statistical test assuming that the premiums have a normal distribution. This gives the sell signal at 2.94% and suggested selling at the end of April with a 289 S&P500 index.

When should one reinvest? According to table 14, at the end of October 1987 the premium declined to 1.97% with the S&P500 at 245.01. Hence the market, though not undervalued was out of the overpriced danger zone. More conservative investors might not have returned to the market until the pendulum swung very much the other way with the premium close to its historical average of -0.36% and certainly below its bull market of the 1980s average of 1.53%. Such reasoning might have put investors back in the market with a 0.59% premium at the end of January 1989 with an S&P500 of 250.48. In any event the 4.14% premium going into October was excessive and indicative of over valuation of stocks.

Table 14
S&P500 index values, yields, PE ratios, government bond yields, and the yield premium over stocks, 1986 to August 1988.

		S&P index	PER	(a) 30-day gov't bond yield	(b) 1/P %	(a)-(b)
1986	Jan	208.19	14.63	9.32	6.84	2.48
	Feb	219.37	15.67	8.28	6.38	1.90
	Mar	232.33	16.50	7.59	6.06	1.53
	Apr	237.98	16.27	7.58	6.15	1.43
	May	238.46	17.03	7.76	5.87	1.89
	Jun	245.30	17.32	7.27	5.77	1.50
	Jul	240.18	16.31	7.42	6.13	1.29
	Aug	245.00	17.47	7.26	5.72	1.54
	Sep	238.27	15.98	7.64	6.26	1.38
	Oct	237.36	16.85	7.61	5.93	1.68
	Nov	245.09	16.99	7.40	5.89	1.51
	Dec	248.60	16.72	7.33	5.98	1.35
1987	Jan	264.51	15.42	7.47	6.49	0.98
	Feb	280.93	15.98	7.46	6.26	1.20
	Mar	292.47	16.41	7.65	6.09	1.56
	Apr	289.32	16.22	9.56	6.17	3.39
	May	289.12	16.32	8.63	6.13	2.50
	Jun	301.38	17.10	8.40	5.85	2.55
	Jul	310.09	17.92	8.89	5.58	3.31
	Aug	329.36	18.55	9.17	5.39	3.78
	Sep	318.66	18.10	9.66	5.52	4.14
	Oct	280.16	14.16	9.03	7.06	1.97
	Nov	245.01	13.78	8.90	7.26	1.64
	Dec	240.96	13.55	9.10	7.38	1.72
1988	Jan	250.48	12.81	8.40	7.81	0.59
	Feb	258.10	13.02	8.33	7.68	0.65
	Mar	265.74	13.42	8.74	7.45	1.29
	Apr	262.61	13.24	9.10	7.55	1.55
	May	256.20	12.92	9.24	7.74	1.50
	Jun	270.68	13.65	8.85	7.33	1.52
	Jul	269.44	13.59	9.18	7.36	1.82
	Aug	263.73	13.30	9.30	7.52	1.78

Source: Yamaichi Research Institute

This model also applies quite well in Japan. Indeed calculations by Shigeru Ishii and William Ziemba at the Yamaichi Research Institute show that it has been an excellent signal for many previous declines in Japan. They studied the twenty declines from 1949 to 1989 listed in Table 7. They found that not all declines began with this spread; but whenever the index was in the danger zone, there was always a decline. Figure 3 shows the spread from 1980 to the end of May 1990. This data shown here is for all of 1980 whereas that in table 14 uses a longer sample hence the numbers are slightly different. Each time the spread exceeded the 4.23 cutoff (which has higher than 95% confidence) there was a decline. The model also indicates that the valuation was still high on May 29, 1990, since the spread was 4.88. Meanwhile, the same calculation for the S&P500 shown in figure 4 indicates that the market was extremely overvalued. Indeed it has been below the mean, since the September 1987 peak of 4.42. The spread value of 1.11 was, however, slightly above the mean level and the highest since the late fall of 1987.

Figure 3: Bond and Stock Yield Differential Model for Japan, 1980-1990

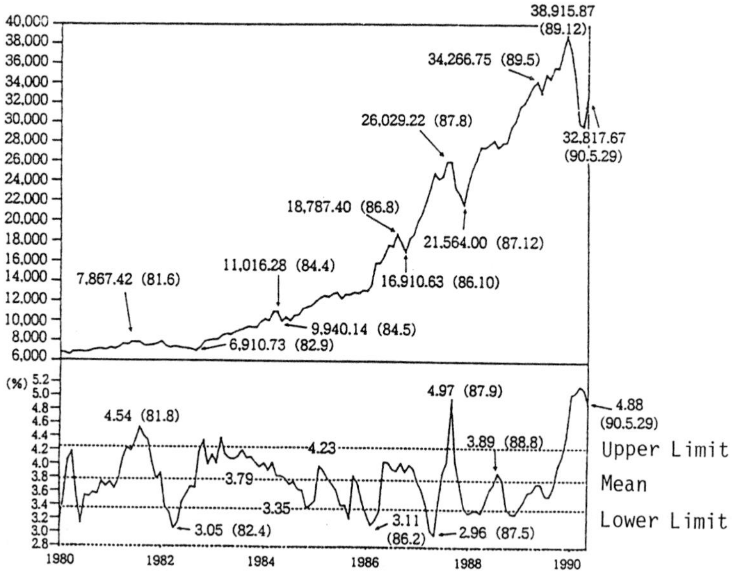

Source: Yamaichi Research Institute

Date/level	Spread	Value of NSA
May 29, 1990	4.88%	32,818
Mean	3.79%	20,022
Upper Limit	4.23%	23,754
Lower Limit	3.35%	17,303

Figure 4: Bond and Stock Yield Differential Model for the S&P500, 1980-1990

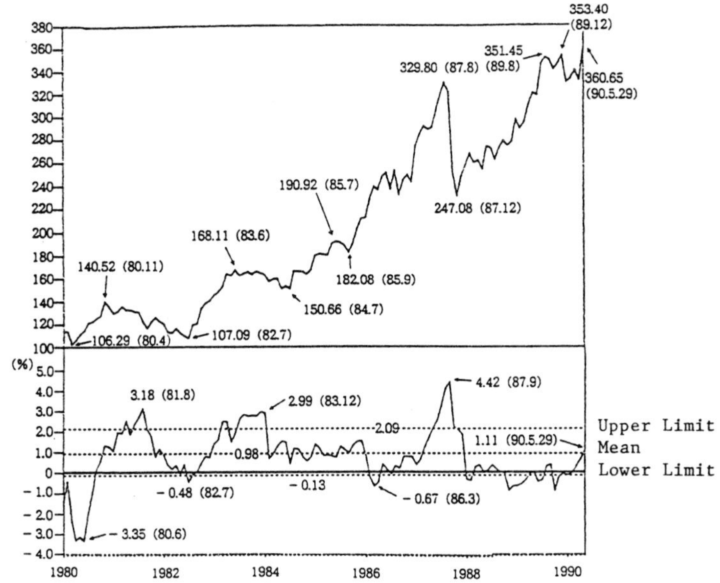

Source: Yamaichi Research Institute

Date/level	Spread	Value of S&P500
May 29, 1990	1.11%	360.65
Mean	0.98%	355
Upper Limit	2.09%	415
Lower Limit	-0.13%	309

REFERENCES

Aron, Paul H. (1981) Are Japanese P/E multiples too high? Daiwa Securities of America, NY.

Aron, Paul H. (1989) Japanese P/E multiples: the tradition continues. Daiwa Securities America Paul Aron Report 35, October 23.

Aron, Paul H. (1990) Japanese P/E multiples in an era of increasing uncertainty. Daiwa Securities America, Paul Aron Report 41, August 31.

French, Kenneth R. and James M. Poterba (1990) Are Japanese stock prices too high? *Journal of Financial Economics*, forthcoming.

Hamao, Yasushi (1991) A standard database for the analysis of Japanese security markets. *Journal of Business 64:* 87-102.

Hamao, Yasushi and Roger Ibbotson (1989) *The Stocks, Bonds and Inflation (SBI) Japan Yearbook,* Ibbotson Associates.

Hayashi, Fumio and Ravi Jagannathan (1990) Ex-day behavior of Japanese stock prices: new insights from new methodology. Working paper No. 3421, National Bureau of Economic Research.

Ibbotson Assoicates (1989) *Stocks, Bonds, Bills and Inflation, 1926-88 Yearbook,* Chicago, IL.

McDonald, Jack (1989) The *Mochiai* Effect: Japanese corporate cross-holdings. *Journal of Portfolio Management 16:* 90-94.

Ziemba, William T. (1991) Japanese security market regularities: monthly, turn of the month and year, holiday and Golden Week effects. *Japan and the World Economy,* forthcoming.

Ziemba, William T. and Sandra L. Schwartz (1991) The growth in the Japanese stock market, 1949-90 and prospects for the future. *Managerial and Decision Economics 12,* 183-195.

Ziemba, William T. and Sandra L. Schwartz (1991) *Invest Japan: The Structure, Performance and Opportunities of Japanese Stock, Bond and Fund Markets,* Chicago: Probus Publishing.

Japanese Financial Market Research
W.T. Ziemba, W. Bailey and Y. Hamao (Editors)

THE CHICKEN OR THE EGG: LAND AND STOCK PRICES IN JAPAN*

William T. Ziemba
Faculty of Commerce, University of British Columbia, Vancouver, B.C. V6T 1Y8

Tsukamoto Sozan Building in Ginza 2-Chome in central Tokyo is built on the most expensive land in the country with one square meter priced at ¥37.7 million or about $279,000 U.S. at the (December 1990) exchange rate of about ¥135 per U.S. dollar.

Abstract
It is well known that land prices in Japan are the world's highest and that the stock market has increased dramatically. This paper explores the relationship between the price levels of these two markets. The results indicate an extraordinarily close relationship, particularly for commercial land. While the prices of land and stocks are highly related, the evidence is that stock prices lead land prices and not the reverse.

Land Prices in Japan are Astronomical

Some 120 million people live in Japan in an area of about 377,800 km^2 which is about the size of Montana. Most of the land is mountainous or is used for agriculture. Indeed, less than 5% of the land is used to house all the people. A breakdown of land use appears in Table 1. Hence, with high incomes, crowded conditions, and an intense desire to invest at home, land prices in the most desirable locations have escalated beyond belief. Almost 30 million people, or a quarter of the population, lives in the greater Tokyo area. Much of the housing in Japan's major cities is owned by the large corporations and their employees receive subsidized rent. However, fully 60% of families in Japan, and 55% in

* Portions of this research were conducted under William T. Ziemba's direction at the Yamaichi Research Institute in Tokyo in 1988/89. Without implicating them I would like to thank my colleagues there, particularly Hirokazu Yuihama and Hitoshi Ishiyama for their help. Thanks are also due to Mr. Motohiko Higashikawa of the Japan Real Estate Institute for supplying data to me. This research was also partially supported by the Centre for International Business Studies, Univeristy of British Columbia and the Social Sciences and Humanities Research Council of Canada.

Tokyo, own their own homes and many individuals invest in raw land or in apartments that they rent to others.

Table 1: Land Use in Japan (1986)

Agriculture	14.5	
Woodlands	66.9	
Moors	0.8	
Rivers	3.5	
Roads	2.9	
Dwellings	4.0	
Other	7.4	
Total	100.0	
Total Area	377.8	(1000 km^2)

Source: National Land Agency, Japan

Table 2 and figure 1 give the Japan Real Estate Institute's land indices for the six largest cities, and for all of Japan for commercial, housing, industrial and total land for each six month period from March 1949 to September 1990. The indices are for March (1) and September (2). Figure 1 also gives the yearly rate of changes as of March of each year. The six largest cities are Tokyo, Osaka, Nagoya, Yokohama, Kobe and Kyoto. The country wide indices are based on 140 cities. The data are appraisal based which tends to smooth the price levels and lag the market. Simple averages of samples of ten lots in each city form the indices which were normalized at 100 as of March 31, 1980. The sampling procedure separates land into high, medium and low grades reflecting location, social circumstances, yield, etc. The sampling procedure selects lots randomly and equally from each of these three classes.

Table 2 also indicates that the price increase has been largest in the six largest cities. Despite large recent rises, the relative gain in the period 1955 to 1970 was much larger than from 1970 to 1990. For land in the whole country, the 1955 to 1970 period produced gains of about 15 times 1955 values. These prices then increased only about four fold in the ensuing twenty years. In the six largest cities, the increase was also much larger in the 1955 to 1970 period versus the past two decades.

Table 2 : Land Indices in Japan 1955-1990

	Nationwide				Six Largest Cities				Consumer Price Index
	All	Commercial	Housing	Industrial	All	Commercial	Housing	Industrial	
1955:1	3.1	3.7	2.5	3.2	2.4	4.9	1.7	2.2	
1955:2	3.3	4.0	2.7	3.4	2.6	5.1	1.9	2.3	
1956:1	3.5	4.3	2.9	3.7	2.8	5.6	1.9	2.6	
1956:2	3.9	4.8	3.2	4.1	3.2	6.1	2.2	3.0	
1957:1	4.5	5.5	3.6	4.8	3.6	6.7	2.6	3.5	
1957:2	5.0	6.1	4.0	5.4	4.2	7.4	2.9	4.1	
1958:1	5.5	6.6	4.5	5.9	4.6	7.8	3.3	4.7	
1958:2	6.1	7.2	5.0	6.5	5.0	7.9	3.6	5.3	
1959:1	6.8	8.1	5.5	7.3	5.5	8.4	4.0	5.9	
1959:2	7.7	9.1	6.2	8.3	6.3	9.6	4.6	6.8	
1960:1	8.7	10.5	6.8	9.5	7.2	11.2	5.2	7.9	
1960:2	10.2	12.4	7.8	11.4	9.3	14.1	6.0	10.6	
1961:1	12.3	14.4	9.3	14.6	12.1	18.0	7.5	14.8	
1961:2	14.5	16.7	10.8	17.4	15.7	22.9	9.5	20.0	
1962:1	15.7	17.9	11.8	19.1	17.3	24.3	10.5	22.2	
1962:2	17.1	19.2	12.8	21.0	19.0	25.4	11.9	24.2	
1963:1	18.4	21.0	13.6	22.7	20.5	27.1	13.1	26.1	
1963.2	19.6	22.1	14.5	24.5	22.3	29.0	14.5	28.4	
1964:1	21.0	23.5	15.5	26.3	24.1	31.1	15.9	30.4	
1964:2	22.5	25.4	16.6	28.0	25.6	32.9	17.1	32.0	
1965:1	23.8	26.6	17.8	29.6	26.4	33.8	17.8	33.1	
1965:2	24.4	27.5	18.2	30.1	26.6	34.1	18.0	33.2	
1966:1	25.0	28.4	18.9	30.5	26.9	34.5	18.4	33.2	
1966:2	25.8	29.5	19.6	30.8	27.2	34.8	18.9	33.2	
1967:1	27.1	31.4	20.8	31.9	28.1	36.3	19.6	34.0	
1967:2	28.8	33.3	22.4	33.2	29.2	37.6	20.7	35.0	
1968:1	30.8	35.7	24.2	35.1	30.5	38.8	22.0	36.3	
1968:2	33.2	38.6	26.3	37.4	32.4	41.1	23.9	38.1	
1969:1	36.1	41.8	29.0	40.2	35.1	44.4	26.1	40.9	
1969:2	39.6	46.1	32.2	43.2	38.1	48.0	28.7	44.1	
1970:1	43.2	49.9	35.5	47.0	41.3	51.4	31.3	47.8	
1970:2	46.8	53.8	38.7	50.7	44.8	54.1	34.4	52.0	
1971:1	50.0	57.0	41.8	54.1	48.0	56.5	37.2	55.8	
1971:2	53.2	59.8	44.9	57.8	51.0	58.8	40.0	59.4	
1972:1	56.5	63.2	47.8	61.8	54.1	61.7	42.8	62.7	
1972:2	61.2	67.8	52.1	66.7	59.6	66.7	48.1	68.6	
1973:1	70.8	76.6	61.6	77.0	71.2	77.0	59.2	80.8	
1973:2	81.1	85.9	71.8	88.5	81.1	85.8	68.5	91.7	
1974:1	87.0	91.4	77.8	94.8	84.1	88.7	71.0	95.3	
1974:2	88.2	92.4	79.1	95.7	84.5	89.1	71.5	95.4	
1975:1	83.3	87.8	74.6	89.7	77.3	82.1	65.6	86.7	100.0
1975:2	83.5	88.0	75.0	89.7	77.5	82.1	66.2	86.8	
1976:1	83.9	88.3	75.7	89.9	78.0	82.4	66.9	86.8	108.3
1976:2	84.7	88.7	77.0	90.2	78.8	82.8	68.3	87.1	
1977:1	85.7	89.3	78.7	90.7	79.9	83.9	69.9	87.4	118.1
1977:2	86.9	90.0	80.5	91.1	80.9	84.5	71.6	87.8	
1978:1	88.1	91.0	82.5	91.8	82.2	85.7	73.6	88.4	112.6
1978:2	89.8	92.2	85.1	92.9	84.5	87.4	77.2	89.7	
1979:1	92.1	93.9	88.7	94.4	88.3	90.3	82.9	92.0	127.0
1979:2	95.5	96.5	93.7	96.8	94.2	95.3	91.6	96.0	

Table 2 Land Indices in Japan 1955-1990 (continued)

| | | Consumer | | | Nationwide | | | | Six Largest Cities |
	All	Com-mercial	Housing	Indus-trial	All	Com-mercial	Housing	Indus-trial	Price Index
1980:1	100.0	100.0	100.0	100.0	100.0	100.0	100.0	100.0	137.2
1980:2	104.6	103.7	106.5	103.5	104.6	104.3	106.2	103.4	
1981:1	108.7	106.9	112.2	106.7	108.5	108.1	110.6	106.7	143.7
1981:2	112.8	110.3	117.6	109.9	112.4	112.5	114.8	109.9	
1982:1	116.4	113.4	122.4	112.6	115.7	116.7	117.9	112.6	147.6
1982:2	119.4	116.0	126.4	115.0	118.5	120.6	120.2	114.8	
1983:1	121.9	118.3	129.5	117.0	121.3	124.6	122.5	116.7	150.5
1983:2	124.0	120.2	131.9	118.9	123.9	128.5	124.6	118.6	
1984:1	125.8	122.0	134.1	120.3	127.6	135.7	126.8	120.6	153.8
1984:2	127.6	123.8	136.0	121.8	132.2	144.4	129.6	123.1	
1985:1	129.3	125.7	137.7	123.2	137.1	153.6	133.8	125.0	157.0
1985:2	131.0	127.8	139.2	124.5	143.3	167.1	138.1	127.1	
1986:1	133.0	130.9	140.7	125.8	156.6	197.9	146.7	131.2	158.1
1986:2	135.6	134.9	142.7	127.3	173.8	229.3	165.3	137.0	
1987:1	140.2	141.1	147.0	130.1	197.2	264.7	186.3	153.6	158.3
1987:2	149.9	153.3	156.1	137.0	234.8	336.7	216.1	175.4	
1988:1	154.2	159.9	159.3	140.1	252.2	375.2	229.4	183.2	159.3
1988:2	159.2	166.9	162.7	144.7	279.9	420.0	240.0	213.1	
1989:1	165.9	175.9	168.1	150.1	318.8	467.5	264.5	243.7	163.4
1989:2	174.8	186.8	176.0	157.7	356.6	528.8	300.7	279.4	
1990:1	189.3	203.9	189.6	170.2	408.2	599.2	253.0	315.7	
1990:2	203.1	220.5	202.9	181.4	429.1	625.9	372.4	331.7	
# times increase in ¥									
1955:1 to 1990:2	65.5	59.6	81.2	56.7	178.8	127.7	219.1	150.8	
1955:1 to 1970:2	15.1	14.5	15.5	15.8	18.7	11.0	20.2	23.6	
1970:2 to 1990:2	4.3	4.1	5.2	3.6	9.6	11.6	10.8	6.4	

Land values in the six largest cities have outpaced the CPI by twenty times since 1955. In the Ginza district of Tokyo each square meter of land is worth over $200,000 U.S. Choice downtown land in Tokyo goes for the equivalent of nearly a billion dollars an acre. At neighboring land prices, the value of land under the Emperor's palace and garden in Tokyo equals that of all California or of Canada. The golf courses of Japan alone are worth more then the entire Australian stock market, some A$250. The total land value in Japan in 1990 was about 4.1 times that of the whole United States. Japanese land was worth some ¥2180 trillion as of the end of 1989. This compares with a value of ¥1050 trillion at the end of 1985. Using an exchange rate of ¥143.76 per dollar at the end of 1989, gives a land value of $15.16 trillion. As of September 1990, all land had an index of 203.1, up 16.2% from September 1989. With an end of 1990 exchange rate of 135.40, total Japanese land values were in the $18.7 trillion range in late 1990. The average acre of land in Japan is worth fully 100 times the average acre in the U.S. So even though the U.S. has about 25 times more land than Japan, its current total value is less than a fourth as much. Essentially half the world's land value at 1987-90 prices is accounted for by Japanese land! It also accounts for about 20% of the total asset value in the world. Simple houses in Tokyo rent for more than $10,000 per month and cost in the millions. Office space for sale in Tokyo's financial district costs nearly $75,000 per square foot. Some luxury apartments in Tokyo rent for well over $20,000 per month. Figure 2 compares land prices throughout Japan, in 1988 with Tokyo normalized at 100. Osaka was then 62, Nagoya, 27, and most other metropolitan areas in the 12 to 18 range. Figure 3 compares land value by region from 1983 to 1987.

Figure 1: Land price indices for industrial, residential, commercial and all land and annual rates of price change for all land, 1955 to 1990

a. In the six largest cities
(semi log scale)

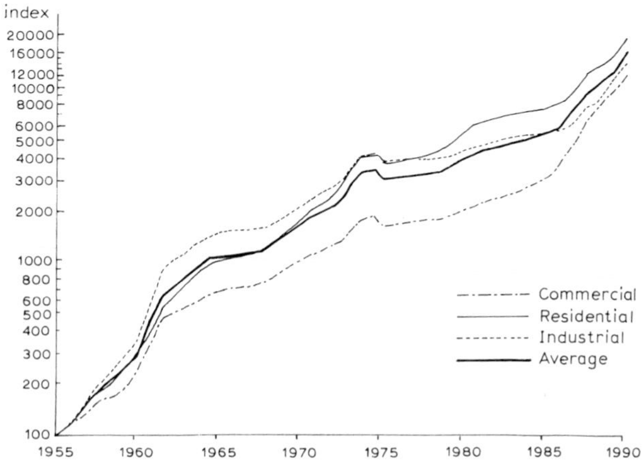

Average annual rates of price change % (6 cities)

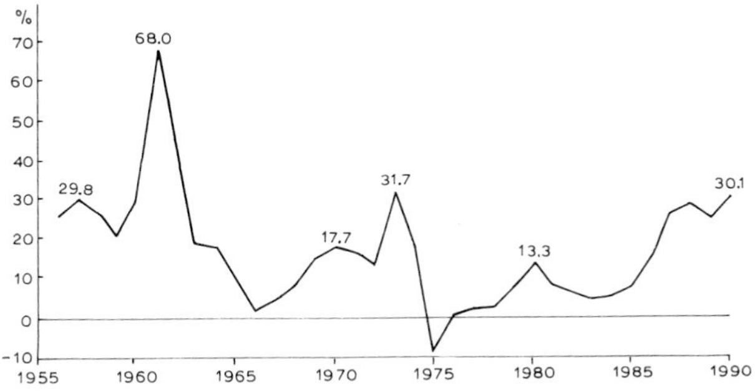

b. In the entire country (140 cities)
(semi log scale)

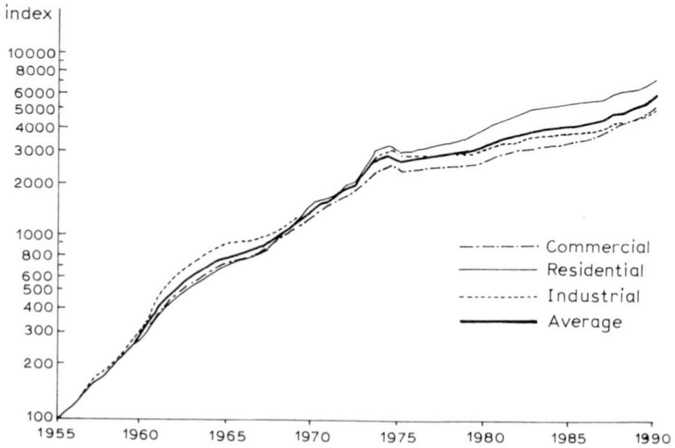

Average annual rates of price change % (140 cities)

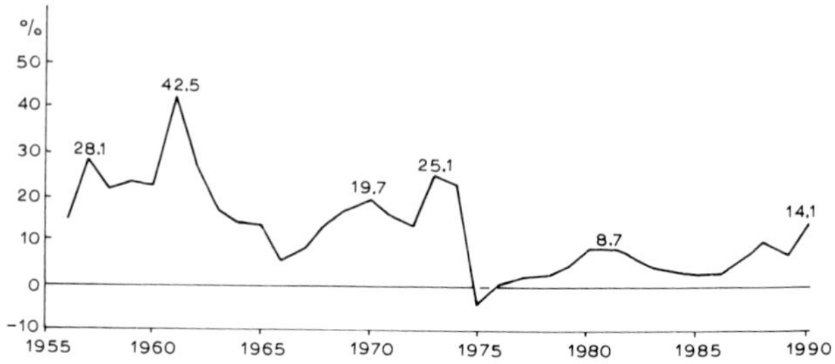

Source: Japan Real Estate Institute

In 1988 Tokyo's land value alone was about $7.7 trillion, or about half the land value of the whole country. To understand how much this is we can do a idealized experiment. Let's borrow on it up to 80% of its value. Banks in Tokyo commonly provided such loans based on land security until the high interest rates of 1990. From 1987 to 1989, the interest rates on loans secured by land were 5.7% and 6.6% for variable and fixed rate loans, respectively. We would then have almost enough money to purchase all the land in the U.S. for $3.7 trillion *and* all the stock on the New York, American and NASDAQ over-the-counter stock exchanges for about $2.6 trillion in an all-cash transaction. Obviously, one could not sell all of Tokyo's land for $7.7 trillion quickly, nor would a group of banks undertake such a large loan, but this was the *value* of land prices in fiscal 1987. In Tokyo about 2% of land changes hand each year. The price is kept up and bid higher because of the excess of demand over supply.

Figure 2: Housing Land Price Index

Tokyo = 100 (¥507,300/m^2), Osaka=62; Nagoya=27; Other Areas=12-18

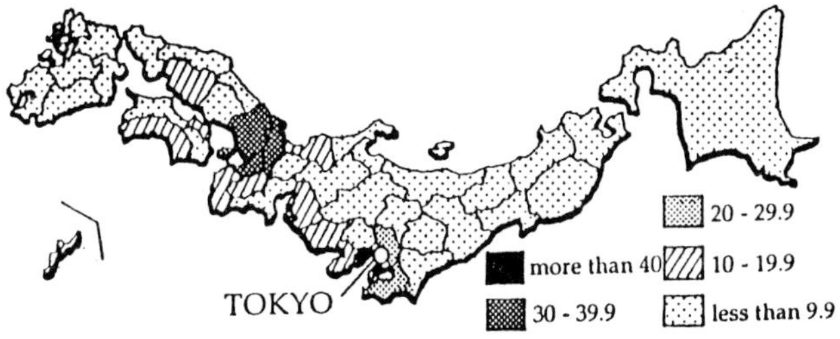

Figure 3: Land Value by Region in Japan

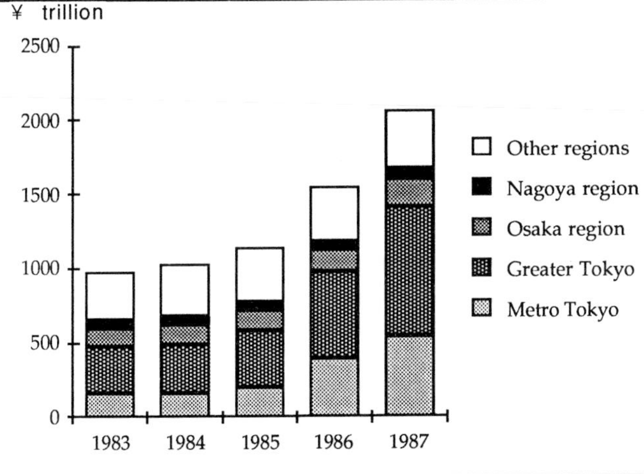

Source: Economic Planning Agency reported in Canaway (1990)

Figure 4 shows that as of 1985 a staggering 56% of the national wealth of Japan was land. The current percentage may be even higher since there was a huge price increase in 1986 and steady rises since then.

Land turnover is very small as the Japanese believe in holding land whenever possible this is reinforced by the tax system which encourages the purchase of more land and discourages land sales. The population in per unit of habitable area is thirty times higher in Japan than the U.S. The GNP and energy consumption per habitable area are also much much higher in Japan than in the U.S. (though the energy per unit GNP is much lower in Japan), see Table 3. This puts upward pressure on land prices.

Figure 4: Composition of National Wealth in Selected Countries

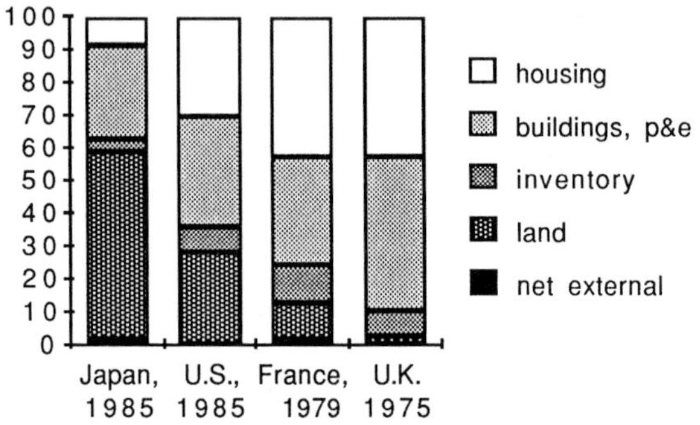

Source: Economic Planning Agency, Japan

Table 3: Comparison of Fundamentals, Japan and the U.S., 1989

	Japan	U.S.	Japan as % of U.S.
Population, millions	120	239	50.21
Total area (1000 sq km)	377	9373	4.02
Habitable area (1000 sq km)	80	4786	1.67
Population per habitable area (pop/sq km)	1500	50	3000.00
GNP per habitable area (million $/sq km)	16.90	0.80	2112.50
Energy consumption (tons oil equivalent/sq km)	4650	390	1192.38

Source: Daiwa Securities America, Inc

If there is to be a major stock market crash in Japan it may well start with or be linked to land values. We study the link between the stock market and land prices in this paper. Central Tokyo land price increases were relatively firm in 1988-1990 but large increases continued in the suburbs and in other cities. Will property prices crash at some later date? It is hard to say, but with the bulk of the property controlled by the major companies and the government, with the tax structure and the incentives favoring land holding, and with buying by both individuals and institutions, the prices may well stay at these lofty levels.

Boone (1989) developed several models in an attempt to rationalize the high land values in Japan from an economic point of view. He found that if Japan's GNP growth exceeds that in the U.S. by about 2% per year forever, then land prices 100 times higher in Japan than in the U.S. are consistent with the economic model. He also developed a simple model for the relative land price in Japan versus that in the U.S.:

$$\text{Relative land price in Japan} = \frac{\text{Land value}}{\text{Rents}} \times \frac{\text{Rents}}{\text{GNP}} \times \frac{\text{GNP}}{\text{Land}}$$

$$= \frac{1}{a} \times 1 \times b,$$

where **a** is essentially the ratio of rents in Japan for comparable properties which are known to be 0.25 to 0.50 in the U.S., **b** is the GNP to land estimate which ranges from 20-30 (Table 2 estimates this at 21 in 1989), and rents/GNP= 1 is consistent with the Cobb-Douglas production model that Boone assumes. Using these a's and b's gives relative land prices close to the actual ratio of 100.

JAPANESE HOUSEHOLDS

The vast majority of the wealth of Japanese households is contained in their land and buildings. This constitutes nearly two thirds of their assets. Various savings deposits amount to about 14%. Rates of return on these savings accounts are regulated, change infrequently and have been low - about 4% for the best investments- but this income is usually not taxed. Deregulation in 1989 and 1990 has made available acounts paying 7% or more, where the income is taxable. Securities, insurance and pension assets are only about 6.9% of the Japanese wealth and the proportion of this that is corporate stock is astonishingly low, some 0.3%. Government bonds and bank debentures each accounts for 0.9%, so the largest bulk of the savings goes into cash savings instruments. This is partially explained by the practice of financing Japanese corporate needs with bank loans rather than equity. Household assets are growing at about $1.83 billion U.S. per day (see Ziemba and Schwartz, 1991b). The excess is going mostly into savings deposits much of which is then made available largely to corporations for loans to purchase assets in the stock market, land, bonds, and overseas investments.

Households in the U.S., in contrast, have their assets concentrated in time deposits (23.2%), insurance and pension funds (13.1%) and securities (19.7%) along with residential (23.4%), with land comprising only 7.1% of total assets. Table 4 details the differences in the household shares in Japan and the U.S. using averages for 1974-83. Consumer durables are one third as widespread in Japan compared to U.S. households, which is not surprising considering the consumer oriented nature of the U.S. economy. Space is a major factor in this. In Japan there simply is little space to store things, hence much less is purchased and stored. Moreover when new items are purchased old ones are trashed or moved out elsewhere.

Table 4: Portfolio Shares of Japanese and U.S. Households, Averages for 1974-83

	Japan	U.S.
Cash	0.8	na
Demand Deposits	1.2	3.4
Time Deposits	7.9	23.2
Postal Saving	4.9	-
Trust	1.8	-
Insurance and Pensions	3.8	13.1
Securities	3.1	19.7
Residential Structures	11.6	23.4
Land	53.4	7.1
Consumer Durables	4.0	11.9
Noncorporate Structures equipment & invent	7.3	6.1

Source: compiled in Noland (1988)

Figure 5 shows the volume of real estate loans. Of particular interest is its variability and predictive power for leveling off periods. Rents shown in figure 6 are rising slower than land prices. Hence one expects increases in valuation to provide profits. That is, the short-run losses which are tax deductible off income will be made up by long-term capital gains which are taxed at lower rates. For additional discussion on these land prices issues, see Boone (1989), Canaway (1990), Cults (1990), Fingleton (1990) and Flack (1990).

High interest rates which led to a sharp fall in stock prices in 1990 have not led to any decline in land prices as shown in Table 2. However, there was a sharp decline in speculative land such as golf course membership and condos, see Figure 13 below and Stone and Ziemba (1990). As interest rates rise, land demand falls but in Tokyo, with virtually no new supply, demand still greatly exceeds supply. At the same time supply declines with higher interest rates as development costs are curtailed. All the incentives favor holding land and not even developing it. As Canaway (1990) has pointed out, land held less than five years is taxed at fully 52% of its sale value. Meanwhile, yearly taxes paid to hold land are about 0.05 to 0.10% of current value. Even upon death it pays to borrow money which is deductible at full value while land is valued at about half its market value. Hence inheritance taxes are minimized. Canaway argues that in a major crash the stock market will go first, then the economy and finally the land markets. The results in the paper are consistent with this view.

Figure 5: Real-Estate Loans in Japan

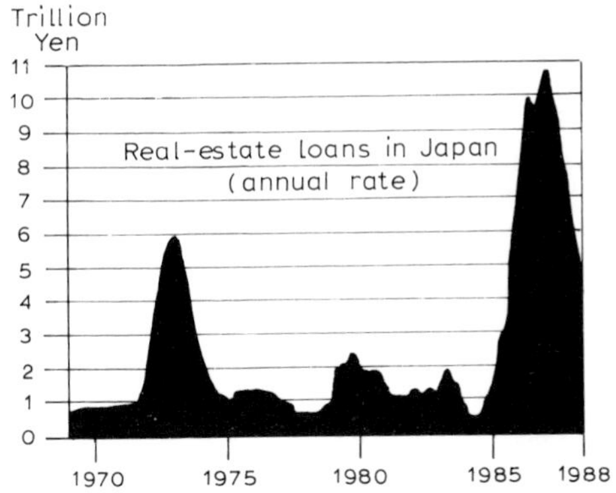

Figure 6: Residential Land Prices vs Rents

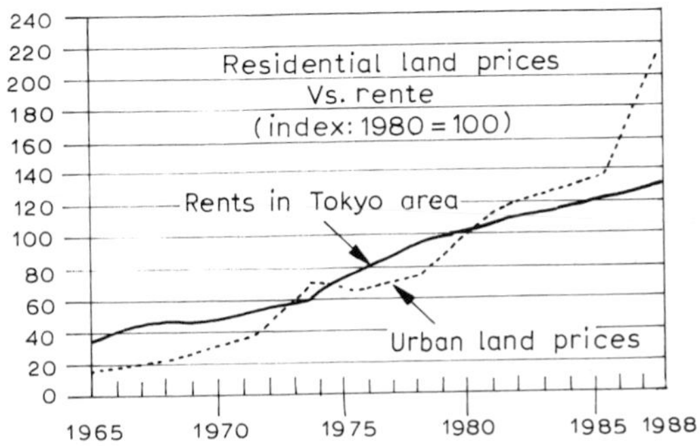

Source: Japan Real Estate Research Institute, Management and Coordination Agency

LAND AND THE NSA CORRELATIONS

The growth in the Nikkei stock average and its declines are discussed by Schwartz and Ziemba in the preceeding article in this volume.

This paper uses the NSA to study the relationship between the levels of stock and land prices in Japan. The NSA is the most popular index and presumably reflects investor sentiment in the economy, so it might relate to land prices at least as well as the Topix. Since the Topix and NSA have a very close correlation, one would not expect the results to be much different anyway. For more details and results on the Japanese stock market, see Elton and Gruber (1989), and Ziemba and Schwartz (1991a), and the papers in this volume.

The biannual data from 1955 to 1988, yields the following correlation matrix for the NSA, and land price indices for all land, all commerical land, housing land, industrial use land throughout Japan and these latter four indices for the six largest cities.

Table 5: Contemporaneous correlations between the NSA and various land indices.

	Nikkei Dow	Land Indices Throughout Japan				Land Indices in 6 Largest Cities			
		ALL	COML	HOUSE	INDL	ALL	COML	HOUSE	INDL
	1	2	3	4	5	6	7	8	9
1	1.000								
2	0.858	1.000							
3	0.857	0.998	1.000						
4	0.874	0.995	0.989	1.000					
5	0.820	0.996	0.997	0.984	1.000				
6	0.963	0.958	0.960	0.961	0.938	1.000			
7	0.988	0.879	0.885	0.885	0.850	0.978	1.000		
8	0.956	0.965	0.962	0.974	0.942	0.996	0.964	1.000	
9	0.889	0.991	0.995	0.981	0.987	0.978	0.919	0.975	1.000

All the correlations of land with the NSA are high. The lowest is 0.82 for industrial land throughout Japan. The six largest cities have the highest land prices and their land values correlate very closely with the NSA. Indeed all land is at 0.963, housing at 0.956 and commerical land at 0.988. Industrial land, much of which is lower priced large acreage away from the major cities, correlates less with the NSA.

The concern is with causality between land and the NSA, so we record the lag behind and future correlations. The six month prior lag behind index values for the land versus the current NSA are shown in Table 6.

Table 6: Correlations between current NSA values and lagged behind land values

	Current NSA	Land Indices Throughout Japan Six Months Before				Land Indices in 6 Largest Cities Six Months Before			
		ALL	COML	HOUSE	INDL	ALL	COML	HOUSE	INDL
	1	2	3	4	5	6	7	8	9
1	1.000								
2	0.853	1.000							
3	0.847	0.998	1.000						
4	0.873	0.995	0.988	1.000					
5	0.816	0.996	0.998	0.983	1.000				
6	0.945	0.970	0.969	0.973	0.953	1.000			
7	0.978	0.905	0.906	0.911	0.881	0.980	1.000		
8	0.940	0.972	0.966	0.982	0.951	0.996	0.968	1.000	
9	0.868	0.993	0.996	0.982	0.992	0.980	0.929	0.974	1.000

These correlations are only slightly lower then the contemparaneous correlations. Again commercial land in the six largest cities has by far the highest correlation.

Lagging forward yields the current NSA and the six month future land index values in Table 7.

Table 7: Correlations between current NSA values and future land values

	Current NSA	Land Indices Throughout Japan Six Months Later ALL	COML	HOUSE	INDL	Land Indices in 6 Largest Cities Six Months Later ALL	COML	HOUSE	INDL
	1	2	3	4	5	6	7	8	9
1	1.000								
2	0.863	1.000							
3	0.868	0.998	1.000						
4	0.875	0.996	0.989	1.000					
5	0.824	0.996	0.996	0.984	1.000				
6	0.976	0.946	0.951	0.948	0.923	1.000			
7	0.993	0.860	0.871	0.864	0.827	0.978	1.000		
8	0.966	0.960	0.960	0.968	0.935	0.995	0.960	1.000	
9	0.915	0.984	0.990	0.975	0.977	0.979	0.923	0.978	1.000

These correlations are higher than the lag behinds and the contemparaneous and suggest that the NSA's current value predicts land values in the future better than the reverse. The correlation with commercial land six months later in the six largest cities is an astounding 0.993, or an R^2 of 0.986 for a regression fit. Hence the level of the NSA explains nearly 99% of the biannual variation of the level of commercial land prices in Japan's six largest cities in the past 34 years!

Table 8 has the correlations with the NSA and commerical and in the six largest cities with lag behind of six (-1) or twelve months (-2), and lag forward of six (+1), twelve (+2) or eighteen (+3) months, plus the contemparaneous values, again with current NSA.

Table 8: Correlations between current NSA values and lagged behind commercial land values

	Current NSA	Commercial Land Indices in Japan's Six Largest Cities -2	-1	Current	+1	+2	+3
	1	2	3	4	5	6	7
1	1.000						
2	0.949	1.000					
3	0.978	0.996	1.000				
4	0.988	0.985	0.996	1.000			
5	0.993	0.964	0.982	0.994	1.000		
6	0.989	0.943	0.966	0.983	0.995	1.000	
7	0.985	0.926	0.950	0.971	0.987	0.996	1.000

The best contemparaneous fit is with commercial land in the six largest cities as shown in Figure 7. The regression equation is (with t statistics in brackets):

$$NSA_t = \underset{(-5.19)}{-818.63} + \underset{(50.70)}{75.23} \text{ Coml Land}_t,$$

with $R^2 = 0.975$, adjusted $R^2 = 0.975$, DW = 0.468, autocorrelation = 0.759, and SS = 891.21. The t-statistic of over 50 indicates the high degree of confidence that this variable's movements relate closely to those of the NSA. However, the Durbin-Wtson statistic is asymptotically equal to $2(1-\rho)$ hence at 0.468 there is significant positive serial correlation.

Figure 7: The NSA and Commercial Land Index Values in the Six Largest Cities, 1955-1988

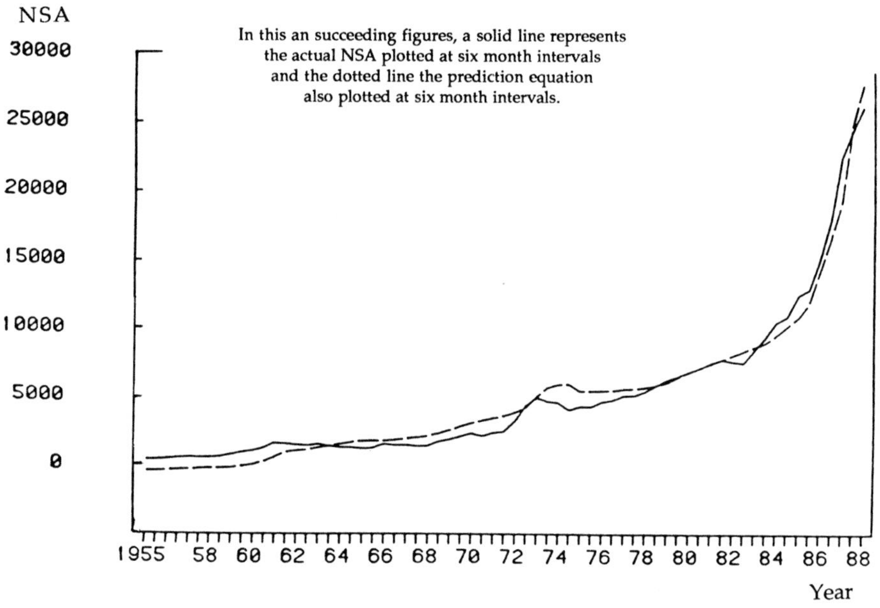

Using commerical land in the six largest cities to explain the level of the NSA leaves little room for earnings to explain much. Indeed, adding earnings six months ahead, which would be a proxy for current earnings estimates, results in an equation with a non-significant earnings variable (although it has the expected sign), a lower R^2, and only a slightly lower sum of squared errors. The equation is:

$$NSA_t = \underset{(-2.79)}{-1297.57} + \underset{(34.60)}{75.77} \text{ Coml Land}_t + \underset{(0.861)}{36.18} \text{ EPS}_{t+1},$$

with $R^2 = 0.971$, adjusted $R^2 = 0.970$, DW = 0.476, autocorrelation = 0.759 and SS = 870.38. Again the low Durbin-Watson value indicates positive serial correlation of errors.

The earnings per share variable is significant with the log model:

$$\log NSA_t = \underset{(10.60)}{3.008} + \underset{(26.60)}{0.8867} \log Coml\ Land_t + \underset{(4.58)}{0.6010} \log EPS_t.$$

However, the fit is not as good, with $R^2 = 0.950$, adjusted $R^2 = 0.948$, DW = 0.172, autocorrelation - 0.913, and SS = 0.24293.

Figure 8 shows how much poorer this fit is compared to Figure 7.

The log model with commerical land in the six largest cities does not fit nearly as well as the linear model. This model is

$$\log NSA_t = \underset{(33.2)}{4.189} + \underset{(31.0)}{0.9734} \log Coml\ Land_t,$$

with $R^2 = 0.936$, adjusted $R^2 = 0.936$, DW = 0.120, autocorrelation = 0.940, and SS = 0.27737.

Figure 8: The NSA and Commercial Land Index Values in the Six Largest Cities and Six Month Future Earnings, Log Model Predictions, 1955-1988

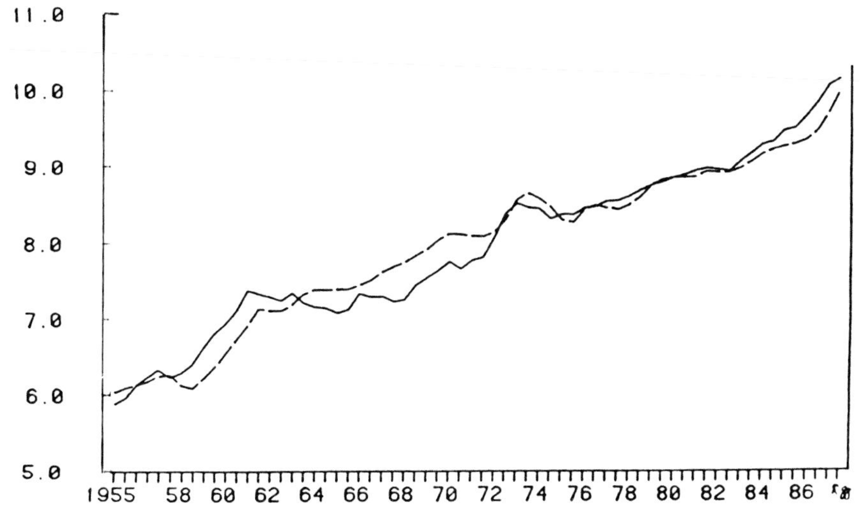

Using commerical land, the wholesale price index is now investigated. The importance of the wholesale price index in Japan can be gleaned from Figure 9

which shows that there is price parity at 1988-89 values of the yen if one uses this index. This is a painful reminder to all consumers in Japan of the extraordinary series of markups before a product the marketplace. The yen at 125-140 is greatly overvalued on a price parity basis for retail items compared to the U.S. dollar. (See Balassa and Noland, 1988, and Ziemba and Schwartz, 1991a, for surveys of these calculations.) See the discussion on a wholesale basis the yen is not overvalued. This should be noted by those who advocate a lower dollar to "solve the trade deficit problem" with Japan. With a higher yen Japanese manufacturers simply modified their operations to make their dollar costs lower. Indeed, as the yen rose in the post-1985 period Japanese manufacturers moved in this direction strongly. It is now commonplace in Japan for companies to list the yen/dollar exchange rate at which they will still be profitable and the percent of capacity at which this would occur. Some companies have their breakeven as low as 70¥/$ with twenty percent capacity. See the discussion in Ziemba and Schwartz (1991a).

Figure 9: Yen-Dollar Exchange Rate and Purchasing Power Parity

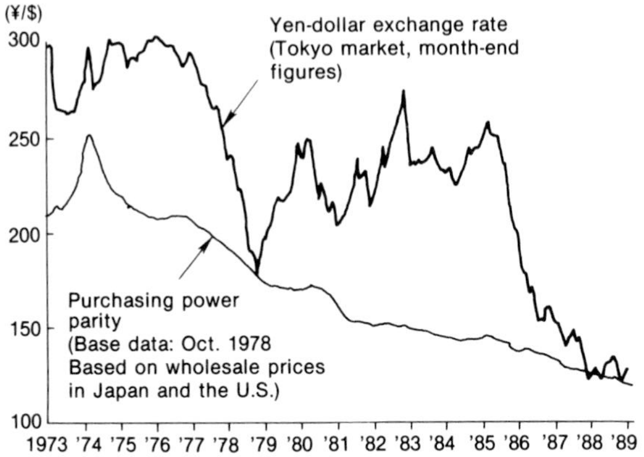

Source: Yamaichi Research Institute, based on "Needs" published by the Nihon Keizai Shimbun Inc. and other data..

The prevailing view is summed up by Akio Morita, the Chairman of Sony, "A stronger yen would not help one jot: they will pay more for the same Japanese products and we will buy up America even more cheaply." For an econometric analysis of the low dollar scenario see Marris (1989, 1987). See also Bergsten (1985). Marris' 1985 "predictions" were remarkably accurate during the fall 1985 to end-1987 period, but the recession he forecast did not come true. From 1988 to 1990 the yen/$ rate has been in a trading range of 120-160. Marris and Bergsten among others are still advocating a weak dollar to help resolve the trade deficit. That may help. But I take the view, held my many Japanese, that the econometrics simply will not work well as the structural characteristics of the Japanese productive economy are changing. What the U.S. needs more than a low dollar are better products that U.S. and foreigners want to buy, more savings and less consumption induced by higher taxes.

Using the wholesale price index and commerical land in the six largest cities one obtains the following equation for the level of the NSA with both coefficients highly significant and an R^2 of 98%:

$$NSA_t = \underset{(-4.40)}{-657.18} - \underset{(-3.84)}{51.37\, WPI_t} + \underset{(55.20)}{74.75\, \text{Coml Land}_t}$$

$R^2 = 0.980$, adjusted $R^2 = 0.979$, $DW = 0.592$, autocorrelation - 0.694, and $SS = 809.57$. This is displayed in Figure 10.

Figure 10: The NSA and Commercial Land Index Values in the Six Largest Cities and Wholesale Price Indices, 1955-1988

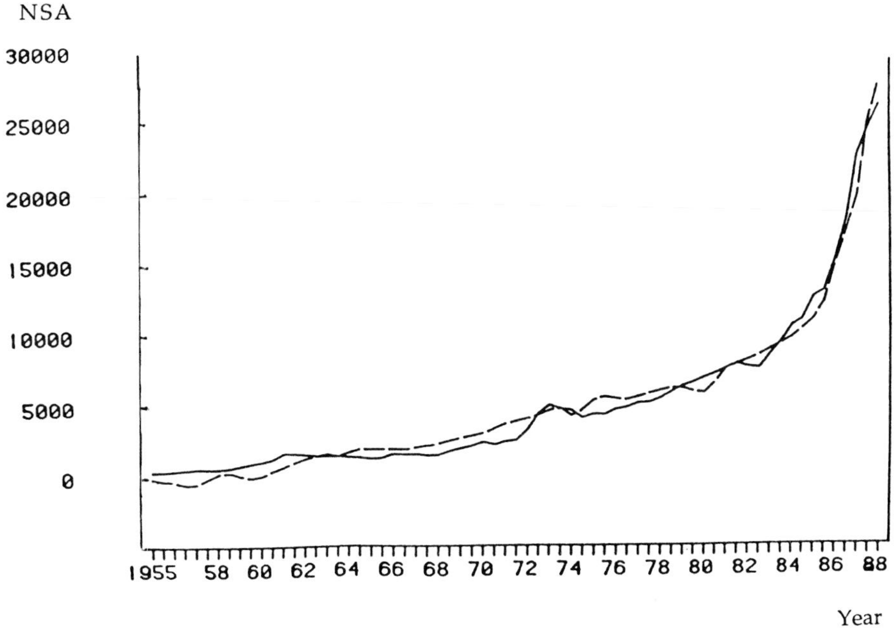

One obtains a slightly better equation, shown in Figure 11 and a near perfect fit from 1985-1988 when there was a steep increase in both land and stock values, by using commerical land lagged six months ahead. One then has

$$NSA_t = -453.85 - 24.30\ WPI_t + 65.94\ Comml\ Land_{t+1}$$
$$(-3.91) \quad (-2.28) \quad (69.8)$$

with $R^2 = 0.987$, adjusted $R^2 = 0.987$, DW = 0.339, autocorrelation = 0.824 and SS = 642.14.

Although not needed to predict the NSA, earnings per share does have the right coefficient sign and the coefficient is significant in both of the latter equations. For example, with contemparaneous commerical land

$$NSA_t = -1581.13 - 62.59\ WPI_t + 72.17\ Comml\ Land_t + 89.58\ EPS_t$$
$$(-3.71) \quad (-4.53) \quad (41.9) \quad (2.30)$$

with $R^2 = 0.9815$, adjusted $R^2 = 0.9806$, DW = 0.683, autcorrelation = 0.650 and SS = 783.63.

Figure 11: The NSA and Commercial Land Index Values in the Six Largest Cities , Lagged Six Months Forward Wholesale Prices and Lagged NSA Indices, 1955-1988

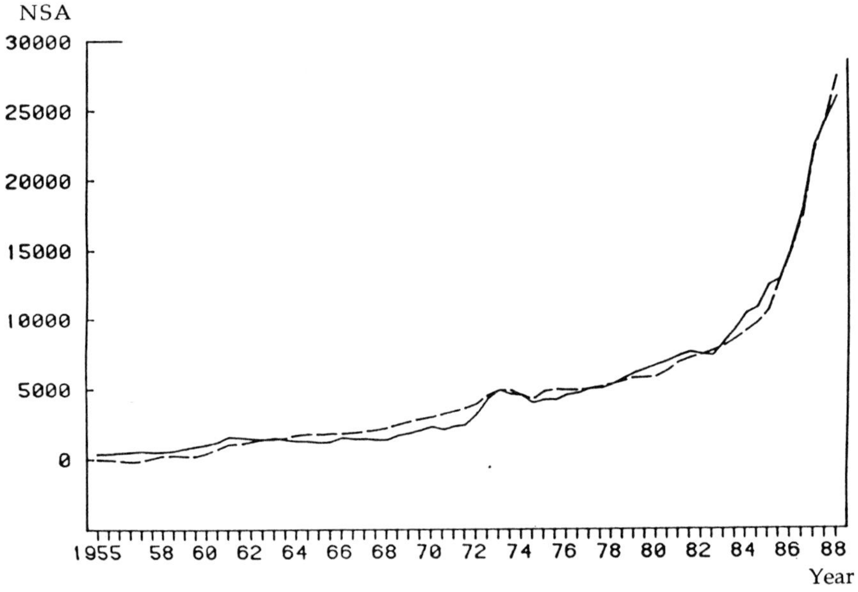

Adding lagged NSA index values to the commerical land and the wholesale price index gives an R^2 above 99%. Leading or lagging or contemparaneous commercial land makes little difference in the R^2 fit but the coefficients change drastically. The commercial land six months ahead has the best fit, with good Durbin Watson statistics, as shown in Figure 12.

The three equations are

$$NSA_t = -287.08 - 26.40\ WPI_t + 23.85\ Coml\ Land_{t+1} + 0.7318\ NSA_{t-1}$$
$$\quad (-3.56) \quad (-4.03) \quad (5.18) \quad (9.56)$$

$R^2 = 0.9942$, adjusted $R^2 = 0.9940$, $DW = 1.51$, autocorrelation $= 0.212$, and $SS = 392.02$.

$$NSA_t = -86.54 - 29.97\ WPI_t + 3.64\ Coml\ Land_t + 1.0567\ NSA_{t-1}$$
$$\quad (-0.817) \quad (-3.64) \quad (0.548) \quad (10.8)$$

$R^2 = 0.9930$, adjusted $R^2 = 0.9927$, $DW = 1.53$, autocorrelation $= 0.209$, and $SS = 483.00$.

$$NSA_t = -46.78 - 31.15\ WPI_t + 0.3425\ Comml\ Land_{t-1} + 1.1043\ NSA_{t-1}$$
$$\quad (-0.429) \quad (-3.53) \quad (0.0575) \quad (14.4)$$

$R^2 = 0.9932$, adjusted $R^2 = 0.9928$, $DW = 1.61$, autocorrelation $= 0.175$, and $SS = 477.09$.

Figure 12: The NSA and Commercial Land Index Valuesin the Six Largest Cities, Lagged Six Months Forward, Wholesale Prices, and Lagged NSA 1955-1988

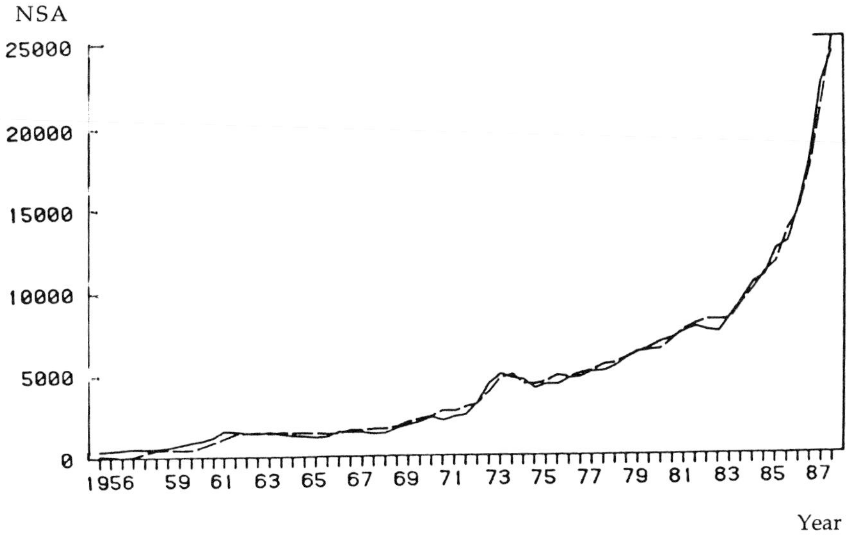

It is not very satisfying to use lagged NSA to predict current NSA. Except when using the future commercial land it takes over the equation. Indeed with lagged behind or contemporaneous commercial land, even that variable becomes insignificant.

We have the strong conclusion that the NSA stock index value is intimitely tied to the values of land in Japan, particularly commerical land in the six largest cities, and where these prices are headed in the next six months. Hence if the commonly discussed crash that many westerners see as inevitable happens, it will likely be tied to a simultaneous crash in land values. However, in 1990 there was a sharp drop in stock prices while land prices increased.

Using bi-yearly data and price levels rather than price changes makes the analysis simpler and the predictions more accurate. This approach can be severely criticized since one is in effect using time as an explanatory variable. Nelson and Kang (1984) discuss this. This bias leads to lower variances and hence greater than true significance. However, the results are so strong that they seem to stand up well. Our purpose is modest, to simply ascertain whether or not land price levels were instrinically related to stock price level and which economic indicator seems to lead the other. The results seem to clearly indicate this dependence and the stocks leading land causality seems clear. But one realizes that the prediction of the changes even over six month periods is not that good by comparing Table 2 and Table 7 in the Ziemba and Schwartz paper in this volume. While there were twenty-two stock price declines of 10% or more there was only one land price decline of about 5% in 1975-77, the second oil crisis period. Roll (1988) discusses the ability to predict stock price changes on daily or monthly basis using CAPM and APT models. The fits measured by R^2 are in the 0.20 and 0.35 range for daily and monthly data, respectively and higher for quarterly returns. Stone and Ziemba (1990) have investigated such price change correlations for land and stock prices using quarterly data. They found that stock price changes do lead land price changes using Granger-Sims causality tests. The P-values for the hypothesis that Topix does not lead all land is only 0.0000149 versus 0.15872 for the reverse hypothesis that all land leads the Topix. Canaway (1990) has estimated that the Topix lead land by eleven months during the period May 1985 to April 1989.

Stone and Ziemba concluded that: (1) stock prices are much more volatile than land prices; (2) despite their high level, the main increase in land prices was before 1971; the 1986-88 rise was high but the earlier rises were cumulatively much larger; (3) in late 1990 land prices were not falling but speculative land investment in condos and golf course membership, etc. fell sharply since March 1990. These investments may be highly related to small stocks; (4) golf course membership price changes do not usually lead the stock market but they did for the 1987 crash; (5) golf course membership price changes do lead land price changes; (6) the golf course membership prices increased more rapidly than stock prices which in turn outpaced land price increases. As of March 1991 there was a considerable gap between Tokyo golf and the overall land market; see Figure 14. In the past the previous gaps particularly in 1987, have been quickly closed; and (7) despite a great desire of the government to cool down the land market and to try to engineer a 20-30% fall, extreme demand cash flows, cultural aspects and unwillingness of the Diet to pass any serious tax laws that would probably generate such a fall, a great crash is unlikely.

Figure 13
The NSA Index versus the Nikkei Golf Membership Index, 1981:4-1991:1

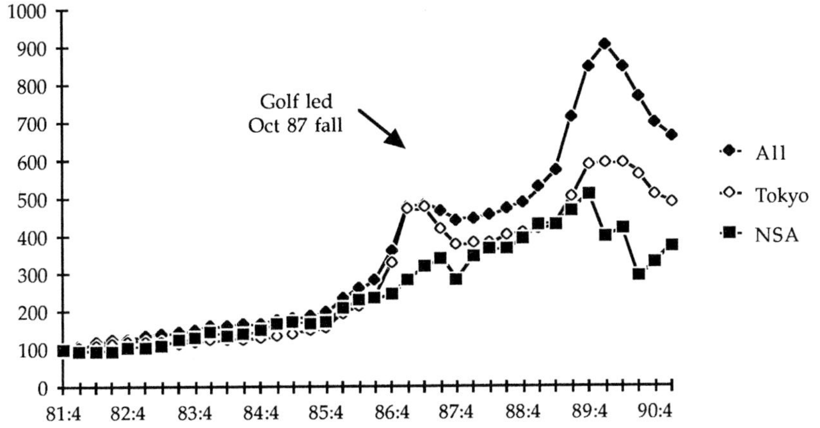

Source: Stone and Ziemba (1990) using data from th Nihon Keizai Shimbun, Inc.

Stone and Ziemba (1990) found that the dynamic regression model shown in Table 9 predicts land price data using past stock price returns.

Table 9
The Dynamic Regression Model to Predict Land Price Changes Using Past Stock Price Returns

Variable	Coefficient	Standard Error	t-Statistic	Significance
Constant	0.9689	0.4041	2.3980	0.0160
Topix (-4)	0.0128	0.0072	1.7880	0.0740
Topix (-3)	0.0355	0.0108	3.2910	0.0010
Topix (-2)	0.0398	0.0108	3.6650	0.0001
Topix (-1)	0.0161	0.0070	2.2920	0.0220
Auto (-1)	1.6509	0.0833	19.7970	0.0001
Auto (-2)	-0.8001	0.0832	-9.6160	0.0001

R2	0.954
Adjusted R2	0.949
Akaike Criterion (AIC)	0.464
Schwarz Criterion (BIC)	0.526
Durbin Watson	1.605
RMS Error	0.411

Source: Stone and Ziemba (1990)

Figure 14 shows the results of the model in the sample estimation period, 1972:2 to 1989:1, and in the forecast period, 1989:2 to 1990:3.

Figure 14
Prediction of Land Price Models In and Out of the Sample Estimation Period, Quarterly Data, 1972:3 to 1989:1 and a Forecast Period of 1989:2 to 1990:3 for the Dynamic Regression Model

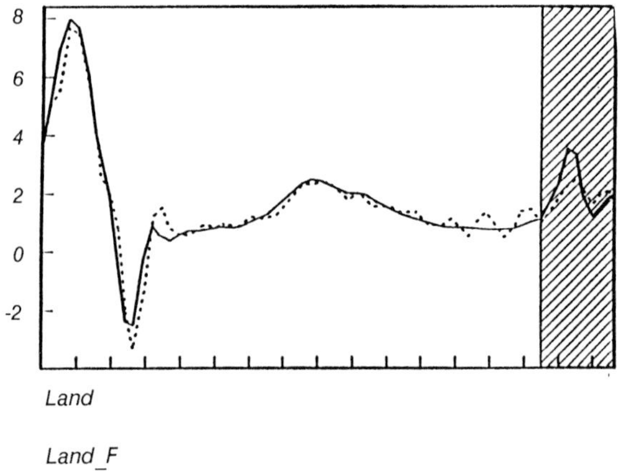

REFERENCES

Bergsten, C. Fred and William R. Cline (1985) *The United States-Japan Economic Problem*, Washington, D.C.: Institute for International Economics.

Boone, P. (1989) High land values in Japan: is the archipelago worth eleven trillion dollars? mimeo, Dept of Economics, Harvard Univ

Canaway, H. (1990) Land prices in Japan: no cause for alarm, Baring Securities, May

Cults, R.L. (1990) Power from the ground up: Japan's land bubble, *Harvard Business Review* (May-June: 164-172.

Elton, Edwin J. and Martin J. Gruber, eds. (1989) *Japanese Financial Markets*, Harper and Row.

Fingleton, E. (1990) Japan's other capital market hits a bunker, *Institutional Investor*, April.

Flack, S. (1990) The land of the setting property values, Forbes, April 30.

French, K.R. and J.M. Poterba (1990) Are Japanese stock prices too high? W.P. No. 547, Dept of Economics, MIT, forthcoming *Journal of Financial Economics.*

Gyourko, J. and D.B. Keim (1990) The risk and return characteristics of stock market-based real estate indices, mimeo, Wharton School, University of Pennsylvania.

Hamao, Yasushi (1989) Japanese stocks, bonds and inflation (SBI) 1973-1987, *Journal of Portfolio Management. 15:* 20-26.

Mankiw, N.G. and D.N. Weil (1988) The baby boom, the baby bust and the housing market, W.P. No 2794 (December), National Bureau of Economic Research, Cambridge, MA

Marris, S. (1985) *Deficits and the dollar: the world economy at risk.* Policy Analyses in International Economics #14. Institute for International Economics. Washington, D.C.

Marris, S. (1987) *Deficits and the dollar: the world economy at risk., Revised Edition* Policy Analyses in International Economics #14. Institute for International Economics. Washington, D.C.

McDonald, Jack (1989) The *Mochiai* Effect: Japanese Corporate Cross-Holdings. *Journal of Portfolio Management* (fall): 90-94.

Nelson, Charles R. and Heejoon Knag (1984) Pitfalls in the use of time as an explanatory variable in regression. *Journal of Business and Economic Statistics 2:* 73-82.

Noland, Marcus (1988) Japanese Household Portfolio Allocation Behavior. *Review of Economics and Statistics 70:* 135-139.

Roll, Richard (1988) R^2, *Journal of Finance*, 63, 541-566.

Stone, Douglas and William T. Ziemba (1990) Land and stock prices in Japan, mimeo, Frank Russell Company and University of British Columbia, presented to the Berkeley Program in Finance in Asia, June.

Ziemba, William T. and Sandra L. Schwartz (1991a) *Invest Japan: The Structure, Performance and Opportunities of Japan's Stock, Bond, and Fund Markets.* Probus Publishing Company.

Ziemba, William T. and Sandra L. Schwartz (1991b) *Power Japan: How and Why the Japanese Economy Works,* Probus Publishing Company.

Japanese Financial Market Research
W.T. Ziemba, W. Bailey and Y. Hamao (Editors)

Japan as a Creditor Nation*

Sandra L. Schwartz

Faculty of Business Administration, Simon Fraser University, Burnaby, B.C.

Abstract
The tremendous development of the Japanese economy over the past forty years has made it the world's largest creditor nation. This paper investigates how Japan attained its position and how it is currently using its new wealth. The dilemma and challenge facing Japan are explored and observations are made concerning the future.

Introduction

Thank you, Japan. The world's biggest creditor has played a similar role in the 1980s to that of America in the 1920s. So far, it has done a better job.
The Economist, December 23, 1989

The Economist praises Japanese participation in the world financial markets. By providing the steady financing for the U.S. twin deficits and funds during the two October stock crises in 1987 and 1989 they helped save the financial system from collapse. Though others take this as signs that the Ministry of Finance manipulates the markets, they instead point to the speed with which they have deregulated the markets.

However *The Economist* expressed other sobering thoughts. At the end of the decade of the 1920s the U.S. was in the same position as Japan with the aftermath of WWI turning it into the major creditor and then came the crash of 1929. They point to the speculative run up in land and stock prices in Japan and call for a

* This research was partially supported by the Social Sciences and Humanities Research Council of Canada and the Center for International Business Studies at the University of British Columbia. I would like to thank Warren Bailey and William Ziemba for helpful comments on earlier drafts of this paper. Additional detail on some of the topics discussed in this paper appear in Ziemba and Schwartz (1991b)

tightening of credit in Japan to head off the problems of the 1930s. This they believe will make Japan a better creditor.

Japan has become the world's largest creditor nation. Many come to Japan seeking more investment and expecting the Japanese to carry on as banker to the world and large contributor to world financial institutions because of the large trade surplus and accumulated reserves. In April 1991 Japan's foreign reserves were about U.S.$67 billion (down from $101 billion at their peak). The major companies were flush with cash and other liquid assets. Meanwhile the land and stock market booms have made millions of people instant millionaires with huge assets. Since stock market profits by individuals in Japan have not been subject to any capital gains taxes (and now only 20% or less) and banks freely lent money at low interest rates based on land collateral (of up to about 80% of appraised value and sometimes 95%) these gains were readily transferrable at low cost into cash that could be used to buy assets elsewhere. With the high prices in Japan and the yen strong, many Japanese institutions and individuals look to the U.S. and elsewhere to make investments. The Japanese are cautious, careful investors who like to invest where they are familiar and comfortable. But they are willing to pay high prices if the proposed deal is attractive over the long horizon, with the relatively low required rates of return that they normally employ.

Times are changing. Higher oil prices briefly cut deeply into the trade surplus. The Japanese knew they were vulnerable and did not see the surpluses as permanent. Japanese manufacturing is well established around the world further cutting into trade surpluses. As the trade surpluses fall, Japanese companies remain wealthy but the concentration of liquid assets has fallen.

Japanese management techniques are having an important effect on industry in the host countries. But they find that the workers need much training. They lack in the words of one Japanese manager *ishin-denshin;* the ability to comprehend without verbal instructions.

Debtors and Creditors

The world financial institutions are undergoing rapid change. The combination of the new age of information and the end of the age of mass production is transforming both real and financial relationships. The world economy is interconnected with fibre optic cables, satellites and satellite dishes. Information flows quickly and takes on a life of its own. Like information, money flows throughout the system; it is potential in the vast computer banks of the financial institutions.

Finance has two faces and financial institutions have two roles. Like a lubricant, finance - the flow of money - maintains the working of the real goods and services in the economy, linking sectors now and through time. Like a veil, finance pursued on its own, can also divert us from the multitude of missions and mechanisms in the economy. Financial institutions serve both to accomodate holding money as a store of value and to help funnel savings to productive investment. These two roles have become mixed as a result of a series of changes in the world economy. The growing overlapping of the roles as conduit of funds for productive and thus risky uses and for secure uses has led to attempts to manage money effectively in the short term to store value long term.

This conflicts with attempts to invest in real production for the long term, and has in turn generated the international debt crisis. To turn this around and differentiate functions will entail an awareness of a continuum of time horizons as well as a refocussing upon the real sectors of the world economic relations.

The debt crises in both the Third World and the U.S. provide both a problem and an opportunity to reshape our institutions and find a role for participation and craft rather than hierarchy, expertise and mechanical mass production. Everyone is either a debtor or a creditor, so no nation can ignore the problems.

Background

The recent epochs that have led to wealth redistribution world wide include:

- post WWII reconstruction efforts plus reliance on the U.S. dollar convertibility led to a U.S. dollar shortage
- Vietnam: U.S. inflation to fight the war without taxation provided stimulus to the rest of world, particularly in Asia, a dollar surplus was created. The U.S. unwillingness to devalue led to flexible exchange rates and a freeing of the U.S. dollar from gold convertibility.
- OPEC I: created a supply shock and also generated masses of funds to OPEC nations. The international banks especially those in the U.S., rose to the challenge and redistributed the surplus by finding outlets for the excessive liquidity of the few. Oil importing countries attempted to inflate out of the problem but the OPEC nations understood that their gains were transitory as long as the price of oil was tied to a declining U.S. dollar.
- OPEC II: everyone came to believe that oil prices would continue to rise. Resource rich countries like Mexico began to borrow on their future. Recession and debt crises began to appear. Japan, fearing the inability to finance sufficient oil imports, encouraged both energy efficiency and exports to earn more foreign exchange.
- Reaganomics and the double deficits: old debts were still a problem, now new ones including the U.S. debt also had to be met. In the early 1980s, the U.S. fiscal program known as Supply Side economics included tax reduction and increased defense spending. Tax revenues were supposed to rise as a result of growth in investment, productivity and income but the true impact was felt with higher consumption resulting in increased imports. Thus a domestic deficit created an international deficit. For an analysis, see Modigliani (1988).

The Mexican debt crisis in 1982 led to easy money. U.S. deficits actually kept other countries growing, including Japan which also benefitted from lower oil prices. Japan's trade balance widened rapidly and Japan became a major creditor.

Japan's rise to creditor status is discussed and the question is posed: can Japan maintain its economic viability and vitality and not give into the illusory wealth of being a creditor? How can it redirect its economy, not so much to turn out more goods but to deepen its services and flow of pleasure from the goods and capital it has? This in the end is the issue. So far Japan has been very flexible and adapted well to the challenges that it faced.

Review of Japan's post WWII history and Rise to Creditor Status

Japan's macroeconomic balances explain its rise to creditor status as shown in Table 1. Japan has had an excess savings *problem* since the early 1970s. In the period of reconstruction and growth, Japan emphasized domestic saving to provide the capital (both real and financial) needed. When the requirements slowed savings did not.

Table 1: Macroeconomic History of Japan, 1950-1991

Period	Savings/ Investment	Taxes/ Government Spending	Exports/ Imports	Exchange Rate
High growth 1950-73 >10%				fixed
	deficit	surplus	zero	till 1971
Lower growth 1974-85 = 4.3%				floating
based on trade to counter oil imports				
1974-79	surplus	rising deficit		small surplus
1980-85	surplus	falling deficit		rising surplus
based on domestic demand to respond to high yen				
1986-87	surplus	≈ zero		falling surplus
1988 (est 6%)	less surplus	rising deficit		rising surplus
1989-91 (est 4.9%)	less surplus	falling deficit		falling surplus
based on rising domestic consumption				

Source: adapted from Lincoln, 1988 and others

The Japanese had much rebuilding and catching up to do after WWII and the people worked hard. They had high savings and high investment needs. A policy decision was made to ensure that investment was from domestic sources so the government ran surpluses to balance their accounts.

Japanese development policies included tight fiscal and expansionary monetary policies (low interest to increase investment), balanced budget or slight surplus so that government did not compete for funds; public works supported business rather than social objectives; import barriers were erected both to protect industry and to avoid too high an import imbalance as the exchange rate was fixed. The world economic environment was supportive, including factors such as falling raw material prices and stable exchange rates. The Japanese valued education, hard work and loyalty. Labor management relations were nonconfrontational as most of the militant unions were wiped out by the early 1960s. The postwar occupation had brought in a number of reforms including land reform.

By the early 1970s Japan had met its driving needs, investment slackened but the custom of sacrifice and saving was ingrained and savings remained high. At this point Japan's economy began undergoing changes and it was set for new changes. The technological gap was closed, the investment requirements slowed, excess labor had been absorbed from agriculture and the retirement age was increased. Then followed a number of economic shocks:

- revaluation of the yen brought a 16% appreciation in 1971 causing a recession followed by rising prices;
- collapse of the Smithsonian agreement and institution of floating exchange rates with further appreciation of the yen;
- soybean embargo from the U.S., with only 6% domestically produced this created a scare even though there were no supply interruptions;
- oil embargo and two oil price shocks;
- growth sustained by public expenditures; and
- U.S. trade deficit and shocks of yen appreciation.

The surplus of savings could have been a potential for a recession if it were not redirected. In part the first oil crisis helped redirect and perhaps reduce it by vastly higher costs of imports. Later the government ran deficits to utilize some of the excess. This was a period of extensive road building. By the 1980s the growing trade surplus was able to absorb the excess. Japan had a current account deficit of $136 million in 1973 and a surplus of $49.2 billion in 1985.

Wage demands have been kept moderate due to the experience in the early 1970s. In 1974 workers negotiated very high wage increases but after the reality of the recession hit, they quickly moderated their demands the next year.

By 1980 the Japanese were confident of continued economic growth and the high quality of their manufactured goods. In fact the reputation for high quality, often speciality goods has enabled exports despite the rise in the value of the yen as described by Lothian in this volume. Official policy now is encouraging more domestic consumption and leisure to deal with the structural oversavings. This policy seems to be working but it is not at all clear how much domestic consumption can rise. There is little space to add appliances and other household goods; parking spaces are limited so two car families are rare; electricity is limited and not many appliances can be used at once; and resort facilities are crowded and airport runways are limited. In the end the true balancer may just be the ageing population. The growth in the elderly population and their need to draw down savings is often written about in the negative showing that this demographic change is not understood. It should not be feared as it could solve the structural problem of over savings!

Japan has proved itself very adaptable to its economic environment. Not only has it met external shocks but it is now coping with the ability to loosen up on its domestic control. The number of transformations in the decades since the war have been dramatic. The yen is attaining the status of an international currency. In 1990, the Japanese yen accounted for 8% of world reserves (up from 4% in 1980). The West German mark accounted for 12%, and the U.S. dollar 80%.

Japan as a country has become the world's largest creditor nation. In 1986, Japan became the largest net investor in the world - $180 billion (versus only $7 billion in 1976).

The major Japanese companies are flush with cash and other liquid assets. This in part is a result of the support of the U.S. dollar. In order to meet G-7 agreements and keep the dollar from falling further the Bank of Japan had to buy surplus dollars. This it did by printing more yen creating extra liquidity. Meanwhile the land and stock market booms have made many people millionaires with huge paper and real assets. Yet the Japanese do not act as if they were rich. They do not seem to act on a wealth effect. They continued high saving. Those who do not own property had to save even more, while those who owned property worry about paying the property sales tax if they were to sell. The extra liquidity went into stocks and more property.

Until 1990, liquidity had been so high that the banks were even selling loans to small businesses in Tokyo that really did not need them. As with the Third World debt crisis, this began to create a strain.

Financial deregulation also played a part. Once the domestic investment requirements were met it became possible to open up financial markets and this process is still incomplete. Post war investment allocation was essentially made by MITI given the huge imbalances. Interest was fixed by the Bank of Japan and also the bank lending was controlled. By the 1980s Japan moved into a freer system but old customs die hard.[1]

Trade balances

Japan's bilateral trade account with the U.S. had been in balance until 1976 when there a $7 billion surplus emerged. This surplus grew except for 1979. Lincoln (1988) notes an asymmetric U.S.-Japan relationship: U.S. exports to Japan have been fairly constant at about 11% of total U.S. exports while Japanese exports to

[1]Some major corporations that had switched to market based financing especially using convertible bonds have regretted this exposure to outside influence and may revert to bank financing. The recent Pickens purchase of 26% stake in Koito is a good example of the problems. Cutting the bounds of relationship may appear profitable in the short run but is often ineffective in the long run, see Schwartz and Sion (1991).

U.S. have risen from 26 to 37% of Japan's exports. In terms of investment, Japan holds about 3-4% of U.S. investment while Japanese investment in the U.S. represents 33% of all Japanese accumulated investment (1985 figures).

Japan's profits began to grow as the US and other countries began to place quotas on Japanese products shifting the economic rent to Japanese producers and pushing up the excess savings gap. In 1977 a quota was placed on TVs; and, in 1982, on autos. The quota raised the U.S. prices above those in Japan. Now money could be made in North America to subsidize domestic sales! Earlier, U.S.-Japan trigger prices on steel had made the U.S. more vulnerable to European steel while not gaining any positive response from the major U.S. steel producers.

Japanese overseas investment booms

The first Japanese overseas investment boom was their U.S. investments which peaked in the 1985-87 period. Banks, insurance firms and brokerage firms set up offices in North America. Some of them established real estate subsidiaries to improve their understanding of the U.S. market and to capitalise on higher U.S. property yields. The investments in U.S. debt and equity from 1970 to 1989 are detailed in Table 1.

Table 1 Net Purchases of U.S. Debt and Equity Securities by Japanese Investors

	Stock $1989M	Stock, % of NYSE	Bonds $1989M
1970	31.9	0.001	6.4
1971	147.0	0.007	5,108.0
1972	471.5	0.019	8,824.8
1973	1382.4	0.064	2,097.4
1974	-113.2	-0.008	-3,314.5
1975	50.7	0.004	-631.3
1976	146.0	0.009	-1,568.8
1977	67.5	0.004	8,875.2
1978	138.8	0.010	9,103.3
1979	217.0	0.015	-466.4
1980	-233.2	-0.015	-2,437.6
1981	160.9	0.010	1,781.1
1982	0.0	0.000	1,034.4
1983	339.9	0.020	3,153.5
1984	-156.4	-0.009	8,958.3
1985	343.5	0.018	27,989.3
1986	3727.6	0.163	15,754.5
1987	12402.7	0.521	2,691.2
1988	2014.7	0.084	30,856.4
1989	3348.0	0.122	8,724.0

Source: French and Poterba (1990)

The second phase was their move into Europe. This began in the early 1980s and is now in full bloom in anticipation of the 1992 European unification. The third phase is the move into Asian equities. The sums so far are less in Europe and Asia because the capital markets are smaller. But with the Asian markets just opening up this investment is increasing rapidly. Yasuhiko Ueyamo, the president of Sumitomo Life, suggested that his firm would like to increase the Asian share of its foreign securities portfolio from 3% to 33% over the next ten years.

As of April 1988 total Japanese direct investments abroad exceeded $180 billion. Of this over $30 billion was invested in the U.S., some 3% of total U.S. assets. In fiscal 1988 these investments totalled $33.4 billion up some 49.5% from 1987 according to JETRO. The U.S. took 46% of the 1988 investments but investment in Asia and Europe is increasing even faster. The yearly increases were 100% and 90%, respectively, in 1987 and 1988. Securities houses and banks held 73% of overall direct investment overseas followed by manufacturers, with 23.5%. The manufacturers' share represented a 200% gain over the previous year. Real estate investment increased 50.7% in the U.S. and 81.7% in Australia. The 1988 investment overseas was $22.8 bilion in the first six months and exceeded $40 billion for fiscal 1988.

In 1988, of 143 acquisitions whose prices were made public by Japanese corporations, 116 were overseas, amounting to $12.65 billion or 97% of the total of $13.07 billion. U.S companies accounted for 67.8%, followed by Australian companies with 8.5%, French with 4.0%, British with 3.4% and Hong Kong with 2.8%. The total investment was higher since a record 229 companies were acquired in 1988 in Japan.

Political turmoil caused more violent price swings leading to a sell off by foreign investors. Foreign investment in Japan is about 0.3% of the gnp and falling compared with Germany the next lowest at 10%. Foreign investors sold a net $1.95 billion in Japanese stocks in April 1989. They had a net purchase of $288 million in March 1989 for the first time since September 1988. They also sold a net $2.98 billion in Japanese public and corporate bonds ($1.1 billion net purchased in March). Japanese investors bought $1.67 billion of foreign stocks in April especially British listed stocks. Japanese investors had been net sellers, $2.31 billion, of foreign bonds in March following net purchases of $11.18 billion in February, 1989.

Japan's direct foreign investment (when foreign interests own or control 10% or more of a U.S. business) rose 35% to $30.82 billion in the six months to September 1989 compared with a year earlier; see Table 2. Finance and insurance represented 24%, real estate 19.3% and services 12.9%. At the same time Japanese investment in Europe increased 90%. The share in Europe increased to 24.9% versus 17.7% with declines in in the U.S. and Latin America. The share in the Asia Pacific rose as well while that in Africa declined.

Table 2: Japan's direct foreign investment, April to Sept 1989

country	investment, billions	growth rate,%
Holland	$2.81	325%
Britain	2.44	23
Germany	0.681	296
France	0.554	272
U.S.	13.13	15
Canada	0.657	93
Asia	3.91	47
Hong Kong	0.940	
Singapore	0.810	
South Korea	0.379	
Indonesia	0.338	
Pacific Region	2.36	90
Australia	2.27	100
Latin America	2.76	-3.7

Why are the Japanese investing much more abroad?

There are many explanations for the acceleration of Japanese investment abroad including:

- The yen was very strong. At ¥125-160 per dollar, assets in the U.S., for example, are inexpensive.
- Japanese investors were willing to consider and purchase investments with relatively low current rates of return because their cost of capital has been extremely low until recently and they have long investment horizons.
- With so much money available they simply had to spend it somewhere - domestic savings far outpace domestic investment needs. Japanese net external assets at the end of 1987 were more than $1 trillion U.S. up 47.3% from 1986. Private savings are accumulating at the rate of about $1.8 billion a day and this is only a part of the growth in wealth.
- The increase of trade protectionism in the U.S. and other countries as trading blocks are formed made it advantageous to buy or build plants and produce in the home market for sale there or elsewhere or even for export to Japan.
- Japanese firms wished to establish overseas operations for long run technological development.
- Many foreign districts such as U.S. states were anxious for the Japanese to build plants and create jobs for their people and to have the resulting highly efficient and productive activities and the positive educational, economic and other benefits. Rather than band together, individual regions compete against each other and further the process of Japanese investment under advantageous terms for the Japanese.

- The foreign operations allowed Japanese firms to expand and capture new markets abroad without fear of quotas, with lower worker costs and a positive reaction by the locals and the host government.
- The global strategy to expand and strengthen overseas production for the long term.
- To secure long run supplies of natural resources and raw materials. This includes large recent purchases of agricultural land for cattle and citrus orchards.
- To develop subsidiaries that could pass on valuable information to the headquarters in R&D, technology, marketing, finance, global trends and the like.
- Corporate tax rates in certain foreign financial centers such as Singapore and Hong Kong were much less than in Japan.
- Profits from subsidiaries in foreign countries could be used to pay dividends to insurance company investors.
- There is a rapid influx of imports from the newly industrialized economies (NICs) particularly those in Asia and it is profitable to simply produce there in Japanese owned facilities for export to Japan.

A survey of 54% of manufacturing companies and 48% of publicly traded companies by the *Oriental Economist* found that Japanese corporations have 15,000 subsidiaries and affiliates in 120 countries. They have 1,540,000 local employees on their payrolls and about 32,000 Japanese employees on overseas assignments.

Though overall Japanese exports are only about 10% of production, for a number of corporations exports are a high or sharply rising percentage of production; for example 99.7% for Uniden, 80.4% for Minolta, 75.5% for Canon, 66.6% for Casio and 62.9% for Honda. Disposing of this production domestically would be extremely hard. Meanwhile overseas production as a percentage of total sales is 30.8% at Nissan and Yakult, 38.2% at Sanyo Electric and 25.7% at Kumagai Gumi.

A new big player in Japan is also about to enter the scene: the massive Japanese pension funds. Until 1989 they were allowed to invest only 3% of their fund assets abroad. Now they are permitted by the Ministry of Finance to invest up to 20%.

Financial Institutions and Their Investments

Japan's financial institutions have overseas activities worth more than twice those of its carmakers and consumer electronics firms together. They went abroad for a variety of reasons:

- following their manufacturing clients

- net outflow of capital (foreign exchange controls were eliminated in 1980, along with less borrowing by government and corporations)
- desire to learn business they were not yet allowed to engage in at home.

Japanese banks are entering the international aircraft leasing and financing business. They are using innovative financing techniques including leveraged leasing. A leasing company sets up a limited partnership with nine investors. The partnership finances 20% and the banks finance 80%. From December 1988 to July 1989, one hundred aircraft were leased this way .

Aircraft are considered less risky than Third World loans as one has the planes as security. It has been projected that 12,500 commercial aircraft will be needed to meet the growing travel demand by the year 2000. Leasing is expected to double to about 25% of the fleet. The largest leasing company is GPA Group based in Ireland of which Mitsubishi Trust & Banking and the Long-Term Credit Bank of Japan are co-owners along with Air Canada. Not only are the loans secured but the banks receive 1-2% of the value in commission and interest.

The power of the Japanese banks was felt when the UAL deal collapsed and sent the U.S. stock market into a 190 point tailspin on the DJIA in the last hour of trading on Friday October 13, 1989. These deals cannot usually be put together without the Japanese. Unsatisfied with the terms offered by the main bankers, Citibank and Chase Manhattan, the Japanese gave only a third of the $3 billion that they were expected to provide. Japanese banks have lent as much as $20 billion to U.S. LBOs and are committed to an additional $15 billion. They provided $5.8 billion for the Kohlberg Kravis Roberts & Co. buy out of RJR Nabisco, and lent to Al Checchi to complete his takeover of NWA Inc.

	outstanding loans billions	total loan commitment of dollars
U.S.	$45.0	$72.0
Japan	20.0	35.0
France	8.5	10.2
Britain	7.5	9.0
Canada	7.0	8.4

Source: *Business Week*, October 30, 1989

Japanese banking institutions in California have experienced dramatic growth. In 1987 they accounted for 21.7% of the California market, their assets reached $76.1 billion. They have one quarter of the market for commercial lending. They accounted for four of the top 10 banks, numbers 6, 7, 8, and 10 as follows: California First Bank with $6.3 billion, Sanwa Bank California, $5.9 billion, Bank of California, $4.9 billion (Misubishi), and Sumitomo Bank of California, $3.5 billion. In 1989 they had five of the top eleven. The Bank of Tokyo owns 76.7% of Union Bank and claims to do business with 80% of the Japanese companies operating in California. After buying Union they merged it with their California

First Bank of San Francisco. The NY Fed estimates that the Japanese control 14% of U.S. banking assets.

Japanese Life Insurance Companies

As of mid 1989 Japan's life insurance companies had combined assets of over ¥95 trillion some $720 billion (see Shale, 1989). This is over twice the combined GNP of Taiwan, Korea, Singapore and Thailand. Nippon Life, by far the world's largest life insurance company alone has assets over $170 billion, some 50% larger than Prudential. Now that postal savings are no longer tax exempt, reducing their effective yields from about 7.6% to 3.7%, about 25% of the ¥30 trillion ($231 billion) expected to flow out of these accounts is destined for the life insurers. The insurers have policies that return most of the investments in the form of guaranteed payments over time plus bonuses in addition to the principal at expiry of the policy. The *seiho* already own about 15% of the TSE. Moreover domestic bonds returned coupons of 4-5% (until the rise in interest rates in 1990 to the 7-8% range). Hence, there is a serious problem about where to put the current and new money (about $26 billion per year for Nippon Life) to return enough - around 10% - to cover their commitments and make a profit. Their commitments include the 5-6% they must pay individuals and policy holders. Unrealized gains cannot be used for this purpose. Neither can realized profits on stock sold in Japan. Bond, money market and stock income as well as income and capital gains from foreign subsidiaries and tokkin accounts do count.

The return of the insurance portfolios is measured in terms of the *dividends* received and not the total return. Dividends include cash received from stock dividends, bond coupons, interest and profits from realized capital gains. This usually amounts to 6-8%. It is difficult to obtain information on total returns. The reported returns do not include unrealized gains from securities, land and other assets held. Since the NSA and TOPIX indices were up about 40% in 1988 and the seiho own 15% of the first section, their total return is well above 6-7%. According to *The Economist*, in 1988 54% of their inflows of ¥6 trillion was invested in securities. In 1988 the inflows totaled about ¥6.3 trillion in the first ten months. Some 39% was invested in stocks and a further 46% in corporate loans. The trust banks generally have returns that exceed those of the seiho because of their emphasis on separate accounts which have high performance in relation to the seiho's pooled accounts.

One way to improve this performance is to move into more risky but higher yielding equities, companies and properties. To improve their know-how they have purchased small stakes in leading foreign brokerage firms and learn investment technology.

Foreign investments are limited to 30% of the total and have been in the 20% range. The seiho have massive losses in unhedged U.S. bonds because of the dollar's fall from 1985-87. These losses were about ¥500 billion in fiscal year ending March 31, 1989. In 1986-88 the losses were even larger. In 1986 they were $17.8 billion. They also had massive losses in U.S. equities during the October 1987 crash. The emphasis then shifted to investments in Australia, Canada, and Europe. For example, Nippon Life's bond portfolio which constitutes 70% of its overseas investments is 52% in the U.S., 16% in Canada, 12% in England, 11% in Australia, 5% in West Germany and 3% in Euroyen, ECU and New Zealand dollar bonds. Their goal is to achieve a total dividend return of at least 8.5% hence low return bonds such as those in Germany are being phased out. With their reluctance to buy bonds with ratings less than AA this may be difficult. Investments in funds run by others such as the Salomon Brothers high yield fund set up for Japanese investors which yielded 10.48% in 1988 are increasing. The vast size of these insurance companies makes investing difficult. For example, the total size of the open Asian markets other than Australia was only ¥60 trillion ($46 billion) about 12% of the TSE's ¥550 trillion and less than a third of the seiho total assets of $170 billion. Real estate and equity markets are underweighted and may well have their exposures increased in subsequent years. The Japanese, like most countries, are still greatly underweighted compared to optimal asset allocation, see French and Poterba (1991) and Jorion (1989). As of December 1989 the equity portfolio weights of non-foreign investment were 82% for British, 94% for U.S. and 98% for Japanese investors; see Table 3.

Table 3
Equity Portfolio Weights for U.S., Japanese and U.K. Investors as of December 1989

	Portfolio Weights		
	U.S.	Japan	U.K
United States	93.8	1.3	5.9
Japan	3.1	98.1	4.8
United Kingdom	1.1	0.2	82.0
France	0.5	0.1	3.2
Germany	0.5	0.1	3.5
Canada	1.0	0.1	0.6

Source: French and Poterba (1991)

Changes in regulations have had a dramatic effect. This market is only now being opened Only recently they had to keep their assets in goverment bonds and domestic equity of certain types. The fall in the yen in 1989 and 1990 has associated with it huge Japanese investment around the world including major investment in Easter and Western Europe and the U.S.

Activities of Japanese Banks

Japanese banks already the biggest in the world based on capitalization are growing larger through mergers. Mitsui and Taiyo Kobe Banks (numbers 7 and 8 in terms of assets) have merged forming the world's second biggest bank. The largest now are Dai-cihi Kangyo, Sumitomo, Fuji, Mitsubishi, Sanwa all with assets of over ¥35 trillion or $250 billion. This was the first big banking merger in Japan in 16 years. The new bank is named Mitsui Taiyo Kobe Bank. The merger was prompted by Mitsui's need for more branches as its shifts from reliance on corporate customers. It also follows on deregulation of deposit rates and growing competition among retail banks. With the growing liquidity in the financial system in Japan, corporations are relying less on banks and more on the capital markets (as well as internal savings) for funds. As well the competition for personal savings is growing with securities firms, insurance companies and the Post Office all competing for customers. Regional banks, such as the Bank of Yokohama, Chiba Bank and Hokuriku Bank, are also growing and have a more secure place in their localities.

Other niches are also giving the banks trouble:

- foreign exchange business: many had large losses due to the dollar's increase against the yen
- bond profits are down in part as the government is issuing fewer bonds and foreign banks and securities dealers have been given a larger share (Mitsui profits of ¥21.7 billion in 1987 went to a loss of ¥5.7 billion in 1988).

The Bank for International Settlements (BIS) risk-asset ratio is forcing Japanese banks to pay more attention to profits. To help this many have issued stock and convertible bonds and sold off stockholdings in other Japanese companies.

MITI will expand its insurance on overseas investment in an attempt to encourage Japanese investment in countries with high investment risks for example wars and civil unrest as well as foreign exchange fluctuations. This will be provided at a risk premium of 0.3 to 1.3% from the current 0.55 to 0.65% and the period of coverage will also be expanded to 3 to 15 years. Insurance will also be available on debt-equity swaps and portfolio investment in developing countries.

Japanese banks may appear to be very conservative but that's because their speculative operations are kept off book in *tokkin* and *kingaishin* accounts (T&K funds) held anonymously by friendly investment firms or trust banks. There are reportedly ¥3 trillion in tokkin accounts (investment pools) the banks set up in 1980 and they are a major force on the TSE. While sales of stock managed in in house portfolios are treated as capital gains, tokkin profits are treated as ordinary income thus they can be used to alter the results of their ordinary business and inflate net operating profit.

New rules will make the accounts more transparent by accounting for a variety of classes of income: revenue from funds management, revenue from service transactions, revenue from non-core businesses and other current revenues. Income from foreign exchange trading, bond trading and bond redemptions will come under non-core while revenue from stock transactions will be entered under other current revenues. The tokkin accounts thus come under the other category. Banks had been disguising bond trading loses by transferring bonds with losses out of trading accounts to portfolio accounts; while revenue from tokkin trusts was used to window-dress banks' accounts making it hard to determine real value from published data.

There are two effects on the market. One will be to more strongly value those banks that are profitable on the basis of their real banking business. The other effect is the fear that the tokkin funds will dry up and cause a decline in the market.

New roles for Japan: foreign aid.

The foreign aid budget of Japan for fiscal 1989 is ¥137 trillion or $11.1 billion (evaluated at ¥123/$) which is higher than the $9.1 billion of the U.S. This amount like that of the U.S. includes grants as well as loans, including ¥804 billion of the latter to developing countries. There are many reasons for such aid: humanitarian, natural disaster relief, good will, investment, repayment of favors, military purposes and the like. Traditionally Japan has used its aid to promote exports and to help secure vital natural resources. Seventy percent of this aid has been given for industrial projects. But because of U.S. pressure Japan is no longer targeting its aid so narrowly and has promised to spend more outside of Asia. Among other things this will remove some of the U.S. aid burden. But internally there is much debate as to how this aid should be spent. Many would like Japan to go its own way and to strengthen itself for possible future trade wars.

Japanese banks are increasing their presence in negotiations on Latin American debt. In part they were concerned by the lack of World Bank guarantees for Brazil's debt restructuring in which they picked up a greater share so they are insisting on guarantees on $500 million of Argentine debt. Japanese banks have about $80 billion in medium and long term loans, second to the U.S.

Japan is expected to be the most important force in Third World development funding in the next decade. However cultural factors are at play here and for Japan to contribute more personnel to international organizations it will need to modify its life time employment expectations or arrange for a special category of personnel.

Japanese loans to and investment in developing countries rose to over ¥1.1 trillion in fiscal year 1988 up 49.2%, making this the largest aid program in the world. Direct loans to governments totaled over ¥1.09 trillion up 51.8% and loans or investments to companies were ¥8.6 billion down 52.6%. Japan is long on yen but short on development experts as the number of personnel has not increased. Aid spending was $1.56 million per staff in 1977 and in 1988, $5.34 million. They do not employ development experts but use personnel from consulting and trading companies.

Turkey is attempting to get Japanese investors. Many there are studying Japanese - urcins, carpet merchants and tycoons! Since 1985 exports to Japan increased 5-fold to $200 mil per year while imports have tripled to about $600 mil. Four joint ventures and 20 representative offices have been established. Japanese are evaluating hotels, golf courses, car, gas lighter and zipper plants. Political stability is seen as important, there is also a concern with inflation (about 65% in 1988) and red tape. Bridgestone making its biggest investment in 1988 paid $60 million for a joint venture in the Turkish tire company Brissa which plans to produce for Middle East and Africa. Toyota is considering producing cars in Turkey via a joint venture with a Turkish financial group. The investment is backed by export credits and government soft loans. Much investment geared to trading.

Japan is the largest supplier of development aid to India since 1987 and India is the fifth largest recipient of Japanese aid

Japanese corporations are becoming more formally involved in aid programs. One hundred Japanese companies have founded the Japan International Development Organization to help provide aid to developing countries.

Resentment and Praise for Japanese Investment Abroad

The Bridgestone case is interesting. It bought a truck tire plant from Firestone Tire and Rubber in LaVergne Tenn in 1983. The plant had labor problems and very poor productivity. Within six years they turned it around and went on to buy the rest of Firestone in May 1988 for $2.6 billion. Firestone, focussing on maximizing return to shareholders, had been cutting back on its manufacturing and concentrating on auto service centers. They halved its labor force, shut down 10 of its 17 North American plants and sold off some of its businesses. It created a mess of problems with inefficient plants, poor labor relations and poor dealer relations as well as poor supplier relations. Productivity at Firestone plants is about half that at Bridgestone. Bridgestone is still 40% held by the founding family. The company began as a manufacturer of tabi, traditional footwear. It has half the replacement tire market in Japan and 35% of the new car tire market. It purchased Firestone in an attempt to follow its customers into North America. But immediately on acquisition, GM, purchasing 20% of its output, dropped Firestone as a supplier. Though they won a contract with Honda, this did not fully compensate.

Atlanta has openly asked Japanese investors to buy their trophy buildings. Kentucky recently took a ¥10 billion loan in yen specifically to give concessions to Japanese corporations relocating there. The Toyota Camry factory in central Kentucky has been a very successful venture for Kentucky as well as for Toyota. On the other hand, communities in the Gold Coast of Australia, in Hawaii, in Ankorage Alaska and elsewhere are up in arms about being priced out of the market and for their land falling in foreign hands.

The Japanese globalization will not come without its costs particularly with the not untypical plan to virtually completely take over and to vertically integrate. Some Australians complain that Japanese never spend any Australian money at all on a vacation there. Everything is paid to Japanese corporations in yen.

The Japanese are increasingly aware of this resentment which is natural for virtually any outsider. A growing number of deals have been cancelled and although this is most publicly discusses in the real estate and mergers and acquisitions area, it happens elsewhere as well. Some Japanese companies have also faced strikes and other frictions with trade unions when they absorbed foreign subsidiaries as well as disputes with local residents and foreign governments. It will be a real challenge for the Japanese expansionists to use the vision necessary to bring out the positive aspects of these acquisitions for the benefit of all.

Japanese companies are usually not vertically integrated but depend on suppliers; for example, the just-in-time inventory system saves considerable resources and gains flexibility. Much of the costs are borne by suppliers that might burden down a large vertically integrated firms. On the other hand, leisure firms tend to be more integrated, with pre sold packages including travel, tours, accomodations, meals paid for in yen and spent in Japanese owned facilities. What really happens is that all the profit is yen based. And it is the profit that provides for regeneration.

The Japanese are attempting to be good neighbors as they follow their investments. In Norman, Oklahoma, the Japanese employees of Hitachi drive U.S. cars and spread themselves around different neighborhoods. Hitachi has set up the Hitachi Foundation in Washington with an endowment of $25 million headed by Eliot Richardson, a former cabinet member. They are buying $350 million annually of capital goods for their Japanese plants.

Mazada's Flat Rock Michigan plant received tax concessions for 12 years with a total incentive package of about $120 million in turn they are giving $100,000/year to the town and an additional $1 million for a sewage project as well as $70,000 to the United Way.

The Japanese government is considering tax deductions for Japanese companies if they give money to hospitals, schools and other charities in the U.S. This would put them on par with U.S. domestic firms and overcome the difference in tax codes in Japan and the U.S.

And the other side, support.

Walter Yetnikoff, president of CBS Record's, interviewed in Forbes, December 11, 1989, believes that Sony has been a good parent (purchased in Jan 1988). First they freed CBS Records from the bureaucracy enabling creative types to begin a turnaround of the company. Over the years the company had come to depend upon superstars and neglected developing new artists. It did have have enough talent coming up to provide income in cycles when the stars were not producing. Interestingly Sony got some negative press. In the year following its purchase, income fell dramatically, but this can be laid to the problem of the lack of new talent that had occured in the years prior to the sale. The whole strategy of development has been revamped. Previously they would put out two songs giving a new artist or group two tries at competing with the superstars at getting on Top 40 and if they failed that was that. Now they start with MTV videos and concert tours and college radio and other promos. Now CBS records is beginning to spawn new labels which will enable them to promote more artists.

The Role of a Creditor Country: Pitfalls and Opportunities

Historically when a country became a major creditor, it had already begun its decline. An economy that cannot use its resources - its skills and what is produced - cannot maintain its level of income and output. This rise and fall from economic power has been discussed by Jacobs (1984), Kennedy (1987), and Olson (1982) from a variety of vantage points. More or less, they all end up saying the same thing.

Kennedy (1988) discusses the rise and fall of nations in terms of finances and wars. In order to fight, countries had to borrow. Well developed and organized finances allowed long drawn out fighting. Surplus countries could lend but the costs of wars were such a drain on the economies of winners and losers alike that rarely was the money repaid. The money was surplus at the time and it may not have mattered to the lender if it were just blown up as long as it wasn't on their territory. Periodically nations would take a break from battle in order to rebuild their economies.

Olson (1982) discusses the same problems in terms of the economic rents and special treatment that grow as stability entrenches special interest groups. The longer a group is in power the more stake it has in maintaining itself and the more it falls prey to interest groups that want to continue strong and wealthy. The distortions created prevent the gains from adaptation and change and the country becomes arthritic.

Jacobs is concerned about cities and how they generate wealth. In her words (1984: 182):

Successful imperialism wins wealth. Yet, historically, successful empires such as Persia, Rome, Byzantium, Turkey, Spain, Portugal, France, Britain, have not remained rich. Indeed, it seems to be the fate of empires to become too poor to sustain the very costs of empire. The longer an empire holds together, the poorer and more economically backward it tends to become.

She sees the paradox as built right into the system of the types of exchanges than occur: military, subsidies to poor regions and investment to aid underdeveloped regions. All are the same in their effects and act as a drain on the economy.

To see why they do not work, consider a benign case similar to what a creditor nation might undertake: a transplant factory. Much of the requirements for the factory are imported as is the financing. And the factory is expected to pay back its capital costs and earn interest and profit.

- if the parent city uses the funds to replenish its own region then there is from its point of view only a temporary deferment
- if they are again reinvested outside the drain continues

Japan's production has outpaced demand creating a surplus. Will Japan lose its vitality as a result? Jacobs thinks so. A country that does not or cannot use what it produces is in trouble and is bound to decline economically. It is not nourishing its flow and the situation cannot be sustained. Economic relations to be sustainable must be reciprocal, to give the group must be willing to receive.

Japanese investment in production abroad may yet be able to defy the historical record. The attempt to make this investment truly global and embedded in each foreign market will help. But of course in turn this will lower the trade surplus and transform Japan.

The spirit of scarcity is a prime motivator of excess economic activity. It can sustain high levels of savings and productive investment. Scarcity can create output where none existed before for people work longer and harder for a transcendent cause. But what comes after scarcity? This will be the challenge for Japan.

Another stress is by way of financial markets. The opening of Japanese financial markets is putting pressure on the social web. This will change decision making perhaps weakening the Japanese economy by cutting at a major advantage: the long time horizon. Finance produces money, a non branded homogeneous good. The time horizons are shorter and one knows sooner whether a strategy has paid off. It will be harder to argue that seniority matters much or that long term loyalty is important, money earned by one firm is the same as money earned by another. There are no special qualities to the output as in producing a Toyota or a Honda. Thus there will be more pressure to reward *individuals* with higher pay and fast advancement. This will be a challenge in a society that has emphasized peer group responsibility.

Will Japan remain a major creditor in the future? This is hard to say. Higher commodity and oil prices could change its requirements for foreign currency. Success in transplanting technology is reducing their exports.

The world of debt and credit has shifted quickly in the past and is likely to again.

References

French, K. R. and J. M. Poterba (1990b) Japanese and U.S. cross-border common stock investments. *Journal of the Japanese and International Economies 4:* 476-493.

French, K. R. and J. M. Poterba (1991) Investor diversification and international equity markets. Working Paper 3609, National Bureau of Economic Research, Inc.

Jacobs, J. (1984) *Cities and the Wealth of Nations.* Vantage Books, New York.

Jorion, P. (1989) Asset allocation with hedged and unhedged foreign stocks and bonds. *Journal of Portfolio Management 15:* 49-54.

Kennedy, P (1987) *The Rise and Fall of the Great Powers.* Vantage Books, New York

Kobayashi, Kaoru (1988) Japanese Corporations Expanding Abroad, in *Top 1500 Japanese Corporations,* Japan Times.

Lincoln, E.J. (1988) *Japan, Facing Economic Maturity,* Washington, D.C.: Brookings Institution.

Modigliani, Franco (1988) Reagan's Economic Policies: A Critique. *Oxford Economic Papers 40:* 397-426.

Olson, M (1982) *The Rise and Decline of Nations.* Yale University Press, New Haven, Conn.

Schale, T. (1989) Too much, too soon, *Global Investor,* July/August.

Schwartz, S. L and E. Sion, (1991) *Athena's Tale: Issues in Social Responsibility and Stakeholder Management,* forthcoming.

Viner, A. (1988) *The Emerging Power of Japanese Money* , Tokyo: *The Japan Times.*

Ziemba, W. T. and S.L. Schwartz (1991a) *Invest Japan: The Sturcture, Performance and Opportunities of Japan's Stock, Bond and Fund Markets,* Probus.

Ziemba, W. T. and S.L. Schwartz (1991b) *Power Japan: How and Why the Japanese Economy Works.* Probus.

PART II:
THE BEHAVIOR OF STOCK PRICES

Japanese Financial Market Research
W.T. Ziemba, W. Bailey and Y. Hamao (Editors)
1991 Elsevier Science Publishers B.V.

PRICE AND VOLUME IN THE TOKYO STOCK EXCHANGE

Y. K. Tse

Department of Economics and Statistics, National University of Singapore, Kent Ridge, Singapore 0511.

Abstract

In this paper we consider the unconditional distributions of market return and trading volume in the Tokyo Stock Exchange. We also examine the relationship between price changes and trading volumes. The problems considered are directed by findings in the U.S. market, with a view to ascertain similarities and differences.

Daily market returns exhibit intra-week periodicity. Returns over daily, weekly and monthly intervals are negatively skewed and leptokurtic. While daily returns are slightly positively autocorrelated, the autocorrelations for weekly and monthly returns are statistically insignificant. There is evidence against the stable Paretian hypothesis for market return; and the empirical results are in support of market returns following a low order mixture of normal distribution. Trading volume is highly positively autocorrelated. This suggests that trading volume is not a good proxy for information. Our results also show that the price-volume relationship is weak and ambiguous.

1. Introduction

Due to the steady growth of the Japanese economy and capital market, together with the rapid appreciation of the Japanese yen against the U.S. dollar in the second half of the 1980s, the Tokyo Stock Exchange (TSE) has emerged as the world's largest stock market in terms of aggregate market capitalization. Academic research in the Japanese market has started to grow. Issues that have been studied include: the size and periodicity anomalies (Jaffe and Westerfield (1985b), Kato and Schallheim (1985), Kato (1988a, 1988b), Kato, Ziemba and Schwartz (1989) and Ziemba (1989)), the multi-index model and the arbitrage pricing theory (Elton and Gruber (1988) and Hamao (1988)), general market characteristics (Hamao (1989)) and the Japanese market in an international perspective (Hamao, Masulis and Ng (1989), Gultekin and Gultekin (1983), Jaffe and Westerfield (1985a) and Poterba and Summers (1988)).

This paper focuses on the structure of price and volume in the TSE. We consider statistical descriptions of the stock market returns and trading volumes.[1] The relationship between the variability of returns and trading volumes is also investigated. Our study is exploratory in nature and is directed by findings in the U.S. market. It is of interest as it examines the international robustness and generality of the empirical results in the U.S. market.

Assumptions concerning the statistical distribution of asset returns are of great importance to certain financial models, such as the mean-variance portfolio selection theory and the pricing of derivative securities. The mean-variance theory can be justified by assumptions of risk aversion and normally distributed asset returns. The celebrated Black-Scholes option pricing formula assumes the returns of the asset upon which the contingent claim is based are normally distributed. Thus testing the normality hypothesis has been a topic of much research interest. In one of the early studies in this area, Fama (1965) found that stock returns have higher kurtosis (fatter tails) than one would predict for a normal distribution. A viable alternative using the stable Paretian distribution had been suggested by Mandelbrot (1963), whose work led to further studies by Fama and Roll (1968, 1971). Although the stable Paretian distribution may explain the "fat tail" findings of stock returns, it introduces the problem of infinite variance in the distribution, except for the special case of normality.[2]

Later studies by Officer (1972) and Hsu, Miller and Wichern (1974) reported evidence that is not consistent with the stable Paretian distribution. Hsu *et al*. suggested a time-varying nonhomogeneous distribution as an explanation for the high kurtosis. This suggestion was supported by Boness, Chen and Jatusipitak (1974). Blattberg and Gonedes (1974) compared the stable law with the Student's *t* distribution and concluded in favor of the latter. Recently Kon (1984) considered a discrete mixture of normal distribution (MND) as an explanation for the observed excess kurtosis and positive skewness of stock returns in the U.S. market.[3] By fitting MND models with orders up to five, he argued that the MND is considerably more descriptive of the data generating process than the simple normal model and the Student's *t* distribution. This finding is congruent with a time-varying nonstationary return process. Periodicity anomalies and varying financial and operating leverages were offered as explanations for the nonstationarity. Additional evidence in support of the MND was provided by Harris (1986) and Hall, Brorsen and Irwin (1989). Recently Affleck-Graves and McDonald (1989) studied the effects of nonnormality on multivariate tests of asset pricing theories. They concluded that the robustness of asset pricing tests are dependent on the skewness and kurtosis of the unconditional distribution of returns.

In comparison, empirical research in the distribution of trading volume *per se* has been very scarce -- volume has been of interest mainly as a covariate in explaining the distribution of asset return. Clark (1973) assumed that asset return follows a subordinated stochastic process in which the directing process is the cumulative volume. Thus the volume in each nonoverlapping period was assumed to be independently distributed. Tauchen and Pitts (1983) suggested a mixing variable model in which price change and volume are simultaneously determined. These two variables are driven by a mixing variable which represents the amount of information reaching the market. As the mixing variable is serially independent, both price change and volume are serially independent. However, while the efficient market hypothesis requires stock return to be serially uncorrelated, it may be too stringent to require trading volume to be also serially uncorrelated. Serial correlation may occur if trading volume is an imperfect proxy for information or if it is not directed by the mixing variable with the given structure.

The earliest empirical examinations of the price-volume relationship were conducted by Granger and Morgenstern (1963) and Godfrey, Granger and Morgenstern (1964). Theoretical models explaining the relationship were suggested by Epps (1975), with further developments in Epps and Epps (1976). Since then, the research output on this topic has become very substantial. The recent survey by Karpoff (1987) provided an excellent review of the literature as well as an extensive bibliography. In particular, he summarized the following stylized facts regarding the price-volume relationship in the U.S. stock market: (i) volume is positively related to the magnitude of the price change, and (ii) volume is positively related to the price change *per se*.[4]

The plan of the rest of the paper is as follows. In Section 2, we briefly survey some features of the Japanese market and describe the data used in this study. The market return is examined in Section 3. It is found that the daily return periodicity has become more similar to that in the U.S. market. Excess kurtosis occurs, but it cannot be explained by the periodicity anomaly. Somewhat surprisingly, the return is found to be negatively skewed. Its distribution can be adequately described by a low order MND; and there is evidence against a stable Paretian distribution. In Section 4, we analyze the volume distribution. Significant serial correlation is found in the trading volume, which raises questions about the use of volume as a proxy for information. The price-volume relationship is examined in Section 5. The results suggest that volume is positively related to price changes *per se*, although the evidence is not very strong. Some concluding comments are given in Section 6.

2. The Japanese Market and the Data

There have been a number of publications that describe and explain the Japanese financial markets; a notable comprehensive introduction is the book by Viner (1988). Other useful references are Hodder and Tschoegl (1985), Hamao (1989) Kato, Ziemba and Schwartz (1989) and Ziemba and Schwartz (1990).[5]

Tradings in TSE are from Monday through Friday. Historically, there was trading on all Saturdays until the end of 1972. Then Saturday trading was gradually phased out until it was completely stopped in February 1989.[6] The most widely used market indicator for the TSE is the Nikkei Stock Average based on 225 issues (N225 hereafter). Apart from this index there is also a Nikkei Stock Average based on 500 representative issues (N500 hereafter). Both N225 and N500 are price-weighted index. Another price indicator is the Topix, which is a value-weighted index of all stocks listed in the First Section of the TSE. The data used in this study were extracted from the NEEDS (Nikkei Economic Electronic Database System) data base provided by Nihon Keizai Shimbun. A description of this data base can be found in Roehl (1985).

Daily, weekly and monthly series for each of the Topix, N225 and N500 indices were extracted. As the weekly and monthly series of the Topix index were given in arithmetic means over the interval (instead of end of the interval), we did not use them in this study. Table 1 summarizes the sampling periods of the data. The market indices were converted to continuously compounded rate of return by calculating the first difference of the logarithm. Trading volume series were also extracted for the same sampling intervals and periods. We considered three measures of volume:

V1 = number of shares traded (in billions);
V2 = (V1 x arithmetic stock price average)/(total market value at end of interval);
V3 = (Sales value during the interval)/(total market value at end of interval).

V3 measures the sales as a proportion (in percent) of the total market value. This is a better measure for the trading volume than V1, which is positively trended due to the increase in the total number of shares over time. However, as V3 was available only monthly, V2 was calculated as a proxy for V3 for the daily and weekly data. The correlation coefficients of the three price series and the three volume series are given in the second last column of Table 1.

The October 1987 crash created some discontinuity jumps in the return series. The Topix index dropped 15.8 percent on October 20 and recovered 9.0 percent on October 21.[7] Including these two observations in the data created some anomalies. For example, when the observations were

Table 1
Data Description and Correlation Coefficients

Sampling Interval	Sampling Period[a]	Variables	Correlation Coefficient	Number of Observations[b]
Panel A: Prices[c]				
Daily	86/1/4 - 89/2/28	(Topix, N225)	0.9529	861
		(Topix, N500)	0.9124	861
		(N225, N500)	0.9455	861
Weekly	83/7/31 - 89/2/19	(N225, N500)	0.8666	288
Monthly	83/8 - 89/2	(N225, N500)	0.8766	66
Panel B: Volumes[d]				
Daily	86/1/4/ - 89/2/28	(V1, V2)	0.9796	864
Weekly	83/7/31 - 89/2/19	(V1, V2)	0.9754	290
Monthly	83/8 - 89/1	(V1, V2)	0.9743	66
		(V1, V3)	0.9241	66
		(V2, V3)	0.9297	66

[a] For weekly data, a week is designated by the date of the first day (Sunday) of the week.

[b] For daily data, the return on October 20 and 21, 1987 are excluded. For weekly data, the returns over the week beginning October 18, 1987 are excluded.

[c] The correlation coefficients calculated are for the first difference in the log price, i.e., the continuously compounded rate of return. The prices refer to the end-of-interval (day, week or month) records.

[d] V1 = number of shares traded (in billions) during the interval;

V2 = (V1 $\times$ arithmetic stock price average)/(total market value at the end of the interval);

V3 = (Sales value during the interval)/(total market value at the end of the interval).

V3 is the sales as a proportion of the total market value. For daily and weekly data, this series is not available and is approximated by V2. Both V2 and V3 are measured in percent.

included, the first order autocorrelation coefficient of the return of the N500 index was 0.0037; and the skewness and kurtosis coefficients were, respectively, -3.88 and 73.26. When these observations were excluded, the autocorrelation increased to 0.1165; and the skewness and kurtosis coefficients became -0.32 and 10.20, respectively. Thus, the extreme return values due to the crash bias the autocorrelation coefficient towards zero, leading to the erroneous conclusion of insignificant autocorrelation, and overstate the higher order moments.

As argued strongly by Greenwald and Stein (1988) in their comments on the Task Force Report, the October 1987 crash should be regarded as a unique event.[8] Thus, we excluded two observations in our data set for all computations involving daily market returns. For weekly data, we also excluded the observation for the week in which the crash occurred.[9] Examining the volume series, we found that the figures during the crash were not abnormally high. Indeed, the trading volumes on October 20 and 21 were below the average of the sample period. Thus, no observation was excluded for computations that involve only the volume series.

3. Price

Table 2 summarizes the first four moments of the return series. To examine the intra-week periodicity, we calculated the summary statistics for different days of the week. Monday was found to have negative return, while returns for all other days were positive, with the return on Tuesday being close to zero. Although trading on Saturday was only for half day, the return was highest among all days of the week. To test the hypotheses: (i) returns are equal Monday through Saturday, and (ii) returns are equal Tuesday through Saturday, we apply the Wald statistics, which are distributed as χ^2. At 5 percent significance level, the first hypothesis is rejected while the second one cannot be rejected.

The above findings are different from others in the recent literature. Kato *et al.* (1989) pointed out that studies in the Japanese market since 1970 indicate typically small losses on Monday and substantial losses on Tuesday.[10] Compared with results in the U.S. market on the day of the week effects (see, e.g., Dimson (1987)), the shift from the "Tuesday effect" to the "Monday effect" found here is more in line with the periodicity in the U.S. market. However, earlier findings for the Japanese market in the 50s and 60s indicated that the heaviest losses were on Monday (see Kato *et al.* (1989, Table 6)). Thus, it is unclear whether the present evidence should be regarded as an indication of the narrowing of differences across national markets, or of the period-specific nature of the intra-week periodicity in the

TSE. The return distributions are negatively skewed and leptokurtic.[11] However, it is often argued that as returns in the equity market are bounded from below but not from above, it is likely that market returns are positively skewed. Studies in the U.S. market (see, e.g., Fielitz and Smith (1972), Fielitz (1976), Simkowitz and Beedles (1980), and Kon (1984)) have ascertained positive skewness in returns, a fact in contrast with the present finding for the TSE. One explanation that has been postulated for the nonnormality of daily market returns is the intra-week periodicity -- the observed skewness and fat tail are caused by pooling different normal distributions characterizing different days of the week.[12] If this hypothesis is correct, we would expect the nonnormality to vanish for returns categorized by day of the week. However, evidence from Table 2 shows that this hypothesis is not supported -- the excess kurtosis does not get smaller for returns thus categorized. If nonnormality is caused by the mixing of distributions, the mixing structure is more complex than a simple intra-week partition.

In Table 3, we summarize the results for testing for autocorrelation in the return as well as the variance of the return. The statistics used are the first and second order autocorrelation coefficients, denoted as r_1 and r_2, respectively, and the runs test and the Box-Pierce portmanteau test.[13]

For the return series, r_1 is significantly different from zero for the daily data for all indices, although its magnitude is quite small. Both the runs test and the Box-Pierce test show evidence of serial correlation. As r_2 and higher order autocorrelation coefficients (not reported in the table) are insignificant, the daily return series appear to be adequately described by a first order moving average process with a small moving average parameter.[14] Residual returns over longer intervals behave like a white noise. For the return variance series, there is significant autocorrelation for the daily and weekly data. A statistical model that may capture the structure of the serial correlation in the variance is the autoregressive conditional heteroskedasticity (ARCH) model due to Engle (1982).[15] However, to pursue our investigation of the robustness of the vast literature on unconditional returns in the U.S. market, we now turn to the problem of modeling the unconditional return distribution in the TSE. In particular, in view of the demonstrated skewness and kurtosis of returns, we consider the stable Paretian law and the MND.[16] The case of conditional modeling will be left for future research.

The full stable Paretian family that allows for asymmetric distributions is characterized by four parameters. We follow the definition proposed by Zolotarev (1957) and adopted by McCulloch (1986), in which the log characteristic function of a stable Paretian distribution has the form

Table 2
Summary Statistics of Returns

Data	Mean[a]	Standard[a] Deviation	Skewness[b] Coefficient	Kurtosis[c] Coefficient	Number of Observations(n)
Panel A: Topix					
All Days	0.106	0.992	−0.065	7.702*	861
Monday	−0.127	0.986	−1.231*	6.964*	153
Tuesday	0.019	0.894	−0.174	6.980*	154
Wednesday	0.171	1.060	0.732*	10.247*	155
Thursday	0.213	0.930	−0.083	4.871*	156
Friday	0.180	1.093	0.168	7.455*	155
Saturday	0.232	0.905	−0.321	4.398*	88

Test mean returns are equal Monday through Saturday, $\chi_5^2 = 14.514^d$.

Test mean returns are equal Tuesday through Saturday, $\chi_4^2 = 4.120^e$.

Panel B: N225					
All Days	0.112	0.940	−0.347*	7.480*	861
Monday	−0.159	0.948	−1.317*	7.210*	153
Tuesday	0.027	0.850	−0.563*	6.385*	154
Wednesday	0.210	0.978	0.239	8.509*	155
Thursday	0.215	0.914	−0.102	4.538*	156
Friday	0.180	0.996	−0.207	9.649*	155
Saturday	0.254	0.866	−0.293	3.833	88
Weekly	0.490	1.795	−0.385*	4.092*	288
Monthly	1.890	4.486	−0.282	4.002	66

Test mean returns are equal Monday through Saturday, $\chi_5^2 = 20.776^d$.

Test mean returns are equal Tuesday through Saturday, $\chi_4^2 = 5.001^e$.

Table 2 (continued)
Summary Statistics of Returns

Data	Mean[a]	Standard[a] Deviation	Skewness[b] Coefficient	Kurtosis[c] Coefficient	Number of Observations(n)
Panel C: N500					
All Days	0.078	0.845	–0.316*	10.199*	861
Monday	–0.156	0.856	–1.886*	11.666*	153
Tuesday	0.007	0.764	–0.821*	7.585*	154
Wednesday	0.154	0.867	0.821*	12.237*	155
Thursday	0.157	0.840	–0.093	5.034*	156
Friday	0.150	0.908	0.086	12.050*	155
Saturday	0.211	0.740	–0.318	5.519*	88
Weekly	0.361	1.717	–0.309*	3.886*	288
Monthly	1.280	4.453	–0.635*	4.564*	66

Test mean returns are equal Monday through Saturday , $\chi_5^2 = 18.989$[d].

Test mean returns are equal Tuesday through Saturday, $\chi_4^2 = 4.487$[e].

[a] Mean and standard deviation are given in percent.

[b] Skewness coefficient is the third sample central moment divided by the third power of the sample standard deviation. An asterisk denotes a case where the skewness coefficient differs from zero by more than twice the standard error, which is approximated by $\sqrt{6/n}$.

[c] Kurtosis is the fourth sample central moment divided by the square of the sample variance. An asterisk denotes a case where the kurtosis coefficient differs from three by more than twice the standard error, which is approximated by $\sqrt{24/n}$.

[d] $\chi^2_{5,0.05} = 11.071$.

[e] $\chi^2_{4,0.05} = 9.488$.

Table 3
Autocorrelation in Returns[a]

Sampling Interval	Index	e_t: r_1 [b]	e_t: r_2 [b]	e_t: Runs Test[c]	e_t: Q(24)[d]	e_t^2: r_1 [b]	e_t^2: r_2 [b]	e_t^2: Runs Test[c]	e_t^2: Q(24)[d]
Daily	Topix	0.18	–0.01	–3.82	57.9	0.13	0.23	–5.45	176.3
		(0.03)	(0.03)			(0.03)	(0.03)		
	N225	0.13	–0.02	–1.91	51.2	0.20	0.31	–6.77	306.0
		(0.03)	(0.03)			(0.03)	(0.03)		
	N500	0.12	–0.02	–2.33	64.7	0.20	0.34	–5.02	378.1
		(0.03)	(0.03)			(0.03)	(0.03)		
Weekly	N225	0.01	0.00	–0.05	8.6	0.10	0.27	–0.56	57.5
		(0.06)	(0.06)			(0.06)	(0.06)		
	N500	–0.01	0.03	–0.10	11.0	0.00	0.08	0.93	40.9
		(0.06)	(0.06)			(0.06)	(0.06)		
Monthly	N225	–0.04	0.00	0.39	18.8	–0.04	0.13	–1.89	6.3
		(0.12)	(0.12)			(0.12)	(0.12)		
	N500	0.07	0.06	–0.87	19.7	–0.10	0.00	1.04	9.0
		(0.12)	(0.12)			(0.12)	(0.12)		

[a] This table summarizes tests for autocorrelation in the residual (deviation from mean) returns, denoted by e_t. Tests for both e_t and e_t^2 are presented. For daily data, the differential return on Monday as against the rest of the week is accounted for. The residuals are obtained from the following regressions:

Topix: $y_t = 0.157 - 0.284 d_t + e_t$

N225: $y_t = 0.170 - 0.330 d_t + e_t$

N500: $y_t = 0.129 - 0.285 d_t + e_t$

where $d_t = 1$ for Monday and zero otherwise.

[b] r_1 and r_2 are, respectively, the first and second order sample autocorrelation coefficients. Figures in parentheses are the standard errors.

[c] The runs test statistic is asymptotically distributed as a standard normal if there is no autocorrelation.

[d] Q(24) is the Box–Pierce portmanteau test statistic for autocorrelation, which is asymptotically distributed as a chi–square with 24 degrees of freedom. At 5 percent significance level, the critical value is 36.4.

$$\Psi(t) = \log E(e^{itX})$$

$$= \begin{cases} it\delta - |ct|^{\alpha}\,[1 - i\beta\, \text{sign}(t) + \tan\frac{\pi\alpha}{2}] & \alpha \neq 1 \\ it\delta - |ct|\,[1 + i\beta\,\frac{2}{\pi}\,\text{sign}(t)\,\log|t|\,] & \alpha = 1, \end{cases} \qquad (1)$$

where X is a stable Paretian variable, t is the parameter of the characteristic function, $i^2 = -1$ and α, β, δ and c are, respectively, the characteristic exponent, the skewness parameter, the location parameter and the scale parameter. The normal distribution is a special member of the stable family with $\alpha = 2$, and is the only stable distribution for which the variance exists. When $\alpha < 2$, absolute moments of order less than α exist, while those of order equal to or greater than α do not.

To estimate the parameters, Fama and Roll (1968, 1971) suggested a fractile method based on order statistics.[17] This method was improved by McCulloch (1986), who extended the Fama-Roll method to take account of asymmetric distributions and a broader range of α. The results reported below were obtained using McCulloch's method.[18]

An important property of the stable Paretian law is that it is invariant under addition. That is, a sum of independently identically distributed stable variables with characteristic exponent α is stable with the same exponent. This property has been used by Fama and Roll (1971) as the basis for a test for the hypothesis that a random variable is stable Paretian. Hsu *et al.* showed that randomizing the stock market return series before summing up the adjacent observations increases the power of the test -- the shift in the characteristic exponent is more prominently demonstrated for the randomized series.[19] Thus, We considered two methods of forming sums of returns. First, we arranged a returns series in chronological order and summed up adjacent observation k terms at a time to form a new series. We defined this method as the chronological sampling scheme, denoted as C. Second, we randomized the returns series and summed up adjacent observations again as above. This method was defined as the randomized sampling scheme, denoted as R. As the summed series had to have sufficient observations for estimation, the value of k was constrained. For daily data, we considered k = 2, 4, 6, and 8; and for weekly data, we considered k = 2. The stable Paretian distribution was estimated for the original series as well as the summed series.[20] Estimates of α are presented in Table 4.

The results show very clearly that, for the randomized series, the estimated characteristic exponent approaches two as the sum size increases. The evidence is thus against the stable Paretian distribution. Similar to findings in the U.S. market, the chronological series fail to detect shifts in α. This would be the case if shifts in return distributions occur over stretches of homogeneous structures, or if the shifts are serially correlated.

Table 4
Estimates of the Characteristic Exponent (α) of the Stable Paretian Distribution for Market Returns[a]

Index	Sampling Scheme[b]	Sum Sizes (k) 1	2	4	6	8
Panel A: Daily Data						
Topix	C	1.544	1.584	1.388	1.749	1.586
	R		1.559	1.729	2.000	2.000
N225	C	1.558	1.758	1.470	1.706	1.371
	R		1.538	1.686	1.708	2.000
N500	C	1.606	1.671	1.798	2.000	1.698
	R		1.869	2.000	1.852	1.905
Number of Observations:		861	430	215	143	107
Panel B: Weekly Data						
N225	C	1.471	1.619			
	R		2.000			
N500	C	1.526	1.626			
	R		2.000			
Number of Observations:		288	144			

[a] Estimates were calculated using McCulloch's (1986) method. Due to insufficient observations, monthly data as well as weekly data with sum size greater than two were not considered.

[b] C denotes chronological sampling and R denotes randomized sampling.

Having rejected the stable Paretian law, we now consider the MND model, in which the market return is assumed to be a random drawing from a set of m normal distributions. Specifically, let x_i be normally distributed with mean μ_i and variance σ_i^2, for i = 1, ..., m. Suppose $\{\lambda_i\}$ represent a discrete probability function defined on i = 1, ..., m such that $1 \geq \lambda_i \geq 0$ and $\lambda_i + ... + \lambda_m = 1$. Then y is said to be a mixture of normal random variable if $y = x_i$ with probability λ_i . Thus, if we denote the density function of x_i by $f(x_i | \theta_i)$ where $\theta_i = (\mu_i, \sigma_i^2)'$, then the density function of y is given by

$$g(y \mid \theta) = \sum_{i=1}^{m} \lambda_i f(y \mid \theta_i), \tag{2}$$

where $\theta = (\mu_1, ..., \mu_m, \sigma_1^2, ..., \sigma_m^2, \lambda_1, ..., \lambda_{m-1})'$ is the vector of parameters with 3m-1 elements. Assuming we have a sample with n independent observations of y denoted by y_1, ..., y_n, we can express the likelihood function of the sample as

$$L(\theta ; m) = \prod_{t=1}^{n} g(y_t \mid \theta)$$

$$= \prod_{t=1}^{n} [\sum_{i=1}^{m} \lambda_i f(y_t \mid \theta_i). \tag{3}$$

Thus, maximum likelihood estimates of θ can be obtained by maximizing $L(\theta ; m)$ (or $\log L(\theta ; m)$) with respect to θ using nonlinear optimization methods.[21]

Kon (1984) estimated the MND model for the U.S. market. However, his optimization procedure did not impose any restrictions on λ_i, so that in some cases the conclusion about the order of the MND model was weakened due to the failure of the numerical optimization procedure to converge to a well-defined distribution.[22] To overcome this difficulty, we use a reparameterization of the quantities representing the probabilities. Thus, we consider m-1 parameters δ_i, for i = 1, ..., m-1, and define

$$\lambda_i = \exp(\delta_i)/(1 + \sum_{i=1}^{m-1} \exp(\delta_i)), \tag{4}$$

for i = 1, ..., m-1 and $\lambda_m = 1/(1 + \sum_{i=1}^{m-1} \exp(\delta_i))$.[23] Although δ_i are unrestricted, the transformation satisfies

Table 5
Estimates of the Mixture of Normal Distribution for Market Returns[a]

	Daily			Weekly		Monthly	
	Topix[b]	N225	N500[b]	N225[c]	N500	N225[d]	N500
Estimated Parameters[e]							
μ_1	0.127	0.172	0.108		0.093	1.890	−12.526
	(0.028)	(0.030)	(0.024)		(0.270)	(0.548)	(1.372)
μ_2		−0.195			0.653		1.697
		(0.183)			(0.155)		(0.474)
σ_1	0.680	0.659	0.607		2.129	4.452	1.728
	(0.035)	(0.035)	(0.026)		(0.214)	(0.387)	(1.085)
σ_2	1.885	1.751	1.953		1.023		3.756
	(0.192)	(0.184)	(0.242)		(0.206)		(0.347)
λ_1	0.831	0.837	0.900		0.520		0.029
Likelihood Ratio Tests[f]							
L_1	5.04	5.88	6.72	1.20	0.28	4.01	2.85
L_2	148.32	138.16	190.58	9.15	14.04		7.84
Implied Moments[g]							
Mean	0.127	0.112	0.108	0.490	0.361	1.890	1.280
	(0.106)	(0.112)	(0.078)	(0.490)	(0.361)	(1.890)	(1.280)
Standard Deviation	0.992	0.940	0.845	1.791	1.714	4.452	4.419
	(0.992)	(0.940)	(0.845)	(1.795)	(1.717)	(4.486)	(4.453)
Skewness	0.000	−0.481	0.000	−0.443	−0.290	0.000	−0.736
	(−0.065)	(−0.347)	(−0.316)	(−0.385)	(−0.309)	(−0.282)	(−0.635)
Kurtosis	7.158	6.890	9.301	4.374	4.044	3.000	4.610
	(7.702)	(7.480)	(10.199)	(4.092)	(3.886)	(4.002)	(4.564)

Table 5 (continued)
Estimates of the Mixture of Normal Distribution for Market Returns

[a] The estimates were obtained using maximum likelihood method. Mixture of normal distributions (MND) were estimated with increasing order until there was no significant increase in the log-likehood, as indicated by the likelihood ratio statistic. Then the accepted MND model was tested for (i) equality of mean, and (ii) equality of variance, separately. The results reported take into account the acceptance (or otherwise) of these hypotheses. Of all models estimated, no nonconvergence was found. Apart from the weekly N225 returns (which follow a third order MND) and the monthly N225 returns (which follow a simple normal distribution), all other returns are described by a second order MND.

[b] For these cases, the hypotheses $H_0 : \mu_1 = \mu_2$ was not rejected at 5 percent level. When this constraint was relaxed, closer fit for the mean was obtained, although this was achieved at the expense of poorer fit for the skewness and kurtosis.

[c] The weekly N225 data follow a MND of third order. The parameter estimates and their standard errors are given below:

μ_1	μ_2	μ_3	σ_1	σ_2	σ_3	λ_1	λ_2
−5.701	0.437	0.795	0.127	1.964	0.801	0.010	0.674
(0.079)	(0.165)	(0.165)	(0.054)	(0.151)	(0.154)		

Tests of the hypotheses (i) $\mu_1 = \mu_2 = \mu_3$ and (ii) $\sigma_1 = \sigma_2 = \sigma_3$ were rejected at 5 percent level.

[d] L_2 is not defined in this case.

[e] Figures in parentheses are standard errors. λ_1 is recovered from Equation (4). The mean and standard deviation are given in percent.

[f] L_1 is the likelihood ratio statistic of testing against a MND of one order higher. L_2 is the likelihood ratio statistic of testing for the acceptability of a MND of one order lower. Both statistics are distributed as χ^2_3, with critical value at 5 percent being 7.82.

[g] These are the moments implied by the estimated MND. Definitions of the skewness and kurtosis coefficients are given in footnotes b and c of Table 2. Figures in parentheses are the sample results extracted from Table 2.

the restrictions $1 > \lambda_i > 0$ and $\lambda_1 + \ldots + \lambda_m = 1$. Maximum likelihood estimates of θ can be obtained by maximizing the likelihood with respect to $\theta_1, \ldots, \theta_m$ and $\delta_1, \ldots, \delta_{m-1}$ and then recovering λ_i from Equation (4). The estimation results for the Japanese market are summarized in Table 5.

To determine the order of the MND model and test the variability of the means and variances across the set of normal distributions, we applied the following procedure. For each of the return series, we fitted the MND model with increasing order until the increase in the log likelihood was insignificant. The criterion for the stopping point was the likelihood ratio statistic, which is distributed as χ^2_3. Thus, m was selected as the smallest integer such that $2\log(L(\theta;\ m+1)/L(\theta;\ m)) < \chi^2_{3,0.05} = 7.82$. Of all the series considered, the MND models fitted are of very low order. Specifically, the monthly N225 series is of order one, the weekly N225 series is of order three and all other series are of order two. The likelihood ratio statistics $L_1 = 2\log(L(\theta;\ m+1)/L(\theta;\ m))$ and $L_2 = 2\log(L(\theta;\ m)/L(\theta;\ m-1))$ are presented in Table 5. For the daily data, the sharp drops from L_2 to L_1 are indicative of the unambiguous specification of m in these cases.[24]

Once m was determined, we tested the following hypotheses separately: (i) μ_i are equal for all i, and (ii) σ_i^2 are equal for all i.[25] Of all the cases considered, the second hypothesis was always rejected. The first hypothesis was rejected for the daily Topix and N500 series. The estimates reported take account of the accepted restrictions. To determine the goodness of fit of the final model for each series, we computed the implied first four moments of the MND and compared them with the sample quantities given in Table 2. These results are given in the last four columns of Table 5, where the figures in parentheses are the sample quantities. For most cases, the agreement of the two sets of figures is surprisingly good.

To sum up, the market return in the TSE exhibits intra-week periodicity. Monday has the lowest return, while returns on all other days of the week are not significantly different from one another. This finding shows a reversal to the periodicity during the 50s and 60s, and coincides with that of the U.S. market. Daily returns are weakly positively autocorrelated and follow a moving average process of order one. Serial correlations for returns over a week and a month are statistically insignificant. Return data are negatively skewed and leptokurtic. These features persist for returns calculated by the day of the week. Thus, nonnormality cannot be explained by intra-week periodicity. Finally, there is evidence against the stable Paretian law as a description of the unconditional return distribution. A better model is the

MND, which fits the data adequately with low order mixtures.[26]

4. Volume

There have been few studies in the statistical distribution of stock market sales volume *per se.* Most studies in stock return and volume focus on the distribution of return and use volume as a covariate in the model. However, the statistical distribution of volume may be of interest for two reasons. First, it is often argued that volume is a proxy for information arrival. As information arrival is random, volume is expected to be serially uncorrelated. Thus, the serial structure of volume may indicate whether volume is a good proxy for information. Second, some models either postulate the price-volume relationship jointly (Tauchen and Pitts (1983)) or explain the return process as a subordinated process driven by a directing process that can be proxied by volume (Clark (1973) and Blattberg and Gonedes (1974)). Knowledge about the marginal distribution of volume can be used to check the implications and assumptions of these models.

Summary statistics of the three volume measures defined in Section 3 are presented in Table 6. Except for V3, of which only monthly data are available, volume statistics were calculated for daily (further categorized by day of the week), weekly and monthly data. The table shows the first four moments and the first order sample autocorrelation coefficients.[27] We observe that volume distributions are positively skewed and slightly leptokurtic. However, as there are large and statistically significant autocorrelations in the volume series, the asymptotic tests for skewness and excess kurtosis conducted in Table 2 are biased and hence are not used here.[28] Point estimates of the mean show that Saturday volume is lower than other days of the week, which is expected because of the shorter trading time on Saturday.

To capture the autocorrelation structures of the volume series, we fitted time series distributed lag regressions for the volume data. Specifically, we considered the following model

$$V_t = \beta_o + \sum_{i=1}^{k} \beta_i V_{t-i} + \beta_{k+1} t^*, \qquad (5)$$

where V_t is the volume and t^* is a time variable. For each series, we selected the model based on the significance of the regression parameters and results of the residual autocorrelation tests. It was found that the order of V_t is at most two. Table 7 summarizes the regression results.

Table 6
Summary Statistics of Volumes

Data	Mean	Standard Deviation	Skewness Coef-ficient[a]	Kurtosis Coef-ficient[a]	r_1 [b]	Number of Obser-vations
Panel A: V1[c]						
All Days	0.902	0.482	1.100	4.264	0.693	863
Monday	0.720	0.344	0.627	3.027	0.460	153
Tuesday	0.885	0.459	0.922	3.586	0.509	155
Wednesday	1.048	0.538	0.964	3.455	0.597	156
Thursday	1.006	0.486	0.966	3.840	0.555	156
Friday	1.039	0.503	1.021	4.038	0.479	155
Saturday	0.565	0.268	1.230	5.129	0.264	88
Weekly	3.558	2.200	1.125	3.815	0.797	289
Monthly	15.317	8.329	0.998	3.404	0.733	65
Panel B: V2[d]						
All Days	0.294	0.150	1.153	4.547	0.674	863
Monday	0.234	0.105	0.556	2.898	0.411	153
Tuesday	0.287	0.142	1.046	4.183	0.462	155
Wednesday	0.341	0.166	1.010	3.804	0.577	156
Thursday	0.328	0.154	1.119	4.331	0.520	156
Friday	0.337	0.153	1.006	3.886	0.438	155
Saturday	0.186	0.082	1.290	5.800	0.201	88
Weekly	1.239	0.647	1.162	4.402	0.741	289
Monthly	5.296	2.351	1.216	4.421	0.649	65
Panel C: V3[d]						
Monthly	4.746	1.544	0.804	2.804	0.593	65

[a] Definitions of the skewness and kurtosis coefficients are given in footnoes b and c of Table 2. In view of the large and highly significant autocorrelation coefficients, tests for significant difference from the normal quantities based on the (uncorrected) asymptotic standard errors (see Tables 2) were not conducted. See Table 7 for the correct test results.

[b] r_1 is the sample first order autocorrelation coefficient. All estimates (except for V2, Saturday) are significantly different from zero.

[c] V1 is the sales in billion shares.

[d] V2 and V3 are the sales as a percentage of the total market value. See footnote d of Table 1.

Table 7
Estimates of the Equation[a]: $V_t = \beta_0 + \beta_1 V_{t-1} + \beta_2 V_{t-2} + \beta_3 t^*$

		Estimates[c]			Residual Analysis			
Sampling Interval	Data[b]	β_1	β_2	β_3	Skewness Coef–ficient	Kurtosis Coef–ficient	r_1	h [d]
Daily	V1	0.71		0.038	1.046	5.920	–0.02	–0.61
		(0.02)		(0.013)	(0.083)	(0.167)		
	V2	0.71			1.057	6.040	–0.01	–0.29
		(0.02)			(0.083)	(0.167)		
Weekly	V1	0.67		0.291	0.819	5.563	–0.05	–1.38
		(0.04)		(0.061)	(0.144)	(0.287)		
	V2	0.65		0.001	0.699	5.197	–0.06	–1.43
		(0.05)		(0.000)	(0.144)	(0.287)		
Monthly	V1	0.63	–0.29	2.479	0.708	6.091	0.03	1.64
		(0.13)	(0.13)	(0.650)	(0.302)	(0.595)		
	V2	0.60	–0.27	0.006	0.848	6.463	0.02	1.57
		(0.13)	(0.13)	(0.002)	(0.302)	(0.595)		
	V3	0.45		0.003	0.255	3.298	0.05	0.95
		(0.12)		(0.001)	(0.302)	(0.595)		

[a] Volume variables were regressed on their lagged values and a time trend. The reported equations were selected based on the following criteria: (i) the residuals pass the autocorrelation test, and (ii) all regression parameter estimates are significant.

[b] See footnote d of Table 1 for the definitions.

[c] For daily data five dummy variables representing different mean values were included. All intercepts and dummies were statistically significant. Furthermore, the dummies were statistically different from one another. The results for the intercepts and dummies are not reported. The time variable was rescaled in such a way that β_3 represents the change in volume over one year. For example, the daily volume as measured by V1 increases by 0.038 billion shares per day in one year and the weekly volume as measured by V2 increases by 0.001 percent per week in one year.

[d] h is Durbin's h–statistic for testing residual autocorrelation. It is approximately distributed as a standard normal if there is no autocorrelation.

Table 8
Regressions of Return on Volume

Price Index	Dependent Variable	Regression Estimates[a] Constant	Dummy	Volume	Diagnostics[b] DW	r_1
Panel A: Daily Data						
Topix	$\triangle \log P_t$	−0.153	−0.211	1.011	1.628	0.185
		(0.078)	(0.089)	(0.226)*		
	$(\triangle \log P_t)^2$	1.042	−0.026	−0.146	1.764	0.118
		(0.205)	(0.232)	(0.591)		
	$\|\triangle \log P_t\|$	0.707	−0.031	0.015	1.546	0.227
		(0.057)	(0.064)	(0.163)		
N225	$\triangle \log P_t$	−0.084	−0.270	0.831	1.740	0.129
		(0.074)	(0.084)	(0.214)*		
	$(\triangle \log P_t)^2$	1.021	−0.002	−0.426	1.609	0.196
		(0.179)	(0.203)	(0.516)		
	$\|\triangle \log P_t\|$	0.707	−0.022	−0.082	1.465	0.267
		(0.053)	(0.060)	(0.153)		
N500	$\triangle \log P_t$	0.033	−0.262	0.313	1.754	0.122
		(0.067)	(0.076)	(0.194)		
	$(\triangle \log P_t)^2$	0.900	−0.004	−0.615	1.622	0.189
		(0.173)	(0.195)	(0.499)		
	$\|\triangle \log P_t\|$	0.655	−0.025	−0.200	1.487	0.257
		(0.049)	(0.055)	(0.141)		
Panel B: Weekly Data						
N225	$\triangle \log P_t$	−0.161	.	0.526	2.023	−0.012
		(0.225)	.	(0.161)*		
	$(\triangle \log P_t)^2$	1.932	.	1.226	1.916	0.041
		(0.701)	.	(0.502)*		
	$\|\triangle \log P_t\|$	0.975	.	0.368	1.880	0.059
		(0.148)	.	(0.106)*		
N500	$\triangle \log P_t$	0.202	.	0.129	2.027	−0.013
		(0.219)	.	(0.156)		
	$(\triangle \log P_t)^2$	3.047	.	0.018	2.072	−0.037
		(0.630)	.	(0.451)		
	$\|\triangle \log P_t\|$	1.227	.	0.095	2.148	−0.077
		(0.143)	.	(0.103)		

Table 8 (continued)
Regressions of Return on Volume

Price Index	Dependent Variable	Regression Estimates[a] Constant	Dummy	Volume	Diagnostics[b] DW	r_1
Panel C: Monthly Data						
N225	$\triangle \log P_t$	0.554		0.254	2.097	-0.051
		(1.389)		(0.240)		
	$(\triangle \log P_t)^2$	13.917		1.852	2.168	-0.085
		(11.227)		(1.940)		
	$\lvert \triangle \log P_t \rvert$	3.036		0.149	2.229	-0.116
		(0.937)		(0.162)		
N500	$\triangle \log P_t$	1.732		-0.079	1.841	0.074
		(1.388)		(0.240)		
	$(\triangle \log P_t)^2$	19.364		0.400	2.281	-0.143
		(11.015)		(1.904)		
	$\lvert \triangle \log P_t \rvert$	3.849		-0.067	2.342	-0.184
		(0.950)		(0.164)		

[a] V2 was used as the measure of volume in the regressions. In accordance with the results of Table 2, a dummy variable to take account of differential mean return was added in the regression for daily data. The dummy is defined as one for Monday and zero otherwise. Estimates of the volume coefficient that are significant at 5 percent level are marked by an asterisk.

[b] DW is the Durbin–Watson statistic and r_1 is the sample first order autocorrelation coefficient.

For the daily series dummy variables that represent different intercepts for different days of the week were included. These dummies were found to be statistically significantly different from one another. To save space, results for the dummies and intercepts are not reported. The time variable t* was scaled in such a way that β_3 represents the change in the volume per sampling interval over a period of one year. For example, the first row in the table shows that V1 increases by 0.0377 billion shares per day over a year; and the last row shows that V3 increases by 0.0027 percentage points per month over a year.

It can be seen that volumes follow low order autoregressive processes. Although t* is statistically significant for most cases, it is economically insignificant. For example, the increase in V1 per month over a year is 16.2 percent (2.474 ÷ 15.317) of the average monthly volume over the sampling period. However, this increase may be largely due to the increase in the number of shares outstanding. The residual analysis shows that there are significant positive skewness and excess kurtosis. This departure from normality is significant for all cases except the monthly V3 series.

To sum up, the volume series follow low order autoregressive processes with statistically significant time trends. The increase in the sales ratio over time is economically insignificant; and, in the case of the number of shares traded, the economically significant time effect may be due to the growing number of shares outstanding. The volume distributions are positively skewed and leptokurtic, except for the monthly V3 series, which is not statistically different from a normal distribution. As V3 is likely to be the best measure for volume, this finding is notable. The negative results in this section may be due to the inappropriateness of V1 and V2 as measures for trading volume. Further research has to be directed to studying V3. To get around the problem of aggregation, it is also desirable to consider the volume of individual stock.

5. Price-Volume Relationship

To find out if there is any empirical regularity in the relationship between price changes and trading volumes in the TSE, we estimated regressions of price changes on trading volumes. Measures of price changes considered were: $\Delta \log P_t$, $(\Delta \log P_t)^2$ and $|\Delta \log P_t|$, where P_t is one of the three market indices. All three volume measures defined in Section 2 were used as regressors. As the results for different volume measures are qualitatively similar, only findings for the regressions on V2 are reported. The estimated equations and residual diagnostics are summarized in Table 8. For the daily data, we included a dummy variable to take account of the different Monday return. The dummy takes a value of one for Monday and zero otherwise.

Karpoff's (1987) asserted "stylized fact" for the U.S. market that trading volume has effects on both $\Delta \log P_t$ and $|\Delta \log P_t|$ is ambiguous for the TSE. Volume is significant for the daily Topix and N225 indices when the dependent variable is $\Delta \log P_t$; and is also significant for the weekly N225 index for all the three price-change measures considered. Otherwise, the effects of volumes on price changes are insignificant. Thus, the results are not only dependent on the sampling intervals, but also on the price indices. It is perhaps safe to conclude that the relationship between price changes and volumes in the market, if there is any, is weak.

In Karpoff's review, most studies in the U.S. market examined individual stocks. The conflicting results for different indices in Table 8 may be due to the aggregation over different stock components. Also, as the volume measures apply to all tradings in the First Section of the TSE, some data incompatibility may occur. In view of these difficulties, it would be interesting to consider the price-volume relationship for individual stocks, which would not be subject to the problems of aggregation and data incompatibility. Future research in this area will be required to ascertain any price-volume regularity.

6. Conclusions

We have examined the unconditional distributions of the market returns and trading volumes in the Tokyo Stock Exchange, as well as the relationship between price changes and volumes. Our results have demonstrated some similarities and differences between the Japanese and U.S. markets.

The intra-week periodicity in daily return in the TSE has shifted from a previous Tuesday loss, as found by many authors, to a Monday loss in the period under this study. Negative skewness and excess kurtosis are found in daily returns; and this evidence of nonnormality persists in data categorized by the day of the week. Daily returns are slightly positively autocorrelated, while returns over a week or a month are not significantly serially correlated. Although the returns are characterized by fat tails, the stable Paretian hypothesis, which was once postulated to account for this problem, is rejected on the basis that the characteristic exponent is unstable under addition. The mixture of normal distribution appears to be a better statistical model. In particular, low order mixtures describe sufficiently well the returns data.

We have measured trading volumes by three quantities and have argued that the sales ratio is the best choice. Trading volumes exhibit positive serial correlation and are unlikely to be good proxies for information arrival. The volumes follow low order autoregressive processes with statistically significant time trends, although the trends are only economically significant for volumes measured by sales in numbers of shares.

The price-volume relationship in the TSE is weak and ambiguous. However, the lack of a strong conclusion in this aspect may be due to the use of aggregate market returns and the incompatibility of the volume measures. Further studies using individual stock data are required to ascertain any regularities of this relationship.

Acknowledgements

This paper was written when I was visiting the University of Illinois at Urbana-Champaign. I thank Josef Lakonishok for stimulation and inspiration. Comments by Bill Ziemba and an anonymous referee are also gratefully acknowledged.

Footnotes

1. In this paper return is defined as the continuously compounded yield computed as the first difference in the log price. We shall use the terms price structure and return structure interchangeably.
2. Normal distribution is a special case of the stable Paretian family. See Mandelbrot (1973) for a discussion of the problem of infinite variance.
3. The MND model was earlier suggested by Fama and Roll (1971). A Poisson mixture of normal distribution was considered by Press (1967).
4. The term "price change" here may be interpreted as price change relative, or continuously compounded rate of return.
5. See also other references in this volume.
6. See Kato *et al.* (1989) for more details.
7. As shown in Table 2 below, the average daily return is only 0.11 percent with a standard deviation of 0.99 percent.
8. Greenwald and Stein (1988, p. 16) concluded that "the stock market crash of October 1987 was fundamentally a unique event, wholly different in character from normal market behavior." If this conclusion is accepted, observations of the crash event should be regarded as outliers.
9. The drop in this week for the N225 index was 12.37 percent. From Table 2, the mean weekly return is 0.49 percent with a standard deviation of 1.80 percent.
10. See Ziemba (1989a, 1989b) for related results.
11. A distribution is said to be leptokurtic if its kurtosis coefficient is greater than three, which is the kurtosis value for a normal distribution. Tests for symmetry and no excess kurtosis are conducted in Table 2; and significance is indicated by an asterisk. These tests assume independent

sample observations. As shown in Table 3 below, the daily return series are slightly positively autocorrelated. This implies that the significance of the tests may be overstated. However, for the kurtosis test, this problem is unlikely to affect the results qualitatively, as the kurtosis coefficients are quite large.

12. See Kon (1984) for discussions of this hypothesis and other possibilities of nonstationarity in the mean and variance.

13. The distribution of the Box-Pierce statistic for the variance of the return was established by McLeod and Li (1983).

14. Hamao *et al.* (1989) also used a moving average process of order one to correct for residual autocorrelation in their study in international market links.

15. See Engle and Bollerslev (1986) for a survey of the ARCH literature.

16. We did not consider student's *t* distribution, as Kon's study suggested that it is likely to be dominated by the MND.

17. As the density function of a stable Paretian distribution in general does not exist in closed form, estimation by maximum likelihood method is very difficult.

18. An alternative method is the iterative regression procedure of Koutrouvelis (1980, 1981). See Akgiray and Lamoureux (1989) for a comparison of the two techniques.

19. The procedure suggested by Fama and Roll is not a significance test in the usual sense. Conclusion is drawn by observing whether there is any "obvious" shift in the estimates of α.

20. Due to insufficient observations, monthly data were not considered in this exercise. Although we also estimated β, the results are not reported here, as our main objective is to test for the stability of α and thus the acceptability of the stable Paretian law. As pointed out by Akgiray and Lamoureux (1989), estimates of β are not robust to small perturbations in the sample and their standard errors are very large. Furthermore, as α approaches two, β loses its effects on the distribution (see McCulloch (1986, p. 1111)).

21. The optimization subroutine used in this study is DUMINF of the IMSL library. Standard errors were calculated by numerically differentiating the Hessian matrix using the DFDHES subroutine. As the daily return series are autocorrelated, the standard errors computed may be downward biased. However, in view of the small magnitude of the autocorrelation coefficient, this problem is unlikely to be serious.

22. Kon reported that when m = 3, only 15 of the 30 stocks considered reached well-defined optimum.

23. This transformation is a particular case of the choice probability of a multinomial logit model (see, e.g., Amemiya (1985, Chapter 9)). Using this transformation, we did not encounter any nonconvergence for all cases considered.

24. As is apparent from the L_2 statistic, rejection of m = 1 against m = 2 for the monthly N500 series is only

marginally significant at 5 percent. Also, rejection of m = 2 against m = 3 for the weekly N225 series is significant at 5 percent but not at 1 percent.

25. Note that when μ_i are equal for all i, the MND is symmetrical.

26. Ikeda and Kanazaki (1989) considered return distributions given by mixed jump log-normal diffusion processes. They assumed that the mixing variable has finite moments up to the sixth order, and fitted the return distributions using a 'cumulant matching method'. Their model has special implications for studying the effects of information release on market returns.

27. For volume classified according to day of the week, r_1 is calculated for the subseries. Although there are gaps in the volume subseries, r_1 is still moderately large and statistically significant.

28. Some correct test results are presented in Table 7 below.

References

Affleck-Graves, J., and B. McDonald, 1989, "Nonnormalities and Tests of Asset Pricing Theories," *Journal of Finance*, 44, 889-908.

Akgiray, V., and C. G. Lamoureux, 1989, "Estimation of Stable-Law Parameters: A Comparative Study," *Journal of Business and Economic Statistics* 7, 85-93.

Amemiya, T., 1985, *Advanced Econometrics*, Cambridge, MA: Harvard University Press.

Blattberg, R. C., and N. J. Gonedes, 1974, "A Comparison of the Stable and Student Distributions as Statistical Models for Stock Prices," *Journal of Business* 47, 244-280.

Boness, A. J., A. H. Chen, and S. Jatusipitak, 1974, "Investigations of Nonstationarity in Prices," *Journal of Business* 47, 518-537.

Clark, P. K., 1973, "A Subordinate Stochastic Process Model with Finite Variance for Speculative Prices," *Econometrica* 41, 135-155.

Dimson, E., 1987, *Stock Markets Anomalies*, Cambridge, U.K.: Cambridge University Press.

Elton, E. J., and M. J. Gruber, 1988, "A Multi-Index Risk Model of the Japanese Stock Market," *Japan and the World Economy* 1, 21-44.

Engle, R. F., 1982, "Autoregressive Conditional Heteroskedasticity with Estimates of the Variance of U.K. Inflation," *Econometrica* 50, 987-1008.

Engle, R. F., and T. Bollerslev, 1986, "Modelling the Persistence of Conditional Variances," *Econometric Reviews* 5, 1-50.

Epps, T. W., 1975, "Security Price Changes and Transaction Volumes: Theory and Evidence," *American Economic Review* 65, 586-597.

Epps, T. W., and M. L. Epps, 1976, "The Stochastic Dependence of Security Price Changes and Transaction Volumes: Implications for the Mixture-of-Distribution Hypothesis," *Econometrica* 44, 305-321.
Fama, E., 1965, "Behavior of Stock Market Prices," *Journal of Business* 38, 34-105.
Fama, E. F., and R. Roll, 1968, "Some Properties of Symmetric Stable Distributions," *Journal of the American Statistical Association* 63, 817-836.
Fama, E. F., and R. Roll, 1971, "Parameter Estimates for Symmetric Stable Distributions," *Journal of the American Statistical Association* 66, 331-338.
Fielitz, B. D., 1976, "Further Results on Asymmetric Stable Distributions of Stock Price Changes," *Journal of Financial and Quantitative Analysis* 11, 39-55.
Fielitz, B. D., and E. W. Smith, 1972, "Asymmetric Stable Distributions of Stock Price Changes," *Journal of the American Statistical Association* 67, 813-814.
Godfrey, M. D., C. W. J. Granger, and O. Morgenstern, 1964, "The Random Walk Hypothesis of Stock Market Behavior," *Kyklos* 17, 1-30.
Granger, C. W. J., and O. Morgenstern, 1963, "Spectral Analysis of New York Stock Market Prices," *Kyklos* 16, 1-27.
Greenwald, B., and J. Stein, 1988, "The Task Force Report: The Reasoning Behind the Recommendations," *Journal of Economic Perspectives* 2, 3-23.
Gultekin, M. N., and N. B. Gultekin, 1983, "Stock Market Seasonality: International Evidence," *Journal of Financial Economics* 12, 469-481.
Hall, J. A., B. W. Brorsen, and S. H. Irwin, 1989, "The Distribution of Futures Prices: A Test of the Stable Paretian and Mixture of Normals Hypotheses," *Journal of Financial and Quantitative Analysis* 24, 105-116.
Hamao, Y., 1988, "An Empirical Examination of the Arbitrage Pricing Theory: Using Japanese Data," *Japan and the World Economy* 1, 45-61.
Hamao, Y., 1989, "Japanese Stocks, Bonds, Bills, and Inflation, 1973-87," *Journal of Portfolio Management* 15, 20-26.
Hamao, Y., R. W. Masulis, and V. Ng, 1989, "Correlations in Price Changes and Volatility Across International Stock Markets," *The Review of Financial Studies* 3, 281-307.
Harris, L., 1986, "Cross-Security Tests of the Mixture of Distributions Hypothesis," *Journal of Financial and Quantitative Analysis* 21, 39-46.
Hodder, J. E., and A. E. Tschoegl, 1985, "Some Aspects of Japanese Corporate Finance," *Journal of Financial and Quantitative Analysis* 20, 173-191.
Hsu, D., R. B. Miller, and D. W. Wichern, 1974, "On the Stable Paretian Behavior of Stock-Market Prices," *Journal of the American Statistical Association* 69. 108-113.

Ikeda, M., and Y. Kanazaki, 1989, "Diffusion-Jump Model to Measure Information Release and Its Effects on Capital Markets," This volume.

Jaffe, J., and R. Westerfield, 1985a, "The Weekend Effect in Common Stock Returns: The International Evidence," *Journal of Finance* 40, 433-454.

Jaffe, J., and R. Westerfield, 1985b, "Patterns in Japanese Common Stock Returns: Day of the Week and Turn of the Year Effects," *Journal of Financial and Quantitative Analysis* 20, 243-260.

Karpoff, J. M., 1987, "The Relation Between Price Changes and Trading Volume: A Survey," *Journal of Financial and Quantitative Analysis* 22, 109-126.

Kato, K., 1988a, "Weekly Patterns in Japanese Stock Returns," This volume.

Kato, K., 1988b, "A Further Investigation of Anomalies on the Tokyo Stock Exchange," Working Paper, Nanzan University, Nagoya, Japan.

Kato, K., and J. S. Schallheim, 1985, "Seasonal and Size Anomalies in the Japanese Stock Market," *Journal of Financial and Quantitative Analysis* 20, 243-272.

Kato, K., W. T. Ziemba, and S. L. Schwartz, 1989, "Day of the Week Effects in Japanese Stocks," mimeo.

Kon, S. J., 1984, "Models of Stock Returns--A Comparison," *Journal of Finance* 39, 147-165.

Koutrouvelis, I., 1980, "Regression-Type Estimation of the Parameters of Stable Laws," *Journal of the American Statistical Association* 75, 918-928.

Koutrouvelis, I., 1981, "An Alternative Procedure for the Estimation of the Parameters of Stable Laws," *Communications in Statistics: Simulation and Computation* 10, 17-28.

Mandelbrot, B. B., 1963, "The Variation of Certain Speculative Prices," *Journal of Business* 36, 394-419.

Mandelbrot, B. B., 1973, "Comments on: 'A Subordinated Stochastic Process Model with Finite Variance for Speculative Prices' by Peter K. Clark," *Econometrica* 41, 157-159.

McCulloch, J. H., 1986, "Simple Consistent Estimators of Stable Distribution Parameters," *Communications in Statistics: Simulation and Computation* 15, 1109-1136.

McLeod, A. I., and W. K. Li, 1983, "Diagnostic Checking ARMA Time Series Models Using Squared-Residual Autocorrelations," *Journal of Time Series Analysis* 4, 269-273.

Officer, R. R., 1972, "The Distribution of Stock Returns," *Journal of the American Statistical Association* 67, 807-812.

Poterba, J. M., and L. H. Summers, 1988, "Mean Reversion in Stock Prices: Evidence and Implications," *Journal of Financial Economics* 22, 27-59.

Press, S. J., 1967, "A Compound Events Model of Security Prices," *Journal of Business* 40, 317-335.

Raiffa, H., and R. Schlaifer, 1961, *Applied Statistical Decision Theory*, Cambridge, MA: Harvard University Press.

Roehl, T., 1985, "Data Sources for Research in Japanese Finance," *Journal of Financial and Quantitative Analysis* 20, 273-276.

Simkowitz, M. A., and W. L. Beedles, 1980, "Asymmetric Stable Distributed Security Returns," *Journal of the American Statistical Association* 75, 306-312.

Tauchen, G. E., and M. Pitts, 1983, "The Price Variability-Volume Relationship on Speculative Markets," *Econometrica* 51, 485-505.

Viner, A., 1988, *Inside Japanese Financial Markets*, Homewood, IL: Dow Jones-Irwin.

Ziemba, W. T., 1989a, "Japanese Security Market Regularities: Monthly, Turn of the Month and Year, Holiday and Golden Week Effects," mimeo.

Ziemba, W. T., 1989b, "Seasonality Effects in Japanese Futures Markets," This volume.

Ziemba, W. T., and S. L. Schwartz, 1990, *Investing in Japan*, forthcoming.

Zolotarev, V. M., 1957, "Mellin-Stieltjes Transforms in Probability Theory," *Theory of Probability and Its Applications* 2, 433-460.

Japanese Financial Market Research
W.T. Ziemba, W. Bailey and Y. Hamao (Editors)

The Volatility of the Japanese Stock Market: Evidence from 1977 to 1990

K.C. Chan and G. Andrew Karolyi[1]

Academic Faculty of Finance, College of Business, The Ohio State University, 1775 College Road, Columbus, Ohio, U.S.A., 43210

Abstract

This study assesses the evolution of Japanese stock market volatility from 1977 to 1990. We document several stylized facts of the pattern of changes in Nikkei Dow Stock Index return volatility over this period. We propose and implement a Generalized Autoregressive Conditionally Heteroscedastic (GARCH) model to the returns series and, in the residual diagnostics, show that this model describes the empirical returns generating process well. We test whether (a) the October, 1987 market crash and (b) the introduction of Nikkei Dow index futures and options trading influenced the pattern of volatility described by these models and find some evidence consistent with only the first hypothesis.

1. INTRODUCTION

There is a widespread public perception that the volatility of financial markets around the world has been increasing over the past decade, a symptom of pervasive economic uncertainty among the major industrialized nations. Focus has recently shifted to the stock markets of the Pacific Rim nations and, in particular, to that of Japan, the premier stock market in the world in terms of trading volume and market capitalization. Several explanations for the alleged increase in volatility in Japanese stock market prices abound. Recent trends toward deregulation and globalization in Japanese financial markets have strengthened the international linkages between stock price movements domestically and abroad. These changes have facilitated a faster and more efficient transmission mechanism through which price shocks experienced abroad would induce similar large price shocks in Japan. An alternative explanation relates the apparent increased volatility to the huge growth in the number and types of derivative security products based on Japanese securities. Since September 1986, numerous index futures and options contracts based on the Tokyo stock price indexes have been introduced, including most recently (since January, 1990) the Nikkei put and call warrants developed and traded on the Toronto and American Stock Exchanges. The financial press and Japanese financial market regulators have alleged that these low cost, speculative vehicles induce transitory bursts of volatility

[1]The authors are grateful for helpful discussions with Bill Ziemba and Warren Bailey, who also kindly provided the data. Errors remain the authors' own responsibility.

that destabilize the workings of the markets in the underlying securities [2].

The objective of this study is to assess the evolution of volatility in the Japanese stock market from 1977 to the present. We document several stylized facts of the pattern of changes in stock return volatility over this period. For this purpose, we propose and implement a Generalized Autoregressive Conditional Heteroscedastic (GARCH) model, as developed by Engle (1982) and Bollerslev (1986) and as utilized by Bollerslev (1987), French, Schwert and Stambaugh (1987), Nelson (1990), Chou (1988), Schwert (1989) and Akgiray (1989) for U.S. stock market returns. We find that this model fits the stock returns for the Nikkei Stock Average (NSA) Index remarkably well. We test several hypotheses regarding changes in the structural process governing the volatility of index returns before and after major influential events such as the market crash of October, 1987 and the introduction of derivative securities in Japan in September, 1986.

After a brief review of the literature in section 2, we discuss the data and some preliminary diagnostics in section 3. We offer motivation for and describe the use of GARCH models in section 4. Estimation results and residual diagnostic analysis are also presented. Section 5 demonstrates the results of the structural break tests related to the two major events: the October, 1987 Crash and the introduction of index futures contracts in September, 1986.

2. REVIEW OF THE LITERATURE

Only recently has the academic community in the United States and elsewhere begun to pay attention to the Japanese stock market and its structure. The focus on the Japanese market is likely related to its growth in relative importance in the world financial markets. The Tokyo Stock Exchange (TSE) has surpassed the New York Stock Exchange in terms of aggregate market values and sales volume. French and Poterba (1990) show that the fraction of total world equity comprised by the TSE has grown from 3.2 percent in 1970 to 29.5 percent in 1988, which represents approximately 3840.2 billions of (U.S.) dollars in equity.

Early[3] analyses of the Japanese stock market have focused on issues uncovered in the U.S. market. For example, Kato and Schallheim (1985) examined and verified that January seasonal and size anomalies prevail in Japanese stock returns. Jaffe and Westerfield (1985) show that a weekly seasonal is also strong in the Japanese market. Moreover, the distributional properties of daily returns in Japan are similar to those for the U.S. in that they exhibit significant positive excess kurtosis ("fat-tailedness") but different in that significant negative skewness is also uncovered[4]. The "day of the week" evidence is

[2]Consider recent publications in (a) *The Economist* "Getting Windy: Japanese Stock Index Futures" (January 21, 1989); (b) *Barron's* "Kamikaze Instruments: Index Futures Wreak Havoc on Japanese Stocks" (April 16, 1990) and (c) *Wall Street Journal*'s "Tokyo Stock Exchange Pushes to Halt Further U.S. Sales of Nikkei Warrants" (April 4, 1990).

[3]Our review considers primarily the English language studies of the Japanese stock market and, of those, only the most closely related to the focus of this study. Refer to the other papers in the Sakakibara, Yamaji, Sakurai, Shiroshita and Fukuda (1988) book and this (Ziemba, Bailey and Hamao (1990)) volume for more extensive references.

[4]See also the essay in Chapter 1 of the Sakakibara et al. (1988) volume for further evidence on non-normality of monthly stock returns on Tokyo Stock Exchange stocks. This study finds that the fat-tailness property is not as pervasive as in Jaffe and Westerfield (1985).

further confirmed in Kato, Schwartz and Ziemba (1989) and Kato (1989).

More recent studies have proposed more general models of the returns generating behavior for Japanese stock returns in light of the evidence above and the patterns in volatility observed in the past few years. For the period 1984 to 1989, Brenner, Subrahmanyam and Uno (1990) examine the changes in monthly standard deviations of daily stock index returns. They find a negative impact on the average volatility of the index returns following the introduction of various stock index futures and options contracts on Japanese securities. The approach they use is simple and assumes that the volatility of index returns is constant over a month and changes over time only in monthly intervals. Hamao, Masulis and Ng (1990) employ a more sophisticated GARCH model of daily stock return volatility in order to evaluate the effect of spill-overs of volatility among the U.S., U.K. and Japanese stock markets. They propose a particular specification for the GARCH model that applies commonly to all three markets[5]. Interestingly, they find that the October, 1987 Crash period is highly influential for the model estimation results. Finally, Tse (1990) has also estimated GARCH models for the Nikkei and TOPIX index returns but has found that their forecast power is limited relative to naive historical average and exponentially weighted moving average models[6].

The current paper differs from these recent studies in several ways. First, a longer sample period is studied. Second, a GARCH model of stock return volatility is proposed, as in Hamao et al. (1990) and Tse (1990), but more detailed specification analysis is provided. In fact, we document, through residual diagnostic analysis, that such models empirically fit the actual returns very well. Third, we test for structural breaks associated with the introduction of index futures and the October, 1987 crash period but find that the influence of these events are mitigated considerably when alternative specifications are employed.

3. DATA AND PRELIMINARY DIAGNOSTICS

This section includes an analysis of the distributional and time series properties of Japanese stock returns. The objective is to determine an appropriate model of the pattern of volatility over the 1977 to 1990 period.

3.1 Data

The data on daily closing values of the NSA Stock Average are obtained jointly from I.P Sharp from January 3, 1986 to February 23, 1990 and hand collected from the *Far Eastern Economic Review* back to January 4, 1977[7]. The NSA consists of 225 stocks traded on the First Section of the Tokyo Stock Exchange[8]. Similar to the Dow-Jones Industrial Average, the NSA represents an unweighted average of the prices of the component stocks[9].

---

[5]Specifically, they use a MA(1)-GARCH(1,1)-in-mean model for open-to-close returns on each market for a period from 1985 to 1988. See section 4 for detailed discussion of these types of model.

[6]Tse (1990) uses a AR(1)-GARCH(1,1) specification for his forecasts.

[7]The authors thank Warren Bailey for providing the data used in his joint study with René Stulz and Simon Yen (1990).

[8]The First Section of the TSE represent the most important listed stocks traded, criteria for which are based on historical dividend yields, number of shares outstanding, trading volume and other factors.

[9]See details on construction of this index in Ziemba and Schwartz (1990).

Table 1

Summary Statistics for Daily Returns on the Nikkei Stock Average Index from January, 1977 to February, 1990. The daily returns series is computed from closing values of the Nikkei Stock Average index and includes Saturday returns when trading occurred on the Tokyo Stock Exchange during the sample (i.e., 9 a.m. to 11 a.m. for all but third Saturday of each month to 1983/7; for all but second Saturday of each month from 1983/8 to 1986/7; for all but second and third Saturday of each month from 1986/8 to 1989/2; and for all Saturdays since 1989/2). The Student-t statistics of the null hypothesis that the sample mean equals zero have critical values of 1.645, 1.960 and 2.576 for 10%, 5% and 1% significance levels. The Kolmogorov-Smirnov Goodness-of-Fit "D" test statistic is computed as the largest absolute deviation between the quantiles of the sample and hypothesized Normal distsribution. The critical values are $1.22/\sqrt{n}$, $1.36/\sqrt{n}$ and $1.63/\sqrt{n}$ for the 10%, 5% and 1% significance levels for n observations. LB(n) is the Ljung-Box statistic at lag n, distributed as a chi-squared variate with n degrees of freedom.

Statistic	77/1 - 81/6	81/7 - 85/12	86/1 - 90/2	77/1 - 90/2
Sample size	1273	1286	996	3557
Mean(000s)	.3562	.3946	.9848	.5463
t(mean=0)	2.482	7.206	2.835	4.279
Std. Dev.(000s)	5.121	6.414	10.96	7.613
Skewness	-.5377	-.2057	-1.456	-1.245
Kurtosis	3.389	5.221	25.18	32.47
Median(000s)	.6526	.5245	1.339	.7215
Range	.0531	.0072	.0095	.0069
Inter-quartile Range	.0052	.0589	.1073	.0927
D-statistic	.0767	.0589	.1073	.0927
LB(6)	22.38	20.43	53.26	99.22
LB(12)	42.42	26.10	69.63	114.6
LB(24)	56.04	38.89	107.3	165.6

The daily returns series for the NSA are computed as the logarithm of the price relatives of daily closing values. That is,

$$r_t = log\left(\frac{I_t}{I_{t-1}}\right) \tag{1}$$

where I_t is the closing NSA index value for day t. Over the sample, trading regularly occurred on Saturdays usually only for the two hour morning session (9 am to 11 am)[10]. We included the closing index values for all available Saturdays in the sample.

3.2 Preliminary Statistics

The daily returns series, r_t, is plotted in Figure 1 and descriptive statistics are reported for the full sample and three equal length subperiods in Table 1. Computed distributional parameters include the mean, median, standard deviation, range, interquartile range, skewness and kurtosis coefficients and the Kolmogorov-Smirnov "D" test of the null hypothesis of normality. Test for the null hypothesis of strict white noise for the returns series include the Ljung-Box "portmanteau" test.

[10]In fact, Saturday trading was closed for the third Saturday of every month to July, 1983; closed the second Saturday of every month from August, 1983 to July, 1986; closed the second and third Saturdays of every month from August, 1986 to February, 1989; and closed every Saturday since February, 1989. See Kato, Ziemba and Schwartz (1989) and Kato (1989) for evidence of the impact of these changes on the weekly seasonal in Japanese stock returns.

FIGURE 1
Returns on the Nikkei 1977:1 - 1990:2

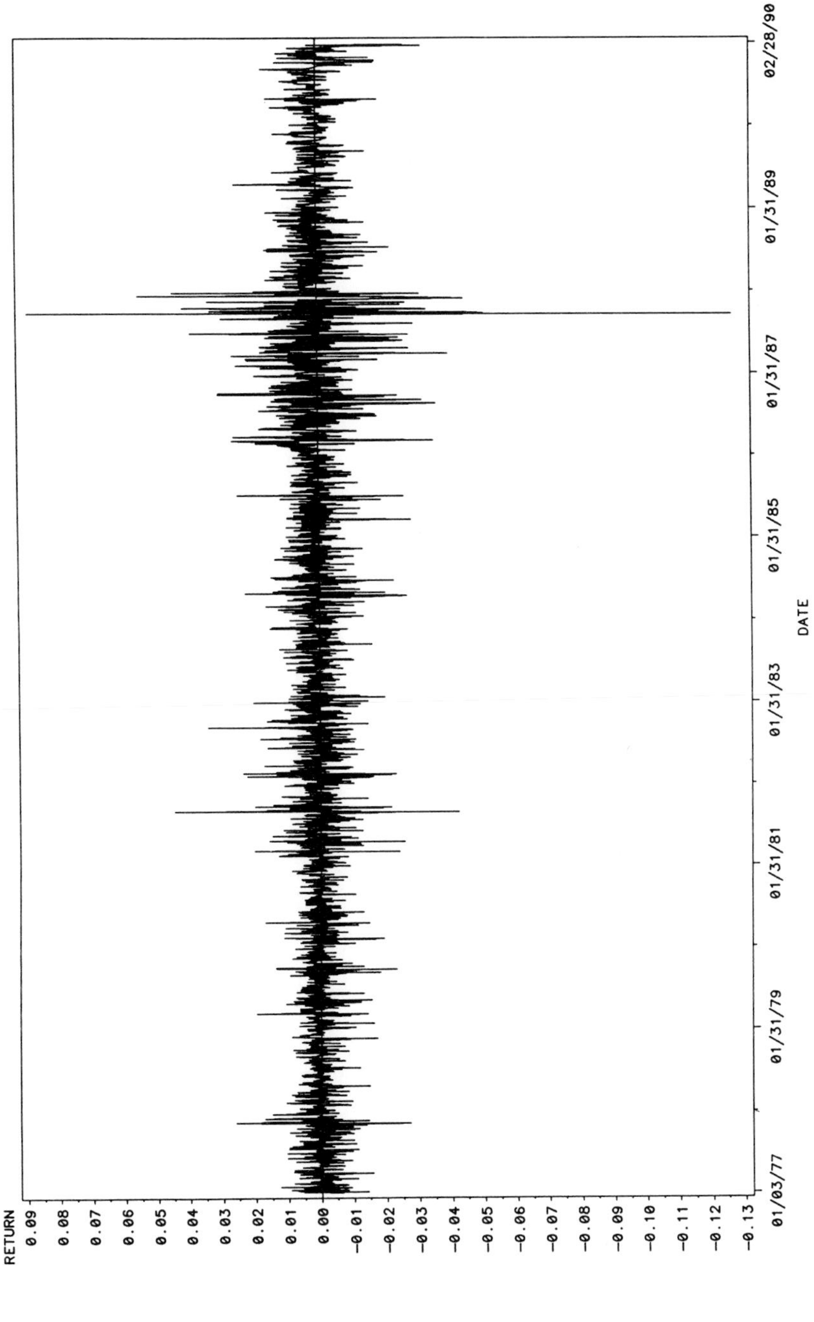

The sample moments in all periods indicate that the empirical distributions have heavy tails and sharp peaks at the center compared to the normal distribution. The Kolmogorov-Smirnov test leads to rejection of normality in every sample. Though, from Figure 1, we expect to observe significant impact of the October, 1987 crash period on the kurtosis coefficients, Table 1 shows that normal zero-excess kurtosis and normal skewness (zero) are rejected in the 1977/1 - 1981/6 and 1981/7 - 1985/12 subperiods also. These results confirm what other studies have already shown for the Japanese stock market[11].

Most popular models of stock returns require that returns be independent random variables and also that they be identically distributed. The Ljung-Box test statistics test the hypothesis of strict white noise or independence and indicate clear rejection at 6, 12 and 24 lags for all sample periods examined. In order to investigate the reasons for lack of independence, the sample autocorrelation functions for the full 1977 - 1990 period are exhibited in Figure 2. In addition to the estimated autocorrelations for the raw returns, r_t, those for the absolute returns, $|r_t|$, and squared returns, r_t^2, are also shown. Significant first and second (and perhaps even fourth) order autocorrelations appear, using the usual asymptotic approximation of $1/\sqrt{T}$ for the standard error of these estimates[12]. There does not seem to be any pattern to the autocorrelation function, especially since autocorrelations beyond four lags do not appear to be significant. The autocorrelations in the absolute and squared returns series are always much higher than those in the raw returns series and are consistently positive up to 24 lags, at least. As the lags increase, both the autocorrelation functions slowly decay and, in the case of the absolute returns series, never go below four standard errors above zero until lag 22. These findings suggest that large price changes are followed by large price changes, small by small. This is similar to the results reported by Fama (1965) and recently Akgiray (1989), among many others, for U.S. stock returns.

3.3 Simple Models for Returns

The linear dependence in daily Japanese returns may be attributed to thin trading in some component stocks in the NSA index, the presence of a common market factor, day-of-the-week effects and other possible reasons. We will attempt in this section to capture these effects in a simple model of stock returns behavior. Non-linear dependence, as evidenced by the significant autocorrelation patterns observed for the absolute and squared returns series, cannot be explained by such phenomena. The well-documented fact of changing volatility may, however, be able to explain these autocorrelation patterns. Moreover, the high levels of kurtosis and possibly the negative skewness observed in Table 1 can possibly be attributed to changing volatility over time. Time varying volatility can be motivated by relating it to the rate of information arrival to the markets, the level of trading activity and corporate financial and operating decisions likely to affect stock prices.

The first step in building a model to describe the returns generating behavior of the NSA is to address the significant first and second autocorrelations. A reasonable strategy is to propose an ARIMA-type model with two lagged MA terms[13]. We also

[11]See Jaffe and Westerfield (1985) and Tse (1989).

[12]This approximation is biased downward due to the non-normality of returns. Yet, the autocorrelations easily exceed by four to five times the usual standard error.

[13]Following a Box-Jenkins type of time series modelling strategy.

FIGURE 2
Autocorrelation Functions for Nikkei Return Series
Raw (star), Absolute (triangle) and Squared (square) Returns

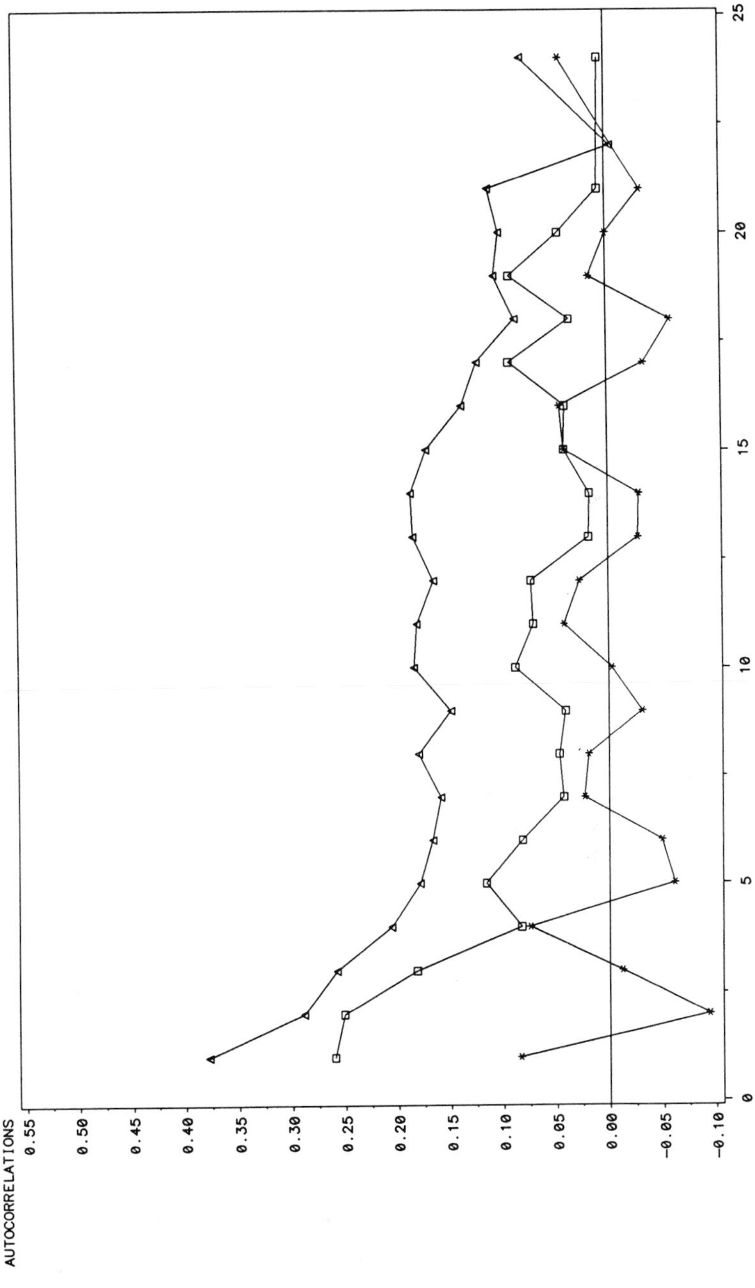

Table 2

Estimates of an ARIMA Time Series Model for Daily Returns on the Nikkei Stock Average Index from January, 1977 to February, 1990. The MA(2) model estimates are obtained for the following equation:

$$r_t = \alpha + \sum_{j=1}^{5} \beta_j D_{j,t} + \epsilon_t + \theta_1 \epsilon_{t-1} + \theta_2 \epsilon_{t-2}$$

r_t denotes the return on the Nikkei Stock Average index on day t, $D_{j,t}$ represents a dummy variable for the day of the week so that $j = 1$ for Tuesday such that $D_{1,t}$ equals one on Tuesdays and zero otherwise; similar construction results for $j = 2$ for Wednesdays,$j = 3$ for Thursdays,..., and $j = 5$ for Saturdays. The values in parentheses are computed standard errors. NOBS represents the number of observations in the sample period.

Coefficient	77/1 - 81/6	81/7 - 85/12	86/1 - 90/2	77/1 - 90/2
α	-.00105	-.00144	.00064	-.00065
	(.00032)	(.00043)	(.00093)	(.00031)
β_1	-.00262	.00352	.00142	.00254
	(.00042)	(.00058)	(.00121)	(.00041)
β_2	.00077	.00108	.00101	.00094
	(.00048)	(.00058)	(.00134)	(.00045)
β_3	.00204	.00194	.00033	.00151
	(.00048)	(.00062)	(.00127)	(.00044)
β_4	.00169	.00222	-.00095	.00099
	(.00049)	(.00065)	(.00112)	(.00041)
β_5	.00126	.00227	.00197	.00131
	(.00049)	(.00067)	(.00010)	(.00062)
θ_1	.13464	.12889	.06269	.09194
	(.01787)	(.01724)	(.01220)	(.00578)
θ_2	-.00124	-.02238	-.12011	-.07684
	(.02135)	(.02195)	(.02016)	(.00831)
σ_ϵ^2(000s)	.02507	.03935	.11529	.05589
Log-likelihood	4939.7	4696.2	3093.42	12355.1
NOBS	1237	1286	996	3557

acknowledge the evidence of Jaffe and Westerfield (1985) and others and include day-of-the-week dummy variables. Consider the simple model,

$$r_t = \alpha + \sum_{j=1}^{5} \beta_j D_{j,t} + \epsilon_t + \theta_1 \epsilon_{t-1} + \theta_2 \epsilon_{t-2} \tag{2}$$

where $D_{j,t}$ represents a dummy variable that equals one for a given day of the week and zero otherwise, so that $j = 1$ for Tuesdays, $j = 2$ for Wednesdays,...,$j = 5$ for Saturdays, and ϵ_t is the normally distributed, zero mean residual with variance σ_ϵ^2.

The estimation results for this model are presented in Table 2. First, the first order MA coefficient is significantly positive in all periods examined ($\theta_1 = .09194$ in the full period) and the estimates are reasonably stable across subperiods. The second order MA coefficient is significantly negative but only in the 1986/1 - 1990/2 period. Second, the day of the week dummies are small and marginally significant in a few cases. Our first subperiod (1977/1 - 1981/6) corresponds very closely with Table 2 of Jaffe and Westerfield (1985) and the results are reasonably similar[14]. Third, the sum of squared

[14]A significant negative return is observed for Tuesday (β_1) and significant positive returns result for

residuals estimated from the models correspond very closely to the unconditional sample variances associated with the returns, as shown in Table 1.

In order to check the hypothesis of independence of the residual series, diagnostics on their distributional properties are presented in the second column of Table 4 and the autocorrelation functions for the residual and the associated absolute and squared series are plotted in Figure 3 (only for the full period results). The negative skewness and significant excess kurtosis prevails in the residuals so that the Kolmogorov-Smirnov "D" test for normality is again easily rejected. The Ljung-Box test statistics of strict white noise are also easily rejected for the residual series. From Figure 3, it appears that although the first and second order correlations are close to zero, the autocorrelations at higher order lags still persist. More significantly, the autocorrelations of the absolute and squared residuals are similar to their counterparts in the returns (Figure 2) being significantly positive at even very long lags.

The residual series from this simple, linear returns generating model is not strict white noise but displays heavy-tailed, peaked non-normal patterns. We need to propose a non-linear process that allows returns to be a function of past values of squared innovations (ϵ_t^2). One such second-order nonlinear process developed by Engle (1982) and generalized by Bollerslev (1986), has become known as Generalized Autoregressive Conditional Heteroscedasticity (GARCH). The process allows first and second moments of r_t to depend explicitly on its past values. It has been shown to fit the empirical distribution of daily stock returns in the U.S.[15], and elsewhere. We explore its appropriateness for daily Japanese NSA index returns in the next section.

4. AN ARCH MODEL OF THE JAPANESE NSA RETURNS

In this section we briefly describe the general family of ARCH models and estimate them for the NSA returns series.

4.1 Description of ARCH Models

A generalized ARCH model of order p and q, denoted as GARCH(p,q), can be described as,

$$\begin{aligned} r_t \mid \Phi_{t-1} &\sim N(\mu_t, h_t) \\ \textit{where} \quad h_t &= a + \sum_{i=1}^{p} b_i h_{t-i} + \sum_{j=1}^{q} c_j \epsilon_{t-j}^2 \\ \textit{and} \quad \epsilon_t &= r_t - \mu_t \end{aligned}$$

where $p > 0$ and $q \geq 0$ and the parameters satisfy the condition that $a > 0$, $b_i, c_j \geq 0$. The function $N(\mu_t, h_t)$ denotes a conditional normal distribution with conditional mean μ_t and variance h_t defined with respect to all information as at time $t-1$, given by Φ_{t-1}. That conditional variances are allowed to depend on past realized variances is particularly

Thursday in our sample but Wednesday and Saturday in their sample.

[15]See Bollerslev (1987), French, Schwert and Stambaugh (1987), Schwert (1989), Chou (1988), Akgiray (1989) and Nelson (1990). A more substantial list can be found in the review by Bollerslev, Chou, Jayaraman and Kroner (1990).

FIGURE 3
Autocorrelation Functions for Residual Series from Nikkei Time Series Model
Raw (star), Absolute (triangle) and Squared (square) Residuals

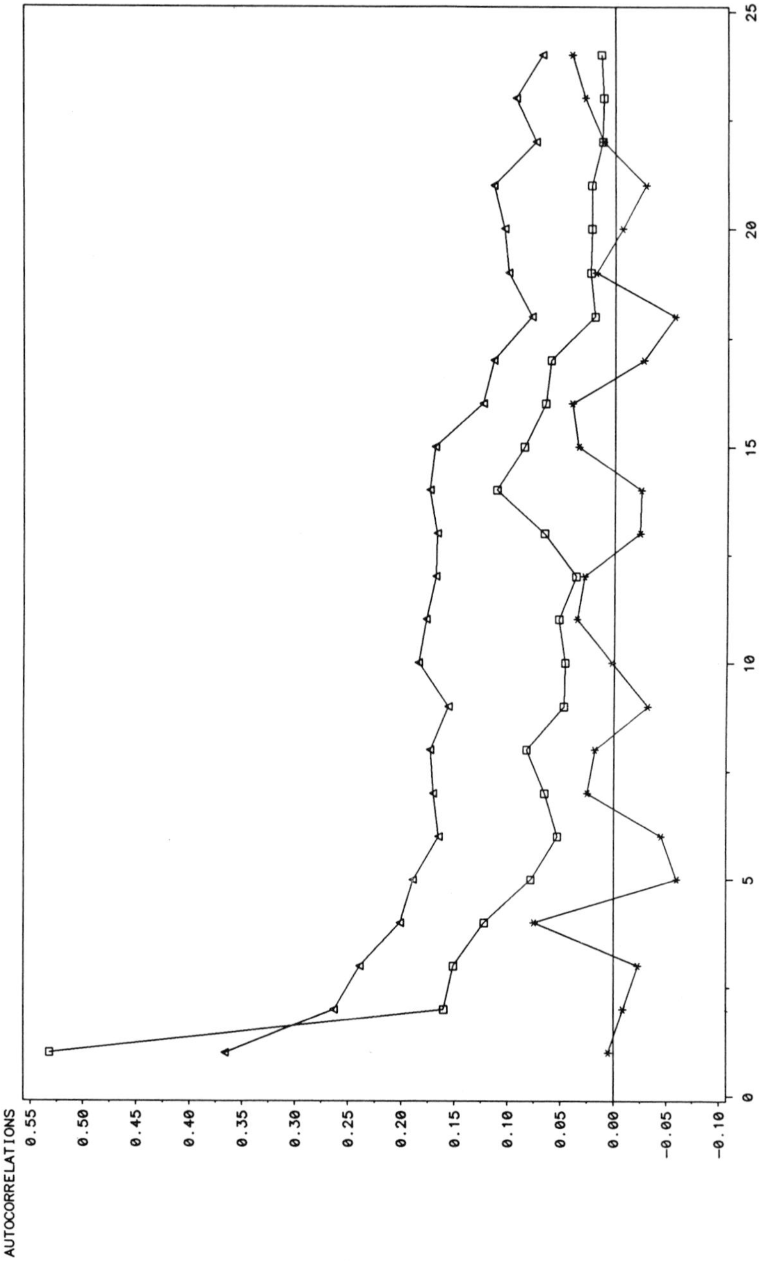

consistent with the stock market which exhibits both stable and unstable periods. Our application of these models for the Japanese NSA daily returns series draws on our results in the previous section in specifying an MA(2) conditional mean returns, μ_t, equation.

$$\mu_t = \alpha + \sum_{j=1}^{5} \beta_j D_{j,t} + \gamma h_t + \epsilon_t + \theta_1 \epsilon_{t-1} + \theta_2 \epsilon_{t-2} \tag{3}$$

where the day-of-the-week dummy variables are as defined above. One adaptation proposed by Bollerslev (1986) and successfully implemented by French, Schwert and Stambaugh (1987), among others, for U.S. returns is the "GARCH(p,q)-in-mean" specification, known as GARCH-M, whereby the conditional mean is allowed to depend also on the conditional volatility. In equation (3), we include the conditional volatility following the GARCH-in-mean specification. We experiment with a number of alternative specifications for the conditional volatility equation, including a MA(2)-GARCH(1,1)-M model and MA(2)-GARCH(1,2)-M model.

To estimate the parameters, $\underline{\phi} = (\mu_t, a, b_i, c_j, ...)$, of the GARCH($p$,$q$) process for a sample of T daily returns, the conditional log likelihood function is evaluated by,

$$L(\underline{\phi}) = \sum_{t=1}^{T} \left[logn(\epsilon_t h_t^{-1}) - log h_t \right] \tag{4}$$

Numerical maximization of the above log likelihood function follows the Berndt, Hall, Hall and Hausmann algorithm.

4.2 Results

Table 3 includes the results of fitting the ARCH processes to the NSA daily returns series for each subperiod as well as the entire sample. We report only the results for the MA(2)-GARCH(1,2)-M model. First, the parameter estimates of the conditional mean returns equation are similar to those reported for the ARIMA model in Table 2. Although some changes in the day-of-the-week dummy variables occur, their joint significance is confirmed. The first MA coefficient is significantly positive and in all periods larger than its counterpart in Table 2. The second MA coefficient is statistically insignificant in all periods unlike those Table 2. It is interesting to note that the serial correlation patterns modelled for the Japanese markets are altered when time variation of the conditional volatility of the markets are incorporated, particularly for the 1986/1 to 1990/2 period.

The parameters estimates associated with the GARCH terms (b, c_1, c_2) are all significant and the likelihood ratio test of the hypothesis that all GARCH coefficients, including the GARCH-in-mean parameter, γ, equal zero indicates sound rejection. Other models such as GARCH(1,1)-M were also tested and statistically significant improvement in goodness-of-fit (via likelihood ratio tests) obtained[16]. The estimates of a are much smaller than the sample variances of ϵ_t in Table 2 showing that, in fact, conditional variances are changing through time. The unconditional volatility of the residuals of the GARCH models, computed as $\sigma_\epsilon^2 = a/(1 - b - \sum_{j=1}^{2} c_j)$, are of similar magnitude to their counterparts

[16]For the three subperiods and full period results, the χ^2 statistic of the null hypothesis that $c_2 = 0$ was 1.4, 3.92, 6.34 and 6.2, respectively.

Table 3

Estimates of a MA(2)-GARCH(1,2)-in-Mean Model for Daily Returns on the Nikkei Stock Average Index from January, 1977 to February, 1990. The model estimated is,

$$r_t = \alpha + \sum_{j=1}^{5} \beta_j D_{j,t} + \epsilon_t + \theta_1 \epsilon_{t-1} + \theta_2 \epsilon_{t-2}$$

$$\epsilon_t | \Phi_{t-1} \sim N(0, h_t)$$

$$h_t = a + bh_{t-1} + \sum_{j=1}^{2} c_j \epsilon_{t-j}^2$$

The values in parentheses are computed asymptotic standard errors. The maximum likelihood estimates of the parameters are obtained numerically using the Berndt-Hall-Hall-Hausman algorithm. The χ_4^2 statistic reports a test of the hypothesis that the GARCH-M parameters are equal to zero (i.e., $b = c_1 = c_2 = \gamma = 0$). See also notes to Table 2.

Coefficient	77/1 - 81/6	81/7 - 85/12	86/1 - 90/2	77/1 - 90/2
α	-.00227	-.00201	.00048	-.00112
	(.00038)	(.00042)	(.00046)	(.00020)
β_1	.00259	.00332	.00133	.00265
	(.00039)	(.00040)	(.00068)	(.00026)
β_2	.00073	.00137	-.00013	.00079
	(.00038)	(.00044)	(.00068)	(.00026)
β_3	.00169	.00173	-.00034	.00138
	(.00039)	(.00049)	(.00073)	(.00027)
β_4	.00145	.00234	-.00033	.00143
	(.00041)	(.00047)	(.00063)	(.00026)
β_5	.00139	.00263	.00115	.00149
	(.00039)	(.00054)	(.00010)	(.00032)
θ_1	.16352	.17209	.14043	.15497
	(.03205)	(.03239)	(.04233)	(.01919)
θ_2	.02633	.03116	.03489	.02198
	(.02908)	(.03240)	(.03577)	(.01709)
γ	64.825	22.809	7.4902	11.454
	(14.559)	(10.274)	(4.5331)	(3.1573)
a(000s)	.00249	.00681	.002785	.00139
	(.00049)	(.00125)	(.00051)	(.00015)
b	.74978	.58687	.86566	.83906
	(.03565)	(.05607)	(.01842)	(.00942)
c_1	.22783	.15441	.23565	.20598
	(.04321)	(.02679)	(.03005)	(.01800)
c_2	-.07445	.08561	-.12439	-.06520
	(.04534)	(.03312)	(.03354)	(.01822)
Log-likelihood	5049.9	4803.8	3321.38	13133.4
χ_4^2 Test	220.5	215.2	455.9	1556.5

Table 4

Comparison of Residual Diagnostics for the ARIMA Time Series and GARCH-in-mean Models for Daily Returns on the Nikkei Stock Average Index from January, 1977 to February, 1990. The ARIMA and GARCH-M model estimates used to generate the residuals are presented in Tables 2 and 3, respectively. The Student-t statistics of the null hypothesis that the sample mean equals zero has critical values of 1.645, 1.960 and 2.576 for 10%, 5% and 1% significance levels. The Kolmogorov-Smirnov Goodness-of-Fit "D" test statistic is computed as the largest absolute deviation between the quantiles of the sample and hypothesized Normal distsribution. The critical values are $1.22/\sqrt{n}$, $1.36/\sqrt{n}$ and $1.63/\sqrt{n}$ for the 10%, 5% and 1% significance levels for n observations. LB(n) is the Ljung-Box statistic at lag n, distributed as a chi-squared variate with n degrees of freedom.

Statistic	ARIMA Model	GARCH-M Model
Sample size	3557	3557
Mean(000s)	-.0119	-.0307
t(mean=0)	-.0952	-1.829
Std. Dev.(000s)	7.504	.9992
Skewness	-.9612	-.6079
Kurtosis	31.04	2.964
Median(000s)	.1603	.0274
Range	.2141	1.187
Inter-quartile Range	.0068	1.155
D-statistic	.0903	.0512
LB(6) for $\hat{\epsilon}_t$	42.57	2.332
LB(12) for $\hat{\epsilon}_t$	56.94	5.867
LB(24) for $\hat{\epsilon}_t$	98.62	20.17
LB(6) for $\lvert\hat{\epsilon}_t\rvert$	1293.	8.042
LB(12) for $\lvert\hat{\epsilon}_t\rvert$	1925.	18.08
LB(24) for $\lvert\hat{\epsilon}_t\rvert$	2546.	30.17
LB(6) for $\hat{\epsilon}_t^2$	1264.	14.74
LB(12) for $\hat{\epsilon}_t^2$	1333.	20.17
LB(24) for $\hat{\epsilon}_t^2$	1454.	37.29

in Table 2. The estimates of $b + c_1 + c_2$ are close to, but statistically less than, unity indicating second-order stationarity for the returns process.

Figure 4 plots the autocorrelation functions for the raw, absolute and squared standardized residuals from the GARCH models estimated in Table 3. The contrast relative to Figure 2 and, especially, Figure 3 is dramatic. Not only do the higher order residual series no longer exhibit any dependence, but also the raw residual series suggests no pattern. A similar result transpires for each subperiod also. The fit of the MA(2)-GARCH(1,2)-M is further evaluated by the residual diagnostics reported in Table 4. The impact of the GARCH specification in reducing the excess negative skewness and especially the positive excess kurtosis (2.94 versus 31.04 for the residuals of the ARIMA model) is evident. The Kolmogorov-Smirnov "D" statistic still rejects the hypothesis of normality for the residuals, however. Finally, the contrast between the Ljung-Box test statistics for the ARIMA and GARCH-M models confirm the striking improvement the latter models offer in absorbing the nonlinear dependence in the NSA returns. Figure 5 plots the time series of conditional volatility implied by the full period GARCH-M model.

FIGURE 4
Autocorrelation Functions for Residual Series from Nikkei GARCH Model
Raw (star), Absolute (triangle) and Squared (square) Residuals

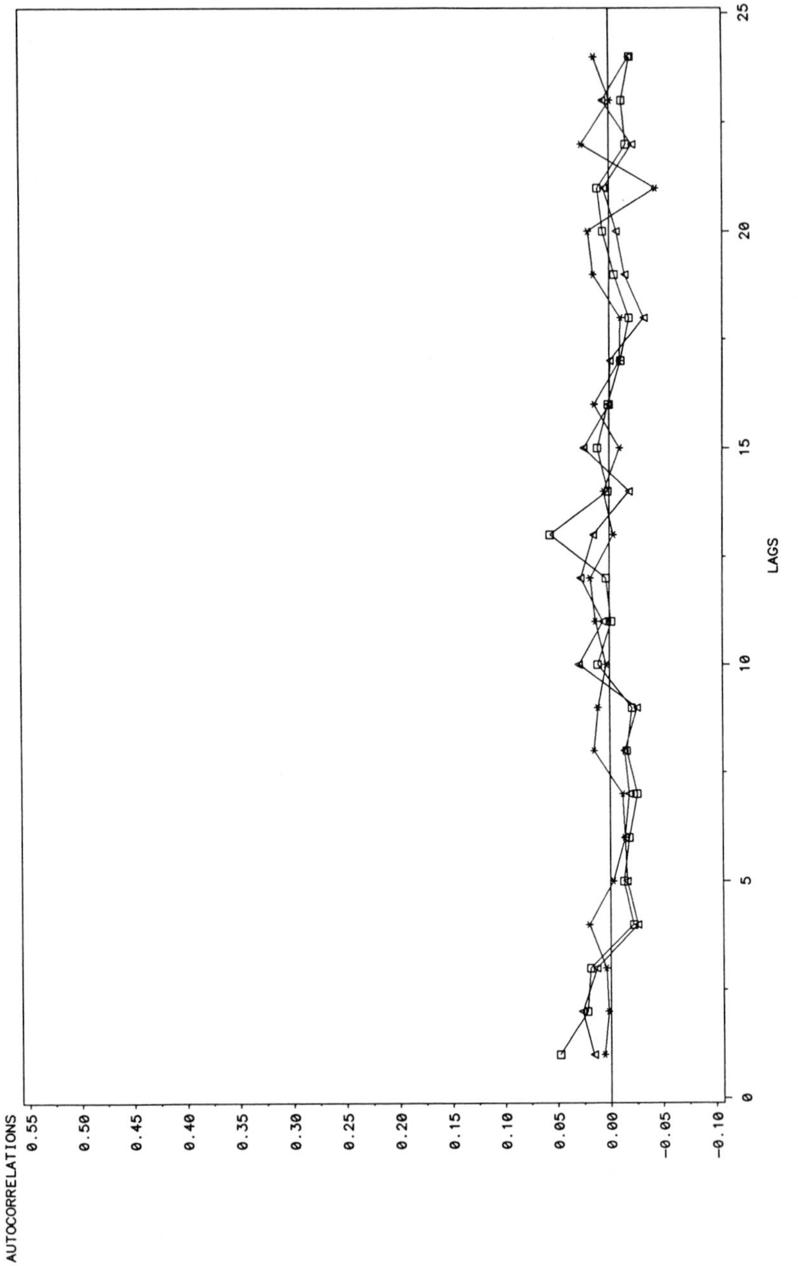

FIGURE 5
Conditional Volatility of Nikkei Returns, 1977:1 - 1990:2

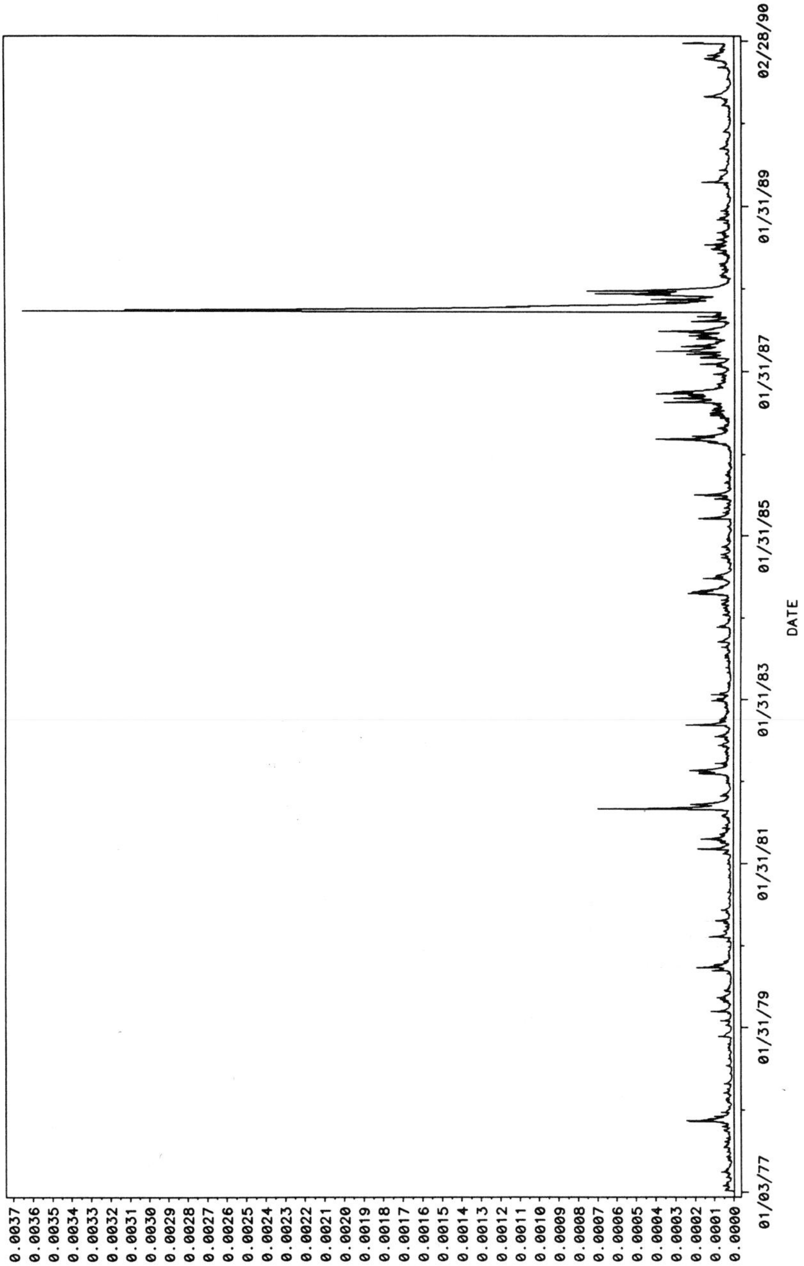

5. TESTS FOR STRUCTURAL BREAKS

This section uses the estimated GARCH-M models as a description of the evolution of volatility in the Japanese NSA index returns to evaluate two hypotheses. First, did the October 1987 crash period cause the overall volatility patterns in the Japanese financial markets to change ? Second, with the introduction of index futures and options trading on the underlying NSA stock index, did the structure of the process governing volatility shift ?

5.1 The October, 1987 Crash

Figure 6 exhibits the path of the NSA index during the two months surrounding the October, 1987 Crash period. A drop of about 16 percent of the index value during the week of October 19, 1987 was smaller than that experienced in the U.S. (twenty percent for the Standard and Poor 500 stock index). Deliberations continue to this day as to the causes and consequences of this event in the financial markets[17]. Our objective here is not to offer a reassessment of these analyses but an evaluation of the impact of the event on the process for the volatility of the NSA index returns. Hamao, Masulis and Ng (1990) provide considerable documentation that the October, 1987 events influence their measure of the spillover of volatility from the U.S. to Japanese markets[18].

Our experiment involves the introduction of a dummy variable for the MA(2)-GARCH (1,2)-M models described above to allow for a shift in the model parameters between the pre- and post-crash period. The dummy variable takes on a value of one after the crash and zero, otherwise. We allow all the parameters of the conditional volatility equation to shift; that is, both the intercept and slope parameters of the volatility process can change. We posit the null hypothesis that the crash period did not disrupt the structure of the volatility of the NSA index returns and perform a likelihood ratio test of the significance of the coefficients associated with the interactive dummy variable terms included.

Table 5 reports the results. Because it is difficult to propose one particular date that defines the potential break in the NSA returns series, we examine two: October 16, 1987 and October 21, 1987. The analysis is restricted to the third subperiod, 1986/1 to 1990/2, so that comparisons of the coefficient estimates should be directed to column four of Table 3. First, the coefficient estimates in the conditional mean equation are well within two standard errors of the original estimates reported in Table 3. Second, the individual estimates of the GARCH parameters in the conditional volatility equation do not shift significantly across the crash period. This finding contrasts that of Hamao, Masulis and Ng (1990). The joint hypothesis that no break occurs (i.e., $d_1 = d_2 = d_3 = d_4 = 0$) is rejected. Third, the inferences are identical for either definition of the break period. Finally, the unconditional variance of the pre- versus post-crash periods indicate a downward shift in volatility (.0001757 (.0001768) pre-crash to .0000536 (.0000535) post-crash for the October 16 (October 21) break).

5.2 Introduction of Index Futures and Options on the NSA Index

In September, 1986 the first stock index futures contract listed on the NSA Index was

[17] See the Brady Commission Report (1988) and Roll (1988).

[18] In fact, the structure of their GARCH-M model is perturbed greatly by the inclusion of the October, 1987 to April, 1988 period. Their GARCH coefficients, b and c_1, for example shift from .78646 and .17861, respectively, to .27809 and .82379, respectively, when the crash period is included.

FIGURE 6
The October, 1987 Crash Period for the Nikkei Index

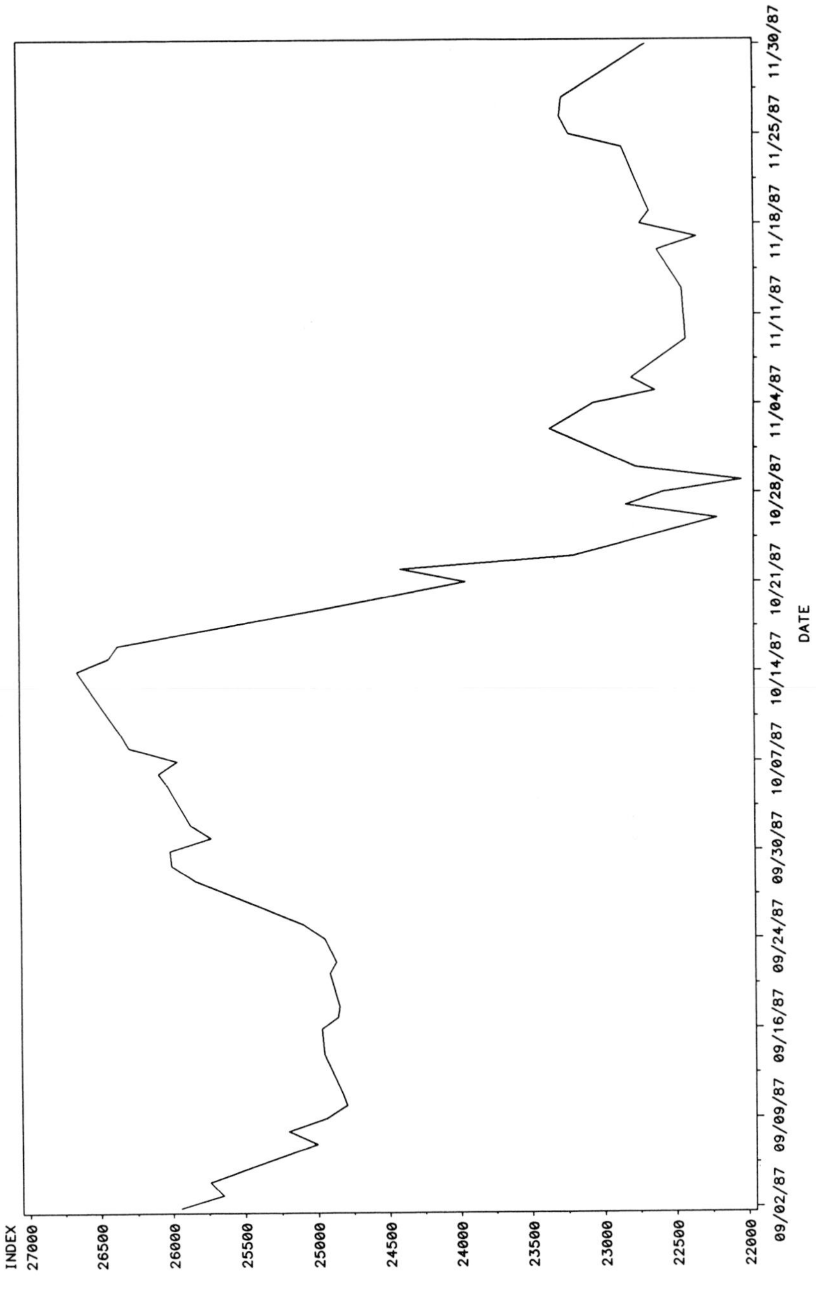

Table 5

Test for Structural Break Around October, 1987 Crash using a GARCH Model for Daily Returns on the Nikkei Stock Average Index from January, 1986 to February, 1990. The MA(2)-GARCH(1,2)-in-mean model estimates are obtained from the following system of equations:

$$r_t = \alpha + \sum_{j=1}^{5} \beta_j D_{j,t} + \gamma h_t + \epsilon_t + \theta_1 \epsilon_{t-1} + \theta_2 \epsilon_{t-2}$$

$$\epsilon_t | \Phi_{t-1} \sim N(0, h_t)$$

$$h_t = (a + d_1 \delta_t) + (b + d_2 \delta_t) h_{t-1} + \sum_{j=1}^{2} (c_j + d_{j+2} \delta_t) \epsilon_{t-j}^2$$

The δ_t dummy variable equals one for all daily returns after the October, 1987 critical date (defined for each model), and zero otherwise. The χ_4^2 statistic reports a test of the hypothesis that the post-Crash period dummy coefficients equal zero (i.e., $d_j = 0 \forall j = 1, 2, 3, 4$). See notes to Table 3.

Coefficient	October 16, 1987 Break	October 21, 1987 Break
α	.00059	.00059
	(.00057)	(.00056)
β_1	.00104	.00104
	(.00071)	(.00070)
β_2	-.00036	-.00041
	(.00073)	(.00073)
β_3	-.00067	-.00068
	(.00078)	(.00077)
β_4	-.00044	-.00045
	(.00069)	(.00067)
β_5	.00139	.00139
	(.00010)	(.00012)
θ_1	.13719	.13225
	(.04369)	(.04289)
θ_2	.03791	.03626
	(.03404)	(.03469)
γ	9.1915	9.5743
	(4.7736)	(5.0427)
a(000s)	.00369	.00388
	(.00121)	(.00133)
b	.91718	.90685
	(.02573)	(.02852)
c_1	.28694	.24021
	(.06756)	(.03351)
c_2	-.22530	-.16908
	(.06904)	(.04307)
d_1	-.00169	-.00174
	(.00133)	(.00146)
d_2	-.02070	-.01631
	(.03226)	(.03508)
d_3	-.05483	-.00702
	(.06599)	(.04930)
d_4	.05919	.00525
	(.06906)	(.05673)
Log-likelihood	3332.10	3332.77
χ_4^2 Test[d]	21.604	22.78

traded at the Singapore International Monetary Exchange (SIMEX). Subsequently, various derivative securities based on Tokyo Stock Exchange stock indices were introduced on the Osaka Securities Exchange and the TSE. Numerous studies in the United States have attempted to assess the impact of the introduction of such contracts on the stability of the underlying stock returns. Market regulators and the popular press have alleged that index futures and options related trading activity destabilizes the stock market by inducing greater volatility. They claim that equity index futures provide a low cost vehicle for trading that attracts predominantly uninformed speculators. Others have maintained that these markets attract rational and differently informed traders that collectively increase trading activity, market liquidity and thus the overall informational efficiency of the capital markets[19].

Brenner, Subrahmanyam and Uno (1990) have examined the impact of the introduction of futures and option related trading for the volatility of the NSA index. They found that the average volatility, measured by sample standard deviations of daily returns, decreased. They assume that the volatility of index returns changes only in monthly intervals. We evaluate the same hypothesis in the context of the GARCH-M models presented above. These models, however, allow the conditional volatility of the returns to change daily. The null hypothesis that no shift in the GARCH parameters occur after the introduction of the SIMEX futures contract in September, 1986 is tested using the same likelihood ratio test methodology with interactive dummy variables as in the previous subsection.

Table 6 presents the results for the MA(2)-GARCH(1,2)-M model with and without the interactive dummy variables. We change the sample period for analysis (September, 1985 to August, 1987) to insulate the results from the October, 1987 crash period and in order to ensure sufficient numbers of observations before and after the event. The stability of the coefficients of the conditional mean returns equation before and after the introduction of the SIMEX futures is remarkable. Only the GARCH-in-mean coefficient appears to go from a marginally significant value of 24.245 to insignificantly different from zero when the dummy shift is introduced. The parameters of the conditional volatility equation do change somewhat, particularly the coefficient of the first lag of squared innovations, c_1. Overall, the null hypothesis that these parameters do not shift over this period (i.e. $d_1 = d_2 = d_3 = d_4$) cannot be rejected at even the 95 percent confidence level ($\chi_4^2 = 12.22$). Interestingly, the results suggest that the unconditional volatility has doubled from .0000649 to .0001274, in contrast to Brenner, Subrahmanyam and Uno (1990).

6. CONCLUSIONS

The objective of this study has been to assess the evolution of volatility in the Japanese stock market from 1977 to the present. We document several stylized facts of the pattern of changes in stock return volatility over this period. We use a Generalized Autoregressive Conditional Heteroscedastic (GARCH) model, as developed by Engle (1982) and Bollerslev (1986), to investigate the pattern of changes in Japanese NSA stock index return

[19]Recent studies include Grossman (1988), Edwards (1988), Harris (1989), Bessembinder and Seguin (1989), Furbush (1989), Neal (1990) and Harris, Sofianos and Shapiro (1990). Papers that have studied the impact of options trading on stock return volatility include Conrad (1989), Skinner (1989).

Table 6

Test for Structural Break Around Introduction of Index Futures Trading using a GARCH Model for Daily Returns on the Nikkei Stock Average Index from September, 1985 to August, 1987. The MA(2)-GARCH(1,2)-in-mean model estimates are obtained from the following system of equations:

$$r_t = \alpha + \sum_{j=1}^{5} \beta_j D_{j,t} + \gamma h_t + \epsilon_t + \theta_1 \epsilon_{t-1} + \theta_2 \epsilon_{t-2}$$

$$\epsilon_t | \Phi_{t-1} \sim N(0, h_t)$$

$$h_t = (a + d_1 \delta_t) + (b + d_2 \delta_t) h_{t-1} + \sum_{j=1}^{2} (c_j + d_{j+2} \delta_t) \epsilon_{t-j}^2$$

The δ_t dummy variable equals one for all daily returns after the September, 1986 date, and zero otherwise. [d] The χ_4^2 statistic reports a test of the hypothesis that the post-event (introduction of index futures contract) dummy coefficients equal zero (i.e., $d_j = 0 \forall j = 1, 2, 3, 4$). See notes to Table 3.

Coefficient	GARCH Model - No Dummy	GARCH Model - Dummy
α	-.00265	-.00187
	(.00064)	(.00073)
β_1	.00377	.00366
	(.00092)	(.00092)
β_2	.00248	.00239
	(.00102)	(.00103)
β_3	.00224	.00199
	(.00093)	(.00094)
β_4	.00263	.00237
	(.00103)	(.00103)
β_5	.00358	.00291
	(.00221)	(.00233)
θ_1	.22663	.20278
	(.05065)	(.05152)
θ_2	.03990	.01227
	(.04927)	(.05024)
γ	24.245	16.414
	(9.5563)	(9.2726)
a(000s)	.00203	.00332
	(.00057)	(.00098)
b	.84696	.74373
	(.03215)	(.06512)
c_1	.15703	.03115
	(.04847)	(.05311)
c_2	-.02523	.17405
	(.05989)	(.10329)
d_1		.00316
		(.00606)
d_2		.12163
		(.12005)
d_3		.17464
		(.09884)
d_4		-.29605
		(.14813)
Log-likelihood	1658.11	1664.22
χ_4^2 Test[d]		12.22

volatility over this period. We find that this model fits the stock returns for the NSA Index remarkably well. We test several hypotheses regarding changes in the structural process governing the volatility of index returns before and after two major influential events: (a) the market crash of October, 1987 and (b) the introduction of derivative securities in Japan in September, 1986. Our results offer evidence consistent with only the first hypothesis.

These results offer important implications for investors. First, although not modelled explicitly in the framework above, these results are consistent with the phenomenon of time variation of a risk premium for Japanese stocks. This fact has been documented widely in the literature for U.S. stocks. Practitioners who follow tactical asset allocation strategies on the basis of market risk premia must acknowledge the pattern of change over time. Second, we present evidence of the success of the GARCH models in capturing not only the higher order dependence in the NSA stock returns but also, surprisingly, the dependence in the raw returns. Some analysts would interpret the simple autocorrelation of returns as evidence of thinness of trading on the Tokyo Stock Exchange. Our results indicate that part of this linear dependence may be due to model misspecification. Third, the strong evidence of time variation in the conditional volatility of the stock market over time recommends that pricing of derivative security instruments based on the index, such as index options and futures, should incorporate some form of stochastic volatility process.

7. REFERENCES

Akgiray, V., 1989, "Conditional Heteroscedasticity in Time Series of Stock Returns: Evidence and Forecasts", *Journal of Business*, 62(1), 55-80

Bailey, W., R. Stulz and S. Yen, 1990, "Properties of Daily Stock Returns from the Pacific Rim Stock Markets: Evidence and Implications", in S. Rhee and R. Chang (eds.), *Pacific Basin Capital Markets Research*, North-Holland, 155-171

Bessembinder, H. and P. Seguin, 1989, "Futures Trading, Liquidity and Stock Price Volatility", working paper, Arizona State University

Bollerslev, T., 1986, "Generalized Autoregressive Conditional Heteroscedasticity", *Journal of Econometrics* 31, 307-327

Bollerslev, T., 1987, "A Conditionally Heteroscedastic Time Series Model of Security Prices and Rates of Return Data", *Review of Economics and Statistics*, 59, 542-547

Bollerslev, T., R. Chou, N. Jayaraman and K. Kroner, 1990, "ARCH Modelling in Finance: A Selective Review of the Theory and Empirical Evidence with Suggestions for Future Research", working paper, University of Arizona

Brenner, M., M. Subrahmanyam and J. Uno, 1990, "The Volatility of the Japanese Stock Indices: Evidence from the Cash and Futures Markets", working paper, New York University

Chou, R., 1988, "Volatility Persistence and Stock Valuations: Some Empirical Evidence using GARCH", *Journal of Applied Econometrics*, 3, 279-294

Conrad, J., 1989, "The Price Effect of Option Introduction", *Journal of Finance* 44, 487-498

Edwards, F., 1988, "Futures Trading and Market Volatility: Stock Index and Interest

Rate Futures", *Journal of Futures Markets* 8, 421-439

Engle, R., 1982, "Autoregressive Conditional Heteroscedasticity with Estimates of the Variance of U.K. Inflation", *Econometrica*, 50, 987-1008

Fama, E., 1965, "The Behaviour of Stock Market Prices", *Journal of Business*, 38, 34-105

French, K. and J. Poterba, 1990, "Are Japanese Stock Prices Too High?", working paper, University of Chicago

French, K., W. Schwert and R. Stambaugh, 1987, "Expected Stock Returns and Volatility", *Journal of Financial Economics*, 19, 137-155

Furbush, D., 1989, "Program Trading and Price Movement: Evidence from the October 1987 Market Crash", *Financial Management*, Autumn, 68-83

Grossman, S., 1988, "An Analysis of the Implications for Stock and Futures Price Volatility of Program Trading and Dynamic Hedging Strategies", *Journal of Business*, 61(3), 275-298

Hamao, Y., R. Masulis and V. Ng, 1990, "Correlations in Price Changes and Volatility Across International Stock Markets", *Review of Financial Studies*, 3, 281-307

Harris, L., 1989, "S & P 500 Cash Stock Price Volatilities", *Journal of Finance*, 44, December, 1155-1175

Harris, L., G. Sofianos and J. Shapiro, 1990, "Program Trading and Intraday Volatility", Working Paper No. 90-03, New York Stock Exchange, Inc.

Jaffe, J. and R. Westerfield, 1985, "Patterns in Japanese Common Stock Returns: Day of the Week and Turn of the Year Effects", *Journal of Financial and Quantitative Analysis* 20, 243-260

Kato, K. and Schallheim, 1985, "Seasonal and Size Anomalies in the Japanese Stock Market", *Journal of Financial and Quantitative Analysis* 20, 243-272

Kato, K., 1989, "Weekly Patterns in Japanese Stock Returns", working paper, Nanzan University

Kato, K., S. Schwartz and W. Ziemba, 1989, "Day of the Week Effects in Japanese Stocks", in *Japanese Capital Markets*, E. Elton and M. Gruber (eds.), Harper and Row Institutional Investor Series in Finance

Neal, R., 1990, "Program Trading on the NYSE: A Descriptive Analysis and Estimates of the Intraday Impact on Stock Returns", working paper, Department of Finance, University of Washington

Nelson, D., 1990, "Conditional Heteroscedasticity in Asset Returns: A New Approach", forthcoming in *Econometrica*

Report of The Presidential Task Force on Market Mechanisms, 1988 (U.S. Government Printing Office, Washington, D.C.)

Roll, R., 1988, "The International Crash of October 1987", *Financial Analysts Journal*, September-October, 19-35

Sakakibara, S., H. Yamaji, H. Sakurai, K. Shiroshita and S. Fukuda, 1988, *The Japanese Stock Market: Pricing Systems and Accounting Information*, Praeger Publishers, New York, NY

Schwert, W., 1989, "Why Does Stock Market Volatility Change Over Time ?", *Journal of Finance*, 44, 1115-1153

Skinner, D., 1989, "Options Markets and Stock Return Volatility", *Journal of Financial Economics* 23(1), 61-78

Tse, Y., 1989, "Price and Volume in the Tokyo Stock Exchange", forthcoming, this volume

Tse, Y., 1990, "Stock Returns Volatility in the Tokyo Stock Exchange", working paper, National University of Singapore

Ziemba, W., W. Bailey and Y. Hamao, 1991, *Japanese Financial Market Research*, North-Holland

Ziemba, W. and S. Schwartz, 1990, *Investing in Japan: The Portfolio Manager's Guide to Stocks, Options, Futures and Mutual Funds*, Dow Jones-Irwin Publishers, Homewood, IL

Japanese Financial Market Research
W.T. Ziemba, W. Bailey and Y. Hamao (Editors)
1991 Elsevier Science Publishers B.V.

Stock Market Rationality and Price Volatility: Tests Using Japanese Data

TAKEO HOSHI*

Massachusetts Institute of Technology, Cambridge, Massachusetts 02139

Received October 20, 1986; revised May 12, 1987

Hoshi, Takeo—Stock Market Rationality and Price Volatility: Tests Using Japanese Data

This paper tests the stock market rationality hypothesis, which implies that a stock price is determined as the discounted sum of optimally forecasted future dividends. Mankiw–Romer–Shapiro volatility tests and new volatility tests which do not use the unobservable "ex post rational price" are applied to the data from a stock market in Japan. A Hausman type specification test of the market rationality hypothesis is also developed and applied to the data. The results suggest that we cannot reject the hypothesis that the Japanese stock market is rational. A couple of variance inequalities are violated by the data but the violation does not seem to be significant. *J. Japan. Int. Econ.*, December 1987, **1**(4), pp. 441–462. Massachusetts Institute of Technology, Cambridge, MA 02139.

Journal of Economic Literature Classification Numbers 023, 211, 521.

I. INTRODUCTION

This paper tests the stock market rationality hypothesis, which implies that a stock price is determined as the discounted sum of optimally expected future dividends. The tests are performed using Japanese stock market data. Two different methods are employed to test the hypothesis. One is the volatility test originally developed by LeRoy and Porter (1981) and Shiller (1979, 1981a). The other is an application of a Hausman (1978) type specification test to the tests of the efficient market model.

The aim of this paper is not only to test the market rationality hypothesis. It also tries to shed some light on the debate about the validity of the

* I am grateful to Olivier Blanchard, Jerry Hausman, Anil Kashyap, Danny Quah, and David Simpson for valuable comments. I thank Hidehiko Ichimura and David Wilcox for helpful discussions at the early stage of this research. I also thank Fumiko Konya and Yasuhiro Yonezawa for providing me with the data. I have also benefited from the comments of two anonymous referees. All remaining errors are my own.

volatility testing. Two points in this paper are worth mentioning. First, tests which are immune to some criticisms of volatility tests are developed below, generalizing the result in Mankiw, Romer, and Shapiro (1985) (abbreviated by MRS henceforth). We use this test in the empirical investigation. Second, Hausman-type specification tests are also used to test the market rationality hypothesis. Some forms of volatility tests are shown to be the tests of a condition which is implied by the null hypothesis of a Hausman-type specification test.

This paper is organized as follows. In the next section, after reviewing the original volatility test by Shiller (1981a) and some criticisms of it, a general implication of the rational expectations concerning the second moments of the variables is stated. The MRS volatility tests are shown to follow from this general result. A new volatility test is constructed using the result, and it is shown to have properties similar to MRS. In Section III, a Hausman-type specification test is applied to the tests of the efficient market model. The relation between the volatility tests and the regression-based specification tests are also discussed. Section IV briefly describes the data employed in this study. Section V reports the results of various tests. In Section VI, we consider some alternative models of stock price determination, and see the implications of our results on these alternatives. Section VII concludes the paper.

II. Volatility Tests

This section begins with a quick overview of discussion concerning the volatility test. Consider the present value relation

$$p_t = \sum_{i=0}^{\infty} \theta^{i+1} E(x_{t+i}|\Omega_t). \tag{1}$$

In a stock market application, p_t and x_t stand for the stock price and the dividend in period t, respectively. In this paper, the stock price p_t is assumed to be measured at the beginning of the period t, and the dividend x_t measures the dividend which belongs to a stockholder at the end of the period t. θ is the discount rate and is assumed to be constant. $E(\cdot|\Omega_t)$ denotes the expectation conditional on some information set, Ω, available at t. Here Ω_t will be assumed to include at least the current and the lagged x's and p's; that is $\Omega_t = \{. . . ; x_0, . . . , x_{t-1}, x_t; p_0, . . . , p_{t-1}, p_t; . . .\}$. $\Omega_t \supset \Omega_{t-j}$, for all $j > 0$ is also assumed. Equation (1) represents the efficient market model to be tested by a volatility test. Here we confine ourselves to the application of the test to a stock market, but the same type of volatility test is applicable to essentially all the economic models which imply the present value relation.[1]

We begin by defining the "ex post rational price" p_t^* as

$$p_t^* = \sum_{i=0}^{\infty} \theta^{i+1} x_{t+i}. \tag{2}$$

Given this definition, the market price p_t is the optimal forecast of the ex post rational price, p_t^*, given the information Ω_t; that is $p_t = E(p_t^* | \Omega_t)$. Next, we define the forecast error $u_t = p_t^* - p_t$. It then follows that, because p_t is the optimal forecast, u_t must be uncorrelated with p_t, so that

$$\mathrm{Var}(p_t^*) = \mathrm{Var}(p_t) + \mathrm{Var}(u_t). \tag{3}$$

Assuming the covariance stationarity of $\{x_t\}$ (and hence $\{p_t\}$),

$$\mathrm{Var}(p^*) \geq \mathrm{Var}(p). \tag{4}$$

This is the most commonly known volatility test, which is used in Shiller (1981a, 1981b) and is attacked by Flavin (1983) and Marsh and Merton (1983, 1986).

Flavin (1983) investigated the small sample distributions of volatility tests. In her example, she found that the possibility of type I error in a volatility test is considerable. For instance she showed that when one used sample mean to calculate the sample variance and when the sample mean of p_t was used as the terminal value in a recursive calculation of p_t^*, the Shiller test rejects the market efficiency hypothesis with probability 0.999, even if the hypothesis is true.

Marsh and Merton (1983, 1986) attack the assumption of stationarity of the dividend process in Shiller (1981a). If the dividend follows a nonstationary process, then Shiller's test may not be valid anymore. Marsh and Merton consider the case where a manager's dividend policy depends on the stock prices. In the extreme case where managers maintain their optimal payout ratio every period, the dividends are shown to follow a random walk, and the inequality (4) will be violated in every sample, even if the market is efficient.

Recently Mankiw *et al.* (1985) devised a volatility test which is immune to the difficulties pointed out by Flavin (1983) and Marsh and Merton (1983, 1986). Here the MRS test is presented in a somewhat generalized

[1] Huang (1981) applied the volatility test to the test of the monetary approach to exchange rate determination. Shiller (1979) and Singleton (1980) tested the expectations hypothesis of the term structure using the volatility tests.

form. First, the following lemma, which is later used to derive both the MRS test and our new test, is proven.

LEMMA 1. *Consider information sets A, B, C, such that $C \supset B \supset A$. Consider two variables p and q, such that $p \notin B$ and $q \in B$. Then*

$$E_A(E_C p - q)^2 = E_A(E_C p - E_B p)^2 + E_A(E_B p - q)^2 \tag{5}$$

where E_I denotes the expectation operator, conditional on the information set I.

Proof. $E_C p - q = E_C p - E_B p + E_B p - q$
$E_A(E_C p - q)^2 = E_A(E_C p - E_B p)^2 + E_A(E_B p - q)^2 + 2E_A\{(E_C p - E_B p)(E_B p - q)\}$. Using the law of iterated projections,

$$\begin{aligned} E_A\{(E_C p - E_B p)(E_B p - q)\} &= E_A\{E_B(E_C p - E_B p)(E_B p - q)\} \\ &= E_A\{(E_B p - E_B p)(E_B p - q)\} \\ &= 0 \end{aligned}$$

since $C \supset B \supset A$. Therefore

$$E_A(E_C p - q)^2 = E_A(E_C p - E_B p)^2 + E_A(E_B p - q)^2. \qquad \text{Q.E.D.}$$

Let I^* be an information set fine enough to give the perfect foresight of dividends from now to infinite future. Then $p_t^* = E(p_t^* | I^*)$. Since $p_t = E(p_t^* | \Omega_t)$ and $I^* \supset \Omega_t$, we get the following proposition from Lemma 1.

PROPOSITION 1. *Let p_t^* be ex post rational price defined in* (2). *Let p_t be market price. If the market is efficient, for any p_t^0 such that $p_t^0 \in \Omega_t$,*

$$E_0(p_t^* - p_t^0)^2 = E_0(p_t^* - p_t)^2 + E_0(p_t - p_t^0)^2, \tag{6}$$

where E_0 denotes the expectation operator, conditional on initial conditions at $t = 0$.

This is the result that MRS used in their tests, and immediately follows from Lemma 1. MRS call p_t^0 a "naive forecast" and specify it as $p_t^0 = \Sigma_{i=0}^{\infty} \theta^{i+1} F_t x_{t+1}$, where F_t denotes the forecast at time t. Proposition 1 is valid as long as p_t^0 lies in the space spanned by Ω_t, and we do not need to specify the form as MRS do.

As a corollary to Proposition 1, the MRS volatility test follows.

COROLLARY 1. *Under the null hypothesis of the market rationality, the following inequalities must hold*:

$$E_0(p_t^* - p_t^0)^2 \geq E_0(p_t^* - p_t)^2 \tag{7}$$

$$E_0(p_t^* - p_t^0)^2 \geq E_0(p_t - p_t^0)^2. \tag{8}$$

From Lemma 1, however, we notice that there are a number of alternative volatility tests which can also be constructed. Noting that $\Omega_t \supset \Omega_{t-1}$, $p_{t-1} \in \Omega_{t-1}$, and $p_t \in \Omega_t$, we get the following proposition.

PROPOSITION 2. *If the market is efficient,*

$$E_0(p_t - p_{t-1})^2 = E_0\{p_t - E(p_t|\Omega_{t-1})\}^2 + E_0\{E(p_t|\Omega_{t-1}) - p_{t-1}\}^2$$

or

$$E_0(\Delta p_t)^2 = E_0(\delta_t p_t)^2 + E_0(E(\Delta p_t|\Omega_{t-1}))^2. \tag{9}$$

Δ is a first difference operator, which is defined as $\Delta z_t = z_t - z_{t-1}$. δ_t is an innovation operator, which is defined as $\delta_t z_t = E(z_t|\Omega_t) - E(z_t|\Omega_{t-1})$.

The proof of the proposition immediately follows from Lemma 1. As a corollary to Proposition 2, a new volatility test follows.

COROLLARY 2. *Under the null hypothesis of the market rationality, the following inequalities must hold*:

$$E_0(\Delta p_t)^2 \geq E_0(\delta_t p_t)^2 \tag{10}$$

$$E_0(\Delta p_t)^2 \geq E_0\{E(\Delta p_t|\Omega_{t-1})\}^2. \tag{11}$$

Equation (10) states that the variation (around zero) of change in prices must be greater than that of the innovation in prices. Equation (11) states that the variation of change in actual prices must be larger than that of the expected change in prices.

Both the MRS test and the new test are unbiased in the sense that the expectation of the sample counterpart satisfies the inequalities to be tested under the efficient market hypothesis. This property is proved using the linearity of the expectation operator.

PROPOSITION 3. *Define*

$$Q1 = T^{-1}\sum_{t=1}^{T}(p_t^* - p_t^0)^2 - T^{-1}\sum_{t=1}^{T}(p_t^* - p_t)^2$$

$$Q2 = T^{-1}\sum_{t=1}^{T}(p_t^* - p_t^0)^2 - T^{-1}\sum_{t=1}^{T}(p_t - p_t^0)^2$$

$$Q3 = T^{-1}\sum_{t=1}^{T}(\Delta p_t)^2 - T^{-1}\sum_{t=1}^{T}(\delta_t p_t)^2$$

$$Q4 = T^{-1}\sum_{t=1}^{T}(\Delta p_t)^2 - T^{-1}\sum_{t=1}^{T}\{E(\Delta p_t|\Omega_{t-1})\}^2.$$

If the market is efficient, $E_0(\mathrm{Q1}) \geq 0$, $E_0(\mathrm{Q2}) \geq 0$, $E_0(\mathrm{Q3}) \geq 0$, *and* $E_0(\mathrm{Q4}) \geq 0$ *in every sample* $\{p_t\}_{t=1}^{T}$, $\{x_t\}_{t=1}^{T}$.

Proof. $E_0(\mathrm{Q1}) \geq 0$ and $E_0(\mathrm{Q3}) \geq 0$ are proved here. $E_0(\mathrm{Q2}) \geq 0$ and $E_0(\mathrm{Q4}) \geq 0$ can be proved similarly.

$$\begin{aligned} E_0(\mathrm{Q1}) &= E_0\left[T^{-1}\sum_{t=1}^{T}(p_t^* - p_t^0)^2 - T^{-1}\sum_{t=1}^{T}(p_t^* - p_t)^2\right] \\ &= T^{-1}\sum_{t=1}^{T}E_0(p_t^* - p_t^0)^2A - AT^{-1}\sum_{t=1}^{T}E_0(p_t^* - p_t)^2 \\ &= T^{-1}\sum_{t=1}^{T}[E_0(p_t^* - p_t^0)^2 - E_0(p_t^* - p_t)^2] \\ &= T^{-1}\sum_{t=1}^{T}E_0(p_t - p_t^0)^2 \geq 0. \end{aligned}$$

The last equality follows from Proposition 1.

$$\begin{aligned} E_0(\mathrm{Q3}) &= E_0\left[T^{-1}\sum_{t=1}^{T}(\Delta p_t)^2 - T^{-1}\sum_{t=1}^{T}(\delta_t p_t)^2\right] \\ &= T^{-1}\sum_{t=1}^{T}[E_0(\Delta p_t)^2 - E_0(\delta_t p_t)^2] \\ &= T^{-1}\sum_{t=1}^{T}E_0\{E(\Delta p_t|\Omega_{t-1})\}^2 \geq 0. \end{aligned}$$

The last equality follows from Proposition 2. Q.E.D.

Thus both the MRS test and the new test are unbiased and are immune to the difficulties that Flavin (1983) and Marsh and Merton (1983, 1986) pointed out. Neither test requires transforming the data to get a stationary series.[2] Moreover the new test has an advantage in that it does not use the

[2] Nonstationarity of the variables still can cause a problem. Using an example in which p_t follows a geometric Brownian motion, Merton (1987) shows that the standard deviations of Q1 and Q2 grow without bound as T gets large and at an exponential rate greater than the growth of $E_0(\mathrm{Q1})$ and $E_0(\mathrm{Q2})$. I have not checked what happens to Q3 and Q4 under Merton's example.

series of ex post rational prices which is calculated using an unobservable terminal condition.

Notice also that Proposition 1 is used to prove the unbiasedness of the MRS test in Proposition 3. Since Proposition 1 turns out to be false when p_t^0 is replaced by $T^{-1}\sum_{t=1}^{T} p_t$ (sample mean of the price), the Shiller test is not unbiased. If it were the case that $T^{-1}\sum_{t=1}^{T} p_t^* = T^{-1}\sum_{t=1}^{T} p_t \in \Omega_t$, $t = 0, 1, \ldots, T$, where p_t^* is a constructed series of the ex post rational prices, then the Shiller test would be unbiased. However, this is typically not the case.

III. Specification Tests of the Efficient Market Model

In the previous section, the result in Mankiw *et al.* (1985) concerning the volatility test was generalized and a new volatility test, which does not use p_t^* (ex post rational price), was developed. In this section, an alternative approach for the test of the market rationality hypothesis is considered. This approach, which uses a Hausman (1978) type specification test, can be used to test the same condition that a volatility test tests, and illuminate the orthogonality condition exploited in the volatility test.

First, some forms of volatility tests are shown to be special forms of a specification test in the sense that the variance bound tested in the volatility test is implied by the null hypothesis of a specification test for a regression model when a certain condition (usually stationarity) obtains. For example, consider the regression model

$$p_t^* = p_t + e_t. \tag{12}$$

Hausman-type specification test tests $H_0: p \lim T^{-1}p'e = 0$, where p and e are T dimensional column vectors $(p_1, \ldots, p_T)'$ and $(e_1, \ldots, e_T)'$. Note that the null hypothesis is an implication of the market rationality hypothesis. Under the market rationality hypothesis, $E(e_t|\Omega_t) = 0$ must hold. Since $p_t \in \Omega_t$, the law of iterated projection implies $E(e_t) = E(e_t|p_t) = E(E(e_t|\Omega_t)|p_t) = 0$, which implies $\mathrm{Cov}(p_t, e_t) = 0$. Under the stationary assumption, $\mathrm{plim}\, T^{-1}p'e = \mathrm{Cov}(p_t, e_t) = 0$, and

$$\mathrm{Var}(p_t^*) = \mathrm{Var}(p_t) + \mathrm{Var}(e_t)$$

or

$$\mathrm{Var}(p^*) \geq \mathrm{Var}(p),$$

which is the Shiller test.

Similarly the MRS test can be shown to be a special form of a specification test.[3]

In fact a volatility test almost always has a corresponding regression-based specification test which tests the same orthogonality condition. Conversely starting from the orthogonality condition assumed in a regression model, a volatility test can be developed. For instance, we might consider the regression

$$p_{t+1} + x_t = \beta p_t + e_t. \tag{13}$$

If the market rationality hypothesis holds, $\mathrm{Cov}(p_t, e_t) = 0$ must hold, β being $1 + r$, where r is the (constant) interest rate.[4] The specification test tests $H_0: \mathrm{Cov}(p_t, e_t) = 0$. A volatility test which exploits the same orthogonality condition can be developed as follows. Under H_0, $\mathrm{Cov}(p_t, e_t) = \mathrm{Cov}(p_t, p_{t+1} - \beta p_t + x_t) = \mathrm{Cov}(p_{t+1}, p_t) + \mathrm{Cov}(x_t, p_t) - (1 + r)\mathrm{Var}(p_t) = 0$. Assuming stationarity, $\mathrm{Var}(\Delta p_t) = \mathrm{Var}(\Delta p_{t+1}) = 2\mathrm{Var}(p_t) - 2\mathrm{Cov}(p_{t+1}, p_t)$. Thus $\mathrm{Cov}(p_{t+1}, p_t) = \mathrm{Var}(p_t) - \frac{1}{2}\mathrm{Var}(\Delta p_t)$. Therefore $-r\mathrm{Var}(p_t) - \frac{1}{2}\mathrm{Var}(\Delta p_t) + \mathrm{Cov}(x_t, p_t) = 0$, or defining ρ as the correlation coefficient between x and p,

$$r\sigma(p)^2 - \rho\sigma(x)\sigma(p) + \tfrac{1}{2}\sigma(\Delta p)^2 = 0,$$

where $\sigma(\cdot)$ denotes the standard deviation. Solving this equation for $\sigma(p)$,

$$\sigma(p) = \left[\rho\sigma(x) \pm \sqrt{\rho^2\sigma(x)^2 - 2r\sigma(\Delta p)^2}\right]/2r.$$

This is real if and only if $\rho^2\sigma(x)^2 - 2r\sigma(\Delta p)^2 \geq 0$, which implies $2r\sigma(\Delta p)^2 \leq \rho^2\sigma(x)^2 \leq \sigma(x)^2$, since $|\rho| \leq 1$. Thus we get the inequality

$$\sigma(\Delta p) \leq \sigma(x)/\sqrt{2r}. \tag{14}$$

In fact, this is the third variance bound tested in Shiller (1981b).

The Hausman-type specification test approach to the market rationality hypothesis has an advantage in that it can give a more powerful test than a volatility test in the following sense. Consider the regression (13) and $H_0: \mathrm{plim}\ T^{-1}p'e = 0$. If H_0 is true, then (14) must hold. However, even if

[3] Consider the regression $(p_t^* - p_t^0) = (p_t - p_t^0) + e_t$. The specification test tests $H_0: \mathrm{Cov}(p_t - p_t^0, e_t) = 0$. With $E(e_t) = 0$, H_0 implies $E_0[e_t(p_t - p_t^0)] = 0$. Thus, $E_0(p_t^* - p_t^0)^2 = E_0(p_t - p_t^0)^2 + E_0(e_t)^2$ or $E_0(p_t^* - p_t^0)^2 \geq E_0(p_t - p_t^0)^2$, which is an inequality in the MRS test. Our new volatility test will be compared to the specification test of the regression model: $(p_t - p_{t-1}) = (E(p_t|\Omega_{t-1}) - p_{t-1}) + e_t$.

[4] Model (13) can be derived from an arbitrage equation: $E(p_{t+1}|\Omega_t) - p_t + x_t = rp_t$.

(14) does hold, H_0 might not be true, since $|\rho|$ could be very small. Under H_0, the exact orthogonality condition implies

$$\sigma(\Delta p) \leq |\rho|\sigma(x)/\sqrt{2r}. \tag{15}$$

Thus it is possible that (15) does not hold but (14) does. In this case, the volatility test will fail to reject H_0, although H_0 is false. Generally speaking, a volatility inequality is weaker than the exact orthogonality condition implied by the model.[5] The Hausman-type specification test, which is more fully discussed below, investigates the exact orthogonality condition, and could be more powerful. In a usual case, then, if a volatility test rejects the null hypothesis for the data, one should expect that the corresponding specification test will also reject the null hypothesis for the data.

Now we discuss how to carry out the specification test. Consider the model (13) again. Defining $y_t = p_{t+1} + x_t$, (13) can be rewritten as

$$y_t = \beta p_t + e_t. \tag{16}$$

The null hypothesis is H_0: plim $T^{-1}p'e = 0$ and the alternative is H_1: plim $T^{-1}p'e \neq 0$. Consider two estimators of β, $\hat{\beta}_0$ and $\hat{\beta}_1$. (I use ^ to denote estimators or estimates.) Let $\hat{\beta}_0$ be the efficient estimator under H_0 in the sense that Var($\hat{\beta}_0$) attains the Cramer–Rao lower bound, but inconsistent under H_1. Let $\hat{\beta}_1$ be a consistent estimator of β under both H_0 and H_1. The difference of the two estimators $\hat{q} = \hat{\beta}_0 - \hat{\beta}_1$ can be used to carry out a specification test. The plim $\hat{q} = 0$ under the null hypothesis, since both $\hat{\beta}_0$ and $\hat{\beta}_1$ are consistent, but the plim $\hat{q} \neq 0$ under the alternative hypothesis. In our case, we can obtain an efficient estimate of β in the regression (16), $\hat{\beta}_0$, using OLS.[6] If we find an instrument w such that plim $T^{-1}w'p = M < \infty$ and plim $T^{-1}w'e = 0$, where M is a nonsingular matrix (in our special case, M is a non-zero scalar), we can construct an instrumental variable estimator, $\hat{\beta}_1$. We let $\sqrt{T}(\hat{\beta}_0 - \beta) \overset{A}{\sim} N(0, V(\hat{\beta}_{OLS}))$ and $\sqrt{T}(\hat{\beta}_1 - \beta) \overset{A}{\sim} N(0, V(\hat{\beta}_{IV}))$ under the null hypothesis. Then $\sqrt{T}\,\hat{q} \overset{A}{\sim} N(0, V(\hat{q}))$ and $V(\hat{q}) = V(\hat{\beta}_{IV}) - V(\hat{\beta}_{OLS})$, since $V(\hat{\beta}_{OLS})$ attains the Cramer–Rao lower bound (see Hausman (1978), p. 1253). Hausman (1978) showed that the statistic $m = T\hat{q}'\hat{V}(\hat{q})^{-1}\hat{q}$ asymptotically distributed as χ^2 with degrees of freedom equal to the rank of $\hat{V}$, which in this case will be the number of right-hand-

[5] This is a general result. See Melino (1983).

[6] Implicitly assuming the homoskedasticity. If the heteroskedasticity presents, we should use GLS or GMM instead. Even if the disturbances are homoskedastic, nonstationarity of p can be a problem. If p is not stationary and plim $T^{-1}p'p$ is not finite, then we cannot discuss the asymptotic property of OLS estimators. I will come back to this point later in this section.

side variables in Eq. (16), i.e., one. $\hat{V}(\hat{q})$ is a consistent estimate (under H_0) of $V(\hat{q}r)$. In our case it is calculated by $\hat{V}(\hat{q}) = \hat{V}(\hat{\beta}_{\mathrm{IV}}) - \hat{V}(\hat{\beta}_{\mathrm{OLS}})$.

Thus we can carry out a specification test of the market rationality hypothesis if we can find a valid instrument. The choice of the instrument is very important in the specification test, since it affects the power of the test. This is easy to see since $\hat{V}(\hat{q})$ depends on $\hat{V}(\hat{\beta}_{\mathrm{IV}})$. Choosing a poor instrument, one which has only small correlation with p, will lead to a large $\hat{V}(\hat{\beta}_{\mathrm{IV}})$, which in turn implies $\hat{V}(\hat{q})^{-1}$ will be small so that the test will have low power.

A candidate of a good instrument is the series of 1's. Let $j = (1, 1, \ldots, 1)$ be a t dimensional column vector of 1's. Then plim $T^{-1}j'p = $ plim $T^{-1}\sum_{t=1}^{T} p_t \neq 0$ and plim $T^{-1}j'e = $ plim $T^{-1}\sum_{t=1}^{T} e_t = 0$. Thus we can use $\hat{\beta}_{\mathrm{IV}} = (T^{-1}\sum_{t=1}^{T} p_t)^{-1}(T^{-1}\sum_{t=1}^{T} y_t)$ as $\hat{\beta}_1$. As for $\hat{\beta}_0$, we can use $\hat{\beta}_{\mathrm{OLS}} = (T^{-1}\sum_{t=1}^{T} p_t^2)^{-1}(T^{-1}\sum_{t=1}^{T} p_t y_t)$. If we restrict the alternative specifications, then other variables can also be used as valid instruments. For example, suppose we maintain the hypothesis that the forecast errors are uncorrelated with the price k or more periods before (say $k = 6$). Then p_{t-s} for $s \geq k$ can be an instrument as long as plim $T^{-1}p_{t-s}'p_t \neq 0$, since we assume plim $T^{-1}p_{t-s}'e_t = 0$. Maintaining the hypothesis of plim $T^{-1}p_{t-s}'e_t = 0$ for $s \geq k$, we could construct a variety of other IV estimators to test our hypothesis.

We need to note some possible caveats in applying the specification test to our data. First, since the specification test exploits the asymptotic properties of estimators, it may cause some problems in small samples. Nonstationarity of the variables can cause a more serious problem. If plim $T^{-1}p'p$ is not finite, the asymptotic argument above does not work.

IV. The Data

The data explored in this paper are from the Tokyo Stock Exchange. This is one of the earliest attempts to apply a volatility test to Japanese data. The data set used here is the same one as that used in Hoshi (1986), and a detailed description of the data is contained in the Appendix.

The data for the dividend series, x_t, show enormous seasonality. Because most dividend payments are made in March and/or in September, the end of an accounting term of many firms, the series x_t, has large peaks at March and September every year. We must decide whether the stock market rationality should be tested using the original data, which contain the seasonal fluctuations, or deseasonalized data, which reflect only the nonseasonal fluctuations. If the decision period of the stock holders is long enough (say, a year), then the use of deseasonalized data will be justified. If the decision period is very short, we should use the original data. I used both the original and the deseasonalized data for the following tests, and found little difference except in the case of Shiller tests.[7] In the next section, I report the results of the tests using the original data, but similar results are obtained using the deseasonalized data.

Since this is an empirical study using Japanese data, some characteristics of the Japanese stock market are in order. Finance by Japanese firms relies more on the borrowings than on issuing stocks. For example, from 1976 to 1980, the proportion of external fund financed through issuing equity was only 3.9% compared to 40.6%, which was financed through borrowings.[8] Further, most of equities are held by parent companies or by some banks through "cross shareholding." As a result the Japanese stock market is a very thin market. Most traditional arguments took this as a reflection of the "backwardness" of the Japanese stock market, and did not even suspect the possibility of its efficiency. Since the thinness of a market does not imply its inefficiency, the efficiency of the Japanese stock market is a question that should be tested empirically.[9]

In order to get some idea about the properties of the Japanese data, the original Shiller tests were performed. This will facilitate a comparison of the Japanese data and the U.S. data, which has been explored by many researchers. (LeRoy and Porter, 1981; Mankiw *et al.*, 1985; Shiller, 1981a, 1981b). The original Shiller tests evaluate the following inequalities (Shiller, 1981a);

$$\sigma(p) \leq \sigma(p^*) \tag{17}$$

$$\sigma(\delta p) \leq \sigma(x)/\sqrt{r_2}; \qquad r_2 \equiv (1 + r)^2 - 1 \tag{18}$$

$$\sigma(\Delta p) \leq \sigma(x)/\sqrt{2r}. \tag{19}$$

These three inequalities impose the variance bounds on the level of prices, the innovations in prices, and the change in prices, respectively. The results are presented in Table I. Since there is a slight upward trend in p_t, the data for p_t and x_t are detrended using the estimated growth rate of

[7] The series x_t and p_t are deseasonalized following Example 9.4 of "RATS Ver. 4.1 User's Manual." First we calculate the Fourier transform of x_t. Then we suppress the spectrum around the seasonal frequencies. Finally we take the inverse Fourier transform, and get the deseasonalized series. I tried to be careful not to extract "too much," so that the spectra of deseasonalized x_t and p_t are smoothed around the seasonal frequencies rather than having sharp dips at the seasonal frequencies.

[8] The calculations are made using Table 2-1 in Kunimara (1986).

[9] There are only a few studies which tested a form of the efficient market hypothesis for the Japanese stock market. Yonezawa and Maru (1984) tested the CAPM model using the data from the Japanese stock market in Chapter 4 and reject CAPM.

TABLE I
SHILLER TESTS

(17)	$\sigma(p) = 178.33$	$\sigma(p^*) = 43.00$
(18)	$\sigma(\delta p) = 35.34$	$\sigma(x)/\sqrt{r_2} = 32.37$
(19)	$\sigma(\Delta p) = 35.26$	$\sigma(x)/\sqrt{2r} = 32.42$

p_t.[10] Following Mankiw *et al.* (1985), the actual value of p_t at the end of the sample, rather than the sample mean, was used as the terminal value of p_t^* in the backward recursion used to construct the p_t^* series. Defining the rate of return $R_t = (p_{t+1} - p_t + x_t)/p_t$, r was estimated as the sample mean of the rate of return, i.e., $r = (T - 1)^{-1} \sum_{t=1}^{T-1} R_t$. As Table I points out, all the three inequalities are violated.[11] Thus, according to the Shiller tests, the Japanese data reject the market rationality hypothesis, just as the data of the U.S. did in Shiller (1981a).

V. EMPIRICAL RESULTS

In this section we apply the volatility test and the specification tests to our data. Overall interpretations are discussed in Subsection D.

A. *MRS Tests*

In order to carry out the MRS tests, the p_t^0 must be chosen. Here p_t^0 is chosen to be "naive forecast" $\sum_{i=0}^{\infty} \theta^{i+1} F_t x_{t+i}$ as in MRS. Furthermore extrapolative and myopic expectations are assumed for the forecast of dividends, namely

$$F_t x_{t+i} = x_t \qquad \text{for all } i. \tag{20}$$

Then p_t^0 is calculated as

$$p_t^0 = x_t/(1 - \theta). \tag{21}$$

[10] Note that a present value relation like (1) holds for the detrended variables. Let T be the base year, and define the detrended data as $\bar{p}_t = p_t/\lambda^{t-T}$ and $\bar{x}_t = x_t/\lambda^{t+1-T}$, where $\lambda = (1 + g)$, and g is the constant growth rate. Then (1) implies $\bar{p}_t = \sum_{i=0}^{\infty} (\theta\lambda)^{i+1} E[\bar{x}_{t+i}|\Omega_t]$.

[11] When the deseasonalized data are used, the violation is more evident for inequalities (18) and (19). The results are as follows:

$$\sigma(p) = 97.66 \qquad \sigma(p^*) = 44.82 \tag{17}$$

$$\sigma(\delta p) = 29.38 \qquad \sigma(x)/\sqrt{r_2} = 8.64 \tag{18}$$

$$\sigma(\Delta p) = 29.32 \qquad \sigma(x)/\sqrt{2r} = 8.65. \tag{19}$$

TABLE II
MRS TESTS

r (% per year)	$E_0(p_t^* - p_t^0)^2$ =	$E_0(p_t^* - p_t)^2$ +	$E_0(p_t - p_t^0)^2$
3	445279	35253	469274
4	263839	20648	271219
5	181932	13606	190184
6	137101	11341	151911
7	109317	12057	132286
8	90579	14596	121786
9	77157	18207	116120
10	67104	22404	113162

p_t^* is calculated backwards using the relation

$$p_t^* = \theta(p_{t+1}^* + x_t), \tag{22}$$

where the terminal value p_T^* is assumed to equal the actual market price p_T. We now can evaluate the two inequalities:

$$E_0(p_t^* - p_t^0)^2 \geq E_0(p_t^* - p_t)^2 \tag{7}$$

$$E_0(p_t^* - p_t^0)^2 \geq E_0(p_t - p_t^0)^2, \tag{8}$$

given some discount rate $r(\theta = (1 + r)^{-1})$.

Table II presents the results for various values of r.[12] Inequality (7) is tested by comparing the first two columns, and inequality (8) by comparing the first and the last columns. Inequality (8) is violated uniformly, although the degree of violation seems to be small. Inequality (7) is accepted uniformly.

Roughly speaking, inequality (7) states that the market price p_t is a better forecast of the ex post rational price p_t^* than the naive forecast p_t^0 in the mean square sense. Inequality (8) states that the ex post rational price moves (around p_t^0) more than the market price (Mankiw *et al.*, 1985, pp. 679–80). Thus the implications of our results are the foilowing. The uniform violation of (8) suggests that the market price fluctuates more than the ex post rational price, contrary to the implication of the market rationality hypothesis. The nonviolation of (7) suggests the naive forecast p_t^0 chosen here is a poor forecast of p_t^* compared with p_t, as the market rationality hypothesis implies.

[12] Since the MRS test does not assume the stationarity, the data were not detrended. This may cause badly behaved asymptotic properties of statistics, but in a finite sample the properties proved in Proposition 3 hold. See also footnote 1 and Merton (1987).

B. *New Tests*

The new tests evaluate the following two inequalities:

$$E_0(\Delta p_t)^2 \geq E_0(\delta_t p_t)^2 \tag{11}$$

$$E_0(\Delta p_t)^2 \geq E_0\{E(\Delta p_t|\Omega_{t-1})\}^2. \tag{10}$$

First we need to calculate the series of innovations $\delta_t p_t$. The present value relation (1) implies $p_t = \theta[x_t + E(p_{t+1}|\Omega_t)]$ and hence $E(p_{t+1}|\Omega_t) = p_t/\theta - x_t$. Then, $\delta_t p_t = E(p_t|\Omega_t) - E(p_t|\Omega_{t-1}) = p_t - p_{t-1}/\theta + x_{t-1}$. Noting that $1/\theta = 1 + r$,

$$\delta_t p_t = \Delta p_t + x_{t-1} - r p_{t-1}. \tag{23}$$

This gives the series of $\delta_t p_t$. Taking the expectation conditional on Ω_{t-1} on both sides of (23), and noting $E(\delta_t p_t|\Omega_{t-1}) = 0$, we obtain

$$E(\Delta p_t|\Omega_{t-1}) = r p_{t-1} - x_{t-1}. \tag{24}$$

This allows us to construct a series for $E(\Delta p_t|\Omega_{t-1})$ from observable variables.

The results of the new tests are presented in Table III. Note that the values of Δp_t do not depend on r. Inequality (10) is tested by comparing the first two columns, and inequality (11) by comparing the first and the last columns. Inequality (10) is uniformly violated, although the degree of violation is small, and inequality (11) holds uniformly.

Inequality (10) states that the fluctuations of actual change in prices should be larger than that of the innovations. Inequality (11) states that the variations of the actual change in prices should be larger than that of the expected change. The results then imply too much variation in unex-

TABLE III
NEW TESTS

r (% per year)	$E_0(\Delta p_t)^2$ =	$E_0(\delta_t p_t)^2$ +	$E_0\{E(\Delta p_t\|\Omega_{t-1})\}^2$
3	352.21	353.13	2.92
4		352.89	3.00
5		352.85	3.28
6		353.03	3.77
7		353.41	4.48
8		354.01	5.38
9		354.81	6.50
10		355.82	7.83

TABLE IV
SPECIFICATION TESTS

IV	Nondetrended series	Detrended series
Constant	4.44	3.42
p_{-1}	6.73	2.60
p_{-2}	10.61	5.80
p_{-3}	8.43	4.24
p_{-4}	6.83	2.10
p_{-5}	4.49	2.56
p_{-6}	3.94	1.72
p_{-7}	6.88	3.88
p_{-8}	7.67	3.81
p_{-9}	6.72	3.40
p_{-10}	7.22	4.02
	$\chi^2_{1,0.05} = 3.84$	$\chi^2_{1,0.01} = 6.63$

pected price changes. The fluctuations of the expected price changes are very small compared with that of the actual price changes.

C. *Specification Tests*

The specification tests are applied to regression model (16):

$$y_t = \beta p_t + e_t, \tag{16}$$

where $y_t = p_{t+1} + x_t$. Since the tests exploit the asymptotic properties of the estimators, nonstationarity is potentially a serious problem. Thus tests are applied to both original and detrended data. The estimated (constant) growth rate of p_t is used in the detrending. As the instruments, the series of 1's (referred to as "constant" henceforth) and the lagged p's are used alternatively. Note that when p_{-k} is used as the instrument, the hypothesis of plim $T^{-1}p_{-k}'e = 0$ is maintained.

The values of $m = T\hat{q}'\hat{V}(\hat{q})^{-1}\hat{q}$ are presented in Table IV. Since $\hat{q}$ is one dimensional, m distributes as χ^2 with one degree of freedom. The critical value of χ_1^2 is 3.84 at the significance level 0.05, and is 6.63 at the significance level 0.01.

The results for the detrended series are considered first. The null hypothesis of correct specification, i.e., plim $T^{-1}p'e = 0$, is rejected in 3 cases at the significance level 0.05, and is uniformly accepted at the significance level 0.01.

The results of the specification tests using the nondetrended data are reported in the first column of Table IV. These results are very different from the results for the detrended data. The null hypothesis is uniformly rejected at the significance level 0.05, and is rejected for 8 out of 11 regressions at the significance level 0.01. As noted earlier, these results must be interpreted with some caution, since the asymptotic argument may not work if the variables exhibit nonstationarity.[13]

D. *Interpretation*

The tests above give seemingly conflicting results about the rationality of the stock market. The MRS test (8), the new test (10), and the specification tests for the nondetrended data rejected the market rationality hypothesis, while the MRS test (7), the new test (11), and the specification test for the detrended data did not reject the hypothesis. It is possible to construct a consistent interpretation if we note that the degree of violation of (8) and (10) is small and that the specification tests for the nondetrended data can be biased as pointed out in footnote 13.

Given these considerations we interpret our results by saying that the rational market hypothesis for the Japanese stock market cannot be rejected; although inequalities (8) and (10) are violated, the degree of violation is small and may be insignificant. We can get some evidence that the violation of (10) is indeed insignificant in the following way. Inequality (10) holds when Q3 > 0, and Q3 > 0 if and only if $E_0(\Delta p_t)(rp_{t-1} - x_{t-1})/E_0(rp_{t-1} - x_{t-1})^2 > \frac{1}{2}$.[14] Thus by running the regression

$$\Delta p_t = \beta(rp_{t-1} - x_{t-1}) + e_t, \tag{25}$$

and checking if $\beta > \frac{1}{2}$ is rejected significantly, we can have some idea if the violation of (10) is significant. Regression (25) on our data yields $\hat{\beta} = 0.22935$ and the standard error of 0.30561. Thus we cannot reject the hypothesis of $\beta > \frac{1}{2}$ with a reasonable significance level. This result suggests that the violation of (10) is also insignificant. I was unable to con-

[13] As a referee has pointed out, this test may be biased toward the rejection of the null hypothesis. For example, the test using the constant as an instrument is equivalent with the t test of $\gamma = 0$ in the following regression: $y_t = \beta p_t + \gamma \bar{p} + e_t$, where $\bar{p}$ is $(1/T)\Sigma_{t=1}^{T} p_t$. Phillips (1986) shows that the t test of $\gamma = 0$ is biased toward the rejection, if y_t and p_t are integrated process. In this case, the tests using the detrended series also suffer from some problems. Another thing we should worry about is the heteroskedasticity. After performing the specification tests, I tested the heteroskedasticity in regression (16) using TR^2 test by White (1980). The results suggest the rejection of homoskedasticity.

[14] I thank a referee for pointing this out.

$$\begin{aligned} Q3 &= E_0(\Delta p_t)^2 - E_0(\delta_t p_t)^2 \\ &= E_0(\Delta p_t)^2 - E_0[\Delta p_t - (rp_{t-1} - x_{t-1})]^2 \\ &= 2E_0(\Delta p_t)(rp_{t-1} - x_{t-1}) - E_0(rp_{t-1} - x_{t-1})^2. \end{aligned}$$

Thus Q3 > 0 iff $E_0(\Delta p_t)(rp_{t-1} - x_{t-1})/E_0(rp_{t-1} - x_{t-1})^2 > \frac{1}{2}$.

struct a similar regression for inequality (8), but the degree of violation is again small except for higher r's. Thus, if we are ready to admit the problem of the specification tests for the nondetrended series pointed out in footnote 13, the results seem to suggest the rationality of the Japanese stock market.

VI. Some Alternative Hypotheses

In this section, we briefly consider some alternative models to (1), and see the implications of our results on those alternatives. Two alternatives are considered here. One is the rational speculative bubbles hypothesis and the other is the "fads" model discussed by Shiller (1984).[15]

A. *Rational Speculative Bubbles Alternative*

The bubbles alternative is formally specified as follows:

$$p_t = f_t + b_t \tag{26}$$

$$f_t = \sum_{i=0}^{\infty} \theta^{i+1} E_t x_{t+i}. \tag{27}$$

$$E_t b_{t+i} = \theta^{-i} b_t. \tag{28}$$

The stock price (p_t) consists of two parts. The first term (f_t) is the present discounted value of the rationally expected future dividends, which is equal to the left hand side of Eq. (1), and is usually called "fundamental." The second term (b_t) is the so-called (rational) "bubbles" term, and is expected to grow at the rate of interest.

What happens to the test statistics in the previous section under the bubbles alternative? We first consider the MRS test. Using a method similar to that in Flood *et al.* (1986), we can show that inequalities (7) and (8) should hold if we calculate the p_t^* using (22). We let $\hat{p}_t$ be the series of p_t^* calculated using (22) and distinguish it from "true" p_t^* which is defined by (2) and unobservable. Then $\hat{p}_t$ can be written as

$$\begin{aligned} \hat{p}_t &= \sum_{i=0}^{T-t-1} x_{t+i} + \theta^{T-t} p_T \\ &= p_t^* - \theta^{T-t} p_T^* + \theta^{T-t} p_T. \end{aligned} \tag{29}$$

[15] Speculative bubbles are discussed by Blanchard and Watson (1982), Diba and Grossman (1983), and Tirole (1982, 1985), among others.

Now we define $u_t = p_t^* - f_t$, and note that u_t is orthogonal to the information at t, Ω_t, since f_t is the optimal forecast of p_t^* given Ω_t. Then,

$$p_t^* = p_t + u_t - b_t. \tag{30}$$

Using (29) and (30), we eliminate p_t^* to get

$$\hat{p}_t - p_t = (u_t - \theta^{T-t} u_T) + (\theta^{T-t} b_T - b_t). \tag{31}$$

Clearly the first term is orthogonal to Ω_t. It is also easy to see that the second term is orthogonal to Ω_t, because

$$E_t(\theta^{T-t} b_T - b_t) = \theta^{T-t}\theta^{-(T-t)} b_t - b_t = 0,$$

using (28). Since both p_t and p_t^0 are included in Ω_t, $\hat{p}_t - p_t$ must be orthogonal to $p_t - p_t^0$, which implies

$$E_0(\hat{p}_t - p_t^0)^2 = E_0(\hat{p}_t - p_t)^2 + E_0(p_t - p_t^0)^2.$$

Thus inequalities (7) and (8) must hold even under the bubbles alternative if we calculate p_t^* using (23).

Similarly, the orthogonality conditions exploited in the new volatility test and in the specification test also must hold under the bubbles alternative. To see this, notice that the condition we used to derive inequalities (10) and (11) is that the innovation in price is orthogonal to Ω_{t-1}. This orthogonality must obtain even under the bubble alternative, since $E_{t-1}(\delta_t p_t) = E_{t-1}[f_t + b_t - E_{t-1}(f_t + b_t)] = 0$.

The condition exploited in the specification test is written as

$$E[(f_t + b_t)(f_{t+1} + b_{t+1} + x_t - \beta f_t - \beta b_t)] = 0$$

if there are bubbles. This condition turns out to hold even under the bubbles alternative, because

$$\begin{aligned} & E[(f_t + b_t)(f_{t+1} + b_{t+1} x_t - \beta f_t - \beta b_t)] \\ &= E[(f_t + b_t) E_t(f_{t+1} + x_t - \beta f_t + b_{t+1} - \beta b_t)] \\ &= E[(f_t + b_t)\{E_t(f_{t+1} + x_t) - \beta f_t + E_t b_{t+1} - \beta b_t\}] \\ &= 0, \end{aligned}$$

using (27) and (28).

Thus our tests do not have any power against the bubbles alternative, and our results could be consistent with the existence of rational bubbles in the Japanese stock market.

B. *Fads Alternative*

Next we consider if the fads model proposed by Shiller (1984) implies the violation of some conditions tested in this paper. The fads model postulates the existence of two types of investors; one type is called smart-money investors while the other type is called ordinary investors. Smart-money investors are assumed to respond to rationally expected returns but to an extent are limited by their wealth. Formally the demand for stocks by smart-money investors is expressed as

$$s_t = (E_t R_t - r)/\phi. \tag{32}$$

Here s_t is the demand by smart-money investors expressed as a portion of the total shares outstanding. R_t is the rate of return $(p_{t+1} - p_t + x_t)/p_t$, and ϕ is constant. ϕ is the risk premium that would induce smart-money investors to hold all the stocks in the market, since $E_t R_t = r + \phi$ when $s_t = 1$. Let Y_t be the total value of stock demand by ordinary investors. Then a market equilibrium is attained when

$$s_t + Y_t/p_t = 1.$$

Solving this using (32), we get

$$p_t = \sum_{i=0}^{\infty} \alpha^{i+1}(E_t x_{t+i} + E_t Y_{t+i}) \qquad \text{where } \alpha \equiv (1 + r + \phi)^{-1}. \tag{33}$$

Notice that Y_t is unrestricted in this model. Thus the orthogonality conditions tested in the previous section need not hold if the stock prices are determined by (33). Therefore, we would expect the rejection of the null in the tests performed in the previous section. Our findings are not consistent with the fads alternative.

VII. Conclusions

This paper has investigated the market rationality hypothesis by volatility and specification tests using Japanese data. The MRS test (8), the new test (10), and the specification tests for the nondetrended data rejected the market rationality hypothesis, while the MRS test (7), the new test (11), and the specification test for the detrended data did not reject the hypothesis. It is possible to construct a consistent interpretation of these seemingly contradictory results, noting that the degree of violation of (8) and (10) are small and that the specification tests for the nondetrended data may have a bias toward the rejection of the null hypothesis. The results seem to be consistent with the rationality of the Japanese stock market.

In the last section we evaluated our results in light of two alternative models of stock price determination. The tests considered in this paper were shown to have no power against the speculative bubbles alternative. The conditions used to derive the inequalities are shown to hold even under the bubbles alternative. The fads model was shown to be inconsistent with our results.

Two directions for the future research seem promising. One direction is to consider an econometric method which can sharply distinguish the failure of orthogonality conditions implied by the market rationality hypothesis and the nonstationarity. If the series are nonstationary, the tests conduct in this paper may yield misleading results. In fact, our specification tests seem to have suffered from this problem (see footnote 13). If we come up with a method which enables us to circumvent this problem, we may be able to get a clearer view of the Japanese stock market rationality.

The other direction is to consider a test for speculative bubbles in the Japanese stock market. In the last section, we saw that our tests have no power against the bubbles alternative. If we maintain the rationality hypothesis, we can test for the speculative bubbles using a method similar to those developed by Casella (1986) and West (1985). Since this paper suggests the rationality of the Japanese stock market, the test for rational speculative bubbles seems to be a natural extension of this study.

Appendix

The data for stock prices is the Tokyo Stock Exchange's stock price index published daily by the Tokyo Stock Exchange. This stock price index is compiled under a total market price method and is a modified stock price which treats the whole stock market as if it were one share. In order to reflect only the changes in stock prices, the index is adjusted to remove changes in the total market value due to factors outside the market, such as the listing of new issues, capital increases, or the delisting of issues. The base date is January 4, 1968, and the index is set equal to 100 at that date (see Japan Securities Research Institute, 1983, pp. 38–42, for details).

As for the data for dividends, we have to use the amount of total dividends which would be generated by the portfolio whose price corresponds to the stock price index above. Unfortunately, such data is unavailable, so we have adjusted our data in the following way. We let v_t, d_t, and p_t be the total market value, the total dividends, and the stock price index, respectively. These three series are available from the Tokyo Stock Exchange. We set the period 0 as the base date for the price index, $p_0 = 100$. d_t/v_t gives the amount of dividend per yen of share. Since the portfolio which corresponds to 1 yen in the period t is different from that in the period 0, we cannot compare d_t/v_t and d_0/v_0. One yen at t is equivalent to $(100/p_t)$ yen at 0. Therefore, we can deflate the amount of total dividends at t to that per 100 yen in the price of period 0 by

$$x_t = p_t d_t / v_t,$$

where x_t expresses the amount of total dividends which would accrue to the imaginary portfolio whose price at the period 0 was 100 (that is the portfolio whose price is expressed as the stock price index).

The data are monthly and span 30 years from January, 1952 to December, 1981. The price index and the total market value in the data are measured at the end of each month. In order to make the timing consistent with the arguments in Sections II and III, we take the price or the total market value at the end of a month t to be those at the beginning of the next month $t + 1$ and denote them by p_{t+1} and v_{t+1}, respectively. The total dividends d_t include all the dividend payments by the listed firms recorded in the month. Both p_t and x_t are deflated by the consumer's price index published by the Statistical Bureau.

References

Blanchard, O. J., and Watson, M. W. (1982). Bubbles, rational expectations and financial markets, *in* "Crises in the Economic and Financial Structure" (P. Wachtel, Ed.), Lexington Books, Washington, D.C.

Casella, A. (1986). "Testing for Price Level Bubbles. The German Hyperinflation Once More," manuscript, Massachusetts Institute of Technology, Cambridge, MA.

Diba, B. T., and Grossman, H. I. (1983). "Rational Asset Price Bubbles," NBER Working Paper No. 1059.

Flavin, M. A. (1983). Excess volatility in the financial markets: A reassessment of the empirical evidence, *J. Polit. Econ.* **91,** 929–956.

Flood, R. P., Hodrick, R. J., and Kaplan, P. (1986). "An Evaluation of Recent Evidence on Stock Market Bubbles," NBER Working Paper No. 1971.

Hausman, J. A. (1978). Specification tests in econometrics, *Econometrica* **46,** 1251–1271.

Hoshi, T. (1986). A test of stock price volatility: The case of Japan, *Japan Financial Rev.* **5,** 1–18.

Huang, R. D. (1981). The monetary approach to exchange rate in an efficient foreign exchange market: Tests based on volatility, *J. Finance* **36,** 31–41.

Japan Securities Research Institute (1983). "Securities Market in Japan 1984," Japan Securities Research Institute, Tokyo.

KUNIMURA, M. (1986). "Gendai Shihon Shijo no Bunseki" ("An Analysis of Modern Capital Market"), Toyo Keizai Shinpou-sha, Tokyo.

LEROY, S. F., AND PORTER, R. D. (1981). The present-value relation: Tests based on implied variance bonds, *Econometrica* **49,** 555–574.

MANKIW, N. G., ROMER, D., AND SHAPIRO, M. D. (1985). An unbiased reexamination of stock market volatility, *J. Finance* **40,** 677–87.

MARSH, T. A., AND MERTON, R. C. (1983). "Aggregate Dividend Behavior and its Implications for Tests of Stock Market Rationality," Sloan School Working Paper No. 1475-83.

MARSH, T. A., AND R. C. MERTON (1986). Dividends variability and variance bounds tests for the rationality of stock market prices, *Amer. Econ. Rev.* **76,** 483–498.

MELINO, A. (1983). A comparison of volatility versus regression tests of the expectational model of the term structure, *in* "Essays on Estimation and Inference in Linear Rational Expectation Models," unpublished Ph.D. dissertation, Harvard University, Boston, MA.

MERTON, R. C. (1987). On the current state of the stock market rationality hypothesis, *in* "Macroeconomics and Finance: Essays in Honor of Franco Modigliani" (R. Dornbusch, S. Fischer, and J. Bossons, Eds.), pp. 93–124, MIT Press, Cambridge, MA.

PHILLIPS, P. C. B. (1986). Understanding spurious regressions in econometrics, *J. Econometrics* **33,** 311–340.

SHILLER, R. J. (1979). The volatility of long-term interest rates and expectations models of the term structure, *J. Polit. Econ.* **87,** 1190–1219.

SHILLER, R. J. (1981a). Do stock prices move too much to be justified by subsequent changes in dividends?, *Amer. Econ. Rev.* **71,** 421–436.

SHILLER, R. J. (1981b). The use of volatility measures in assessing market efficiency, *J. Finance* **36,** 291–304.

SHILLER, R. J. (1984). Stock prices and social dynamics, *Brookings Pap. Econ. Act.* **2,** 457–498.

SINGLETON, K. J. (1980). Expectations models of the term structure and implied variance bounds, *J. Polit. Econ.* **88,** 1159–1176.

TIROLE, J. (1982). On the possibility of speculation under rational expectations, *Econometrica* **50,** 1163–1181.

TIROLE, J. (1985). Asset bubbles and overlapping generations, *Econometrica* **53,** 1499–1528.

WEST, K. D. (1985). "A specification Test for Speculative Bubbles," manuscript, Princeton University, Princeton, NJ.

WHITE, H. (1980). A heteroskedasticity-consistent covariance matrix estimator and a direct test for heteroskedasticity, *Econometrica* **48,** 817–838.

YONEZAWA, Y., AND MARU, J. (1984). "Nihon no Kabushiki Shijo" ("Japanese Stock Market"), Toyo Keizai Shinpou-sha, Tokyo.

Japanese Financial Market Research
W.T. Ziemba, W. Bailey and Y. Hamao (Editors)

MARKET MICROSTRUCTURE AND PRICE DISCOVERY ON THE TOKYO STOCK EXCHANGE *

Yakov AMIHUD

Leonard N. Stern School of Business, New York University, New York, NY 10006, USA
Tel-Aviv University, Tel Aviv, Israel

Haim MENDELSON

Stanford University, Stanford, CA 94305, USA

Received January 1989, final version received June 1989

This paper compares the price discovery processes at the opening and closing transactions for the fifty largest stocks trading on the Tokyo Stock Exchange. Open-to-open returns are found to have a greater volatility and a more negative autocorrelation pattern than close-to-close returns, similar to the pattern we found on the New York Stock Exchange. The results are consistent with pricing over-reaction at the opening and partial price-adjustment at the close. These patterns persist over time and prevail when estimated for returns conditional on the contemporaneous market effect. Our analysis of daytime and overnight returns suggests that pricing errors at the opening are corrected over the trading day. We present a new measure of volatility – the relative dispersion of stock returns around the market return – and find that it is greater at the opening, consistent with a more noisy price discovery process.

Keywords: Price discovery process, Tokyo Stock Exchange, open-to-open returns, close-to-close returns, price adjustment.

1. Introduction

The Tokyo Stock Exchange (TSE) is one of the most important financial centers of the world. The average daily monetary value of traded shares is similar to that of the New York Stock Exchange, and the value of equity listed on the TSE already exceeds New York Stock Exchange listed equity value. The TSE operates as a two-sided semi-continuous market where buy and sell orders are directly matched. Unlike the New York Stock Exchange, where trading is performed through specialists that directly participate in the trading process and take active inventory positions, the Tokyo Stock Exchange's *Saitori* perform primarily a clerical function. They cannot accept orders directly, nor can they trade for their own account.

* The authors acknowledge helpful comments and suggestions by an anonymous referee, programming assistance by Edgar Gorres, and partial financial support by the Center for Japan–U.S. Business and Economics Studies of New York University.

The TSE uses a number of trading mechanisms for different securities and at different times. For all but the most liquid stocks, orders are submitted for execution to a computer-based system which displays current bid and ask quotes. The most liquid stocks are traded on the exchange floor, where the *Saitori* use a manual order book to manage the trading process. Trading on the TSE takes place in two daily sessions. Each session is opened by a batched clearing process known as *Itayose* and followed by a continuous two-sided trading process called *Zaraba*.

This paper compares the price behavior of heavily traded stocks on the TSE in the opening transaction with the price behavior of the same stocks at the closing transaction. Since both prices are affected by the very same information, differences in price behavior can stem from the differences in the trading method applied in each of these transactions, from the period of no-trade which precedes the opening transaction, or from both. In this paper we analyze the differences between the price discovery processes [1] in the opening and closing transactions and the effects of these market microstructure factors on stock price behavior.

Following Amihud and Mendelson (1987), we distinguish between the intrinsic *value* of a security and its observed *price*, with the differences being attributed to two market microstructure factors: (i) the price-adjustment process, and (ii) trading noise [Black (1986)]. The first factor pertains to the speed of adjustment of market prices to new information, and the second to transitory price fluctuations generated by friction in the trading process.

We study and compare the operation of the *Itayose* to that of the *Zaraba*, focusing on the volatility and autocorrelation of stock returns. Volatility is naturally of interest to any risk-averse trader. In addition, volatility induced by trading noise makes it more difficult for market participants to extract signals from stock prices and reduces the information content of these prices. Thus, a market with more noisy price signals is less informationally efficient. Further, when greater volatility reduces the liquidity of the market, it should also lead to higher required returns, thus lowering security prices [Amihud and Mendelson (1986a, b, 1988a, b, 1989a)]. The pattern of return autocorrelation is also associated with market efficiency [Fama (1970)] and trading friction. [2] These two measures – volatility and autocorrelation – enable us to compare the efficiency of pricing in the opening and closing transactions on the Tokyo Stock Exchange. We present here estimates of these measures for the open-to-open and close-to-close returns, which demonstrate the existence of significant differences between the two return series. These differences are consistent over

[1] See Schwartz (1988).

[2] See, e.g., West and Tinic (1971), Cohen et al. (1979), Cohen et al. (1980), Schwartz and Whitcomb (1977).

time and prevail when estimated conditional on the common market index.

Our tests reveal that most of the return volatility occurs during the daytime trading. Then, investors also correct pricing errors made at the opening transaction, where greater volatility (due to noise and overreaction) exists. We also introduce and analyze a new volatility measure: the Relative Return Dispersion (RRD) *across* stocks. The RRD is a cross-sectional measure of volatility which characterizes the extent to which inferences can be made from the behavior of the market as a whole on the behavior of individual security returns. We also examine the difference in the RRD between the *Itayose* and the *Zaraba,* focusing on its variation over time.

In what follows, we discuss the trading mechanisms employed by the TSE in section 2. Our model of price adjustment is presented in section 3, and the data used in our analysis is discussed in section 4. Section 5 presents our results on the variances and autocorrelations of the open-to-open and close-to-close returns in the TSE, and section 6 studies the behavior of residual returns and compares daily to overnight returns. Section 7 discusses our new measure of relative return dispersion and examines its unusual behavior during the stock market crash, and our concluding remarks are offered in Section 8.

2. Trading regimes in the Tokyo Stock Exchange

The TSE is a two-sided market where buy and sell orders are directly matched. The matching process is facilitated by the *Saitori,* who control the trading process. Unlike the New York Stock Exchange specialists, the *Saitori* do not trade for their own account and do not take an inventory position; rather, they passively control the process of matching buyers and sellers and manage the order book. There are two basic types of orders submitted to the exchange and managed by the *Saitori*: (i) limit orders, which state the order quantity and the minimum selling price or the maximum purchase price at which the order is to be executed; and (ii) market orders, which specify only the quantity to be sold or bought with no price limits. Quantities are quoted in thousands of shares, and prices in yen. [3] Market orders are executed if possible; limit orders are recorded on the *Saitori*'s order book and await execution against matching orders.

The *Saitori*'s order book is computer-based for all but the most heavily-traded stocks, such as the ones in our sample. In addition to the clerical function of managing the book and matching orders according to the exchange rules, the *Saitori* sometimes plays the role of auctioneer using 'special quotes': When there is a major order imbalance, the *Saitori* will announce a price inside the current bid and ask quotes, attempting to attract orders to reduce

[3] The minimum price increment for many stocks has recently been increased to ten yen.

Table 1
The *Saitori*'s limit order book just prior to the *Itayose* procedure. Each order is written in the row corresponding to its price. Within this row, the order identifies the securities company (A through J in this example) and the order quantity in lots of 1,000 shares (written above the company identification).

Sell orders	Price (yen)	Buy orders
2 5 H A	Market	2 4 C I
	1353	
3 1 G A	1352	1 1 E F
1 2 B A	1351	4 E
3 2 B A	1350	4 C
5 D	1349	3 C
	1348	4 J

the imbalance. Further, the *Saitori* is responsible for enforcing the daily price limits instituted by the TSE.

There are two market mechanisms operating in the TSE: the *Itayose* mechanism, which governs the opening transaction, and the *Zaraba* mechanism for continuous trading, which also governs the closing transaction. Both trading methods are managed by the *Saitori*, who uses an order sheet which lists the orders by decreasing price, as in table 1. Buy orders are listed on the right-hand side of the order sheet, and sell orders on the left-hand side. The sequence of order arrival (which is important for maintaining time priority in the *Zaraba* method of trading) is indicated by the distance of the order from the price column at the center of the order sheet.

Trading at the opening transaction (following the *Itayose* method) is performed by batching together all orders submitted prior to the opening and determining the corresponding market clearing price, if one exists. This is done by determining the cumulative quantity offered and bid at each feasible price, thus effectively constructing the supply and demand schedules from the orders submitted to the market (see fig. 1). These schedules are then intersected at the market-clearing price at which all exchanges are executed. Thus, the *Itayose* resembles the clearing house studied by Mendelson (1982a, 1985, 1987) and

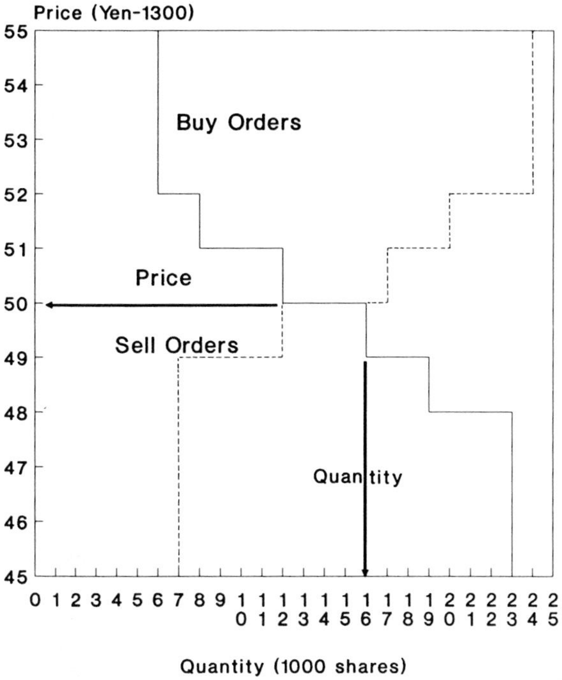

Fig. 1. Market-clearing at the opening – *Itayose*. The market-clearing price is 1350 yen, and the quantity traded is 16,000 shares.

proposed to be incorporated in an integrated computerized trading system by Amihud and Mendelson (1985, 1988a). For example, considering the orders in table 1, the market clearing price at the opening may be determined by examining the demand and supply schedules in table 2 and fig. 1. Clearly, the market clearing price in this example is 1350 yen, with 16,000 shares exchanged at that price. This will require filling only part of the 3,000-share sell order of securities company B with limit price 1350.

Table 2
The supply and demand schedules corresponding to the orders in table 1. A quantity of 16,000 shares will be exchanged at a price of 1350 yen.

Quantity supplied (thousands)	Price (yen)	Quantity demanded (thousands)
24	1353	6
24	1352	8
20	1351	12
17	*1350*	*16*
12	1349	19
7	1348	23

Table 3
The *Saitori*'s order sheet immediately following the opening.

Quantity supplied (thousands)	Price (yen)	Quantity demanded (thousands)
	1353	
3 1 G A	1352	
1 2 B A	1351	
1 B	1350	
	1349	3 C
	1348	4 J

Once the market has opened, trading continues by the *Zaraba* method. The marginal unexecuted orders remaining on the *Saitori*'s book determine the bid and ask prices as well as the corresponding quantities. For the example of table 1, the remaining orders following the *Itayose* are shown in table 3; the current bid is 1349 yen with a depth of 3,000 shares, and the ask is 1350 yen with depth 1,000 shares. An order to sell 3,000 shares at market will be executed at price 1349, reducing the bid price to 1348 yen. Over time, additional orders will be added to the book or executed, and the process will continue up to the closing transaction, which is also part of the continuous *Zaraba* market.

3. A model of price adjustment

Amihud and Mendelson (1987) have analyzed a simple model of price adjustment which is useful for studying stock price behavior. The model distinguishes between the *value* of a security at time t, V_t, and its observed *price*, P_t. Security prices follow a partial-adjustment process with noise:

$$P_t - P_{t-1} = g \cdot [V_t - P_{t-1}] + u_t, \tag{1}$$

where V_t and P_t are in logarithms. Eq. (1) posits a partial-adjustment model with adjustment coefficient $0 < g < 2$ and a 'white noise' sequence $\{u_t\}$ of i.i.d. random variables with zero mean and finite variance σ^2. The noise, which pushes the observed price of the security away from its value, reflects factors such as transitory order imbalances, price fluctuations between the bid and the ask and idiosyncratic liquidity-motivated transactions. The adjustment-coefficient g measures the speed of adjustment of transaction prices to changes in the security's value. In particular, $0 < g < 1$ represents partial price adjustment, $g = 1$ represents full price adjustment and $g > 1$ corresponds to *over-shooting* or *over-reaction* of prices to new information about the value of the security [see Amihud and Mendelson (1982)].

We assume that the logarithms of security values $\{V_t\}$ follow a random walk process with drift m:

$$V_t = V_{t-1} + e_t + m, \tag{2}$$

where $\{e_t\}$ are i.i.d. random variables, independent of u_t, ,with zero mean and finite variance ν^2; the differences $(V_t - V_{t-1})$ are the *value returns* of the security. The *observed* security returns are defined by $R_t = P_t - P_{t-1}$.

Amihud and Mendelson (1987) showed that the observed return variance is given by

$$\mathrm{Var}(R_t) = \frac{g}{2-g}\nu^2 + \frac{2}{2-g}\sigma^2, \tag{3}$$

where the first term is due to the value return variance, ν^2, and the second represents the contribution of the noise. When $0 < g < 1$, only part of the value return variance is incorporated in the observed returns, reflecting the smoothing effect of the partial adjustment process. In the over-reaction case ($g > 1$), the first term of (3) (and hence certainly the overall variance) becomes greater than the value return variance, since then value fluctuations are amplified by traders' over-reaction. The second term in (3) represents the contribution of the noise to the observed return variance. It increases in both the noise variance σ^2 and the adjustment coefficient g.

The first-order *autocovariance* of the observed returns is given by

$$\mathrm{Cov}(R_t, R_{t-1}) = \frac{g}{2-g} \cdot \left[(1-g)\nu^2 - \sigma^2\right], \tag{4}$$

which can also be written in the form

$$\mathrm{Cov}(R_t, R_{t-1}) = (1-g) \cdot \mathrm{Var}(R_t) - \sigma^2, \tag{5}$$

where the contribution of the adjustment-process itself to the covariance is proportional to $(1 - g)$, and the contribution of the noise is $-\sigma^2$. If stock prices follow a random walk with noise due only to fluctuations between the bid and ask prices, the return autocovariance is negative and the square root of its absolute value is proportional to the bid–ask spread [Roll (1984)]. [4] However, when $g < 1$, as is usually the case, the autocovariance can be positive despite the existence of noise-inducing factors such as the bid–ask spread [Amihud and Mendelson (1987, p. 547)].

[4] See also Cohen et al. (1979) and Cohen et al. (1980) on the serial correlation induced by market microstructure and trading friction.

By (3)–(5), the first-order return autocorrelation is given by

$$\rho(R_t) = \frac{g(1-g)\nu^2 - g\sigma^2}{g\nu^2 + 2\sigma^2} = (1-g) - \frac{\sigma^2}{\operatorname{Var}(R_t)}. \tag{6}$$

The contribution of the noise to the autocorrelation is always negative, whereas the contribution of the adjustment process is positive when $0 < g < 1$ (the case of partial price adjustment) and negative when $g > 1$ (the over-reaction case).

Our formulation (6) highlights the factors which contribute to non-zero autocorrelation: the deviation of the adjustment-coefficient g from unity, and the deviation of the noise variance σ^2 from zero. Since zero autocorrelation of returns is consistent with the random walk model of prices, return autocorrelation has been used to test the market efficiency hypothesis [see Fama (1970)]. However, our formulation shows that this type of test may fail to reject the hypothesis that prices evolve as a random walk even if in fact they do not: If $(1-g)$ is close to $\sigma^2/\operatorname{Var}(R_t)$, $\rho(R_t)$ may be close to zero since the two opposite effects of the partial price-adjustment and the noise will approximately cancel out. This casts doubt on this test procedure of market efficiency, and questions the results obtained in some previous studies.

One way to resolve this problem is to examine the autocorrelations of stock *portfolios*. Amihud and Mendelson (1989b) have shown that when the returns R_t represent a well-diversified portfolio of stocks with the same adjustment-coefficient g and independent noise components, the noise term of the portfolio return covariance tends to zero. Then, (5) reduces to

$$\operatorname{Cov}(R_t, R_{t-1}) = (1-g) \cdot \operatorname{Var}(R_t), \tag{7}$$

and the autocorrelation coefficient of the portfolio returns is $(1-g)$. In particular, the portfolio autocorrelation should be negative when $g > 1$ and positive when $g < 1$. The latter will hold even if the autocorrelation of the underlying returns on the individual securities is zero or negative due to a large noise variance.

Note that the above result shows that the return autocorrelations of individual stocks are expected to behave quite differently from those of stock portfolios. For an individual security, the return autocorrelation given by (6) reflects two different factors:

(i) A *price-adjustment* effect, which induces a *positive* autocorrelation when $g < 1$ (the partial-adjustment case) and a *negative* autocorrelation when $g > 1$ (the over-reaction case).
(ii) A *noise* effect, which always induces a *negative* autocorrelation.

Since the noise variance is diversified away in a portfolio, we obtain (7) where the only remaining effect is that of partial price-adjustment. When $g < 1$ and the 'noise' variance is sufficiently high, we obtain that while the

Table 4
Tokyo Stock Exchange stocks included in the sample and their stock symbols. Stocks are ranked by their trading volume in 1987.

Stock symbol	Stock	Annual trading volume [a]
5401	Nippon Steel	29,241,292
5403	Kawasaki Steel	10,327,528
5404	NKK	7,901,628
7011	Mitsubishi Heavy Ind	6,417,124
5405	Sumitomo Metal Ind.	5,970,479
7013	IHI	5,125,284
5406	Kobe Steel	4,989,778
5407	Nisshin Steel	4,594,115
6502	Toshiba	3,895,143
6501	Hitachi	3,413,462
6503	Mitsubishi Electric	3,289,096
4005	Sumitomo Chemical	2,964,449
9531	Tokyo Gas	2,959,396
4001	Mitsui Toatsu Chemic	2,577,739
7003	Mitsui Engin & Ship	2,426,753
6702	Fujitsu	2,120,964
4004	Showa Denko	2,095,041
5711	Mitsubishi Metal	2,001,761
9101	Nippon Yusen	1,829,709
9103	Japan Line	1,820,589
7012	Kawasaki Heavy Industries	1,792,233
6752	Matsushita Electric Industrial	1,787,006
3402	Toray Industries	1,709,522
8031	Mitsui	1,626,098
6701	NEC	1,525,186
7004	Hitachi Zosen	1,451,788
1801	Taisei	1,358,725
6504	Fuji Electric	1,332,730
5801	Furukawa Electric	1,283,998
6302	Sumitomo Heavy Ind.	1,277,924
3407	Asahi Chemical Ind.	1,249,023
3401	Teijin	1,203,559
4061	Denki Kagaku Kogyo	1,183,932
5712	Nippon Mining	1,135,943
8751	Tokio Marine & Fire	1,128,438
6764	Sanyo Electric	1,096,240
3101	Toyobo	1,066,407
5631	The Japan Steel Work	1,035,887
4208	Ube Industries	1,034,984
4010	Mitsubishi Kasei	1,014,578
8604	Nomura Securities	1,005,617
1802	Ohbayashi	976,876
8802	Mitsubishi Estate	966,545
3702	Sanyo–Kokusaku Pulp	942,812
9062	Nippon Express	921,637
9001	Tobu Railway	915,975
8058	Mitsubishi	877,500
9005	Tokyu	872,792
8801	Mitsui Real Estate	827,688
3103	Unitika	804,177

[a] In thousands of shares (1987).

autocorrelations of individual security returns are negative, those of well–diversified portfolios will be positive. This phenomenon, which was considered a puzzle [Lo and MacKinlay (1988)] is resolved by our model.

We shall now present the evidence on stock return behavior, focusing on their variance and autocorrelation, and apply the model analyzed in this section to interpret the results.

4. The data

Our data consist of the opening and closing prices of the fifty largest stocks traded on the TSE over the period June 1, 1985 to August 19, 1988, excluding the unusual week of the crash (October 19 through October 23 of 1987). The stocks, their stock symbols and their 1987 trading volumes (in thousands of shares) are listed in table 4.

Our empirical study considers the open-to-open returns,

$$R_{o,t} = P_{o,t} - P_{o,t-1} \text{ (in logarithms)} \tag{8a}$$

where $P_{o,t}$ is the day-t opening price. Similarly, the close-to-close returns are defined by

$$R_{c,t} = P_{c,t} - P_{c,t-1} \text{ (in logarithms)} \tag{8b}$$

where $P_{c,t}$ is the day-t closing price. [5] The sample consists of 891 open-to-open returns $\{R_{o,t}\}$ and the corresponding 891 close-to-close returns $\{R_{c,t}\}$ which cover the same period of time. All information which changes the values of the examined stocks is equally reflected in both $R_{o,t}$ and $R_{c,t}$. Hence, observed differences in the distributions of $R_{o,t}$ and $R_{c,t}$ may be attributed to the different price discovery processes in the opening and the closing of the TSE. Such differences can result from the period of 'no trade' which precedes the opening transaction, whereas the closing transaction is preceded by active trading which provides traders with information. Or, they can be due to the two alternative trading mechanisms, the *Itayose* and *Zaraba*, applied in the opening and in the closing.

5. Stock return variances and autocorrelations

Eqs. (3) and (4) suggest that the measured variances and autocovariances of stock returns may be different under different price-discovery processes (characterized by the parameters g and σ^2) even when the underlying value-returns are the same. Thus, if the nature of price discovery in the *Itayose* (the

[5] Due to the unavailability of data, we could not adjust the returns for dividends. However, this should not affect the comparison between the opening and closing returns. Further, dividends in Japan are small compared to the U.S.

opening) is different from that of the *Zaraba*, which governs the close, this will be reflected in differences in the variances and autocovariances of the observed returns.

Table 5 compares the variances and autocorrelations for the open-to-open and close-to-close return series. [6] The table shows distinct differences between the *Itayose* and the *Zaraba*: the open-to-open return variance exceeds the close-to-close return variance for 49 out of 50 stocks. On average, the variance of the open-to-open returns is 15% greater than that of the close-to-close returns. Thus, traders who choose to transact at the opening are usually exposed to greater volatility than those who trade at the closing. This result is similar to the behavior of stock returns on the New York Stock Exchange obtained by Amihud and Mendelson (1987). In fact, the average variance ratio for the 30 stocks on the Dow Jones Industrial list was even higher (21%), possibly reflecting the effects of price-stabilization at the closing by the NYSE specialists.

The greater variance at the opening transaction, both on the New York Stock Exchange and in Tokyo, suggests that the different price-discovery processes at the opening and the closing have a significant impact on the corresponding price behavior. Prior to the closing, the stocks are traded in a continuous market (the *Zaraba*) where traders can monitor prices continuously and infer from these prices the impact of new information as soon as it arrives to the market. The current quotes as well as the sequence of transaction prices signal the current value of the security to public traders and reduce estimation errors, since traders have at their disposal the most recently available information set. In contrast, there is likely to be at the opening a greater amount of information which has accumulated since the last transaction. Thus, there may be a relationship between the size of the pricing error and the amount of accumulated information, leading to greater price dispersion in the opening.

The first-order autocorrelations of both the open-to-open and close-to-close return series are presented in table 5. The open-to-open autocorrelations show a distinct negative pattern: 44 out of the 50 stocks have negative open-to-open return autocorrelations of which 21 are statistically-significant at the 5% level, and the average autocorrelation is -0.0565 (standard error $= 0.0070$). The autocorrelation coefficients for the close-to-close returns are mixed in sign: 21 are negative and 29 positive, and their mean is positive but very small, 0.0131 (standard error = 0.0088). While 16 of these autocorrelations are significantly different from zero, 7 are negative and 9 are positive. Thus, the close-to-close returns show no clear pattern of autocorrelation. However, the *difference* between the close-to-close and open-to-open autocorrelations shows a clear

[6] The statistics are not independent across stocks. We later analyze the residual returns, conditional on a common market index.

Table 5
Open-to-open and close-to-close return variances and autocorrelations.

Stock symbol	Variance			Autocorrelation		
	Open $Var(R_t^o)$	Close $Var(R_t^c)$	$\frac{Var(R_t^o)}{Var(R_t^c)}$	Open $\rho(R_t^o)$	Close $\rho(R_t^c)$	$\rho(R_t^c t) - \rho(R_t^o)$
5401	0.0006834	0.0005937	1.1510670	−0.0233650	0.0578591	0.0812241
5403	0.0009527	0.0007762	1.2273860	−0.0969967 [a]	0.0205012	0.1174979
5404	0.0009036	0.0007892	1.1449200	−0.0610048	0.0094298	0.0704346
7011	0.0007517	0.0006125	1.2272880	−0.0842978 [a]	0.0285165	0.1128144
5405	0.0008182	0.0006138	1.3329820	−0.1404034 [a]	−0.0137942	0.1266092
7013	0.0009999	0.0009150	1.0928280	−0.0500334	−0.0314707	0.0185628
5406	0.0008807	0.0006986	1.2605950	−0.0970712 [a]	0.0096963	0.1067674
5407	0.0007696	0.0007443	1.0339130	−0.0271366	−0.0135128	0.0136238
6502	0.0006344	0.0005429	1.1685460	−0.0794130 [a]	−0.0022221	0.0771909
6501	0.0005933	0.0005404	1.0979650	−0.0584832	−0.0180714	0.0404118
6503	0.0006445	0.0005135	1.2550770	−0.1235714 [a]	−0.0288973	0.0946740
4005	0.0006022	0.0005323	1.1314340	0.0211155	0.0395810	0.0184655
9531	0.0009176	0.0008218	1.1166550	0.0041982	0.0427946	0.0385964
4001	0.0006243	0.0005252	1.1887400	−0.0220352	0.0259770	0.0480122
7003	0.0008100	0.0006978	1.1607990	−0.1437788 [a]	−0.0703491 [a]	0.0734297
6702	0.0006624	0.0005869	1.1286950	−0.0639359	0.0001068	0.0640426
4004	0.0006925	0.0006252	1.1077690	−0.0737347 [a]	−0.0268983	0.0468364
5711	0.0004339	0.0003739	1.1606380	−0.0609168	0.0169023	0.0778192
9101	0.0006705	0.0005949	1.1270480	−0.0820215 [a]	0.0004960	0.0825175
9103	0.0011820	0.0012410	0.9524856	−0.0344354	−0.0810596 [a]	−0.0466242
7012	0.0011227	0.0008473	1.3249160	−0.0804546 [a]	0.0643238	0.1447783
6752	0.0005881	0.0005277	1.1144630	0.0149631	0.0827180 [a]	0.0677549
3402	0.0004665	0.0003844	1.2134680	−0.0922228 [a]	0.0198933	0.1121161
8031	0.0005717	0.0005136	1.1131110	−0.0183041	0.0282814	0.0465855
6701	0.0006903	0.0005840	1.1820230	0.0130971	0.0575690	0.0444718
7004	0.0008185	0.0006978	1.1729860	−0.1499009 [a]	−0.0987361 [a]	0.0511648
1801	0.0007154	0.0005930	1.2063780	−0.0717331 [a]	0.0146270	0.0863601
6504	0.0006622	0.0005791	1.1435550	−0.1595618 [a]	−0.0858020 [a]	0.0737598
5801	0.0004811	0.0004250	1.1320230	−0.0226484	0.0659043 [a]	0.0885527
6302	0.0007460	0.0007302	1.0216640	−0.0339217	−0.0512504	−0.0173287
3407	0.0005038	0.0003957	1.2730760	−0.1153402 [a]	−0.0125114	0.1028288
3401	0.0004614	0.0003855	1.1968020	−0.0546368	0.0572837	0.1119205
4061	0.0005361	0.0004949	1.0833360	0.0291330	0.0738455 [a]	0.0447126
5712	0.0004870	0.0004706	1.0347560	−0.0422276	−0.0951891 [a]	−0.0529614
8751	0.0007287	0.0005756	1.2659750	−0.0085959	0.1517105 [a]	0.1603064
6764	0.0003563	0.0003553	1.0028250	−0.0064544	−0.0154273	−0.0089729
3101	0.0005004	0.0004484	1.1160880	−0.0956098 [a]	0.0236926	0.1193024
5631	0.0009268	0.0008579	1.0802480	−0.0367183	−0.0152080	0.0215103
4208	0.0006467	0.0005711	1.1323960	−0.1082756 [a]	−0.0795779 [a]	0.0286977
4010	0.0004571	0.0004058	1.1264660	−0.0235556	0.0114925	0.0350481
8604	0.0007418	0.0005832	1.2719510	−0.0130572	0.1664712 [a]	0.1795284
1802	0.0007600	0.0006006	1.2653630	−0.1214228 [a]	−0.0102491	0.1111737
8802	0.0007256	0.0006721	1.0796360	0.0351352	0.1377451 [a]	0.1026099
3702	0.0004225	0.0003809	1.1092680	−0.1235992 [a]	−0.0344447	0.0891546

Table 5 (continued)

Stock symbol	Variance			Autocorrelation		
	Open $\text{Var}(R_t^o)$	Close $\text{Var}(R_t^c)$	$\frac{\text{Var}(R_t^o)}{\text{Var}(R_t^c)}$	Open $\rho(R_t^o)$	Close $\rho(R_t^c)$	$\rho(R_t^c t) - \rho(R_t^o)$
9062	0.0007148	0.0006092	1.1733660	−0.0445852	0.0758585 [a]	0.1204437
9001	0.0006897	0.0005551	1.2425630	−0.0419534	0.1049040 [a]	0.1468574
8058	0.0006450	0.0005986	1.0776190	−0.0687421 [a]	−0.0255351	0.0432070
9005	0.0008261	0.0006996	1.1809430	−0.0103918	0.1070431 [a]	0.1174349
8801	0.0007749	0.0006791	1.1410300	−0.0064327	0.0520158	0.0584486
3103	0.0004454	0.0004450	1.0009070	−0.0687110 [a]	−0.0797074 [a]	−0.0109963
Mean	0.0006888	0.0006001	1.150921	−0.0564810	0.0131465	0.0696275
S.D.	0.0001797	0.0001642	0.083512	0.0491645	0.0621730	0.0506613

[a] Significant at the 5% level.

pattern: their mean is 0.0696 (the standard error is 0.0072), and 45 of them are positive.

To interpret these results, we re-examine eqs. (3) and (4) for the return variance and covariance. By (3), the return variance is an increasing function of the adjustment coefficient g. As for the effect of an increase in g on the return autocovariance, we note that $g(1-g)/(2-g)$ is a decreasing function of g for $2-\sqrt{2} < g < 2$, whereas $g/(2-g)$ is an increasing function of g. Thus, by (4), the return autocovariance is a decreasing function of g for all $2-\sqrt{2} < g < 2$. It follows that if g_0, the adjustment-coefficient at the opening, is greater than g_c, the adjustment-coefficient at the close, then the open-to-open return variance will be *higher* than the close-to-close return variance *and* the open-to-open return autocovariance will be *lower* than the close-to-close return autocovariance.[7] Similarly, an increase in the 'noise' variance σ^2 increases the return variance and decreases the return autocovariance. This is because for a given g, the partial derivative of $\text{Var}(R_t)$ with respect to σ^2 is $2/(2-g)$, which is positive for all $g < 2$, whereas the partial derivative of $\text{Cov}(R_t, R_{t-1})$ with respect to σ^2 is $-g/(2-g)$, which is negative.

The effect of g on the return autocorrelation is given by the function

$$\frac{g(1-g)\nu^2 - g\sigma^2}{g\nu^2 + 2\sigma^2} = 1 - \frac{g^2\nu^2 + g\sigma^2 + 2\sigma^2}{g\nu^2 + 2\sigma^2}, \tag{9}$$

whose derivative with respect to g is negative as long as $g > 1/2$. Thus, for $2 > g > 2-\sqrt{2}$, the autocorrelation and the first-order autocovariance are decreasing functions of g. Further, differentiating (9) with respect to σ^2, we observe that the autocorrelation is a decreasing function of σ^2 for all $g < 2$. Turning to the results in table 5, the open-to-open returns have higher

[7] Assuming $g > 2-\sqrt{2}$.

variances *and* lower (negative) autocorrelations than the close-to-close returns. As shown above, both the higher variance and the lower autocorrelation may reflect a higher value of g and/or a higher 'noise' variance. Thus, the relationship between the variances and autocorrelations shown in table 5 is consistent with a higher adjustment coefficient g at the opening, greater 'noise' variance at the opening, or both.

In summary, an increase in the noise variance σ^2 or in the adjustment coefficient g increases the return variance and reduces the return autocovariance (possibly to a more negative level), ceteris paribus. That is, the same factors that drive up the variance differential between the open-to-open and close-to-close returns, defined by

$$\Delta V_i = \mathrm{Var}\left(R^i_{\mathrm{o},t}\right) - \mathrm{Var}\left(R^i_{\mathrm{c},t}\right)$$

also drive up the covariance differential between the close-to-close and open-to-open returns,

$$\Delta C_i = \mathrm{Cov}\left(R^i_{\mathrm{c},t},\ R^i_{\mathrm{c},t-1}\right) - \mathrm{Cov}\left(R^i_{\mathrm{o},t},\ R^i_{\mathrm{o},t-1}\right).$$

This suggests that ΔV_i should be positively related to ΔC_i across securities. To test this hypothesis, we regressed ΔV_i on ΔC_i, obtaining

$$\Delta V_i = 0.000024 + \underset{(15.39)}{1.40\,\Delta C_i} \qquad R^2 = 0.83, \tag{10}$$

where the t-ratio for the covariance-differential coefficient ΔC_i, 15.39, indicates a positive and strongly significant relation. Note that since ΔC_i are only sample estimates, we encounter here the 'errors in the variables' problem which biases the regression coefficient downward, against rejecting the null hypothesis of no relationship between ΔV and ΔC. Still, the null is strongly rejected.

As discussed in section 3, we can infer the value of the adjustment-coefficient g from the autocorrelation coefficient of a well-diversified portfolio of securities, using (7). The results in table 5 suggest that $g_{\mathrm{o}} > g_{\mathrm{c}}$, consistent with a higher variance and a lower autocorrelation of the open-to-open returns compared to the close-to-close returns. To test the hypothesis that $g_{\mathrm{o}} > g_{\mathrm{c}}$, we grouped the stocks randomly into five portfolios with ten stocks in each and calculated the equally-weighted open-to-open and close-to-close portfolio returns and the corresponding autocorrelations. By (7), the autocorrelation coefficient of a well diversified portfolio p is equal to $(1 - g^p)$, where g^p is the adjustment-coefficient of the stocks in the portfolio.[8] Thus, we obtained five estimates $\{g^p_{\mathrm{o}}\}^5_{p=1}$ of g_{o}, and five estimates $\{g^p_{\mathrm{c}}\}^5_{p=1}$ of g_{c}. Under the null hypothesis of no difference between the opening and closing returns, the

[8] Due to data limitations, we used portfolios of ten stocks, which may not be sufficiently well diversified. Hence, our estimates of g may reflect some of the noise.

Table 6
Variances and autocorrelations for the five 'thinness'-based portfolios. Portfolio 5 is the 'thinnest'.

Portfolio p	$\mathrm{Var}(R_t^{\mathrm{o}})$	$\mathrm{Var}(R_t^{\mathrm{c}})$	$\dfrac{\mathrm{Var}(R_t^{\mathrm{o}})}{\mathrm{Var}(R_t^{\mathrm{c}})}$	$\rho(R_t^{\mathrm{o}})$	$\rho(R_t^{\mathrm{c}})$
1	0.0004666	0.0003617	1.29	−0.089353	0.033708
2	0.0002512	0.0001958	1.28	−0.104818	0.009784
3	0.0002292	0.0001738	1.32	−0.123324	0.032179
4	0.0001919	0.0001485	1.29	−0.049595	0.151510
5	0.0003707	0.0002814	1.32	−0.014059	0.193296

differences $\Delta g^p = g_{\mathrm{o}}^p - g_{\mathrm{c}}^p$ should reflect only sampling errors, hypothesized to be a random sample from a population with zero mean. We obtained for Δg^p the five values, 0.154, 0.159, 0.191, 0.191 and 0.1556, all of which are positive. Applying a binomial test, the probability that this is due to chance is $(1/2)^5 = 0.03125$, implying significance. In addition, all the open-to-open portfolio autocorrelations were negative and all the close-to-close return autocorrelations were positive, implying $g_{\mathrm{o}}^p > 1$ and $g_{\mathrm{c}}^p < 1$ for all $p = 1, 2, \ldots, 5$. This leads to a rejection of the null hypothesis that $g_{\mathrm{o}} = 1$ by the alternative hypothesis $g_{\mathrm{o}} > 1$ and it similarly supports the hypothesis $g_{\mathrm{c}} < 1$ against the null $g_{\mathrm{c}} = 1$. The result $g_{\mathrm{o}} > 1 > g_{\mathrm{c}} > 0$ suggests that the nature of price discovery in the opening is substantively different from that at the close: traders' behavior at the opening can be characterized as over-reaction, whereas their behavior at the close reflects gradual price adjustment.

The adjustment coefficient g may depend on the 'thinness' in trading of the stock. In our sample, there are differences in trading volume between the stocks at the top of the list and those at the bottom (see table 4). Thus, we can make an inference about the dependence of g on the 'thinness' of the stock by comparing the return autocorrelations of portfolios formed from stocks in different sections of the list. We grouped our stocks into five portfolios of ten stocks in each based on the order of table 4 (portfolio 1 consists of the first ten stocks in the list, which are the most heavily-traded, and portfolio 5 – of the last ten, which are the 'thinnest'), and calculated the equally-weighted returns for each portfolio. We then estimated the return variance and autocorrelation for each of the five 'thinness'-based portfolios. The results are shown in table 6.

The results show that for the close-to-close returns, the adjustment-coefficient g_{c} is (generally) a decreasing function of stock 'thinness'. That is, g_{c} is smaller (and, correspondingly, the first-order autocorrelation is higher) for thinly-traded stocks.[9] This may reflect the fact that for thinly-traded securi-

[9] The caveat of the previous footnote applies here as well.

ties, the lags in price-adjustment are larger because of the difficulties in disseminating information about them and the smaller number of orders and transactions which serve to update the market price to reflect the arrival of new information [see Amihud and Mendelson (1989b)]. At the opening, the autocorrelations generally decline as we move from portfolio 1 to portfolio 3, but then they move up again. In general, the first three and the last two portfolios seem to constitute two different groups, with the adjustment coefficients g_0 and g_c being lower for the second group. Finally, consistent with our previous results, we find that for all five portfolios, $g_o^p > 1 > g_c^p$.

The pattern of the variances of the portfolio returns is similar to that of the individual stocks. For all five portfolios, $\mathrm{Var}(R_t^o) > \mathrm{Var}(R_t^c)$. However, the average ratio of $\mathrm{Var}(R_t^o)/\mathrm{Var}(R_t^c)$ is much larger for the portfolios, amounting to 1.30 compared to 1.15 for the individual stocks. This is because the security-specific variances as well as the noise variances σ_i^2 are diversified away in the portfolios, thus heightening the effects of the adjustment-coefficient g. Indeed, by (3), if the noise variance is fully diversified in the portfolio, and given that ν^2 is the same for both R_t^o and R_t^c, the variance ratio should equal

$$\frac{g_o}{2-g_o} \cdot \frac{2-g_c}{g_c}.$$

For the orders of magnitude at hand, this expression is larger than the ratio $\mathrm{Var}(R_t^o)/\mathrm{Var}(R_t^c)$ when the noise variances are included, unless the noise variance at the opening is much larger than the noise variance at the close. In general, the higher variance ratio for the portfolios implies, by (3), that it is mainly the overshooting phenomenon which accounts for the larger variance at the opening.

Finally, we examined the behavior of the index returns $R_{o,t}^m$ and $R_{c,t}^m$ as a function of the day of the week, distinguishing between the open and the close. The results are summarized in table 7. They show that on every day of the week except for Monday, the variance of the open-to-open returns is greater than that for the close-to-close returns. It is interesting to note that on Monday, not only is the inequality between the return variances reversed, but also the opening volatility is smaller than on any other opening, whereas the closing volatility is about average.

Jaffe and Westerfield (1985a, b) estimated the mean returns for the Nikkei-Dow index for the period 1970–1983, which precedes our estimation period. Their estimations naturally reflect the closing prices, whereas ours pertain to both opening and closing prices. They note that the day with the lowest mean return for the week was not Monday, as in the U.S., but rather Tuesday, which follows the U.S. Monday. Our estimates show this to be the case for the Tuesday open-to-open return. This, in fact, corroborates the suggestion of Jaffe and Westerfield (1985a, b) about the effect of the U.S. market: while the

Table 7
Day-of-the-week statistics for the open-to-open and close-to-close market indices, $R^m_{0,t}$ and $R^m_{c,t}$.

	Trading days	Average return		Standard deviation		Variance ratio
		Open	Close	Open	Close	
Monday	155	0.00305	−0.00132	0.01179	0.01257	0.88
Tuesday	157	−0.00315	0.00076	0.01543	0.01269	1.48
Wednesday	159	0.00313	0.00193	0.01606	0.01502	1.14
Thursday	160	0.00202	0.00325	0.01508	0.01300	1.34
Friday	160	0.00295	0.00120	0.01598	0.01242	1.66
Saturday	100	−0.00150	0.00223	0.01575	0.01020	2.39
All days	891	0.00126	0.00130	0.01522	0.01292	1.39

Monday close-to-close return is negative in our study as in Jaffe and Westerfield, the open-to-open return on Monday is positive and significant, indicating that the low Monday return takes place primarily during the trading day.

To verify the robustness of the results derived in this section, we examined their persistence through time by dividing our time series into two equal subperiods and repeating our analysis for each subperiod. The results were virtually intact.

6. Residual returns, day and overnight returns

In this section we further elaborate on the results derived in section 5. We first examine the robustness of these results by repeating our estimations while controlling for the common market factor. We estimated the market model regressions for the opening and closing returns of each stock,

$$\begin{aligned} R^i_{o,t} &= \alpha^i_o + \beta^i_o R^m_{o,t} + \epsilon^i_{o,t} \\ R^i_{c,t} &= \alpha^i_c + \beta^i_c R^m_{c,t} + \epsilon^i_{c,t}, \end{aligned} \tag{11}$$

where $R^m_{o,t}$ and $R^m_{c,t}$ are the opening and closing equally-weighted portfolio returns of our sample stocks. We recomputed table 5 using the market-model residuals of (11) instead of the raw returns, to correct for the cross-security dependence introduced by the common market index. [10] The results are shown in table 8.

The behavior of the residuals corroborates the results obtained for the unadjusted returns. The open-to-open residual variance is higher than the close-to-close residual variance for 39 stocks out of 50. A binomial test of the

[10] We follow the common practice of neglecting the slight dependence due to the fact that all assets are included in the index.

Table 8
Open-to-open and close-to-close variances and autocorrelations of the residuals from the market model.

Stock symbol	Variance			Autocorrelation		
	Open $\mathrm{Var}(\epsilon_t^o)$	Close $\mathrm{Var}(\epsilon_t^c)$	$\frac{\mathrm{Var}(\epsilon_t^o)}{\mathrm{Var}(\epsilon_t^c)}$	Open $\rho(\epsilon_t^o)$	Close $\rho(\epsilon_t^c)$	$\rho(\epsilon_t^c)-\rho(\epsilon_t^o)$
5401	0.00028793	0.00029290	0.98304900	−0.01268671	0.01244273	0.02512944
5403	0.00042894	0.00038103	1.12571900	−0.07149483 [a]	0.03476148	0.10625630
5404	0.00040793	0.00037673	1.08280700	−0.02841161	0.02590999	0.05432161
7011	0.00027942	0.00028071	0.99541210	−0.08786581 [a]	−0.04356766	0.04429815
5405	0.00041180	0.00035807	1.15005300	−0.11746830 [a]	−0.02443561	0.09303272
7013	0.00048881	0.00048672	1.00430400	−0.00064589	−0.02575498	−0.02510908
5406	0.00049551	0.00043775	1.13196200	−0.10280040 [a]	−0.02429795	0.07850243
5407	0.00044639	0.00046210	0.96599440	−0.00898580	−0.04957639	−0.04059058
6502	0.00043144	0.00040507	1.06510500	−0.03618935	−0.01893730	0.01725206
6501	0.00045992	0.00045226	1.01694400	0.02598960	0.01725484	−0.00873476
6503	0.00042919	0.00036140	1.18758300	−0.04409714	0.01028589	0.05438302
4005	0.00035592	0.00036152	0.98450220	−0.01291307	−0.04458057	−0.03166750
9531	0.00050970	0.00048032	1.06115100	0.06664770 [a]	0.08292725 [a]	0.01627955
4001	0.00038103	0.00033934	1.12285300	−0.05897362	−0.08455002 [a]	−0.02557639
7003	0.00051877	0.00051089	1.01542600	−0.14119030 [a]	−0.11071380 [a]	0.03047644
6702	0.00057392	0.00053690	1.06895500	0.00379739	0.04600864	0.04221125
4004	0.00046636	0.00045089	1.03430000	−0.07188781 [a]	−0.08197028 [a]	−0.01008247
5711	0.00037916	0.00033514	1.13132600	−0.04195793	0.00328276	0.04524069
9101	0.00036046	0.00033902	1.06323400	−0.12871810 [a]	−0.10143590 [a]	0.02728216
9103	0.00102535	0.00114527	0.89529100	0.00737646	−0.07540105 [a]	−0.08277752
7012	0.00062382	0.00052106	1.19720200	−0.05416273	0.02297396	0.07713668
6752	0.00051554	0.00047677	1.08130900	0.05976987	0.11431590 [a]	0.05454607
3402	0.00030599	0.00028131	1.08775000	−0.07975309 [a]	−0.06321655	0.01653653
8031	0.00035409	0.00034862	1.01570500	0.01362082	−0.00171193	−0.01533276
6701	0.00058879	0.00051660	1.13973200	0.06574002	0.09119429 [a]	0.02545428
7004	0.00056831	0.00052378	1.08501600	−0.17100370 [a]	−0.13129330 [a]	0.03971042
1801	0.00043332	0.00040122	1.08000900	−0.03459571	−0.02532394	0.00927177
6504	0.00053981	0.00048775	1.10674800	−0.12529120 [a]	−0.07719175 [a]	0.04809948
5801	0.00034666	0.00032010	1.08299700	0.00387392	0.01555802	0.01168410
6302	0.00053875	0.00055221	0.97562240	−0.03663418	−0.11364730 [a]	−0.07701311
3407	0.00039454	0.00033769	1.16835700	−0.08380152 [a]	−0.04720059	0.03660093
3401	0.00033274	0.00027464	1.21154600	−0.09780440 [a]	−0.03054848	0.06725593
4061	0.00043194	0.00042970	1.00521000	0.03328462	0.02561450	−0.00767012
5712	0.00044764	0.00044102	1.01050100	−0.01944384	−0.10331180 [a]	−0.08386801
8751	0.00037033	0.00034026	1.08836200	0.00317745	0.07685872 [a]	0.07368127
6764	0.00030084	0.00030651	0.98148670	0.00062188	−0.03541381	−0.03603569
3101	0.00036652	0.00034395	1.06561700	−0.11034910 [a]	−0.05486306	0.05548606
5631	0.00070210	0.00067826	1.03514200	−0.02053396	−0.04389581	−0.02336186
4208	0.00043625	0.00044158	0.98793110	−0.07030322 [a]	−0.13308510 [a]	−0.06278187
4010	0.00031290	0.00029603	1.05698900	−0.04994824	−0.07295052 [a]	−0.02300228
8604	0.00033211	0.00032184	1.03190400	−0.00375731	0.07940835 [a]	0.08316565
1802	0.00045648	0.00039224	1.16379300	−0.08842058 [a]	−0.03400152	0.05441907
8802	0.00041559	0.00041564	0.99987140	0.06618787	0.07740133 [a]	0.01121345

Table 8 (continued)

Stock symbol	Variance			Autocorrelation		
	Open $Var(\epsilon_t^o)$	Close $Var(\epsilon_t^c)$	$\frac{Var(\epsilon_t^o)}{Var(\epsilon_t^c)}$	Open $\rho(\epsilon_t^o)$	Close $\rho(\epsilon_t^c)$	$\rho(\epsilon_t^c)-\rho(\epsilon_t^o)$
3702	0.00033132	0.00032247	1.02744100	−0.11336730 [a]	−0.09714237 [a]	0.01622490
9062	0.00034863	0.00034461	1.01164400	−0.06016063	0.00199787	0.06215850
9001	0.00036195	0.00034165	1.05941700	−0.02542527	0.01448052	0.03990579
8058	0.00038013	0.00041312	0.92015150	−0.03618842	−0.07876646 [a]	−0.04257804
9005	0.00045162	0.00042941	1.05172400	−0.04447723	0.00681505	0.05129229
8801	0.00045179	0.00043383	1.04138400	−0.01910613 [a]	−0.02988355	−0.01077742
3103	0.00036046	0.00038555	0.93490720	−0.07745141 [a]	−0.14961070 [a]	−0.07215926
Mean:	0.00043878	0.00041827	1.0559190	−0.04076356	−0.02497576	0.01578780
S.D:	0.00012444	0.00013474	0.0711523	0.05581535	0.06325608	0.04793087

[a] Significant at the 5% level.

null hypothesis that the opening variance is equally likely to be greater or smaller than the closing variance produces a probability $p < 10^{-3}$. This strongly rejects the hypothesis that the open-to-open residual return variance is equal to its close-to-close counterpart in favor of the alternative hypothesis that the variance of the open-to-open residual return is higher. A standard t-test of the hypothesis that the residual variance ratio is unity against the alternative that it is greater than unity results in a t-value of 5.61, highly significant.

Turning to the autocorrelations, they were negative for 38 stocks in the case of open-to-open returns (18 of these are significant) and for 31 stocks in the close-to-close residual return series (14 of these are significant; there are also 6 positively significant autocorrelations). The difference $\Delta\rho = \rho(\epsilon_t^o) - \rho(\epsilon_t^c)$ was on average 0.0158, with a standard error of 0.0068 and $t = 2.33$, indicating a high level of significance. The binomial probability that $\Delta\rho > 0$ due to chance was $p = 0.025$.

We also estimated regression (10) to test the cross-security relationship between the residual variance differential $\Delta V_i(\epsilon)$ and the corresponding autocovariance differential, $\Delta C_i(\epsilon)$. The resulting regression equation was

$$\Delta V_i(\epsilon) = 0.000014 + \underset{(10.01)}{1.114} \cdot \Delta C_i(\epsilon), \qquad R^2 = 0.68. \tag{12}$$

This corroborates our previous results and reaffirms the robustness of our model.

We have suggested that the behavior of the open-to-open returns reflects the existence of over-reaction and noise, while the behavior of the close-to-close returns reflect partial price adjustment with possibly a lower level of noise. This implies that the over-reaction should occur between the closing of one

Table 9
Variances and autocorrelations for the day and overnight returns.

Stock	$\mathrm{Var}(RN_t)$	$\mathrm{Var}(RD_t)$	$\frac{\mathrm{Var}(RD_t)}{\mathrm{Var}(RN_t)}$	$\rho(RN_t, RD_t)$
5401	0.0001549	0.0004189	2.70	0.0402720
5403	0.0001928	0.0006213	3.22	−0.0535260
5404	0.0001723	0.0006512	3.78	−0.0498020
7011	0.0001777	0.0004522	2.54	−0.0295280
5405	0.0001933	0.0005092	2.63	−0.1402560
7013	0.0001837	0.0007252	3.95	0.0097300
5406	0.0002266	0.0005611	2.48	−0.1238550
5407	0.0002135	0.0005468	2.56	−0.0222460
6502	0.0001635	0.0004096	2.51	−0.0572450
6501	0.0001887	0.0003554	1.89	−0.0061210
6503	0.0001756	0.0004174	2.38	−0.1456960
4005	0.0001474	0.0004076	2.77	−0.0450160
9531	0.0001806	0.0006700	3.71	−0.0401120
4001	0.0001858	0.0003879	2.09	−0.0893690
7003	0.0002272	0.0005401	2.38	−0.0980840
6702	0.0001854	0.0003968	2.14	0.0096870
4004	0.0001918	0.0004495	2.34	−0.0262090
5711	0.0001277	0.0002903	2.27	−0.1135090
9101	0.0001467	0.0004648	3.17	−0.0304820
9103	0.0004399	0.0007863	1.79	0.0137500
7012	0.0002462	0.0006975	2.83	−0.1150960
6752	0.0001944	0.0003416	1.76	−0.0150380
3402	0.0001614	0.0002850	1.77	−0.1433510
8031	0.0001572	0.0003824	2.43	−0.0518810
6701	0.0002201	0.0003799	1.73	−0.0264350
7004	0.0002103	0.0005914	2.81	−0.1462730
1801	0.0001584	0.0004697	2.97	−0.0631490
6504	0.0001918	0.0004265	2.22	−0.0674150
5801	0.0001546	0.0002831	1.83	−0.0291740
6302	0.0003137	0.0004773	1.52	−0.0774940
3407	0.0001588	0.0003017	1.90	−0.1470930
3401	0.0001174	0.0003096	2.64	−0.1075750
4061	0.0001771	0.0003323	1.88	−0.0287640
5712	0.0001620	0.0003327	2.05	−0.0506670
8751	0.0002148	0.0003976	1.85	−0.0618410
6764	0.0001241	0.0002324	1.87	−0.0023520
3101	0.0001588	0.0003373	2.12	−0.1021100
5631	0.0001907	0.0006831	3.58	−0.0206640
4208	0.0001695	0.0004387	2.59	−0.0668930
4010	0.0001417	0.0003029	2.14	−0.0926240
8604	0.0002537	0.0003823	1.51	−0.0836650
1802	0.0001870	0.0004867	2.60	−0.1200710
8802	0.0001817	0.0004830	2.66	0.0137510
3702	0.0001454	0.0002771	1.91	−0.1026030
9062	0.0001878	0.0004724	2.52	−0.0845270
9001	0.0001938	0.0004109	2.12	−0.0867700

Table 9 (continued).

Stock	$\text{Var}(RN_t)$	$\text{Var}(RD_t)$	$\frac{\text{Var}(RD_t)}{\text{Var}(RN_t)}$	$\rho(RN_t, RD_t)$
8058	0.0001928	0.0004257	2.21	−0.0335850
9005	0.0002202	0.0005111	2.32	−0.0460180
8801	0.0002290	0.0004889	2.14	−0.0567340
3103	0.0001353	0.0003363	2.49	−0.0610130
Mean	0.0001885	0.0004468	2.40	−0.0614948
S.D.	0.0000510	0.0001287	0.57	0.0474793

day and the opening on the following trading day, and that the overreaction and the noise of the opening are perhaps 'corrected' during daytime trading. That is, if investors have over-estimated the price change between the closing and the following opening, they *reverse* the direction of the price change later in the day in order to bring the stock price closer to its estimated value.

The empirical implications of this hypothesis is as follows. Define

$$RN_t = \log(P_{o,t}) - \log(P_{c,t-1})$$

as the overnight return between the closing and the following opening, and

$$RD_t = \log(P_{c,t}) - \log(P_{o,t})$$

as the daytime return between the opening and the closing. The hypothesis that there is an overreaction or noise (or both) at the opening which is 'corrected' later during the day predicts that

$$\rho ND = \rho(RN_t, RD_t) < 0.$$

Table 9 presents the variances of the daytime returns RD_t, the overnight returns RN_t, and the correlations between them, ρND. The results strongly support our hypothesis, since the correlations between the returns over the two periods are predominantly negative. For all but five of the 50 stocks, $\rho ND < 0$, with 20 of the estimated correlation coefficients significantly negative, and the mean of ρND is -0.0615. This shows that during the course of daytime trading, investors reverse price changes at the opening which they consider to have been excessive and erroneous.

The results regarding the variances of RN_t and RD_t are also of interest. Despite the fact that the night period is substantially longer than the daytime period, the overnight return variances are substantially lower: on average, the daytime variance is about 2.4 times larger than the overnight variance. This is consistent with French and Roll's (1988) finding that most of the observed stock return volatility takes place during the trading period, with Black's (1986) hypothesis that some of the volatility reflects interaction between traders and is thus related to the trading period itself, and with the notion that much of the arrival of new information takes place during the trading day.

7. Relative return dispersion (RRD)

In the previous sections, we used the time-series return variance as a measure of volatility. To the extent that volatility does not reflect underlying changes in the value returns, it is undesirable since it leads to a reduction in market liquidity and in the informativeness of the price signals provided by the market to the economy as a whole. [11] This applies both to the provision of information about the value of a single security, and to the inference made from the prices of a set of securities on the values of *different* securities.

We now introduce another measure of volatility: the relative return dispersion across stocks (*RRD*). The *RRD* measures, for each time period, the extent to which the market 'moves together', that is, the dispersion of the individual stock returns around the return on the market index. Naturally, we expect the returns on individual stocks to deviate from the market return because of differences in the elasticities of individual stock prices to the factors which affect the market as a whole. In addition, however, there are idiosyncratic shocks which cause deviations of the return on a single stock from the market-induced return. These shocks may result either from stock-specific information or from friction and noise in the trading process. As before, the information-induced shocks should affect the opening and closing prices equally. It is the additional cause of idiosyncratic change in price, associated with the price discovery process, which we focus on here. If the price discovery process in the opening is less efficient and more noisy than that at the close, we would expect the *RRD* to be higher at the opening even after accounting for the effects of market-wide shocks.

The *RRD*, which measures the volatility across stocks, is defined for the open-to-open return series as

$$RRD_{\mathrm{o},t} = \frac{1}{N} \sum_{i=1}^{N} \left(R^{i}_{\mathrm{o},t} - R^{m}_{\mathrm{o},t} \right)^2, \tag{13}$$

where $N = 50$ is the number of stocks. Similarly, for the close-to-close returns,

$$RRD_{\mathrm{c},t} = \frac{1}{N} \sum_{i=1}^{N} \left(R^{i}_{\mathrm{c},t} - R^{m}_{\mathrm{c},t} \right)^2. \tag{14}$$

Since the relative return dispersion measures given by (13)–(14) are cross-sectional, we computed them also for the week of the stock market crash. [12]

The *RRD* thus measures for every day t the dispersion of the returns on the individual stocks around the market return for that day. The general phenomenon of dispersion in relative price changes has been analyzed theoretically by Amihud and Mendelson (1982), who proved (for the prices of storable

[11] See Mendelson (1982, 1985, 1987), Amihud and Mendelson (1988), Bernstein (1987).
[12] This period has been excluded from subsequent time-series estimations.

commodities) that aggregate economic shocks are transmitted into individual commodity prices in a way which generates relative price dispersion. As a result, the relative price dispersion is an increasing function of the variance of the aggregate shocks.

A similar result holds for stock prices as well. Our focus here, however, is on the *differences* in RRD between the opening and the closing. That is, we wish to examine whether the differences in the price discovery processes in the opening and at the close generate differences in RRD after controlling for its response to aggregate shocks.

For the whole sample period, the average of RRD_o is 0.00048 ($S.D.$ = 0.00040), whereas the average of RRD_c is 0.00045 ($S.D.$ = 0.00035). To obtain an estimate of the order of magnitude of RRD relative to its mean, we calculated the ratio $\sqrt{RRD}/|R^m|$ (which is the absolute coefficient of variation of the individual stock returns) for both the opening and the closing. The mean ratio was 17.01 for the opening and 14.44 for the closing. Since the stock-specific volatilities are diversified away in the market portfolio, the market return is substantially less volatile than the individual stock returns; this is reflected in the high values of the coefficient of variation. The above statistics indicate that the RRD at the opening is also of a greater magnitude relative to the size of market-wide shocks than at the close.

The time-series pattern of the relative return dispersions, RRD_t, over the the whole sample period is demonstrated in fig. 2, for the open-to-open and in fig. 3 for the close-to-close return series. The figures show that the time series of RRD_t has a great deal of volatility over time. The time-series behavior of the RRD_t series is made clearer in fig. 4, which shows for each day t ($t \geqslant 50$) the 50-day moving average of $RRD_{o,t}$ and $RRD_{c,t}$ up to and including day t:

$$MA_o(t) = \tfrac{1}{50} \sum_{s=t-49}^{t} RRD_{o,s} \tag{15}$$

and

$$MA_c(t) = \tfrac{1}{50} \sum_{s=t-49}^{t} RRD_{c,s}. \tag{16}$$

Interestingly, the RRD's were generally higher in the last quarter of 1986 and in the first half of 1987 rather than in October of 1987 and the period which followed. While there is an increase in the relative return dispersion in the period following October 19, 1987, it is still low compared to the last quarter of 1986 and the first half of 1987.

The moving averages show that the open-to-open relative return dispersion tends to be higher than its close-to-close counterpart, especially in the second half of the sample period. In fact, if we view ΔRRD ($= RRD_o - RRD_c$) as a random sample of 896 observations, its sample mean is 0.0000278 with a

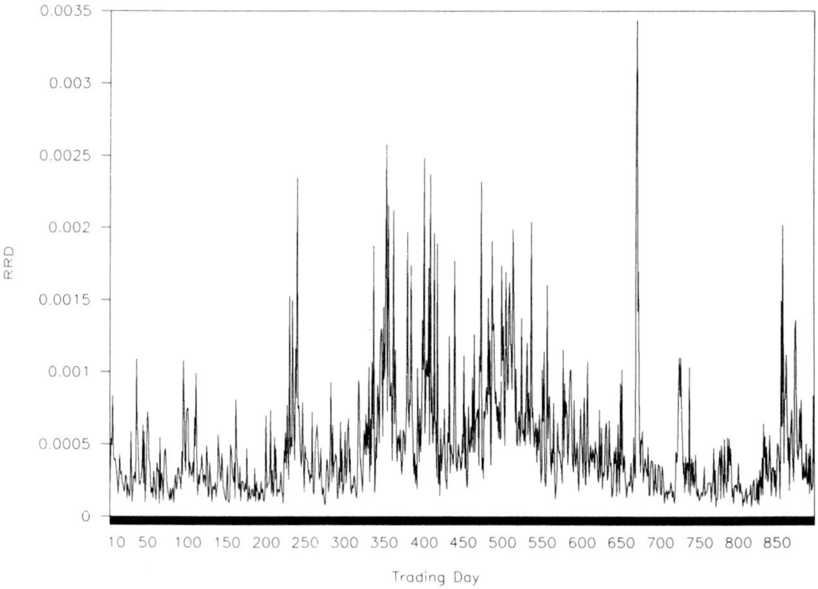

Fig. 2. Open-to-open relative return dispersion, $RRD_o(t)$.

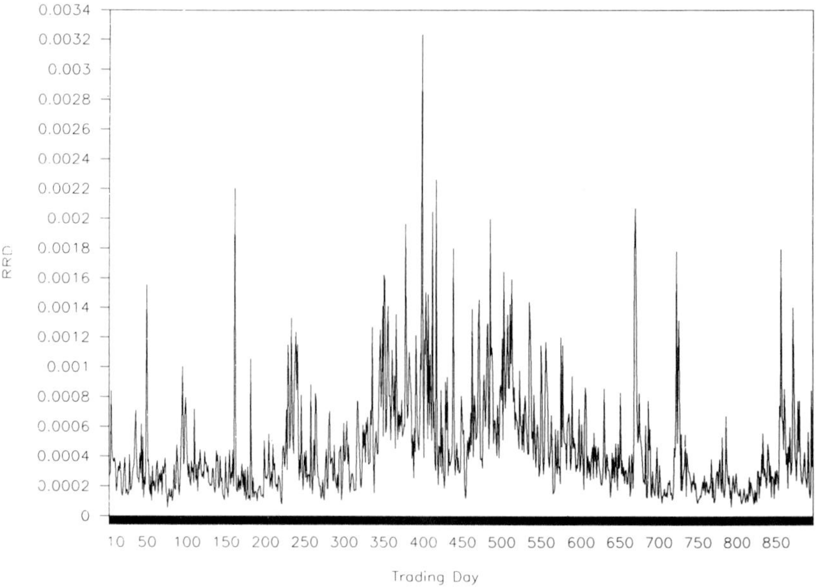

Fig. 3. Close-to-close relative return dispersion, $RRD_c(t)$.

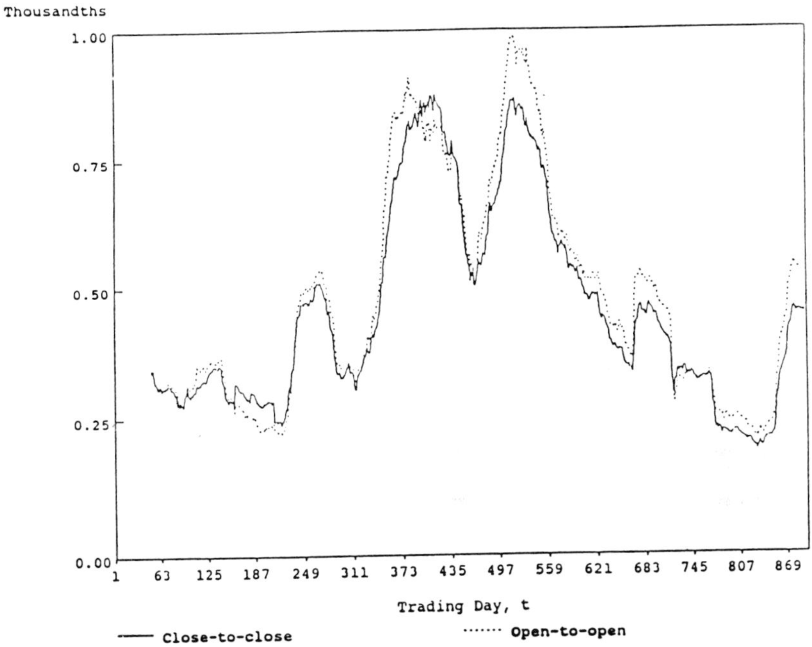

Fig. 4. 50-day moving averages of the opening and closing *RRD*, $MA_o(t)$ (dotted line) and $MA_c(t)$ (solid line). Trading-day 668 is October 19, 1987.

standard deviation of 0.0003389, leading to a significant t-statistic. Also, $RRD_{o,t} > RRD_{c,t}$ for 480 out of our 896 data points, leading to a statistically significant binomial difference between the opening and the close.[13]

Next, we conducted a test on the difference between the *RRD* in the opening and at the close, conditional on the contemporaneous differences in the aggregate market shocks. Again, we emphasize that we are not concerned here with the general level of volatility, but rather with the differences in *RRD* between the opening and the closing. Our dependent variable is thus $\Delta RRD = RRD_0 - RRD_c$. We estimated the following model:

$$\Delta RRD_t = \alpha + \beta \cdot \left[\left(R^m_{o,t} \right)^2 - \left(R^m_{c,t} \right)^2 \right] + u_t. \tag{17}$$

In (17), we expect β to be positive, since *RRD* is positively associated with market-wide shocks [see Amihud and Mendelson (1982b)]. The constant coefficient α in (17) estimates the difference in the level of *RRD* which is not attributable to market-wide shocks, and reflects the noise in price discovery across stocks.

[13] This test ignores, however, the ramifications of dependence patterns (see below).

We estimated model (17) over our sample period, excluding the week of the crash, October 19, 1987 – October 23, 1987. We corrected for autocorrelations in the residuals, obtaining the regression

$$\Delta RRD_t = \underset{(2.05)}{0.000016} + \underset{(6.70)}{0.132} \cdot \left[(R^m_{o,t})^2 - (R^m_{c,t})^2 \right],$$

$$R^2 = 0.05, \quad DW = 2.03, \quad \rho = \underset{(9.82)}{-0.31}. \tag{18}$$

As can be seen, the unconditional difference in RRD is positive and significant.

The week of the stock market crash, which was excluded from our sample in estimating model (18), is naturally of interest. It is well known that overall, the return volatility has increased on that week; our focus here, however, is on the difference between the open and the close. For each trading day of the week (October 19, 1987 – October 23, 1987), we calculated the abnormal difference in RRD between the open and the close as follows: We used the estimated parameters of (18) to calculate $\widehat{\Delta RRD_t} = (RRD_{o,t} - RRD_{c,t})$ for every trading day in the excluded week, and then calculated the 'abnormal' differences using the estimated residuals $\hat{u}_t = \Delta RRD_t - \widehat{\Delta RRD_t}$. We then divided the estimated residuals $\hat{u}_t$ by the estimated standard error of the residuals in (18), obtaining the number of standard deviations of $\hat{u}_t$ from zero on the days of the crash. The results, presented in table 10, indeed show abnormal and significant values of $\hat{u}_t$ on October 20 and 21, even after accounting for the unusual market shocks in those days (recall that the October 19 stock market crash in the U.S. was first reflected in Japan trading on October 20). Thus, we obtain that the price discovery process during the week of the October crash was significantly more turbulent at the opening than at the close.

Table 10
Abnormal differences in RRD_t, $\hat{u}_t = \Delta RRD_t - \widehat{\Delta RRD_t}$, in the week of the 1987 stock market crash.

Date	Abnormal ΔRRD_t, $\hat{u}_t$	Standard deviations from zero
10/19/87	−0.0025	−0.81
10/20/87	0.00176	5.68
10/21/87	0.00299	9.65
10/22/87	−0.00011	−0.35
10/23/87	0.00049	1.58

8. Concluding remarks

This paper has examined the impact of differences in trading mechanisms on the price discovery processes in the Tokyo Stock Exchange. Specifically, we examined the differences between the *Itayose* method applied at the opening and the *Zaraba* method used at the close. The comparison involves both the impact of the different operational procedures and the different timing of transactions, both of which are important design parameters of the trading mechanism.

We find that open-to-open return variances are higher than their close-to-close counterparts and that the open-to-open autocorrelations are lower at the opening, when they tend to be negative. Interpreting these results in light of our price-adjustment model, we conclude that the return behavior at the opening is consistent with an over-reaction of traders to new information, whereas the behavior at the close is consistent with partial price adjustment. We also show that during the trading day, investors correct pricing errors they have made at the opening by reversing the opening price changes which they perceive to have been excessive.

Finally, we introduce a new measure of market volatility, the relative return dispersion (*RRD*) around the market return. Such a dispersion is naturally expected, but our interest is in the differences in *RRD* between the opening and the closing transaction. We obtained that the *RRD* is positively associated with general market shocks, and is usually greater in the opening even after controlling for differences in market shocks, again indicating that the price discovery process at the opening is less efficient. Altogether we find that the *Zaraba* tends to be associated with a more orderly price discovery process than the *Itayose*.

Our results demonstrate the usefulness of Amihud and Mendelson's (1987) model of price-adjustment when studying stock price behavior, particularly when the focus is on market-microstructure effects. The model enables us to study and interpret phenomena that would be considered enigmatic and elusive from the perspective of classical models: the serial correlation patterns of returns on portfolios and individual stocks, factors affecting volatility and the relation between alternative measures of efficiency.

Having focused on volatility as a measure of market performance, it is useful to consider the tradeoff between volatility and efficiency in the context of our price-adjustment model. A sluggish adjustment of stock prices to changes in their underlying values – having an adjustment coefficient $g < 1$ – dampens return volatility but causes a deviation of observed prices from values. A prompt adjustment of prices to value changes ($g = 1$) is considered a desirable property of an efficient market, but it also increases observed price volatility. This suggests that in some circumstances, an increase in the volatility of observed returns is associated with the market moving towards greater informational efficiency. If, however, the adjustment of prices to value changes follows an over-reaction process ($g > 1$), as indicated by our results for the *Itayose*, the elimination of over-reaction will simultaneously reduce volatility and increase efficiency.

The results here are consistent with those we have obtained for the New York Stock Exchange, adding credence to the proposition that the existence of continuous markets improves price discovery. This seems to hold regardless of the specific continuous trading procedure employed by the Exchange. If the results on the greater return volatility in the opening transaction are due to the non-trading period which precedes it, they bear on the recent proposals to institute 'trading halts' in the stock market following a sizable price movement. Our results show that the overnight trading halt results in a relatively inefficient price discovery process when trading resumes. [14]

The greater extent of pricing errors made at the opening can also reflect a shortcoming in the prevailing *Itayose* method. At the opening, investors cannot observe the stock price just before making the transaction, as they can during the day (and at the closing), when they observe a price prior to triggering an execution. This problem is partially resolved by traders' ability to make their orders at the opening contingent on price, using limit orders. With such conditioning, they can trade as if they first observed the price and then transacted on it. However, by the current trading method, a limit order at the opening (and in general) can be contingent only on the price of the same stock for which the order is made, but it cannot be contingent on the prices of other stocks. That is, *simultaneous conditioning* of limit orders is impossible. Thus, while an investor can enter an order during the day after having observed the prices (as well as volume and other pertinent information) of *all* stocks, an order at the opening can be made contingent only on *one* stock's price, resulting in greater pricing errors. Indeed, our results show that as the information about the market as a whole is unraveled over the trading day, investors 'correct' the errors they have made at the opening. It follows that if simultaneous conditioning were available at the opening, that is, if limit orders could be made contingent on more information, pricing errors could be reduced.

The simultaneous conditioning of limit orders was proposed by Amihud and Mendelson (1985, 1988a) in the context of an integrated computerized trading system. In that system there will be, side by side, both periodic clearing and continuous trading. However, unlike the *Itayose*, limit orders in the periodic clearing will be allowed to depend on the price of the stock for which the order is placed as well as on the clearing prices of other stocks and possibly other information. This could help reduce the pricing errors which occur under current systems.

[14] This insight is due to Fischer Black.

A question which still remains open is whether our results are due primarily to the timing of transactions or to the trading procedure itself. If periodic market-clearing procedures were to operate *while* the continuous market is functioning, as suggested by Amihud and Mendelson (1985, 1988a), rather than *prior* to it, we cannot predict whether or not they will induce greater volatility. This interesting issue will be the subject of future research.

References

Amihud, Y. and H. Mendelson, 1982a, Asset price behavior in a dealership market, Financial Analysts Journal, May/June, 50–59.

Amihud, Y. and H. Mendelson, 1982b. Relative price dispersion and economic shocks: An inventory-adjustment approach, Journal of Money, Credit and Banking 14, 390–398.

Amihud, Y. and H. Mendelson, 1985, An integrated computerized trading system, in: Y. Amihud, T. Ho and R. Schwartz, eds., Market making and the charging structure of the securities industry (Lexington Books, Lexington, MA).

Amihud, Y. and H. Mendelson, 1986a, Asset pricing and the bid–ask spread, Journal of Financial Economics 17, 223–249.

Amihud, Y. and H. Mendelson, 1986b, Liquidity and stock returns, Financial Analysts Journal 42, May/June, 43–48.

Amihud, Y. and H. Mendelson, 1987, Trading mechanisms and stock returns: An empirical investigation, The Journal of Finance 62, July, 533–553.

Amihud, Y. and H. Mendelson, 1988a, Liquidity, volatility and exchange automation, Journal of Accounting, Auditing and Finance 3, Fall, 369–395.

Amihud, Y. and H. Mendelson, 1988b, Liquidity, maturity, and the yields on treasury securities, Working paper (The William E. Simon Graduate School of Business Administration, University of Rochester, Rochester, NY).

Amihud, Y. and H. Mendelson, 1989a, The effects of beta, bid–ask spread, residual risk and size on stock returns, The Journal of Finance 44, June, 479–486.

Amihud, Y. and H. Mendelson, 1989b, Index and index-futures returns, Journal of Accounting, Auditing and Finance 4, Fall.

Bernstein, Peter, 1987, Liquidity, stock markets and market makers, Financial Management, Summer, 54–62.

Black, Fischer, 1986, Noise, Journal of Finance 41, July, 529–543.

Cohen, Kalman, Steven Maier, Robert Schwartz and David Whitcomb, 1979, On the existence of serial correlation in an efficient securities market, TIMS Studies in the Management Science 11, 151–168.

Cohen, Kalman, Gabriel Hawawini, Steven Maier, Robert Schwartz and David Whitcomb, 1980, Implications of microstructure theory for empirical research on stock price behavior, Journal of Finance 35, May, 249–257.

Fama, Eugene F., 1970, Efficient capital markets: A review of theory and empirical work, Journal of Finance 25, 383–417.

French, Kenneth and Richard Roll, 1988, Stock return variances: The arrival of information and the reaction of traders, Journal of Financial Economics Sep., 5–26.

Jaffe, Jeffery and Randolph Westerfield, 1985a, The week-end effect in common stock returns: The international evidence, Journal of Finance, June 433–454.

Jaffe, Jeffery and Randolph Westerfield, 1985b, Patterns in Japanese common stock returns: Day of the week and turn of the year effects, Journal of Financial and Quantitative Analysis June, 261–272.

Japan Securities Research Institute, 1988, Securities market in Japan (JSRT, Tokyo).

Lo, Andrew and A. Craig MacKinlay, 1988, Stock market prices do not follow random walks: Evidence from a simple specification test, Review of Financial Studies 1, 41–66.

Mendelson, Haim, 1982, Market behavior in a clearing house, Econometrica 50, Nov., 1505–1524.

Mendelson, Haim, 1985, Random competitive exchange: Price distributions and gains from trade, Journal of Economic Theory 37, 254–280.
Mendelson, Haim, 1987, Consolidation, fragmentation and market performance, Journal of Financial and Quantitative Analysis 22, June, 189–207.
Schwartz, Robert A, 1988, Equity markets (Harper & Row, New York).
Schwartz, Robert A. and David K. Whitcomb, 1977a, Evidence on the presence and causes of serial correlation in market model residuals, Journal of Financial and Quantitative Analysis, June, 291–313.
Schwartz, Robert A. and David K. Whitcomb, 1977b, The time-variance relationship: Evidence on autocorrelation in common stock returns, Journal of Finance, March, 41–55.
West, Richard R. and Seha M. Tinic, 1971, The economics of the stock market (Praeger, New York).
Whitcomb, David K., 1985, An international comparison of stock exchange trading structures, in: Y. Amihud, T. Ho and R. Schwartz, eds., Market making and the changing structure of the securities industry (Lexington Books, Lexington, MA) 237–255.

Japanese Financial Market Research
W.T. Ziemba, W. Bailey and Y. Hamao (Editors)

Do Management Forecasts of Earnings Affect Stock Prices in Japan?

Masako N. Darrough and Trevor S. Harris [1]

Graduate School of Business, Uris Hall, Columbia University, New York NY 10027

Abstract

Japanese companies are requested to provide management forecasts of earnings simultaneously with their announcement of annual earnings. The announcements are made separately for parent and consolidated earnings. This research tests whether the management forecasts have incremental information content in the announcement period. The findings show that: (i) "analysts" forecasts provide the most accurate measure of expected parent-only earnings, (ii) investors do react to unexpected parent-only earnings, (iii) investors also react to the management forecasts of next period's parent-only earnings, (iv) investors' reaction to unexpected consolidated earnings occurs but is not monotonic, and (v) investors react to the management forecasts of consolidated earnings.

These results suggest that (i) investors in Japanese stocks should pay attention to management's forecasts of both parent and consolidated earnings, and (ii) those interested in understanding the relatively high Japanese price/earnings ratios should consider the management forecasts. Furthermore, as Japanese influence on international capital markets grows, we might see additional pressure on non-Japanese managers to provide management forecasts.

1. Introduction

Capital markets in Japan have played a crucial role in the recent globalization

[1] We are grateful to Jim Haggard for significant programming assistance, Vic Bernard and Joshua Livnat for helpful comments, the Center on Japanese Economy and Business at Columbia University for their financial assistance in obtaining the data, and the participants at the seminar at Purdue University. We also acknowledge the cooperation provided by Nihon Keizai Shimbun, in particular H. Tanaka and J. Uno for hours of conversation with invaluable wisdom.

process of international capital markets. For anybody interested in the international capital markets, it is important to understand the similarities and differences in the way Japanese markets operate in comparison to the more familiar Anglo-American environment.

One of the major differences that has attracted a great deal of attention is the relatively high average price/earnings [PE] ratio for the stocks listed on the Tokyo Stock Exchange (Viner [1988]). A question often raised in the popular press is whether the difference in PEs suggests that US stocks are undervalued or Japanese stocks are overvalued.[2] Of course, such a question cannot be answered without understanding how stocks are valued as well as how earnings are determined. Stock prices are formed and earnings are calculated in possibly quite different institutional environments that exist in Japan and the United States. This paper considers one such institutional characteristic; a routine practice of disclosing management forecasts in Japan.

The securities exchanges in Japan request that management provide (annual and semiannual) forecasts of sales, earnings and dividends. Although the forecasts are technically voluntary, almost all Japanese companies provide them. In contrast, relatively few US firms seem to publish forecasts.[3] While the evaluation of the relevance of management forecasts is only one piece of a complex puzzle, we believe it is important in understanding the factors influencing the Japanese stock market. For example, if we find that management forecasts influence investors' expectations, we expect that Japanese PEs can be explained better by incorporating forecasted earnings in addition to current earnings. There is no consensus so far as to whether the PEs are really different once "proper" adjustments are made. For example, Aron [1987, 1989] has consistently argued that "adjusted" PE ratios are virtually identical in the two countries.[4] Others such as Scheinemann [1988, 1989], and Poterba and French [1989] arrive at the opposite conclusion, despite making similar adjustments. All these calculations are based on historic earnings. Yet, if prices reflect expected earnings, and management forecasts of earnings are relevant in Japan, then it is necessary to examine how these forecasts affect stock prices.[5]

Two questions must be answered in order to assess the relevance of Japanese management forecasts. First, how accurate are the management forecasts? If the forecasts are inaccurate we should not expect them to be useful to investors. We

[2] For a recent example, see "Abreast of the Market" in *The Wall Street Journal*, September 6, 1989 pp. C1-C2.

[3] For example, the survey by Lees [1981] found that only 10.4% of the surveyed firms (total of 397 firms) disclosed forecasts. See also the samples in Waymire [1984] or Baginski [1987].

[4] Aron's claim is based mainly on two types of adjustments. First, he uses aggregate data to adjust Japanese earnings to conform more closely to US generally accepted accounting principles. Second, he incorporates different growth and discount rates into a capitalization rate. He has made these calculations periodically since 1979.

[5] Both Value-Line Investment Service and IBES provide PEs for US companies with expected earnings (from analysts) in the denominator.

compare the predictive accuracy of management forecasts with a simple random walk model. All the research we have found on the association between unexpected earnings and security returns in Japan has used such a model as the benchmark (e.g. Kunimura [1986], Ito [1988] and Sakakibara, et al. [1988]).

Clearly, while predictive accuracy is presumably necessary (Penman [1980]), it is not sufficient in order to claim that management forecasts are important for investors. Thus the second question considered is whether investors actually use these forecasts in pricing securities. To answer this question we investigate whether management forecasts provide additional "news" at the time of their release, by estimating the price reaction around the date of forecast announcement.

The procedure we follow requires a careful sorting of various information releases by Japanese companies. Two disclosure practices must be noted: (1) many companies disclose parent and consolidated financial statements at different times; and (2) those that provide forecasts announce both realized historical earnings and forecasts of next period's earnings simultaneously. Disclosure of both parent and consolidated values suggests that there are two potential earnings "news" dates. Simultaneous announcement of both historical and forecast data necessitates that we first discriminate and control for the reaction to the realized earnings. To provide the maximum control for tests of the reaction to forecast earnings, we consider unexpected earnings measures based on historic and forecast earnings as well as the latest "analyst" forecasts.[6] Consequently, the study also provides some evidence on the relevance of these analyst forecasts.

The evidence we provide in this paper suggests (1) that management forecasts of both parent and consolidated earnings are generally more accurate than the widely used random walk model, and (2) that investors appear to use both management forecasts in pricing securities.

Section 2 of the paper discusses some institutional background and presents the basic hypotheses. We describe the sample and test procedures in Section 3. The predictive accuracy tests and results are reported in Section 4, and the price reaction studies are presented in Section 5. We summarize the findings and conclude the paper in Section 6.

2. Background Information and Hypotheses

Japan's Commercial Code requires companies to prepare unconsolidated annual reports within three months of the fiscal year end (FYE). The Securities and Exchange Law, which covers companies listed on the securities exchanges, has also required listed companies to submit consolidated reports since FYE March 31, 1978.[7] These consolidated reports are generally submitted after the parent-only

[6] The term "analyst" forecast should not be interpreted as being equivalent to that in the U. S. As explained in Section 3 of the paper we use the forecasts provided by Nihon Keizai Shimbun (Nikkei) analysts. Their officials explained that the forecasts are not made in a manner similar to a detailed US forecast, and are frequently based on management's own estimates.

[7] Although consolidated reports were required from 1978, the use of equity accounting for un-

reports, and are required to be published within four months of the FYE.[8]

These two are the only reports legally required, but the securities exchanges require companies to announce a brief summary of current financial information including sales, earnings and dividends in a press release (*Kessan Tanshin*). In addition, they *request* management to provide forecasts and most companies comply.[9] These announcements are made for both parent and consolidated results so that we frequently have two separate announcements and forecasts. Figure 1 provides a summary of the disclosures and their timing for a typical company.

The parent-only report submitted to the Ministry of Finance (Yuka Shoken Hokokusho) is a document with detailed disclosures, while the equivalent consolidated report (Renketsu Yuka Shoken Hokokusho) contains considerably less detail. The parent-only report has generally been considered to be the one on which many users rely (Viner [1988]).[10] Thus, a question arises as to whether consolidated earnings have any marginal information over the parent-only earnings. Using small samples with historical data, Ishizuka [1987] (event period of one week) and Ito [1988] (event period of three months) show that both the changes in consolidated and in parent-only earnings explain some of the variation in market-adjusted (abnormal) returns. Thus consolidated earnings would appear to have marginal information content. A problem with these, and most other information content studies using Japanese data, is that they ignore the forecasts when measuring unexpected earnings (UE). Although Kunimura [1986] and Ishizuka [1987] have performed some preliminary analysis on the relevance of parent-only management forecasts, the question of earnings expectation models and the relevance of forecasts in Japan has largely been ignored and remains unresolved (Ito [1988] p.8).

As mentioned in the introduction, interest in the relevance of management forecasts (MFs) of earnings goes beyond the methodological choice of an earnings expectations model. We believe it is an important question because the answer will not only provide insights for the analysis of the high Japanese PEs, but may also influence the institutional setup of capital markets in other countries, as regulators understand better the information needs of the potential suppliers of capital.

The basic question of interest is whether Japanese management forecasts are relevant to investors. This question is broken down into separate pieces that are formulated into three hypotheses. The first relates to the degree of MF accuracy. If MFs have a higher predictive accuracy than a simple random walk model, then we should expect the forecasts to provide a better measure of UE than the naive

---

consolidated affiliates has only been required since 1983. Equity accounting is not used in the parent-only report.

[8]As of FYE March 31, 1988, listed companies will be required to submit the parent and consolidated reports simultaneously.

[9]Kunimura [1986] reports a survey that found more than 90 percent of firms (March 31, 1981 FYEs and listed on the Tokyo Stock Exchange) provided management forecasts of sales and earnings.

[10]Interestingly, the widely publicized PE ratios (e.g., as in *Morgan Stanley Capital International Perspectives*) are usually based on the parent-only earnings.

model generally used. Thus the first hypothesis to be tested is:

H_1^N: Management forecasts of earnings are no more accurate than forecasts based on a simple random walk model.

The alternative hypothesis is that the MFs are more accurate. This null hypothesis is evaluated separately for parent and consolidated earnings.

Of course, predictive accuracy alone is not sufficient to conclude that investors use the information. Hence we consider next whether MFs provide incremental information in explaining the association between unexpected earnings and (unexpected) security returns at the announcement dates. Unfortunately, Japanese MFs are disclosed simultaneously with the other earnings data. Consequently, it is not possible to control for other events in the manner employed by Waymire [1984] or Jennings [1987]. To assess the incremental relevance of MFs, however, we need to control for the "news" in UE.

The available research on Japanese securities markets does not provide us with clear guidance as to which UE model to use. In addition to the random walk (RW) and MF models, we have periodic analyst forecasts (AFs) reported in the Nihon Keizai Shimbun (Nikkei).[11] Security analysis in Japan has not developed in the same way as in the US or Britain. As a result, these forecasts frequently reflect the most recent MFs as extracted from interviews or other management disclosures. At the very least these AFs should reflect the MFs provided with the announcement of mid-year interim results. Possibly as a reflection of the relative importance of the parent-only statements, AFs are only available in machine-readable form from Nikkei for the parent earnings. We were also informed that analysts rarely provide forecasts of consolidated earnings.

Based on the studies we have seen, it appears that there is little understanding of the relationship between (unexpected) returns and the different measures of UE.[12] Consequently, we choose to analyze the question of MFs relevance for investors in two steps.

First, we consider the impact of annual earnings announcements on returns using different measures of UE. Specifically we determine which of the three measures provides the strongest association between (abnormal) returns and UE. Brown, Foster and Noreen [1985] have shown that "the more timely the expectations model, the stronger the association between average cumulative abnormal returns and earnings forecast errors" (p.8). Hence, the second null hypothesis to be tested is that there is no difference in the association between the different measures of unexpected earnings and unexpected returns. The hypothesis will be formally specified in Section 5.

[11]Nikkei is one of two major sources of analyst forecasts. The other is the rival publisher, the Toyo Keizai Shimbun. We do not have access to these forecasts in machine readable form, but do not expect that they would be very different given the nature of security analysis in Japan.

[12]For a small sample of firms in the period 1976-1978, Kunimura [1986] shows that AFs are more accurate than the estimates based on interim earnings forecasts.

Second, once the results of tests of the first step are obtained, we examine whether the MFs for the next period's earnings have any impact on the unexpected returns after controlling for the effect of UE. Again this question will be considered for both parent and consolidated forecasts, with the latter tests controlling for the results from tests of parent-only forecasts. Thus, formal specification of the hypothesis is also deferred to Section 5.

3. Data and Sample Selection

The primary research question is whether MFs of both parent and consolidated earnings contain marginal information for investors. Since consolidated data are relatively recent in Japan, the availability of MFs of consolidated earnings is the major constraint in selecting a sample.

The Center on Japanese Economy and Business at Columbia University has a data base of parent and consolidated financial statement data, security prices and "attribute" data (including dividends and parent forecasts) compiled by Nikkei. The data base covers a maximum of 10 years (for prices) ending with August 1987.

We first extracted all companies available on the consolidated data file, which runs from FYEs March 31, 1978 through May 31, 1987. As 59% of all the companies on the consolidated data file have March 31 FYEs we focussed our collection procedures on this subset of firms. We hand- collected the announcement dates and management (consolidated) forecasts released at the time, for all companies with March 31 FYEs, as well as for companies with any other FYE whose announcements are published in the daily Nihon Keizai Shimbun in May, June or July of the relevant years. The Nikkei newspaper publication date is one day after the actual release of the Kessan Tanshin.

The "attribute" files from Nikkei contain monthly parent-only forecasts and "update dates," representing the dates on which Nikkei has discussed the company's potential results. In principle the forecasts represent AFs and the update dates reflect the dates on which the forecasts are first announced. However, we were told that the first update after the FYE represents the date of the announcement of earnings (i.e., the date of the Kessan Tanshin) and that this date's forecast is in fact the MF. Therefore, we selected the first update date at least 30 days after the FYE as the parent-only announcement date, and the forecast on that date as the MF for the parent-only earnings. Given that these are monthly data files and that the update date represents the last update in the month, we checked the dates and forecasts against those reported in the daily Nihon Keizai Shimbun to ensure that our information is accurate. We found and corrected numerous differences in announcement dates, as a result of an announcement being earlier than the last update in a month, but found no differences in the forecasts. Thus even when there is an apparent update in AFs after the announcement of MFs in the same month the actual values of the forecasts do not change.

Given that we are interested in both the parent and consolidated data, we exclude observations for which the parent and consolidated announcement dates are less than 12 trading days apart.[13]

The attribute data files are also used to extract the AFs. We select the last update date and forecast prior to the FYE as the most recent AF prior to the announcement of earnings. Although many of these dates are within the month prior to the FYE, the forecasts may not have been revised since the interim forecast by managers.[14] As previously indicated, even when the AF is more recent it is possible that the AF is based on some updated information from management, so that the reference to AFs should be interpreted cautiously.

The final criterion used is that the price and attribute files contain data to calculate a sufficient number of returns to estimate the coefficients in the standard market model used in the abnormal returns analysis.[15] The market model used is

$$R_{it} = \alpha_i + \beta_i R_{mt} + \epsilon_{it}, \tag{1}$$

where :

R_{it} is the return (including dividends and adjustment factors) for firm i for day t,

R_{mt} is the return on the equally-weighted index of all firms in the first section of the Tokyo Stock Exchange for day t,

α_i and β_i are firm specific parameters, and

ϵ_{it} is the residual and is assumed to behave according to the standard assumptions.

The model is estimated over the 180 days immediately preceding the maximum event window (-4 to +4 days) considered for the announcement of parent-only earnings. Observations are dropped if there are less than 90 days of returns available to estimate the market model parameters. The event window is chosen to ensure that we minimize the impact of confounding signals between parent and consolidated announcements.

The imposition of all the filters leads to a final sample of 1,300 observations. Table 1 shows the impact of the different selection criteria, while Table 2 provides some description of the characteristics of the sample. Panel A of Table 2 indicates that most of the observations are in fiscal years 1985 through 1987, which reflects the

[13]A twelve day period is chosen because the event study part of this research considers a maximum window of -4 to +4 days.

[14]The AFs and interim MFs relate only to parent earnings. In our sample period a majority of companies did *not* provide interim MFs of consolidated earnings.

[15]Although several studies using daily returns have used returns based on simple price changes (e.g., Chap. 4 in Sakakibara, et al. [1988]), the returns in this study include all dividends and appropriate adjustment factors.

increased presentation of consolidated data once the equity method was required. This period is characterized by unusually high increases in Japanese stock prices.[16] Panel A also shows that there is a widespread distribution of observations across industries. The electronics industry, which has the largest number of firms, covers a range of specializations including general and heavy electric equipment, appliances, electronic controls and electric auto parts.

The descriptive statistics presented in Panel B of Table 2 indicates, as we would expect, that the consolidated earnings are higher (by about 15%) than parent-only earnings. It is also apparent that managers are generally optimistic in their forecasts.

4. The Predictive Accuracy of Japanese Management Forecasts

The first stage of our analysis of Japanese MFs considers their forecast accuracy. Separately for parent-only and consolidated earnings, we estimate random walk ($RWFE$) and management (MFE) forecast errors:

$$RWFE^r_{it} = \frac{A^r_{it} - A^r_{it-1}}{|A^r_{it}|}, \tag{2}$$

and

$$MFE^r_{it} = \frac{A^r_{it} - MFA^r_{it}}{|A^r_{it}|}, \tag{3}$$

where:

A^r_{it} is the accounting earnings for the r type report [r = parent (p) or consolidated (c)] for firm i at year t, and

MFA^r_{it} is the management forecast of year t earnings for the r type report for firm i made at $t-1$.

For each firm-year observation we also calculate the difference between the absolute value of the two forecast errors:

$$d^r_{it} = |RWFE^r_{it}| - |MFE^r_{it}|. \tag{4}$$

We compute both parametric and nonparametric tests from d^r_{it}. To reduce the influence of outliers we truncate d^r_{it} at 1 (i.e., 100 percent).[17] The mean of d^r_{it} is the mean absolute forecast error frequently used as the test of forecast accuracy in other studies (e.g., Brown et al. [1987a]). Despite truncation, the parametric tests are sensitive to violations of the normality assumption. Thus we also compute

[16]The TOPIX (Tokyo Stock Price Index) during this period started at a year-end high of 913.37 on December 28, 1984 and went up to 2,258.56 on June 11, 1987. TOPIX is the index (100 on January 4, 1968) of the total market value of the stocks listed on the first section of the Tokyo Stock Exchange.

[17]The substance of the results is not affected by different truncation rules.

the nonparametric Wilcoxon Signed Rank Test (Lehman [1975]) and the Fisher Sign Test (Hollander and Wolfe [1973]). The Sign Test ignores the magnitudes and reflects only the direction of predictive ability.

Table 3 reports the results of the tests of predictive accuracy. For parent-only earnings all mean and median differences are positive, and for the pooled as well as several yearly samples these differences are statistically significant. In three of the years the median difference is more than 5 percent, so that on average, we can expect these differences to be economically significant.

The results based on consolidated earnings have a similar pattern, although the mean differences are generally lower than in the parent-only case. The differences for the pooled sample of 5.7 percent for the mean and 1.7 percent for the median are statistically significant. Also in four years the median difference is more than 5 percent.[18] Interestingly the only year in which the Fisher Test indicates a significant number of negative differences (i.e., less accurate MFs) is in 1986. Given the concentration of March 31 FYEs, this probably reflects the unexpected appreciation of the yen in the last three quarters of 1985 and in early 1986, which we might expect to add noise relative to a RW model if MFs had been anticipating a continued yen deprecation.[19]

The results presented in Table 3 clearly indicate that management forecasts are more accurate measures of expected earnings in most cases. Thus we can reasonably expect that investors use the MFs and that the correlation with security returns is higher for MFUE than for RWUE.

5. The Relation between Unexpected Earnings, Management Forecasts and Security Returns

Before we can assert that management forecasts are indeed relevant, we have to consider whether investors actually utilize them. As the MFs are released simultaneously with historic earnings, we must first understand and control for any reaction to the (unexpected) earnings signals. Traditionally, the information content of an earnings signal has been evaluated by the association between a measure of unexpected earnings and unexpected returns (UR) (e.g., Beaver [1968]). The association tests are more complex in Japan because of the separate disclosures of parent-only and consolidated information, coupled with the availability of different measures of expected earnings. Thus we have to consider potential information sources in the following order: (1) unexpected parent-only (historic) earnings, (2) MF of next period parent-only earnings, (3) unexpected consolidated (historic)

[18]The forecast errors are unlikely to be cross-sectionally independent in each period. However, each period's mean difference reflects an independent observation. Taking the 't-statistic' for the annual means is 4.36 for the parent-only and 3.65 for the consolidated differences. Each is statistically significant at all reasonable probability levels so that the potential cross-sectional dependence will not affect our inferences (Bernard [1987]).

[19]This period of rapid yen appreciation began in early 1985, but was given significant impetus by the meeting of the "Group of Seven" finance ministers in September 1985.

earnings, and (4) MF of next-period consolidated earnings.

5.1. Tests pf an Association between (Unexpected) Returns and Unexpected Parent-only Earnings

We first examine the associations around the time of the announcement of parent-only earnings. We have three measures of unexpected parent-only earnings:

$$RWUE^p_{it} = \frac{A^p_{it} - A^p_{it-1}}{P^p_{is-5}}; \quad MFUE^p_{it} = \frac{A^p_{it} - MFA^p_{it}}{P^p_{is-5}}; \quad AFUE^p_{it} = \frac{A^p_{it} - AFA^p_{it}}{P^p_{is-5}},$$

where:

AFA^p_{it} is the last "analysts" forecast of year t parent-only earnings for firm i prior to the FYE, and

P^p_{is-5} is the price times shares outstanding for firm i on the day before the first date of the -4 to +4 day event window, i.e., 5 days prior to day s, the announcement date of parent-only earnings.[20]

The null hypothesis tested is:

H^N_{2p}: There is no association between unexpected earnings and (unexpected) security returns so that there is no difference for random walk ($RWUE^p_{it}$), annual management forecast ($MFUE^p_{it}$) or latest analyst forecast ($AFUE^p_{it}$) based measures of unexpected earnings.

The alternative hypothesis is that an association exists and that there is a difference. We expect that the association is highest for $AFUE^p_{it}$ and lowest for $RWUE^p_{it}$.

In all the return related tests, we have to define an appropriate measure of returns. In similar tests using US data, the preference has been to use abnormal (unexpected) returns (AR_{it}) calculated as:

$$AR_{it} = R_{it} - (\hat{\alpha}_i + \hat{\beta}_i R_{mt}), \tag{5}$$

where $\hat{\alpha}_i$ and $\hat{\beta}_i$ are estimated from a standard market model as in equation (1) (e.g., Waymire [1984] and Baginski [1987]). AR_{it} is also frequently cumulated over a test period to obtain

$$CAR_{it} = \sum_{t=1}^{T} AR_{it}, \tag{6}$$

where T is the length of the test period. CAR_{it} has also been estimated using standardized abnormal returns (e.g., Morse [1981], Ishizuka [1987] and Burgstahler

[20]We deflate by the price times shares outstanding at the first day prior to the event window to reduce the potential measurement error in unexpected earnings and to be consistent with the valuation relation implicit in these tests (See Christie [1987]). We also ran the tests using alternative denominators. These are: $|A_{it}|$ (i.e., as in equations (2) and (3)) and the price two days prior to the announcement date for the $(-1, +1)$ event period tests, with little difference in the results.

et al. [1989]), i.e.,

$$SCAR_{it} = \sum_{t=1}^{T} \frac{AR_{it}}{S_{\epsilon_i}}, \tag{7}$$

where S_{ϵ_i} is the standard deviation of the residuals for the market model in the estimation period (equation (1)).

We performed association tests using AR_{it}, CAR_{it} and $SCAR_{it}$ where $\hat{\alpha}_i$ and $\hat{\beta}_i$ are estimated as described in Section 3. Unfortunately, the market model does not seem to have much explanatory power in Japan (Sakakibara et al. [1988], Ch. 2; Maru et al. [1986], Ch. 4), particularly in certain periods. Looking at our own estimations for each firm, we often find a high variance from year to year in both $\bar{R}^2$ and the parameter estimates of the model. For example, Mitsui Mining has $\bar{R}^2 = 0.10$ and $\hat{\beta} = 2.75$ for announcement date 5/23/86 and $\bar{R}^2 = -0.01$ and $\hat{\beta} = -0.17$ for announcement date 5/22/87. For the sample as a whole the mean beta is 1.32, the median is 0.60 and more than 10% of the sample has a beta of greater than 2.5.[21]

As a result of the poor explanatory power of the market model for our sample we also considered the correlations between the unexpected earnings measures and raw returns, cumulative raw returns ($CR_{it} = \sum_{t=1}^{T} R_{it}$), market adjusted returns ($MAR_{it} = R_{it} - R_{mt}$) and cumulative market adjusted returns ($CMAR_{it} = \sum_{t=1}^{T} MAR_{it}$), as well as these measures standardized by the appropriate standard deviations calculated in the estimation period (e.g., $SCMAR_{it} = \sum MAR_{it}/S_{MAR_i}$, where S_{MAR_i} is the standard deviation of MAR_{it} for firm i.).

To test H^N_{2p}, the firms are initially placed into ten portfolios based on a ranking by UE. Different portfolios are established for each of the UE measures. We then calculate the mean and median cumulative (abnormal) returns within each portfolio, for four different event windows; (-4,+1), (-4,+4), (-1,+1) and (0,+4). We consider the four event windows because of the perception that there is information leakage of the announcement and also a potential for slow adjustment to news (Sakakibara et al. [1988]). However the purpose of testing H^N_{2p} is to ensure that we have adequately controlled for news in current earnings announced simultaneously with MF^p_{it+1}. Consequently, we are not really concerned with the vagaries of the event window, *per se*. Having considered all four event windows, we choose to report only the results for the (-1,+1) window as this minimizes the omitted variable problem and provides qualitatively equivalent results to those for other event windows.[22] The results of the parent-only test are reported in Table 4. We

[21]Sakakibara et al. [1988] in their test of annual earnings announcements find similar results for their sample. In their full sample the average beta is 1.1, but when they remove observations for which the market model $\bar{R}^2 < 0.05$, the average beta jumps to 1.79.

[22]Of course information leakage or a post-announcement drift may exist if one looks outside the -4 to +4 day period, but this is beyond the scope of this paper as we are considering the market reaction to current earnings solely as a control for other information around the announcement of MF.

report only the results using the standardized set of return measures ($SCAR_{it}^{p}$ and $SCMAR_{it}^{p}$), as the other measures yield qualitatively similar results.

The results provide evidence in favor of the alternative hypothesis that there is an association between UE and UR at the time of parent-only earnings announcements, and that the best measure of expected earnings is AF_{it}^{p}. The rank correlation between $AFUE_{it}^{p}$ and $SCAR_{it}^{p}$ ($SCMAR_{it}^{p}$) is 0.059 (0.060), which is statistically significant and is higher than the equivalent correlations for the other UE measures. The pattern of abnormal returns across portfolios follows a pattern that can be viewed as broadly consistent with UE, but does not appear to be monotonic. For example, while the average of the abnormal returns is clearly higher for the top five portfolios compared to the bottom five, portfolio 5 has a higher mean abnormal return than portfolios 2, 3 and 4. Similarly portfolio 8 has a large positive return despite negative unexpected earnings. This last result partially reflects positive outliers as the $SCAR_{t}^{p}$ ($SCMAR_{t}^{p}$) for $AFUE_{t}^{p}$ portfolio 8 is 0.002 (0.198).[23] Nevertheless, the results reported in Table 4 suggest that we have an omitted variable or that there is a problem with short window association tests.

Given the concerns about market model estimation expressed previously, one possibility is a misspecified model, so we recommend caution in interpreting the $SCAR_{it}^{p}$ results. But other cumulative return measures provide similar patterns. Another possibility is that net income contains transitory components that are discounted by investors.[24] As previously indicated, we may not have a long enough window to capture information leakage or a post-announcement drift. Nevertheless, the purpose of the test is to control for news in UE. Thus, having found that $AFUE_{it}^{p}$ is the best measure of unexpected earnings we can now consider the information content of parent-only MFs, and see whether this is a candidate omitted variable.

5.2. Tests of the Information Content of Management Forecasts of Parent-only Earnings

The third null hypotheses (for parent MFs) is:

H_{3p}^{N}: There is no information in management forecasts of next-period parent-only earnings.

The alternative hypothesis is that there is information in the MFs such that forecasted increases (decreases) in earnings lead to higher (lower) URs.

As already stated, the MF of next period earnings are provided in the Kessan Tanshin, simultaneously with the announcement of historic earnings. Consequently,

[23]When we refer to portfolios we drop the i subscript from all earnings and return description.

[24]Although some Japanese researchers have used ordinary income as their measure of income for association tests, in Japan the difference between ordinary income and net income includes several items which would not be classified as extraordinary in many other countries including the United States. Consequently we choose to focus on net income.

to test for the information content in MFs we must control for "news" in the current earnings announcement.

To test the third hypothesis we first partition the observations into ten portfolios based on the magnitude of $AFUE^p_{it}$ as reported in Table 4. Then within each $AFUE^p_t$ portfolio we repartition the firms based on whether the MF predicts an increase or decrease in parent-only earnings for the next year. We compute the change in earnings using MF as:

$$\Delta MFA^p_{it+1} = MFA^p_{it+1} - A^p_{it}.$$

Within each $AFUE^p_t$ based portfolio, we expect

$$\left\{SCAR^p_t \,|\Delta MFA^p_{it+1} \geq 0\right\} > \left\{SCAR^p_t \,|\Delta MFA^p_{it+1} < 0\right\},$$

and equivalently for $SCMAR^p_t$. These results are reported in Table 5. We see that for each $AFUE^p_t$ portfolio except portfolio 5 the abnormal returns for the subgroup of firms with positive ΔMFA^p_{it+1} are higher than for those firms with negative ΔMFA^p_{it+1}. For the sample as a whole, the rank order correlations of ΔMFA^p_{it+1} and abnormal returns are more than double those for $AFUE^p_{it}$ (0.140 vs. 0.059 for $SCAR^p_{it}$ and 0.174 vs. 0.060 for $SCMAR^p_{it}$).[25] The results also show that for eight of the ten $AFUE^p_t$ portfolios the negative ΔMFA^p_{t+1} sub-portfolios have negative $SCAR^p_t$ ($SCMAR^p_t$) and all the positive ΔMFE^p_{t+1} sub-portfolios have positive $SCAR^p_t$ (eight out of ten portfolios for $SCMAR^p_t$). Of particular interest is the result for portfolio 8. In Table 4 we report a surprisingly high positive mean $SCAR^p_t$ ($SCMAR^p_t$). When we partition using ΔMFA^p_{it+1}, we see that positive means reflect, at least in part, a reaction to good news in the MF.

The results presented in Table 5 clearly indicate that parent-only MFs have information content. This finding is consistent with the aforementioned belief that parent-only reports are important for users of Japanese financial reports.

An alternative test of H^N_{3p} is to include ΔMFA^p_{it+1} and $AFUE^p_{it}$ as independent variables in a regression model with cumulative (abnormal) returns as the dependent variable. The portfolio results reported in Tables 4 and 5 suggest that the relationship between these variables may not be linear so that standard linear models will yield a poor fit. The results from a regression analysis reflects this poor fit.[26] An observer of the almost exponential rise in Japanese stock prices since 1985 should not be surprised by this result, as earnings did not reflect an equivalent increase.

Having established the relevance of parent-only earnings announcements and MFs we next consider the corresponding questions for consolidated earnings.

5.3. Tests of an Association between (Unexpected) Returns and Unexpected Consolidated Earnings

[25] The rank order correlation between $AFUE^p_{it}$ and ΔMFE^p_{it+1} is -0.175.

[26] The regression models resulted in insignificant $\bar{R}^2$.

Similarly to the analysis in Section 5.1, before we can consider the information content of MFs of consolidated earnings, we need to control for any information in the announcement of current earnings. As indicated, we have no analysts forecasts for consolidated income as these are rarely made. Therefore, the two basic measures of unexpected earnings available are:

$$RWUE_{it}^{c} = \frac{A_{it}^{c} - A_{it-1}^{c}}{P_{is-5}^{c}}; \qquad MFUE_{it}^{c} = \frac{A_{it}^{c} - MFA_{it}^{c}}{P_{is-5}^{c}},$$

where superscript c denotes consolidated and P_{is-5}^{c} is the price times shares outstanding on the day before the first date of the -4 to +4 day window for the consolidated earnings announcement. Consequently the second part of H_2^N is:

H_{2c}^N: There is no association between unexpected consolidated earnings and (unexpected) security returns so that there is no difference for random walk ($RWUE_{it}^{c}$) or annual management forecast ($MFUE_{it}^{c}$) based measures of unexpected earnings.

The alternative hypothesis is that an association exists and that there is a difference with a higher association expected for $MFUE_{it}^{c}$.

We use the same return measures as in the parent-only tests. Given the time pattern of disclosures (Figure 1), it is an open question as to how to partition the firms to test H_{2c}^N. Ito [1988], in a study of annual return associations, partitions observations based on the sign of $A_{it}^{p} - A_{it-1}^{p}$ and then on the sign of $A_{it}^{c} - A_{it-1}^{c}$. Using a short-event period, Ishizuka [1987], Komura [1988] and Sakakibara et al. [1988] consider the change in consolidated earnings as an independent signal but do not control for other information.[27] Based on our use of a short-event window with the sample partitioned so as to ensure that there are no overlapping days between the parent and consolidated windows, in Table 6 Panel A, we present mean values of $SCAR_{it}^{c}$ and $SCMAR_{it}^{c}$ (for event window -1 to +1) for 10 portfolios partitioned using $MFUE_{it}^{c}$ and $RWUE_{it}^{c}$. This provides us with a basis of comparison with the parent-only results presented in Table 4.

The mean abnormal returns suggest that there is no clear pattern in the association between the returns and unexpected consolidated earnings measures. The results using $SCAR_{it}^{c}$ and $MFUE_{it}^{c}$ show that three of the five highest $MFUE_{t}^{c}$ portfolios have negative abnormal returns while only two of the five lowest $MFUE_{t}^{c}$ portfolios have negative abnormal returns. Even if we consider the averages of the top five and the bottom five portfolios, we find that these are indistinguishable. When we use $RWUE_{t}^{c}$ as the measure of unexpected earnings the pattern improves in that three of the five highest (four of the five lowest) $RWUE_{t}^{c}$ portfolios have positive (negative) abnormal returns. However, the order of the magnitudes of

[27] Sakakibara et al. actually use $A_{t-1}^{c} \times 1.05$ as their measure of expected earnings.

abnormal returns across the portfolios does not follow the pattern of the size of unexpected earnings. This is reflected in the small negative rank order correlations of - 0.009 for $MFUE^c_{it}$ and - 0.011 for $RWUE^c_{it}$. When we consider the associations for $SCMAR^c_{it}$ there is slightly more consistency as reflected in the positive rank order correlations of 0.038 for $MFUE^c_{it}$ and a marginally significant ($p = 0.058$) 0.053 for $RWUE^c_{it}$.

Given the poor associations between traditional measures of unexpected earnings and abnormal returns, and the time pattern of earnings releases, we constructed a third unexpected consolidated earnings variable imputed from the parent-only information. If the ratio between parent and consolidated earnings is reasonably stable, then it should be simple for investors to use the current parent-only earnings to estimate the forthcoming consolidated earnings. Using this logic we compute:

$$PFUE^c_{it} = \frac{A^c_{it} - \left[\left(\frac{A^c_{it-1}}{A^p_{it-1}}\right) A^p_{it}\right]}{P^c_{is-5}} \quad .$$

The mean abnormal returns for ten portfolios partitioned on the basis of $PFUE^c_{it}$ are reported in the columns 8 and 9 of Table 6, Panel A. While the rank correlations are statistically significant at a 5 percent level for both return measures, the pattern of returns is not monotonic across portfolios.

The natural question that arises is why we find such poor associations between unexpected consolidated earnings and abnormal returns. As the disclosure of consolidated earnings is so recent, when looking for comparative results in the literature, we could find only three previous studies dealing with reactions to the announcement of consolidated earnings and all considered the period 1978–1984. Komura [1988] uses monthly returns and cannot reject a null hypothesis of no announcement effect. Ishizuka [1987] considers weekly returns and finds an announcement effect using squared $SCAR^c_{it}$ but does not differentiate according to the sign of unexpected earnings. Sakakibara et al. [1988] find an association using daily *CAR*s and a simple good news/bad news split. However, they find that "the price adjustment to the consolidated earnings occurs on and after the announcement day" (p. 83), which, they suggest, "provides conclusive evidence that the Tokyo Stock Exchange is not all that efficient with respect to consolidated earnings information" (p. 90). Ishizuka's results also suggest that the market reacts slowly to consolidated earnings announcements. Consequently, we next consider whether a post-announcement window of 0 to +4 days provides us with a more clearly discernible pattern of associations between UR and UE.[28] These results are reported in Panel B of Table 6. We report results only for $MFUE^c_t$ and $PFUE^c_t$ portfolios in the interest of parsimony.

The rank order correlations and the inconsistent pattern of mean values

[28]For the - 4 to +1 event window the rank order correlations for $SCMAR^c_{it}$ ($SCAR^c_{it}$) are 0.026 (-0.006) with $MFUE^c_{it}$, 0.048 (- 0.000) with $RWUE^c_{it}$, and 0.041 (0.025) with $PFUE^c_t$.

within each portfolio suggest that the results may be sensitive to outliers. Since this was found to be partially true, we only report the median values for the abnormal returns for the 0 to +4 event window. We also found that portfolio 10, i.e., the worst UE, seemed idiosyncratic, so we eliminated firms with negative consolidated earnings from all portfolios considered in Table 6, Panel B.[29]

Looking first at the rank order correlations, we see that for $MFUE_{it}^{c}(PFUE_{it}^{c})$ the correlations are 0.040 (0.035) for $SCAR_{it}^{c}$ and 0.075 (0.068) for $SCMAR_{it}^{c}$, with the latter being statistically significant. The median value of $SCMAR_{it}^{c}$ is negative for all $PFUE_{t}^{p}$ (nine out of ten for $MFUE_{t}^{c}$) portfolios, but in general the returns are lower for lower UE portfolios. The average $SCMAR_{it}^{c}$ of the top five portfolios is higher than the average of the bottom five. Similar results exist for the $SCAR_{t}^{c}$ portfolios. Thus, there still appears to be some other information affecting the returns.

One possibility is the relevance of MFs of next period earnings, which is the primary issue in this paper. However, another possibility is that unexpected parent-only earnings and ΔMFA_{t+1}^{p} are omitted variables, that is, we are capturing a post-announcement effect from the parent-only values. To test this we partitioned the sample into eight portfolios based on a 4-way partition on $AFUE_{it}^{p}$ and then a sub-partition on the sign of ΔMFE_{it+1}^{p}, similar to the process discussed in Section 5.2 and reported in Table 5.[30] We then considered the abnormal returns around the consolidated earnings announcement date for these portfolios as well as new portfolios based on a further partition using (separately) the magnitudes of $MFUE_{it}^{c}$, $PFUE_{it}^{c}$ and $RWUE_{it}^{c}$ (e.g., the eight $AFUE_{t}^{p}/\Delta MFE_{t+1}^{p}$ portfolios were sub-partitioned using $MFUE_{it}^{c}$ rankings). These results are not reported in the paper because they provide no additional insights. The χ^2 statistic for the frequency distribution based on the signs of $SCAR_{it}^{c}$ (0,+4) ($SCMAR_{it}^{c}$ (0,+4)) and $AFUE_{it}^{p}$ is 1.30 (2.19), which is not significant.[31] Other partitions using first ΔMFE_{it+1}^{p} then the consolidated unexpected earnings measures also added no additional insights.

To summarize, we can (weakly) reject the H_{2c}^{N} in that both $RWUE_{it}^{c}$ and $MFUE_{it}^{c}$ provide measures of unexpected earnings that are associated with unexpected returns, although it is difficult to distinguish between the two traditional UE measures.[32] However, the unexpected returns are not consistent with the magnitudes of either UE measure or the third UE measure imputed from the parent information ($PFUE_{it}^{c}$). As the objective of the analysis in this subsection is to

[29]Neither the median values nor removal of firms with negative earnings provided any clearer pattern of associations for the -1 to +1 event window so we have not reported these values. There was also no material impact on the parent-only results from these adjustments.

[30]We used an initial 4-way partition to ensure that we did not have too few observations in the final portfolios.

[31]We also partitioned the sample into different years and evaluated the UE and UR association by year. There are differences across years, but the qualitative conclusions remain. Thus, we do no not report these statistics.

[32]The rank order correlation between $RWUE_{it}^{c}$ and $MFUE_{it}^{c}$ is 0.69.

establish the control variables to use in the test of the information content of MFs, the strength of the association between UE and unexpected returns is important but not itself critical. Consequently we consider next whether MFs of next period consolidated earnings are relevant, and whether they reduce the inconsistency.

5.4. Tests of the Information Content of Management Forecasts of Consolidated Earnings

The third hypothesis for consolidated earnings can be simply stated as:

H_{3c}^{N}: There is no information in management forecasts of next-period consolidated earnings.

The alternative hypothesis is that there is information in the MFs such that forecasted increases (decreases) in earnings lead to higher (lower) unexpected returns.

To test this hypothesis we partition each of the ten portfolios formed using $MFUE_{it}^{c}$ ($PFUE_{it}^{c}$) reported in Table 6 Panel B, based on whether the MF predicts an increase or decrease in consolidated earnings for the next year. We compute the change in consolidated earnings using MF as:

$$\Delta MFA_{it+1}^{c} = MFA_{it+1}^{c} - A_{it}^{c}.$$

Then within each $MFUE_{t}^{c}$ ($PFUE_{t}^{c}$) portfolio, we expect

$$\left\{SCAR_{t}^{c} | \Delta MFA_{it+1}^{c} \geq 0\right\} > \left\{SCAR_{t}^{c} | \Delta MFA_{it+1}^{c} < 0\right\},$$

and equivalently for $SCMAR_{t}^{c}$.

The results for the 0 through +4 day window are reported in Panels A and B of Table 7. For portfolios originally partitioned on the magnitude of $MFUE_{it}^{c}$ (i.e., in Panel A) we see that for $SCAR_{t}^{c}$, in nine of the ten portfolios the median unexpected return is higher for the positive ΔMFA_{t+1}^{c} than for the negative ΔMFA_{t+1}^{c} portfolios. Similar, though less pronounced, differences exist for $SCMAR_{t}^{c}$. Of particular interest in the $SCAR_{t}^{c}$ associations is the split for portfolios 2, 4, 5 and 9. In the high $MFUE_{t}^{c}$ portfolios (2, 4 and 5), we see that the negative ΔMFA_{t+1}^{c} sub-portfolios (column 1 in Table 7, Panel A) actually have negative median values of -0.391, -0.516 and -0.601 respectively, while the positive ΔMFA_{t+1}^{c} sub-portfolios (column 2 in Table 7, Panel A) have positive median values of 0.182, 0.008 and 0.049 respectively. A similar effect is seen in low $MFUE_{t}^{c}$ portfolio 9. However, a note of caution is warranted as there are portfolios, in particular portfolio 7, in which the ΔMFA_{it+1}^{c} has the opposite effect.

Considering portfolios initially partitioned on the magnitude of $PFUE_{t}^{c}$ (Table 7 Panel B) we see that for seven of the ten $PFUE_{it}^{c}$ portfolios, the median $SCAR_{t}^{c}$ values are higher for positive ΔMFA_{t+1}^{c} sub-portfolios. Once again in portfolios 1, 3, 7, 8 and 9 we find negative (positive) medians of $SCAR_{t}^{c}$ for the negative (positive) ΔMFA_{t}^{c} sub-portfolios. The results for the $SCMAR_{t}^{c}$ values are similar although the size of the differences are smaller.

Taken as a whole, we feel comfortable in rejecting H_{3c}^{N}, as the results in Table 7 provide reasonable evidence that management forecasts of consolidated earnings are associated with unexpected security returns. However, the conclusion would possibly be stronger if we could more easily unravel the associations between unexpected returns and unexpected current earnings. We believe that there are several factors at work that cannot be easily separated. First, it is possible that consolidated information may take longer to be incorporated. We can then expect more noise in short-window association tests between UR and UE. This can be easily tested by extending the event window, however, acceptance of the notion of delayed pricing of information introduces a different set of concerns because it brings into question the relevance of a market price based association test. It also becomes more difficult to ensure that we have controlled for other information.[33]

Second, and somewhat related, we have most of our observations in the period from 1985–1987 (see Table 2). As noted earlier, this is a period of extraordinary growth in security prices (approximately 150 percent) without the same growth in earnings. Clearly, either the market was reacting to information other than earnings or an anomaly (e.g., a speculative bubble) was occurring. Furthermore, in part of this time Japan was faced with a potential crisis in its export industries because of the rapid appreciation of the yen, so we should expect increased earnings uncertainty. Thus, overall, we can reasonably expect the return series to be more noisy in this period than in the 1978–1984 test period of Ishizuka [1987] or Sakakibara et al. [1988].[34] However, this problem should affect both parent and consolidated earnings unless the latter included a higher proportion of export-oriented or foreign subsidiaries.

Third, we use net income as our measure of earnings. As previously explained, an alternative earnings number, ordinary income, excludes items that would reasonably be included as operating income in other countries. On the other hand, net income may include extraordinary items that can add noise to the UE classification. It is also possible that we could improve our associations by using the management forecast from the interim consolidated report. Unfortunately, based on information from Nikkei representatives as well as our own random checks, it seems that most companies do not provide interim forecasts of consolidated income. Given the specific objective of this research we did not feel it was necessary to try to improve the association between unexpected earnings and unexpected returns by focusing on these two issues.

Fourth, there may be firm or industry characteristics that distort the associ-

[33]Extending the event window by one day to (0,+5) reduced the rank order correlations in all combinations of UE and UR, e.g., the correlation between $SCMAR_{it}^{c}$ and $MFUE_{it}^{c}$ went from 0.075 to 0.070.

[34]For example, recall from Section 4 that RW outperformed MF for 1986. Removal of 1986 increases χ^2 statistics from frequency distributions based on the signs of the UE and UR measures. However, as indicated the qualitative conclusions remain the same so in the interests of parsimony we do not report these tests.

ation patterns, for example the historical accuracy of managers' forecasts. We shall begin investigating these possibilities in future research.

Finally, given that the problems do not appear to be as serious for parent-only earnings, it is possible that Japanese investors do not yet rely on consolidated earnings for most companies. However, we need to conduct a more detailed investigation to make such a conclusion. It is possible that the announcement of consolidated information does not have as much impact for timing reasons. Since most consolidated figures are disclosed more than one month after the parent-only figures, it is quite possible that more detailed information about the firms may have been made public during the interval (e.g., shareholders meetings), thereby reducing the information content. This delay in consolidated announcement is expected to be shortened in the future, as firms are now required to file parent-only and consolidated annual reports to the Ministry of Finance simultaneously. This is also a question for additional research.

6. Summary and Conclusions

In this paper we have evaluated the information content of management forecasts in the Japanese stock market. Given the typical practice of simultaneous announcement of actual and forecast earnings but separate disclosures of parent-only and consolidated figures, a careful investigation is necessary to determine the impact of management forecasts. We believe that this is the first thorough study to sort out different pieces of information. The empirical findings demonstrate that (1) management forecasts of both parent and consolidated earnings are generally more accurate than a simple random walk model; (2) the "analysts" forecast of parent-only earnings preceding the announcement date is the most accurate measure of unexpected earnings and is most closely associated with unexpected returns; (3) it is difficult to distinguish between management forecast, imputed (parent-earnings-based), and random walk measures of unexpected consolidated earnings relative to their associations with unexpected returns; and (4) the sign of management forecasts of next period earnings are associated with unexpected returns for both parent and consolidated earnings.

These findings have potential implications for both academics and market participants. First, for academics, we believe it is naive to use simple random walk models as measures of unexpected earnings in studies of Japanese capital markets. Further, if one is interested in considering price reactions to accounting information, one should control for the concurrent (or, at least, latest) management and analyst forecast.

Second, for market participants, we believe the results indicate a need to consider management and analyst forecasts in their investment decisions. Further, it would be foolish to ignore the parent-only accounting data, as these appear still to be relevant to Japanese investors.

Third, studies of the PE anomaly should consider the management forecast, particularly if it indicates a large increase or decrease. Finally, for those interested in the globalization of financial markets, it seems reasonable to suggest that as Japanese influence continues to develop, it is possible that we shall see increasing interest in non-Japanese companies presenting some form of management forecast.

Figure 1: Flow of Information
Mitsui Mining for 1986

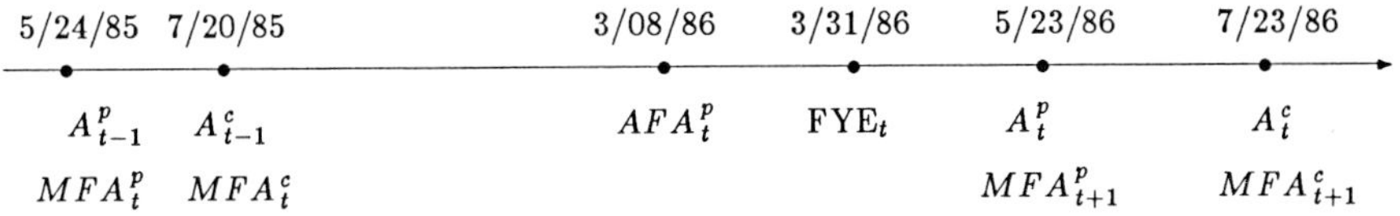

A^c_t is the actual consolidated earnings for fiscal year t.
A^p_t is the actual parent-only earnings for fiscal year t.
MFA^c_t is the management forecast of consolidated earnings for year t made at $t-1$.
MFA^p_t is the management forecast of parent-only earnings for year t made at $t-1$.
AFA^p_t is the last analyst forecast of parent-only earnings year t prior to FYE_{t-1}.
FYE_t is the fiscal year end for t.

Table 1: Summary of Sample Selection Procedure

Observations available on consolidated data base	3,488
Observations for which forecasts are not collected	(1,205)
Observations lost by lagging to obtain forecast errors	(752)
Observations lost from lack of parent forecast or consolidated and parent forecasts being too close	(150)
Observations without a sufficient return series	(81)
Final number of observations	1,300

Table 2: Description of the Sample of Firms

Panel A: Industry and Annual Distribution

Industry	87	86	85	84	83	82	81	80	79
Foods	21	23	21	2	2	2	2	2	2
Textile Products	13	26	19	1	1	1	1	1	1
Paper & Pulp	7	10	8	–	–	–	–	–	–
Chemicals	29	40	39	3	2	2	1	–	–
Drugs	5	8	6	1	1	–	–	–	–
Petroleum	3	4	3	–	–	–	1	1	1
Tires	3	5	4	–	–	–	–	–	–
Clay and Glass Products	11	13	12	1	–	–	–	–	–
Iron and Steel	16	19	18	1	–	–	1	1	1
Metal Products	17	27	27	2	1	–	–	–	–
Machinery	20	35	30	5	3	1	1	1	1
Electric Equipment	45	66	56	16	16	13	16	14	10
Shipbuilding	2	5	4	1	1	1	1	1	1
Motor Vehicles & Parts	11	14	12	3	3	2	2	2	2
Transportation Equipment	3	3	3	–	–	–	1	1	1
Precision Instruments	9	15	14	4	3	3	3	3	2
Other Manufacturing	5	6	6	–	–	–	–	–	–
Marine Products	3	3	1	–	–	–	–	–	–
Mining	3	5	5	–	–	–	–	–	–
Construction	9	13	11	1	2	2	1	1	1
Trading and Wholesale	27	30	28	10	11	11	10	3	–
Retail Stores	1	2	1	1	–	–	–	–	–
Credit & Leasing	3	3	2	1	1	1	–	–	–
Real Estate	7	7	4	–	–	–	–	–	–
Railroad & Bus	9	13	12	–	–	–	–	–	–
Trucking	7	8	7	–	–	–	–	–	–
Sea Transportation	2	8	8	–	–	–	–	–	–
Entertainment & Service	1	1	1	–	–	–	–	–	–
Total	292	412	362	53	47	39	41	31	23

Table 2 (continued)

Panel B: Descriptive Statistics for Earnings Variables

	1st Quartile	Median	3rd Quartile	Mean	SD
1. Parent-only					
A_t^p	6.73	13.70	24.81	19.40	30.21
MFA_t^p	7.67	14.42	26.77	22.40	34.25
MFA_{t+1}^p	7.23	13.66	25.44	20.34	32.06
AFA_t^p	6.33	13.19	25.01	19.01	29.21
2. Consolidated					
A_t^c	7.65	15.67	28.94	22.21	35.40
MFA_t^c	9.30	17.62	31.80	26.53	40.70
MFA_{t+1}^c	8.63	15.79	29.80	23.96	37.23

A_t is the earnings per share for year t.
MFA_t is the management forecast of year t earnings made at $t-1$.
AFA_t is the last analyst forecast of year t earnings per share prior to the fiscal year end.
SD is the standard deviation.
p (c) denotes parent (consolidated)

Table 3: Results for Tests of Predictive Accuracy of Annual Management Forecasts Relative to a Random Walk Model (in %)[1]

	Mean Difference	't' Value	1st Quartile	Median Difference	3rd Quartile	Sign of Wilcoxon Test Statistics	Fisher Test Statistic
			PARENT-ONLY				
Pooled	6.4	8.94**	- 2.6	2.6	13.4	+**	7.4**
1987	9.2	6.06**	- 1.7	3.1	15.6	+**	4.1**
1986	1.4	1.03	- 10.8	0.0	8.6	+	- 1.6
1985	10.6	7.70**	0.0	7.0	19.6	+**	7.1**
1984	7.0	2.00*	0.1	4.1	12.7	+**	4.0**
1983	2.1	0.87	- 3.7	1.2	9.1	+	0.4
1982	4.4	1.03	- 2.6	2.1	7.1	+	1.4
1981	0.9	0.28	- 4.5	1.7	11.2	+	1.7
1980	13.1	3.46**	4.5	8.4	18.2	+**	4.9**
1979	8.4	1.84	0.2	4.6	10.8	+	2.7*
Aggregate[2]	6.3	4.36**					
			CONSOLIDATED				
Pooled	5.5	7.45**	- 2.8	1.6	13.6	+**	3.4**
1987	8.3	4.88**	- 0.1	2.2	16.4	+**	2.7
1986	0.8	0.63	- 7.5	0.0	8.6	+	- 4.3**
1985	9.4	6.17**	- 0.5	5.5	18.7	+**	5.6**
1984	8.3	2.79**	0.1	6.9	18.6	+**	3.7**
1983	0.8	0.24	- 3.4	1.3	6.4	+	0.7
1982	0.0	0.13	- 3.0	0.0	3.9	+	- 0.8
1981	1.5	0.46	- 7.7	0.8	10.6	+	0.5
1980	9.2	2.38*	2.8	7.1	17.1	+**	3.4**
1979	6.5	1.32	- 1.4	6.7	14.0	+	1.9
Aggregate	5.0	3.65**					

* $p < 0.05$ ** $p < 0.01$

[1] The differences in forecast errors are based on the random walk minus management forecast. Thus a positive (negative) sign indicates a more accurate management (random walk) forecast.

[2] The aggregate mean and 't' value are based on the annual observations that are assumed to be independent. This test is done to ensure that cross-sectional dependence within each year does not affect the inferences made.

Table 4: Means and Rank Correlations for Portfolios Partitioned on the Basis of Different Measures of Unexpected Parent-only Earnings (N=1,300)

	$AFUE_t^p$			$MFUE_t^p$			$RWUE_t^p$		
Portfolio #	UE_t^p (×100) (1)	$SCAR_t^p$ (-1,+1) (2)	$SCMAR_t^p$ (-1,+1) (3)	UE_t^p (×100) (4)	$SCAR_t^p$ (-1,+1) (5)	$SCMAR_t^p$ (-1,+1) (6)	UE_t^p (×100) (7)	$SCAR_t^p$ (-1,+1) (8)	$SCMAR_t^p$ (-1,+1) (9)
1	1.90	0.451*	0.284	2.76	0.264	0.135	6.43	0.147	0.077
2	0.39	0.245	0.066	0.65	0.133	0.054	1.31	0.377*	0.227
3	0.21	0.387**	0.143	0.34	0.422**	0.128	0.70	0.327*	0.073
4	0.11	0.206	0.004	0.13	0.364*	0.125	0.40	0.195	- 0.022
5	0.05	0.424**	0.148	0.03	0.159	0.038	0.19	0.265	0.050
6	0.01	0.348*	0.211	- 0.07	0.109	- 0.313	0.06	0.085	- 0.059
7	- 0.01	0.081	- 0.239	- 0.29	0.224	- 0.012	- 0.14	0.192	0.047
8	- 0.13	0.498**	0.259	- 0.62	0.294	- 0.010	- 0.56	0.264	- 0.010
9	- 0.29	- 0.090	- 0.229	- 1.18	0.100	- 0.062	- 1.32	0.319*	0.087
10	- 1.74	0.100	0.043	- 5.15	0.581**	0.340*	-6.03	0.478**	0.219
Rank Order Correlation[a]		0.059*	0.060*		0.005	0.036		- 0.014	0.021

$AFUE_t^p$ is the difference between actual and latest "analyst" forecast of parent-only earnings year t divided by price times shares outstanding at time $s-5$, where s is the day of announcement.
$MFUE_t^p$ is the difference between actual and management forecast of parent-only earnings for year t divided by price times shares outstanding at time $s-5$.
$RWUE_t^p$ is the difference between actual (for year t) and last year's actual parent-only earnings divided by price times shares outstanding at time $s-5$.
$SCAR_t^p$ is the standardized cumulative abnormal return for year t.
$SCMAR_t^p$ is the standardized cumulative market adjusted return for year t.
* $p < 0.05$, ** $p < 0.01$ for mean not equal to 0.
[a]The rank order correlations are based on the full sample of 1,300 observations.

Table 5: Means and Rank Correlation of Adjusted Returns for Portfolios based on Analyst Forecast of Unexpected Earnings and the Management Forecast of Changes in Next Period Earnings
Parent-only
(N=1,300)

	$SCAR_t^p$ (-1,+1)			$SCMAR_t^p$ (-1,+1)		
	ΔMFA_{it+1}^p			ΔMFA_{it+1}^p		
Portfolio #	Negative (1)	Positive (2)	Difference (2)-(1)	Negative (3)	Positive (4)	Difference (4)-(3)
1	0.383	0.545	0.162	0.171	0.442	0.271
2	- 0.570	0.806	1.376	- 0.668	0.585	1.271
3	- 0.095	0.641	0.736	- 0.307	0.382	0.689
4	- 0.036	0.298	0.334	- 0.106	0.074	0.180
5	0.482	0.401	- 0.081	0.235	0.118	- 0.117
6	- 0.164	0.470	0.634	- 0.167	0.301	0.468
7	- 0.541	0.348	0.889	- 0.723	- 0.032	0.691
8	- 0.305	0.882	1.187	- 0.395	0.571	0.966
9	- 0.619	0.120	0.739	- 0.732	- 0.030	0.702
10	- 0.288	0.222	0.500	- 0.210	0.122	0.332
Rank Order Correlation[a] (with ΔMFA_{it+1}^p)	0.140**			0.174**		

$SCAR_t^p$ is the (portfolio) standardized cumulative abnormal return in year t.
$SCMAR_t^p$ is the (portfolio) standardized cumulative market adjusted return in year t.
ΔMFA_{it+1}^p is the difference between management forecast of parent-only earnings for firm i for year $t+1$ and actual earnings in year t.

** $p < 0.01$

[a]The rank order correlations are based on the full sample of 1,300 observations.

Table 6: Summary Statistics for Portfolios Partitioned on the Basis of Different Measures of Unexpected Consolidated Earnings

Panel A: Rank Correlations and Portfolio Means for the Full Sample (N=1,300)

	$MFUE_t^c$			$RWUE_t^c$			$PFUE_t^c$		
Portfolio #	UE_t^c (×100) (1)	$SCAR_t^c$ (-1,+1) (2)	$SCMAR_t^c$ (-1,+1) (3)	UE_t^c (×100) (4)	$SCAR_t^c$ (-1,+1) (5)	$SCMAR_t^c$ (-1,+1) (6)	UE_t^c (×100) (7)	$SCAR_t^c$ (-1,+1) (8)	$SCMAR_t^c$ (-1,+1) (9)
1	3.59	0.251	0.229	7.73	- 0.099	0.119	5.36	- 0.039	0.109
2	0.95	- 0.283	- 0.125	1.81	0.071	0.066	0.73	0.016	0.048
3	0.44	- 0.047	- 0.036	0.97	0.132	- 0.015	0.32	0.279	0.161
4	0.18	0.097	- 0.054	0.53	0.191	0.060	0.13	- 0.043	- 0.076
5	0.00	- 0.392*	- 0.181	0.24	- 0.152	- 0.113	0.02	0.143	0.085
6	- 0.17	0.246	0.163	0.05	- 0.330*	- 0.207	- 0.07	- 0.138	- 0.179
7	- 0.50	0.005	- 0.119	- 0.25	- 0.119	- 0.115	- 0.20	- 0.038	- 0.154
8	- 1.01	- 0.001	- 0.025	- 0.81	0.224	0.092	- 0.45	0.130	0.082
9	- 1.83	0.071	- 0.001	- 1.85	- 0.111	- 0.074	- 0.95	- 0.291*	- 0.251*
10	- 6.66	- 0.242	- 0.157	- 6.78	- 0.119	-0.121	- 6.90	- 0.312	- 0.131
Rank Order Correlation[a]		0.009	0.038		- 0.011	0.053		0.064*	0.076**

Table 6 continued

Panel B: Summary Statistics
for Portfolios from Sample without Negative Consolidated Earnings
(N=1,190)

	$MFUE_t^c$			$PFUE_t^c$		
Portfolio #	Mean UE_t^c (×100) (1)	Median $SCAR_t^c$ (0,+4) (2)	$SCMAR_t^c$ (0,+4) (3)	Mean UE_t^c (×100) (4)	Median $SCAR^c$ (0,+4) (5)	$SCMAR^c$ (0,+4) (6)
1	3.77	0. 133	- 0.086	5.20	0.007	- 0.094
2	1.04	- 0.167	0.002	0.72	0.028	- 0.068
3	0.50	0.018	- 0.094	0.32	0.051	- 0.100
4	0.24	- 0.048	- 0.113	0.14	- 0.390	- 0.139
5	0.06	- 0.326	- 0 .143	0.03	- 0.312	- 0.144
6	- 0.09	- 0.078	- 0.180	- 0.04	- 0.104	- 0.070
7	- 0.31	- 0.200	- 0.197	- 0.16	- 0.018	- 0.248
8	- 0.71	- 0.352	- 0.327	- 0.37	- 0.137	- 0.304
9	- 1.34	0.030	- 0.212	- 0.78	- 0.133	- 0.144
10	- 3.33	- 0.439	- 0.156	- 4.82	- 0.357	- 0.227
Rank Order Correlation[b]		0.040	0.075**		0.035	0.068*

$MFUE_t^c$ is the difference between actual and management forecast of consolidated earnings divided by price at time $s-5$.

$RWUE_t^c$ is the difference between actual and last year's actual consolidated earnings divided by price at time $s-5$.

$PFUE_t^c$ is the difference between actual and imputed expected consolidated earnings divided by price at time $s-5$. Imputed expected earnings is based on current parent earnings multiplied by the ratio of consolidated to parent earnings in the prior period.

$SCAR_t^c$ is the standardized cumulative abnormal return for year t.

$SCMAR_t^c$ is the standardized cumulative market adjusted return for year t.

[a]The rank order correlations are based on the full sample of 1,300 observations.

[b]The rank order correlations are based on the sample of 1,190 observations, i.e., firms without negative consolidated earnings.

* $p < 0.05$ ** $p < 0.01$

Table 7 Medians and Rank Correlations of Adjusted Returns for Portfolios based on Unexpected Earnings and the Management Forecast of Changes in Next Period Earnings Consolidated (N=1,190)

Panel A: Management Forecast of Unexpected Earnings

Portfolio #	$SCAR_i^c$ (0,+4) ΔMFA_{it+1}^c Negative (1)	Positive (2)	Difference (2)-(1)	$SCMAR_i^c$ (0,+4) ΔMFA_{it+1}^c Negative (3)	Positive (4)	Difference (4)-(3)
1	- 0.080	0.288	0.368	- 0.143	- 0.072	0.071
2	- 0.391	0.182	0.573	- 0.058	0.023	0.081
3	- 0.225	0.020	0.245	- 0.019	- 0.103	- 0.084
4	- 0.516	0.008	0.524	- 0.142	- 0.058	0.084
5	- 0.601	0.049	0.650	- 0.322	- 0.116	0.206
6	- 0.310	- 0.002	0.308	- 0.150	- 0.183	- 0.033
7	0.525	- 0.376	- 0.901	0.131	- 0.300	- 0.431
8	- 0.460	- 0.337	0.123	- 0.348	- 0.327	0.021
9	- 0.339	0.180	0.519	- 0.450	- 0.199	0.251
10	- 0.779	- 0.289	0.490	- 0.657	- 0.126	0.531
Rank Order Correlation[a] (with ΔMFA_{it+1}^c)	0.042			0.052		

Table 7 continued

Panel B: Imputed Unexpected Earnings

	$SCAR_t^c$ (0,+4) ΔMFA_{it+1}^c			$SCMAR_t^c$ (0,+4) ΔMFA_{it+1}^c		
Portfolio #	negative (1)	positive (2)	Difference (2)-(1)	negative (3)	positive (4)	Difference (4)-(3)
1	- 0.361	0.213	0.574	- 0.167	- 0.055	0.112
2	0.106	0.028	- 0.078	- 0.027	- 0.070	- 0.043
3	- 0.015	0.058	0.073	- 0.128	- 0.076	0.052
4	- 0.541	- 0.269	0.271	- 0.232	- 0.120	0.112
5	- 0.297	- 0.312	- 0.015	0.131	- 0.150	- 0.281
6	0.063	- 0.150	- 0.213	0.014	- 0.134	- 0.148
7	- 0.259	0.124	0.383	- 0.349	- 0.180	0.169
8	- 1.147	0.034	1.181	- 0.650	- 0.234	0.366
9	- 0.472	0.155	0.627	- 0.312	- 0.091	0.221
10	- 0.444	- 0.324	0.120	- 0.109	- 0.239	- 0.130

$SCAR_t^c$ is the standardized cumulative abnormal return in year t.
$SCMAR_t^c$ is the standardized cumulative market adjusted return in year t.
ΔMFA_{it+1}^c is the difference between management forecast of consolidated earnings for firm i for year $t+1$ and actual earnings in year t.

[a]The rank order correlations are based on the sample of 1,190 observations, i.e., firms with positive consolidated earnings.

References

[1] Aron, Paul [1987], "Japanese Price Earnings Multiples: Refined and Updated," Daiwa Securities America Inc. May 28.

[2] Aron, Paul [1989], "Japanese P/E Ratios and Accountancy II: Rhetoric and Reality," Daiwa Securities America Inc., August 22.

[3] Baginski, Stephen P. [1987], "Intraindustry Information Transfers Associated with Management Forecasts of Earnings," *Journal of Accounting Research*, 25(2), Autumn: 196–216.

[4] Beaver, William [1968], "The Information Content of Annual Earnings Announcements," *Journal of Accounting Research*, Supplement: 67–92.

[5] Bernard, Victor L. [1987], "Cross-Sectional Dependence and Problems in Inference in Market-Based Accounting Research," *Journal of Accounting Research*, 25(1), Spring: 1–48.

[6] Brown, Larry, Robert L Hagerman, Paul A. Griffin and Mark E. Zmijewski [1987a], "Security Analyst Superiority Relative to Univariate Time-Series Models in Forecasting Quarterly Earnings," *Journal of Accounting and Economics*, 9: 61–87.

[7] ——— [1987b], "An Evaluation of Alternative proxies for the Market's Assessment of Unexpected Earnings," *Journal of Accounting and Economics*, 9: 159–193.

[8] Brown, Philip, George Foster and Eric Noreen [1985], *Security Analyst Multi-year Earnings Forecasts and the Capital Market*, Studies in Accounting Research #21, American Accounting Association.

[9] Burgstahler, David, Marilyn F. Johnson and Terry Shevlin [1989], "Informational Efficiency and the Information Content of Earnings during the Market Crash of October 1987," *Journal of Accounting and Economics*, 11 (2): 207–224.

[10] Christie, Andrew A. [1987], "On Cross-sectional Analysis in Accounting Research," *Journal of Accounting and Economics*, December: 229–230.

[11] Hollander, M. and D. A. Wolfe [1973], *Nonparametric Statistical Methods*, New York: John Wiley.

[12] Ishizuka, Hiroshi [1987], ed. *Jissho Kaikei Joho to Kabuka* (Accounting Information and Stock Prices), Dobun Sha: Tokyo (In Japanese).

[13] Ito, Kunio [1988], "The Relative and Incremental Information Content of Consolidated Earnings Data," mimeo.

[14] Jennings, Robert [1987], "Unsystematic Security Price Movements, Management Earnings Forecasts, and Revisions in Consensus Analyst Earnings Forecasts," *Journal of Accounting Research*, Vol 25(1), Spring: 90–110.

[15] Komura, Mitsuo [1988], *Gendai Kigyo Kaikei to Shoken Shijo* (Modern Corporate Accounting and Securities Market), Tokyo: Dobun Sha (In Japanese).

[16] Kunimura, Michio [1986], *Gendai Shion Shijo no Bunseki* (An Analysis of Modern Capital Market), Toyo Keizai Shinpo Sha (In Japanese).

[17] Lees, F. A. [1981], *Public Disclosure of Corporate Earnings Forecasts*, The Conference Board.

[18] Lehman, E. L. [1975], *Nonparametric Statistical Methods Based on Ranks*, Oakland: Holden-Day.

[19] Maru, Junko, Megumi Sutoh and Midori Komine [1986], *Gendai Shoken Shijo Bunseki* (An Analysis of Modern Securities Market), Tokyo: Toyo Keizai Shinpo Sha (In Japanese).

[20] Morse, Dale [1981], "Price and Trading Volume Reaction Surrounding Earnings Announcements: A Closer Examination," *Journal of Accounting Research*, 19 (2): 374–383.

[21] Penman, Steven [1984], "An Empirical Investigation of Voluntary Disclosure of Corporate Earnings Forecasts," *Journal of Accounting Research*, Spring: 132–60.

[22] Poterba, James and Ken French [1989], "Are Japanese Stock Prices Too High?" February, mimeo.

[23] Sakakibara, Shigeki, Hidetoshi Yamaji, Hisakatsu Sakurai, Kengo Shiroshita and Shimon Fukuda [1988], *The Japanese Stock Market: Pricing Systems and Accounting Information*, New York: Praeger Publishers.

[24] Schieneman, Gary S. [1988], "Japanese P/E Ratios: Are They Overstated by Conservative Accounting Practices," in *International Accounting and Investment Review*, Prudential-Bache Securities, July 20.

[25] ——— [1989], "Japanese P/E Ratios II: Myth and Reality," in *International Accounting and Investment Review*, Prudential-Bache Securities, March 30.

[26] Viner, Aron [1988], *Inside Japanese Financial Markets*, Dow Jones–Irwin: Homewood, Illinois.

[27] Waymire, Greg [1984], "Additional Evidence on the Information Content of Management Earnings Forecasts," *Journal of Accounting Research*, Autumn: 703–18.

Japanese Financial Market Research
W.T. Ziemba, W. Bailey and Y. Hamao (Editors)

STOCK MARKET ANOMALIES AND THE PRICING OF EQUITY ON THE TOKYO STOCK EXCHANGE

Gabriel A. Hawawini

Yamaichi Professor of Finance, Euro-Asia Centre of INSEAD
77309 Fontainebleau, France

Abstract

The relationship between the average return and the risk of a sample of common stocks traded on the Tokyo Stock Exchange (TSE) exhibits a significant monthly seasonality pattern. We show that the capital asset pricing model (CAPM) does not provide a valid framework to predicting common stock returns on the TSE unless adjustment is made for firm size and prediction is limited to the month of January. During the other eleven months of the year, the CAPM fails to predict common stock returns on the TSE. These results are similar to those observed in the US and Canadian markets as well as various European exchanges.

1. INTRODUCTION

The purpose of this study is to examine the relationship between the average return and the risk of a sample of common stocks traded on the Tokyo Stock Exchange (TSE). Specifically, the study addresses the following question: Is the capital asset pricing model (CAPM) a valid *predictor* of common stock returns on the TSE given that this market exhibits two well-known "anomalies?" These are the size effect and the seasonal behavior of monthly common stock returns. They are both described below following a brief presentation of the CAPM and a review of the first test of that model on the TSE.

According to the CAPM (Sharpe 1964) the expected return of a risky asset [$(E(R_i)$] is equal to the return of a riskfree asset (R_F) plus a risk premium equal to the expected return of the market portfolio in excess of the riskfree rate [$E(R_m) - R_F$)] multiplied by the relative risk (or beta coefficient) of that asset (β_i).

We can write this equilibrium pricing equation as:

$$E(R_i) = R_F + [E(R_m) - R_F].\beta_i , \qquad (1)$$

where the market portfolio is a portfolio that contains all outstanding assets in proportion to their market value. The beta coefficient of asset i is the risk of that asset relative to the risk of the market portfolio. It is a measure of the "market," or systematic risk of asset i. Risk not related to the market, or unsystematic risk, is assumed to be eliminated through portfolio diversification. It is thus not priced in the market and hence does not appear in the equilibrium pricing equation.

The first test of the CAPM on the TSE was performed by Lau, Quay and Ramsey (1974). They estimated the cross sectional relationship between the average monthly return of 10 portfolios and their corresponding beta coefficient over the 5-year period from October 1964 to September 1969. They found a positive and linear relationship between average portfolio returns and betas and concluded that the CAPM is applicable on the TSE.

Is this conclusion still valid in light of the size effect and the seasonal behavior of monthly common stock returns? The size effect refers to the observed *inverse* relationship between common stock returns and firms' size (measured by the market value of firms' shares outstanding): small-capitalization firms seem to earn, on average, excess returns after controlling for the difference in systematic risk that may exist between small and large firms. This phenomenon, which is inconsistent with equity pricing according to the CAPM, has been observed in most stock markets around the world (Hawawini (1988)). Evidence of its existence on the TSE has been documented by Nakamura and Terada (1984), Kato and Schallheim (1985) and others.

The other so-called "anomaly" is the seasonal behavior of monthly returns: most stock market indices exhibit, on average, higher returns in January than during the other months of the year. Nakamura and Terada (1984) as well as Kato and Schallheim (1985) report a significant "January effect" on the TSE. There are no definitive explanations of these two phenomena. We do know, however, that they are related. Most of the excess return earned by small firms on the TSE occurs during the month of January (see Nakamura and Terada).

Seasonality and size have also been shown to affect the estimated CAPM-risk premium, that is, the estimated slope of the equilibrium pricing equation (1). In other words, not only do common stock returns exhibit monthly seasonality but so does the entire risk-return relationship. This phenomenon has been documented by Tinic and

West (1984, 1986) in the U.S. equity market, by Tinic and Barone-Adesi (1988) in the Canadian equity market and by Corhay, Hawawini and Michel (1987) in the Belgian, French and U.K. equity markets.

In what follows we examine the seasonal behavior of the risk-return relationship on the TSE and show that it displays a significant monthly seasonality pattern. The next section describes the data and the methodology we employ to carry out our empirical tests. Section 3 presents evidence of seasonality in the estimated risk premia inferred from alternative models of equity pricing. Section 4 reports evidence of a size effect and shows that it displays monthly seasonality. Section 5 re-examines the validity of the CAPM in light of seasonality and the size effect and looks at the implications for portfolio management. Section 6 presents evidence indicating that risk does not exhibit seasonality. Section 7 contains the concluding remarks.

2. DATA AND METHODOLOGY

2.1. Data

The data on monthly common stock returns is extracted from a tape compiled by the Japanese Securities Research Institute. Monthly returns for common stocks listed on the first section of the TSE begin on January 1955 and end on December 1985, providing a maximum of 372 consecutive monthly returns per common stock. The number of firms in the sample varies from a minimum of 373 (which traded continuously from January 1955 to December 1985) to a maximum of 566 (which traded continuously from January 1970 to December 1985). Monthly returns are adjusted for all changes in capitalization including dividend payments.

Two market indexes are calculated, a value-weighted index of all firms in the sample and an equally-weighted index of all firms in the sample. Their seasonal behavior is reported in Table 1 and discussed in Section 3.7.

2.2. Methodology

The methodology employed to test the validity of the CAPM is similar to that found in Fama and MacBeth (1973) and Banz (1981). It allows us to test the CAPM as a *predictive* model of portfolio returns instead of a *descriptive* model of portfolio returns. Note that the early test of the CAPM on the TSE, performed by Lau et al (1974) and reported above, is of the second type: descriptive rather than predictive. They examined the relationship between average portfolio returns and beta coefficients estimated over

TABLE 1
Average Monthly Returns on a Portfolio Containing All the Stocks in the Sample (from 373 to 566 stocks) Over the Period January 1955 - December 1985

Average Monthly Return Over	Sample Size	Equally-Weighted Portfolio		Value-Weighted Portfolio	
		Average Return	t-statistics	Average Return	t-statistics
All Months	372	**1.60%**[a]	6.40	**1.84%**	7.55
All Months but January	341	**1.24%**	4.75	**1.61%**	6.22
January	31	**5.58%**	13.17	**4.36%**	9.85
February	31	1.00%	1.85	0.99%	1.73
March	31	**2.90%**	3.77	**3.85%**	4.48
April	31	0.51%	0.57	1.01%	1.23
May	31	0.18%	0.20	0.86%	0.91
June	31	**2.51%**	4.59	**2.43%**	4.09
July	31	0.65%	0.75	0.44%	0.51
August	31	0.92%	0.85	1.05%	1.09
September	31	0.13%	0.17	**1.28%**	1.85
October	31	0.52%	0.48	0.49%	0.56
November	31	1.81%	1.76	**2.42%**	2.27
December	31	**2.48%**	3.02	**2.87%**	3.25

a. Average return in bold are significantly different from zero at the 5 percent level.

the *same* sample period. A test of the predictive power of the CAPM should examine the relationship between beta coefficients estimated over a given period and the return of portfolios realized during a *subsequent* period. With such a procedure one can find out, for example, if a strategy that consists in holding a high-beta portfolio constructed in period 1 yields a higher than average return in period 2.

To test the CAPM as a predictive model of portfolio returns, we proceed as follows. An initial 2-year period of monthly returns is used to construct portfolios on the basis of size and risk (2-year construction period). The following three years of monthly returns are employed to estimate the risk of the portfolios constructed over the previous 2-year period (3-year risk estimation period). Finally, the examination of the risk-return relationship and the investigation of seasonality and size effects are performed over the sixth year of data (1-year test period). The entire procedure is then repeated after dropping the first year of data. The approach is explained below in more detail.

2.3. Portfolio construction

The first 2 years of monthly returns (1955 and 1956) are used to construct *five* equally-weighted portfolios ranked according to size (market capitalization). Each one of these size-portfolios is then divided into *four* subportfolios ranked according to the magnitude of their beta coefficient. This method yields a total of *twenty* equally weighted portfolios constructed according to size and risk.

2.4. Risk estimation

The following 3 years of monthly returns (1957 to 1959) are used to estimate the risk of each stock in the sample. Two measures of risk are considered: systematic risk (beta coefficient) and unsystematic risk. They are both estimated using the following regression, known as the market model (Fama (1976)):

$$\tilde{R}_{it} = \alpha_i + \beta_i . \tilde{R}_{mt} + \tilde{e}_{it} , \qquad (2)$$

where the beta coefficient is the estimated slope coefficient β_i and unsystematic risk is the standard error of residual returns ($\sigma(\tilde{e}_{it})$). Both risk measures are estimated either with the equally-weighted index or the value-weighted index ($\tilde{R}_{mt}$). The risk of the portfolios is calculated by taking the arithmetic average of the risk of the individual securities that make up the portfolio.

2.5. Model testing

Finally, the sixth-year of monthly returns (1960) is used to estimate the following five pricing models:

$$R_{pt} = \gamma_{0t} + \gamma_{1t}.\beta_{p,t-1} + \mu_{p,t} \tag{3}$$

$$R_{pt} = \gamma'_{0t} + \gamma'_{1t} \cdot \beta_{p,t-1} + \gamma_{2t} \cdot \beta^2_{p,t-1} + \gamma_{3t} \cdot \sigma(e)_{p,t-1} + \mu'_{p,t} \tag{4}$$

$$R_{pt} = \gamma^s_{0t} + \gamma_{4t} \cdot \left[\frac{V_p - V_m}{V_m}\right]_{t-1} + \mu^s_{p,t} \tag{5}$$

$$R_{pt} = \gamma''_{0t} + \gamma''_{1t} \cdot \beta_{p,t-1} + \gamma''_{4t} \cdot \left[\frac{V_p - V_m}{V_m}\right]_{t-1} + \mu''_{p,t} \tag{6}$$

$$R_{pt} = \gamma^*_{0t} + \gamma^*_{1t} . \beta_{p,t-1} + \gamma^*_{2t} . \beta^2_{p,t-1} + \gamma^*_{3t} . \sigma(e)_{p,t-1} + \gamma^*_{4t} . \left[\frac{V_p - V_m}{V_m}\right]_{t-1} + \mu^*_{p,t} \tag{7}$$

where:

R_{pt} = realized return of portfolio p in month t;

γ_{1t} = systematic risk premium in month t;

γ_{3t} = unsystematic risk premium in month t;

γ_{4t} = size premium in month t;

$\beta_{p,t-1}$ = the beta coefficient of portfolio p estimated with regression (2) over the 36 month estimation period ending in the calendar year preceding month t and updated yearly;

$\sigma(e)_{p,t-1}$ = the unsystematic risk of portfolio p estimated with regression (2) over the 36-month estimation period ending in the calendar year preceding month t and updated yearly;

$\left[\frac{V_p - V_m}{V_m}\right]_{t-1}$ = the size of portfolio p relative to the size of the market at the end of the calendar year preceding month t and updated yearly.

Regression (3) is the standard two-parameter capital asset pricing model according to which security holders are compensated only for bearing systematic risk with a linear risk-return relationship.

Regression (4) is the Fama-MacBeth (1973) version of a four-parameter capital asset pricing model. This specification provides a direct test of the linearity assumption (if the risk-return relationship is linear γ_{2t} should be statistically equal to zero) as well as a direct test of the marginal contribution of unsystematic risk to asset pricing (if unsystematic risk is not priced in the market γ_{3t} should be statistically equal to zero).

Regression (5) is run to determine if there is a size premium on the TSE. If portfolios constructed according to relative size at the end of a calendar year have different average returns over the following year, then γ_{4t} will be statistically different from zero. If portfolios of smaller firms outperform portfolios of larger firms γ_{4t} will be negative.

Regression (6) allows us to examine the combined effect of systematic risk and size on average returns. If γ''_{4t} is significantly negative, there is a size effect on the TSE even after controlling for the difference in risk than may exist between small and large firms.

Finally, regression (7) is the four-parameter capital asset pricing model in which we have added a size variable.

2.6. Model validity and seasonal behavior

For each *month* of the 12-month test period, we calculate the realized return of each one of the 20 portfolio (R_{pt}). These 20 portfolio returns are then cross sectionally regressed on beta (regression (3)); beta, beta squared and unsystematic risk (regression (4)); size (regression (5)); beta and size (regression (6)); and beta, beta squared, unsystematic risk and size (regression (7). From the 12 monthly cross-sectional regressions we get 12 monthly estimates of the risk premia $\gamma_1, \gamma'_1, \gamma''_1, \gamma^*_1, \gamma_2, \gamma^*_2, \gamma_3$ and γ^*_3 and the size premia γ_4 γ''_4 and γ^*_4

The entire procedure is then repeated using the second and third years of monthly returns (1956 and 1957) to construct portfolios, the fourth, fifth and sixth years of monthly returns (1958 to 1960) to estimate risk, and the seven year of monthly returns (1961) to estimate the monthly relationships between realized returns, risk and size. Dropping one year of early data and adding a new one to estimate the risk and size premia, we keep on repeating the entire procedure until we reach the last year of data, 1985. This approach provides a total of 312 monthly estimates of risk and size premia ; 26 estimates for each of the 12 months of the year (from January 1960 to December 1985). By examining the average value of the estimated monthly risk and size premia either over the entire period or over specific months of the year, we can test the pricing models (3) to (7) and find out whether these premia exhibit monthly seasonality.

2.7. Seasonality in the monthly returns of the market indexes

As mentioned earlier, in this study we use two proxies for the market: an equally-weighted index (EWI) and a value-weighted index (VWI). The average monthly returns for these two indexes is reported in Table 1. When average returns are calculated over the entire 372 months, the EWI has a monthly return of 1.60% and the VWI a monthly return of 1.84%. Both are significantly different from zero at the 5% level, but they are not significantly different from each other. When average returns are calculated over each of the 12 months of the year, we notice that returns exhibit monthly seasonality.

Average returns are the highest during January and higher for the EWI than for the VWI. Higher January return for the EWI than for the VWI is the manifestation of the January size premium. Since the EWI gives a relatively larger weight to smaller firms than does the VWI, the latter will exhibit a higher return than the former during January, a month where small firms outperform their larger counterparts. Note that market returns are also significantly positive in March, June, September and December. These are the last months of the first, second, third and fourth quarter of the year, respectively. This quarterly seasonality may reflect the activity of institutional investors who tend to rebalance their portfolios every quarter.

3. EVIDENCE OF MONTHLY RISK-PREMIA SEASONALITY

3.1. Systematic risk-premia

The average values of the estimated coefficients of regression (3) are reported in Table 2. The third and fourth columns give the average values of the coefficients in the case where the beta coefficients are estimated using a value-weighted index in the market model (regression (2)). The last two columns give the average values of the

TABLE 2

Average Values of the Fama-MacBeth Estimates of the Intercept (γ_0) and Slope (γ_1) Coefficients of the Two-Paramater Model [a]:

$$R_{pt} = \gamma_{0t} + \gamma_{1t} \cdot \beta_{p,t-1} + \mu_{p,t}$$

Average Over	Sample Size	Value-Weighted Index[b] $\bar{\gamma}_0$	Value-Weighted Index[b] $\bar{\gamma}_1$	Equally-Weighted Index[c] $\bar{\gamma}_0$	Equally-Weighted Index[c] $\bar{\gamma}_1$
All months	312	**0.0150**[d] **4.90**	-0.0046 1.45	**0.0109** **3.63**	0.0002 0.05
All months but January	286	**0.0138** **4.28**	**-0.0070** **2.14**	**0.0119** **3.78**	**-0.0047** **1.86**
January	26	**0.0279** **3.00**	**0.0220** **2.09**	-0.0009 0.10	**0.0543** **5.36**
February	26	**0.0207** **2.79**	**-0.0185** **2.22**	0.0073 0.63	-0.0029 0.28
March	26	**0.0261** **3.01**	0.0016 0.14	0.0247 2.24	0.0005 0.05
April	26	0.0061 0.45	-0.0082 0.64	-0.0011 0.12	-0.0007 0.06
May	26	0.0014 0.15	-0.0041 0.40	0.0119 1.43	-0.0127 1.21
June	26	**0.0226** **2.33**	-0.0011 0.10	0.0035 0.40	**0.0195** **1.92**
July	26	0.0121 1.28	-0.0109 0.97	**-0.0168** **1.90**	**0.0220** **2.15**
August	26	0.0015 0.15	0.0002 0.01	0.0104 1.29	-0.0102 0.74
September	26	0.0130 1.21	0.0158 1.56	**0.0276** **3.72**	**-0.0318** **4.15**
October	26	-0.0022 0.15	0.0001 0.01	-0.0021 0.20	-0.0008 0.06
November	26	**0.0359** **4.14**	-0.0249 0.83	**0.0351** **2.24**	-0.0224 1.52
December	26	**0.0150** **4.66**	0.0054 1.63	**0.0308** **2.93**	0.0128 1.24

a. Estimated with monthly data from January 1955 to December 1985.

b. Beta coefficients estimated with a value-weighted index of all stocks in the sample.

c. Beta coefficients estimated with an equally-weighted index of all stocks in the sample.

d. Absolute values of t-statistics are below the corresponding average values. Coefficients in bold are significantly different from zero at the 5 percent level.

coefficients in the case where the beta coefficients are estimated using an equally-weighted index in the market model.

We observe the following:

(1) When all 312 months are considered (from January 1960 to 1985) the relationship between average portfolio returns and estimated systematic risk is *not* significantly different from zero at the 0.05 level, irrespective of whether the index is equally-weighted or value-weighted.

(2) When the year is split in two parts, that is, the month of January and the rest of the year, another picture emerges: the relationship between average portfolio returns and estimated systematic risk is significantly *positive* in January and significantly *negative* during the rest of the year.

(3) When the value-weighted index is used to estimate systematic risk, the systematic risk premium is significantly negative in February. When the equally-weighted index is used to estimate systematic risk, the systematic risk premium is significantly positive in June and July and significantly negative in September. The negative September effect outweighs the positive June and July effects resulting in a negative risk-return relationship over the 11 months from February to December.

We have a clear seasonality pattern in the estimated risk-return relationship on the TSE. This phenomenon is similar to that observed in the United States (Tinic and West (1984)), Canada (Tinic and Barone-Adesi (1988)) and Europe (Corhay, Hawawini and Michel (1987)). We do not have an explanation of this phenomenon. We should note, however, that it is not the manifestation of the monthly seasonality in the returns of the market indexes. Indeed, the pattern of monthly return seasonality in the market indexes reported in Table 1 does not correspond with the pattern of monthly return seasonality in the systematic risk premium reported in Table 2, although the month of January has the highest estimates in both cases.

3.2. Linearity and the pricing of unsystematic risk

The average values of the estimated coefficients of regression (4) are reported in Table 3 with risk estimated using the value-weighted index. Qualitatively similar results were obtained with the equally-weighted index.

A look at the results reported in Table 3 shows that when unsystematic risk is introduced as an independent variable in the regression, systematic risk (beta) is no longer priced. Over the entire period, neither beta nor unsystematic risk are related to average portfolio returns. But during the months of January and June, portfolios with high levels of unsystematic risk tend to earn higher returns. The opposite occurs during the month of September where the relationship between average portfolio returns and unsystematic is negative.

The results reported in Table 3 provide no support for the CAPM as a predictor of common stock returns on the TSE: systematic risk is not priced and unsystematic risk is priced during some months of the year. We now turn to the size effect and its implication for equity pricing on the TSE.

4. THE SIZE EFFECT AND ITS SEASONAL BEHAVIOR

4.1. Size premia

Is there a size effect on the TSE and is it seasonal? The answer is found in Table 4 where the average values of the estimated coefficients of regression (5) are reported using the value-weighted index. When all months are considered, there is no significant size effect. The month-to-month results, however, reveal another picture. There is significant size effect during the months of January, June and July but it is strongest during January. For September we have a reverse size effect: large firms outperform their smaller counterparts.

Two observations should be made. First, the absence of a size effect when all months are considered may be due to the fact that our sample tends to be biased toward larger firms. Our largest number of firms is 566 which are concentrated among the top third of all firms listed on the first section of the TSE. Despite this bias toward large firms, we do report a significant January risk premium. Second, note that two of the months where we report a size effect (January and June) are the two months where the unsystematic risk premium is positive, and the month where we report a reverse size effect (September) is the month where the unsystematic risk premium is negative. In other words, unsystematic risk and firm size are inversely correlated (the smaller the

TABLE 3
Average Values of the Fama-MacBeth Estimates of the Coefficients of the Four-Parameter Model [a]:

$$R_{pt} = \gamma'_{0t} + \gamma'_{1t} \cdot \beta_{p,t-1} + \gamma_{2t} \cdot \beta^2_{p,t-1} + \gamma_{3t} \cdot \sigma(e)_{p,t-1} + \mu'_{p,t}$$

Average Over	Sample Size	$\bar{\gamma}'_0$ (Intercept)	$\bar{\gamma}'_1$ (Systematic Risk)	$\bar{\gamma}_2$ (Systematic Risk)^2	$\bar{\gamma}_3$ (Unsystematic Risk)
All months	312	0.0078 1.78	- 0.0029 0.30	- 0.0011 0.23	0.0947 1.56
All months but January	286	**0.0114**[b] **2.55**	- 0.0042 0.43	- 0.0002 0.03	0.0017 0.03
January	26	- 0.0315 1.75	0.017 0.31	- 0.0110 0.58	**1.1176** **4.62**
February	26	0.0037 0.26	- 0.067 0.36	- 0.0014 0.17	0.0504 0.337
March	26	**0.0033** **2.25**	- 0.0066 0.22	0.0062 0.41	- 0.1104 0.57
April	26	- 0.0123 1.11	0.0206 0.71	- 0.0106 0.71	0.0102 0.051
May	26	0.0134 1.29	- 0.0087 0.33	0.0084 0.85	- 0.2281 1.21
June	26	0.0012 0.07	0.0082 0.228	- 0.0104 0.61	**0.3540** **2.13**
July	26	0.0087 0.56	- 0.0479 1.28	0.0179 0.95	0.2259 1.43
August	26	- 0.0096 0.79	0.0156 0.53	- 0.0097 0.68	0.1769 0.80
September	26	**0.0371** **4.82**	- 0.0058 0.23	0.0025 0.18	**0.4900** **3.24**
October	26	0.0004 0.02	0.0274 0.58	0.0118 0.52	0.1914 0.75
November	26	0.0167 0.84	0.0397 0.92	- 0.0315 1.48	- 0.0694 0.28
December	26	**0.0359** **2.40**	- 0.0269 1.15	0.0152 1.14	- 0.0921 0.53

a. Estimated with monthly data from January 1955 to December 1985 with the independent variables estimated with a value-weighted index of all stocks in the sample.

b. Absolute values of t-statistics are below the corresponding average values. Coefficients in bold are significantly different from zero at the 5 percent level.

TABLE 4
Average Values of the Estimated Intercept and Slope
Coefficients of the Regression [a]:

$$R_{pt} = \gamma_{0t}^{s} + \gamma_{4t} \cdot \left[\frac{V_p - V_m}{V_m}\right]_{t-1} + \mu_{p,t}^{s} ,$$

Average Over	Sample Size	$\bar{\gamma}_0^s$ (Intercept)	$\bar{\gamma}_4$ (Relative Size)
All months	312	0.0476 1.41	-0.0010 1.16
All months but January	286	-0.0058 0.17	0.0003 0.35
January	26	**0.6359** [b] **5.96**	**-0.0160** **5.52**
February	26	0.0930 0.98	-0.0024 0.94
March	26	-0.0621 0.52	0.0022 0.69
April	26	-0.0775 0.59	0.0021 0.59
May	26	-0.0846 0.84	0.0024 0.88
June	26	**0.1878** **2.13**	**-0.0045** **1.98**
July	26	**0.2236** **2.54**	**-0.0060** **2.52**
August	26	0.0003 0.00	-0.0002 0.05
September	26	**-0.2468** **3.17**	**0.0067** **3.26**
October	26	-0.0186 0.12	0.0005 0.11
November	26	-0.0645 0.47	0.0021 0.57
December	26	-0.0148 0.16	0.0008 0.31

a. Estimated with monthly data and a value-weighted index from January 1955 to December 1985 where V_p and V_m are the market values of porfolio p and the market, respectively.

b. Absolute values of t-statistics are below the corresponding average values. Coefficients in bold are significantly different from zero at the 5 percent level.

firm, the higher its unsystematic risk) and one variable may act as proxy for the other. Which is a proxy for the other will be examined in section 6.

4.2. Risk-adjusted size premia

The size premia reported in Table 4 do not adjust portfolio returns for differences in systematic risk. This adjustment is done in regression (6) whose average estimated coefficients are reported in Table 5. Here, January emerges as the only month of the year where average returns are directly related to systematic risk and inversely related to firm size (we do not report in Table 5 the results for each of the 11 months from February to December because they are all insignificant).

The above results imply that a high-risk, small-capitalization portfolio will outperform any other portfolio and particularly so during the month of January. Indeed, the results in Table 7 show that the smallest portfolio in our sample with the highest beta (it has a size 5,337 million Yens and a beta of 1.648) earned an average *monthly* return of 11.65% during January over the 26-year period from January 1960 to December 1985. The results reported in Table 7 are discussed in more detail in Section 7.

5. SEASONALITY, SIZE EFFECT AND EQUITY PRICING ON THE TSE

We have seen that average portfolio returns are directly related to systematic risk and inversely related to size only during the month of January. During the other 11 months of the year, and over the entire sample period, there is no significant relationship between average portfolio returns on one hand and systematic risk and size on the other.

Is this conclusion modified when we introduce unsystematic risk as a variable in the regression? The answer is found in Table 6 where the average values of the coefficients of regression (7) are reported. Again, January emerges as the only month of the year where average portfolio returns are directly related to systematic risk and inversely related to size. Unsystematic risk is no longer priced and the relationship between average portfolio returns and systematic risk is linear. Note, however, that there is still a pure size effect during the month of July.

What can we conclude from these results? The CAPM is obviously not a valid predictor of common stock returns on the TSE unless we make an adjustment for size and limit ourselves to predicting returns during the month of January. During the other 11 months of the year, the CAPM is not a useful tool to predict common stock returns on the TSE.

TABLE 5
Average Values of the Estimated Intercept and the Slope Coefficients of the Regression:

$$R_{pt} = \ddot{\gamma}_{0t} + \ddot{\gamma}_{1t} \cdot \beta_{p,t-1} + \ddot{\gamma}_{4t} \cdot \left[\frac{V_p - V_m}{V_m}\right]_{t-1} + \ddot{\mu}_{p,t}$$

where V_p and V_m are the Market Value of Portfolio p and the Market, Respectively.[a]

Average Over	Sample Size	$\bar{\ddot{\gamma}}_0$ (Intercept)	$\bar{\ddot{\gamma}}_1$ (Systematic Risk)	$\bar{\ddot{\gamma}}_4$ (Size)
All months	312	0.0518 1.53	-0.0030 0.99	-0.0011 1.20
All months but January	286	0.0046 0.14	-0.0048 1.52	0.0002 0.17
January	26	**0.5715**[b] **4.87**	**0.0171** **2.01**	**-0.0148** **4.60**

a. Estimated with monthly data from January 1955 to December 1985 with systematic risk (beta coefficient) estimated with a value-weighted index of all stocks in the sample.

b. Absolute values of t-statistics are below the corresponding average values. Coefficients in bold are significantly different from zero at the 5 percent level.

TABLE 6
Average Values of the Estimated Intercept and
Slope Coefficients of the Regression [a]:

$$R_{pt} = \gamma^*_{0t} + \gamma^*_{1t}\cdot\beta_{p,t-1} + \gamma^*_{2t}\cdot\beta^2_{p,t-1} + \gamma^*_{3t}\cdot\sigma(e)_{p,t-1} + \gamma^*_{4t}\cdot\left[\frac{V_p - V_m}{V_m}\right]_{t-1} + \mu^*_{p,t}$$

Average Over	Sample Size	$\overline{\gamma}^*_0$ (Intercept)	$\overline{\gamma}^*_1$ (Systematic Risk)	$\overline{\gamma}^*_2$ (Systematic Risk)^2	$\overline{\gamma}^*_3$ (Unsystematic risk)	$\overline{\gamma}^*_4$ (Size)
All months	312	0.0427 0.99	-0.0055 0.61	0.0011 0.25	0.0205 0.33	-0.0008 0.74
All months but January	286	0.0086 0.19	-0.0087 0.94	0.0023 0.50	-0.0112 0.17	0.0001 0.09
January	26	**0.4171** [b] **2.89**	**0.0293** **2.10**	-0.0122 0.67	0.0369 0.56	**-0.0111** **2.95**
February	26	0.1499 0.93	0.0137 0.66	-0.0070 0.74	-0.2521 1.11	-0.0039 0.93
March	26	0.0109 0.09	-0.0055 0.16	0.0051 0.30	-0.0942 0.49	0.0004 0.13
April	26	-0.1819 1.24	-0.0104 0.38	0.0062 0.46	0.3179 2.22	0.0044 1.16
May	26	-0.0945 0.68	-0.0331 1.89	0.0176 1.76	0.0138 0.08	0.0030 0.86
June	26	0.1512 1.13	0.0087 0.26	-0.0066 0.40	0.0591 0.30	-0.0037 1.09
July	26	**0.3033** **2.51**	-0.0361 1.04	0.0202 1.03	-0.1551 0.75	**-0.0073** **2.47**
August	26	-0.1547 0.99	0.0046 0.21	-0.0106 0.89	0.2751 1.21	0.0037 0.95
September	26	-0.1298 0.96	-0.0231 0.95	0.0055 0.40	-0.1523 0.94	0.0042 1.27
October	26	0.0207 0.11	-0.0212 0.43	0.0083 0.36	0.1217 0.47	-0.0004 0.08
November	26	-0.1307 0.82	0.0186 0.51	-0.0250 1.25	0.1490 0.54	0.0038 0.91
December	26	0.1477 0.92	-0.0091 0.40	0.0121 0.89	-0.3785 1.51	-0.0032 0.76

a Estimated with monthly data from January 1955 to December 1985 with the independent variables estimated with a value-weighted index of all stocks in the sample. V_p and V_m are the market value of portfolio p and the market, respectively.

b Absolute values of t-statistics are below the corresponding average values. Coefficients in bold are significantly different from zero at the 5 percent level.

6. DO RISK MEASURES EXHIBIT A JANUARY SEASONAL?

The return of common stocks is higher in certain months of the year because their risk may be higher during those months. Also, the seasonal behavior of the risk-return relationship may be partly due to the fact that we do not measure risk during particular months of the year. The results presented in the previous sections are based on measures of risk estimated over a 3-year period. These estimated risk-measures are then regressed against realized returns during particular months of the year. In other words, we explicitly recognize the seasonal behavior of returns but ignore the possibility that risk may also exhibit a monthly seasonal behavior.

In order to find out whether measures of risk display monthly seasonality on the TSE, we estimate the systematic risk of common stocks using only a particular month of the year instead of 36 consecutive months. For example, to estimate the January beta of common stock i we regress the 31 January returns of that common stock (from January 1955 to January 1985) against the 31 January returns of the value-weighted index. This is one for the subsample of firms for which we have 31 years of consecutive trading. One drawback of this method is that 31 years is too long a period and hence the assumption that a firm's beta is stable over the estimation period may be violated. We have also estimated betas over the 15 most recent years (thus reducing the estimation period by half). Reducing the estimation period did not significantly modify the results presented in Table 7.

Table 7 gives several characteristics of 20 portfolios constructed on the basis of size and systematic risk (beta). The securities in our sample are first used to construct 5 size portfolios (group 1 to group 5 in the first column of Table 7). Each size portfolio is then divided into 4 risk portfolios according to their magnitude of beta (see the third column in Table 7). For a given size we have a wide range of portfolio betas from about 0.20 to about 1.70 (see the third column in Table 7). The fifth column in Table 7 gives the estimated January beta for the portfolio. We do not report the estimated betas for the other 11 months of the year but we have found that they are not significantly different from January betas. Also, January betas do not significantly differ from all-month betas. Note that large portfolios tend to have *higher* January betas than all-month betas, and small portfolios tend to have *lower* January betas than all-month betas. Turning to the variance of portfolio returns, note that the January variance generally differs from the all-month variance, but the differences are not significant (the statistical tests are not reported in Table 7). It seems that the January seasonal exhibited by common stock returns and estimated risk premia cannot be explained by differences between January risk-measures and all-month risk-measures.

Table 7
Risk and Return Characteristics of 20 Portfolios Partitioned According to Size (Market Value) and Systematic Risk (Beta): January versus All Months
(January 1955 - December 1985)

Porfolio Size in Million [b]	Number of Stocks in Portfolio	Estimated Systematic Risk (Beta)				Return Variance		Average Monthly Return			
		All Months	t-stat.	January	t-stat.	All Months	January	All Months	t-stat.	January	t-stat.
Group 1											
178735	29	1.692	53.96	1.920	8.11	0.0069	0.0031	2.16%	4.95	5.82%	5.74
174412	29	1.072	46.10	1.453	7.27	0.0029	0.0019	1.36%	4.81	3.52%	4.42
156259	28	0.681	29.47	0.631	2.99	0.0014	0.0010	1.46%	7.42	2.65%	4.66
141787	28	0.260	9.31	0.143	0.76[a]	0.0007	0.0006	1.10%	7.69	1.58%	3.54
Group 2											
48791	29	1.660	38.71	1.655	4.77	0.0073	0.0036	1.98%	4.41	6.97%	6.37
48753	28	1.068	41.01	0.745	4.11	0.0029	0.0009	1.07%	3.73	4.09%	7.60
49791	28	0.673	24.97	0.504	3.03	0.0015	0.0006	1.20%	5.83	2.95%	6.57
48304	28	0.197	5.79	-0.288	1.29[a]	0.0010	0.0009	1.15%	7.00	1.81%	3.36
Group 3											
24655	29	1.713	36.40	1.475	4.32	0.0079	0.0032	1.76%	3.75	8.83%	8.54
24384	28	1.090	31.08	0.933	4.00	0.0035	0.0014	0.97%	7.55	5.14%	7.50
24936	28	0.691	21.52	0.423	2.28	0.0069	0.0007	1.15%	5.15	3.97%	8.37
24560	28	0.198	4.92	-0.034	0.11[a]	0.0029	0.0014	1.02%	5.31	2.79%	4.07
Group 4											
12950	29	1.676	30.73	1.187	3.27	0.0014	0.0030	1.56%	3.25	10.09%	10.08
12611	28	1.096	24.93	0.646	2.36	0.0007	0.0015	0.94%	2.82	6.37%	9.07
12577	28	0.734	17.37	0.294	1.16[a]	0.073	0.0001	0.87%	3.31	4.66%	7.66
12720	28	0.250	5.15	-0.429	1.60[a]	0.0029	0.0013	1.08%	4.65	2.96%	4.50
Group 5											
5337	29	1.648	24.38	1.284	2.47	0.0015	0.0054	1.20%	2.37	11.65%	7.94
4890	28	1.069	18.88	0.529	1.47[a]	0.0010	0.0023	0.64%	1.94	8.11%	9.26
4944	28	0.711	13.30	0.184	0.61[a]	0.0079	0.0015	0.60%	2.00	5.78%	8.09
4664	29	0.204	3.50	-0.298	1.07[a]	0.0035	0.0013	0.87%	3.19	3.85%	5.77

a. Estimated beta coefficient not significantly different from zero at the 5 percent level.
b. Millions of Yens.

Finally, recall our earlier observation: the small portfolio (5,337 million Yens) with the highest beta (1.648) achieved the highest return during the month of January (a *monthly* return of 11.65%). This relatively large January return cannot be explained by higher January risk for smaller firms. Indeed, the January beta of the small-size, high-risk portfolios is actually *smaller* than the all-month beta (1.284 compared to 1.648).

7. CONCLUDING REMARKS

For this study, we examined the relationship between the average return and the risk of portfolios of common stocks traded on the TSE. We wanted to find out whether the CAPM is a valid predictor of common stock returns in light of the seasonal and size anomalies. We showed that the CAPM does not provide a valid framework to predict common stock returns on the TSE unless we make an adjustment for firm size and limit ourselves to predicting returns during the month of January. During the other 11 months of the year, the CAPM fails to predict common stock returns on the TSE. How is the phenomenon explained and are there alternative models to predict common stock returns on the TSE are questions for further research on the pricing of Japanese equity.

REFERENCES

1 Banz, R. (1981) "The relationship between return and market value of common stocks," **Journal of Financial Economics**, 9 (June), 3-18.

2 Corhay, A., G. Hawawini and P. Michel (1987) "Seasonality in the risk-return relationship: Some international evidence," **Journal of Finance**, 42 (March), 49-68.

3 Fama, E. (1976) **Foundations of Finance**, New York: Basic Books.

4 Fama, E. and J. MacBeth (1973) "Risk, return and equilibrium: Empirical tests," **Journal of Political Economy,** 71 (May/June), 607-636.

5 Hawawini, G. (1988) "Market efficiency and equity pricing: International evidence and implications for global investing", unpublished working paper.

6 Kato, K. and J. Schallheim (1985) "Seasonal and size anomalies in the Japanese stock market," **Journal of Financial and Quantitative Analysis**, 20 (June), 243-260.

7 Lau, S., S. Quay and C. Ramsey (1974) "The Tokyo Stock Exchange and the capital asset pricing model," **Journal of Finance,** 28 (May), 507-514.

8 Nakamura, T. and N. Terada (1984) "The size effect and seasonality in Japanese stock returns" unpublished manuscript (Institute for Quantitative Research in Finance).

9 Sharpe, W. (1964) "Capital asset prices: A theory of market equilibrium under conditions of risk," **Journal of Finance**, 19 (September), 425-442.

10 Tinic, S and G. Barone-Adesi (1988) "Stock return seasonality and the tests of asset pricing models: Canadian evidence" in E. Dimson (ed.) **Stock Market Anomalies**, Cambridge University Press.

12 Tinic, S. and R. West (1984) "Risk and return: January versus the rest of the year," **Journal of Financial Economics**, 13 (December), 561-574.

13 Tinic, S. and R. West (1986) "Risk, return and equilibrium: A revisit," **Journal of Political Economy**, 94 (February), 126-147.

Japanese Financial Market Research
W.T. Ziemba, W. Bailey and Y. Hamao (Editors)
1991 Elsevier Science Publishers B.V.

WEEKLY PATTERNS IN JAPANESE STOCK RETURNS*

KIYOSHI KATO

School of Business Administration, Nanzan University, Nagoya, Japan

This study investigates the day of the week effect in the Japanese stock returns. Low Tuesday and high Wednesday returns are observed. Most of the positive returns arise during the nontrading period. The Monday effect is also observed in the week whose previous week is closed by Friday trading. Low Tuesday returns appear to be related to low Monday returns in the U.S. The weekly pattern is more pronounced for the returns of smaller firms. A reverse size effect is observed during the trading period.
(ANOMALY; PATTERN; SEASONALITY)

Considerable attention has been paid to the discovery of anomalous patterns in stock price movements. These anomalies include the January effect, the size effect, the P/E effect, the monthly effect and the weekend effect. This paper examines one of these anomalies, the day of the week effect for Japanese stock returns.

Some empirical studies using daily stock returns assume that the distribution of stock returns is stationary for all days of the week. This has been shown to be incorrect by numerous studies which report a day of the week effect. Cross (1973) and French (1980) document that the average return for Monday is significantly negative and the other days of the week have positive returns of varying magnitude. The average return for Friday is higher than that of the other days of the week.

Several studies attempt to identify its cause. Gibbons and Hess (1981) propose and test the settlement hypothesis. Lakonishok and Levi (1982) add the check clearing process to this settlement procedure. However, the results of neither study completely support the settlement hypothesis. Furthermore, Dyl and Martin (1985) provide evidence against the settlement hypothesis. Keim and Stambaugh (1984) investigate a specialist related bias by examining the stocks in the over-the-counter market. Their results are not consistent with a specialist related bias. Measurement error is also examined by Gibbons and Hess (1981) and Keim and Stambaugh (1984).[1] Neither study supports the measurement error hypothesis.

These previous papers focus on daily returns measured from the previous day's close to the current day's close. Recent studies have employed intraday data by decomposing daily returns into shorter periods. Rogalski (1984) documents a nontrading weekend effect. All of the average negative returns from Friday closes to Monday closes documented in the literature take place during the nontrading period from Friday close to Monday open. Smirlock and Starks (1986) extend Rogalski's study by decomposing daily returns into six hourly return measures and extending the time periods. Their results indicate that the day of the week effect is time variant. Harris (1986) documents that the Monday effect accrues for the first 45 minutes after the market opens.

* Accepted by William T. Ziemba; received March 1989. This paper has been with the author 3 months for 2 revisions.

[1] Negative correlations between returns on Saturday and the following Monday would suggest a random type error.

Keim and Stambaugh (1984) and Keim (1987) investigate the relationship between the January-size effect and the day of the week effect. Friday returns are strongly related to firm size and Monday returns are consistently negative across all size portfolios. Cornell (1985) examines whether the same weekly pattern is present in the futures markets for the S&P 500 and reports no such patterns.

Connolly (1989) analyzes the robustness of the day-of-the-week effects to alternative estimation and testing procedures. Connolly concludes that the strength of the day-of-the-week effects appears to depend on the estimation and testing method.

Few studies have been conducted regarding this anomalous effect outside the U.S. including Japan. Pettway and Tapley (1984) first document the weekly pattern in the Japanese stock market using three market indices and stock data from five major Japanese firms from 1979 through 1982. Their findings are different from those in the U.S. Tuesday returns are the lowest and Wednesday returns are the highest.

Jaffe and Westerfield (1985a, b) examine the daily stock indices for Australia, Canada, Great Britain and Japan. Their results for Japan are similar to Pettway and Tapley's results for their longer sample period. In addition, the structure of institutional correlations of the weekly patterns is examined. The relationship between two major stock markets, the Tokyo Stock Exchange and the New York Stock Exchange, does not appear to be linked during the period 1970 through 1983.[2] Measurement errors are also examined and the evidence does not appear to be influenced by measurement errors.

Ikeda (1988) replicates several U.S. studies using the index of the Tokyo Stock Exchange. Similar results to Pettway and Tapley's are obtained regarding the day of the week effect. In addition, the weekly pattern also exists for skewness and kurtosis of the daily returns in Japan. Furthermore, high Wednesday returns are partly the result of the settlement effect according to Ikeda. However, low Tuesday returns are not satisfactorily explained.

These three studies utilize indices of the Tokyo Stock Exchange. The relationship between the day of the week effect and firm size has not been examined. In addition, the Tokyo Stock Exchange has sometimes been closed on Saturdays since 1973. This infrequent Saturday trading provides an opportunity to examine the weekend effect in more detail. Furthermore, we are aware of no analysis regarding the intraday stock returns for the Tokyo Stock Exchange.

This paper attempts to further investigate the nature of the day of the week effect on the Japanese stock returns. In §1, the day of the week effect is examined using the stock index of the Tokyo Stock Exchange. The intraday effect and the effect of infrequent Saturday trading on the weekly pattern are examined as is the relationship between the Tokyo and the New York market. In §2, the relationship between the January-size effects and the day of the week effect is analyzed. The paper closes with a summary and conclusions.

1. Analysis of the Japanese Stock Index

A. *The Data*

The Value Weighted Index (TOPIX) of the Tokyo Stock Exchange is mainly used to

[2] There is a recent study by Hamao, Masulis and Ng (1989) that reports the evidence of price volatility spillovers from New York to Tokyo. No similar spillover effect in the other direction.

examine the day of the week effect.[3] Data consist of the daily return observations of the TOPIX from April 1978 through June 1987 and the intraday return observations of the TOPIX from January 1982 through December 1987. Daily returns are computed as the percentage change in the value of the index from the previous day (using the closing price) to the closing price of the current day. Likewise, the intraday returns are calculated as the percentage change in the value of the index in the following six time periods: at the beginning of the previous day's close to the ending of 9:15 a.m., 10:00 a.m., 11:00 a.m., 1:15 p.m., 2:00 p.m., 3:00 p.m. These intra-daily prices of the index are collected from *Nihon Shoken Shimbun* (The Japanese Securities Newspaper).

During the sample period, the Tokyo Stock Exchange was open from Monday through Friday from 9 to 11 a.m. and from 1 to 3 p.m. The market was also open on Saturday from 9 to 11 a.m. until 1972. During the period January 1973 through July 1983, the market was closed on the third Saturday of each month. During the period August 1983 through July 1986, the market was closed on the second Saturday of each month. Since then, the market has been closed on the second and third Saturday of each month until January 1989. Since February 1989, all Saturdays are closed. These changes offer an additional opportunity to examine the weekly pattern of Japanese stock returns.

B. *Closing Returns*

In this section, we reinvestigate the results of previous studies regarding the Japanese daily stock returns using more recent data. The close-to-close returns of the TOPIX is used to identify the weekly patterns of the daily stock returns. To formally test the timing and existence of weekly patterns, the following regression model is used:

$$R_t = \sum_{k=1}^{6} a_k D_{kt} + u_t \qquad (1)$$

where D_{kt} are day-of-the-week dummy variables such that $D_{1t} = 1$ if day t is a Monday, and $D_{1t} = 0$ otherwise; $D_{2t} = 1$ if t is a Tuesday, etc. The coefficients of equation (1) are the mean returns for Monday through Saturday. The equality of these coefficients is tested using an F-test.[4]

Table 1 presents the results. The distribution of daily returns displays a pattern similar to that observed by Jaffe and Westerfield (1985a, b). The hypothesis of equal expected returns for each day of the week is rejected for this sample period. Tuesday returns are the lowest and Wednesday returns are the highest. There also appears to be a weekly pattern for kurtosis and skewness as Ikeda (1987) noted. During the period 1978 through 1981, a significantly high kurtosis is observed for Monday and Tuesday returns. Figure 1 exhibits the histograms of the daily returns of six days of the week. Tuesday returns are skewed to the right. All other returns are skewed to the left. Saturday returns are the highest during the period between 1982 through 1987. This finding is similar to that of Keim and Stambaugh (1984) during the time the New York Stock Exchange was open

[3] The Value Weighted Index consists of all stocks on the First Section of the Tokyo Stock Exchange. The TOPIX is weighted by the market capitalization. The same analysis is conducted using the Nikkei Stock Average. Since the results are not substantially changed, we only report the analysis of the VWI except §E. The Nikkei Dow is a price weighted index of 225 securities of the First Section of the Tokyo Stock Exchange.

[4] We compute the autocorrelation function up to 14 lags during this sample period. Most of these estimates of the autocorrelations are not significantly different from zero.

TABLE 1

Summary Statistics of the Percent Return of the Tokyo Stock Exchange Index from the Close of the Previous Trading Day to the Close of the Day Indicated

Tokyo Stock Exchange Index (TOPIX) April 4, 1978–June 18, 1987									
Period	Statistic	Monday	Tuesday	Wednesday	Thursday	Friday	Saturday	All Days	*F*
1978–1987	Mean	0.0039	−0.0902	0.1449	0.0648	0.1049	0.1397	0.0581	11.47**
	t-value	(0.13)	(−3.08)	(4.95)	(2.22)	(3.60)	(4.11)	(4.72)	
	Standard Deviation	0.64	0.65	0.62	0.69	0.66	0.46	0.63	
	Skewness	−1.66	−0.08	−0.59	0.37	0.66	0.07	−0.22	
	Kurtosis	8.78	9.37	3.71	5.15	5.45	3.74	6.48	
	Observations	449	464	464	465	467	343	2652	
1978–1981	Mean	0.0007	−0.0852	0.1283	−0.0273	0.0834	0.0957	0.0302	5.90**
	t-value	(0.02)	(−2.58)	(3.89)	(−0.83)	(2.54)	(2.54)	(2.17)	
	Standard Deviation	0.53	0.48	0.47	0.44	0.41	0.31	0.45	
	Skewness	−2.33	1.02	−0.15	−0.85	−0.75	0.17	−0.71	
	Kurtosis	16.78	15.02	2.43	3.42	3.03	0.92	9.64	
	Observations	182	185	186	189	188	142	1072	
1982–1987	Mean	0.0061	−0.0935	0.1561	0.1279	0.1195	0.1707	0.0771	7.44**
	t-value	(0.14)	(−2.15)	(3.58)	(2.92)	(2.74)	(3.33)	(4.19)	
	Standard Deviation	0.71	0.74	0.71	0.81	0.78	0.55	0.73	
	Skewness	−1.43	−0.27	−0.67	0.31	0.69	−0.06	−0.17	
	Kurtosis	6.28	7.16	3.09	3.65	3.75	2.81	4.75	
	Observations	267	279	278	276	279	201	1580	

** Significant at the one percent level.

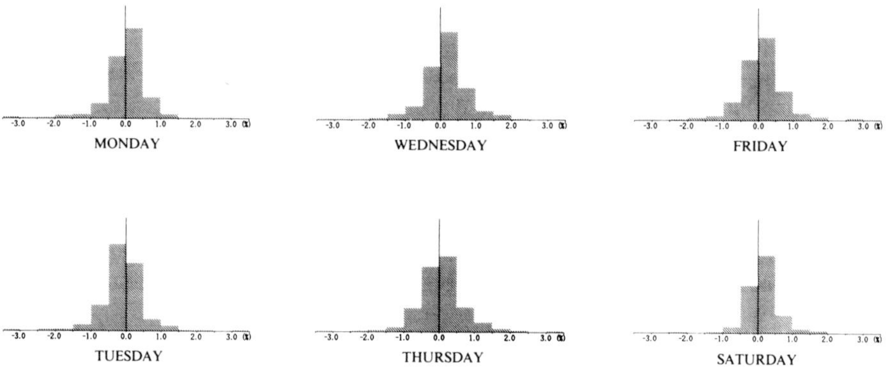

FIGURE 1. Histograms of Returns of the TOPIX, in Percent, from 1978 through 1987.

on Saturday mornings. The effect of Saturday trading is examined in more detail in the following section.

The markets are, on average, depressed in the first two days of the week and rise in the remaining three or four days in Japan during this sample period.[5] The results in this section are mostly consistent with the previous findings.

[5] The existence of National holidays may affect the results. We delete the days after holidays from our data and then conduct the same analysis. However, this adjustment does not alter our inferences.

C. *Intraday Returns*

We now attempt to provide additional insight into the characterization of the weekly patterns in the Japanese stock returns by employing intraday returns of the TOPIX of the Tokyo Stock Exchange. One of the most important questions is: In what time period do the negative Tuesday returns and high positive Wednesday returns take place?

To address the pattern of intraday returns, the same regression analysis in equation (1) is conducted.[6] Summary statistics for the seven intraday return measures across days of the week during the period from 1982 through 1987 are presented in Table 2. Weekly patterns exist for both nontrading and trading periods (R11 and R12). Significantly higher *F*-values are observed during the nontrading period. Mean nontrading period returns are positive for all six days of the week.[7] Indeed, most of the positive returns arise during the nontrading period.[8] During the trading period, both Monday and Tuesday experience negative returns. The average returns for other days of the week are close to zero excluding Saturday returns.

Figure 2 presents the cumulated mean intraday returns by week. One noticeable observation is the downward slope of Monday returns. In the morning, the Monday return

TABLE 2

Summary Statistics for Intraday Returns of the Tokyo Stock Exchange Index

Tokyo Stock Exchange Index (TOPIX) Jan. 4, 1982–Dec. 25, 1987											
Period	Variable[a]	Statistic	Monday	Tuesday	Wednesday	Thursday	Friday	Saturday	All Days	*F*
1982–1987	R	Mean	−0.0213	−0.1331	0.1792	0.1201	0.1212	0.1983	0.0723	6.88**
		t-value	(−0.41)	(−2.60)	(3.52)	(2.35)	(2.38)	(3.28)	(3.350)	
	R11	Mean	0.1002	0.0013	0.1177	0.1211	0.1134	0.0487	0.0855	23.58**
		t-value	(5.08)	(0.07)	(6.11)	(6.26)	(5.88)	(2.13)	(10.466)	
	R12	Mean	−0.1217	−0.1344	0.0611	−0.0017	0.0069	0.1490	−0.0135	4.54**
		t-value	(−2.73)	(−3.07)	(1.41)	(−0.04)	(0.16)	(2.89)	(−0.735)	
	R1	Mean	−0.0040	−0.0671	0.0114	0.0065	0.0237	0.0278	−0.0016	3.67**
		t-value	(−0.24)	(−4.13)	(0.70)	(0.40)	(1.47)	(1.45)	(−0.230)	
	R2	Mean	−0.0543	−0.0589	−0.0457	−0.0546	−0.0627	0.1210	−0.0330	10.46**
		t-value	(−0.262)	(−2.90)	(−2.26)	(−2.69)	(−3.11)	(5.05)	(−3.837)	
	R3	Mean	−0.0514	−0.0097	0.0232	0.0029	0.0019		−0.0070	4.47**
		t-value	(−4.22)	(−0.81)	(1.95)	(0.24)	(−0.16)		(−1.295)	
	R4	Mean	−0.0516	−0.0251	−0.0160	−0.0035	0.0070		−0.0175	3.24**
		t-value	(−3.44)	(−1.71)	(−1.09)	(−0.24)	(0.48)		(−2.651)	
	R5	Mean	0.0387	0.0215	0.0885	0.0466	0.0407		0.0473	8.55**
		t-value	(2.12)	(1.20)	(4.97)	(2.62)	(2.29)		(5.902)	

[a] R is defined as close-to-close return, in percent. R11 is defined as close-to-open return. R12 is defined as open-to-close return. R1 is defined as the percentage change from 9:15 a.m. to 10 a.m. R2 is defined as the percentage change from 10 a.m. to 11 a.m. R3 is defined as the percentage change from 11 a.m. to 1:15 p.m. R4 is defined as the percentage change from 1:15 p.m. to 2 p.m. R5 is defined as the percentage change from 2 p.m. to 3 p.m.

** Significant at the one percent level.

[6] The intraday returns are used instead of the daily close-to-close returns. The regression analysis is conducted for R, R11, R12, R1, R2, R3, R4, and R5, respectively as a dependent variable in equation (1).

[7] Contrary to our results, Smirlock and Starks (1986) report that mean trading period return of the Dow Jones Industrial Average is 0.007 percent and mean nontrading period return is 0.003 percent during the period 1963 through 1983.

[8] However, another nontrading period (R3) from 11 a.m. to 1 p.m. does not appear to exhibit the same pattern. Mean return of this period in Table 3 is close to zero for all days of the week except Monday.

is similar to the other three days (Wednesday, Thursday and Friday). However, after the morning trade is closed, Monday returns exhibit a different pattern which is similar to Tuesday returns. Tuesday returns reveal the comparable pattern to Monday returns

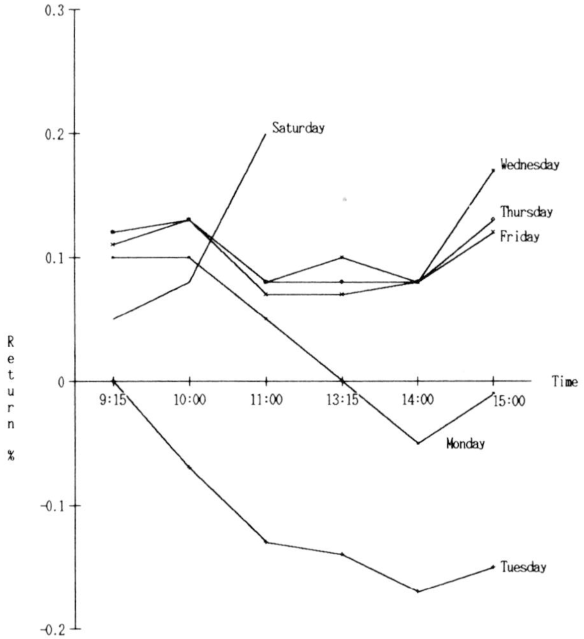

FIGURE 2. Cumulated mean intra-day returns by week, in percent. The accrued return is the average rate of return experienced by the TOPIX of the Tokyo Stock Exchange. The starting points are overnight returns.

in the U.S., as reported by Harris (1986).[9] In addition, during the time period from 10 to 11 a.m. the market is depressed on average except on Saturdays. Since the market on average rises during the last trading period, the high Saturday return during the period from 10 to 11 a.m. is consistent.

D. *Saturday Effect?*

To further investigate systematic weekday differences, we examine how infrequent Saturday trading is related to the returns of the other days of the week.[10] The weekly pattern may be related to Saturday trading. The weekend effect of high Friday and low Monday returns found in the U.S. may be observed in Japan when the week is closed by Friday trading. This conjecture is tested by dividing the data into the following four groups: Group A contains the weeks closed by Saturday trading. Group B contains the

[9] Although Harris uses intraday returns at 15-minute intervals, this study employs an hourly return.
[10] Most of the previous research regarding the Japanese market overlook this infrequent Saturday trading.

weeks closed by Friday trading. Then Group A is divided into two subgroups A1 and A2. A1 includes the weeks whose previous week is closed by Saturday trading. A2 contains the weeks whose previous week is closed by Friday trading. In the same manner, Group B is divided into two groups, B1 (previous week is closed by Saturday trading) and B2 (previous week is closed by Friday trading). The same regression analysis presented in equation (1) is conducted for each group. The results are presented in Table 3.

The most interesting feature of the results in Table 3 is that large negative returns are observed on Monday in the weeks whose previous week is closed by Friday (A2 and B2).[11] Conversely, the Tuesday effect almost disappears in the weeks closed by Friday trading. This finding indicates that negative Monday and Tuesday returns in Japan are closely related to Saturday trading.

Infrequent Saturday trading also provides an opportunity to test the settlement effect hypothesis. Jaffe and Westerfield (1985a) misspecified the settlement process in Japan. Since October 7, 1972, no cash settlement has occurred on Saturday even when the market is open. The delivery of securities and receipt of payment takes place on the third business day after the day of transaction. According to the settlement effect hypothesis, Thursday returns in the week closed by Friday trading should be higher than Thursday

TABLE 3

Mean Return of the Tokyo Stock Exchange Index for Each Day of the Week by Four Groups Classified by Saturday Trading

Tokyo Stock Exchange Index (Value Weighted) April 4, 1978–June 18, 1987

Group	Monday	Tuesday	Wednesday	Thursday	Friday	Saturday	F(day)[b]	N
A1	0.0198	−0.1072	0.1790	0.0581	0.0605	0.1678	8.67**	1406
(S–S)[a]	(0.50)[c]	(−2.76)	(4.59)	(1.49)	(1.55)	(4.30)		
A2	−0.1008	−0.1102	0.1074	0.0306	0.1582	0.0793	2.53*	649
(NS–S)	(−1.50)	(−1.66)	(1.63)	(0.46)	(2.42)	(1.20)		
B1	0.1135	−0.0649	0.0980	0.0933	0.1341		4.05**	539
(S–NS)	(2.15)	(−1.27)	(1.92)	(1.84)	(2.63)			
B2	−0.3489	0.1931	0.2479	0.2609	0.2193		0.46	58
(NS–NS)	(−0.90)	(0.52)	(0.67)	(0.67)	(0.59)			
F(group)	2.36	2.93*	6.74**	1.38	3.58**	16.93**		
N	449	464	464	465	467	343		

[a] (S–S) means Saturday trading in previous week as well as this week. (NS–S) means no Saturday trading in previous week and Saturday trading in this week. (S–NS) means Saturday trading in previous week and no Saturday trading in this week. (NS–NS) means no Saturday trading in previous week as well as this week.

[b] The F(day) statistic tests the equality of mean return difference across days of the week. The F(group) statistic tests the equality of mean return difference across four groups for a particular day of the week.

[c] t-statistics are shown in parentheses.

* Significant at the five percent level.

** Significant at the one percent level.

[11] This finding is different from the U.S. finding by Keim and Stambaugh (1984). Monday effect was observed for both Saturday trading and non-Saturday trading periods.

TABLE 4

Correlation Coefficients Between the Dow Jones Industrial Average of the New York Stock Exchange ($t = -1$ and 0) and the Nikkei Stock Average of the Tokyo Stock Exchange ($t = 0$) During the Period, 1980 Through 1987

			Tokyo ($t = 0$)		
			Close-to-Open	Open-to-Close	Close-to-Close
New York					
($t = -1$)	close-to-open	r	0.3306	0.2817	0.3721
		p-value	(0.0001)	(0.0001)	(0.0001)
	open-to-close	r	0.3823	0.1091	0.2453
		p-value	(0.0001)	(0.0006)	(0.0001)
	close-to-close	r	0.5363	0.2551	0.4313
		p-value	(0.0001)	(0.0001)	(0.0001)
($t = 0$)	close-to-open	r	0.1556	0.0565	0.1096
		p-value	(0.0001)	(0.0138)	(0.0001)
	open-to-close	r	−0.0057	0.0591	0.0484
		p-value	(0.8031)	(0.0099)	(0.0348)
	close-to-close	r	0.0887	0.0929	0.1145
		p-value	(0.0001)	(0.0001)	(0.0001)

returns in the week closed by Saturday trading.[12] The results presented in Table 3 regarding Thursday are consistent with this hypothesis.[13] In addition, as Ikeda (1988) noted, high Wednesday returns are also consistent with this hypothesis. However, low Monday and Tuesday returns as well as high Saturday returns are not consistent with this hypothesis.

E. *New York Effect?*

Low Tuesday returns may be related to the Monday effect in the U.S. Since Tokyo is 14 hours ahead of New York, the Japanese weekly pattern may be analogous to the American pattern led by one day. To examine this hypothesis, correlation coefficients are computed between the Dow in the New York Stock Exchange and the Nikkei Stock Average in the Tokyo Stock Exchange during the period 1980 through 1987. The results appear in Table 4. High correlation is observed between previous day returns ($t = -1$) of the New York Dow and the day close-to-open returns ($t = 0$) of the Nikkei Stock Average. This finding is consistent with the hypothesis that the opening price of the Tokyo market is strongly related to the previous day's New York market. Lower correlation coefficients between previous day returns ($t = -1$) of the New York Dow and the day open-to-close returns ($t = 0$) of the Nikkei Stock Average may indicate that the stock price reflects information quickly.[14,15]

[12] The settlement procedure is presented in more detail in the Appendix.

[13] Statistical tests are also performed. Mean Thursday return of group B is statistically significantly greater than that of group A.

[14] We also divide the entire period into four subperiods. The particular time series pattern is not observed for correlation coefficients between the returns of the Nikkei Stock Average and the previous day returns of the New York Dow.

[15] Contemporaneous dependence between the New York Dow and the Nikkei Stock Average is also reported. Although most correlation coefficients are significant between returns ($t = 0$) of the New York and returns ($t = 0$) of the Tokyo, the magnitude is much smaller. This result may indicate that the New York market is still the seismic center of information.

The result described above is tested more formally in the same manner as Jaffe and Westerfield (1985b). To investigate whether the weekly pattern in Japan differs from the U.S. pattern, infrequent Saturday trading should be considered. We divide the data into two groups. The first data set consists of the weeks whose previous week has Saturday trading.[16] The second data set contains the remaining weeks.[17] The following regression is conducted for both groups:

$$R_{JAP,t} - R_{US,t-1} = \sum_{k=1}^{6} a_k D_{kt} + u_t, \quad (2)$$

where $R_{JAP,t}$ is the close-to-close return of the Nikkei Stock Average on the Tokyo market and $R_{US,t-1}$ is the previous days' close-to-close return of the New York Dow. D_{kt} is a dummy variable as defined in equation (1).

The results are striking. The F statistic of the first data set is 0.32 which is not significant at the 10 percent level.[18] However, the F statistic of the second data set is 3.48 which is significant at the 1 percent level. The significant F statistic for the second data set is mainly caused by the low Monday return of the Nikkei Stock Average relative to high Friday return of the New York Dow.[19]

Considering the possibilities of release of new information in Japan during the weekend, the match of the Monday return of the Nikkei Stock Average and the Friday return of the New York Dow may not be appropriate.[20] In the first data set, the Monday return of the Nikkei Stock Average is automatically excluded because of no matched day. Thus, when we exclude the Monday returns from the Japanese stock returns, we are not able to reject the hypothesis that the weekly pattern of two markets are the same. This finding is consistent with our conjecture that the Japanese Tuesday effect is really a reflection of the Monday effect in the U.S.[21] In addition, the Monday effect seems to exist in the Japanese daily stock returns.

2. Analysis of Individual Stocks

A. *Data and Portfolio Formation*

The data are the daily stock returns of all common stocks listed on the First Section

[16] In this data set, the Tuesday return of the Nikkei Dow corresponds to the Monday return of the New York Dow, the Wednesday return of the Nikkei Stock Average to the Tuesday return of the New York Dow, the Thursday return of the Nikkei Stock Average to the Wednesday return of the New York Dow, the Friday return of the Nikkei Stock Average to the Thursday return of the New York Dow and the Saturday return of the Nikkei Stock Average to the Friday return of the New York Dow. The Monday return of the Nikkei Stock Average is excluded.

[17] In this data set, the Monday return of the Nikkei Stock Average corresponds to the Friday return of the New York Dow in the previous week. The Tuesday of the Nikkei corresponds to the Monday of the New York Dow, the Wednesday of the Nikkei to the Tuesday of the New York, the Thursday of the Nikkei to the Wednesday of the New York and the Friday of the Nikkei to the Thursday of the New York. No day is excluded.

[18] We also ran the regression using the close-to-open returns on the Japanese index and the open-to-close returns on the U.S. index. The results are not substantially changed.

[19] In order to confirm our conclusion, we drop Friday returns of New York and Monday returns of Tokyo from the second data set and conduct the same regression. An insignificant F statistic is obtained.

[20] Saturday was still not a holiday for a relatively large number of Japanese corporations during this sample period.

[21] The results in this section are somewhat different from those of Jaffe and Westerfield (1985b) as the time period chosen in this study is more current.

of the Tokyo Stock Exchange for the 14-year period from 1974 through 1987.[22] The number of sample firms ranges from 806 in 1974 to 1069 in 1987.

In the previous section, intraday returns are examined using the TOPIX of the Tokyo Stock Exchange. Since the nontrading period exhibits a different pattern from the trading period, the daily returns in this section are also decomposed into two periods, nontrading and trading. Then, the analysis is performed for three different time periods, close-to-close, close-to-open and open-to-close.[23]

Kato and Schallheim (1985) document the January-size effects in the Japanese stock market. The weekly pattern in Japan may be related to the January-size effects. In order to investigate the relationship between firm size and the weekly pattern, five size related portfolios are constructed based upon the year end market value of equity. Each year end, all stocks are ranked based upon their market value. Then all stocks are equally divided into five groups. Portfolio 1 contains the smallest firms and Portfolio 5 contains the largest firms. This ranking and portfolio formation procedure is repeated each year. Summary statistics for the five portfolios are presented in Table 5.

B. *January-Size Effect*

The regression analysis in equation (1) is conducted to examine whether the weekly pattern exists for five size related portfolios. The results are presented in Table 6. Panels A, B and C exhibit the results of close-to-close, close-to-open and open-to-close returns respectively. Several interesting results emerge from Table 6.[24]

All F statistics are significant. A size effect is observed for both close-to-close and close-to-open returns. However, a reversal size effect is observed for open-to-close returns. The F(size) statistics indicate that both the size and reversal size effects are significant, although the magnitude of the size effect is much larger. The returns on the nontrading period are all positive except for the Tuesday returns of the largest portfolio. On the other hand, the returns on the trading period are mostly negative except for Wednesday and Saturday. Monday's close-to-open return is the highest for the smallest portfolio.[25] Low Monday close-to-close returns mainly emerge from the trading period. Finally, the F(day) statistics indicate that the day of the week effect for close-to-open returns is stronger for smaller firms in the portfolio. The same pattern is not observed for open-to-close returns.

Since the size effect is concentrated in January, we examine the results described above

[22] The Yamaichi Research Institute generously provides the daily stock return file containing all common stocks listed on the First Section of the Tokyo Stock Exchange. This data file consists of close-to-close returns, close-to-open returns and open-to-close returns.

[23] If trade has not occurred, the closing price is the same as opening price. Small firm stocks are likely to be candidates. As a result, we observe multi-day return after no trade and zero return for the day of no transaction. In order to avoid this infrequent trading bias, we assign the missing values for the following day of no transaction as well as the days of no transaction. To be complete, we also perform the same analysis using the data without this alteration. Since similar weekly pattern is observed for both data sets, we only report the result of missing value adjustment.

[24] The data are decomposed into three subperiods, 1974 through 1977, 1978 through 1981, and 1982 through 1987. Then the same analysis is performed. The same pattern exists for all three subperiods. However, the weekly pattern of close-to-close returns is more severe during the most recent period.

[25] The effect of infrequent Saturday trading is also examined using five size related portfolios. The similar pattern exists for all five size related portfolios.

TABLE 5

Mean Returns for Size Related Portfolios

Firm Size	Market Value[a] (¥ Millions)	Mean Return Close-to-Close	Close-to-Open	Open-to-Close
Smallest	773	0.1492	0.1784	−0.0295
2	1,716	0.1058	0.1545	−0.0489
3	3,275	0.0859	0.1354	−0.0495
4	6,554	0.0764	0.0976	−0.0213
Largest	32,689	0.0653	0.0483	0.0168

[a] Market value for a portfolio is measured by the average, across all years, of the mean market values of that size related portfolio in each year.

TABLE 6

Mean Portfolio Close-to-Close, Close-to-Open and Open-to-Close Returns by Week and Firm Size During the Period January 4, 1974 *Through June* 18, 1987

Panel A: Close-to-Close Returns

Firm Size	Monday	Tuesday	Wednesday	Thursday	Friday	Saturday	F(day)
All firms	0.0544	−0.0406	0.2188	0.0604	0.1119	0.1489	30.67**
	(2.48)	(−1.89)	(10.19)	(2.81)	(5.22)	(5.94)	
Smallest	0.1249	0.0240	0.2803	0.1157	0.1583	0.2059	51.73**
	(5.33)	(1.04)	(12.20)	(5.03)	(6.90)	(7.68)	
2	0.0855	−0.0277	0.2325	0.0574	0.1348	0.1674	34.15**
	(3.72)	(−1.23)	(10.32)	(2.55)	(5.99)	(6.37)	
3	0.0519	−0.0472	0.2114	0.0287	0.1297	0.1590	27.80**
	(2.25)	(−2.08)	(9.32)	(1.26)	(5.73)	(6.01)	
4	0.0500	−0.0491	0.1899	0.0321	0.1067	0.1459	24.10**
	(2.25)	(−2.25)	(8.70)	(1.47)	(4.89)	(5.73)	
Largest	0.0340	−0.0672	0.1591	0.0357	0.1053	0.1447	17.41**
	(1.41)	(−2.84)	(6.71)	(1.50)	(4.45)	(5.23)	
F(size)	10.20**	4.00**	83.32**	7.20**	31.23**	61.86**	
N	3,225	3,350	3,350	3,340	3,360	2,460	

Panel B: Close-to-Open Returns

Firm Size	Monday	Tuesday	Wednesday	Thursday	Friday	Saturday	F(day)
All firms	0.1776	0.0483	0.1176	0.1510	0.1252	0.0534	116.95**
	(15.64)	(4.34)	(10.35)	(13.54)	(11.26)	(4.11)	
Smallest	0.2616	0.1030	0.1844	0.2084	0.1673	0.1381	191.77**
	(19.68)	(7.89)	(14.13)	(15.95)	(12.84)	(9.07)	
2	0.2324	0.0805	0.1537	0.1942	0.1577	0.0961	174.54**
	(18.96)	(6.69)	(12.78)	(16.13)	(13.13)	(6.85)	
3	0.2039	0.0679	0.1325	0.1639	0.1509	0.0813	144.77**
	(17.26)	(5.86)	(11.43)	(14.12)	(13.04)	(6.01)	
4	0.1661	0.0393	0.0952	0.1207	0.1106	0.0409	87.02**
	(14.58)	(3.51)	(8.52)	(10.79)	(9.91)	(3.14)	
Largest	0.0959	−0.0113	0.0425	0.0793	0.0707	0.0022	23.25**
	(7.48)	(−0.90)	(3.38)	(6.30)	(5.62)	(0.15)	
F(size)	234.77**	33.92**	127.10**	197.06**	102.22**	43.91**	
N	3,225	3,350	3,350	3,340	3,360	2,460	

** Significant at the one percent level.

separately for January from the rest of the year.[26] The returns are on average larger and exhibit a stronger relationship to firm size in January than in the other months for each day of the week. The weekly pattern is stronger in non-January months. As the size decreases, the weekly pattern tends to be larger. These results are consistent with the U.S. findings. The size effect is observed for close-to-open returns of both January and non-January months. The reversal size effect during the trading period does not occur in January. One noticeable observation is that negative Tuesday returns mainly occur in non-January months.[27]

3. Summary and Conclusion

The weekly pattern of Japanese stock returns is examined. Low Tuesday and high Wednesday returns are observed for the close-to-close returns. This finding is similar to the findings of the previous studies. Intraday returns are also used to examine this anomalous effect. Most of the positive returns arise during the nontrading period. Both Mondays and Tuesdays experience negative returns during the trading period, especially the last trading period in the morning. Positive returns are observed for the last trading period of the day.

Saturday trading also affects the weekly pattern. The Monday effect is observed when the previous week concludes with Friday trading. The Tuesday effect in Japan is related to the Monday effect in the U.S. The weekly pattern is related to the size effect. The weekly pattern decreases as the size of the firm increases concerning close-to-close returns. A reversal size effect is observed during the trading period which is inconsistent with our common sense, that small firms' stocks are, on average, riskier than large firms' stocks and as a result, experience higher mean returns. The relationship between the January effect and the weekly pattern is also investigated. The weekly pattern is more severe in non-January months, which is similar to the U.S. findings.

An interesting weekly pattern is observed in Japanese stock returns. No conclusive explanation is presented in this paper. Even if we accept the settlement effect hypothesis, we still must investigate why low Monday returns in Japan as well as in the U.S. occur. In addition, we must provide an explanation of why Saturday trading affects the weekly patterns. These questions are open for future research.[28]

[26] The same analysis is conducted for three subperiods. The results are essentially the same. One noticeable observation in this analysis is that the weekly pattern of close-to-open returns is stronger for non-January months as the time progresses. This is especially true for the smallest portfolio. The same pattern does not exist for open-to-close returns. The effect of infrequent Saturday trading is also examined for both January and non-January months. A similar pattern is observed.

[27] Keim (1987) reports that negative Monday returns are observed in the U.S. in non-January months. Negative Tuesday returns in non-January months is consistent with New York effect hypothesis.

[28] Some preliminary findings appear in Komatsu and Ziemba (1989).

This paper was presented at the American Finance Association Meeting in New York in December of 1988. I would like to thank Yoshio Iihara, Jim Schallheim, Rene Stulz and Bill Ziemba who read and commented on earlier version of the paper. I also acknowledge research assistance by Kyoko Ito and Sadae Muramatsu. Excellent computer programming by Hiroshi Mouri at the SAS Software is also appreciated. This research is supported by the Yamaichi Research Institute, the Institute for Statistical Research and the Japan–U.S. Friendship Commission. All remaining errors are mine.

Appendix. Settlement Procedure for Each Day of the Week of the Tokyo Stock Exchange

In order to earn Tuesday's return, for example, an investor must purchase stocks at the closing price of Monday and sell them at the closing price of Tuesday. The same principle applies to the returns of the remaining

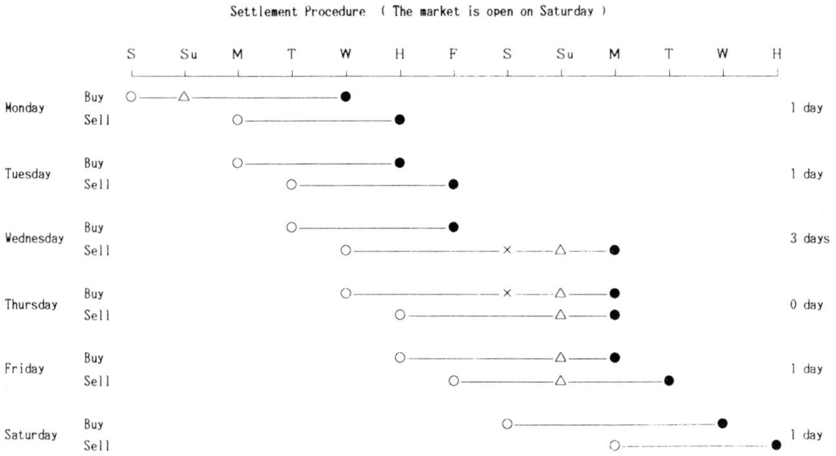

APPENDIX. Settlement procedure for each day of the week of the Tokyo Stock Exchange. This diagram is adapted from Ikeda (1988).

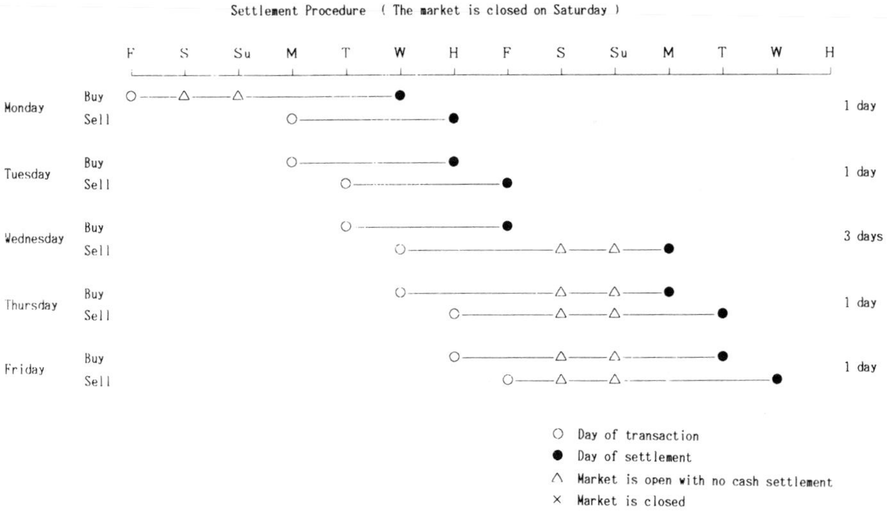

days of the week. However, cash settlement occurs after three business days. The following table describes this procedure for each day of the week for the week with Saturday trading and without Saturday trading.

When the market is open on Saturday, an investor who purchases stocks on Wednesday and sells them on Thursday can make a cash settlement on the same day, the following Monday. However, if the market is closed on Saturday, an investor must pay money on the following Monday and receive money on the following Tuesday.

References

ARIEL, R., "Monthly Effect in Stock Returns," *J. Financial Economics*, 18 (March 1987), 164–174.

BLUME, M. AND R. STAMBAUGH, "Biases in Computed Returns: An Application to the Size Effect," *J. Financial Economics*, 12 (June 1983), 387–404.

CONNOLLY, R., "An Examination of the Robustness of the Weekend Effect," *J. Financial Quantitative Anal.*, 24 (June 1989).

CORNELL, B., "The Weekly Pattern in Stock Returns: Cash versus Futures: A Note," *J. Finance*, 40 (June 1985), 583–588.

CROSS, F., "The Behavior of Stock Prices on Fridays and Mondays," *Financial Analysts J.*, 27 (November–December 1973), 67–69.

DYL, E. AND S. MARTIN, "Weekend Effects on Stock Returns: A Comment," *J. Finance*, 40 (March 1985), 347-349.

FRENCH, K., "Stock Returns and the Weekend Effect," *J. Financial Economics*, 8 (March 1980), 55–69.

GIBBONS, M. AND P. HESS, "Day of the Week Effects and Asset Returns," *J. Business*, 54 (October 1981), 579–596.

HAMAO, Y., R. MASULIS AND V. NG, "Correlations in Price Changes and Volatility across International Stock Markets," Unpublished manuscript, 1989.

HARRIS, L., "A Transaction Data Study of Weekly and Intradaily Patterns in Stock Returns," *J. Financial Economics*, 16 (March 1986), 99–117.

IKEDA, M., "Day of the Week Effect and Mixture of Normal Distribution Hypothesis," *Japan Financial Rev.*, 18 (1988), 27–54.

JAFFE, J. AND R. WESTERFIELD, "The Weekend Effect in Common Stock Returns: The International Evidence," *J. Finance*, 40 (June 1985a), 433–454.

——— AND ———, "Patterns in Japanese Common Stock Returns: Day of the Week and Turn of the Year Effects," *J. Financial Quantitative Anal.*, 20 (June 1985b), 261–272.

KATO, K., "Being a Winner in the Tokyo Stock Market: The Case for an Anomaly Fund," *J. Portfolio Management*, forthcoming.

——— AND J. SCHALLHEIM, "Seasonal and Size Anomalies in the Japanese Stock Market," *J. Financial Quantitative Anal.*, 22 (June 1985), 243–260.

KATO, K., S. SCHWARTZ AND W. ZIEMBA, "Day of the Week Effects in Japanese Stocks," To appear in *Japanese Capital Markets*, E. Elton and M. Gruber (Eds.), Ballinger, Boston, 1989.

KEIM, D. B., "Size-Related Anomalies and Stock Return Seasonality: Further Empirical Evidence," *J. Financial Economics*, 12 (June 1983), 13–32.

———, "Daily Returns and Size-Related Premiums: One More Time," *J. Portfolio Management*, (Winter 1987), 41–47.

——— AND R. STAMBAUGH, "A Further Investigation of the Weekend Effect in Stock Returns," *J. Finance*, 39 (July 1984), 819–835.

KOMATSU, A. AND W. ZIEMBA, "Some Tests of Plausible Causes for Anomalous Behavior in Japanese Security Markets," unpublished manuscript, Yamaichi Research Institute, 1989.

LAKONISHOCK, J. AND M. LEVI, "Weekend Effects on Stock Returns: A Note," *J. Finance*, 37 (June 1982), 883–889.

——— AND ———, "Weekend Effects on Stock Returns: A Reply," *J. Finance*, 40 (March 1985), 351–352.

PETTWAY, R. AND T. TAPLEY, "The Tokyo Stock Exchange: An Analysis of Stock Market Prices," *Keio Business Rev.*, (1984), 75–93.

ROGALSKI, R., "New Findings Regarding Day-of-the-Week Returns over Trading and Non-Trading Periods: A Note," *J. Finance*, 39 (December 1984), 1603–1614.

SMIRLOCK, M. AND L. STARKS, "Day-of-the-Week and Intraday Effects in Stock Returns," *J. Financial Economics*, 17 (June 1986), 197–210.

PART III:
EXCHANGE RATES AND HEDGING

Japanese Financial Market Research
W.T. Ziemba, W. Bailey and Y. Hamao (Editors)

A history of yen exchange rates

James R. Lothian[a]

Abstract

The history of Japanese exchange rates, though short by British or American standards, is exceedingly rich, both from the standpoint of variation in the data and in the institutions governing exchange rate arrangements and Japanese monetary conditions. This paper reviews that history and traces the evolution of yen-dollar and yen-sterling exchange rates from 1874 until the present, comparing their behavior to that of the dollar-sterling rate. It shows the relationships of all three nominal exchange rates to indexes of purchasing power parity, and it investigates the links among exchange-rate regimes, exchange rates themselves and other macroeconomic variables. Two conclusions emerge: (1) Purchasing power parity – at least in relative form – held remarkably well for the yen over the longer run. (2) The variability of real yen exchange rates under the current float does not, in fact, differ greatly from the often substantial and largely self-reversing movements observed historically.

1. INTRODUCTION

The history of Japanese exchange rates, though short by British or American standards, is exceedingly rich, both from the standpoint of variation in the data and in the institutions governing exchange rate arrangements and Japanese monetary conditions. In the approximate century and a quarter that followed the Meiji restoration of 1867, Japan experienced three episodes of floating exchange rates, two episodes – one very brief – on the gold standard, a period of heavily managed floating rates during the interwar years, the dollar peg of the Bretton Woods era, and the exceptionally severe inflation and accompanying substantial yen depreciation of the World War II years.

In this paper I review that history. I trace the evolution of yen-dollar and yen-sterling exchange rates from 1874 until the present and compare the behavior of both to that of the dollar-sterling rate. I go on to analyze the relationship of all three to indexes of purchasing power parity and to

---

[a]Fordham University, Graduate School of Business Administration, New York, NY, 10023, USA. I would like to thank Cornelia McCarthy for comments on and assistance in the preparation of this paper, and Kyung-Won Lee and Dario Werthein for their computational help. Most important is the debt that I owe to the late John Metcalf who stimulated my interest in Japanese monetary issues and directed me to what had then been a largely unexploited body of data. This paper extends and in several places draws upon my earlier paper "A Century Plus of Yen Exchange Rate Behavior," written under the sponsorship of the Japan-U.S. Center for Business and Economic Studies of New York University and published in Japan and the World Economy.

examine the links among exchange-rate regimes and the behavior of exchange rates themselves and of other important macroeconomic variables.

2. HISTORICAL DESCRIPTION OF EXCHANGE-RATE BEHAVIOR

Following the Meiji restoration, Japanese trade with the rest of the world increased dramatically. From a base of essentially nil at the time of Admiral Perry's first visit in 1853, exports rose to approximately 15% of GDP shortly after the turn of the century and to over 20% of GDP by the 1920s.[1]

For most of the nineteenth century, however, Japan was not on the gold standard. From 1867 to 1878, the Japanese monetary system was effectively a system of fiat currency and floating exchange rates. From 1878 until 1897, when Japan did finally adopt gold, Japan both *de jure* and *de facto* was on a silver standard. The result was a continuation of floating rates relative to the gold standard world.[2]

This flexibility in exchange rates enabled Japan to avoid the deflation that prevailed in Britain, America, and other countries on gold during these years. We can see this in Table 1.[3] Over the subperiod 1874 to 1887 Japanese wholesale prices showed virtually no net change, earlier inflation being offset by later deflation. Over the later subperiod 1888 to 1896, they actually rose by 35%. In the United States, wholesale prices declined by slightly over 40% between 1874 and 1887 and by another 21% between 1888 and 1896. In Britain, the deflation followed a largely similar pattern, cumulative declines in wholesale prices of 41% and 11% in the two subperiods, respectively.

In the foreign exchange market, the yen depreciated relative to both the dollar and sterling. For the full period 1874 to 1896, the increase in the yen-dollar rate averaged 3.15% per year and the increase in the yen-sterling rate, 3.03% per year. In both instances, the declines were more or less in line with the cross-country differences in inflation rates, but in neither case was the offset exact. In real terms, the yen appreciated somewhat against both currencies, while the dollar fell slightly against sterling. We can see this in the figures presented in the last three columns of Table 1 showing the average annual percentage changes in real exchange rates and in the plot of the real yen-dollar and real pound-dollar rates shown in Figure 1.[4]

Purchasing power parity, therefore, held tolerably well as a first approximation. But for Japan in particular it was only that. One possibility for the slack in the relationship between changes in nominal exchange rates and the differential in inflation rates is measurement error in the Japanese price data, an overstatement of the levels of wholesale prices in the later relative to the later years of the period. An alternative is a shift in the equilibrium real exchange rate, resulting perhaps from increased productivity in the Japanese tradeable goods sector.[5]

In addition to these trend-like movements, both yen real rates exhibited fairly sizable year-to-year variability, well in excess of the variability of dollar-sterling, particularly in the subperiod from 1888 to 1896. This variability, however, had no obviously adverse effects on other real variables, either real trade flows or real output. Exports and imports increased substantially as already noted. Rates of growth of Japanese real income and industrial production were comparable to or higher than the rates in Britain and America. Between 1885 and 1900, real income in Japan

Fig 1: Indexes of Real Exchange Rate

(1980 = 100)

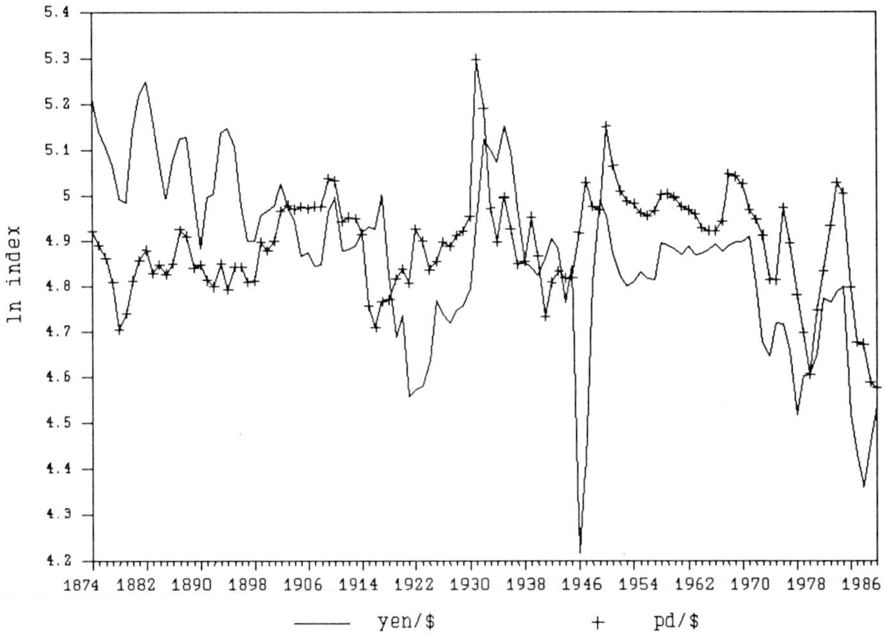

Note: 1990 estimated from partial data

increased at an average annual rate of 3.1% versus 2.35% in the United Kingdom and 2.79 in the United States. Over the longer period 1874-1896, industrial production increased by 4.75% per year in Japan versus 1.96% per year and 4.44% per year in the United Kingdom and the United States respectively.[6]

The difference between Japanese and U.S. and U.K. price behavior in this last quarter of the nineteenth century appears to a large extent to mirror international developments rather than domestic monetary policy actions in Japan. Throughout these years, countries were continually shifting from silver to a gold standard. At the same time that this shift in the relative demands for the two precious metals was taking place, discoveries of silver in the United States were increasing its supply. The result, as Irving Fisher (1911) documented, was an upward trend in the price levels of the

Table 1
Rates of change of wholesale prices, nominal exchange rates and real exchange rates in Japan, the United States and the United Kingdom, 1875-1989

	Wholesale prices			Nominal rates			Real rates		
Period	Japan	U.S.	U.K.	¥/$	¥/£	£/$	¥/$	¥/£	£/$
1875-1896	1.43	-2.77	-2.30	3.15	3.03	0.12	-1.07	-0.71	-0.36
1875-1887	-0.27	-3.10	-3.03	2.16	2.06	0.10	-0.66	-0.69	0.03
1888-1896	3.91	-2.30	-1.24	4.56	4.41	0.15	-1.65	-0.74	-0.91
1897-1914	2.67	2.15	1.58	0.17	0.34	-0.17	-0.34	-0.74	0.40
1915-1940	3.76	0.54	1.96	2.86	1.62	1.24	-0.36	-0.17	-0.19
1915-1921	10.58	5.10	9.90	0.35	-2.91	3.26	-5.13	-3.59	-1.55
1922-1928	-5.21	-5.81	-9.77	0.51	3.72	-3.21	2.69	1.20	1.49
1929-1940	3.29	-1.76	1.27	5.69	3.03	2.66	0.64	1.01	-0.37
1941-1953	40.24	5.92	6.74	34.13	32.37	1.76	-0.18	-1.13	0.94
1954-1973	1.37	2.16	3.24	-1.42	-2.11	0.69	-0.62	-0.24	-0.38
1974-1989	2.85	5.71	9.74	-4.24	-6.23	1.99	-1.37	0.67	-2.04

Source: See endnote 3.
Note: Figures are continuously compounded per cent per annum rates of change.

countries that remained on silver and a downward trend in the price levels of countries on gold.

When Japan did make the switch to gold in 1897, price movements in the gold-standard world had begun to reverse. Gold discoveries, coupled with the introduction of improved methods of refining, led to a more than doubling of the world's gold stock from 1890 to 1914. (Friedman and Schwartz, 1963, p. 137). This in turn increased growth in money supplies and thus caused prices to rise. In Japan, the inflation exceeded that of the rest of the world. Given the fixed nominal exchange rate, the yen therefore depreciated against both the dollar and sterling in real terms. Government borrowing abroad and the drawing down of the gold balances received as an indemnity payment following the war with China in 1893 and 1894 are the likely reasons for this disparity in price behavior.[7] These enabled Japan to insulate itself from the operation of international gold-standard forces and thus to pursue inflationary policies domestically.

In 1914, with the outbreak of war in Europe, the worldwide gold standard broke down, most countries blocking its workings by placing embargoes on gold exports, some leaving gold completely. Japan took the former route until 1917, at which point it left gold officially. Unlike Britain and America, Japan remained off the gold standard throughout the 1920s, not returning until the beginning of 1930, and then only to leave a scant two years later.

The twenties were not, however, years of completely free floating yen exchange rates. An initial attempt to peg the yen against the dollar (1919 to 1920) was followed by controlled depreciation and then two planned, but aborted, moves to return to gold. The first attempt failed in the wake of the Great Kanto Earthquake of 1923 and the large trade deficits that resulted. The second, after a year of preliminary stabilization of the yen, was abandoned following the financial panic of March 1927 (Takagi, 1989). The years 1932 to 1934 were marked by a more or less free yen float, but the five years that followed by a peg of the yen to sterling.

What stands out during the 1915-1940 period is the volatility of real exchange rates. Judged in terms of both the subperiod-average rates of change shown in Table 1 and the yearly standard deviations shown below in Table 2, it was at record highs, far greater than under the gold standard and, in the main, even greater than under the post-Bretton Woods float. The only sense in which this is not the case is for the period viewed as a whole. The average annual rates of change of all three real rates over the years 1915 to 1940 were in fact less than the respective averages for the years prior to 1914. In each instance, protracted movements of the real exchange rate in one direction during WWI and the years immediately thereafter were very nearly offset by subsequent protracted movements in the opposite direction. Over the longest period, therefore, purchasing power parity again appears to have held, despite substantial departures for long periods in between.

With World War II came the disruption of international transactions, breaks in the official yen exchange-rate data and substantial increases in price levels around the world. In Japan, the inflation was severe. Between 1940 and 1949 Japanese wholesale prices increased by a multiple of 127, or at a continuously compounded average annual rate of increase of 53.8%. Relative to American and British wholesale prices, this translated into (continuously compounded) cumulative increases in excess of 400%.

In 1948, when official data for yen exchange rates become available, its value relative to the dollar had fallen from the 4.35 yen per dollar rate in place in 1940 to 160 yen per dollar. By 1950, in the face of continued strong inflation, it reached 361 yen per dollar, roughly the rate maintained for the remainder of the Bretton Woods era.

Then in 1971, in the face of monetary excesses in the United States, the reserve-currency country, the Bretton Woods system broke down and the current float began. Since then the yen has shown a trend-like nominal appreciation against the dollar and sterling, a similar real appreciation against the dollar, though somewhat surprisingly, not sterling, and a series of alternating sharp shorter term real appreciations and depreciations against both currencies.

The monetary part of the picture during the early years of the float can be divided into three episodes, all of which show evidence of links to U.S. policy. In the mid 1970s, Japan in part as a spillover from policy in the United States, experienced both high money growth and inflation (Darby and Lothian, 1983b). In its aftermath, however, Japanese policy became considerably tighter than policy in the United States and remained so longer. Despite renewed expansionary effects emanating from the United States via the balance of payments, Japan therefore escaped the double-digit inflation that plagued America and Britain at the start of the last decade.[8] In the latter part of the 1980s, Japan appears to have again been led into expansive policy as the Bank of Japan, along with the U.S. Federal Reserve, sought to halt the depreciation of the dollar.

Of particular interest in these episodes is the pattern of volatility of real exchange rates and of inflation. Over time, fluctuations in inflation have become more muted in Japan while fluctuations in the real yen- dollar rate have remained substantial. This, coupled with the longer term downward trend in the yen-dollar real exchange rate have been a source of increased skepticism about both purchasing power parity as an equilibrium condition and the functioning of the floating rate system.

3. PPP, REAL EXCHANGE RATES AND EXCHANGE-RATE REGIMES

The historical overview highlights several sets of important issues. One has to do with the purchasing power parity relationship. The other centers around the links between exchange-rate regimes, exchange-rate variability and the behavior of other macroeconomic variables. The specific question that arises with regard to PPP is whether the tendency for nominal exchange rates to move in line with relative price levels that is apparent in the longer term comparisons presented in Table 1 is a behavioral phenomenon or simply a statistical quirk, the spurious correlation that can arise between two trended series.

The theoretical rationale for PPP and modified PPP relationships is as a macroeconomic equilibrium condition. In the simplest theoretical models, which ignore the effects of real variables like productivity and differences in relative prices of traded and non-traded goods, absolute PPP holds. It is the open-economy analogue of the classical closed-economy neutrality proposition as in in the monetary-approach models of the type developed in Frenkel and Johnson (1976). Expressed in log form, the absolute PPP relationship is

$$p_t - e_t = p_t^* \, , \tag{1}$$

where p, and p^* represent the logarithms of the price levels in the home country and the foreign country respectively, e represents the logarithm of the nominal exchange rate (the price in the home country's currency of a unit of the foreign country's currency), and t is an index of time.

There is now abundant empirical evidence suggesting that to the extent that purchasing power parity holds, it does so only over longer time periods, and that even then there may be disturbances to the relationship that are highly persistent in their effects. Two general classes of models have evolved to explain this phenomenon. In one, which is an extension of the monetary-approach model, such deviations are purely transient, the result of sluggish adjustment of prices to monetary shocks. (See, e.g., Dornbusch, 1976). In the other, which assumes instantaneous adjustment of goods prices and thus the price level, deviations from PPP can be permanent, the result of real shocks that affect the equilibrium real exchange rate (See Stockman, 1980). Models of this class preserve the long-run neutrality (or super-neutrality) of money but see absolute PPP as a highly special case that would only exist in the limit, in situations in which real influences were of no practical significance. Relative PPP does, however, potentially fare better in these models. Real shocks have one-time effects on levels. As the time period lengthens, the effect on rates of change therefore progressively diminishes.

Extending the concept of neutrality in another direction, Stockman (1983) demonstrated that within the context of an equilibrium model similar to the one developed in his earlier (1980) paper, and as intuition might suggest, the (nominal) exchange-rate regime should have no effect on the equilibrium behavior of real variables, including that of the real exchange rate.

Like continuous PPP, this insight does not appear to carry over to the actual data. Real exchange rates, as Stockman went on to show and as evidence in Mussa (1986) confirms, have been more variable under floating rates than fixed rates during the post-WWII period. The behavior of other real variables, however, appears to be invariant across the two regimes (Baxter and Stockman, 1989; Baxter, 1991).

The major difficulty that arises in interpreting these results is that the regime is essentially an endogenous variable. The choice of regime very likely is influenced by factors that, in turn, affect monetary and price-level behavior, and also by the behavior of real variables, including the real exchange rate itself.[9] How real exchange rates behave under different regimes, as well as the choice of the regime, may be two aspects of the same general question.

Below I examine these issues, the time-series behavior of PPP and the relationships between exchange-rate regimes and the variability of real exchange-rates. I begin with the analysis of real-exchange rate variability since it is more heavily descriptive and thus serves as useful introduction to the time-series analysis of PPP that follows.

3.1 REAL-EXCHANGE-RATE VARIABILITY AND EXCHANGE-RATE REGIMES

The data in Table 2 showing standard deviations of the log real exchange rates and their first differences for various subperiods appear fully consistent with the hypothesis of greater variability under floating than fixed exchange rates. Standard deviations for the current floating rate period, for the interwar period and the Japanese nineteenth century float are indeed greater than the standard deviations for the Bretton Woods and gold standard periods in most instances.[10]

This, however, does not appear to be the full story. One hint that more is involved than a simple fixed-floating dichotomy is provided by experience during the Japanese float in the latter decades of the nineteenth century. In this episode there is a marked difference in variability - particularly in the variability of the differenced data - between the subperiods 1875-1887 and 1888-1896. In the first of these subperiods, Japanese real exchange rates were noticeably less variable than in the second and not appreciably more variable than the real pound-dollar rate. Quite interestingly, this first subperiod saw much greater stability of Japanese inflation rates than the second.

A more serious problem is posed by the interwar years. This was a period of managed floats alternating with pegs of various sorts, over various time spans, depending upon the currency. Real exchange rates, however, were even less stable during the interwar years than under the current float. Hence, if there is a behavioral-type relationship between the degree of exchange rate flexibility and the variability of real exchange rates it is certainly not monotonic. Alternatively, it may be that the relationship is largely statistical, economic conditions that give rise to variability in real exchange rates also strongly influencing the choice of regime.

Table 2
Standard deviations of real exchange rates, 1875-1989

Period	Countries					
	Levels of logs			Differences in logs		
	JA/US	JA/UK	UK/US	JA/US	JA/UK	UK/US
1875-1896	8.80	7.71	4.95	8.77	6.95	4.77
1875-1887	8.31	6.29	5.89	7.90	5.26	5.28
1888-1896	8.22	7.74	3.47	10.38	9.24	4.15
1897-1914	5.50	7.93	6.31	5.52	3.82	3.95
1915-1940	17.67	18.03	12.46	9.14	11.88	10.53
1921-1928	8.72	8.83	4.07	8.83	9.62	5.57
1929-1940	14.38	16.69	13.39	9.31	13.07	14.20
1954-1973	5.43	5.03	3.89	4.37	4.45	3.23
1974-1989	13.64	9.12	13.71	10.15	10.00	10.82

Note: Figures are multiplied by 100 to convert to per cent terms.

To investigate these issues further, I computed standard deviations of the changes in the log real exchange rates and of the three countries' inflation rates for five-year periods. I then used these as the observations in a series of dummy-variable regressions. These regressions took the general form:

$$\sigma_{xj} = \gamma_0 + \gamma_1 \text{ DFIX} + \gamma_2 \text{ DIW} + \gamma_3 \text{ DWW} + \epsilon_j , \qquad (2)$$

where σ_x is the standard deviation of variable x, DFIX is a dummy taking the value 1 for fixed-rate periods (the gold-standard years and the years of greatest stability under Bretton Woods) and 0 otherwise, DIW is a dummy taking the value 1 for the interwar period and 0 otherwise, DWW is a dummy taking the value 1 for the two world wars and 0 otherwise, the γs are coefficients to be estimated, ϵ is the error term, and j is an index for the period. Table 3 contains the results of these regressions.

Under the hypothesis that the regime *per se* is the determinant of real-exchange-rate variability, γ_1, γ_2 and γ_3 should all be negative, and γ_2 and γ_3 should each be less in absolute value than γ_1. The data, in general, do not support these predictions.

In all three instances, DFIX has a negative sign, which is consistent with the view that the variability of real exchange rates is low under fixed rates. But only in the case of the pound-dollar rate is the difference statistically significant. For the two yen rates only DWW is significant. Much more important, in all three cases there appears to be little difference statistically between the interwar period and periods of relatively free float: DIW is insignificant and slightly positive in all three instances. Certainly, there is no evidence of lower variability then as would be the case if the degree of variability of real exchange rates were directly related to the degree of flexibility of nominal exchange rates.

Table 3
Regressions to analyze the variability of real exchange rates and inflation rates across regimes

Countries	γ_0	γ_1	γ_2	γ_3	R^2	SEE

$$\sigma_{xj} = \gamma_0 + \gamma_1 \text{ DFIX} + \gamma_2 \text{ DIW} + \gamma_3 \text{ DWW} + \epsilon_j,$$

Countries	γ_0	γ_1	γ_2	γ_3	R^2	SEE
ΔLog real exchange rate						
JA/US	.081	-.042	.002	.086	.294	.068
	(3.517)	(-1.311)	(0.048)	(2.216)		
JA/UK	.086	-.060	.032	.134	.413	.081
	(3.152)	(-1.577)	(0.665)	(2.899)		
UK/US	.087	-.051	.031	.015	.490	.036
	(4.534)	(-2.145)	(0.886)	(.778)		
Inflation rate						
JA	.051	-.018	.062	.182	.386	.098
	(1.554)	(-.395)	(1.056)	(3.256)		
US	.052	-.023	.054	.040	.395	.039
	(3.917)	(1.264)	(2.279)	(1.798)		
UK	.043	-.010	.069	.048	.378	.045
	(1.840)	(-.402)	(2.113)	(1.631)		

Source: Observations are standard deviations of annual data for non-overlapping five-year periods.
Note: σ_x is the standard deviation of the variable x, DFIX is a dummy for fixed-rate periods, DIW is a dummy for the interwar period, DWW is a dummy taking the value 1 for the two world wars and 0 otherwise. Figures in parentheses are t statistics.

The inflation-rate regressions provide a partial clue to what underlies these results. For all three countries, DWW is significantly positive and for Japan especially so. For the United States and the United Kingdom, so also is DIW. DFIX is negative in all three instances but in none is it significant.

Both bodies of data, therefore, show somewhat similar temporal patterns. and, in the case of Japan, a similarity that is particularly pronounced. The close association observed between movements in nominal and real exchange rates since the advent of floating exchange rates in the early 1970s is, therefore, clearly not a general phenomenon. Over the long span of years covered by these data, variability in inflation rates very often has accompanied variability in real exchange rates. This continued association between the two suggests the need for a common explanation.

3.2 PPP: Evidence from tests of cointegration

The implications of the theoretical models of exchange rate determination reviewed above translate into competing hypotheses about the nature of the disturbances that affect the PPP relationship.

To illustrate, let us first amend equation (1) to include a disturbance term and also, since it will be of use empirically, consider an alternate version written in terms of the real exchange rate.

As the empirical counterpart of equation (1), we get:

$$p_t^a = a + p_t^* + u_t \ , \tag{3}$$

and as the real-exchange-rate equation,

$$q_t = a' + u_t' \ , \tag{4}$$

where $p_t^a \equiv p_t - e_t$, $q_t \equiv (e_t - p_t + p_t^*)$, p and p^* now represent logarithms of price indexes rather than price levels, a and a′ are normalizing constants, and u and u′ are error terms.

Particularly well suited to analyzing the processes governing these errors are the tests of cointegration developed by Engle and Granger (1987). According to Engle and Granger, two series which themselves have to be differenced n times to be stationary, are said to be cointegrated of order n-1 if some linear combination of their nth differences is stationary.[11] Cointegrated variables have the property that even though, for example, the levels of both may be subject to drift, there is some linear combination of the two that is not. Tests for cointegration are therefore essentially unit-root tests applied to the errors in these equations, or to suitably differenced versions thereof.

To see the connection between the tests and the hypotheses about exchange rate behavior suggested by theory, let us first consider the (instantaneous) equilibrium model. Since in this model both goods prices and the nominal exchange rate adjust fully within the period to monetary shocks, deviations from PPP are solely the result of real shocks. These real shocks both have permanent effects and provoke full within-period adjustment. Accordingly, the equilibrium model predicts: non-stationary of the u_ts (or u_t's) and hence non-cointegration of p_t^a and p_t^*; the necessity of differencing to achieve stationarity; and an extremely rapid pattern of adjustment.

In the monetary overshooting model, real shocks play no role. Deviations from PPP are solely the result of lagged adjustment to monetary shocks. In the long run, the adjustment of nominal exchange rates and the price level to such shocks is complete, but in the short run the exchange rate overshoots to maintain covered interest rate parity, while the price level adjusts slowly. The overshooting model, therefore, predicts: stationarity of the u_ts and, hence, cointegration of the levels of p_t^a and p_t^*; and a pattern of adjustment that corresponds to that of the price level.

A third more general class of models admits the possibilities of both real shocks influencing the equilibrium exchange rate and sluggish adjustments of prices (see e.g. Mussa, 1982). The predictions of these models are, therefore, a mixture of those of the other two: stationarity of the errors, at least after differencing or adjustment for a deterministic trend in the real exchange rate; and a pattern of adjustment to residual errors that again mimics that of the price level following a monetary shock.

To test these hypotheses, I followed two related procedures. One was the two-step method outlined by Engle and Granger (1987); the other was simply to apply unit-root tests in the context of simple univariate models of the real exchange rate.

In the two-step procedure, the first step was to estimate the cointegrating regression based on equation (3):

$$p_t^a = a + b\, p_t^* + u_t \,, \tag{5}$$

where a and b are the coefficients to be estimated and where the slope coefficient b, which in theory should be unity, is included as an allowance for measurement error (Taylor, 1988).[12]

The second step uses variants of the Dickey-Fuller (1979) test to examine the stationarity of the u_ts.[13] The equations underlying these tests took the general form:

$$\Delta u_t = \beta_1\, u_{t-1} + \sum_{k=1}^{K} \beta_{k-1}\, \Delta u_{t-k} + v_t. \tag{6}$$

Here the parameter of interest is β_1, the coefficient on the level of the lagged error term from the cointegrating regression. A negative and statistically significant value of β_1 leads to rejection of the hypothesis of non-stationarity. This, in turn, implies that p^a and p^* are cointegrated and hence is evidence in favor of long-run PPP. In one variant of the test, the coefficients on the lagged differences of the errors were constrained to zero. This is referred to as the DF (Dickey-Fuller) test. In the other, no such constraint was imposed. This variant of the test is referred to as ADF (augmented Dickey-Fuller) test.[14]

The alternative procedure, in which I examined the stationarity of the real exchange rate directly, is essentially a test of cointegration subject to the constraint that b, the slope coefficient in the cointegrating regression, is unity. Given this constraint, the two steps collapse into one and the following general equation serves as the basis for our tests:

$$\Delta q_t = \mu_0 + \mu_1\, q_{t-1} + \sum_{k=1}^{K} \lambda_k\, \Delta q_{t-k} + v_t \,. \tag{7}$$

Again the focus of the tests is on the coefficient of the lagged level, a value of μ_1 significantly less than zero providing evidence in favor of the hypothesis of stationarity of the real exchange rate. In the DF tests, the λ_k again were assumed to be zero; in the ADF tests, the number of such coefficients to be included in the regression was chosen empirically.

To investigate the influence of real variables and other factors that might cause the real exchange rate to undergo permanent shifts, I conducted two further series of tests. In the first, I estimated a variant of (7) that included a deterministic time trend as an additional regressor. In the second, I allowed for a stochastic trend by substituting log differences of the real exchange rate data in place of the log levels used initially. In both instances, I conducted unit-root tests similar to those used above.

The equations underlying these additional tests took the respective forms:

$$\Delta q_t = \mu_0 + \mu_1 q_{t-1} + \mu_2 t + \sum_{k=1}^{K} \lambda_k \Delta q_{t-k} + v_t , \tag{8}$$

and

$$\Delta q_t - \Delta q_{t-1} = \mu_0 + \mu_1 \Delta q_{t-1} + \sum_{k=1}^{K} \lambda_k (\Delta q_{t-k} - \Delta q_{t-k-1}) + v_t . \tag{9}$$

Table 4 contains the results of the cointegration tests based on the two-step procedure, both the DF and ADF t-like statistics and the Durbin-Watson statistic from the cointegrating regression. Table 5 contains the statistics for the analogous unit root tests for the real exchange rates. In each instance in Table 4, we are able to reject the hypothesis of no cointegration between p_t^a and p_t^*. The same is true for the third test proposed by Engle and Granger based upon the Durbin-Watson statistic. Correspondingly, we are able to reject the hypothesis of non-stationarity of the real exchange rate, or put another way, of no cointegration given the constraint of a unit coefficient in the cointegrating regression linking p_t^a and p_t^*.

Estimated speeds of adjustments to equilibrium are rather lengthy in both instances.[15] For the pound-dollar the estimated half lives range from 2.1 to 2.3 years based on the results reported in Table 4 and from 2.2 to 2.9 years based on those reported in Table 5. These are not the rapid speeds of adjustment envisioned in the equilibrium models, but they are not out of line with the estimated speeds of adjustment of price levels to monetary shocks in the United States and the United Kingdom.[16]

For the yen rates, the situation is similar when we confine our attention to Table 4. The estimated half lives range from 2.1 to 2.4 years for the yen-pound and from 2.1 to 2.3 years for the yen-dollar. The picture changes, however, when we look at the results reported in the top panel of Table 5. For the yen-dollar the estimates range from 3.7 to 4.2 years, and for the yen-pound from 3.0 to 3.7 years.

The difference in the two sets of estimates for the yen exchange rates, I believe, reflects the imposition of the constraint b=1 that is implicit in the real-rate formulation. For the pound-dollar the constraint appears to be reasonable. The estimate of b reported in Table 4 is virtually unity and reversing the order of the variables in the cointegrating regression does not alter this result. In the cointegrating regressions for the two yen rates, in contrast, the estimates of b are both somewhat removed from unity, 1.16 and 1.09 for the yen-dollar and yen-pound, respectively. This, coupled with the visual impression of a long-term drift in the yen-dollar rate that one gets from Figure 1, raise questions about the importance of other than transient shocks.

Table 4
Tests for cointegration between the logarithms of exchange-rate-adjusted price levels: 1875-1989

Countries	$\frac{b}{sb}$	DW	$\frac{1-\beta_1}{s\beta_1}$	DF	$\frac{1-\beta_1}{s\beta_1}$	ADF(K)	K
JA/US	1.164	.540* (.019)	.714	-4.486* (.064)	.741	-4.663* (.077)	2
JA/UK	1.091	.553* (.014)	.715	-4.421* (.065)	.747	-3.392** (.075)	2
US/UK	1.016	.474** (.014)	.779	-3.495** (.063)	.723	-3.583** (.077)	3

Notes: The slope coefficient in the cointegrating regression is denoted by b and its standard error by sb. The coefficient in the test regression of the lagged residual from the cointegrating regression, u_{t-1}, is denoted by β_1 and its standard error by $s\beta_1$. DW is the Durbin-Watson statistic from the cointegrating regression, DF is the Dickey-Fuller test statistic and ADF(K) is the augmented Dickey-Fuller test statistic from a regression with K lagged values of the differenced residuals. One, two, and three asterisks denote significance at the .01, .05 and .10 levels, respectively in this and the next table.

One possibility is outright measurement error, particularly for the price series, but perhaps also for the early exchange rate data since these were derived as midpoints of the yearly highs and lows published by the Bank of Japan. The other obvious possibility is that real variables are affecting these real exchange rates. As already noted, a number of researchers have used differences in productivity growth in the United States and Japan to account for the drift in the yen dollar rate over the post-WWII period (see Marston, 1986; and Yoshikawa, 1990). In light of the rapid growth of the Japanese traded goods sector prior to WWII, it is plausible to believe that productivity differences may have been important then also. Given the somewhat low power of unit-root tests, we may therefore be incorrectly rejecting the hypothesis of non-stationarity.

To investigate this possibility, I ran the additional tests based on equations (8) and (9). In the middle panel of Table 5, I show the results of the tests in which a deterministic trend is included in the regression. In the bottom panel, I show the results for the first differences in q. In both cases, we can reject non-stationarity, and generally at high levels of significance. Real yen rates may be subject to permanent influences - either stochastic shocks or forces that follow a trend-like pattern - but there is a decided tendency to return to equilibrium otherwise. Over long periods PPP appears to hold at least for rates of change, and perhaps also for levels, albeit with the possible need for adjustment for a dterministic trend in the real exchange rate.[17]

Table 5
Unit root tests of real exchange rates: 1875-1989

Countries	$\frac{1-\mu_1}{s\mu_1}$	DF	$\frac{1-\mu_1}{s\mu_1}$	ADF(K)	K
Levels					
$\Delta q_t = \mu_0 + \mu_1 q_{t-1} + \sum_{k=1}^{K} \lambda_k \Delta q_{t-k} + v_t$					
JA/US	.847 (.051)	-2.987**	.829 (.059)	-2.887**	2
JA/UK	.792 (.056)	-3.727*	.828 (.062)	-2.789**	2
UK/US	.786 (.064)	-3.364*	.729 (.073)	-3.443*	3

Levels with trend

$$\Delta q_t = \mu_0 + \mu_1 q_{t-1} + \mu_2 t + \sum_{k=1}^{K} \lambda_k \Delta q_{t-k} + v_t$$

Countries	$\frac{1-\mu_1}{s\mu_1}$	$\frac{\mu_3}{s\mu_3}$	DF	$\frac{1-\mu_1}{s\mu_1}$	$\frac{\mu_3}{s\mu_3}$	ADF(K)	K
JA/US	.741 (.064)	-.0009 (.0003)	-4.040*	.668 (.077)	-.0012 (.0004)	-4.308*	2
JA/UK	.646 (.072)	-.0013 (.0004)	-4.903*	.663 (.088)	-.0012 (.0005)	3.847**	2
UK/US	.788 (.065)	.0000 (.0002)	-3.291***	.733 (.082)	.0000 (.0002)	3.277***	3

Differences

$$\Delta q_t - \Delta q_{t-1} = \mu_0 + \mu_1 \Delta q_{t-1} + \sum_{k=1}^{K} \lambda_k (\Delta q_{t-k} - \Delta q_{t-k-1}) + v_t$$

Countries	DF	ADF(K)	K
JA/US	-9.808*	-7.704*	3
JA/UK	-10.750*	-7.586*	2
UK/US	-9.394*	-6.026*	3

Notes: The symbols $s\mu_1$ and $s\mu_3$ represent the standard errors of the regression coefficients μ_1 and μ_3. DF is the Dickey-Fuller test; ADF(K) is the augmented Dickey-Fuller test based on a regression using n lagged differences of the dependent variable.

4. CONCLUSIONS

For the study of exchange-rate behavior, Japanese historical experience offers a nearly ideal laboratory. Over the 115 years for which data are available, the yen has floated with much greater frequency than either sterling or the dollar, while the Japanese price level has been subject to considerably greater variability than either the British or the American price level.

Despite this volatility, however, purchasing power parity - at least in relative form - has held remarkably well for the yen over the longer run. Using an expanded body of data relative to that in my earlier (1990) study, I can always reject the hypotheses of non-trend stationarity and non-difference-stationarity of real yen exchange rates at high levels of significance. Relaxing the constraint of a unit cointegrating factor between the exchange-rate-adjusted Japanese price level and the foreign price level, I can do the same for the hypothesis of non-stationarity of the absolute levels.

These results stand in sharp contrast both to casual impressions gained from experience under the current float and to much scholarly evidence derived from it. The difference, I believe, is due in the main to the difference in the spans of data. Given the existence of long-lived deviations of exchange rates from PPP, a long historical series is a virtual necessity if we are to distinguish persistent, but transient, deviations from permanent ones.

Viewed from the perspective of this study, the continued emphasis by the Bank of Japan and by business economists on PPP as a macroeconomic equilibrium condition no longer appears anomalous.[18] The fluctuations in the real yen-dollar rate over the past decade that made it seem such turn out to not differ much from the often substantial and largely self-reversing movements observed historically. Relative to the fluctuations in the years surrounding World War II they are, in fact, rather small.

Not directly identifiable are the factors producing such fluctuations. For the sterling-dollar rate they appear to have been largely transitory in their impact. For the two yen rates, both permanent and transitory factors appear to have mattered. Productivity-related influences may well have been important over much of the sample period. In addition, the close association between variability in yen real exchange rates and variability in the Japanese inflation rate suggests a major role for monetary influences.[19]

REFERENCES

Abuaf, Niso and Phillipe Jorion, 1990, Purchasing power parity in the long run, Journal of Finance, 45, 157-174.

Baillie, Richard T. and Tim Bollerslev, 1989, Common stochastic trends in a system of exchange rates, Journal of finance 44, 167-181.

Bank of Japan, Statistics Department, 1966. Hundred year statistics of the Japanese economy (Bank of Japan, Tokyo).

Baxter, Marianne, 1991, Business cycles, stylized facts and the exchange rate regime: Evidence from the United States, Journal of international money and finance 10, forthcoming.

Baxter, Marianne and Alan C. Stockman, 1988, Business cycles and the exchange rate system: some international evidence, Journal of monetary economics, 23, 377-400.

Darby, Michael R., 1983, Movements in purchasing power parity: The short and long runs, in Michael R. Darby, James R. Lothian, et al., The international transmission of inflation (University of Chicago Press for the NBER, Chicago, IL).

Darby, Michael R. and James R. Lothian, 1983a, British economic policy under Margaret Thatcher: A midterm examination, Carnegie Rochester conference series on public policy, 18, 157-208.

Darby, Michael R. and James R. Lothian, 1983b, Conclusions, in Michael R. Darby, James R. Lothian, et al., The international transmission of inflation (University of Chicago Press for the NBER, Chicago, IL).

Darby, Michael R. and James R. Lothian, 1989, International transmission afloat, in Michael D. Bordo, ed., Money, history and international finance: Essays in honor of Anna J. Schwartz (University of Chicago Press for the NBER, Chicago, IL).

Dickey, David A. and Wayne A. Fuller, 1979, Distribution of the estimators for autoregressive time series with a unit root, Journal of the American statistical association 74, 427-431.

Diebold, Francis X., Stephen Husted and Mark Rush, "Real exchange rates under the gold standard, unpublished manuscript, 1990.

Dornbusch, Rudiger, 1976, Expectations and exchange rate dynamics, Journal of political economy 84, 1161-1176.

Enders, Walter, 1988, ARIMA and cointegration tests of purchasing power parity, Review of economics and statistics 70, 504-508.

Enders, Walter, 1989, Unit roots and the real exchange rate before World War I: The case of Britain and the United States, Journal of international money and finance 8, 59-73.

Engle, Robert F. and Clive W.J. Granger, 1987, Cointegration and error correction: Representation, estimation and testing, Econometrica 55, 251-287.

Engle, Robert F. and Byung Sam Yoo, 1987, Forecasting and testing in cointegrated systems, Journal of econometrics 35, 143-159.

Feinstein, C.H., 1972, National income, expenditure and output of the United Kingdom, 1855-1965 (Cambridge University Press, Cambridge).

Fisher, Irving, The purchasing power of money (Augustus Kelley, New York). [a reprint of the 1922 second revised edition of the 1911 original]

Frenkel, Jacob A., and Harry G. Johnson, 1976, eds, The monetary approach to the balance of payments (University of Toronto, Toronto).

Friedman, Milton and Anna J. Schwartz, 1963, A monetary history of the United States: 1867-1960 (Princeton University for the NBER, Princeton, NJ).
Friedman, Milton and Anna J. Schwartz, 1982, Monetary trends in the United States and the United Kingdom (University of Chicago for the NBER, Chicago, IL).
Fuller, Wayne A.,1976, Introduction to statistical time series (John Wiley and Sons, New York, NY).
Gandolfi, Arthur E. and James R. Lothian, 1983, Price behavior and the demand for money, in Michael R. Darby, James R. Lothian, et al., The international transmission of inflation (University of Chicago Press for the NBER, Chicago, IL).
Hakkio, Craig S. and Mark Rush, 1989, Market efficiency and cointegration: an application to the sterling and deutschemark exchange markets, Journal of international money and finance 8, 75-88.
International Monetary Fund, International financial statistics, various issues.
Lockwood, William W., 1954, The economic development of Japan: Growth and structural change, 1868-1938 (Princeton University, Princeton, NJ).
Lothian, James R., 1986, Real dollar exchange rates under the Bretton-Woods and floating-rate systems, Journal of international money and finance 5, 429-448.
Lothian, James R., 1990, A century plus of Japanese exchange rate behavior, Japan and the world economy, 2, 47-70.
Lothian, James R., Michael R. Darby and Michael Tindall, 1990, Buffer stock models of the demand for money and the conduct of monetary policy, Journal of policy modeling, 12, 325-345.
Marston, Richard, 1986, real exchange rates and productivity growth in the United States and Japan, NBER working paper no. 1922.
McNown, Robert and Myles S. Wallace, 1989, National price levels, purchasing power parity and cointegration: A test of four high inflation economies, Journal of international money and finance 8, 533-545.
Mitchell, B. R., 1975, European historical statistics, 1750-1970 (Columbia University Press: New York, NY).
Moulton, Harold G., 1931, Japan: An economic and financial appraisal (Brookings, Washington, DC).
Mussa, Michael, 1982, A model of exchange rate dynamics, Journal of political economy 90, 74-104.
Mussa, Michael, 1986, Nominal exchange rate regimes and the behavior of real exchange rates: Evidence and implications, in Karl Brunner and Allan H. Meltzer, eds., Carnegie-Rochester conference series on public policy 26 (North Holland, Amsterdam).
Nakamura, Takafusa, 1983, Economic growth in prewar Japan (Yale University Press, New Haven). [a translation by Robert A. Feldman of Senzenki nihon keizai seicho no bunseki (An analysis of economic growth in prewar Japan) IWANI SHOTEN publishers, Tokyo 1971].
Ohkawa, Kazushi and Henry Rosovsky, 1973, Japanese economic growth (Stanford University, Stanford, CA).
Ohta, Takeshi, 1983, Exchange-rate management and the conduct of monetary policy, in Paul Meek, ed., Central bank views on monetary targetting (Federal Reserve Bank of New York, New York, NY).

Savvides, Andreas, 1991, Real exchange rate variability and the choice of exchange rate regime, Journal of international money and finance, 9, forthcoming.
Shinjo, Hiroshi, 1962, History of the yen (Tokyo, Kinokuniya Bookstore Co., Ltd. for the Research Institute for Economic and Business Administration of Kobe University).
Stockman, Alan C., 1980, A theory of exchange rate determination, Journal of political economy, 88, 673-698.
Stockman, Alan C., 1983, Real exchange rates under alternative monetary systems, Journal of international money and finance 2, 147-166.
Stockman, Alan C., 1988, Real exchange rate variability under pegged and floating nominal exchange rate systems: An equilibrium theory, University of Rochester, Working paper no. 128 .
Sturm, Frederick W., 1990, The yen, the dollar and the pull to parity, Fuji Securities, Inc., Perspectives, March 30.
Suzuki, Yoshio, 1988, Prospects for the future of the international monetary system: A Japanese perspective, paper presented at the New York University conference on international financial markets.
Takagi, Shinji, 1989, Floating exchange rates in interwar Japan, unpublished, International Monetary Fund.
Taylor, Mark P., 1988, An empirical examination of long-run purchasing power parity using cointegration techniques, Applied economics 20, 1369-1381.
Taylor, Mark P., and P.C. McMahon, 1988, Long-run purchasing power parity in the 1920s, European economic review, 32, 179-197.
United States Department of Commerce, 1973, Long term economic trends (United States Government Printing Office, Washington, DC).
Yoshikawa, Hiroshi, 1990, On the equilibrium yen-dollar rate, American economic review 3, 576-583.

NOTES

1. Data for Japanese nominal exports and imports came from Ohkawa and Rosovsky (1973). I divided these figures by the estimates of nominal GDP in Nakamura (1983) to convert them to ratio form.

2. The silver yen became legal tender in May of 1878. See the discussions of this period in Moulton (1931) and Shinjo (1962) and the references cited therein.

3. The exchange rate data for the period ending in 1965 are annual series for the yen relative to the currencies of the other three countries as reported in the Bank of Japan's Hundred Year Statistics of the Japanese Economy. For the years 1880 to 1914, these are midpoints of the range between the reported yearly high and low exchange rates for each currency; for 1874 to 1879 and for the years after 1914, they are yearly averaged data. These series were used directly to compute yen-other country real exchange rates and to derive the sterling-dollar real exchange rate.

The published figures for 1894 contained what appears to be two errors. I corrected the yen-dollar rate using the alternative estimate of Nakamura (1983, p. 34) and derived the yen-sterling rate using that corrected figure and the estimate of the dollar-pound exchange rate for 1894 in Friedman and Schwartz (1982).

Observations for yen exchange rates for the years 1941 to 1947 were not reported by the Bank of Japan. For these years, I used Swiss quotes of yen-dollar rates from Abuaf and Jorion (1990) that Phillipe Jorion graciously provided me, and the dollar-sterling figures reported in Friedman and Schwartz (1982) to fill in the missing observations for the yen-sterling and pound-dollar rates and to derive the yen-pound rate.

I updated the nominal exchange rate series for the years after 1965 using the basis of the annual average yen-dollar and dollar-pound rates reported in the International Financial Statistics (IFS) and derived the yen-pound rate from these figures.

The data for wholesale prices came from a variety of sources: for the United States, the U.S. Department of Commerce's Long Term Trends for the years 1873 to 1970, and the IFS thereafter; for the United Kingdom, European Historical Statistics for the years 1873 to 1975 and IFS thereafter; and for Japan, the Bank of Japan's Hundred Year Statistics for the years 1873 to 1965 and the IFS thereafter. These subseries were linked either by regression or by multiplying the earlier series by the ratio of the overlapping observations. The resultant series were then rebased to 1980.

4. I define the real exchange rate as the ratio of the nominal exchange rate (the price of a unit of the foreign currency) divided by the ratio of the home-country price index to the foreign-country price index.

5. This explanation has been widely applied to explain the behavior of the yen-dollar rate in the post-WWII period. See, for example, Marston (1986) and Yoshikawa (1990).

6. Japanese real income (GDP) and industrial production data came from Nakamura (1983); U.S. and U.K. real income (NNP) data from Friedman and Schwartz, (1982); U.S. industrial production from U.S. Department of Commerce (1973); and U.K. industrial production from Feinstein (1972).

7. See the discussion of this episode in Lockwood (1954, pp. 36-37) and the references cited therein.

8. This short-run spillover of expansive U.S. policies to Japan is evident in data for Japanese balance of payments and high-powered money growth. Japan's official settlements surplus increased sharply in 1977 and remained high in 1978 in the face of substantial U.S. official settlements deficits in these years. Japanese high-powered money growth in this environment rose from 8.1% per year on average in 1976 and 1977 to 13.9% per year in 1978.

See Darby and Lothian (1989) on the difference between long-run and short-run price behavior among OECD countries since the advent of floating rates and Ohta (1983) for a discussion of Japanese policy during the late 1970s and early 1980s.

9. Stockman (1988) attributes the greater stability of real exchange rates under fixed rates to government actions in the goods and capital markets that affect both the price level and the nominal exchange rate. Mussa (1986), in contrast, attributes the variability under floating exchange rates to the non-instantaneous adjustment of goods prices.

Savvides (1991) using a simultaneous model estimated for a group of 39 developing countries over the period 1976 to 1984 studies the relationship between the exchange-rate regime and the behavior of real exchange rates. He finds no independent effect of the regime on the variability of real exchange rates.

10. The definition of the gold-standard period varies with the countries being compared. For Japan it begins in 1897 and for the United States in 1879.

11. See the discussion of cointegration in Engle and Granger, 1987. I apply this technique to long-term time series data for Japan, the United States, the United Kingdom and France in my earlier (1990) paper. Unlike the data used here those data excluded the WWII and immediate postwar years.

Other applications to exchange rate data are contained in Abuaf and Jorion (1990), Baillie and Bollerslev (1989), Diebold, Husted and Rush (1990), Enders (1988, 1989), Hakkio and Rush (1989), McNown and Wallace (1989), Taylor (1988) and Taylor and McMahon (1988).

12. As I point out below, an estimate different from unity may also be an indication of omitted variables that affect the equilibrium real exchange rate.

13. Since there is no way *a priori* to choose the ordering of the variables, I also ran the reverse set of regressions and conducted the corresponding tests for cointegration. These resulted in no appreciable change in the results reported below.

14. Significance levels for the t-statistics used in these tests are those of Engle and Yoo (1987).

15. These estimated adjustment speeds are derived from the coefficients on the lagged level terms in equations (6) and (7). The estimated half lives of adjustment are $\ln(.5)/\ln(1-\beta_1)$ and $\ln(.5)/\ln(1-\mu_1)$ for the two equations respectively.

16. For the United States and the United Kingdom, the lag before the effects of a monetary shock become apparent in prices is often described as being on the order of two years. Full adjustment - including overshooting - appears to take longer, however. See Darby and Lothian (1983a) for a discussion of this issue and for estimates of the adjustment process for the United Kingdom that takes overshooting into account.

17. A similar phenomenon appears to characterize money-price relationships. (See Gandolfi and Lothian, 1983; and Lothian, Darby and Tindall, 1990).

18. See Yoshio Suzuki (1988) of the Bank of Japan's research department for an analysis based on long-run purchasing power parity of movements in the yen exchange rates under the current float. Frederick W. Sturm (1989) of Fuji Securities presents a similar analysis of recent movements in the yen-dollar, DM-dollar, and dollar-pound exchange rates.

19. Evidence suggesting that this is also the case under the current float is presented in my (1986) study of the real dollar exchange rates of 11 OECD countries.

Japanese Financial Market Research
W.T. Ziemba, W. Bailey and Y. Hamao (Editors)

NEWS FROM THE U.S. AND JAPAN

Which Moves The Yen / Dollar Exchange Rate?*

Takatoshi ITO

University of Minnesota, Minneapolis, MN 55455, USA
National Bureau of Economic Research, Cambridge, MA 02138, USA

V. Vance ROLEY*

University of Washington, Seattle, WA 98195, USA
National Bureau of Economic Research, Cambridge, MA 02138, USA

Intra-daily movements in the yen/dollar exchange rate are examined in four non-overlapping segments within each business day from January 1980 to September 1985. The results indicate that the dollar tended to appreciate in the New York segment and depreciate in the European segment. In three of the four subsamples considered, the Tokyo segment made virtually no contribution to annual yen/dollar rate movements. The volatility of the exchange rate also differed across markets. Finally, in examining the relative effects of news from the U.S. and Japan explicitly, U.S. money announcement surprises had the most consistent effects.

1. Introduction

The pre-eminence of the efficient markets hypothesis has led to a number of studies on the effect of news on asset prices. Many of these studies further employ finely observed data, usually a change in an asset's price during a 24-hour period containing potentially important 'news'. In this context, 'news' refers to an unexpected change in a fundamental variable relevant to the asset's price determination. By examining the response to news, different hypotheses about an asset's price behavior can be evaluated.

Among the recent studies examining the effect of news, the response of foreign exchange rates has received considerable attention. The response to the

*The authors are grateful to Jacob Frenkel, John Huzinga, Sule Ozler, Charles Pigott, Charles Plosser, James Poterba, Christopher Sims, Lawrence Summers, and Simon Wheatley for helpful discussions and comments. The authors also benefited from the comments received from participants of seminars at the Japanese Ministry of Finance, the Bank of Japan, the University of Chicago, and the University of Minnesota. Kenichi Ohno performed outstanding research assistance. Financial assistance from the Hoover Institution (National Fellowship to the first author), the National Science Foundation (Grant No. SES 8408603 to the second author), the National Institute for Research Advancement in Tokyo, the National Bureau of Economic Research, and the University of Washington's Graduate School of Business Administration (Affiliate Program Professorship to the second author) is gratefully acknowledged. The data and related documentation are available in the USJNEWS data archive from the authors.

Federal Reserve's weekly money announcements is investigated by Cornell (1982, 1983), Frankel and Hardouvelis (1985), Engel and Frankel (1984), Hardouvelis (1984), and Roley (1986b), among others. Most of the evidence is consistent with the so-called policy-anticipations (or Keynesian) hypothesis in that a positive money announcement surprise causes dollar appreciation. Under this hypothesis, the observed positive response of U.S. interest rates to positive money announcement surprises represents a real interest-rate response, leading to an appreciation of the dollar in foreign exchange markets. The real rate rises due to the expectation of future tightening by the Federal Reserve as a reaction to the unanticipated increase in money.[1]

The response of exchange rates to other economic announcements also has been considered. Batten and Thornton (1984) examine the response to U.S. discount rate changes. They conclude that unexpected discount rate changes implemented with international considerations, most notably on November 1, 1978, are significant in explaining exchange rate movements. Hakkio and Pearce (1985) consider the response of exchange rates to U.S. announcements of inflation, industrial production, and the unemployment rate, in addition to weekly money announcements. Their results suggest that only money surprises affect exchange rates significantly.

While not focusing on economic announcements, Mussa (1979), Dornbusch (1980), and Frenkel (1981) also consider the effect of unanticipated changes in economic variables on exchange rates. Edwards (1982, 1983, 1984) and Longworth (1984) further attempt to formalize a method to explain the deviations between the forward rate and the realized spot rate using the unanticipated components of money, interest rates, and output. Since their data consist of monthly changes, the immediate responses of exchange rates to news announcements are not measured. A novelty of their approach, however, is to take into account foreign (non-U.S.) news as well as domestic (U.S.) news.

As is recognized in the literature on the response of asset prices to economic announcements, it is desirable to take the shortest interval possible around potential news since other shocks may dilute the estimated effect over one month. However, Edward's idea that exchange rates should respond to not only U.S. news but foreign news, implying correlated error terms in the various currency equations, is well taken. This point leads to the question of how to measure exchange rate responses to foreign (non-U.S.) news. Since an exchange rate is the relative price of two assets (i.e., currencies), it is important to recognize that the rate could respond to domestic and/or foreign news. However, if exchange rate responses to domestic and foreign news are to be

[1]For discussions of both the policy anticipations and expected inflation hypotheses, see Urich and Wachtel (1981), Cornell (1983), and Roley and Walsh (1985).

separated, a 24-hour segment, not to mention one month, as a data unit is not fine enough since it involves reactions to both domestic and foreign news.

Most studies investigating the effects of announcements measure the change in exchange rates over 24 hours (e.g., a change from a close to a close). In contrast, Hakkio and Pearce (1985) examine exchange rate responses in the New York market over two sub-intervals, but they do not consider exchange rate movements in the rest of the world. As noted above, it is important to recognize that not only domestic but also foreign news is very relevant in the determination of the exchange rate, and that the foreign exchange market is open almost continually somewhere in the world. Therefore, an analysis of the effects of news on exchange rates needs to be carried out with respect to the other country's news as well as U.S. news.

This paper distinguishes itself in several aspects from the other studies mentioned above. Most advantages come from the data set, which consists of the opening and closing quotes of the yen/dollar exchange rate in the Tokyo market and the 9 a.m., noon, and 4:30 p.m. (or later) quotes in the New York market for each business day from January 1980 through September 1985. In addition, announcements of the money supply, industrial production, and wholesale (producers) prices are collected both for the U.S. and Japan. Using this data set, the responses of the exchange rate to U.S. and Japanese economic news can be differentiated. Because of the 14-hour (13-hour during daylight saving time) time difference between Tokyo and New York, the business hours of the two markets do not overlap. (See the appendix for data sources and timing.) As a consequence, exchange rate changes in the New York market (9 a.m. to 4:30 p.m.) can be regarded as responses to U.S. news, and the changes in the Tokyo market (9 a.m. to 3:30 p.m.) as responses to Japanese news. Since the exchange rate should reflect not only U.S. news but also Japanese news, it is very interesting to consider how Japanese economic announcements compare with U.S. economic announcements with respect to the exchange rate response.

The features of this investigation outlined above also are extremely useful in addressing recent policy issues. By identifying whether Japanese news or U.S. news influences the exchange rate more, and also by identifying what kind of news in each market moves the exchange rate, this analysis sheds light from a new angle on the controversy of the cause of the 'overvalued dollar in the 1980s'. If the 'cause' of the strong dollar was tight monetary policy of the U.S., the exchange rate should exhibit relatively large responses to U.S. money announcement surprises. Alternatively, if the dollar's strength, particularly from 1982 through 1985, was a reflection of the strength of the U.S. economy relative to that of Japan, then other kinds of news such as industrial production announcements in both countries should have significant effects on the exchange rate.

To analyze the effects of changes in policy as well as deregulation further, several possible break points are considered within the 1980–1985 sample. First, December 1980 should be noted for the sweeping deregulation that occurred with respect to Japanese capital controls both into and out of Japan.[2] Second, in October 1982, the Federal Reserve announced the abandonment of its previous monetary-control procedure and also indicated that targets for the narrowly-defined money stock (M1) would be deemphasized. Third, in February 1984, the Federal Reserve adopted a different reserve requirement system, and as a consequence the behavior of money and interest rates in the U.S. may have changed.[3]

Following this introductory section, the second section examines the relative volatility of the yen/dollar rate in the New York and Tokyo markets. The relative contributions of these markets in determining longer-run movements also are considered. In the third section, the response of the yen/dollar rate to economic news announcements in both the U.S. and Japan is estimated. The main conclusions are summarized in the final section.

2. Trend and volatility analysis

To compare movements of the yen/dollar exchange rate in different markets throughout the world, four major segments are considered within each day. (The timing of different markets is explained further in the appendix.) First, exchange rate movements from the opening (9 a.m.), TKO, to the close (3:30 p.m.), TKC, of the Tokyo market mainly reflect traders' responses to news originating in Japan. Both the London and New York markets are closed during business hours in Tokyo. This segment is denoted as the 'Tokyo' segment of the day. Second, from the close of Tokyo market to the opening of the New York market, news and actions in the European markets are thought to be responsible for the changes in the yen/dollar exchange rate through cross arbitrage with European currencies. This segment is referred to as 'Europe'. Third, changes of the yen/dollar rate from 9 a.m., NYO, to 4:30 p.m. (or later), NYC, in the New York market mainly reflect the effects of U.S. news, although the London market is still open concurrently at the very beginning hours of New York market trading.[4] This segment is denoted as 'New York'. The fourth segment of the day differs from the others. In particular, there is no major market between New York and Tokyo. For $3\frac{1}{2}$ hours ($2\frac{1}{2}$ during daylight saving time), most of the Japanese, American and

[2] See Ito (1986) for the effect of the December 1980 changes on covered interest parity.

[3] The effects of these changes in Federal Reserve policy are considered in detail by Roley (1986a, c). The response of interest rates to money announcement surprises is found to change significantly over the different regimes.

[4] As discussed in the next section, the Federal Reserve occasionally collected quotes after 4:30 p.m. to take the effects of money announcements into account.

European market participants are not trading. For convenience, this period is referred to as the 'Pacific' market.

A summary of yen/dollar exchange rate movements for each market is presented in table 1. This table indicates which market was most influential in determining exchange rate changes and volatility. Several stylized facts are apparent in this table. First, the exchange rate at the end of the sample, September 20, 1985, happened to be about the same as that of the start of the sample period, January 1, 1980. That is, total net changes summed over all markets for the entire sample period are less than one yen. However, when they are decomposed into separate markets and potential policy regimes, differences are apparent. In particular, accumulated changes in the New York market during the second subperiod reflect yen depreciation, and those for Europe in the first, second, and third subperiods reflect yen appreciation. The drift of the exchange rate in the Tokyo market appears to be 'trendless' except for a mild depreciation in the second subperiod. The data are consistent with the view that U.S. economic activity and policies led toward an 'over-valued' dollar, while the European markets recorded opposite effects.

It also is of interest to examine whether an average daily change was statistically different from zero in any market during any subperiod. As indicated in table 1, the daily exchange rate movement in the New York market during subperiod II (464 observations) was not a random walk in the sense that the hypothesis that the mean change is equal to zero is rejected at the 1 percent significance level. Similarly, in the European market during subperiods I and III, mean changes are significant at the 5 percent level. However, the mean change is slightly more than $\frac{1}{10}$ of one yen, which is approximately the same magnitude as the bid–ask spread. Moreover, some portion of the yen/dollar rate's movement could be due to interest-rate differentials between the two countries.

The volatility of the exchange rate measured by variances and mean absolute changes also is reported in table 1. The Pacific market consistently had low volatility, about a half to a third that of any other market in terms of mean absolute changes.[5] As is shown below, this result is robust even when correcting for the different number of hours in the segments.

The volatilities of the Tokyo and New York markets changed significantly over the sample. In the first subperiod, the Tokyo market was slightly more volatile than both the New York and European markets. However, the New York market was most volatile from the second to the fourth subperiods. Since October 1982, the New York market has been about twice as volatile as the Tokyo market in terms of the variances, due mainly to the major decline in the

[5] For the entire sample, for example, the hypotheses that the Pacific segment's variance is the same as those in the Tokyo, Europe, and New York segments can be rejected at the 5 percent level in each case. The relevant F-statistics (degrees of freedom) are 3.96 (1426, 1375), 4.41 (1323, 1375), and 6.03 (1433, 1375), respectively.

Table 1

Summary of yen/dollar exchange rate movements in four markets.[a]

	Tokyo	Europe	New York	Pacific	Total
Entire sample: January 1, 1980 to September 20, 1985					
Accumulated change	14.16	−72.12	70.92	−4.65	0.60
Mean	0.00992	−0.05447	0.04946	−0.00338	
Variance	0.63625	0.70969	0.96987	0.16079	
Mean absolute change	0.55923	0.59154	0.72035	0.25552	
Standard error (mean)	0.02111	0.02269	0.02601	0.01082	
t-statistic (mean = 0)	0.47	−2.40[b]	1.90	−0.31	
Period I: January 1, 1980 to November 30, 1980					
Accumulated change	−3.40	−29.41	1.75	10.06	−21.40
Mean	−0.01504	−0.13553	0.00764	0.04615	
Variance	1.01821	0.88533	0.85011	0.11837	
Mean absolute change	0.71584	0.61544	0.62450	0.23670	
Standard error (mean)	0.06712	0.06387	0.06093	0.02330	
t-statistic (mean = 0)	−0.22	−2.12[b]	0.12	1.98[b]	
Period II: December 1, 1980 to October 4, 1982					
Accumulated change	20.42	−21.81	60.69	−4.05	56.95
Mean	0.04430	−0.04879	0.13079	−0.00910	
Variance	0.88640	0.85735	1.15799	0.17612	
Mean absolute change	0.71037	0.68387	0.84356	0.25638	
Standard error (mean)	0.04385	0.04380	0.04996	0.01989	
t-statistic (mean = 0)	1.01	−1.11	2.62[b]	−0.46	
Period III: October 5, 1982 to January 31, 1984					
Accumulated change	−2.89	−32.47	4.33	0.13	−39.60
Mean	−0.00878	−0.10211	0.01304	0.00041	
Variance	0.50246	0.64401	1.17537	0.17180	
Mean absolute change	0.50009	0.59223	0.80883	0.26912	
Standard error (mean)	0.03908	0.04500	0.05950	0.02395	
t-statistic (mean = 0)	−0.22	2.27[b]	0.22	0.02	
Period IV: February 1, 1984 to September 20, 1985					
Accumulated change	0.03	8.57	4.15	−10.79	4.35
Mean	0.00007	0.02159	0.01015	−0.02739	
Variance	0.25656	0.49428	0.65259	0.14925	
Mean absolute change	0.35143	0.47408	0.56242	0.25404	
Standard error (mean)	0.02495	0.03529	0.03994	0.01946	
t-statistic (mean = 0)	0.00	0.61	0.25	−1.41	

[a]Accumulated changes are sums of all observed daily changes in the respective markets for the specified period. Because of occasional missing observations due to holidays in both countries, accumulated changes for the four markets do not necessarily add up to the total changes. If one market is closed because of a holiday, then not only that market but also the adjacent markets become missing observations. For the same reason, the numbers of observations in each segment are different even for the same subperiod. The number of observations can be calculated by dividing the accumulated change by the mean for a particular market for a particular subperiod.

[b]Significant at the 5 percent level.

Tokyo market's volatility. In terms of variances, the volatility of the third subperiod is a half of the first period's in the Tokyo market, and the fourth period's volatility is again half that of the third period.[6]

The decline in the volatility in the Tokyo market may be partially explained by deregulation.[7] In particular, most of the capital controls on flows into and out of Japan were eliminated on December 1, 1980. In addition, the so-called 'real demand principle' was eliminated on April 1, 1984. Prior to that date, positions in the forward market without 'real demands' were prohibited. Both measures contributed to the broadening of the Tokyo market, which in turn may have increased its stability.

2.1. Volatility per hour

In the preceding subsection, the difference in the number of hours for different segments was ignored. If one segment is longer than another, its apparent volatility may be artificially high. To correct for the difference in segment hours, 'per hour' variances are calculated below.[8] The market hours in Tokyo and New York are constant for all observations. The hours between two markets, however, vary depending on whether the U.S. is on the daylight saving time. In addition, the Pacific segment, hours from New York closing to Tokyo opening, includes a weekend (an extra 48 hours) once every five observations.

Table 2 shows per hour variances calculated from the volatility measures reported in table 1. Even on a per hour basis, the volatility ranking between

[6] The hypothesis that the Tokyo market's variance is the same over adjacent subsamples cannot be rejected at the 5 percent level only for subsamples I and II. The F-statistics are 1.15 (225, 460) for subsamples I and II, 1.76 (460, 328) for subsamples II and III, and 1.96 (328, 428) for subsamples III and IV. For the New York market, F-statistics for the same periods are 1.36 (463, 228), 1.02 (331, 464), and 1.80 (331, 408). The null hypothesis of equal variances cannot be rejected only for subsamples II and III in this case. The hypothesis that the variances in the Tokyo and New York markets are equal cannot be rejected at the 5 percent level in subsample I, but it can be rejected in the remaining subsamples. The F-statistics are 1.20 (225, 228), 1.31 (463, 460), 2.34 (331, 328), and 2.54 (408, 428).

[7] An alternative explanation is that the Japanese economy was highly volatile after the second oil crisis in 1980. Three more reasons for the volatility differences have been suggested to us by the Japanese traders. First, Japanese traders are on salaries, while U.S. traders are on commissions. This, however, does not explain why Japanese volatility has been decreasing. Second, the Tokyo market has a higher proportion of 'real demands' than the New York market. The buy and sell orders based on real demands, that is leads and lags, may occur with the change in the level and be stabilizing, while speculative demands could be destabilizing. This explanation is at odds with the fact that the volatility has been decreasing since the abolition of the 'real demand principle' in the forward market. Third, traders have self-fulfilling expectations that Tokyo is stable and New York is volatile. If the market is thought to be stable, profit-taking (and squaring the position) occurs with a small change, and loss-taking (and squaring the position) does not occur until the change becomes large. Both actions would stabilize the market. This explanation cannot, however, account for the changes which occurred over time in both of the markets.

[8] French and Roll (1984) discuss the use of 'per hour' volatility in the context of stock prices.

Table 2

Volatility per hour.[a]

Period	Tokyo	Europe	New York		Pacific	
			All day	9–12 only	Weekday	Weekend
Jan. 1, 1980 to Nov. 30, 1980	0.1476	0.1212	0.1119	0.1828	0.0519	0.0039
Dec. 1, 1980 to Oct. 4, 1982	0.1364	0.1201	0.1553	0.2063	0.0397	0.0087
Oct. 5, 1982 to Jan. 31, 1984	0.0780	0.0952	0.1579	0.1813	0.0543	0.0073
Feb. 1, 1984 to Sept. 20, 1985	0.0396	0.0716	0.0873	0.0919	0.0474	0.0036

[a]Variances divided by the number of hours of the respective market. The number of hours for both Europe and Pacific is different from the last Sunday in April to the last Sunday in October due to daylight savings time in the New York market. (See the appendix.) The reported numbers are adjusted for the difference due to daylight savings time by taking a weighted average, with the weights being the number of observations for the summer and winter, respectively.

Tokyo and New York does not change. The Tokyo market was more volatile in 1980, while the New York market was more volatile than Tokyo beginning in the second subperiod.[9]

Turning to the Pacific segment, volatility per hour is expected to be very small since all major markets in the world are closed during these hours. Moreover, if this segment contains a weekend, it extends more than 50 hours without trading activities. As indicated in table 2, the per hour variance of the weekday Pacific segment is a third to a half that of its New York counterpart as expected.

The low per hour volatility of the Pacific market may be interpreted as evidence for the lack of news. To examine this hypothesis further, the Pacific segment of the day can be compared to the most 'active' segment of the day, namely 9 a.m. to 12 noon in the New York market. The London market is still open during some part of the New York morning session. The three hours which would reflect New York and European news are obviously more volatile than the comparable hours in the Pacific segment of the day.[10]

As alternative explanation of the lower volatility during the Pacific segment could be its lack of 'self-generating' trading rather than the lack of news. French and Roll (1984) propose that trades self-generate volatility based on

[9]The hypothesis that the per hour variances in the Tokyo and New York markets are equal cannot be rejected at the 5 percent level in subsample II, but it can be rejected in the remaining subsamples. The F-statistics are 1.32 (225,228), 1.14 (463,460), 2.02 (331,328), and 2.20 (408,428).

[10]Since both segments extend about three hours, the comparison is immune from a possible bias from per hour correction. The hypothesis that the per hour variances in the New York 9–12 and the Pacific weekday segments are equal can be rejected at the 5 percent level in each subsample. The F-statistics are 3.52 (228,174), 5.20 (463,356), 3.34 (331,254), and 1.94 (408,315).

evidence that when the stock market is closed during regular business hours, the volatility between closing and opening quotes is significantly less than during other times. Unfortunately, because the foreign exchange market is almost always open somewhere in the world (except the Pacific segment) and ready to process relevant news, the maintained hypothesis that it is news which determines volatility cannot be differentiated from an alternative hypothesis that the mere existence of trading generates the volatility.

3. Responses to economic news announcements

In this section, the response of the yen/dollar exchange rate to announcements of important economic news is examined. Announcements of the money supply, industrial production, and producers (wholesale, in Japan) prices are considered for both the U.S. and Japan across potential policy regimes. Previous research in this area is extended in at least two ways. First, by considering foreign exchange trading each day in several segments throughout the world, competing hypotheses about factors which determine the exchange rate (critical fundamentals) can be better differentiated. Second, Japanese announcements are analyzed in parallel with U.S. announcements. Since the exchange rate could be influenced by either economy, parallel effects from Japanese news announcements might be expected. However, due to the differences in monetary policy rules, regulations, institutions, and economic structures, announcement effects may not be symmetric between the two countries.

3.1. Specification and data

The usual efficient markets model is used to estimate the response of the yen/dollar exchange rate to economic news announcements. This model may be represented as

$$YD(k) = a(k) + b_1(k) \cdot SX_1 + b_2(k) \cdot SX_2 + b_3(k) \cdot SX_3$$
$$+ c_1(k) \cdot EX_1 + c_2(k) \cdot EX_2 + c_3(k) \cdot EX_3 + e(k), \qquad (1)$$

where

$YD(k)$ = change in the yen/dollar rate in the kth segment after the announcement,
SX_i = surprise part of the announcement for variable X_i ($i = 1, 2, 3$),
EX_i = expected part of the announcement for variable X_i ($i = 1, 2, 3$).

Under the null hypothesis of market efficiency, the coefficients on the expected announced values, $c_i(k)$ for $i = 1, 2, 3$, should equal zero. Moreover, if the market incorporates news rapidly, the coefficients on the surprise components of the announcements, $b_i(k)$ for $i=1,2,3$, should equal zero in segments following that of the announcement. Alternatively, if one segment of the market either over- or under-reacts to news, subsequent segments may exhibit significant responses.

The announcement data are defined in the appendix. All announcement data are monthly with the exception of the weekly money announcements in the U.S. None of the Japanese announcements occurred on the same day in the sample. In contrast, two or more U.S. announcements did occasionally fall on the same day. In estimating announcement effects, all three economic variables for each country are included in the estimated equations, as in eq. (1).[11]

Variables representing expected values of announcements differ depending on the country. For the U.S., expected announced values are constructed using the survey compiled by Money Market Services, Inc. These survey data are adjusted by regressing actual announced values on a constant, the survey measure, and the change in the 3-month Treasury bill yield over the subsequent four business days [see Roley (1983, 1986b)]. To insure the robustness of the results, three other measures of expectations also were considered for the U.S.: the unadjusted survey data, the survey data adjusted for the effects of social security weeks on expected money [Clark, Joines and Phillips (1985)], and fitted values from simple time-series models.[12] Differences due to the different expectations measures are discussed below.

Survey data for economic announcements are not available in Japan. As an alternative, a rolling vector autoregression is used, including money, industrial production, wholesale prices, the yen/dollar exchange rate, and the Gensaki interest rate. The announcement surprises generated by this model are confirmed to have means insignificantly different from zero and no significant serial correlation.[13]

3.2. Estimation results

The estimation results of eq. (1) for each country's three economic announcements are summarized in table 3. Eq. (1) is estimated over the entire

[11] The effects of the individual announcements also were estimated separately. The results were qualitatively the same as those reported in the tables.

[12] To adjust the survey data for social security weeks, the specification presented by Clark, Joines and Phillips (1985) was used. Social security weeks occur if the third day of a month falls on a weekend, a Monday holiday, or a Friday holiday. To construct time-series measures of expected money, autoregressions were estimated over the 1980:2–1982:10 and 1982:10–1985:9 sample periods. To construct similar measures for industrial production and inflation, two variable VAR models were estimated over the same subsamples.

[13] Results reported in tables 3 through 6 are robust with respect to several modifications in the data set: a change in lag length, the deletion of the Gensaki rate, and/or the deletion of the exchange rate.

1980–85 sample as well as several subsamples corresponding to possible changes in policy regimes in both the U.S. and Japan. For U.S. announcements, the first segment ($k = 0$) is calculated from the closing quote in the Tokyo market to the 12:00 noon quote in the New York market. The 9:00 a.m. New York quote is not used because both U.S. industrial production and producer price index announcements were made at either 8:30 a.m. or 9:00 a.m. throughout the 1980–85 period. The second New York segment ($k = 1$) is measured from 12:00 noon to closing in the New York market, and it captures the effects of U.S. money announcements.[14] The total response regressions for both the U.S. and Japan represent the cumulative one-day response across markets.[15] The remaining segments for the U.S. and Japan are as defined previously.

In addition to summary statistics, test statistics for the hypothesis that coefficients on expected values of economic values equal zero [$c_1(k) = c_2(k) = c_3(k) = 0$] are reported. In only one case is this hypothesis rejected at the 5 percent level in either country. In particular, this hypothesis is rejected in the $k = 1$ segment for U.S. announcements when the responses are estimated over the entire 1980–85 sample. The results for the subsamples of the $k = 1$ segment, however, do not reject the null hypothesis at the 5 percent level. As a consequence, the results as a whole lend support to this implication of efficient markets.

Two of the three alternative measures of expectations considered for the U.S. yield similar results with respect to both the efficiency tests reported in table 3 and the estimated response coefficients reported in subsequent tables. In particular, using the time-series measures of expectations, the null hypothesis that $c_1(k) = c_2(k) = c_3(k) = 0$ cannot be rejected at the 5 percent level in any of the segments across subsamples. For the unadjusted survey data, the same hypothesis can be rejected at the 5 percent level only in the $k = 1$ segment for the entire sample and the 1980 : 12–1982 : 10 subsample. The rejections occur mainly because of the statistical significance of expected money. The results using the adjusted survey data reported in table 3 do not suffer from this problem in any of the segments across subsamples.

The third alternative measure of expectations involving adjustments due to social security weeks yields results somewhat different from those of the other

[14] Beginning on November 29, 1982, money announcements were made at 4:15 p.m. They were previously made at 4:10 p.m. Starting on March 22, 1984, money announcements were made at 4:30 p.m. On money announcement days following March 22, 1984, the Federal Reserve began collecting closing foreign exchange rate quotes after 4:30 p.m. to reflect any effects from money announcements.

[15] For the U.S., the total response is measured from the closing quote in Tokyo in day T to the opening quote in New York in day $T + 1$. For Japan, the total response is measured from Tokyo opening in day T to Tokyo opening in day $T + 1$. The individual segment response coefficients reported in subsequent tables may not sum to the total because of different numbers of missing observations in the segments due to holidays.

Table 3. Summary of estimation results.[a]

U.S. announcements

Sample	$k=0$ New York Morning $\bar{R}^2$	SE	$F(m,n)$	$k=1$ New York Afternoon $\bar{R}^2$	SE	$F(m,n)$
80:1–85:9	0.01	0.97	2.24 (3,376)	0.10	0.59	3.24[b] (3,388)
80:1–80:11	0.01	0.93	1.44 (3,53)	0.04	0.41	1.95 (3,55)
80:12–82:10	0.02	1.05	0.95 (3,121)	0.17	0.61	1.72 (3,125)
82:10–84:1	−0.04	1.11	0.72 (3,81)	0.07	0.72	0.00 (3,85)
84:2–85:9	0.01	0.80	0.76 (3,100)	0.07	0.51	1.11 (3,102)

Sample	$k=2$ Pacific $\bar{R}^2$	SE	$F(m,n)$	$k=3$ Tokyo $\bar{R}^2$	SE	$F(m,n)$
80:1–85:9	0.06	0.47	0.11 (3,372)	−0.01	0.86	0.56 (3,376)
80:1–80:11	−0.07	0.42	0.56 (3,51)	−0.06	0.99	0.49 (3,51)
80:12–82:10	0.10	0.55	0.19 (3,121)	−0.03	1.07	0.74 (3,123)
82:10–84:1	0.13	0.46	1.68 (3,79)	−0.00	0.78	1.23 (3,79)
84:2–85:9	−0.04	0.36	0.47 (3,100)	−0.03	0.53	0.23 (3,102)

Sample	$k=4$ Europe $\bar{R}^2$	SE	$F(m,n)$	Total $\bar{R}^2$	SE	$F(m,n)$
80:1–85:9	0.01	0.85	0.85 (3,356)	0.04	1.88	1.45 (3,358)
80:1–80:11	−0.03	0.78	0.57 (3,47)	0.09	1.63	1.90 (3,50)
80:12–82:10	0.02	0.84	1.11 (3,114)	0.07	2.17	1.01 (3,116)
82:10–84:1	0.00	0.91	0.79 (3,74)	−0.05	2.19	0.15 (3,73)
84:2–85:9	−0.01	0.85	0.53 (3,100)	−0.02	1.39	0.44 (3,98)

Japan announcements

Sample	$k=0$ Tokyo $\bar{R}^2$	SE	$F(m,n)$	$k=1$ Europe $\bar{R}^2$	SE	$F(m,n)$
80:1–85:9	0.05	0.67	2.08 (3,200)	0.01	0.89	2.47 (3,192)
80:1–80:11	0.08	0.99	0.86 (3,26)	−0.11	0.79	0.70 (3,23)
80:12–82:10	0.03	0.63	1.09 (3,59)	0.02	0.93	1.36 (3,58)
82:10–84:1	0.11	0.54	0.08 (3,41)	0.02	1.03	1.40 (3,38)
84:2–85:9	−0.07	0.58	0.70 (3,50)	−0.05	0.81	0.87 (3,49)

Sample	$k=2$ New York $\bar{R}^2$	SE	$F(m,n)$	$k=3$ Pacific $\bar{R}^2$	SE	$F(m,n)$
80:1–85:9	−0.01	0.95	0.85 (3,192)	−0.02	0.47	0.17 (3,185)
80:1–80:11	0.11	0.78	1.29 (3,23)	−0.20	0.34	0.43 (3,22)
80:12–82:10	−0.02	1.06	1.35 (3,58)	−0.04	0.54	0.90 (3,57)
82:10–84:1	−0.13	1.23	0.18 (3,38)	−0.08	0.54	0.15 (3,35)
84:2–85:9	−0.02	0.69	1.29 (3,49)	−0.03	0.44	0.95 (3,47)

Sample	Total $\bar{R}^2$	SE	$F(m,n)$
80:1–85:9	−0.01	1.58	0.49 (3,193)
80:1–80:11	−0.01	1.64	0.36 (3,25)
80:12–82:10	0.02	1.52	1.19 (3,58)
82:10–84:1	−0.04	1.59	1.12 (3,38)
84:2–85:9	−0.02	1.62	1.27 (3,48)

[a] The estimation results are for eq. (1),

$$YD(k) = a(k) + b_1(k)\cdot SX_1 + b_2(k)\cdot SX_2 + b_3(k)\cdot SX_3 + c_1(k)\cdot EX_1 + c_2(k)\cdot EX_2 + c_3(k)\cdot EX_3 + e(k),$$

where SX_i and EX_i are the surprise and expected part of the announcement for variable X_i ($i = 1,2,3$), respectively, and $YD(k)$ is the change in the yen/dollar rate in the kth segment after the announcement.

$F(m,n)$ is an F-statistic with (m,n) degrees of freedom. The null hypothesis is that $c_1(k) = c_2(k) = c_3(k) = 0$ in eq. (1). $\bar{R}^2$ is the multiple correlation coefficient corrected for degrees of freedom. SE is the standard error.

[b] Significant at the 5 percent level.

measures. In particular, social security week adjustments to the measure of expected money used in table 3 cause expected money to have estimated coefficients significantly different from zero for the $k = 0$ and $k = 1$ segments, as well as for the total, during the 1980:1–1980:11 subsample. Moreover, in contrast to results focusing on the response of U.S. interest rates to money announcement surprises [Clark, Joines and Phillips (1985)], the addition of this information also causes the estimated response of the yen/dollar rate to be insignificantly different from zero at high significant levels for all segments during the 1980:1–1980:11 subsample. Additional empirical results indicated that the survey measure of expected money incorporated virtually all of the information about social security weeks by 1982:10, and all of the information by 1984:2. During the 1980:1–1980:11 subsample, however, this information was not incorporated in the survey measure. Together, these results suggest that the expectations data used in table 3 reflect the information set used by currency traders with respect to social security weeks, and that the effects of social security weeks were at least partially unanticipated in the 1980:1–1980:11 subsample.[16]

The estimated coefficients on announcement surprises are discussed below. For each country, the responses are estimated jointly in equations corresponding to those summarized in table 3.

3.3. Response to money announcement surprises

The estimated response of the yen/dollar exchange rate to weekly U.S. money announcement surprises is reported in table 4. As reflected in the table, these announcements occur during the second segment ($k = 1$) of the New York market. While similar estimates of the initial response in the New York market are reported elsewhere, the results in table 4 are obtained both for a more recent sample and for more highly disaggregated segments within a 24-hour period.

The initial response to U.S. money announcement surprises in the New York market is positive and statistically significant at the 5 percent level for the overall sample and in two of the four subsamples. In these instances, the response is consistent with the expectation of higher real interest rates in the U.S., for example, as the Federal Reserve attempts to offset a positive money surprise. The estimated response is not significant at even the 10 percent level in the February 1984 to September 1985 period, corresponding to the adoption of contemporaneous reserve requirements by the Federal Reserve. Roley (1986c) finds that the response of the 3-month Treasury bill yield also is insignificantly different from zero in the post-February 1984 period. As a

[16]Estimation and test results analogous to those reported in tables 3 through 6 using the three alternative expectations measures are available from the authors upon request.

Table 4

Response to money announcement surprises; response coefficient $b_1(k)$ estimates.[a]

	U.S.				
Sample	$k=1$ New York	$k=2$ Pacific	$k=3$ Tokyo	$k=4$ Europe	Total[b]
80:1–85:9	0.11[c] (6.25)	0.08[c] (5.19)	0.01 (0.44)	−0.02 (−0.82)	0.22[c] (3.73)
80:1–80:11	0.06 (1.94)	0.03 (0.88)	0.06 (0.84)	0.08 (1.22)	0.27[c] (2.16)
80:12–82:10	0.14[c] (5.01)	0.12[c] (4.37)	0.01 (0.21)	−0.04 (−1.01)	0.30[c] (2.90)
82:10–84:1	0.14[c] (3.07)	0.10[c] (3.37)	−0.03 (−0.59)	−0.09 (−1.44)	0.11 (0.75)
84:2–85:9	0.05 (1.37)	0.01 (0.45)	0.00 (0.08)	−0.00 (−0.05)	0.06 (0.64)

	Japan				
Sample	$k=0$ Tokyo	$k=1$ Europe	$k=2$ New York	$k=3$ Pacific	Total[b]
80:1–85:9	0.07 (0.43)	−0.05 (−0.22)	−0.08 (−0.32)	−0.02 (−0.15)	−0.23 (−0.59)
80:1–80:11	−0.74 (−0.89)	−0.06 (−0.07)	−0.21 (−0.22)	−0.21 (−0.50)	−1.39 (−1.01)
80:12–82:10	0.10 (0.45)	−0.36 (−1.11)	−0.34 (−0.94)	−0.04 (−0.22)	−0.64 (−1.22)
82:10–84:1	0.96[c] (1.98)	0.60 (0.55)	0.05 (0.04)	−0.68 (−1.08)	0.19 (0.12)
84:2–85:9	−0.26 (−0.67)	−0.08 (−0.15)	−0.04 (−0.09)	0.16 (0.55)	−0.29 (−0.27)

[a] The estimation results are for eq. (1),

$$YD(k) = a(k) + b_1(k) \cdot SX_1 + b_2(k) \cdot SX_2 + b_3(k) \cdot SX_3 + c_1(k) \cdot EX_1 + c_2(k) \cdot EX_2 + c_3(k) \cdot EX_3 + e(k),$$

where SX_i and EX_i are the surprise and expected part of the announcement for variable X_i ($i = 1, 2, 3$), respectively, and $YD(k)$ is the change in the yen/dollar rate in the kth segment after the announcement.

Numbers in parentheses below the coefficient estimates are t-statistics. For U.S. money announcements, the response in the New York market is measured in the second New York segment ($k = 1$), which corresponds to the period from 12:00 noon to closing (after 4:30 p.m.). For Japanese money announcements, the response in the New York market is measured from 9:00 a.m. to closing.

[b] Total response from $k=0$ to $k=4$ for U.S. announcements and from $k=0$ to $k=3$ for Japan announcements.

[c] Significant at the 5 percent level.

consequence, it is not surprising that the response of the yen/dollar exchange rate is insignificant.

Similar to the response in the New York market, the response in the Pacific segment is statistically significant in two subsamples. These results, which have not been reported previously, indicate that the yen/dollar exchange rate does not adjust fully by the measured closing quotes in the New York market. Instead, a response of almost equal magnitude is incorporated in the opening Tokyo quote as reflected by the response in the Pacific segment. U.S. money announcement surprises have no further effects in the subsequent Tokyo and Europe segments.

The total one-day response is significant at the 5 percent level in three instances. In the initial subsample ending in November 1980, the response accumulates across markets to yield a significant total response. The total response in the subsequent subsample is about the same magnitude, but it reflects the estimated responses during the first two segments. In contrast, in the October 1982 to January 1984 subsample, the responses in the first two segments are partially offset in the Tokyo and Europe segments to yield a total response insignificantly different from zero. Nevertheless, the hypothesis that the response is the same as that in the previous subsample cannot be rejected at low significance levels. As a whole, the results in table 4 suggest that U.S. monetary information has affected the yen/dollar exchange rate significantly, particularly within the three to four hours following an announcement.

If the Bank of Japan operates under the same policy rule as the Federal Reserve, a symmetric effect to Japanese money announcements would be expected. However, it is widely suspected that the Bank of Japan does not emphasize the money supply as its policy target. Thus, Japanese money announcements may influence the exchange rate differently.

In contrast to the U.S., money announcements are made monthly in Japan. In particular, the Bank of Japan announces every month the growth rate of the money supply for 12 months ending in the month preceding the announcement. The monthly average of M2 + CD is used for the definition of money supply.

The response of the yen/dollar exchange rate to Japanese money announcement surprises is summarized in the right-hand side of table 4. As is apparent in the table, a significant response of the exchange rate after a money announcement is detected in only one instance. In particular, during the October 1982 to January 1984 subsample, a positive money surprise is associated with yen depreciation. This response does not persist, however, as is apparent from the estimated total response. Moreover, the estimated response for the entire sample is not significantly different from zero. The results therefore suggest that money announcements in Japan have, at most, limited information value for traders about the future course of the economy or economic policies. Traders must believe that the Bank of Japan does not respond to any surprise increase or decrease in the money supply. Thus, the money supply is apparently not a primary or intermediate target of the Bank of Japan.

3.4. Response to industrial production announcement surprises

The unanticipated component of industrial production announcements could affect exchange rates through at least two channels. First, the announcement may embody information about the future course of the economy. A surprise increase in industrial production, for example, may indicate that the future growth of the economy will be stronger than previously expected. In turn, expectations about real interest rates and capital inflows will be revised upward. As a consequence, the surprise increase would induce an appreciation of this country's currency. Moreover, the monetary or fiscal authorities may react to the industrial production surprise by implementing countercyclical policies. Under these circumstances, the effect on the exchange rate could be reinforced.

Second, a surprise increase in industrial production may imply higher future inflation which should have a depreciating effect on a country's currency. If traders think this scenario is more plausible, the exchange rate should depreciate at the time of the announcement.

The estimated response of the yen/dollar exchange rate to U.S. industrial production announcement surprises is exhibited on the left-hand side of table 5.[17] The response again is estimated using eq. (1). Because U.S. industrial production announcements were made at either 8:30 or 9:00 a.m., the initial response should appear during the first segment ($k=0$) of the New York market.

During the segment in which the U.S. announcement is made, the estimated response is insignificantly different from zero at the 5 percent level. In the afternoon following the announcement, however, there is some evidence that the dollar depreciates in response to a positive surprise. For the entire sample, the significant negative response in this segment is more than offset to yield a significant positive total response. The positive response in the Europe segment, as well as that in the initial New York segment, contributes to this total effect. Thus, despite the significant negative response in the second New York segment, the evidence appears to be consistent with dollar appreciation in response to positive industrial production surprises, perhaps reflecting traders' assessments of higher economic growth.

Turning to industrial production announcements in Japan, the estimated response of the yen/dollar exchange rate is reported on the right-hand side of table 5. The yen appreciates significantly in response to positive industrial

[17]For both the U.S. and Japan, surprises in industrial production and producer (wholesale) prices are calculated from announced percentage changes.

Table 5

Response to industrial production announcement surprises; response coefficient $b_2(k)$ estimates.[a]

	U.S.					
Sample	$k=0$ New York	$k=1$ New York	$k=2$ Pacific	$k=3$ Tokyo	$k=4$ Europe	Total
80:1–85:9	0.51	−0.39[c]	0.18	0.16	0.62[c]	1.29[c]
	(1.54)	(−2.01)	(1.12)	(0.52)	(2.07)	(2.03)
80:1–80:11	−0.44	0.05	−0.02	0.75	0.75	0.32
	(−0.56)	(0.15)	(−0.06)	(0.90)	(1.80)	(0.23)
80:12–82:10	0.75	−0.41	0.13	0.02	−0.16	1.63
	(1.55)	(−1.52)	(0.50)	(0.03)	(−0.20)	(1.64)
82:10–84:1	0.07	0.17	0.70	−0.05	0.32	0.79
	(0.07)	(0.27)	(1.70)	(−0.07)	(0.23)	(0.42)
84:2–85:9	1.07	−1.35[c]	0.06	0.57	1.42	1.76
	(1.43)	(−2.87)	(0.18)	(1.17)	(1.82)	(1.35)

	Japan				
Sample	$k=0$ Tokyo	$k=1$ Europe	$k=2$ New York	$k=3$ Pacific	Total
80:1–85:9	−0.044	0.05	0.08	0.05	0.12
	(−0.72)	(0.61)	(0.95)	(1.20)	(0.84)
80:1–80:11	−0.05	0.02	−0.06	0.04	−0.05
	(−0.28)	(0.14)	(−0.40)	(0.62)	(−0.17)
80:12–82:10	0.05	0.16	0.26	0.04	0.50
	(0.40)	(0.86)	(1.21)	(0.35)	(1.65)
82:10–84:1	−0.26[c]	0.11	0.10	0.10	0.02
	(−2.65)	(0.57)	(0.42)	(1.00)	(0.08)
84:2–85:9	0.08	−0.03	0.14	0.03	0.17
	(0.68)	(−0.19)	(0.89)	(0.27)	(0.48)

[a] The estimation results are for eq. (1),

$$YD(k) = a(k) + b_1(k)\cdot SX_1 + b_2(k)\cdot SX_2 + b_3(k)\cdot SX_3 + c_1(k)\cdot EX_1 + c_2(k)\cdot EX_2 + c_3(k)\cdot EX_3 + e(k),$$

where SX_i and EX_i are the surprise and expected part of the announcement for variable X_i $(i = 1,2,3)$, respectively, and $YD(k)$ is the change in the yen/dollar rate in the kth segment after the announcement.

Numbers in parentheses below the coefficient estimates are t-statistics. For U.S. announcements, the initial response in the New York market $(k = 0)$ is measured from the closing quote in Tokyo to the 12:00 noon quote in New York. The response in the subsequent segment $(k = 1)$ is measured from 12:00 noon to closing in New York. For Japanese announcements, the response in the New York market is measured from 9:00 a.m. to closing.

[b] Total response from $k = 0$ to $k = 4$ for U.S. announcements and from $k = 0$ to $k = 3$ for Japan announcements.

[c] Significant at the 5 percent level.

production surprises in one subsample. This estimated response also is consistent with traders' assessments of a stronger economy and higher real interest rates, which leads to appreciation of the yen. This behavior appears to be reasonable given the popular belief in Japan that the economic growth rate is an important policy target. However, even this effect is offset in other markets by the end of one day.

3.5. Response to inflation announcement surprises

As was the case for money announcements, there are two main competing hypotheses concerning the response of exchange rates to a surprise in an inflation announcement. Suppose that traders believe that a surprise increase in prices is a signal of future inflation, then it has a depreciating effect on the exchange rate through Purchasing Power Parity. Alternatively, if traders think that the central bank will tighten its policy in response to a surprise price increase, the exchange rate could appreciate due to higher real interest rates and an increased inflow of capital.

The response of the yen/dollar exchange rate to inflation surprises is exhibited in table 6. Results using producer (wholesale) prices are reported for both the U.S. and Japan in the table. Movements in producer prices are generally considered to provide more relevant information about future inflation than observed movements in consumer prices.

For surprises in U.S. producer prices, which again are announced at either 8:30 or 9:00 a.m., the response of the yen/dollar rate is uniformly insignificant at the 5 percent level. This result suggests that producer price index surprises were not useful in forecasting future inflation and that U.S. policymakers were not expected to respond to such surprises. Traders in other segments also did not act on this new information.

For surprises in Japanese wholesale prices, the response of the yen/dollar rate also is uniformly insignificant at the 5 percent level. This non-reaction is perhaps more plausible for Japan. In particular, the Bank of Japan focuses more attention than U.S. policymakers on real interest rates and the exchange rate.

4. Summary of conclusions

This paper examined yen/dollar exchange rate movements from a new perspective. In particular, movements in the yen/dollar rate were examined in disaggregated segments within each business day from 1980 through 1985. This disaggregation allowed within-day movements in New York and Tokyo to be considered separately. In investigating the behavior of the yen/dollar rate during these segments, two factors were considered. First, both the volatility of the markets and the contributions of the respective markets in

Table 6

Response to inflation announcement surprises; response coefficient $b_3(k)$ estimates.[a]

	U.S.					
Sample	$k=0$ New York	$k=1$ New York	$k=2$ Pacific	$k=3$ Tokyo	$k=4$ Europe	Total
80:1–85:9	0.23	−0.16	0.13	0.47	−0.01	0.55
	(0.55)	(−0.63)	(0.64)	(1.20)	(−0.03)	(0.68)
80:1–80:11	0.11	0.03	0.21	0.22	0.39	0.97
	(0.17)	(0.11)	(0.73)	(0.31)	(0.71)	(0.86)
80:12–82:10	0.38	0.40	0.08	0.52	0.29	1.52
	(0.36)	(0.66)	(0.14)	(0.48)	(0.34)	(0.69)
82:10–84:1	−1.02	−0.88	−0.07	1.51	−1.66	−1.89
	(−1.01)	(−1.34)	(−0.14)	(1.66)	(−1.56)	(−0.95)
84:2–85:9	1.29	−0.14	0.04	0.24	−0.36	1.12
	(1.68)	(−0.28)	(0.12)	(0.44)	(−0.41)	(0.81)

	Japan				
Sample	$k=0$ Tokyo	$k=1$ Europe	$k=2$ New York	$k=3$ Pacific	Total
80:1–85:9	−0.15	−0.25	−0.16	−0.10	−0.48
	(−1.14)	(−1.22)	(−0.72)	(−0.87)	(−1.49)
80:1–80:11	−0.19	−0.23	−0.16	0.00	−0.39
	(−0.79)	(−1.00)	(−0.69)	(0.03)	(−0.97)
80:12–82:10	−0.12	−0.26	−0.29	−0.32	−0.99
	(−0.37)	(−0.54)	(−0.52)	(−1.16)	(−1.25)
82:10–84:1	0.18	0.19	0.08	−0.33	−0.10
	(0.50)	(0.25)	(0.09)	(−0.81)	(−0.10)
84:2–85:9	−0.07	−0.84	−0.45	0.00	−1.36
	(−0.13)	(−1.10)	(−0.70)	(0.01)	(−0.89)

[a] The estimation results are for eq. (1)

$$YD(k) = a(k) + b_1(k)\cdot SX_1 + b_2(k)\cdot SX_2 + b_3(k)\cdot SX_3 + c_1(k)\cdot EX_1$$
$$+ c_2(k)\cdot EX_2 + c_3(k)\cdot EX_3 + e(k),$$

where SX_i and EX_i are the surprise and expected part of the announcement for variable X_i $(i = 1, 2, 3)$, respectively, and $YD(k)$ is the change in the yen/dollar rate in the kth segment after the announcement.

Numbers in parentheses below the coefficient estimates are t-statistics. For U.S. announcements, the initial response in the New York market ($k=0$) is measured from the closing quote in Tokyo to the 12:00 noon quote in New York. The response in the subsequent segment ($k=1$) is measured from 12:00 noon to closing in New York. For Japanese announcements, the response in the New York market is measured from 9:00 a.m. to closing.

[b] Total response from $k=0$ to $k=4$ for U.S. announcements and from $k=0$ to $k=3$ for Japan announcements.

[c] Significant at the 5 percent level.

determining longer-run exchange rate movements were compared. Second, the relative effects of news from the U.S. and Japan were examined explicitly with respect to the response of the yen/dollar rate to particular economic announcements in both countries.

The empirical results yielded conclusions in two principal areas. First, in terms of the general characteristics of daily yen/dollar movements, the data indicated that the New York market was typically more volatile, perhaps reflecting a greater presence of relevant news. Moreover, the volatility in the Tokyo market has been dramatically decreasing. Also, in the first half of the 1980s, the dollar tended to appreciate in the New York market and depreciate in the European market. In three of the four subperiods considered, the Tokyo market made virtually no contribution to annual yen/dollar rate movements.

Second, among the economic announcements considered, U.S. money announcement surprises had the most consistent effects, at least prior to February 1984. Positive surprises were found to result in dollar appreciation. Additional evidence suggested that positive industrial production surprises also may have resulted in dollar appreciation. For Japanese economic announcements, significant responses were recorded in only one period. These responses again were associated with industrial production and money announcements in the Tokyo market. By the end of one day, even these effects were offset in other markets.

As a whole, the results indicate that the source of the dollar's strength relative to the yen during the 1980–1985 period emanated from the New York market. In turn, information related to U.S. monetary policy affected the yen/dollar rate significantly. European markets, however, tended to reverse the longer-run effects originating in New York. The evidence is nevertheless suggestive that U.S. economic policies and the behavior of the U.S. economy were at least partly responsible for the behavior of the yen/dollar rate over this period.

Appendix

A.1. Exchange rate quotes

TKO = 9 a.m. quote in the Tokyo foreign exchange market,
TKC = 3:30 p.m. quote in the Tokyo foreign exchange market,
NYO = 9 a.m. quote in the New York foreign exchange market,
NYN = 12 noon quote in the New York foreign exchange market,
NYC = 4:30 p.m. quote in the New York foreign exchange market (on money announcement days, the quote is taken after 4:30 p.m. to capture any effects from money announcements).

All quotes are in yen/dollar. Tokyo quotes were collected from a daily newspaper, *Nihon Keizai Shinbun*. New York quotes were obtained from the Federal Reserve Bank of New York.

A.2. Data timing

	Tokyo		New York	
Day	Time	Day	EST	EDT
T	9:00 a.m. (opening), TKO	$T-1$	7:00 p.m. (closed)	8:00 p.m. (closed)
T	3:30 p.m. (closing), TKC	T	1:30 a.m. (closed)	2:30 a.m. (closed)
T	10:00 p.m. (closed)	T	8:00 a.m. (closed)	9:00 a.m. (opening), NYO
T	11:00 p.m. (closed)	T	9:00 a.m. (opening), NYO	10:00 a.m. (open)
$T+1$	5:30 a.m. (closed)	T	3:30 p.m. (open)	4:30 p.m. (closing), NYC
$T+1$	6:30 a.m. (closed)	T	4:30 p.m. (closing), NYC	5:30 p.m. (closed)
$T+1$	9:00 a.m. (opening), TKO	T	7:00 p.m. (closed)	8:00 p.m. (closed)

The New York foreign exchange market, unlike its Tokyo counterpart, does not have well-defined business hours. Therefore, 9 a.m. and 4:30 p.m. quotes are only approximations of the opening and closing rates for the day.

The number of hours between opening (O) and closing (C) quotes is the following:

Tokyo (O) – Tokyo (C): 6.5 hrs. (with 1.5 hr: lunch break)
Tokyo (C) – N.Y. (O): 7.5 hrs. (EST)/6.5 hrs. (EDT)
N.Y. (O) – N.Y. (C): 7.5 hrs.
N.Y. (C) – Tokyo (O): 2.5 hrs. (EST)/3.5 hrs. (EDT)

A.3. Japanese announcement and surprise data

M2 + CD = growth rate of the monthly average of M2 + CD over the past 12 months ending two months before the announcement month. The announcement is usually made on Tuesday or Friday of the first or second week. (Source: Bank of Japan, reported in *Nihon Keizai Shinbun*.)

IP = percentage change in the industrial production index, seasonally adjusted, for one month before the announcement month. The announcement is usually made sometime toward the end of the month. (Source: Ministry of Industry and International Trade, reported in *Nihon Keizai Shinbun*.)

WPI = percentage change in the wholesale price index, seasonally adjusted, for one month before the announcement month. The announcement is made during the second or third week. (Source: Bank of Japan, reported in *Nihon Keizai Shinbun*.)

The base year for WPI and IP changed during the sample period. Announced values during the old base year samples are deflated by the ratio of the new series to the old series.

A rolling vector autoregression model, including M2 + CD, IP, WPI, TKC, and the end of month Gensaki interest rate (3-month repurchase agreement) is used to create one-step (month) ahead predictions (expected values). The information set contains a constant and three lagged endogenous values which are available at the time of prediction. The deviations of expected values from realized values are confirmed to have zero means and no serial correlation.

A.4. U. S. announcement and surprise data

M1 = weekly change in the narrowly defined money stock, seasonally adjusted, in billions of dollars. The data are for the statement week ended about $1\frac{1}{2}$ weeks previously. Each week's announcement was typically made on a Thursday or Friday. (Source: Board of Governors of the Federal Reserve System, H.6.)

IP = percentage change in the industrial production index, seasonally adjusted, for the month before the announcement month. (Source: Board of Governors of the Federal Reserve System, the *Federal Reserve Bulletin*.)

PPI = percentage change in the producer price index, seasonally adjusted, for the month before the announcement month. (Source: Bureau of Labor Statistics.)

Expectations are measured using the medians of the weekly market survey conducted by Money Market Services, Inc. The change in the 3-month Treasury bill yield during the four business days prior to an announcement is used to update the survey measure.

References

Batten, Douglas S. and Daniel L. Thornton, 1984, Discount rate changes and the foreign exchange market, Journal of International Money and Finance 3, 279–292.

Clark, Truman A., Douglas H. Joines and G. Michael Phillips, 1985, Social security payments, money supply announcements, and interest rates, Mimeo. (University of Southern California, Los Angeles, CA).

Cornell, Bradford, 1982, Money supply announcements, interest rates, and foreign exchange, Journal of International Money and Finance 1, 201–208.

Cornell, Bradford, 1983, The money supply announcements puzzle: Review and interpretation, American Economic Review 73, 644–657.

Dornbusch, Rudiger, 1980, Exchange rate economics: Where do we stand?, Brookings Papers on Economic Activity, 143–185.

Edwards, Sebastian, 1982, Exchange rates and 'news': A multi-currency approach, Journal of International Money and Finance 1, 211–224.

Edwards, Sebastian, 1983, Floating exchange rates, expectations and new information, Journal of Monetary Economics 11, 321–336.

Edwards, Sebastian, 1984, Exchange rates and 'news': Reply, Journal of International Money and Finance 3, 123–126.

Engel, Charles and Jeffrey Frankel, 1984, Why interest rates react to money announcements: An explanation from the foreign exchange market, Journal of Monetary Economics 13, 31–39.

Frankel, Jeffrey A. and Gikas A. Hardouvelis, 1985, Commodity prices, money surprises, and fed credibility, Journal of Money, Credit and Banking 17, 425–438.

French, Kenneth R. and Richard Roll, 1984, Is trading self-generating?, Working paper no. 121 (University of Chicago, Chicago, IL).

Frenkel, Jacob A., 1981, Flexible exchange rates, prices and the role of 'news': Lessons from the 1970s, Journal of Political Economy 89, 665–705.

Hakkio, Craig S. and Douglas K. Pearce, 1985, The reaction of exchange rates to economic news, Economic Inquiry 23, 621–636.

Hardouvelis, Gikas A., 1984, Market perceptions of Federal Reserve policy and the weekly monetary announcements, Journal of Monetary Economics 14, 225–240.

Ito, Takatoshi, 1986, Capital controls and covered interest parity, Economic Studies Quarterly 37, 223–241.

Longworth, David, 1984, Exchange rates and 'news': A comment, Journal of International Money and Finance 3, 119–121.

Mussa, Michael L., 1979, Empirical regularities in the behavior of exchange rates and theories of the foreign exchange market, Carnegie–Rochester Conference Series on Public Policy 11, 9–57.

Roley, V. Vance, 1983, The response of short-term interest rates to weekly money announcements, Journal of Money, Credit and Banking 15, 344–354.

Roley, V. Vance, 1986a, The response of interest rates to money announcements under alternative operating procedures and reserve requirement systems, National Bureau of Economic Research working paper no. 1812.

Roley, V. Vance, 1986b, U.S. monetary policy regimes and U.S.–Japan financial relationships, National Bureau of Economic Research working paper no. 1858.

Roley, V. Vance, 1986c, Market perceptions of U.S. monetary policy since 1982, Federal Reserve Bank of Kansas City Economic Review 71, 27–40.

Roley, V. Vance and Carl E. Walsh, 1985, Monetary policy regimes, expected inflation, and the response of interest rates to money announcements, Quarterly Journal of Economics 100, 1011–1039.

Urich, Thomas J. and Paul Wachtel, 1981, Market responses to the weekly money supply announcements in the 1970s, Journal of Finance 36, 1063–1072.

Japanese Financial Market Research
W.T. Ziemba, W. Bailey and Y. Hamao (Editors)

Currency Hedging Strategies for U.S. Investment in Japan and Japanese Investment in the U.S*

William T. Ziemba

Faculty of Commerce, University of British Columbia, Vancouver, B.C. V6T 1Y8

Abstract

Investment to and from Japan can be very profitable. For example, a dollar invested in the Nikkei Stock Average in 1949 was worth over $500 at the end of 1989. In recent years there has been much Japanese investment in the U.S. particularly in bonds, stocks and real estate. The drop in the yen dollar rate from the 260 range in the fall of 1985 to the 120 range at the end of 1987 and its sharp rise back to 160 in mid 1989 and back under 130 in late 1990 shows the extreme risk involved in these investments. This paper investigates currency hedging strategies for Japanese investors making investments in U.S. assets and Americans investing in Japan. The traditional approach is to fully eliminate the currency risk using forward or futures contracts to offset the long exposure to the foreign currency. For the American investing in Japanese stocks the hedge often provides a bonus: an essentially risk free gain of 1-4% per year due to the difference in interest rates between the two countries. Although improvements adding risk are conceivably possible this approach is a very satisfactory resolution of this problem. The situation has been much more difficult and complicated for Japanese investment in the U.S. The forward/futures hedge eliminated the currency risk but at a cost of 1-4% per year until 1990. Strategies that do not lose this interest rate differential and in fact collect positive premiums are available by selling and buying yen put and call options. Simulations using an investment in three year Treasury bonds investigate this using recent currency movements and Black-Scholes estimated prices for plausible future scenarios to evaluate the risk-

*Presented at the conference on Financial Optimization held at the Wharton School, University of Pennsylvania, November 10-11, 1989. Without implicating them I would like to thank Warren Bailey, Yuko Beppu, Andy Turner and my colleagues at the Yamaichi Research Institute particularly A. Komatsu and H. Shintani for their help and useful discussions. Mr. H. Maruyama performed the simulation calculations in the empirical part of the paper. Part of this research was conducted at the Yamaichi Research Institute with the advice of William T. Ziemba. I thank the Yamaichi Research Institute for permission to publish those results. This research was also partially supported by the Social Sciences and Humanities Research Council of Canada, and the Centre for International Business Studies, University of British Columbia.

reward tradeoffs and the worst possible outcome using the various strategies. The added risk seems well worth taking for many investors to achieve substantial expected gains.

1. Introduction

Futures and options can be used for hedging-risk reduction purposes as well as for speculation. For the yen, there are active options markets as well as futures markets around the world. Long term yen currency warrants are traded on the American Stock Exchange. Yen futures markets in Japan began in June 1989. For the stock market, only index futures were available for use in Japan until the new NSA index options contracts began trading in Osaka in June 1989. Futures options contracts on the Topix on the TSE and the Nagoya 25 began trading in October 1989. However, long term puts and calls on the NSA and Topix have been trading for some time in markets outside Japan. There are no futures or options contracts in existence or planned regarding individual stocks or for small stocks. Hence, hedging strategies involving individual stock portfolios using the index derivative instruments will be subject to tracking error, which must be considered in the design of such strategies. The paper by Bailey and Ziemba in this volume discusses many of these index options and warrant contracts.

When the yen strengthened from 260 in the fall of 1985 to its low near 120 in 1987 and 1988, the *seibo* (life insurance companies) lost some $50 billion from their U.S. Treasury bond investments by not hedging. During 1989 and 1990, the yen has fallen back to the 150-160 range and then to the 125-135 range. Hence they have made back some of these losses. The strategy discussed here is a simple one that utilizes short-term puts and calls. Other instruments that could be used for currency hedging are put warrants as well as currency swaps, foreign exchange annuity swaps, foreign currency borrowing, interest rate caps and floors, investment or deposit in foreign currencies (such as dollar deposits with reverse floating rates against option contracts), hybrid capital market instruments (such as index bonds), etc.

The *seiho* have generally neglected the currency risk for investing long-run in the higher interest rates in the U.S. and for international diversification of their portfolios. The main reason is that their capacity to take large risks has come from the soaring prices of their accumulated real estate, stocks, and bonds in the domestic markets since 1985. Altman and Minowa (1989) discuss risks and returns from Japanese investment in high yield corporate (junk) bonds using futures hedging strategies. Obviously with so much at stake, strategies to protect this investment against unfavorable currency movements is of considerable interest.

2. Hedging a U.S. Stock Portfolio Against a Possible Increase in the Value of the Yen for a Japanese Investor

To begin our discussion, let's consider the case of a Japanese individual or institutional investor with a U.S. denominated portfolio that is either owned or contemplated. To make the case simplest, suppose the investor has $10 million in yen or about 1271.5 million yen at the spot rate of 127.15¥/$ in late October 1988. It does not matter if the money is in dollars from earnings in the U.S., or in yen because this sum can be immediately converted at very low cost from one currency to the other.

Strategies for Making and Keeping Excess Profits in the Stock Market (Ziemba, 1991) provides strategies and suggestions for investment in the U.S., so we will not discuss how to wisely invest there. Assume that you are about to purchase the $10 million in U.S. denominated stocks, bonds, and treasuries. How can you protect against the chance that the yen will keep rising and possibly go to 100 against the dollar?[1]

Table 1. October 20, 1988 Futures for Japanese Yen

JAPANESE YEN (MM) 12.5 million yen; $ per yen (.00)

	Open	High	Low	Settle	Change	Lifetime High	Lifetime Low	Open Interest	Yen/ US$
Dec 78	.7931	.7948	.7908	.7911	+ .0013	.8530	.7115	46,621	126.41
Mar 89	.8007	.8019	.7981	.7982	+ .0013	.8590	.7439	2,094	125.28
June 89	.8093	.8096	.8065	.8065	+ .0013	.8400	.7500	785	123.99
Sept 89	.8150	.8180	.8145	.8140	+ .0014	.8180	.7690	174	122.85

Est Vol 28,556; vol Wed 27,380; open into 49,674, -1,104.

A hedge involves the purchase of yen futures to match the sale of yen on day 0 - the conversion day - into dollars and the sale of these futures on day τ - the day you sell all or part of your stock in dollars and convert it back into Yen. On Thursday, October 20, 1988 the futures displayed in table 1 were available. The spot price was 0.7865 U.S. dollars per 100 yen, or 127.15 yen per dollar. The futures price of the yen is such that it is expected that the dollar will fall more than one yen in each three month period. Over a twelve month period, the dollar will fall in the futures market hedge by about 4.75 Yen or about 3.75%. This difference is the amount that it must fall in the futures market to account for the difference in interest rates in Japan and the United States. For example, the U.S. discount rate in late October 1988 was 6.5%, and the Japanese was 2.5% for a 4% difference.[2] If

[1]Most of this paper was written in the fall of 1988 and the winter of 1989 when the yen was in the 125-130 range and many predicted the it would increase further due to the U.S twin trade and budget deficits. The fear then was about a ¥100 per dollar rate. In May 1990 we had a 150-160 yen and the possibility of further falls. Hence, in recent times hedging may not have been the best strategy *expost*. At these and higher levels it may soon be very wise again. And it was as the yen was about 130 when we went to press in December 1990.

[2]In December 1990, the U.S. discount rate was 7.0% and that in Japan 6.00% for a 1% difference.

the futures were not priced this way then risk-free arbitrage would be possible by buying dollars with borrowed yen and investing them in U.S. dollars at the higher interest rates, meanwhile guaranteeing no loss by selling these dollars at high rates in the futures market.

The point is that an investor will lose about 3.75% per year by using this type of hedge. One buys

$$\frac{\$10 \text{ million U.S.} \times 127.15\ ¥/\$}{12.5 \text{ million } ¥/\text{contract}} = 101.7$$

or about 102 futures contracts and sells them when the stock is sold and the proceeds are converted back into yen. Since the 101.7 is not exactly 102 and one may not get exactly the same selling price for the futures contract as the spot price equivalent, except on an exact delivery date (because the futures price involves expectations, the so called basis risk, as well as interest rate differentials) there may be some additional small costs or benefits from this transaction.

The percentage gain on the portfolio in yen will be approximately

$$\left(100 + \begin{array}{c}\text{Rate of increase}\\ \text{in the portfolio in}\\ \text{U.S. dollars in percent}\end{array}\right)(0.9625) - 100.$$

So if the portfolio gains 25% in dollars it will gain only about 20% in yen. Hence a full 5% of the gain is lost just to manage the hedge. Can one avoid this loss? Yes, to some extent, but not without bearing some currency risk.

3. A Partial Hedge: The Basic Idea

One way is to partially hedge by selling put options on the yen. The short position in puts is equivalent to a long position in yen that pays a premium. This strategy eliminates the 3.75% annual loss because the yen is projected to strengthen in the futures markets and indeed provides a similar premium. So instead of losing 3.75% per year you gain about 7.60% per year (using the data below). The actual premium depends upon the usual factors that affect option prices: current volatility, time to expiry, the difference between the current yen price and the nearest strike price, the interest rates, and current market expectations regarding the yen-dollar exchange rate.

But this gain does not come for free, because you are only partially protected against falls in the dollar to the tune of the 7.60% or 11.35% per year in comparison to the futures approach. The spot price was 78.65 U.S. cents per 100 yen on October 20, 1988. The options were priced as listed in table 2. With options one has many choices of how to do the partial hedge but let us sell

December puts.[1] They are the most liquid and have about two months to expiry. Since the yen is expected to strengthen and the spot price is already 78.65 we can sell the 79 puts for about 1.00¢.

Table 2. October 20, 1988 Options on Japanese Yen

Strike		Calls - Settle			Puts-Settle	
Price	Nov-c	Dec-c	Jan-c	Nov-p	Dec-p	Jan-p
77	2.15	2.43	----	0.06	0.34	0.42
78	1.27	1.70	2.46	0.17	0.61	0.67
79	0.60	1.11	----	0.48	1.00	----
80	0.22	0.69	1.29	1.09	1.57	----
81	0.07	0.41	0.90	----	2.27	----
82	0.02	0.23	0.60	----	3.09	----

Let's see how this works out. Assume that in the ensuing two months the portfolio, including dividends goes up 3% - a roughly 20% yearly rate of return which is similar to the historical returns from the TOPIX or NSA. The investor will leave some of this stock as collateral for the margin required and invest the premium proceeds in T-bills and interest-bearing accounts with the brokerage firm to cover losses on the short calls.

The investor will collect the premiums, which, with rolling over every few months, amount to the roughly 7.6% per year and do not lose the 3.75% interest premium decay in the futures markets. So if the time horizon is long, say three years, then the investor has more than 25% to play with in possible drops in the dollar against the yen in comparison with the futures hedge. So assuming one rolls up and dynamically updates this hedge you are better off with the partial hedge over the three year horizon as long as the dollar stays above 95 yen.

It's not so simple, though, because whipsawing volatility is hazardous to this strategy. For example, when the dollar falls our investor loses all the gains in the yen above about 2/3% per month premiums and the about 1/3% per month from the interest rate differential. Also the investor does not participate in the gains in the dollar since he or she is protecting again falls in the dollar. So if there are sharp falls, such as the five yen fall in table 3, they will take a while to recoup the losses. However, the five yen fall or 4% in only two months still results in a gain of 1.42% on the partially hedged yen, which is less than 1% worse than the straight hedge.

This strategy is appropriate for a market with a yen that is slightly on the increase against the dollar. After the fall to the lower end of the Group of Seven target area for the yen of a reputed 120 to140 this may not be too risky a strategy. At some stage, the already grossly over-valued yen in price-parity terms will, once

[1]We could buy calls, such as the 79's for 1.11¢ but that would get us back into the interest rate loss situation as in the futures markets at roughly similar costs. At-the money calls would eliminate the currency risks as the futures hedge did and out-of-the-money puts would partially protect against large losses with lower costs.

the U.S. twin deficits are held in check, start falling and then one will want to participate in its rise more fully than you can with the covered call strategy. You can then simply go long in the stocks or protect the other way by selling yen futures option puts.

Table 3. Results of the Short Put, Partial Hedging Strategy on the U.S. Portfolio for a Japanese Investor, Gains and Losses in U.S. $ on December 1988 Expiry (on Second Friday)

Day 0	Hedge Comparison	Dollar Remains Constant @ 127.15¥/$ or $0.7865/100¥	Dollar Rises 1.75¥ to 129¥/$ or $0.7750/100¥	Dollar Rises 5¥ to 132.15¥/$ or 79.90¢/100¥	Dollar Falls 2¥ to 125.15¥/$ or 79.90¢/100¥	Dollar Falls 5¥ to 122.15¥/$ or 81.87¢/100¥
Convert 127,150,000¥ into $10 mil US @ $0.7865/100 ¥ or 127.15¥/$	$300,000 (gains on stock with dividends less 0.625% loss on hedge or $62,500	$300,000 (gains on stock with dividends)	$300,000 (gains on stock with dividends)	$300,000 (gains on stock with dividends)	$300,000 (gains on stock with dividends)	$300,000 (gains on stock with dividends)
Sell 102 Dec 79 puts @ 1.00¢/100¥ Collect $125,000 less commissions of about $2040 (assuming $20/contract)		$122,800 (in premiums $1228 (interest on premiums at 6%/year	$122,800 (in premiums $1228 (interest on premiums at 6%/year	$122,800 (in premiums $1228 (interest on premiums at 6%/year	$122,800 (in premiums $1228 (interest on premiums at 6%/year	$122,800 (in premiums $1228 (interest on premiums at 6%/year
		-0, since short puts expired worthless	a loss of $161,400, short puts 0.0125¢ in the money, with commission	a loss of $426,595, short puts 0.0333¢ in the money, with commission	-0, since short puts expired worthless	-0, since short puts expired worthless
Total Gain is in $ % Gain in $ % Gain in ¥	$1237,500 2.38% 2.38%	$424,028 4.24% 4.24%	$262,628 2.63% 4.12%	($2567) (0.026%) 3.91%	$424,028 4.24% 2.60%	$424,028 4.24% 1.4%

As with all option positions they must be carefully monitored because sudden movements in the spot price are magnified in the options markets. Still, with proper management, the short-put partial hedge strategy with dynamic adjustments can provide a useful way to hedge against possible future dollar drops again the yen.

4. Testing out the partial hedge idea: Japanese investment in U.S. Treasury Bonds[1]

The short put strategy discussed above is useful for an investor especially if the dollar does not fall too much. But it does not participate in possible rises in the dollar. We discuss some related strategies that do participate in dollar advances and limit the loss for yen gains. These strategies are then compared by simulation to ascertain how good they really are.

[1]Mr. H. Maruyama of the Yamaichi Research Institute assisted in this test by performing the simulation calculations that follow.

First let's look at the various strategies. For the context and calculations, we move to Wednesday, November 23, 1988, when the yen was trading at 82.41¢ per 100¥ or 121.34¥/$ near its low for the year. At this time the U.S. interest rates had risen to protect the dollar so the spread in the futures markets was about $4\frac{1}{2}$% per year. Figure 1 compares the various strategies. In these graphs the profits or losses from the option trading are kept separate from the asset returns. You may think of the underlying asset as being in U.S. currency with zero mean return and no variance. This simplifies these diagrams. The most risky strategy, called N and shown in figure 1a is simply to not hedge at all. This, of course, is what is done most frequently by investors. By not hedging one does not lose the roughly $4\frac{1}{2}$% annual futures discount but there is no protection if the yen rises. All gains in the dollar against the yen are captured. But all losses from gains in the yen are lost. If the yen rises less than $4\frac{1}{2}$% per year this strategy beats the hedge.

Figure 1b shows the futures hedge, called H. This strategy is essentially riskless. One receives the same return, a loss of about -$4\frac{1}{2}$%/12 per month or about -0.75% over two months, namely -0.91¥ or 0.618¢ per 100¥.

Strategy 0, shown in figure 1c is the short put partial hedge described in the previous section. This strategy is the next most risky procedure. The investor sells yen puts near the money. The investor collects the premium of say 7% per year and does not pay for the $4\frac{1}{2}$% discount. So if the yen rises less than 11 $\frac{1}{2}$% per year this strategy provides higher mean returns than the futures hedge. This strategy does not participate in dollar gains. It is only protected against yen gains by the roughly $11\frac{1}{2}$% per year.

The five new strategies limit the down-side risk of yen rises and participate in dollar rises in various ways. Figure 1d describes strategy: A1 Sell put near the money, buy put 2¢ out of the money. The related strategy was also tested: A2 Sell put near the money, buy put 3¢ out of the money.

These strategies are less risky than strategy 0. They participate in the dollar rise once it moves 2¢ or 3¢, respectively, but the protection against the yen's rise is limited to the premium. This strategy is the opposite of strategy C described below and has similar risk, assuming one worries about yen falls as well as rises. It is more risky against yen rises than C. The net premiums collected are less, say 4-5% per year than with strategy 0 because the deep out put must be purchased.[1]

Strategies B1 and B2 are the least risky. B1, which is shown in figure 1e, has the investor buy a call 2¢ out of the money in addition to strategy A1. So the full position is to sell a put near the money, buy a put 2¢ out and a call 2¢ out. The related strategy B2, which corresponds to A2 but with the extra 2¢ out call with the at the money short put and the 3¢ out long put was tested as well.

---

[1]Strategies like this would have worked well *ex post* during the dollar's rise in 1989 and 1990 while at the same time protecting against a sudden drop in the dollar.

Figure 1. The Various Hedging Strategies Compared
N, H, O, A, B and C

a: Case N: No Hedge

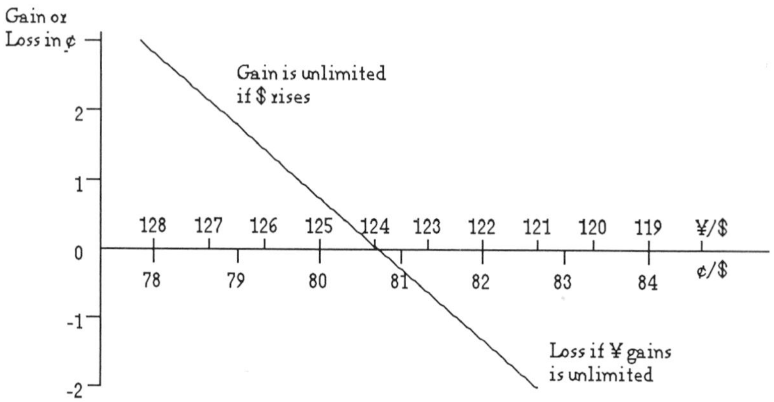

b: Case H: Futures Hedge

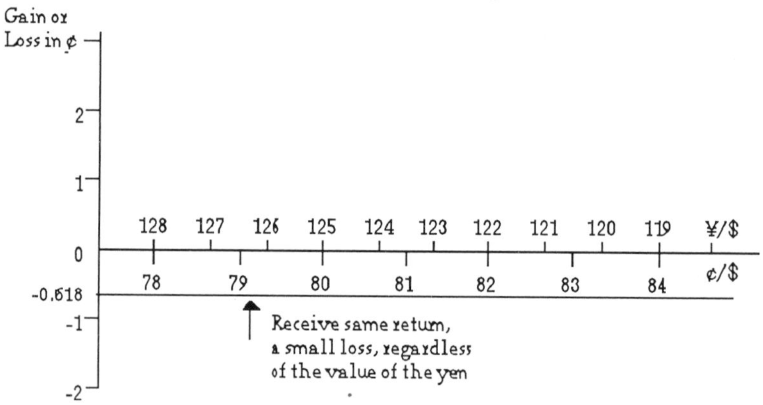

c: Case O: The Partial Hedge with Put Sold Near Money, at 81¢/100¥

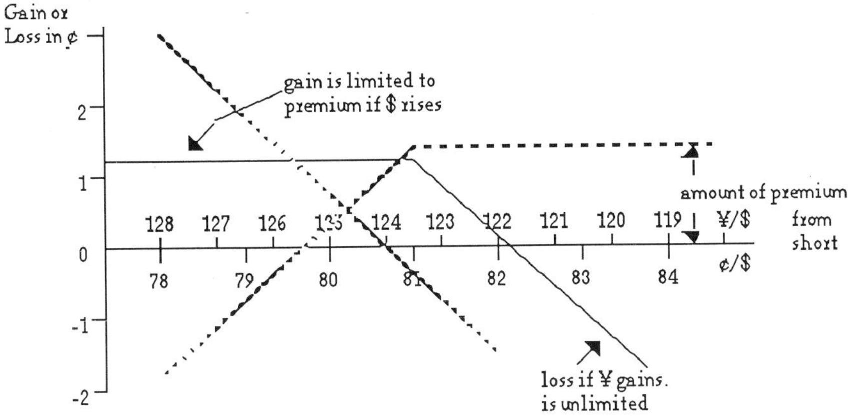

d: Case A1: The Partial Hedge with Put Sold Near Money at 81¢/100¥
and Put Bought out of Money, at 79¢/100¥

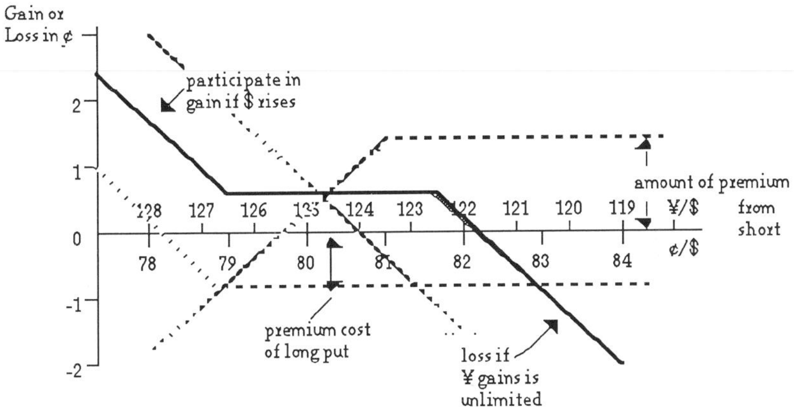

e: Case B1: The Partial Hedge with Put Sold Near Money, Put Bought 2¢ out of Money and Call Bought 2¢ Out of the Money

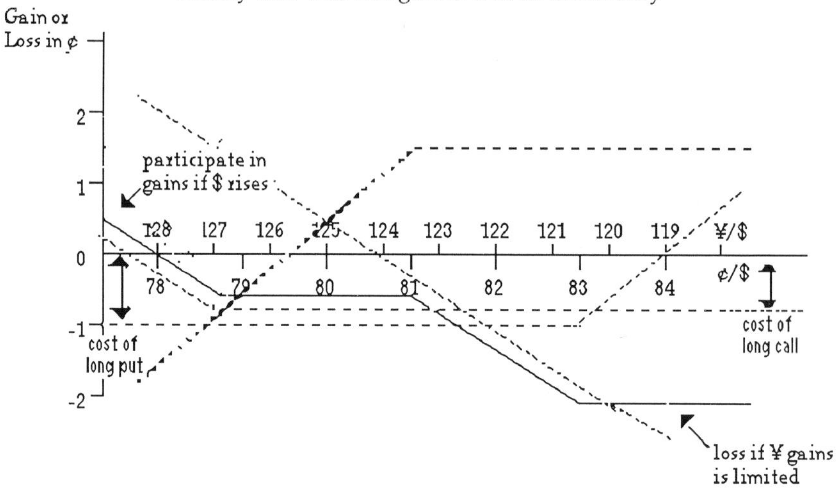

f: Case C: The Partial Hedge with Put Sold Near Money, at 81¢/100¥ and Call Bought Out of Money, at 83¢/100¥

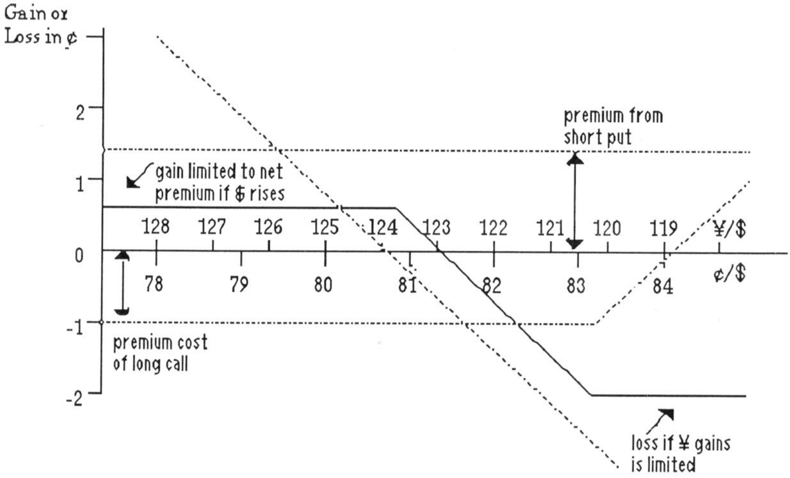

Figure 2: ¥/$ Exchange Rate, July 31, 1986 to Jan 19, 1989

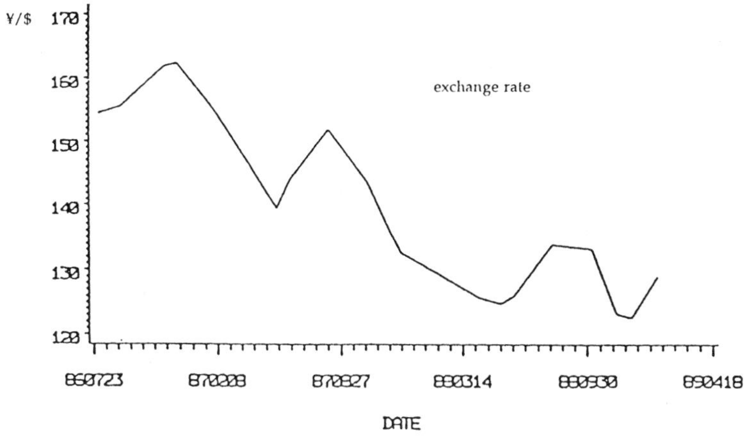

Figure 3. Results of Various Strategies ,July 23, 1986 to January 19, 1989, U.S. T-bonds yielding 6-7% and a Reinvestment Rate of 6%

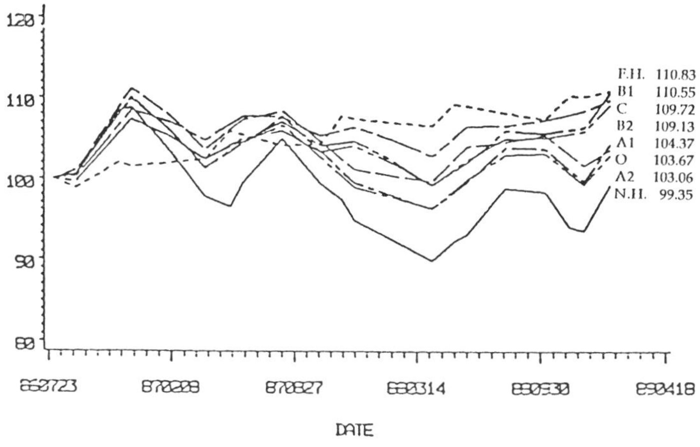

The investor is now protected on both sides and participates in dollar rises once it moves through the strike price and the losses on the yen's rise are limited to 2¢ less the net premiums. The net premiums collected are from the short put minus the out of the money puts and calls. This will not be very much, maybe $\frac{1}{2}$% to 3% per year depending on volatility, execution, etc.

The final strategy, C is shown in figure 1f. In this strategy the at-the-money put is sold and a deep out call is purchased. This is a cheaper strategy cost wise than B1 since the deep out put is not purchased. What you gain is to limit the maximum loss in any 2 month period if the yen rises sharply to a ¥2 change in the ¥/$ rate. So you have protection against the yen rising. But you do not participate in dollar gains. The risk of this strategy is less than with A1. For this strategy you collect less premium because a call is bought as well as the put sold. The options sold provide more money than those bought so the total return is about 4-5% per year.

These strategies are compared by investigating how they would have performed in the previous two or more years and simulating their likely future performance. The context used for the future simulations was investment in U.S. Treasury bonds with a fixed rate and a 3 year maturity. The specifics being:

Nov 1991 8 $\frac{1}{2}$ Bid 98-02 Ask 98-06 yield 9.23%, and
coupons received on stream were assumed invested at 8% per year.

An amount ¥A=¥100 is converted into US$ at time 0 and invested in U.S. assets at time 0. At time τ the proceeds are converted back into ¥B. The data were from July 23, 1986 to Jan 19, 1989. The test used a T-bond with a yield of 6.7% and it was assumed that the coupons were reinvested at 6%. This was a period of sharp increase for the yen except during 1988. As shown in figure 2, the yen started at about 154 and ended up about 128. The first year and a half the yen rose over 25% (154 $\rightarrow$ 120). Then it stayed in a volatile trading range of 120-135. With such a large gain in the yen one would expect the futures hedge to work the best. It did, returning 110.83 without risk. Strategies B1, B2 and C were only about 1% behind, but they had more risk. The other strategies were 5-10% worse. Figure 3 shows the results.

The conclusion is: if the yen rises 15-20% in a year or so, the futures hedge will be the best strategy. You have to have the yen rise no more than say 10% per year for the other strategies to possibly be better. So over three years the rise in the yen must be less than, say, 30-35%. Given the dollar's sharp fall since 1985 a further 30% drop would take it under 90¥/$, an event that may or may not occur. Obviously, the yen cannot keep rising forever. Indeed the dollar rose to the ¥150 level in 1989 and to ¥160 in April 1990 before it fell to the ¥125 to ¥135 range in late 1990. Hence, there may well be use for the partial hedge strategies that are now investigated with the simulation of possible futures for the ¥/$ exchange rate.

A Black-Scholes simulation shows how the strategies might do in various possible futures. The idea was to assume that the put and call prices were well estimated by their Black-Scholes options prices. Volatility was assumed to be 11.8% which was that of 1988.[1] For interest rates we used 9% for the U.S. (the federal funds rate) and 3.9% for Japan (the call rate). The yen/dollar rate evolves day by day as[2]

$$(¥/\$)t{+}1 = (¥/\$)t \exp\left(-\frac{d}{252} + \sigma\delta\right)$$

d = the assumed yearly drift of the scenario over the 252 trading days

σ = the assumed volatility = 11.8% but double for the weeks with shocks

$\delta = \begin{cases} +1 \\ -1 \end{cases}$ for increases and decreases, for the binominal model with drift.

The two month options are bought and sold at their Black Scholes prices and held to maturity when they either expire worthless or are covered at the then in the money price assuming no bid-ask spread.

The following scenarios were tested:

1 The yen rises at 4% per year in each of the three years. This is roughly what the futures market expected (d=-0.04)

1' The same as 1 but every three months there is a shock and for one week the volatility doubles.

2 The yen has a zero (d=0) drift in the first year. In the second and third years the yen falls with a drift of 5% per year (d=0.05). This is a mildly stronger dollar scenario.

3 The yen drifts up 4% in year 1 (d=-0.04) but then the $ drifts up 15% in the second year (d=0.15) and 20% in the third year (d=0.20). This is the U.S. trade and budget improvement scenario moving close to price parity in 3 years.[3]

---

[1]Constant volatility is a requirement of the Black-Scholes model inputs. Obviously, volatility is not constant, so this is simply a convenient simplification. There is much scope to consider alternative currency option pricing models here.

[2]This is a binomial currency change model and it was convenient to utilize when analyzing broad currency trends as I wished to do. There are alternative theories of currency movements such as those based on the Fisher effect, purchasing power parity and expectation theory that could be utilized and compared as well.

[3]This is the scenario that is closest to what has actually happened before the yen firmed again in mid 1990.

4 The yen drifts up 10% in the first year then 5% more in year 2 and 10% more in the third year. This is the hard landing for the dollar with the $/¥ rate falling to less than 100.

These five scenarios seem to span the range of possibilities reasonably well. There could be more violent moves in the market, but it seems doubtful that the yen would fall much below 95-100 (scenario 4) or rise much above about 165 (scenario 3). For some of the simulation outcomes, the ¥/$ rate is outside these bands so we do have estimates of the strategic performances of these cases also.

Observations

1 The mean yen/dollar rate was 120.4 with a minimum of 47.6 and a maximum of 254.1.

2 The future hedge returns 114.96 without risk.

3 The other strategies return more on average but they have more risk. Additonal mean return is approximately linear in standard deviation risk with a slope of 0.334 units of mean return per unit of standard deviation. Figure 4 shows this tradeoff. B1 is slightly above the curve but more or less you get what you pay for in a Markowitz mean-standard deviation sense. Another measure of risk is the lowest payoff. Figure 5 shows the minimum payoffs, the specific numbers appear in table 4.

The strategies N, O, A1 and A2 have very low minimum values. These are with very low dollar values. Assuming that the dollar cannot fall below 90¥ then the minimum values are (starting with 100 in year 0)

No Hedge	96
0	89
A1	99
A2	99

So you could lose money with these strategies.

B1 and B1 and C have minimum payoffs of 95, 97 and 102, respectively, with all scenarios. With the yen no lower than 90, the minimum payoffs for these strategies are

B1	102	with ¥/$ at 93	¥/$ = 74 before loss of 5
B2	104	" at 94	¥/$ = 60 before loss of 2
C	105	" at 102	Never losses, its minimum is 102 when the exchange rate is 83¥/$

So C compares favorably with the hedge. Its mean is 3.5% higher. Its lowest return with yen at 92 is 105 versus the 115 with the futures hedge. Its standard deviation is low. Strategies B1 and B2 look promising as well. These strategies seem to promise a 2% minimum return per year and get more mean return 5.7% with B1 and 4.4% with B2 versus the futures hedge.

Table 4. Summary of the 125 simulation runs, 25 per scenarios times 5 scenarios for each of the eight strategies, both in total and individual.

Variable Strategy	Sample Size	Mean Return	St Dev of Return	Min Return	Max Return	St Error of Mean Ret
Exchange Rate	125	120.42	37.46	47.60	254.08	3.35
N	125	128.29	39.91	50.71	270.67	3.57
H	125	114.96	0.00	114.96	114.96	0.00
O	125	120.24	22.13	60.01	170.47	1.92
A1	125	124.16	30.68	54.15	226.77	2.74
A2	125	122.48	27.35	55.21	205.31	2.45
B1	125	121.61	17.71	95.02	189.80	1.58
B2	125	120.12	14.31	97.66	171.69	1.28
C	125	118.53	8.06	102.24	148.48	0.72

Scenario	N	O	A1	A2	B1	B2	C
1	113.14	115.13	113.25	113.37	113.31	113.48	115.6
1'	114.05	111.69	113.29	112.50	117.44	116.68	116.7
2	140.96	129.18	135.11	132.46	126.46	124.05	121.1
3	173.92	138.57	157.25	151.22	143.36	137.88	126.3
4	99.37	106.61	101.88	102.88	107.44	108.53	113.0
Total	128.29	120.24	124.16	122.48	121.61	120.12	118.5

Scenario	STD N	STD O	STD A1	STD A2	STD B1	STD B2	STD C
1	25.69	18.79	22.07	20.48	10.10	8.31	6.12
1'	28.58	19.62	24.34	22.58	12.01	10.15	6.35
2	32.01	19.27	24.85	22.16	13.72	10.82	7.33
3	39.50	18.76	26.94	22.64	17.22	13.05	7.70
4	22.57	18.41	20.28	19.41	8.54	7.42	5.53
Total	39.91	22.13	30.68	27.35	17.71	14.31	8.06

Table 5 gives the minimum returns for the various strategies given a variety of low final values for the dollar/yen exchange.

This study was oriented toward the concern that the yen would strengthen to provide poor returns on the investment. Should the dollar neither fall nor strengthen, then all of the partial or no hedge strategies will beat the futures hedge. Hence at final exchange rates of ¥120+ for the dollar one sees this effect. Not surprisingly, the no hedge strategy is then best but the partial hedge strategies that were good protection against a fall in the dollar are pretty good should the yen fall.[1]

[1]The yen did in fact fall to the 150-160 range and the no hedge strategy did the best *ex post* returning 170 vs. 153 for strategy A1 and 176 versus 168 if the dollar rises past 170.

Figure 4: Mean-Standard Deviation Tradeoff of the Scenario Results for the Various Strategies.

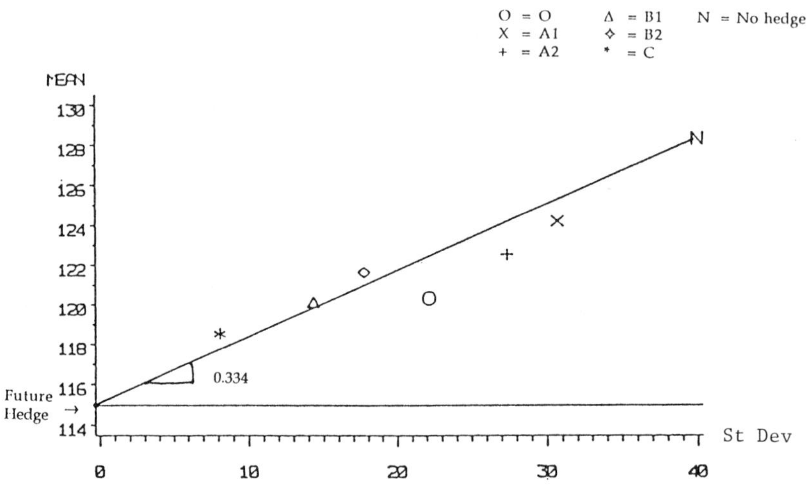

Figure 5: Mean-Standard Deviation Tradeoff plus Ranges of the Scenario Results for the Various Strategies

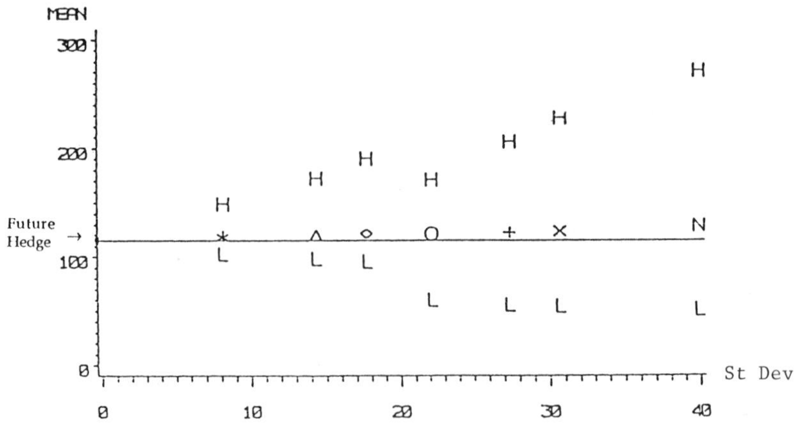

Table 5: Minimum returns for the various strategies for various minimum final values for the dollar in yen.

Value of $ in ¥	NH	0	A1	A2	B1	B2	C	Futures Hedge
90+	96	89	99	99	102	104	105	115
95+	100	107	105	105	106	105	110	115
100+	106	108	109	110	108	112	112	115
105+	112	108	112	111	108	112	112	115
110+	117	101	115	113	108	110	111	115
115+	121	115	120	118	118	112	112	115
120+	127	126	126	124	119	117	118	115
125+	132	128	130	129	121	120	119	115
130+	138	132	139	137	126	126	119	115
135+	142	131	142	139	127	125	118	115
140+	147	130	138	138	130	130	121	115
145+	154	131	144	144	144	139	135	115
150+	159	148	145	144	125	123	127	115
160+	170	132	153	142	148	138	131	115
170+	176	150	168	159	140	132	123	115
Mean Returns	128	120	124	122	121	120	119	115

This simulation used 25 histories for each strategy. Each result is path dependent so that the outcome depends upon how the yen/dollar rate reached its final value. For professional application one might do several things in addition to more model development and simulations to decide on a preferred strategy, such as:

1 Using a market maker prices can be obtained that are better than those estimated from the Black-Scholes equations. One can sell at the ask and buy at the bid. That is worth a few percent over the three years.

2 These calculations use a 2 month rollover period with no dynamics. There is room for some improvement by altering slightly the strategy as the outcomes unfold. One also might be able to buy back shorts if prices are low and combine a little market timing on the margin.

3 The interest on the shorts is worth more than calculated here as are the coupons. The latter benefits the futures hedge as well.

More mathematical analyses emphasizing continuous time strategies using futures are discussed by Adler and Detemple (1988), Duffie and Jackson (1986), Duffie and Richardson (1989), Eaker and Grant (1987), Solnik (1989) Svensson

(1988) and references therein. The goals of these authors differed from those here. We are searching for a way to attempt to minimize the effects of the deep futures discount on the yen, while they were more concerned with minimizing the variance of returns over time. See also Jorion (1989), Stone and Hensel (1989) and Perold and Schulman (1988).

The analysis here and in most other literature assumes that stock prices and currency movements are uncorrelated. This is definitely not the case with the yen and the Tokyo market. Indeed the Tokyo market generally reacts favorably to higher yen values and negatively to the reverse. This was especially true in the 1990 correction when the yen and the indices fell sharply, and then turned around together in late April and May. It is not simple though, during 1989 there was a sharp rise in the NSA coupled with a falling yen. It was higher interest rates that triggered the stock market fall in 1990. The point of this for a complete analysis is that one needs to consider the relationship between currency and stock price movements and their relationship with interest rates and other macro variables such as inflation. Such is the depth of difficulty of this problem.

5. Hedging a Japanese Portfolio Against a Possible Drop in the Value of the Yen for a U.S. Investor

This situation is the reverse of the previous case, except now the interest rate differential works in the investor's favor. Hence, the futures prices of the dollar are higher than the spot prices. In addition, because the dollar is expected to fall, the prices of the puts you would have to sell to produce the partial hedge are not as high as the calls. Hence, the futures hedge seems like the preferable way to protect against possible gains in the dollar. Let's look at it with some numbers.

Assume that U.S.$10 million has been invested in Japanese securities at the October 20, 1988 spot exchange rate of 78.65 cents per 100 yen or 127.15 ¥/$. The dollar can fall about 3.75% or about 4.75 yen to 122.40 ¥/$ before the advantage of the hedge ceases to give you an edge over the status quo considering a one year horizon.

The futures hedge allows you to change your yen back into dollars at the currently favorable rate of 122.40 ¥/$. So your U.S.$10 million is really worth $10,375,000 as long as the stock market performance in yen matches the performance in the U.S. stock market. This $375,000 edge provides a cushion for the yen tracking error risk as well as the market risk and transactions costs.

A short call partial hedge is illustrated in table 6 and compared with the futures hedge. Assuming the stock portfolio plus dividends increases by 3% in the two month period from October 20, 1988, until the options expire on the third Friday in December, the hedge gains 3.63%; the 3% gain plus the two month bonus of 0.63% from the interest rate differential. If the exchange rate stays constant then the partial hedge returns 4.40% in yen as well as in dollars. You do not gain much extra with dollar falls because you have sold the calls short. The gains of 4.88% and 4.99% with dollar falls of 2 and 5 yen, respectively, differ slightly from the 4.40% of the constant exchange rate case because of transactions costs, the fact that the 102 short calls is not the exact cover for the partial hedge and the basis difference beween the spot and strike prices of the options.

Table 6: Results of the Short Call, Partial Hedging Strategy on a Japanese Portfolio for a U.S. Investor, Gains and Losses in Yen on December 1988 Expiry (Second Friday in December)

Day 0	Hedge Comparison	Dollar Remains Constant at 127.15¥/$ or $0.7865/100¥	Dollar Rises 1.75¥ to 129¥/$ or $0.7750/100¥	Dollar Rises 5¥ to 132.15¥/$ or 79.90¢/100¥	Dollar Falls 2¥ to 125.15¥/$ or 79.90¢/100¥	Dollar Falls 5¥ to 122.15¥/$ or 81.87¢/100¥
Convert $10 million US into 127,150,000¥ @ $0.7865/100 ¥ or 127.15¥/$	3,814,500¥ (gains on stock with dividends) gain on hedge of 0.625% or 794,688¥	38,145,000¥	38,145,000¥	,145,000¥	38,145,000¥	38,145,000¥
Sell 102 Dec 79 calls @ 1.11¢/100¥ Collect $140,250 less commissions of $2040		$138,210 or 17,573,402¥	$138,210 or 17,573,402¥	$138,210 or 17,573,402¥	$138,210 or 17,573,402¥	$138,210 or 17,573,402¥
		-0, since short calls expired worthless	-0, since short calls expired worthless	-0, since short calls expired worthless	a loss of $116,790 or 14,849,849¥ short calls 0.009¢ in the money with commission	a loss of $367,965 or 44,946,625¥ short calls 0.0287¢ in the money with commission
Total Gain in $	46,091,880¥	55,894,123¥	55,894,123¥	55,894,123¥	41,041,274¥	10,944,198¥
% Gain in $	3.63%	4.40%	4.40%	4.40%	3.23%	0.86%
% Gain in ¥	3.63%	4.40%	2.90%	0.45%	4.88%	4.99%

The investor is pretty well fully protected on this side but does not participate in any further gains. When the dollar rises, the investor is only partially protected to the tune of the options premium for unlike the yen into dollars play, investor does not gain the interest differential in comparison with the futures hedge. In addition, because the yen is projected to increase in value in the futures market, the calls are not as valuable to sell as the puts were. Still, our investor makes 2.90% when the dollar rises 1.75¥ and 0.45% when it rises 5¥ in this two month period. On balance the straight hedge seems preferable for this investor. The advantage of the essentially riskless 3.75% per year makes this strategy a hard one not to employ. The U.S. investor in Japan does not need to use the complicated strategies that the Japanese investor in the U.S. might wish to utilize.[1]

[1]In May 1990, this differential against the U.S. dollar was more on the order of 1% per year rather than the 3.75% it was in the fall of 1988 and in December it was slightly negative. Given this, one may wish to consider more risky strategies, such as those discussed above for Japanese investment in the U.S.

The Canadian investor or those from countries such as England, France, Italy and Switzerland, that have higher interest rates than in the U.S. have even more advantages investing in Japan. Figure 6 shows this with four different approaches. In figure 6a the portfolio value in yen is displayed with its typical volatility assuming an upward trend in prices. The portfolio value in Canadian dollars is much more volatile as shown in figure 6b. Huge jumps in value of the portfolio have occured often in these markets. For example, on Friday, May 11, 1990, the Canadian dollar fell 5 yen from 135 to 130. Since currency and stock price movements are highly correlated one will have large moves in both directions from the trend line in yen. Figure 6c hedges the currency and the Canadian investor is able as of December 1990 to eliminate the Canadian/yen risk and gain over 5% essentially risk free. Given this edge the investor may well be wise to spend some of it on portfolio insurance protection through Nikkei put warrants or some other scheme. The situation is shown in figure 16.6d where there is a floor on the minimum portfolio return that is above the nominal investment with a positive drift of 1-2% per year. Given the poor performance of Canadian portfolios and managers over the past twenty years they would likely benefit from strategies like figure 4d. The difference between hedged and unhedged returns is explored more fully after we discuss adjusting the amount of the hedge.

6. Adjusting the Amount of the Hedge

The U.S. investor in Japan does need to adjust the number of contracts in the hedge as the portfolio of Japanese stocks varies in value. Since each yen currency contract is for ¥12.5 million the number of contract required to hedge the position when the currency is exchanged is

$$\text{int}\left[\frac{S_0 A}{\text{¥12.5M per contract}}\right] = c_0$$

where S_0 is the current spot exchange rate say ¥140/\$, A is the investment, say \$10 milion, and int means that one takes the largest integer that is less than the quantity in the brackets. With these data c_0=112 contracts exactly but usually one will have to round down so as not to over hedge. To update the hedge, one simply keeps the number of contracts sold on day t equal to

$$\text{int}\left[\frac{S_t A(1+r_t)}{\text{¥12.5M per contract}}\right] = c_0$$

where S_t is the yen/dollar spot exchange rate on day t and r_t is the gross rate of return on the portfolio from the start up to day t.

So if St is 150 and r_t=16% then

$$\text{int}\left[\frac{150(10 \text{ million})(1.16)}{¥12.5 \text{ million}}\right] = \text{int}(139.2)=139.$$

Hence one needs 27 more contracts. This day-by-day adjustment procedure works well in general. Problems can occur from basis risk when the futures gets out of whack with the spot rate or when there is a sharp move in stock or currency values. The former rarely amounts to more than on half yen so the tracking error is less than 0.5% which is small in comparison with the interest differential futures discount gain. The latter, a sharp move in the stock portfolio value or the yen/dollar rate can cause hedging losses. Like portfolio insurance strategies used in the October 1987 stock market crash, one must dynamically adjust in a continuous fashion. Since one is not dealing with stock futures premiums that can get 5% or more out of whack with the cash indices but with currency futures the risk from the potential basis change does not seem that great.

7. Hedged and Unhedged Returns[1]

The mean return from hedged and unhedged returns is the same for an investment from one country to another as long as the returns from investments and from currency changes are uncorrelated. The difference in actual returns is then equal to this mean return plus the return in the local currency plus the currency surprise. This is shown as follows. Let

r_u = the unhedged return
r_h = the hedged return
r_c = the currency return
r_e = the return in the local currency
S_t = the spot currency exchange rate to change local into foreign returns
F_t = the forward/futures rate local to foreign currencies
V_t = the asset values in the local currency

$$1 + r_u = \frac{S_tV_t}{S_{t-1}V_{t-1}} = \left(\frac{S_t}{S_{t-1}}\right)\left(\frac{V_t}{V_{t-1}}\right) = (1+r_c)\ (1+r_e)$$

$$1+r_h = \frac{F_tV_{t-1}+(V_t - V_{t-1})\ S_t}{S_{t-1}\ V_{t-1}}$$

$$= \frac{(F_t - S_{t-1})\ V_{t-1} - (S_t-S_{t-1})\ V_{t-1} + S_tV_t}{S_{t-1}\ V_{t-1}}$$

---

[1]Thanks to Andy Turner for his help on this section. See also Gillies and Turner (1990).

$$= 1+r_e \quad + \underbrace{\left(\frac{F_t - S_{t-1}}{S_{t-1}}\right)}_{p} - \underbrace{\left(\frac{S_t - S_{t-1}}{S_{t-1}}\right)}_{r_c} .$$

The actual return of the hedged portfolio equals that of the unhedged portfolio plus the futures hedge premium p minus the currency return. If we let $\varepsilon = r_c - p$ then the return of the hedged portfolio equals that of the unhedged portfolio plus the currency surprise ε. Taking expectations yields

$$E(r_h) = E(r_u) + E(\varepsilon) = E(r_u)$$

since currency surprise has mean zero.

In terms of local returns and currency returns one has

$$\begin{aligned} 1+ r_h &= 1+ r_u - \varepsilon \\ &= (1 + r_c)(1+re) - \varepsilon \\ &= 1 + re + r_c + r_c r_e - \varepsilon \end{aligned}$$

So $r_h = r_e + p + r_c r_e$ and $E(r_h = E(r_e) + p + \mathrm{cov}(r_c, r_e)$.
If $\mathrm{Cov}(r_c, r_e) = 0$, then $E(r_h) = E(r_e) + p = E(r_u)$.

In practice, the currency returns and the local returns have low correlation[1] so the expected hedged return equals the expected local return plus the futures hedge premium.

Figure 6 shows the typical behavior of the various portfolios for a Canadian investor. For a U.S. investor the situation is similar except that the drift in figure 16.6 is about 1% and the floor in figure 6d has a slight negative drift of 1-2% per year.[2] The return in local currency r_e shown in (a) has the same volatility as the hedged portfolio (b), namely $\sigma(r_e)$. The hedged portfolio has return r_e+p with volatility $\sigma(r_e)$. The unhedged portfolio has return r_e+p+ε which has the same mean return as the hedged portfolio but higher volatility assuming $\sigma^2(\varepsilon)$ is positive but $\mathrm{cov}(r_e,\varepsilon) = \mathrm{cov}(r_e,r_c) = 0$.

---

[1]This assumption, as discussed above, is not particularly valid for Japan.

[2]In December 1990 the Cdn$/yen futures was at a discount of about 4.5% per year so that the investor could hedge currency and stock price level risks and still have a floor well above Long term NSA put warrants had costs much less than this per year. For U.S. investors the currency difference was actually slightly negative. Hence the floor is slightly below A.

Figure 6: Typical portfolio values in yen and dollars over time.

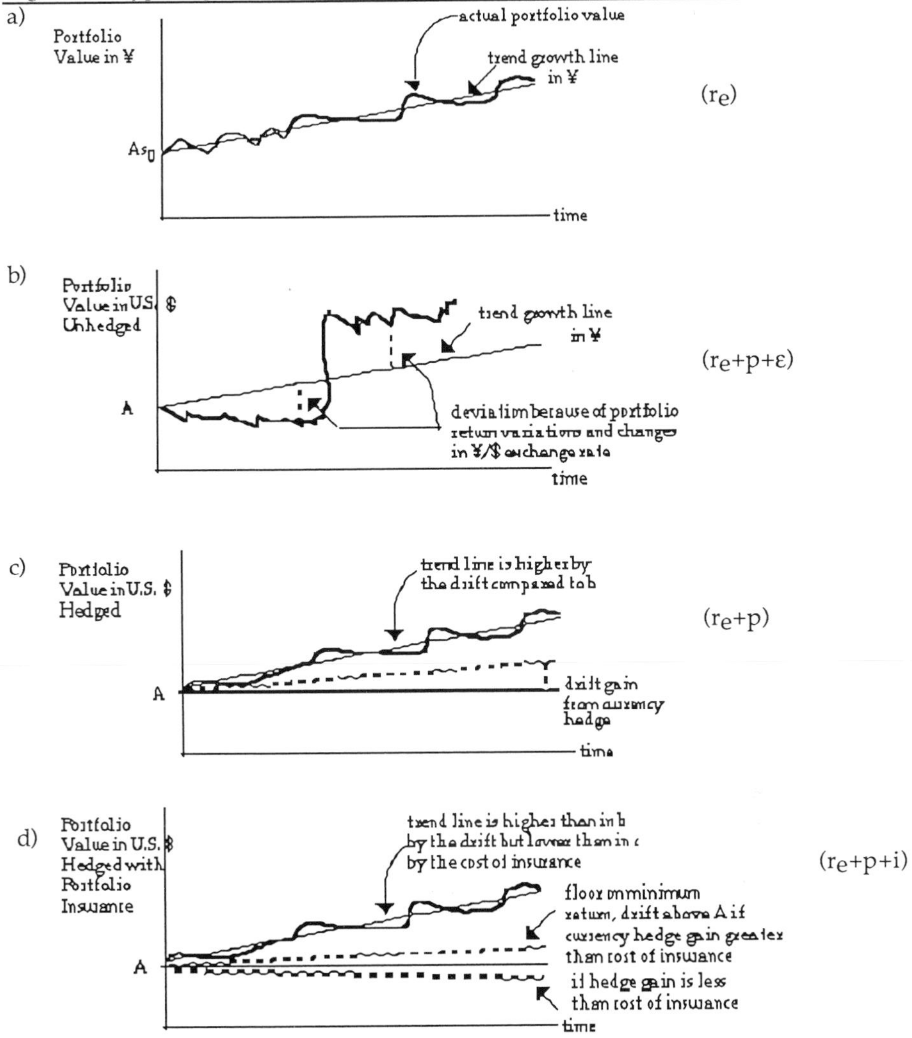

References

Adler, M. and J. Detemple (1988) Hedging with futures in an intertemporal portfolio context. *Journal of Futures Markets 8:* 249-269.

Altman, Edward J. and Yoshiki Minowa (1989) Analyzing risks and returns and potential interest in the U.S. high yield corporate debt market for Japanese investors, *Japan and the World Economy 13:* 163-86.

Duffie, Darrell and M. Jackson (1986) Optimal hedging and equilibrium in a dynamic futures market, Research Paper 814, Graduate School of Business, Stanford University.

Duffie, Darrell and Henry R. Richardson (1989) Mean-variance hedging in continuous-time, Working Paper.

Eaker, M. and D. Grant (1987) Cross-hedging foreign currency risks. *Journal of International Money and Finance:*

Gillies, John M. and Andrew L. Turner (1990) On the relationship between currency hedged and local rates of return. *Russell Technical Notes* (March).

Jorion, Philippe (1989) Asset allocation with hedged and unhedged foreign stocks and bonds. *Journal of Portfolio Management* (Summer): 49-54.

Perold, Andre F. and Evan C. Schulman (1988) The free lunch in currency hedging: impolications for investment policy and performance standards. *Financial Analysts Journal* (May-June): 45-50.

Solnik, Bruno (1989) Optimal currency hedge ratios: the influence of the interest rate differential, in S. G. Rhee and R. P. Chang, eds *Pacific-Basin Capital Markets Research* , Amsterdam, North Holland, 441-465.

Stone, Douglas and Chris R. Hensel (1989) Strategic currency hedging non-U.S. investments for U.S.-based investor. *Russell White Paper* (August).

Svensson, L.E.O. (1988) Portfolio choice and asset pricing with non-traded assets, Working Paper, Institute for International Economic Studies, University of Stockholm.

Ziemba, William T. (1991) *Strategies for Making and Keeping Excess Profits in the Stock Market* , William Morrow, forthcoming.

PART IV: DERIVATIVE SECURITY MARKETS

Japanese Financial Market Research
W.T. Ziemba, W. Bailey and Y. Hamao (Editors)

The Development of Organized Futures Trading: The Osaka Rice Bill Market of 1730[1]

Ulrike Schaede
Japan-Zentrum der Universität Marburg
Wilhelm-Röpke-Str. 6E, 3550 Marburg
Federal Republic of Germany

Abstract

The Dojima rice market of 1730 is the oldest thoroughly organized futures market we have detailed information about. Futures were traded on standardized rice bills and the system also provided for daily mark-to-market and clearing houses. This market did not build on prior economic insight of the authorities, but materialized according to the traders' needs. Therefore, differences in trading practices, the most important of which is the "multiple clearing system" in Osaka, hint at alternative ways of futures market microstructure.

1. INTRODUCTION

The first thoroughly organized futures exchanges are said to be those established in 1867 in Frankfurt, and in 1877 in London. In 1848, the Chicago Board of Trade was founded, but the Great Fire destroyed all records that could have shown the exact nature of the Chicago futures market prior to 1871. The New York Cotton Exchange, incorporated in 1872, did not provide for clearing facilities before 1892 (Seki 1985:10, Kaufmann 1984:11, Kolb 1985:3).

In Japan, however, an organized futures exchange with a standardized clearing system was officially permitted in Dojima, a section of the city of Osaka, as early as in

---

[1] The author is Research Associate at the Center for Japanese Studies, Universität Marburg. She is highly indebted to Shinji Takagi, Adrian E. Tschoegl, Matao Miyamoto and many others for insightful comments. However, the author alone is responsible for all remaining errors.

1730. It has been suggested that this was a full-fledged futures markets (e.g., Sansom 1964/III:126); some have even claimed that it was a financial futures market (Shimamoto 1969, Sakudō 1961:345). This paper will examine the exact operations of the Osaka rice market during the Tokugawa period (1603-1867) and evaluate how closely it corresponded to the technical requirements of a modern futures markets as stated in the modern literature of finance. It will show that Osaka indeed was a futures market, and that it therefore is the oldest organized futures exchange about which we have detailed information and material.

The underlying assumption of the paper is that rational behavior of market participants is the reason for the development of an organized futures market; i.e., the major motive for organizing trade is the minimization of transaction costs (cf. Telser and Higinbotham 1977). Dojima developed without any guidance from financial authorities. Thus, this was a market that materialized solely in response to the needs of market participants, who made up their own rules in a way that best suited their needs. This contrasts sharply with today's markets. The fundamental question to be raised in view of this development of the market is what the economic implications of the difference are in practice. Differences between contemporary trading practices and those in the 18th century might either imply that the Dojima market was imperfect or that contemporary rules do not meet the economic needs of market participants. For an evaluation of Edo-period trading practices, the following criteria, necessary components of a futures market today, are used as a standard:

1) only exchange members can participate in the market;
2) contracts traded are standardized;
3) for each position, 'good-faith'-money (a margin) has to be deposited at the clearinghouse;
4) trading is not bilateral, but the clearinghouse enters each transaction as a third party and guarantees the fulfillment of all contracts;
5) the contract runs for a certain trading period and open positions are reassessed daily in accordance with price fluctuations (mark-to-market); and
6) positions dissolved before the end of the trading period are cleared by cash settlement.

The paper will show that the Dojima market practices generally satisfied these criteria except that it had different margin rules and a different mark-to-market mechanism. However, both were modified when a new system was introduced in the 1860s and are therefore of little substantive importance. More importantly, there were several clearinghouses at the Osaka exchange. This raises questions in regard to the efficiency of the clearing system we know today, and it may also offer a solution to problems we are facing today with coordinating different clearing systems.

The analysis builds on primary material (as reprinted in Shimamoto 1969, 1970) as well as on early Japanese research (Suzuki 1940, Shimamoto 1953, Tanaka 1910) and on the pioneering work of Miyamoto (1972, 1977a,1977b, 1982, 1986). The lack of reliable data, however, did not allow for a more quantitative examination of these issues.

The paper is organized as follows. Section 2 describes the evolution of Osaka as the so-called "kitchen of the country" (Dohi 1981:69). Section 3 presents the organization of the Dojima market, and Section 4 outlines the rice price policy by the government. Sections 5 and 6 describe the trading systems in forwards and futures respectively.

Section 7 will give final concluding remarks in regard to a) the categorization of Dojima trading practices into commodities and financial futures, and b) the practice of "multiple clearing".

2. THE EMERGENCE OF OSAKA AS A TRADING CENTER

During the years 1603 through 1868, 15 successive heads of the Tokugawa family, situated in Edo (present-day Tokyo), reigned the country as shoguns, while the emperor in Kyoto had no political power. Since 1639, the country was secluded, and there was no political and almost no economic exchange with the rest of the world. Therefore, the Tokugawa period comes close to the idea of a "closed economy" as stipulated in modern textbooks of economics, and everything that developed during this period emerged from "the inside".

In the 250 years of the Tokugawa period, Japan's population is estimated to have been remarkably stable at roughly 30 million people. Of this total, 87% were farmers, 5% were 'warriors' (*bushi*), who actually were the public servants of feudal domains (*han*), and 8% were merchants and artisans living in the cities (Sekiyama 1957:247). The population of the city of Osaka was an estimated 200 000 in 1609; it doubled to 400 000 by the 1750s (Dohi 1983:18)[2]. When Toyotomi Hideyoshi, the second of the three great unifiers of the country, placed his castle in Osaka, the city became the commercial heart of the country: In his attempt to unify the then divided country, Hideyoshi faced strong opposition from the nearby city of Sakai which had been the dominant trading city since the 14th century. In order to make his castle town, Osaka, into the principal commercial base of the country, Hideyoshi lured merchants away from independently-minded Sakai by improving the infrastructure of the city. He provided for a closely-knit canal system and requested the merchants to gather on a single spot in the center, called Senba (see Figure 1). An active market soon evolved in Senba and attracted Sakai merchants, thus eventually contributing to the fall of the former trading center.

The physical characteristics of Osaka contributed to the city's development into the most important rice market. Not only was Osaka located on the arterial roads connecting the east and the west of the country, but it was also important as a port. As losses were high when transporting rice on horseback through the untraversed country, territorial lords (*daimyō*) built their own ships, which they could easily unload in Osaka because of its many rivers and canals. In the 1670s, all important feudal lords had built their own warehouses along the Osaka waterfront for rice shipments from their domains.

Rice, as the most important product of an agrarian economy, was officially regarded to be the basic accounting unit. Because rice was largely homogeneous, it was the basic unit for taxation by the shogunate, and the feudal domains, i.e., the basis of

---

[2] Throughout the paper, dates are given in accordance with the primary sources, some of which are based on the old Japanese (lunar) calendar. However, this differed only slightly from the Western calendar.

Fig.1: City Map of Osaka in the 1880s
(Source: Osaka-shi shiyakusho 1980/I)

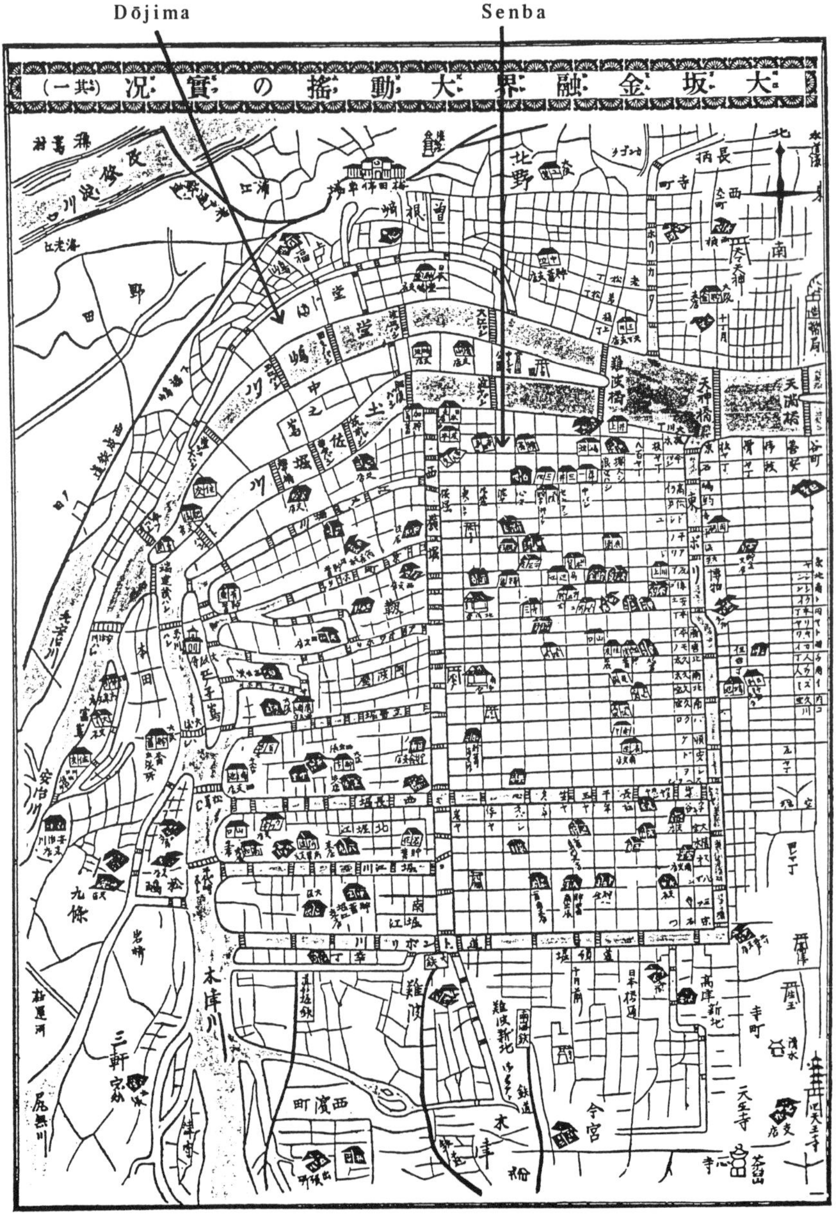

national income. The value of a certain parcel of land was measured in *koku*[3] of rice theoretically producable on it, taxes were levied in rice, and *bushi* were paid in rice. However, it was only in the very beginning of the Tokugawa-period that rice was used as a means of payment. Farmers had to give a certain percentage of their annual rice harvest as tax to their feudal lords. What was left after the farmers' own consumption they sold to rice merchants on local markets. The local rice merchants in turn brought the rice to Osaka where all the large merchants were located. Similarly, the feudal lords used the rice they levied as tax for their own consumption and to pay their retainers, and sent the surplus to Osaka. There the rice was stored in warehouses (*kurayashiki*) until the sellers' trading agents in the city could bring it to the market.

Although rice was officially regarded as the general means of accounting, money became more and more important over the years. In the 17th century Japan used gold coins, quantities of silver, and copper or iron coins[4]. Silver money was not coined, but had to be weighed for each transaction. As weighing was a great bother, uncoined silver went out of circulation in the 18th century, but it remained as an accounting unit, because the silver system used decimal division.

In addition to the Osaka merchants, Osaka already had money changers (*ryōgae-ya*). Because the feudal lords needed to smooth out expenditures throughout the whole year out of annual shipments of rice, they developed a special relation with the money changers, who became the financial agents of the feudal lords and supplied credit against future rice transport.

The feudal lords, who had their own warehouses in Osaka, sold rice by issuing a certificate of title to a certain amount of rice in the warehouse in exchange for money. The certificates were called rice bills and initially were traded in an occasional fashion in front of the house of Yodoya, the outstanding trading house at the time. Because the crowd of merchants who would gather there daily disturbed the traffic, in 1688 the authorities asked the merchants to gather in Dojima, a small island at the delta of the three main rivers in the northern part of the city (see Figure 1). In 1697, Yodoya himself moved to Dojima and thereby established the island as the central trading place. In 1730, the authorities officially acknowledged the market place as an exchange. It was at the same site that a modern commodities exchange was established in 1871[5] .

---

[3] 1 *koku* = 10 to = 180 liters

[4] On the monetary system of Tokugawa-period Japan see Crawcour 1961, Crawcour and Yamamura 1971, and BOJ 1974/III

[5] The city of Edo, which had become the seat of the shogunate in 1603, only started to develop when Osaka was already a full-fledged trading center. In the 18th century, Edo began to catch up with Osaka in its size and role as an important rice market, because rice harvests of shogunate-owned domains and from some of the northern domains were sent there. However, advanced trading practices as known in Osaka were never officially permitted in Edo.

3. ORGANISATION OF THE MARKET

3.1. Warehouses

Osaka had 91 warehouses in 1673, and 124 in 1730 (Suzuki 1940:6). The functions of a warehouse belonging to a particular domain were (1) to sell goods on hand (most importantly rice); (2) to buy goods not available in the domain; and (3) to arrange credit to the domain. Management was in the hands of the warehouse superintendent (*kuramoto*), who was responsible for organizing auctions in order to sell the rice. Initially, a *bushi* was sent from the domain, but as early as in the 1660s, Osaka merchants took over the tasks of the superintendent (*chōnin-kuramoto*). In addition, the warehouses had a special financial agent (*kakeya*, lit.: "money raiser") whose business very closely resembled that of a modern bank: he kept the books on all transactions by recording such items as assets obtained from selling rice, credits granted to the feudal lord, and money transfers to the government in Edo on behalf of the domain. These were standing orders, i.e., they were automatic credit extensions to the domain. Furthermore, raising fees and delivering certificates became the task of the financial agents who expeditiously took over all of the auction proceedings (Suzuki 1940:7-8, Miyamoto 1982:53).

3.2. Rice Bills

While in most of Japan, including Edo, rice dealings were exclusively done on a spot basis, the dealing in Osaka was made through rice bills (*kome-tegata* or *kome-gitte*). Rice bills were introduced as a means to minimize the transaction costs of trading large volumes of rice that arrived in Osaka during a short period of time. Without the securitization of rice trading, it would have been difficult to smoothe out rice consumption over the year and over Japan, and large temporal price fluctuations could have resulted.

When rice bills came to be traded in the early 17th century, they were a receipt on the delivery of a certain amount of rice to be made within 30 days[6]. The receipt was delivered upon payment of a fraction of total value as a good-faith deposit, which varied according to the rules of the various warehouses and to the kind of bills issued. An initial payment of 30% seems to have been the usual practice from the 1650s onward.

---

[6] In the beginning, the rice bill was a warehouse receipt. The issuer of a warehouse receipt in general cedes right of ownership to the purchaser and remains in charge of storage only, while the bearer takes the risk of damages and losses. In Osaka, however, the question of responsibility for safe storage was not settled until 1716, when a fire burnt down the warehouses of the domains Kaga and Murakami (Echigo). The Kaga domain insisted that no guarantee was given, but the sharp protest put the domain's political prestige at stake. The Kaga domain had to replace the non-guarantee clause on its bills by a full guarantee (Miyamoto 1982:54). Because of this shift of guarantee to the warehouses, rice bills could be traded without consideration to guarantee and creditworthiness.

In time, the scope of rice bills expanded to cover any bill written on any rice, and the bills' period of validity was extended from 30 days to more than a year. This enabled the warehouses to issue unbacked bills, i.e., bills on rice which was not on storage. In order to facilitate trading, rice bills were standardized in terms of 10 *koku* of rice counted in number of rice bales at around 1700[7].

Fig.2: Delivering Bill (left) and "Empty Bill" (right) Issued by the Domain Kaga (Source: Suzuki 1940)

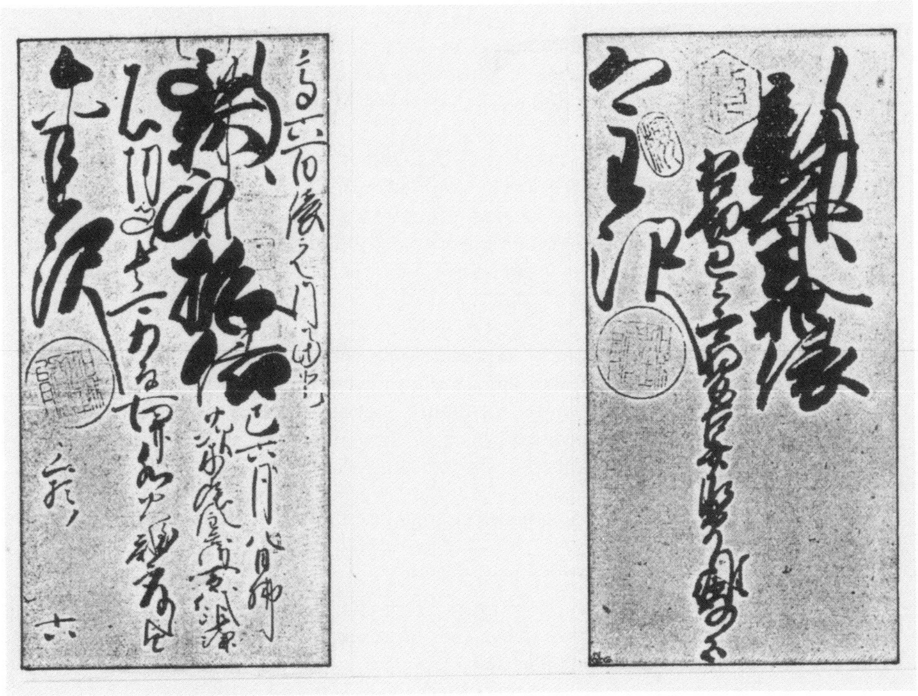

[7] Moreover, some of the warehouses began to issue interest-bearing bills, i.e., the initial payment for the bill was one third of the face value plus interest on the remaining two thirds (Suzuki 1940:10).

With the issuance of unbacked rice bills and the further development of the market, bills with different rights and features appeared. One way to categorize bills is a division into two types according to inscription. Bills that were issued after the arrival and immediate sale of rice, i.e. the backed and wholly paid-for bills, were called "delivering bill" (*dashi-kitte*)(see Figure 2). They gave the running number of the bill, name of the buyer, number of bales, name of the auctioneer (financial agent), date of the auction and name of the warehouse. Bills that were issued without rice being on stock, i.e., unsecured bills, were called "monk bills" (*bōzu-kitte*). The monk bill derived its name from the fact that Buddhist monks follow the practice of tonsure and are therefore bald-headed, just as monk bills were bald in that neither the name of the purchaser nor the date were inscribed on the unsecured bills. Thus, monk bills are analogous to bearer bonds.

In general, securities can be divided into debt securities (such as bonds and mortgages) and ownership securities (such as stock certificates and titles to marketable assets). Depending on the manner in which they were issued, the rice bills traded in Tokugawa-period Dojima took the shape of either a debt security or an ownership security.

"Delivering bills" and "monk bills", together referred to as auction bills (*rakusatsu-kitte*), were sold by way of auction and were in effect ownership securities. Auction bills were delivered upon paying a "good-faith" deposit, the amount of which varied according to the respective warehouse's rules and to the kind of bill issued. Such a bill represented evidence of a property right in a certain amount of rice which was stored in the warehouse. On the other hand, "prepayment bills" (*sennō-kitte*), issued without auction on payment, were closer to debt securities. These bills were also called "empty (rice) bills" (*kūmai-kitte*), overdraft bills (*kamai-kitte*), or financial bills (*chōtatsu-kitte*, lit. "(money) raising bills"), each implying that they were issued without connection to the issuing warehouse's inventory. Neither the issuer nor the purchaser regarded them as titles to physical rice. Instead, these bills were more like an evidence of credit extended by a merchant to a warehouse. In case the warehouse was not able to repay the credit after one year the bill was converted into an auction bill, with the interest being payed either independently or added to the total sum (Miyamoto 1982:54, Suzuki 1940:200, Shimamoto 1953:15). In 1749, bills in circulation were estimated to have represented more than 110000 bales of rice, whereas the inventory at that time only amounted to approximately 30000 bales (Yagi-chō, April 7th, 1749, in: Shimamoto 1970); i.e., the outstanding balance of rice bills represented almost four times the actual quantity of rice available for physical delivery.

The differences in the type of rice bills mean differences in the way the bills were traded. If the buyer had to furnish the whole amount of money on the day he bought a bill that was unbacked, he actually bought a bond. On the other hand, if the rice merchant bought a backed rice bill, he entered a forward contract. If this rice bill was standardized and being traded on the futures market, he effectively entered into a futures contract.

3.3. Rice merchants

Rice merchants were divided into "rice traders" (*kome-donya*) and "rice brokers" (*kome-nakagai*). Whereas brokers in Edo typically bought their goods from the wholesalers and sold them on the market, brokers in Osaka had a totally different function. When Dojima was officially acknowledged as a rice exchange in 1730, rice merchants were registered. In order to keep the number of rice merchants within controllable limits, the shogunate sold licenses (*kabu*): 500 in 1731, another 500 in April 1732, and 300 in November 1732. The first 500 licensed merchants obtained the most privileged position of rice traders (*tonya*), the remaining 800 became brokers (Shimamoto 1953:57, Honjō 1954:591).

Tonya had the legal right to deal on the spot market as well as on the futures market. Some of the *tonya* were also active in warehouse rice delivery or rice transportation, even though most of them specialized in one field or another. A further privilege of the 500 *tonya* was their "primary dealers" status: only they were permitted to participate in rice bill auctions at the warehouses. In this function, they were called *kura-namae*, lit. "warehouse names". Brokers, who had bought the exchange license in 1732, were confined to only one of the activities in the market. On the exchange in Dojima, they dealt in the rice bills previously bought at auction by the *tonya*.

Both types of merchants were required to pay an annual fee for the license, called *myōgakin* (lit. "thanks-money"). This fee was in effect a trading license tax, which in return granted controlled market access in rice trading at the exchange. By issuing these licenses, the shogunate could exercise close surveillance over the Osaka rice market and, at the same time, earn rents on the market. Also, the licence system implied that access to the exchange was limited to a certain group of participants of high standing. Therefore, the futures market that materialized in the 18th century was guaranteed by the fact that only market participants with high creditworthiness could trade in futures directly[8].

3.4. The Exchange

The development and formalization of trading practices was not a government-led process but emanated from the market's own dynamics. The exchange

---

[8] The same is true for futures on bonds and stocks that were introduced to Japan in 1985 and 1989: the market is not guaranteed by a clearinghouse, but through the creditworthiness of a restricted number of market participants who need a licence from the Ministry of Finance.

A second parallel between the Tokugawa-period and the 1980s is the market participants' self-regulation. In the 1730s, the rice merchants formed groups or guilds (*kumiai, nakama*) based on the ward they lived in. The merchants of the same area and business who would not join the group were required to close their shops. In the 1980s, rules on arbitrage, broking and also on trading behavior (e.g., no extensive trading during the last 30 minutes of a day's trading session) are set up and monitored by the Association of Securities Dealers (*Shōkengyō-kyōkai*).

was an autonomous, voluntary, non-profit association of its members, and its main function was to supervise everyday trading, regulate brokers and auctions, settle disputes, and register official daily closing prices (Tanaka 1910:29, Suzuki 1940:53).

The staff of the exchange consisted of five so-called "annual directors" (*nengyōji*), five "monthly directors" (*tsukigyōji*), 14 "watermen"(*mizukata*, whose function will be explained in section 6.3.) and other officials with special responsibilities such as supervising daily trading practices. The board of directors was elected annualy by the exchange members. During their honorary term of office, directors were not allowed to trade by themselves. Before the exchange building was completed in 1783, the house of the head of the board served as the office building. However, even though the annual directors enjoyed several benefits (e.g., tax exemption), it was a rather unpopular job. Therefore, directors often reported sick, or else engaged in active trading precisely because this would result in suspension from the board. In 1774, the system was revised so that directors in office nominated their successors (Suzuki 1940:57, Shimamoto 1953:52).

The exchange members of every ward of the city elected a head each month. Out of approximately 35 such heads, the five representing the largest groups made up the board of "monthly directors". These directors were intermediaries between the rice merchants and the board of "annual directors".

3.5. Clearinghouses

The original function of clearinghouses (*komegata-ryōgae* or *yarikuri-ryōgae*, lit. "rice-merchants' money changer" or "matchmaking agents") was to change rice into money and keep the deposits of rice merchants. The more actively rice bills were traded, the more difficult it was for a merchant to keep an eye on all his open interests in the futures market and settle all his transactions with a huge number of different trading partners. Therefore, he entrusted the settlement of his daily transactions to a special money changer.

In 1731, 50 special licenses (*kabu*) were issued for money changers and another 10 in 1746. These houses were not permitted to trade in their own interest, and their clientele was restricted to the licensed exchange members. On receiving margin payment, the clearinghouses took responsibility for the fulfillment of the contract (Suzuki 1940:79). Thus, the merchants paid a margin and fees on their open positions and in turn settled their positions at the clearinghouse without regard to the creditworthiness of the ultimate counterparty. In this interpretation, the clearinghouse provided intermediation services for futures market participants. This intermediation service is one of the key features of a modern clearinghouse.

The final clearing between the several clearinghouses was arranged at the clearing center (*keshiai-ba*, lit."settlement place"). The clearinghouses registered the open futures positions of their customers and settled them in total on liquidation days (see section 6.4.). The cost of maintaining the central clearing place was paid for by the several clearinghouses, i.e., the clearing center was an association of individual clearinghouses.

Commissions on long-term transactions were regulated by the exchange[9], but the clearinghouses were not allowed to charge for clearing of daily trading positions. Probably because daily clearing constituted a highly labor-intensive business, the houses suffered a loss in this part of their business; of the original sixty houses that were established in the first half of the 18th century, only four survived into the 19th century. However, it is still remarkable that Osaka had four clearing institutions towards the end of the Tokugawa-period, while a modern exchange has only one clearinghouse.

4. GOVERNMENT RICE POLICY

As rice played the paramount role in the economy of the Tokugawa period, the shogunate in Edo pursued an active rice policy by issuing official decrees (*o-fure*) since the 1650s. Because the shogunate considered the expansion of unbacked rice bills to be the main cause of inflation, it prohibited unbacked rice bills in 1652[10] . In 1660, the shogunate prohibited trading in rice bills altogether and limited the maximum term of a bill to 30 days, and to 10 days in 1663. The decrees, however, did not have the desired effect: the merchants now paid the total amount of the bill within 10 days, while the rice continued to remain in the warehouses and bills were traded as actively as before (Sakudō 961:348, Miyamoto 1972:207). The shogunate seems to have abandoned the 10-day restriction a few years later.

Since decrees were of no effect, the shogunate looked for other ways to regulate rice prices. The major reason for rising prices was soon - rightly or wrongly - traced back to the trading of unbacked rice bills "on the book" (i.e., as forwards and futures, see section 6) in front of Yodoya's house that was said to be nothing but gambling. In 1705, Yodoya's house was closed and his impressive wealth was confiscated. The official reason was Yodoya's violation of sumptuary restrictions, while in reality the shogunate hoped that dissolving the "fictitous" gambling would stop the increase in rice prices (Sugie 1984:17). In spite of these restrictive shogunate measures, book trading kept flourishing under cover in front of Yodoya's closed house.

The Kyōho era (1716-1735) under Tokugawa Yoshimune, who was also called the "rice shogun", saw a 180 degree reversal in government rice policy. The

---

[9] Until today, commissions for bond and stock trading are prescribed by the stock exchanges. When stock index futures were introduced in September 1989, commissions were deregulated for the new market segment. In reality, however, they are still coordinated by "guidance rates" proposed by the stock exchange.

[10] One of the most important decrees at that time was issued in 1654, when the word bill (*tegata*) was mentioned by the officials for the first time. According to the decree, these bills were issued on payment of only a part of the total sum and "passed through more than ten hands a day" (Ōsaka-shi shiyakusho 1927/III:47).

Kyōho-reforms consisted, among others, of attempts to increase tax revenue by encouraging rice land cultivation, a revision of the tax system and of sumptuary regulations. Furthermore, the shogunate revalved the currency so that one *koku* of rice which sold for 200 *monme*[11] in 1714 sold for about 30 *monme* in 1718 (Sugie 1984:24). Rice prices fell not only in nominal terms, but also in real terms because of a series of good harvest years. What the shogunate aimed at now was to simultaneously reduce the general price level and raise rice prices. Because the trading practices of the Dojima rice merchants were regarded to be "ficititious" and "price-hiking", the shogunate officially authorized "prolonged transactions" (see section 5.1.) in 1728; in 1730, the Dojima rice market became the only officially acknowledged and organized futures exchange in Japan.

In recognizing the futures market, the decree of 1730 specifically stated (Shimamoto 1953:9-10):
1. the aim of officially allowing the market was to increase rice prices;
2. "book transactions" must be conducted only according to conventional practices;
3. clearing business was restricted to the 50 clearinghouses that had been active in this business before [1730];
4. exchange members had to follow market rules; and
5. only Dojima, and no other market, could deal in book transactions.

The wording suggests that "book transactions" had already been in existence as an established system with well-defined trading patterns before they were officially acknowledged in 1730. Also, the authorization of an organized "rice futures" market was meant to be temporary, because the shogunate initially intended to prohibit trading on the book as soon as rice prices rose again. However, once the market was formally established, the shogunate could not shut it down again.

In the 1770s, the government gave up its futile attempts to regulate the size of the rice bill market. In realizing that the whole credit system had come to rely on rice bills and that a breakdown of the rice bill-system would topple the entire economy, the shogunate in 1773 introduced "suing-days" that allowed merchants to bring suits in connection with fraud or default in rice bill trading to the governor of Osaka (*Ōsaka machi-bugyō*). If the suit was justified, the government paid out the claims. The bills were also safe even if the government confiscated the possession of a merchant or financial agent[12], because the merchant's rice bill holdings were transferred to his wife or children (Shimamoto 1953:19,22). The effect was that rice bills became equivalent to local bonds or shogunate-backed bonds, except that rice bills were denominated in rice, whether or not physically defined. As a result, next to the guarantee on storage which was taken over by the warehouses, risk in trading rice bills was further diminished by a government guarantee in case of default of the issuer; these guarantees provided for the stability in trading objects which is a prerequisite for a futures market.

---

[11] 1 *monme* of silver was 17,36 grains

[12] This happened quite often for several reasons, one being that a feudal lord or the shogunate itself was heavily indebted to a merchant.

5. THE FORWARD MARKET

On-the-spot trading in rice bills developed into trading rice bills as futures in a trial-and-error manner. The process was based (1) on the development of "prolonged transactions" (*nobemai-akinai*), and (2) on the further sophisitication of these transactions into the so-called *shōmai-akinai*, lit.:"dealings in real rice". Although this name is suggestive of spot transactions, the transactions so designated were in fact forwards.

5.1. "Prolonged Transactions"

The origin of forward transactions was the so-called prolonged trading (*nobeuri-nobegai*, lit.: "prolonged selling - prolonged buying"), which developed as early as in the 1620s. Two parties contracted to exchange a certain amount of rice while extending delivery as well as payment to a specified future time; i.e. such a transaction was an agreement to complete trade at a future time and price specified when the agreement was made. The bills used for this kind of transactions were called "prolongation bills" (*nobe-tegata*). They were drafts drawn on the buyer by the seller, but were not presented for payment before the contract matured (Honjō 1959:1293).

Prolonged transactions were "empty" dealings, that is, the seller did not have the rice on hand at the time of the forward sale. This kind of transactions is said to have originated in an incident that occurred between 1616 and 1621. A rice merchant from Nagoya frequently met a colleague from Sendai on his business trips to Edo and exchanged information on harvest, weather conditions etc. in their hometowns. One day the Nagoya merchant learned of an impending bad harvest in the northern parts of Japan which would reduce rice shipments to Edo by about 50%. At the same time he knew that the Nagoya area would have a good harvest. Recognizing the potential profit opportunity, the Nagoya merchant bought the future harvest of his region by paying approximately 10% to the farmers and writing drafts for the rest of the negotiated amount. These drafts were not to be presented for payment before the rice was actually sold. When the harvest came in, he stored it and after three or four months sold it with a profit of 30-40%, as prices had climbed in the meantime (Sugie 1984:5). The benefit for the seller (i.e., the farmer) was the advance payment of 10% and the guarantee he had about the future revenue, i.e., he could hedge his future income against rice price fluctuations. Other merchants copied the system, which became the prevailing trading practice and remained so until the 1650s.

This practice of buying in advance, i.e., taking a long position on unharvested rice without the money to pay for it, is the earliest form of forward transactions in Japan. However, prolonged transactions gradually lost their importance with the development of the rice bill market.

5.2. The Trading System of Forwards

The increase of outstanding volume of rice bills in the second half of the 17th century meant that hedging against and speculating on rice price fluctuations could be more efficiently (i.e., with minimized transaction costs) pursued on the rice bill market in Osaka. The basic pattern of the trading system of forwards in the first half of the 17th century appears to have been as follows:

For instance, a rice trader (*tonya*) would buy a bill on seven *koku* rice from a warehouse with a maturity of, e.g., 30 days, by paying about 30% (i.e., the margin) of the market price of the auction day. The balance of the price would be due in 30 days from the day he purchased the bill at the latest. Thus, the bill represented a contract between two trading partners on the delivery of seven *koku* rice in 30 days at the price of the day on which the contract was made. This type of rice trading was a forward transaction.

Fig.3: Forward and Futures Market Transactions

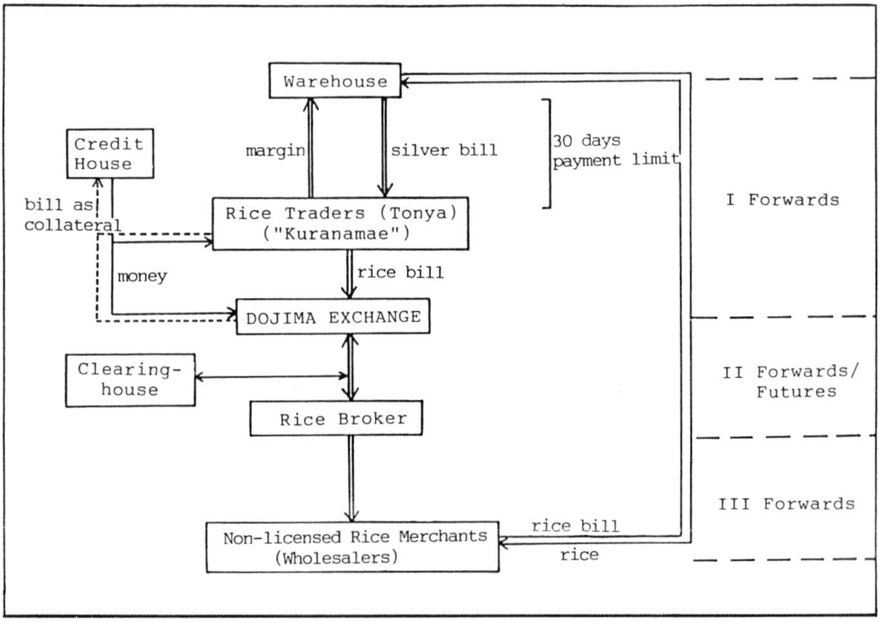

In the second half of the 17th century, the trading system became more intricate. With the standardization of rice bills, trading in futures became common (see Figure 3). The *tonya*, who were admitted to warehouse auctions, deposited 30% of the total sum as "good-faith" and for this received a margin receipt called silverbill (*gin-gitte*), which quoted the total price of the transaction in silver units. The *tonya* had to pay the 70% balance due within the next 30 days and received the rice bill (phase 1 in Figure 3), which he could then sell on the futures market in Dojima (phase 2 in Figure 3)[13]. At some point, an exchange member might buy the rice for resale to a wholesale rice merchant who, in contrast to the exchange members, would buy the bill with the intention of taking possession of the underlying rice (phase 3). As the maturity of the rice bill was extended to more than one year, the bill could remain on the market for some time.

The *tonya* could, of course, trade his silverbills before maturity and thus speculate on daily price fluctuations. A full-fledged trading system emerged out of such practice, with so-called credit houses developing into financing institutions.

5.3. Credit Houses and Margin Transactions

Credit houses (*irikae-ryōgae*, lit.: "pay and convert"-money changers) resemble today's securities financing firms (*shōken-kinyū gaisha*) which finance margin transactions. The credit houses were wealthy money changers who extended credit against rice bills, silverbills or commodities as collateral. There were 20 houses of this kind, although only the largest six took part in volume business where credit sums exceeded 100 *koku* rice. In addition to charging interest, the credit houses earned profits by trading the collateral bills, and for this reason, they accepted bearer bills (monk bills) as collateral only (Shimamoto 1953:35, 25-26; Honjō 1959:69).

The credit houses financed and traded with participants in the futures markets as well as the *tonya* depicted in phase 1 of Figure 3. The *tonya* would deposit his silverbills at the credit house and in turn receive a credit[14].

---

[13] The actual amount of lending could also have been smaller than 70% of the face value of the silverbill (the margin certificate) by the amount of interest to be paid to the credit house.

[14] The credit house either returned the bill on repayment of the credit sum or paid the outstanding balance to the financial agent and receive the rice bill itself. Thus, the credit house would lend either the face amount of the bill minus interest or just the margin.

6. THE FUTURES MARKET

The further development of the original spot and forward market into a rice bill futures market was accomplished by (1) the emergence of a full-fledged secondary market for rice bills, (2) the increased issues of standardized bearer bills, and (3) the growing importance of the overall clearing center in the trading process (phase 2 in Figure 3).

Trading futures was called "(rice) book transactions" (*chōaimai-akinai*). It can be reasonably assumed that trading on the book (i.e. settling positions without delivering contracts or goods) emerged in order to reduce transaction costs: having an organized exchange where all transactions in standardized contracts were settled by a central clearing institution allowed participants on the market to trade without regard for the credit standing of the counterparty.

6.1. The Mechanics of Trading

Trading periods A year was divided into three periods:
1) 4th day of 1st month - 8th day of 4th month,
2) 17th day of 4th month - 8th day of 10th month, and
3) 17th day of 10th month - 24th day of 12th month[15].

The market was closed for about 10 days between two succeeding trading periods in order to make a rollover of open positions to the following period impossible. The last day of every trading period was the liquidation day (*kiri-ichi*, lit.: "closing the market"), when all positions had to be settled. During the last three days of a trading period no new positions could be taken.

Standard rice (*tatemono-mai*) The underlying rice for the futures contracts changed with every period. The so-called "winter-standard" (*fuyu-tate*) and "spring standard" (*haru-tate*) were chosen from the harvest of the feudal domains of Chikuzen, Higo, Chūgoku, and Hiroshima, depending on which of the four had the best harvest. The "summer standard" (*natsu-tate*) was rice from Kaga (or, if the harvest was poor, Yonago). A feudal domain benefited from furnishing the standard rice, because the standard commanded a premium price. In turn, the domain was willing to bear the expenses of the exchange for the period.

---

[15] In the lunar calendar, the first month of the year need not necessarily be equivalent to January, but the span of time covered by a trading period does not change substantially if translated into the solar calendar.

Various sources give different dates for the three trading periods. The other dates are 8th day of 1st month through 27th day of 4th month; 7th day of 5th month through 8th day of 10th month; and 17th day of 10th month through 23rd day of 12th month.

Trading unit In principle, one contract (*ichi-mai*, lit.: "one sheet [of paper]") was written on 100 *koku* rice[16]. 100 *koku* rice was quoted by the number of rice bales which differed in size from region to region, such as 200 bales of 5 *to*, 250 bales of 4 *to*, or 300 bales of 3 *to*. Trading was quoted by the number of contracts. For example, "3 *mai* (bills) for 23" would have been 300 *koku* rice for 23 *monme* per *koku*.

Tick Minimum price movements were measured in the market price for one hundredth of a unit of the standard contract, hence the price for 1 *koku*.

Margin For taking a futures position, the trader had to deposit up to one third of the total amount traded as good-faith at a clearinghouse. This margin was not an individual deposit with the broker at the clearinghouse, and therefore the margin did not vary in line with a trader's positions; instead, the margin was traded with the contract, i.e., it was taken over by the next purchaser. The reason for this seems to be that, in the formative years of the system, the bilateral element in each transaction was still prevalent, and only later did margin practices change into what they are today. Nevertheless, the underlying function was the same: in return for the margin, the clearinghouse guaranteed the fulfillment of the contract. We can only guess what the exact margin requirements were. They seem to have fluctuated around 30% of the value traded, depending on the credit standing of the client as well as on prevailing market conditions[17].

Accounting There was no central book in which all transactions were registered. Instead, each exchange member had his own "trading notebook" (*baibai-techō*), in which he made an entry on every contract detailing the amount traded as well as the counterparty. Every evening exchange members would pass the notebooks on to their clearinghouses, which would then collectively register all transactions of the day.

6.2. Price Fixing

Trading began at 8 a.m. for futures and at 10 a.m. for forwards and spot transactions. The futures price at 10 a.m. was written on a board and was the opening

---

[16] It is not clear whether a contract could be written on higher amounts in 10 *koku* units, such as 130 *koku*.

[17] An entry in "*ina no ho*" ("On Rice") evidences that margin requirements were lowered to one to two *monme* of silber per *koku* of rice in 1770 (Ōsaka-shi shiyakusho 1927/V). This means 200 to 300 *monme* per trading contract of 100 *koku*, hence a minimal margin requirement of only 5%. This suggests that margin practices were not standardized, at least not over the entire the Tokugawa period.

price for forwards. At 12 a.m., the exchange closed for a lunch break[18].

The closing price at the end of the afternoon trading session was fixed in a sophisticated method called *ruiyō* system (lit. "establish and use" [19]). A wooden box containing a "fire cord" (*hinawa*, a sort of a wick) was hung at the ridgepole of the exchange building. Exchange officials put fire on the cord and allowed trading to continue as long as the box was on fire. The prevailing price at the moment the fire went out became the day's official closing price, called the "fire cord price" (*hinawa-nedan*). This price became the official opening price of the following day's session.

However, traders were little impressed by the official closing of the market and had to be stopped from continuing their transactions by the "watermen" (*mizukata*) who splashed water all over the market place in order to disperse the trading crowd (see Figure 4). Because splashing was also of limited effectiveness, in their second attempt the watermen would dash whole buckets of water over the crowd, which usually stopped the day's trading. The prevailing price at this time, the "bucket price" (*oke-nedan*), was the actual daily trading price which was registered in the books and used for mark-to-market or settlement (Shimamoto 1953:41, Suzuki 1940:100-101).

The price fixing system included two restrictions: if no price was found at the time the fire went out, or if the box did not burn down completely by itself for some reason, all transactions of the day were declared void and open positions that had been kept overnight had to be cleared by the fire cord price of the preceeding trading day (Sugie 1984:46).

This rule had both positive and negative effects. On the positive side, the clearing obligation made hoarding or dumping practices almost impossible. For example, if a broker engaged in hoarding purchases and other market participants became aware of this, they simply stopped trading and left him standing alone on the market place. No fire cord price could be found, as there was no trading, and all transactions of the day were nullified. In this way, the *ruiyō-system* ruled out cornering.

On the negative side, the clearing obligation encouraged riotous behavior. A broker who had suffered great losses during the day could certainly try to disturb trading at the market closing time, e.g. by charging through the market place on a horse. Or else, he could try to extinguish the fire before the box had burnt down. Brokers who had a 'big day' certainly wanted to see the box burn down without interference and have a fire cord price established for the day, so that they could finalize their gains. Therefore, it often happened that brokers - not unlike two basketball teams - ended up fighting

[18] Until today, Japanese stock exchanges close for one hour at lunchtime. At times of market upheaval, the lunch break functions as a circuit breaker, as it gives traders time to reorganize their trading strategies. At the Stock Market Crash of October 1987, the lunch break was one of the stabilizing factors at the Tokyo Stock Exchange.

[19] The original meaning of this word is not clear. It could as well be interpreted as "to burn out and use".

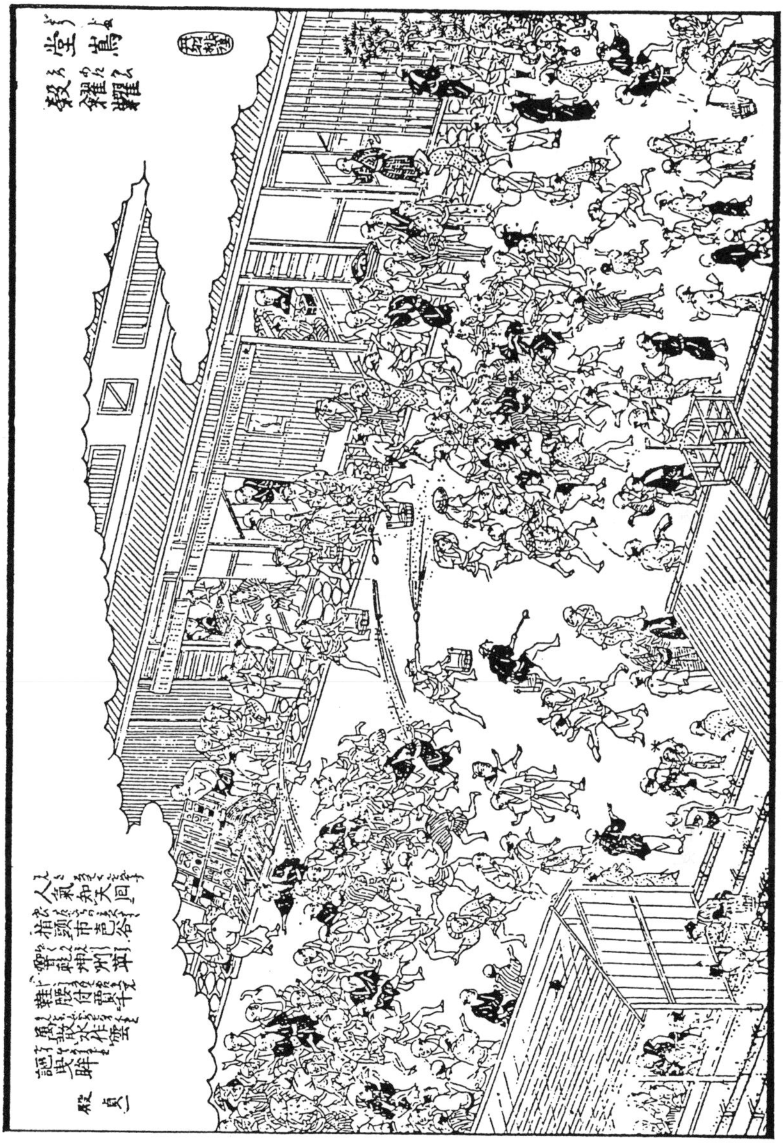

Fig.4: The Dojima Market at the End of a Trading Day
(Source: Suzuki 1940)

over the burning wooden box at the ridgepole of the exchange building at the end of the afternoon session.

Market disturbances of this type became more and more frequent during the second half of the Tokugawa-period, and they became the rule at the end of the period. Frequently, there was no fire cord price for several days in a row, and finally these disturbances lead to the breakdown of the system. It should be stressed, however, that the system of fixing exchange prices by use of a wooden box was very effective in preventing market manipulation and hoarding for a substantial period of time. Moreover, the obligation to register all positions at the end of the trading day at the clearinghouse at the bucket price was equivalent in function to today's mark-to-market mechanism, i.e., the daily reassessment of all open positions.

6.3. The Clearing System

In the 17th century, traders seem to have settled positions at the end of each trading day. If this was impossible, they could hold a position at the clearinghouse overnight. At the end of the 17th century, however, it became common to retain positions over longer periods, as evidenced by the system of "10-day-clearing" (*keshiai-hi*, lit.: "liquidation day"): Every evening brokers went to their clearinghouses and transcribed their transactions of the day into the trading book of the house. Every ten days the secretaries of the clearinghouses met at the central clearing place and assessed the positions of their customers on an overall basis. If they found the total of open positions unbalanced, they asked their customers for settlement on the following day. In particular, those who had suffered losses were asked to pay the difference (maintenance margin) and those who had gained profits received disbursements from the clearing center (Shimamoto 1953:73, Tanaka 1910:42, Suzuki 1940:103-104). This system thus represented a ten-day mark-to-market mechanism.

When the futures exchange was officially acknowledged and contract specifications were outlined in detail in 1730, an overall settlement system was also imperative. In 1737, the so-called "Cash-or-Carry" system (*shōgin-shōmai*, lit. "real silver-real rice") was introduced for settling all positions at the end of a trading period, i.e., three times a year. This system allowed for settlement by physical delivery as well as in cash during the last three days of each trading period. As the standard rice changed with every period, the purpose was to clear all positions, close the exchange and then start again with new rice. Although positions were still supposed to be settled according to the ten-day pattern, those traders who had kept open positions or had not yet paid for their losses had to clear all obligations during the last three days of the period either in cash or in rice (Tanaka 1910:52, Miyamoto 1982:55). In practice, only few contracts were settled by physical delivery except at the very end of the Tokugawa period.

There also existed futures transactions without clearing at the central place, "in-house" or "retail" futures. "In-house" futures were possible because of the existence of four clearinghouses (and even more in the first half of the 18th century). A clearinghouse could settle futures transactions of its own clientele without taking it to the market or contacting other clearinghouses[20] (cf. for details Tanaka 1910:42, Suzuki 1840:107). Although these "in-house" transactions, which were not settled at the central clearing place, comprised only a small fraction of the total value of all futures transactions, they are important in that they cast a new light on the existence of multiple clearinghouses which allowed such "in-house" transactions that are not usually associated with the current characterization of a futures market; they might suggest an alternative for trading systems of OTC futures.

6.4. The "Small Futures" Market

What was called small futures or "*koku* futures" (*ko-akinai*, *kokudate-akinai*, lit. "trading per *koku*") began as early as book-rice transactions, but did not come into widespread use before the end of the Tokugawa period. The *koku* futures market derived its name from the standard contract size: it was not written on the usual 100 but on 20 (later 10) *koku*.

According to early-18th century records, the trading year was divided into six trading periods; trading in the following period's contract began 15 days before the running contract matured. Thus, the strict division of periods as known in the book-rice market was abandoned. The settlement price was the mean of the forward closing prices of the preceeding three days. If the small futures prices deviated from forward prices by more than 15 *monme*, all open positions had to be settled by taking up reverse positions or by physical delivery. Thus, the system provided for a price limit which, in contrast to present-day practices, was linked to price movements on the cash market[21]. Daily transactions were registered at the clearing center and mark-to-market was done the next morning, with margins being disbursed or replenished. Unlike book transactions, the margin was not traded, but was a "good-faith" deposit of one market participant with his clearinghouse, as it is known today (Sugie 1984:55, Shimamoto 1953:47). The reason for this change in system probably was that market participants realized an opportunity for reducing transaction costs by keeping individual margins.

The Tenpō-years (1830-1843) saw an economic downturn resulting from a series

---

[20] Today, in-house clearing of customers' positions by a securities company (*baikai*), i.e., settlement without transferring orders to the exchange, is still possible with bonds; it is thus a special form of OTC-transactions. For stocks, in-house clearing was prohibited in 1968, because settlement within the company ran counter to the stock exchange rule of time and price priority as designated in the *zaraba*-trading method. Present-day futures on stocks and bonds, although traded without clearinghouse, do not allow for in-house clearing (see Schaede 1990, Chapter 7.5.).

[21] It is noteworthy in the context of futures markets in the 1980s and especially concerning the discussions following the October-1987 Crash that, in a period of economic deterioration, price limits were introduced to the market.

of bad harvests, rice riots, and an increasing indebtedness of the shogunate and domains to the merchant class. Although the spot and forward prices of rice rose along with the general price level, futures prices did not rise because the fire cord-system made regular price fixing impossible. The result was a wide spread between spot and futures prices, and the market in book transactions collapsed altogether. Also, clearinghouses raised commissions and margin requirements in order to minimize the risk of guaranteeing futures positions. By April 1866, the authorities had to close the market for forward and book-rice transactions (Sugie 1984:56, Shimamoto 1953: 56,49).

Meanwhile, the small futures system had been revised and simplified in 1863: the trading unit was 10 *koku*; a trading period lasted for one month; settlement day was the last day of the month; and all remaining open positions were cleared at the price valid ten days before settlement (Shimamoto 1953:49). Small futures trading under the new system was active between 1866 and April 1869, when the authorities closed the Dojima rice market following the Meiji-Restoration. The significance of the small futures market lies not so much in the actual trading during this period as in its impact on the new trading rules adopted for the Dojima commodities exchange opened in 1871: the trading system meets all the criteria of a modern futures market and had an important influence on the shape of the Meiji-period Dojima commodities exchange.

7. SUMMARY AND CONCLUSIONS

Futures trading in rice, i.e., trading a certain kind of rice "on the book" based on a cash settlement system, materialized soon after the domains began to build their rice warehouses in Osaka. Rice bills were perfectly suited for futures trading, because (1) the increased size of rice shipments to the warehouses in the mid-17th century provided market liquidity, and (2) there were sharp seasonal fluctuations in these rice shipments.

Feudal lords who were typically in constant financial need, obtained financing in Osaka in two ways. One was the direct credit of an Osaka merchant. The second, indirect, was the issue of 'unbacked' rice bills that were empty promises of rice delivery. Because of the crucial role of this credit system in the economy, the shogunate guaranteed all rice bills in 1773, effectively changing the deficit financing bills of domains into shogunate-backed bonds.

In the 17th century, rice bills were traded as forwards. Maximum maturity was gradually extended to 18 months from the officially prescribed three weeks. When traders standardized bills in order to facilitate transactions, it sufficed to write all commitments in a personal trading book instead of exchanging the actual bill with each transaction. As trading became less bilateral, the merchants entrusted accounting and settlement procedures to one of the special settlement institutions, the clearinghouses. These houses in turn constituted an interdealer-market with a central clearing place and charged for registering, clearing and guaranteeing the fulfilment of the contracts. The margin requirement was between 5 and 30% of the total trading sum.

Judged against the integral features of a present-day futures market (see the introduction), "book-rice" trading in Dojima was undoubtedly trading in futures: it had a limited number of participants; all contracts traded as futures were standardized;

traders had to deposit a margin as a "good-faith deposit" at the warehouse or at a clearinghouse; on the last day of the period all positions had to be cleared, either in cash or by physical delivery at one of the clearinghouses; and, finally, the central clearing place, which was an institution made up of a number of individual clearinghouses, assumed contract obligations when a default occured.

It was not because of abstract insight or prior economic reasoning that the rice bill market in Dojima was organized as a futures exchange. Rather, the market was a natural result of the given economic necessities of the time and its evolution was shaped in a trial-and-error manner by the market participants, who traded bills in order either to speculate on price fluctuations or to shift the risk of price fluctuations onto those who were willing to bear it.

Successful risk shifting requires that there be speculators who are willing to take the risk. There was no lack of profit-seeking rice brokers in Osaka, especially because the seasonality of prices made rice an ideal object for speculation. Furthermore, rice is an agricultural product whose output is much more vulnerable to natural conditions (weather, floods, plagues, etc.) than to the marketing strategies of its producers. Thus, the variability of price changes increased the need for hedging by some traders and also created ample scope for speculation by others.

In a series of papers, Miyamoto (1977a, 1979, 1986) demonstrated a high correlation between spot prices and futures prices from 1751 through to the 1830s on the basis of annual and quarterly average price fluctuations. He concluded that the market was efficient until around 1830, when the hedging function of the market began to deteriorate. Although the lack of reliable data precludes a more vigorous testing of the efficiency hypothesis, the very fact that the Dojima futures market showed a constant high trading volume for more than 100 years must indicate that the market fulfilled its purposes.

Regarding the mechanics of trading, one can classify the different types of transactions on the Dojima rice market into forwards and futures according to the system of Figure 5.

1) The issue of a rice bill by the warehouse represented a promise to deliver a specified amount of rice at a certain time in the future at the price of the day of settling the contract; this was a forward transaction.

2) Trading (standardized) rice bills on the exchange, with a clearinghouse in charge of the settlement procedure and guaranteeing fulfillment of contracts, was a futures transactions.

3) A rice bill that served as collateral at a credit house became a collateralized credit bill, but it regained its original character as a rice bill if it was then traded on the market; trading such a bill was thus a forward.

4) The settlement of trading in credit bills, financing bills, or silverbills on the exchange was entrusted to clearinghouses; thus these were futures transactions.

Because the bills traded at the exchange were not bought (sold) in order to buy (sell) rice, there was hardly a connection to actual rice. However, the underlying commodity of all these bills, i.e., the commodity the bills were written on and priced in, was rice. In this sense, the Dojima rice market was a market for commodities forwards and futures.

Fig.5: The Division of Trading Practices on the Dojima Exchange into Forwards and Futures

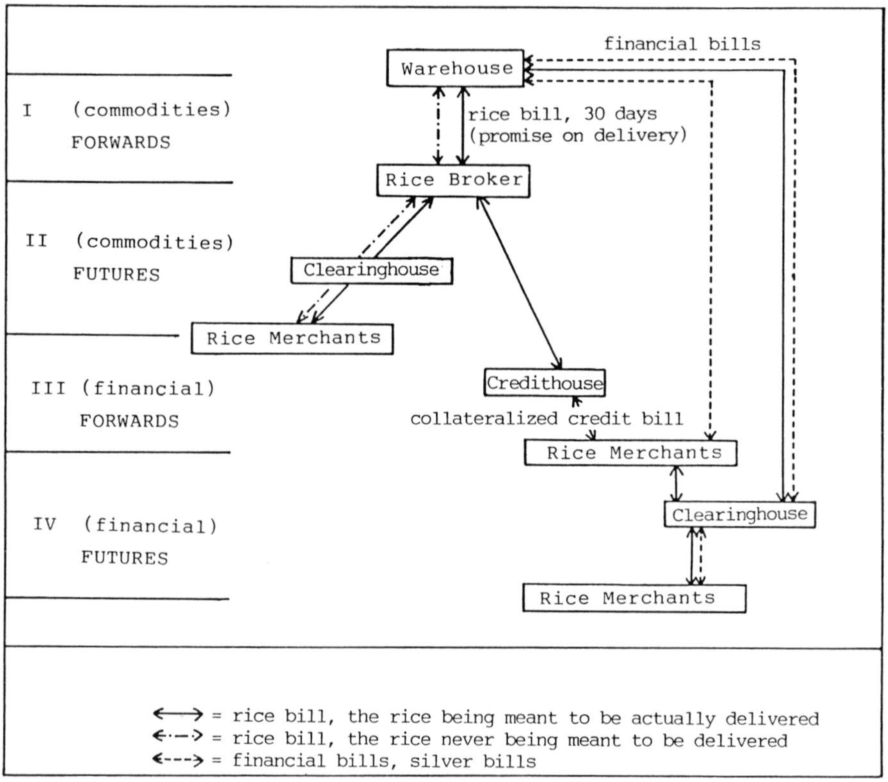

Shimamoto (1953, 1969) and Sakudō (1961:345) claim that the Tokugawa-period Dojima market was not a commodities exchange but was in fact a securities exchange. This claim is based on the assumption that no bill traded at Dojima had any connection to its underlying commodity, and especially so the financing bills that made up the greater part of the contracts. As a logical extension of this assumption, trading practices in Dojima would have to be categorized as financial futures.

However, this is only true if the role of rice in the Tokugawa period is ackowledged to be monetary, because it remains a fact that the underlying commodity of all contracts was rice. If rice had a hybrid nature of both "money" and commodity, rice bills could be categorized into commodity bills and securities, according to the way they were used[22]. Figure 5 then has to be divided into trading in commodities forwards and futures and trading in financial forwards and futures. In particular, financial forwards and futures would include transactions based on financial bills, credit bills, and silverbills as well as all unbacked bills (phases three and four in Figure 5). Under this interpretation, the Dojima market was both, a commodities exchange and a securities exchange that offered forwards and futures in both parts of the market.

Although the Dojima market undoubtedly was a futures market, it had three features that distinguished it from contemporary markets. First, daily reassessment of positions entailed settlement of the entire position until the 18th century, but the system changed into the Cash-or-Carry system, when contract specifications were detailed in 1730. Second, the margin differed from the later 'small' futures system and current practices in that a margin was not an individual account of a client at his clearinghouse, but was traded along with his specific position; this practice changed into the present-day mechanism, when the small futures market was reorganized in 1863.

Finally, the coexistence of several clearinghouses in an organized "multiple clearing system" - which developed in reaction to the needs of market participants - may cast doubt on the modern assumption that the system of one clearinghouse at one exchange is the most efficient solution. The multiple clearing system offers four propositions which are of interest for the structure of modern futures markets:

1. Multiple clearinghouses need not necessarily be inefficient, even if existent on one single market, provided that there is a central clearing institution. However, a futures market with multiple clearing has to be guaranteed by the creditworthiness of market participants, which must be restricted in number, and by an underlying guarantee on the trading object (as nowadays known for government bonds, GNMAs or treasury bills).
2. The second alternative to a single clearinghouse is no clearinghouse at all, as can be observed with the futures contracts traded at the Tokyo and Osaka Stock Exchanges since the 1980s, where the exchange is responsible for clearing, but where no clearinghouse exists. Again, the market has to be guaranteed by the creditworthiness of market participants.
3. Multiple clearing also offers a solution to the question of how to combine several futures exchanges which trade the same underlying object, e.g. Yen or T-Bonds, either in one country or on the international level (e.g., Tokyo, Singapore and Chicago): instead of standardizing clearing systems and computer technology at the exchanges concerned, a clearing center could be established which coordinates the individual clearing systems of its member exchanges.

---

[22] This hybrid nature of rice both as "money" and as a commodity can be regarded as a reflection of the nature of financial systems prior to high degrees of specialization and the developments of fiat money replacing metals. The very same ambiguity can be observed in recent discussions as to whether gold should be considered simply as a commodity or as a monetary asset, and, accordingly, as to whether futures on gold are to be classified as commodities or financial futures.

4. Finally, multiple clearing suggests one possibility of how to organize OTC-futures, i.e., thoroughly standardized contracts traded outside the exchange: these futures could be organized under a central clearing institution, so that market liquidty and overall mark-to-market are assured.

Considering the high level of sophistication of the Osaka rice futures of the 18th century, it is important to recognize that the spontaneous development of an organized exchange at which standardized contracts were traded seems to support the view that there is an economic need for such a standardized market as a mechanism to reduce transaction costs and provide market liquidity. Also, the development of the Dojima rice market is a reflection of the ingenuity of Tokugawa-period Japanese merchants, which has influenced the Japanese futures market on bonds and stocks of today 24: not only does the modern market show traditional features, such as a lunch break or fixed commissions, and a clearing system that is markedly different from what modern literature of finance suggests. The modern market is also based on an restricted membership system, added by monitoring of financial authorities, so that a market guarantee is granted - just as the Osaka merchants and the Tokugawa shogunate designed a market guarantee to be.

REFERENCES

Bank of Japan, Research Department (BOJ, Nihon ginkō chōsa-kyoku), 1974, *Nihon no kahei, 3: Kinsei heisei no hatten* (The currencies of Japan, Vol.3: The development of a currency system in the Tokugawa period); Tokyo: Tōyō-keizai shinpō-sha

Crawcour, E.S., 1961, The Development of a Credit System in Seventeenth Century Japan, *Journal of Economic History*, Vol.21 No.3, 342-360

Crawcour, E.S. and K. Yamamura, 1970, The Tokugawa Monetary System: 1787-1868, *Economic Development and Cultural Change*, Vol.18 No.4, 489-518

Dohi Noritaka, 1981, *Edo no komeya* (Rice merchants in Edo), "Edo"-sensho 7; Tokyo: Yoshikawa-kōbunsha

Dohi Noritaka, 1983, *Kome to edo-jidai - kome-shōnin to torihiki no jittai* (Rice in the Edo- period - rice merchants and rice trading), 3rd ed.; Tokyo: Yūsankaku-shuppan

Hara Makoto and I. Arai (eds.), 1986, *Sakimono-torihiki* (Futures Transactions); Tokyo: Yūhikaku-bijinesu 9

Honjō Eijirō, 1954, *Nihon keizai-shi jiten* (Dictionary of Japanese Economic History); Tokyo: Nihon-hyōron shinsha

Kaufman, Perry J.(ed.), 1984, *Handbook of Futures Markets - Commodity, Financial Stock Index, and Options*; New York: John Wiley & Sons

Kolb, Robert W., 1985, *Understanding Futures Markets*; London: Glenview/ Illinois

Matsuyoshi Sadao, 1932, *Nihon ryōgae-kinyū-shi ron* (History of Money Changers and Finance in Japan); Tokyo: Bungei-shunjū-sha

Miyamoto Matao, 1972, *Kinsei Ōsaka-kurayashiki ni okeru haraigome-shihō* (Rice Payment Methods in Tokugawa-period Warehouses in Osaka), Kōbe daigaku keizaigaku-kenkyū nenpō 19, 188-219

Miyamoto Matao, 1975, Kinsei-kōki Ōsaka ni okeru beika-hendō to beikoku-torihiki kikō - shōmai-kakaku to chōaimai-kakaku no ugoki (Rice Price Fluctuations and Mechanisms of Rice Trading in Osaka in the Late Tokugawa Period - Fluctuations of Spot and Futures Prices), *Keizai-kenkyū*, Vol.26 No.4, 359-368

Miyamoto Matao, 1977a, "Kakaku to shijō no keisei" (Prices and Market Formation), Keizai-shakai-shi gakkai (ed.), *Atarashii edo-jidai-shizō o motomete* (In Search for a New Perception of Tokugawa-period History), 199-223; Tokyo: Tōyō-keizai shinpō-sha

Miyamoto Matao, 1977b, Ōsaka kurayashiki no kome-gitte kyōkyū-kansū (Demand and supply functions for rice bills of the Osaka warehouses), in: Hidemura Senzō et al.(eds.), *Kindai-keizai no rekishiteki kiban* (Historical Foundations of the Modern Economy), 29-44; Tokyo: Minerva-shobō

Miyamoto Matao, 1982, Edo-jidai no kome-shijō - sono kōzō to kinō (The Rice Market in Edo-period Japan: Its Structure and Function), *Kikan-Gendai-keizai*, Spring 1982, 48-63

Miyamoto Matao, 1986, "Emergence of National Market and Commercial Activities in Tokugawa Japan - With Special Reference to the Development of the Rice Market", *Osaka Economic Papers*, Vol.36 No.1,2

Ōsaka-shi Shiyakusho (Osaka City Office), 1927, *Ōsaka-shi shi* (History of the city of Osaka); Osaka: Seibundō

Ōsaka-shi Shiyakusho (Osaka City Office), 1980, *Ōsaka-shi shi* (History of the city of Osaka), revised and reprinted edition; Osaka: Seibundō

Sakudō Yōtarō, 1961, *Nihon no kahei-kinyū-shi no kenkyū* (Research on the History of Japanese Currencies and Finance); Tokyo: Miraisha

Sansom, George, 1964, *A History of Japan*, Vol.3: 1615-1867; London: The Cresset Press

Schaede, Ulrike, 1990, *Der neue japanische Kapitalmarkt - Finanzfutures in Japan* (The new Japanese capital market - Financial futures in Japan); Wiesbaden: Gabler

Seki Kaname, 1985, *Saiken-sakimono-torihiki to zaimu-senryaku* (Bond Futures Trading and Financial Strategies); Tokyo: Kinyū-zaisei

Sekiyama Naotarō, 1957, *Kinsei Nihon no jinkō-kōzō* (The Population of Japan during the Tokugawa period); Tokyo: Yoshikawa Kōbunkan

Shimamoto Tokuichi, 1953, *Tokugawa-jidai no shōken-shijō no kenkyū* (Research on the Tokugawa-period Securities Market); Osaka: Sangyō-keizai

Shimamoto Tokuichi, 1969, *Dōjima kome-kaisho kobunken - sekai saiko no shōken-shijō* (Early Records on the Dojima Rice Exchange - the Oldest Securities Market of the World), Kinki daigaku sekai-keizai kenkyujo, Sekai-keizai mondai kenkyū-sōsho 9, Osaka

Shimamoto Tokuichi, 1970, *Dōjima kome-kaisho kobunken* (Early Records on the Dojima Rice Exchange)

Sugie Masahiko, 1984, *Tōki to sakimono-torihiki no riron* (The Theory of Speculation and Futures); Tokyo: Chikuma shobō

Suzuki Shōhei, 1940, *Dōjima kome-shijō-shi* (History of the Dōjima rice market); Tokyo: Nihon hyōron-sha

Tanaka Tashichirō, 1910, *Nihon-torihikijo ron* (On exchanges in Japan); Tokyo : Yūhikaku-shobō

Telser, Lester G. and Harlow H. Higinbotham, 1977, "Organized Futures Markets: Costs and Benefits", in: *Journal of Political Economy*, Vol.85 No.5, pp.969-1000

Japanese Financial Market Research
W.T. Ziemba, W. Bailey and Y. Hamao (Editors)
1991 Elsevier Science Publishers B.V.

The Market for Japanese Stock Index Futures: Some Preliminary Evidence

Warren Bailey

Recent years have witnessed an explosion in the variety of derivative assets traded on securities markets. Interestingly, financial futures trading has only recently established a toehold in Japan. This is surprising because, by some measures, Japan's equity markets are the world's largest and the country is home to enormous institutional investors. However, regulatory barriers are gradually being dismantled and several futures markets based on Japanese stocks and government bonds are already operating.

This paper examines available data on Japanese stock index contracts and provides preliminary empirical evidence on a variety of pricing relationships. An understanding of the behavior of the new Japanese markets is essential because the international investment community is likely to find Japanese stock index contracts increasingly popular and important in coming years. The paper is organized as follows. Section I describes the history and institutional details of the Nikkei 225 and Stock 50 contracts. Section II describes the data set of market prices and trading volumes and presents summary information on futures trading volumes and returns on the underlying stock averages. Section III investigates the relationship between changes in the stock averages and futures contract trading volume. Section IV examines the power of cost-of-carry and continuous-time futures pricing models to predict market prices. Section V tests the effectiveness of the contracts in hedging against changes in the value of the underlying index.

I. Japanese Index Contracts: History and Institutional Details

Commodity futures have a long history in Japan. An informal market for rice warehouse receipts in Osaka evolved into an organized rice futures market in 1730.[1] Rice, soybeans, dried silkworm cocoons, and other commodities have traded on established exchanges for several decades.[2] Financial futures have a less distinguished history and reputation due to a series of futures markets collapses in the 1930's.[3]

I thank Lee Soo Bailey, James N. Bodurtha, Jr., Eduardo Lemgruber, Der-Ming Lieu, Edward Ng, and two anonymous referees for their assistance. Citicorp N. A. I. B., The Osaka Securities Exchange, the City of Osaka's Chicago office, and The Singapore Monetary Exchange graciously supplied much of the data used in this study.

[1]*The Economist*, May 21st 1987, p. 69, *The Economist*, June 18th 1988, p. 84., and Osaka Securities Exchange (1987), p. 14.

[2]See Roberts (1985).

[3]*The Economist*, May 9th 1987, p. 73, and June 18th 1988, p. 84.

Warren Bailey is an Assistant Professor of Finance at The Ohio State University.

The first Japanese stock index contract appeared in an "offshore" market. Futures contracts based on the Nikkei 225 Stock Index began trading on the Singapore Monetary Exchange (Simex) on September 3rd, 1986.[4] The Nikkei 225 stock index is a simple, equally-weighted average similar to the Dow Jones Industrials: the sum of the prices of the component shares is scaled and adjusted for stock splits with a divisor factor. The index includes two-hundred and twenty-five companies from all sectors of the Japanese economy including industrials, trading companies, and financial institutions.

The first stock index contract offered in Japan, the Stock 50 contract, requires delivery of the underlying stock at maturity because the Japanese Securities Trading Law had prohibited cash settlement contracts. The Osaka Securities Exchange began trading Stock 50 futures contracts on June 9th, 1987. The Stock 50 index is an equally-weighted average of share prices for fifty companies listed on the Osaka exchange. The Exchange states that the Stock 50 average has been designed to mimic the Nikkei 225: all but four of the fifty companies are also included in the Nikkei 225 index. If a Stock 50 contract is held to maturity, the short investor delivers one thousand shares of each of the component shares of the index and pays one-way stock commissions and transfer tax.[5]

Table I illustrates details of the two contracts. Information on the Chicago Mercantile Exchange's $S + P$ 500 contract is included for comparison. The Stock 50 contract's value is substantially larger than the Nikkei or $S + P$ 500 contracts. Furthermore, the Stock 50 trades in a more structured market which includes standard commission rates and daily price limit moves. The Nikkei 225 contract is very similar to the $S + P$ 500 contract. Both Japanese-based contracts differ from the $S + P$ 500 in that they trade on Saturday mornings, to match the trading hours of the Tokyo and Osaka stock exchanges.

II. DATA AND SUMMARY STATISTICS ON INDEX RETURNS

Daily data from the Nikkei 225 market for the period from September 3rd, 1986 to March 31st, 1987 were supplied by the Singapore Monetary Exchange. The data consist of open, high, low, and close prices for all futures contracts and the underlying stock index, plus settle prices and volumes for the futures. Daily closing futures prices and volumes from the Stock 50 market for the period from June 9th to October 31st, 1987 were supplied by the Osaka Securities Exchange and the City of Osaka's office in Chicago. The daily closing level of the Stock 50 index was obtained from the business pages of *The Japan Times*. Records of short-term Japanese interest rates needed to test pricing models were also obtained.[6]

Figures 1 and 2 plot daily volume for the two contracts. The Simex averaged 9430 Nikkei contracts traded per month while the Osaka exchange averaged 17302 Stock 50 contracts traded per month during the time periods in the sample. Volume, particularly for the Stock 50 contract, appears to have increased with time. However, volume for both contracts is small relative to U. S. index markets. For example, Chicago Mercantile

[4]The Singapore Monetary Exchange operates under rules similar to those of the Chicago Mercantile Exchange. Currently, the Simex trades futures contracts on German marks, Japanese yen, UK pounds, Eurodollars, and gold, in addition to the Nikkei 225.

[5]Offsetting trades can be initiated prior to maturity to avoid delivery of the underlying shares.

[6]Euroyen rates are used with the Nikkei contracts which, like Euroyen deposits, are traded offshore. Yields on Japanese Treasury bills are used with the Osaka contracts.

Table I
SUMMARY OF CONTRACT AND MARKET FEATURES

	Simex Nikkei 225	Osaka Stock 50	CME S + P 500
Underlying Index:	225 shares, equally-weighted	50 shares, equally-weighted	500 shares, capitalization-weighted
Contract Value:	futures price times *Y*500	futures price times *Y*50,000	futures price times $500
Maturity:	third Wednesday of March, June September, December, and current month	fifteenth day of March, June September, and December	third Friday of March, June September, and December
Settlement:	cash	delivery	cash
Minimum Price Move Per Contract:	*Y*2500 (≈ $20)	*Y*5000 (≈ $40)	$25
Limit Move:	none	3%	none
Futures Commissions:	negotiable, comparable to U.S.	varies from .03% to .09% plus .0125% tax (about 1.5 index points)	negotiable, generally less than $100
Stock Commissions:	.15% to 1.25% plus .5% tax	.15% to 1.25% plus .5% tax	negotiable
Initial Margin:	*Y*750,000	9%	negotiable
Typical Contract Value:	20,000 (futures price) × *Y*500 = *Y*10,000,000 (≈ $75,000)	1,400 (futures price) × *Y*50,000 = *Y*70,000,000 (≈ $500,000)	250 (futures price) × $500 = $125,000

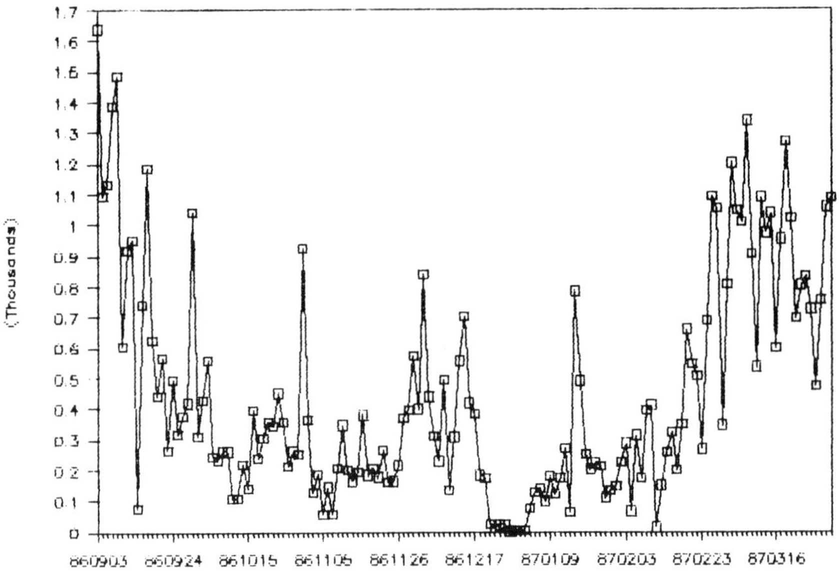

Figure 1
Nikkei 225, Total Daily Volume.

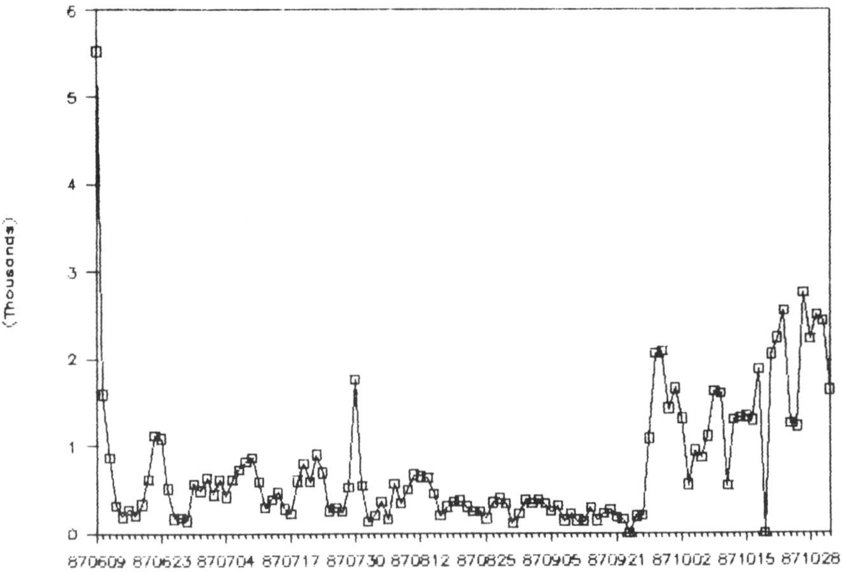

Figure 2
Osaka Stock 50 Total Daily Volume.

Table II
SUMMARY STATISTICS FOR DAILY STOCK INDEX RETURNS

Variable	Nikkei 225	Osaka Stock-50
Observations	153	114
Time Span	3/9/86 to 31/3/87	9/6/87 to 31/10/87
Mean (standard deviation) of daily index return:		
Close-to-Close	0.001007 (0.01017)	−0.001016 (0.02477)
Close-to-Close, Monday to Friday or Saturday[a]	0.002133 (0.009898)	0.0004739 (0.02597)
Close-to-Close, Friday or Saturday to Monday	−0.003767 (0.01008)	−0.007943 (0.01703)
Close-to-Close, Tuesday	−0.0009497 (0.01063)	−0.003044 (0.04180)
Close-to-Open	0.0000445 (0.001138)	– *
Close-to-Open Weekend only	0.0000964 (0.000649)	– *
Open-to-Close	0.0008900 (0.009942)	– *
Open-to-Close, Monday through Friday	0.0006478 (0.01005)	– *
Open-to-Close, Saturday	0.003295 (0.00879)	– *
1st Order Correlation (p-test) of Close-to-Close Returns	0.195 (.016)	−.206 (.029)

[a]"Friday or Saturday" uses Saturday price on Saturdays when market is open, Friday otherwise
*open prices for the Osaka average were not available

Exchange (1986, 1987) indicated that the $S + P$ 500 futures market averaged over one-and-a-half million contracts traded per month during the time periods in the sample.

Table II presents summary statistics on the daily returns of the two stock averages. The information in the table can be compared to existing evidence on U. S. and Japanese stock prices. French (1980) reports a statistically significant "weekend effect" in U. S. common stock returns: returns measured from Friday close to Monday close are, on average, smaller than those measured across other times of the week. Jaffe and Westerfield (1985) report a "Tuesday effect" (lower close-to-close returns than at other times of the week) for Japanese stock averages. This also appears to be exhibited by the sample of Nikkei 225 and Stock 50 returns.

French and Roll (1986) report that the volatility of U. S. common stock returns is, on average, greater during times when stock markets are open than overnight or across weekends and holidays. The data summarized in Table II suggests that similar effects prevail in Japanese stock markets. Weekday close-to-close returns span a twenty-four hour period while weekend close-to-close returns span a period of two to three days. Therefore, the weekend close-to-close standard deviation should be bigger than the weekday close-to-close standard deviation by a factor of $\sqrt{2}$ to $\sqrt{3}$ if index volatility is the same across the two times of the week. However, the data indicate that the weekend close-to-close standard deviation is only 1% higher than the weekday standard deviation for the Nikkei and is 35 percent lower for the Stock 50. Clearly, price volatility is greater when Japan's markets are open.

The opening prices available for the Nikkei average provide further illustration of this point. The open-to-close period spans about six hours while close-to-open spans about eighteen hours on weekdays and two to three days on weekends. Given identical volatility across periods, the close-to-open standard deviation should be larger than the open-to-close standard deviation by a factor of at least $\sqrt{3}$. However, the data show that the close-to-open standard deviation is only about 11 percent of the size of the open-to-close standard deviation, that is, one-fifteenth as large as predicted. The table also reports summary statistics on returns measured close-to-open over the weekend only. Given a weekend of forty-eight to seventy-two hours' length, the weekend close-to-open standard deviation should be many times larger than the weekday open-to-close standard deviation. However, the data indicate that the weekend close-to-open standard deviation is only 6.5% of the size of the weekday open-to-close standard deviation.

The stochastic behavior of Japanese stock averages varies considerably across different times of the week and appears to exhibit many of the peculiarities of U. S. markets that have been documented by other authors. The evidence presented in Table II also suggests that i.), open-to-close returns during the short Saturday session are higher and more volatile, and ii.), there is a small but significant degree of autocorrelation in the stock average returns.

III. FUTURES VOLUME AND CHANGES IN THE STOCK AVERAGES

Many studies have found a positive correlation between price changes and trading volume in securities markets. In particular, both returns and absolute values of returns of U. S. stock indices have been found to be correlated with trading volume. Links between price changes and trading volume highlight how information is trasmitted to (and incorporated by) securities markets, the effect of short sale contraints, and other aspects of market structure. Karpoff (1987) provides a summary of theory and empirical evidence.

Using non-parametric correlation coefficients, the sum of trading volume in index contracts is related to various measures of the change in the spot index. Tests are run separately for the Nikkei and Osaka markets and are reported in Table III. There is no evidence of correlation between price changes and futures volume. There is, however, considerable evidence of correlation between the absolute value of price changes and futures volume. The correlation is highly significant for the Stock 50 measured close-to-close and the Nikkei 225 measured high-to-low. It is marginally significant for the Nikkei measured open-to-close and close-to-close.

The evidence suggests that futures volume increases as speculators and hedgers react to the arrival of new information and resulting price changes. Furthermore, the lack of short sale constraints in futures markets is apparent: volume increases with any price change, regardless of its sign. In equity markets, short sale rules and margin requirements can impede selling in a bearish market. However, futures markets do not distinguish between long and short positions with uptick rules or differential margins. As a result, futures volume can react freely to any change in the underlying index, regardless of its sign.

IV. TESTS OF TWO FUTURES PRICING MODELS

Changes in the underlying index have a direct impact on index futures prices in an efficient market. This section describes two models which price index futures contracts relative to the value of the underlying index, then tests their power to predict market prices for Japanese index contracts.[7]

In a frictionless market with non-stochastic interest rates and a non-stochastic index dividend yield, the futures price is related to the level of the underlying index, the interest rate, and the dividend yield on the index through the simple cost-of-carry model:

$$F = S \exp\{\tau(r - \delta)\} \tag{1}$$

F and S represent the futures price and the level of the index, r the riskless interest rate spanning the life of the contract, δ the dividend yield on the index,[8] and τ the time until the contract matures. If market frictions are significant, the futures price lies in a range equal to the right-hand side of equation (1), plus or minus transactions costs. Variations of the model have been tested with U.S. index futures data by French and Cornell (1983), Modest and Sundaresan (1983), and other authors.

If interest rates are stochastic, the continuous-time model presented in Ramaswamy and Sundaresan (1985) can be used to price index futures contracts. The model assumes that the stock index follows a log-normal process:

$$dS = (\alpha - \delta)Sdt + \sigma_1 S\, dz_1 \tag{2}$$

[7]Chung (1988), MacKinlay and Ramaswamy (1987), and Stoll and Whaley (1986) examine "program trading" and the efficiency of U.S. index futures markets using transactions data. Such tests are beyond the scope of this paper.

[8]The model assumes the dividend yield is a constant flow. Brenner, Subrahmanyam, and Uno (1987) find that ex-dividend dates for Japanese shares are clustered at the end of March and September. They note, however, that the impact on futures prices is probably insignificant: Japanese dividend yields are small and the maturity cycle of futures contracts ensures that no short maturity contracts span the end of March or September.

Table III
TESTS OF PRICE-VOLUME EFFECTS: THE CORRELATION BETWEEN FUTURES MARKET VOLUME, CHANGES IN THE STOCK INDEX, AND THE ABSOLUTE VALUE OF CHANGES IN THE STOCK INDEX[a]

Variable	Nikkei 225 Average	Osaka Stock-50 Index
Observations	153	114
Time Span	3/9/86 to 31/3/87	9/6/87 to 31/10/87
Correlation Between:		
Close-to-Close Price Change and Volume	.020 (.810)	.121 (.201)
Absolute Value of Close-to-Close Price Change and Volume	.135 (.095)	.380 (<.001)
Open-to-Close Price Change and Volume	−.007 (.933)	– *
Absolute Value of Open-to-Close Price Change and Volume	.140 (.084)	– *
High-Low Price Difference and Volume	.255 (.001)	– *

[a]the statistic reported is Spearman's rank correlation, with p test reported in parentheses next to each correlation estimate

*open, high, and low prices for the Osaka average were not available

Parameters α and σ_1 are the drift and volatility of the stochastic process, δ is the dividend yield of the index, and dz_1 is a standard Wiener process. The model also assumes that the instantaneous riskless interest rate, r, follows a mean-reverting process:

$$dr = \kappa(\mu - r)\,dt + \sigma_2\sqrt{r}\,dz_2 \tag{3}$$

Parameters κ, μ, and σ_2 are the speed of adjustment, long run mean, and volatility of the stochastic process while dz_2 is a standard Wiener process. The covariance between dz_1 and dz_2 is ρdt. If the Local Expectations Hypothesis of Cox, Ingersoll, and Ross (1981) holds, the following partial differential equation governs the futures price:

$$\frac{1}{2}\sigma_2^2 rF_{rr} + \frac{1}{2}\sigma_1^2 S^2 F_{SS} + \rho\sigma_1\sigma_2 S\sqrt{r}F_{rS} + \kappa(\mu - r)F_r + (r - \delta)SF_S = F_\tau \tag{4}$$

The line hopscotch method, a finite difference technique presented in Gourlay and McKee (1977), is used to numerically solve the partial differential equation with appropriate boundary conditions. The time step size is set at $1/52$. The index and interest rate step sizes are set to yield one-hundred steps in the price direction and twenty-five steps in the interest rate direction.[9]

The procedure outlined in Dietrich-Campbell and Schwartz (1986) is used to estimate the parameters κ, μ, σ_1, σ_2, and ρ.[10] The transformations $S' = \log\{S\}$ and $r' = \sqrt{r}$ yield a system of equations with homoscedastic errors:

$$dS' = [\alpha - \delta - \sigma_1^2/2]\,dt + \sigma_1\,dz_1 \quad (5)$$

$$dr' = [(\kappa\mu - \sigma_2^2/4)/2r') - (\kappa r'/2)\,dt + (\sigma_2/2)\,dz_2 \quad (6)$$

Because S' and r' are not continuously observable, discrete first differences, $r'(t + h) - r'(t)$ and $S'(t + h) - S'(t)$, are employed in the estimation. Assuming the drift of process (6) is constant between observations, the parameters are jointly estimated by maximizing the bivariate conditionally normal likelihood function. Beginning of period drift (r' equals $r'(t)$) and the substitution $\beta = \kappa\mu - \sigma_2^2/4$ are used in equation (6). The resulting parameter estimates are $\hat{\sigma}_1$ equal to .146, $\hat{\kappa}$ equal to .627, $\hat{\beta}$ equal to .0344, $\hat{\sigma}_2$ equal to .019, and $\hat{\rho}$ equal to $-.193$. The estimated long run mean, $\hat{\mu}$, implied by $\hat{\kappa}$ and $\hat{\sigma}_2$ is .055.

Cost-of-carry and continuous-time model values are computed for each futures contract in the sample and compared to the closing market prices in the dataset.[11] Tables IV and V present summary statistics on model pricing errors measured in index points. The cost-of-carry model overprices Nikkei contracts by an average of Y51.3 and underprices Stock 50 contracts by an average of Y9.7. Given average Nikkei prices of about Y20,000 and average Stock 50 prices of about Y1400, the mispricings represent about $-.25\%$ and .7% of a typical contract price respectively. The average absolute value of cost-of-carry mispricings is Y158.8 for Nikkei and Y19.3 for Osaka, roughly .8% and 1.4% of the contract price respectively. For all contracts and maturities, the standard deviations of errors suggest that the mispricings are not significantly different from zero.

The small differences between cost-of-carry and market prices reported in the table are easily explained by observation errors, trading costs, short sale constraints, different borrowing and lending rates, and other market imperfections.[12] The data also indicate that the pricing errors from the continuous time model are not substantially different

[9]The hopscotch program matched simulations published in Ramaswamy and Sundaresan (1985) with errors of only a few cents. Doubling the grid fineness does not increase precision significantly and raises the cost, in CPU seconds, about 350%. Simulation results are available from the author.

[10]Parameters are estimated with end-of-month quotes for the Nikkei average and short maturity Euroyen from January 1981 to August 1986.

[11]The dividend yield, δ, on both the Nikkei 225 and the Stock 50 is assumed to equal the estimate of .86% provided by the Simex (1986). Because Japanese dividend yields are small, pricing errors due to variation in the dividend yield are likely to be insignificant. Out-of-sample quotes for the Stock 50 average were not available because the index level was not published in *The Japan Times* prior to the introduction of the futures contract. Therefore, continuous-time values for Stock 50 futures are computed using the parameters estimated for the Nikkei average and Euroyen yield. This is unlikely to produce significant errors because the Nikkei and Stock 50 averages are highly correlated and, as Takagi (1987) notes, Japanese T-bill and Euroyen term structures have converged in recent years.

[12]Traders have no incentive to undertake an arbitrage unless profits exceed transactions costs. Mispricings of only 1% or so are likely to be too small: Brenner, Subrahmanyam, and Uno (1987) estimate total arbitrage transactions costs of 1.01% for a broker and 2.77% for an institutional investor.

Table IV
MEAN (STANDARD DEVIATION) OF PRICING ERROR, ξ, AND ABSOLUTE VALUE OF PRICING ERROR, $|\xi|$: CLOSING MARKET PRICES MINUS MODEL PRICES ESTIMATED FOR NIKKEI 225 FUTURES CONTRACTS

		Cost-of-Carry Model			Continuous Time Model		
Contract	N[a]	ξ	No. Pos.[b]	$\lvert\xi\rvert$	ξ	No. Pos.	$\lvert\xi\rvert$
All	244	−51.3 (225.6)	110	158.8 (167.9)	−50.4 (225.0)	111	159.2 (166.4)
9/86	10	−2.9 (47.1)	5	37.5 (25.9)	4.8 (48.5)	6	37.6 (28.4)
11/86	4	91.0 (273.3)	2	190.9 (192.8)	97.1 (275.5)	2	192.7 (197.3)
12/86	71	−189.9 (263.5)	17	237.1 (221.4)	−184.5 (263.4)	17	234.7 (219.3)
1/87	11	22.8 (60.2)	7	53.6 (32.1)	30.3 (59.8)	8	56.0 (33.8)
2/87	2	7.0 (156.0)	1	110.3 (9.9)	13.3 (148.6)	1	105.1 (18.8)
3/87	87	−33.3 (163.8)	45	122.2 (133.4)	−31.5 (165.6)	45	124.2 (113.2)
6/87	48	41.4 (159.9)	27	128.1 (102.6)	36.9 (162.5)	26	129.0 (103.9)
9/87	8	206.4 (348.5)	5	272.2 (292.3)	185.1 (350.1)	5	268.3 (281.7)
12/87	3	−116.6 (405.5)	1	340.7 (103.2)	−165.0 (402.9)	1	356.1 (113.4)
$\tau < 1/4$[c]	159	−52.5 (235.0)	80	163.3 (176.6)	−47.5 (234.7)	82	163.1 (174.9)
$1/4 < \tau < 1/2$	81	−44.0 (202.0)	29	142.4 (149.1)	−49.2 (199.7)	28	143.1 (146.9)
$1/2 < \tau$	4	−147.1 (336.6)	1	315.2 (98.5)	−187.3 (332.0)	1	330.7 (105.6)

[a]number of observations
[b]number of deviations greater than zero
[c]τ is time, in years, until contract maturity

Table V
MEAN (STANDARD DEVIATION) OF PRICING ERROR, ξ, AND ABSOLUTE VALUE OF PRICING ERROR, $|\xi|$: CLOSING MARKET PRICES MINUS MODEL PRICES ESTIMATED FOR STOCK 50 FUTURES CONTRACTS

		Cost-of-Carry Model			Continuous Time Model		
Contract	N[a]	ξ	no. pos.[b]	$\lvert\xi\rvert$	ξ	no. pos.	$\lvert\xi\rvert$
All	209	9.7 (28.6)	122	19.3 (22.5)	9.3 (27.3)	119	18.9 (21.7)
9/87	72	11.9 (22.1)	45	18.5 (16.8)	12.0 (21.9)	45	18.4 (16.8)
12/87	106	9.8 (24.5)	65	18.4 (18.7)	9.0 (24.0)	63	17.9 (18.3)
3/88	26	1.5 (22.3)	10	15.7 (15.6)	1.5 (21.8)	9	15.2 (15.4)
6/88	5	19.1 (106.2)	2	67.0 (78.3)	15.7 (107.0)	2	67.5 (77.8)
$\tau < 1/4$[c]	104	7.3 (21.4)	53	16.8 (15.1)	7.4 (21.2)	53	16.7 (15.0)
$1/4 < \tau < 1/2$	92	10.5 (25.5)	59	19.1 (19.8)	9.8 (24.9)	57	18.5 (19.4)
$1/2 < \tau$	13	22.9 (159.0)	10	41.3 (66.1)	20.1 (64.3)	9	40.1 (53.3)

[a]number of observations
[b]number of deviations greater than zero
[c]τ is time, in years, until contract maturity

from those reported for the simpler cost-of-carry model. Although the more complex model allows for interest rate volatility and correlation between the interest rate and the stock index, it offer no improvement over the cost-of-carry model, perhaps because the volatility of Japanese interest rates is very low. Plots of market versus cost-of-carry prices (available from the author) indicates that most pricing errors occur near the inauguration of trading, the fall of 1986 for the Nikkei market and the middle of 1987 for the Osaka market. As the futures markets have matured, prices have tended to converge to theoretical values.

V. TESTS OF HEDGING EFFECTIVENESS

The evidence presented in the previous section indicates that futures pricing models closely approximate market prices conditional on the level of the underlying index. However, a model which accurately captures the dynamics of the spread between index

Table VI
TESTS OF HEDGING EFFECTIVENESS OF THE NIKKEI 225 AND OSAKA STOCK 50 CONTRACTS

	N[a]	Mean (standard deviation) of daily portfolio return:[b] Unhedged	Cost-of Carry Hedge[c]	Empirical Hedge[d]	Correlation (p test) of percentage changes in spot and futures prices
Nikkei 225:					
12/86	71	.0002619 (.01251)	.0002084 (.007618)	.0002123 (.008552)	.823 (<.001)
3/87	87	.002518 (.01193)	.0001117 (.005490)	−.0002878 (.006092)	.890 (<.001)
6/87	48	.004196 (.01224)	.0004194 (.006918)	−.0003222 (.007579)	.834 (<.001)
Osaka Stock 50:					
9/87	72	−.0006931 (.01396)	.0005825 (.008884)	.001294 (.01154)	.770 (<.001)
12/87	106	−.001093 (.02104)	.0003285 (.01554)	.001244 (.02235)	.688 (<.001)

[a]number of observations
[b]portfolio returns are computed close-to-close
[c]the cost-of-carry hedge is $-\exp\{-\tau(r - \delta)\}$ futures contracts
[d]the empirical hedge is $-(1/\beta)$ futures contracts, where β is the estimated slope from a regression of percentage futures price changes on percentage index changes; estimated slopes are .863, .849, and .796 for the Nikkei contracts and .619 and .554 for the Osaka contracts

and index futures price is required to construct hedge portfolios. Hedging effectiveness depends on the strength and stability of the correlation between index level and future price, that is, the degree of basis variability.

This section reports tests of the hedging effectiveness of the Nikkei 225 and Stock 50 contracts. A hedge portfolio is assumed to consist of one unit of the underlying index and a short futures position. The size of the futures position is computed in two ways. First, the derivative of the cost-of-carry futures price with respect to the spot value of the index is employed:

$$\partial F/\partial S = \exp\{\tau(r - \delta)\} \tag{7}$$

One unit of the underlying index is hedged with $-1/(\partial F/\partial S)$ futures contracts. Second, an empirical hedge ratio of the type used by Ederington (1979) is employed. One unit of the underlying index is hedged with short futures contracts equal in number to the inverse of the slope coefficient from a regression of futures price changes on spot price changes. For both types of hedges, daily portfolio returns are computed and summarized.

Table VI presents summary statistics on the hedge portfolio returns and on the correlation between spot and futures prices. Only the more active futures contracts, which have enough of a time series of data available, are studied. Returns from unhedged portfolios are included for comparison. The statistics on hedge portfolio returns suggest that the futures contracts perform poorly in hedging the underlying index. A riskless rate of return of .02% per day is consistent with the annualized rate of about 6% prevailing during the time period. The hedge portfolio returns are, on average, statistically close to .02%. However, the standard deviations of hedged portfolio returns are large, about one-half to three-quarters of the size of the standard deviations of unhedged returns. This is equilvalent to an annualized standard deviation of 10% to 15%. The results indicate considerable basis variability, though the standard deviations are no larger those reported by Figlewski (1985) for U. S. index contracts. The sizeable basis risk of the futures contracts is confirmed by the correlation coefficients presented in the table. Although the correlation between futures prices and underlying stock averages is highly significant, it is considerably less than one.

Given the short time series of data currently available, it was necessary to conduct hedging tests with daily portfolio returns. Longer horizon tests would be more representative of actual investor strategies. They would also alleviate the effects of bid-ask spreads and non-synchronous data (which are compounded with the use of daily returns) and produce lower standard deviations of returns. Nonetheless, it appears that the Japanese index futures markets have not matured enough to be a reliable medium for hedging Japanese stock portfolios.

VI. SUMMARY AND CONCLUSION

This paper reports the results of a variety of empirical tests based on a small sample of prices and volumes from the newly-created Japanese stock index futures markets. The evidence is similar to that presented in studies of U. S. index markets. There are strong links between the stochastic behavior of the underlying stock averages and futures prices and volumes. Weekly seasonals exhibited by the stock averages are significant. Theoretical pricing models are reasonably accurate in predicting futures prices. However, the basis variability of the new contracts reduces their usefulness as hedging instruments. Nonetheless, the pace of deregulation and growing investor interest are leading to greater trading activity in existing Japanese stock index contracts and development of new contracts. The size of the Japanese capital market and the gradual dismantling of regulatory constraints insure that Japanese stock index contracts will grow in importance in coming years.

Bibliography

Brenner, M., Subrahmanyam, M. G.; and J. Uno (1987): "Arbitrage Opportunities in the Nikkei Spot and Futures Markets," Working Paper, New York University.

Chicago Mercantile Exchange (1986, 1987): *Statistical Yearbook*.

Chung, Y. Peter (1988): "A Transactions Data Test of Stock Index Futures Market Efficiency and Program Trading Profitability," Working Paper, Ohio State University.

Cox, J. C., Ingersoll, J. E.; and S. A. Ross (1981): "A Reexamination of Traditional Hypotheses about the Term Structure of Interest Rates," *Journal of Finance,* 36: 769–799.

Dietrich-Campbell, B., and E. Schwartz (1986): "Valuing Debt Options: Empirical Evidence," *Journal of Financial Economics,* 16: 321–343.

Ederington, Louis H (1979) "The Hedging Performance of the New Futures Markets," *Journal of Finance,* 34: 157–70.

The Economist, numerous issues.

Figlewski, Stephen (1985): " Hedging with Stock Index Futures: Theory and Application in a New Market," *Journal of Futures Ma*rkets, 5: 183–199.

French, Kenneth R (1980): "Stock Returns and the Weekend Effect," *Journal of Financial Economics,* 8: 55–70.

French, K. R. and B. Cornell (1983): "The Pricing of Stock Index Futures," *Journal of Futures Markets,* 3: 1–14.

French, K. R. and R. W. Roll (1986): "Stock Return Variances: The Arrival of Information and the Reaction of Traders," *Journal of Financial Economics,* 17: 5–26.

Gourlay, A. R., and S. McKee (1977): "The Construction of Hopscotch Methods for Parabolic and Elliptic Equations in Two Space Dimensions with a Mixed Derivative," *Journal of Computational an Applied Mathematics,* 3: 201–206.

Jaffee, J., and R. Westerfield (1985): "Patterns in Japanese Common Stock Returns: Day of the Week and Turn of the Year Effects," *Journal of Financial and Quantitative Analysis,* 20: 267–72.

Karpoff, J. M. (1987): "The Relation between Price Changes and Trading Volume: A Survey." *Journal of Financial and Quantitative Analysis,* 22: 109–23.

MacKinlay, A. C., and K. Ramaswamy (1987): "Program Trading and the Behavior of Stock Index Futures Prices," Working Paper, University of Pennsylvania.

Modest, D. M. and M. Sundaresan (1983): "The Relationship Between Spot and Futures Prices in Stock Index Futures Markets: Some Preliminary Evidence," *Journal of Futures Markets,* 3: 15–41.

Osaka Securities Exchange (1987): "Stock Futures 50: A New Investment Strategy for Japanese Stocks," pamphlet.

Osaka Securities Exchange, and Japan Securities Dealers Association: "Stock Futures (OSF50): Its Systems and Characteristics," undated pamphlet.

Ramaswamy K., and S. Sundaresan (1985): "The Valuation of Options on Futures Contracts," *Journal of Finance,* 40: 1319–40.

Roberts, Gerald (1985): *Guide to World Commodity Markets,* Kogan Page, Ltd., London.

Singapore Monetary Exchange, Ltd (1985): "Nikkei Stock Average Futures," pamphlet.

Stoll, H. R., and R. E. Whaley (1986): "Expiration Day Effects of Index Options and Futures," New York University Salomon Brothers Center Monograph.

Takagi, Shinji (1987): "Transactions Costs and the Term Structure of Interest Rates in the OTC Bond Market in Japan," *Journal of Money, Credit, and Banking,* 19: 515–27.

Japanese Financial Market Research
W.T. Ziemba, W. Bailey and Y. Hamao (Editors)

SEASONALITY EFFECTS IN JAPANESE FUTURES MARKETS*

William T. Ziemba

Yamaichi Research Institute, Tokyo
University of Tsukuba and
University of British Columbia

This paper investigates seasonal regularities in the security price returns on the first section of the Tokyo Stock Exchange. The research uses data from the futures markets in Singapore for the Nikkei Dow 225 index and in Osaka for the Kabusaki 50 index. The questions of main concern are whether or not the seasonal anomalies observed in the spot markets are maintained, are they anticipated in the futures markets, and do the futures market anticipations alter the character of the seasonal regularity. Results are presented concerning day of the week, monthly, holiday, turn of the month and year and first half of the month effects. The conclusions are tentative because the futures markets have only a short history to date.

1. INTRODUCTION

The Japanese country and economy were devastated in WWII. After the war the country was occupied and plans were set for a rebuilding. The stock markets reopened in 1949. The early years were difficult but the hard work and internal savings for investment paid off as the country's products gained more and more acceptance abroad. The full fruits of the economic miracle of Japan are now well known and feared in the west. Since 1980 the transfer of wealth to Japan from the U.S and others has been very large indeed. Figure 1 shows this through the world stock market capitalizations in October 1980 and September 1988. Europe's share of the world's stock markets has stayed about constant (21% in 1988 versus 20% in 1980), the U.S. share has dropped from

*Without implicating them I would like to thank my colleagues at the Yamaichi Research Institute particularly A. Komatsu and H. Shintani for their help and useful discussions on anomalous behavior in Japanese security markets. Thanks are also due to Warren Bailey and Sandra Schwartz for helpful comments on an earlier draft of this paper. This research was conducted at the Yamaichi Research Institute with the advice of William T. Ziemba. All the rights to the research belong to the Yamaichi Research Institute. I thank the Yamaichi Research Institute for permission to publish the results. This research was also partially supported by the Social Sciences and Humanities Research Council of Canada, and the Centre for International Business Studies, University of British Columbia.

53% to 31% and the rest of the world's is now 6% compared to 12% in 1980. Meanwhile, Japan's share has increased from 15% to 42% Net assets of Japan were $11.5 billion at the end of 1980 and those of the U.S. were $106.3 billion. By 1987 Japan's net assets grew over 20 fold to $240.7 billion. Meanwhile U.S. private and public assets fell by a negative $368.2 billion. There is much talk in the press about the U.S. trade and budget deficits. Indeed the public's deficit was $148.9 billion at the end of 1987. But the private sector of the U.S. is also $219.3 billion in the red.

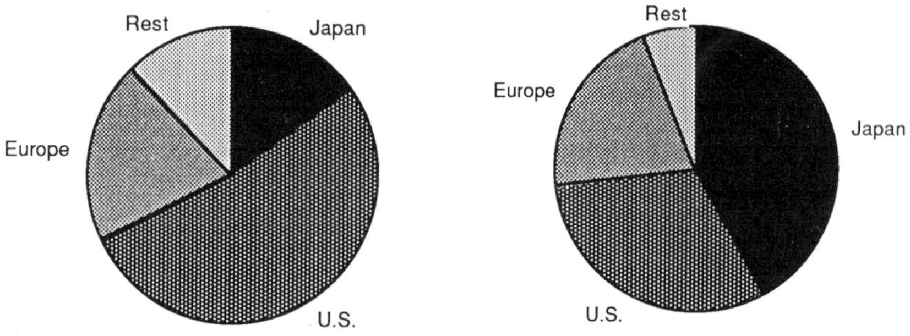

October 1980 September 1988

Figure 1: Stock Market Capitalizations

There has been a huge increase in Japanese stock prices. A standard measure of the market is the Nikkei Dow index. This index is analogous to the Dow Jones Industrial Average in the U.S. Its value at any time is the sum of the prices of the 225 stocks in the index divided by the current divisor which is adjusted over time to account for stock splits, rights offerings, etc. The index stood at ¥176.21 on the date of its original investment, May 16, 1949. By the end of the year the index had fallen to ¥109.9. But by the end of December 1988 the index had increased to ¥30,159. The divisor which began at 225 was then 10.289. The increase over the 38+ years was 171.15 times not counting dividends and taxes. In U.S. dollars the increase was a remarkable 489.59 times. The increase has not been straight up. Over this period there have been twenty corrections of 10% or more and nine of over 20%. For details see Ziemba and Schwartz (1990). Table 1 shows the closing prices of the ND index plus the value of the yen/dollar exchange rate year by year plus the gains in yen and dollars for the ND index.

The major stock market in Japan is the Tokyo Stock Exchange. The TSE has over 85% of the value and trading volume of the whole market which is also traded in Osaka, Nagoya and five other smaller exchanges. The stocks in the Nikkei Dow comprise about 50% of the market value and about 75% of the

Table 1: Yearly Yen Closing Prices of the Nikkei Dow and Yen/Dollar Exchange Rates, 1949-88

End of Year	ND	Yen/$	Current Value of 1¥ invested in 1949 in ¥	Current Value of 1$ invested in 1949 in$
1949	109.9	360.00	0.62	0.62
1950	101.9	360.00	0.58	0.58
1951	166.1	360.00	0.94	0.94
1952	362.6	360.00	2.06	2.06
1953	377.9	360.00	2.14	2.14
1954	356.1	360.00	2.02	2.02
1955	425.7	360.00	2.42	2.42
1956	549.1	360.00	3.12	3.12
1957	474.5	360.00	2.69	2.69
1958	666.5	360.00	3.78	3.78
1959	874.9	360.00	4.97	4.97
1960	1356.7	360.00	7.70	7.70
1961	1432.6	360.00	8.13	8.13
1962	1420.4	360.00	8.06	8.06
1963	1225.1	360.00	6.95	6.95
1964	1216.5	360.00	6.90	6.90
1965	1417.8	360.00	8.05	8.05
1966	1452.1	360.00	8.24	8.24
1967	1283.5	360.00	7.28	7.28
1968	1714.9	360.00	9.73	9.73
1969	2359.0	360.00	13.39	13.39
1970	1987.1	360.00	11.28	11.28
1971	2713.7	314.80	15.40	17.61
1972	5207.9	302.00	29.56	35.23
1973	4306.8	280.00	24.44	31.42
1974	3817.2	300.95	21.66	25.91
1975	4358.6	305.15	24.74	29.18
1976	4990.8	292.80	28.32	34.82
1977	4865.6	240.00	27.61	41.42
1978	6001.8	194.60	34.06	63.01
1979	6569.5	239.70	37.28	55.99
1980	7116.4	203.00	40.39	71.62
1981	7681.8	219.90	43.59	71.37
1982	8016.7	235.00	45.50	69.69
1983	9893.8	232.20	56.15	87.05
1984	11542.6	251.10	65.50	93.91
1985	13113.3	200.50	74.42	133.62
1986	18701.3	160.05	106.13	238.72
1987	21564.0	123.00	122.38	358.18
1988	30159.0	125.85	171.15	489.59
April 19. 1989	33185.15	132.36	188.32	512.22

trading volume on the first section of the TSE. The second section has only a few percent of the value and volume so the first section and the Nikkei Dow give onea good indication of the whole market. The first section's capitalization is currently about Y490 trillion which is more than all the stock exchanges in the U.S. The ND index suffers from the same problems as the DJIA. A more representative index of the whole market is the TOPIX which is a value weighted index of all, some 1135, stocks on the first section. It is analogus to the NYFE index in the U.S. Relative to the TOPIX, the ND has a beta (using data from Octover 1983 to October 1988) of about 0.84 so it is less variable than the overall market. The TSE is highly regulated with detailed and cumbersome listing procedures, price and margin limits and the like. Trading is dominated by the institutions including the life insurance companies and made largely through the big four: Nomura, Nikko, Daiwa and Yamaichi. Although there are some 45 foreign brokerage firms in Japan they handle only about 2% of the trading volume. In contrast, Nomura alone has about 30% of the trading volume. Although the foreign firms are very active in program trading and the like the lack of commission business has led to massive losses. Only ten of the 45 had profits in 1988 and the profits of these were small compared to those of the big four.[1]

The Japanese stock market is not well understood and is therefore avoided in the U.S. Despite sharply rising prices and a firming yen, there was net selling by foreigners from 1984 to mid 1988. Fears of extraordinary high PE ratios, land prices beyond belief and the like abound as has been described in Ziemba and Schwartz (1990). A few key points are:

- there are extraordinary high correlations between land prices particularly of commercial land and stock prices, see also Ziemba (1989b)
- much of the stock holdings are to cement business relationships and are never traded
- there is a great preference by the Japanese corporations and individuals to accumulate land and a strong feeling not to sell it ever
- the value of the stocks is much less, even with their high PE ratios based on trailing earnings of some 50-70 times, than the value of the land and stock holdings they own not to mention the value of the assets in businesses they are in. Tobin's Q, the percent of the assets that the stocks are worth is about 70% for the ND.
- the PE ratios are not generally as useful a measure of stock value as in the U.S. because of the nontrading, undervaluation of land and other buildings, stock holding and other assets. Still there is a small but significant low PE effect separate from other valuation descriptors

The impending crash that many U.S. and other foreign observers see as inevitable may take a while to materialize if at all. The confidence level of the Japanese in their markets is high and for good reason. Sharply rising earnings growth, GNP growth of about 6% in 1988, 4.5% in 1989 (estimated), low

[1] Japanese firms are not doing well in the U.S either.

interest and inflation rates, a strong yen, huge balance of trade and the like are cited as reasons (and used as explanatory variables in econometric prediction equations) for this strength. Japanese investors prefer to buy on weakness rather than on strength. That is the reverse of the majority of U.S. investors.

The stock market is opening up quickly with a whole host of derivative instruments[2] recently added and planned. There are now four index futures contracts trading and options on futures indices are scheduled to be traded later in 1989. Details on these contracts and their early histories appear in Ziemba and Schwartz (1990).

There is not much literature yet on Japanese anomalies.[3] Part of the reason for this is a lack of interest in such studies by the big Japanese brokerage firms who are unaware and suspicious of their potential use. Also these firms do not generally publish much of their research findings even in Japanese. Recently, however, U.S. and Japanese researchers have been studying these markets. The thrust has been mainly to ascertain the similarities and differences with the analogous results in U.S. markets. Some of the main references are Hawawani (1988a,b), Jaffe and Westerfield (1985a,b), Kato (1988a,b), Kato and Schallheim (1985), Kunimura (1984), Ikeda (1985, 1988) and Nakumura and Terada (1984). Kato, Schwartz, and Ziemba (1989) have surveyed the research and presented new results on day of the week effects in Japanese security markets. Other research works on the Japanese stockmarket are Bailey (1989), Brenner, Subrahmanyam and Uno (1987, 1988), Elton and Gruber (1988, 1989), Hamao (1988, 1989), Kunimura (1984), Hiraki, Aggarwal and Rao (1988), Komatsu and Ziemba (1989), Lau, Quay and Ramsey (1974), Roehl (1985), Pettway and Tapley (1984), Suzuki (1988) and Schoenfeld (1988).

Ziemba (1989a) had access to data on the entire 38+ years of the ND and TOPIX indices and used it to study holiday, monthly, turn of the month and year, first half of the month and Golden Week effects on the first section of the TSE. There are strong and pervasive security market regularities that with some changes because of the institutions involved are analogous to many U.S. findings. The purpose of this paper is to investigate how the new index futures markets are affecting these anomalies. The specific data used are from two of these futures contracts: the SIMEX, ND225 futures traded on the Singapore International Monetary Exchange and the Kabusaki 50 index traded on the Osaka Stock Exchange. These contracts began trading on September 3, 1986 and June 6, 1987, respectively. The newest futures contracts, based on the TOPIX traded on the TSE, and the ND traded on the OSE began trading on September

---

[2]For a survey of the U.S. derivative instruments and some of the theory behind them see Rubinstein (1987).

[3]The U.S. literature on seasonal regularities is now extremely voluminous. Surveys and list of references appear in Schwert (1983), Keim (1986), Jacobs and Levy (1988) and the books by Dimson (1988) and Ziemba (1990).

3, 1988. In this paper we investigate the SIMEX, and Kabusaki data up to September 19 and 20, respectively, which is 557 trading days for the SIMEX and 552 for the Kabusaki.

Figure 2 shows the volume on the SIMEX and Kabusaki 50 during and after the period of this study. Similarly, Figure 3 shows the volume of the two new contracts. The main point is that the new contracts essentially replaced the Kabusaki 50 and its trading volume shrank to almost nothing and it has remained at this low level of activity. Meanwhile the SIMEX had an increase in volume part of which is increased programmed trading. The papers by Brenner, Subrahmanyam and Uno (1987, 1988) study arbitrage programmed trading strategies between the SIMEX and Kabusaki for the early part of the history before September 1988. See also Chapter 13 in Ziemba and Schwartz (1990). The Kabusaki is a price weighted package of 50 stocks traded on the TSE and OSE designed to track the ND. It has a daily limit price move of 3% in either direction. Hence in a market crash, it does not trade. The SIMEX has no such price limits and had a huge fall on crash day October 20, 1987. It now has a daily price limit change of 15%

Singapore time is one hour behind Tokyo time, hence to correspond to Tokyo's 9:00 a.m. opening, the SIMEX begins trading at 8 a.m. During the time of this study, the TSE was open for trading from 9:00-11:00 a.m. and 1:00-3:00 p.m., and 9:00-11:00 a.m. on the first, fourth and fifth (if there is one) Saturdays of the month. As of the beginning of February 1989 there was no Saturday trading on the TSE with trading in the afternoon from 12:30-3:00 pm with extra trading on the previously closed days December 28 and 29. SIMEX does not close for lunch and trades continuously from 8 a.m. to 2:15, an extra fifteen minutes after Tokyo's close. This is much the same as the extra time futures on the S&P 500 and other indices trade following the close of the New York Stock Exchange. Most of the trading days on the TSE and SIMEX are comparable but occasionally one of them has a different holiday. In the initial period until May 23, 1987 SIMEX did not trade on Saturdays.

The SIMEX has a spot contract for the ND that is rarely traded, plus four futures contracts that mature on the quarter months, as do the Kabusaki and U.S. futures contracts, of March, June, September and December. The contracts mature on the third Wednesday of the month and they are settled in cash based on the closing value of the ND. The Kabusaki is settled on the fifteenth day of each contract month with the delivery of the basket of stocks. Throughout most of its trading history the SIMEX traded at a discount from fair value and often the Kabusaki was at a premium. There simply was not enough arbitrage trading to keep the prices in line. I refer the reader to the cited references and also Schoenfeld (1988) who among other accomplishments was the first westerner to trade on the SIMEX.

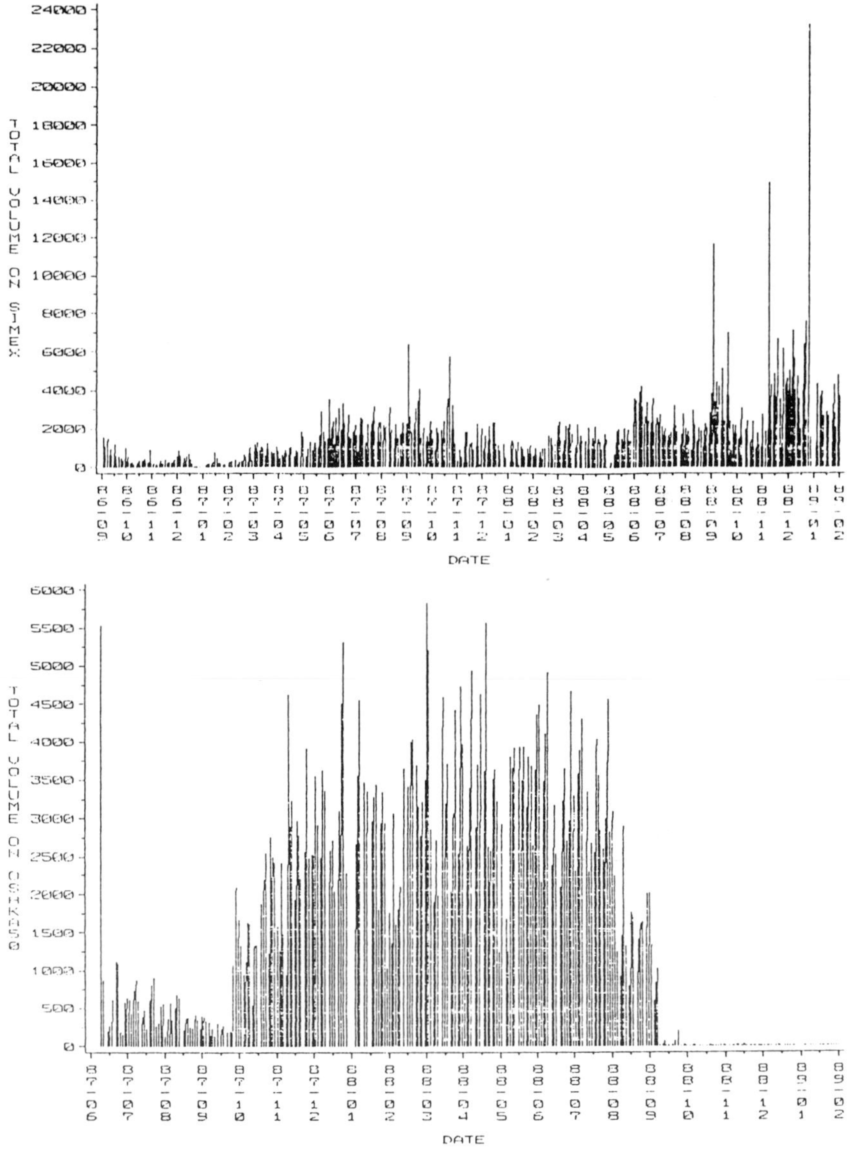

Figure 2: Trading Volume of the SIMEX and Kabusaki Futures Contracts for their Inception through the End of January 1989.

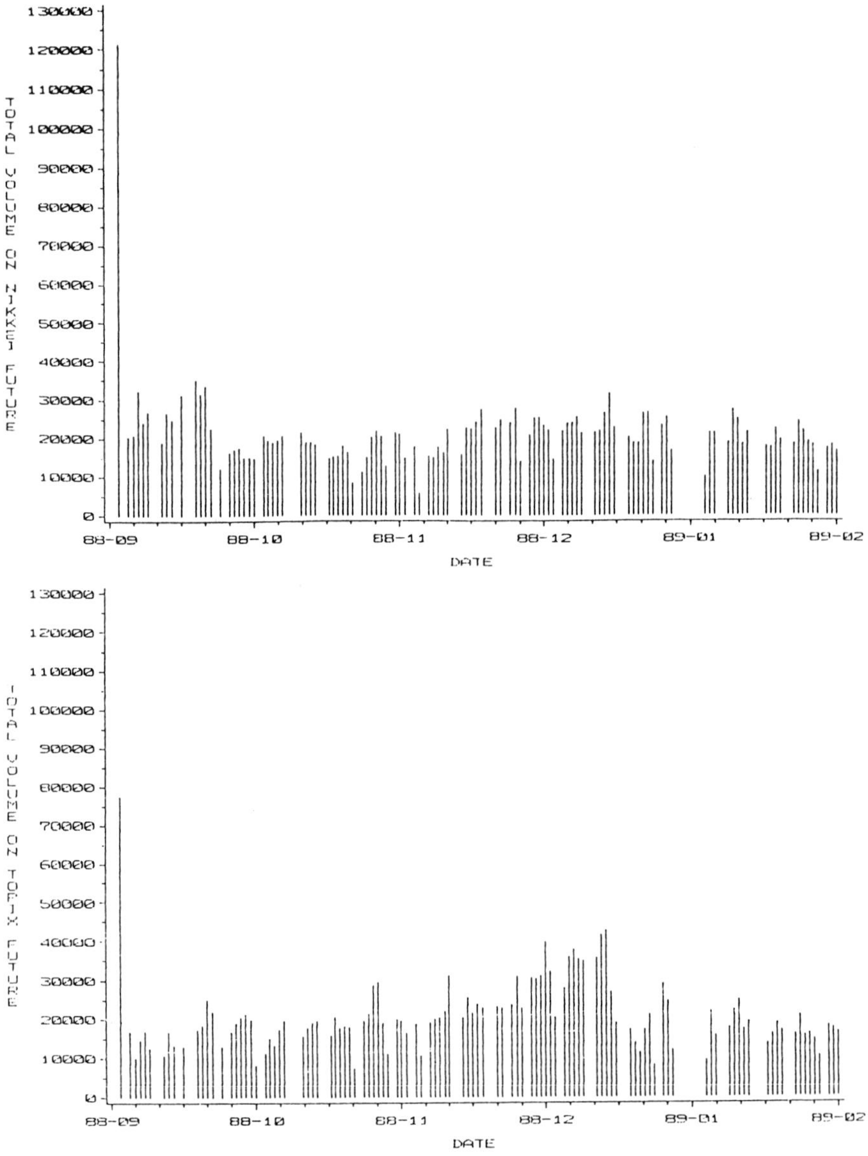

Figure 3: Trading Volume of the ND and TOPIX Futures Contracts Traded on the OSE and TSE, September 3, 1988 to January 31, 1989.

The plan of the paper is to describe in turn each of the spot anomalies and then investigate their current effects in the futures and spot markets. The conclusions reached are tentative because these data sets are still small but they are suggestive. In general, the anomalies still seem to be there, although they are anticipated in the markets to some extent and this has shifted their effects somewhat.

2. Days of the Week Effect

A survey of the days of the week effect in the spot Japanese stock markets along with some new results investigating the ND and TOPIX indices for the entire 1949-88 period appears in Kato, Schwartz and Ziemba (1989). The major research papers investigating the day of the week effects using data from the 1970s and 1980s are Ikeda (1985, 1988) in Japanese, Kato (1988a,b), Kato and Schallheim (1988), and Jaffe and Westerfield (1985a,b). Some of the main conclusions of this research are:

- There is a strong day of the week effect. Wednesdays and Saturdays are strongly positive, Thursdays and Fridays are mildly positive, Mondays are about neutral, and Tuesdays are especially negative. Until the end of January 1989, Saturday trading occurs for a half day on the first, fourth, and (if applicable) the fifth week of the month.

- For the period 1978-87, Wednesdays gain 0.145% and Saturdays 0.14% each about triple the average gain of 0.058%. This is counterbalanced by the nearly even Mondays which return 0.004% on average and a loss of 0.09% on Tuesdays. Thursdays and Fridays return 0.065% and 0.105%, respectively.

- Except for Saturdays which open up and rise all day, on average, most of the gains occur at night. Except for a brief rise early in the day and a little kick at the end all the other days have negative returns during trading hours.

- Saturday trading affects the market in significant ways. Indeed the market seems affected by whether or not Saturday trading occurs. For example, with Saturday trading on the first, fourth and fifth weeks of the month during the sample period, the following Mondays are positive. But without Saturday trading Mondays are negative. Tuesdays are always negative except in the third week of the month when there is no Saturday trading both in this week and the proceeding week. In this case Mondays are especially negative losing 0.35% on average while Tuesdays gain back 0.19% of this.

- In total, Monday-Tuesday trading losses in Japan are about 0.09% which is similar to the Monday losses coupled with Tuesday's mildly positive gain in New York for a Monday-Tuesday return of about -.11%. Correlations between the New York and Tokyo's Dow's vary by time period but these relationships are more or less becoming stronger over time. What is consistent is that New York's effect on Tokyo is stronger than the reverse. For the period 1980-87 the correlation between the previous day's return in New York and the close-to-open returns in Tokyo was 53.6%. The reverse effect, the correlation between Tokyo's close-to-close and New York's close-to-open is only about 11%.

Table 2 sumarizes the recent effects using 1978-87 data and the effects of Saturday trading.

Table 2: Effects of Saturday Trading on the TOPIX, April 4, 1978-June 18, 1987

Week	Trading Ends This Week	Trading Ends Last Week	Mon	Tues	Wed	Thur	Fri	Sat	Sample Size
1st,5th A1	Sat	Sat	0.0198	-0.1072	0.1790	0.0581	0.0605	0.1678	1406
4th A2	Sat	Fri	-0.1008	-0.1102	0.1074	0.0306	0.1582	0.0793	649
2nd B1	Fri	Sat	0.1135	-0.0649	0.0980	0.0933	0.1341		539
3rd B2	Fri	Fri	-0.3489	0.1931	0.2479	0.2609	0.2193		58
	All Weeks		0.0039	-0.0902	0.1449	0.0648	0.1049	0.1397	2652
Sample Size			449	464	464	465	467	343	2652

(Source: Kato 1988a)

Pieptea and Prisman (1988) and others such as Cornell (1985) have found that in the U.S. markets Mondays fall is fully anticipated in the futures markets using the S&P500 index. The futures market tends to fall in the last hour or so of trading so that even as the spot market is rising the futures are moving lower to anticipate Monday's decline. For the period March 18, 1983 to June 27, 1986 Pieptea and Prisman found the following results:

	Mon	Tues	Wed	Thur	Fri
Mean Annualized Return in Spot Market	-4.93	42.33	3.16	23.50	32.59
its Standard Deviation	2.11	2.45	2.41	1.97	2.23
Mean Annualized Return in Futures Market of the Nearest Contract	19.35	9.10	4.83	23.57	6.75
its Standard Deviation	2.09	2.46	2.48	2.07	2.12

Figure 4 and Table 3 compare the day of the week effects on the spot ND in Tokyo with the futures market on the Nikkei Dow at the SIMEX in Singapore. Similarly Figure 5 and Table 4 compare the effects on the Osaka 50 futures, the Osaka 50 spot and the Nikkei Dow spot.

Table 3: Days of the Week Effects in the ND Spot Market in Tokyo and the SIMEX Futures Markets in Singapore, Sept 3, 1986 to Sept 19, 1988

	SIMEX futures				*ND spot*			
	Sample	Mean		%	Sample	Mean		%
Day	Size	Return	t-Statistic	Positive	Size	Return	t-Statistic	Positive
All	532	0.094	1.00	56.8	557	0.082	1.50	56.6
Mon	102	-0.223	-1.52	46.1	100	-0.301*	-2.93	44.0
Tues	104	-0.137	-0.47	57.7	99	-0.120	-0.68	50.5
Wed	101	0.029	0.20	58.4	100	0.251	1.74	60.0
Thur	101	0.534	1.90	59.4	101	0.305*	3.08	64.4
Fri	99	0.207	1.39	62.6	102	0.174	1.54	59.8
Sat	25	0.383	1.09	56.0	55	0.258*	1.96	63.6

In this and succeeding tables, * indicates that a coefficient is significantly different from zero at the 5% level, ** at 1% and *** at 0.1%.

Figure 4: Days of the Week Effects in the ND Spot Market in Tokyo and the SIMEX Futures Markets in Singapore, Sept 3, 1986 to Sept 19, 1988

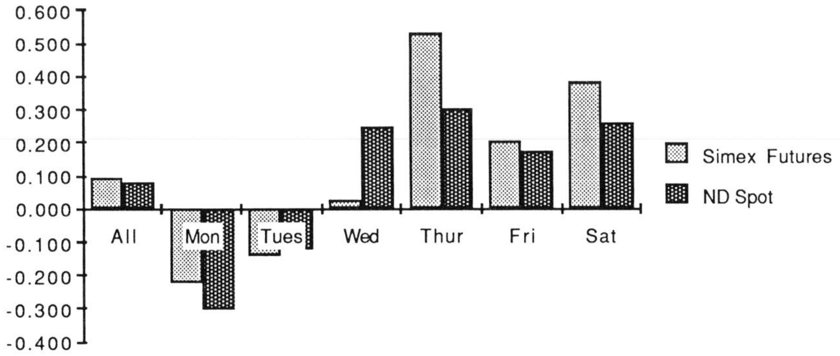

Table 4: Days of the Week Effects in the ND Spot Market and the Osaka 50 Spot Market in Tokyo and the Osaka 50 Kabusaki Futures in Osaka, June 6, 1987 to Sept 20, 1988

	Osaka 50 Futures				*Osaka 50 Spot*			
Day	Sample Size	Mean Return	t-Statistic	% Positive	Sample Size	Mean Return	t-Statistic	% Positive
All	352	-0.020	-0.30	49.4	353	0.000	0.00	52.1
Mon	65	-0.329*	-2.35	38.5	65	-0.347*	-2.50	38.5
Tues	62	0.205	1.20	54.8	63	-0.173	-0.62	60.3
Wed	64	0.018	0.10	51.6	64	0.275	1.15	53.1
Thur	63	-0.012	-0.09	50.8	63	0.173	1.31	55.6
Fri	64	0.007	0.04	46.9	64	-0.025	-0.15	46.9
Sat	34	0.018	0.08	58.8	34	0.190	0.90	64.7

	ND Spot			
Day	Sample Size	Mean Return %	t-Statistic	% Positive
All	353	0.033	0.45	56.4
Mon	65	-0.254	-1.93	46.1
Tues	63	-0.196	-0.75	52.4
Wed	64	0.318	1.57	59.4
Thur	63	0.204	1.79	63.5
Fri	64	0.059	0.39	56.3
Sat	34	0.107	0.62	64.7

Figure 5: Days of the Week Effects in the ND Spot Market and the Osaka 50 Spot Market in Tokyo and the Osaka 50 Kabusaki Futures in Osaka, June 6, 1987 to Sept 20, 1988

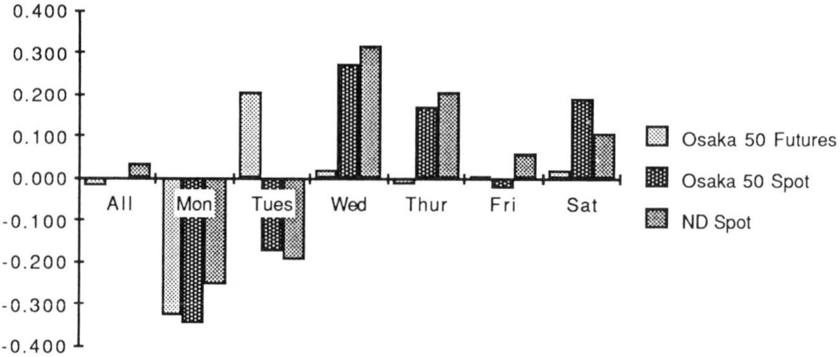

The spot effect of weak Mondays and Tuesdays and strong Wednesday to Saturday is continuing. Wednesdays are the strongest days followed by Thursdays and Saturdays in the spot market. The Simex futures in Singapore look just like the spot market in Tokyo except in the Wednesday -Thursday period. Possibly this market is following rather than leading, although other evidence suggests the leading hypothesis. The futures seem to rise and fall with the spot. The Osaka 50 seems to anticipate the days of the week effect. Saturdays hardly rise at all in the futures markets despite the spot gains thus anticipating Monday's fall. Then these futures fall on Monday to anticipate a further fall on Tuesday. They then rise on Tuesday to anticipate the gains on Wednesday, Thursday, Friday and Saturday. They are then flat until the fall the next Monday.

3. HOLIDAY EFFECTS

The main references on the holiday effect in U.S. spot markets are Ariel (1988), Lakonishok and Smidt (1989), Zweig (1986) and the survey in Ziemba (1990). These authors found a very strong effect: days before holidays have significantly higher returns than other days. The effect is relatively strongest for large capitalized stocks although the total preholiday returns is higher for the small stocks because of the small firm effect. Indeed for the 90 year Lakonishok and Smidt DJIA sample from 1897-1986 these eight or so days return more than half the non-dividend return over the whole year. Trading days before the preholiday and after the holiday do not have significantly higher returns. Indeed these days particularly the post holidays have lower returns on average. Ziemba (1989a) has investigated similar effects on the TSE. In Japan there are about twelve holidays each year compared with about eight in the U.S. For the Nikkei Dow from 1949-88, I found that the mean daily returns could be estimated by

$$R = \underset{(3.745)}{0.0352} + \underset{(1.491)}{0.0799}\, Day_{-3} + \underset{(0.424)}{0.0222}\, Day_{-2} + \underset{(3.709)}{0.1894}\, Day_{-1} - \underset{(-1.334)}{0.0663}\, Day_{+1} + \underset{(0.023)}{0.00114}\, Day_{+2},$$

where Day_{-3} is the dummy for the separate effect of trading day -3, etc. The pre-holiday with an extra mean return of 0.1894% per day is statistically significant with a t-static of 3.709 and none of the other days have returns that are significantly different from b_0. The effect of the +1 day is negative, although the coefficient is not significant. Their total returns are slightly positive, 0.0068% which is less than a typical day. In total, the preholidays return 0.2246 per day versus 0.049% on a typical non-preholiday with lower risk measured by the standard deviation, 0.794% versus 0.979%. The preholidays also improve every day of the week, for the Japanese stocks see Ziemba (1989a), just as Lakonishok and Smidt (1989) found for the DJIA.

Figure 6 and Table 5 show the spot holiday effect on the ND and on the SIMEX futures market for the period of the SIMEX data, September 3, 1986 to September 19, 1988 some 557 trading days. The preholidays have gains on 78% of the days which is much higher than for the other days. The mean returns are high, averaging 0.276% per day which is nearly four times the return on other days. However, the t statistic of 1.57 is not significant except at the 13% level. Moreover, the third day before the holiday has even higher returns. The other days around the preholiday have low returns as expected.

In the futures markets the SIMEX anticipates the holiday effect on the 3rd day before the holiday. This anticipation seems to affect the spot market so the spot prices rise on -3 taking out some of the gains that would normally occur on the preholiday. The return in the SIMEX futures market on the preholiday is in fact slightly negative again reinforcing the fact that the preholiday effect is anticipated.

Table 5: Holiday Effect on SIMEX Sept 1986-Sept 1988

	ND Spot on TSE				*ND Futures on SIMEX*			
Day	Sample Size	Mean Return %	t-statistic	% Positive	Sample Size	Mean Return %	t-statistic	% Positive
All	557	0.082	1.50	56.6	508	0.098	1.00	56.9
3rd PH	21	0.370	1.38	57.1	17	0.684	1.62	64.7
2nd PH	22	-0.083	-0.30	50.0	20	0.014	0.04	45.0
PH	23	0.276	1.57	78.3	18	0.225	0.48	66.7
AH	23	-0.001	0.00	56.5	21	0.445	1.25	61.9
2nd AH	21	0.092	0.48	52.4	21	0.320	1.07	66.7
Others	447	0.071	1.12	55.9	411	0.063	0.55	56.0

Figure 6: Holiday Effect on SIMEX Sept 1986-Sept 1988

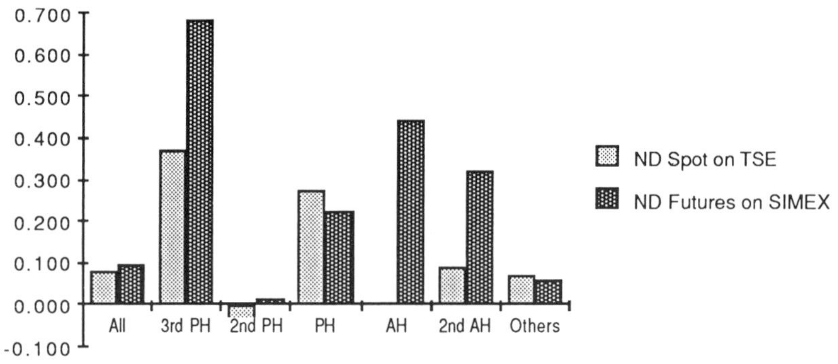

Figure 7 and Table 6 investigate the holiday effect from the Kabusaki Osaka 50 index for the period June 6, 1987 to September 20, 1988. In the spot market on the TSE the effect is similar to the historical record. The preholiday returns average 0.50% per day and the index increases 75% of the time. The gain is significant at the 5% level. The third trading day before the holiday has high returns but they are not significant. In the futures markets the return is only significant at the 5% level on the preholiday. The returns were high around the holiday periods in this sample with the days outside the pre and post holidays having negative returns. There is no evidence of the future market anticipating the holiday effect.

Table 6: Holiday Effect on the Kabusaki 50 Sept 1986-Sept 1988

	Kabusaki 50 Spot on TSE				Kabusaki 50 Future on TSE			
Day	Sample Size	Mean Return	t-Statistic	% Positive	Sample Size	Mean Return	t-Statistic	% Positive
All	353	-0.001	0.00	52.1	352	-0.020	-0.30	49.4
3rd PH	12	0.340	0.68	58.3	12	0.324	0.61	41.7
2nd PH	11	0.021	0.04	45.5	11	-0.206	-0.42	45.5
PH	12	0.499**	3.68	75.0	12	0.391*	2.27	66.7
AH	12	-0.022	-0.07	50.0	12	0.284	1.03	50.0
2nd AH	11	0.243	0.74	63.6	11	0.324	0.68	63.6
Others	295	-0.043	-0.46	50.8	294	-0.070	-0.94	48.6

In the spot market, the holiday effect for this sample of data of a year plus is not working in the usual fashion. The preholiday is strong but not dominant compared to the other days around the holiday. In fact for the SIMEX trading period the ND spot has risen most on the 3rd day before the holiday not on the preholiday. For the period that the Osaka 50 has been trading, the preholiday has the highest returns on the ND and these results are highly significant. The Osaka 50 also seems to have a strongly positive effect on the -3 preholiday trading day although these coefficients are not significant. So there may be some anticipation of the effect but with the small sample one cannot conclude much.

Figure 7: Holiday Effect on the Kabusaki 50 Sept 1986-Sept 1988

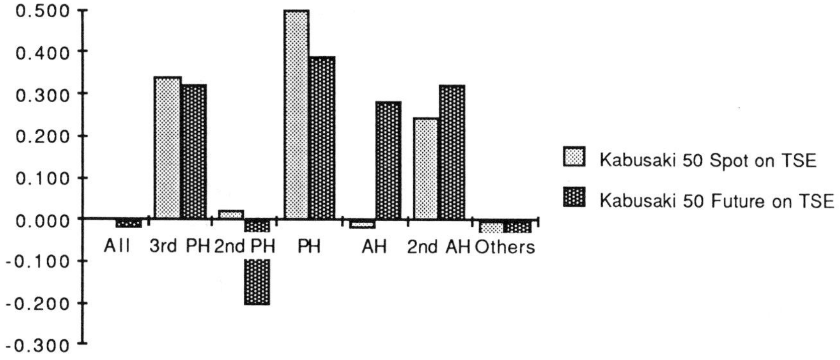

4. TURN OF THE MONTH AND FIRST HALF OF THE MONTH EFFECTS

The U.S. turn of the month effect occurs on trading days -1 to +4, see Ariel (1987) for an analysis of the spot data from 1963-82 and Sick and Ziemba (1989) for an analysis of futures data from 1982-88. The gains in this period are very high and contribute a very large percentage of the total monthly returns. The return in this *week*, coupled with that in the second week of the month, roughly trading days +5 to +8 or +10, essentially amounts to *all* the gains in the spot stock market during 1960-88. The rest of the month is essentially noise and at best provides zero returns. The reason(s) for this effect are not fully known but part of the story is that people receive their salaries on or around the -1 day as well as their stock account statements so they have funds to invest in stocks. There are also the portfolio balancing and renewal effects. When would one expect the turn-of-the-month to be in Japan? Many companies pay their salaries around the 25th of the month. Indeed, Ziemba (1989a) found similar turn of the month and first half of the month effects on the TSE. These effects are in the trading periods -5 to +2 and +3 to +7. For the ND from 1949-88 the period with trading days -5 to +2 receives the bulk of the month's return and each of these day's return is significant at the 5% level or better. Days +3 to +7 have positive returns and the rest of the month is noise; see Table 7 and Figure 8. Because of the pecularities of the Japanese market including Saturday trading day, +22 corresponds to a -5 day once a year or for 39 times in that many years. Since Japan had more trading days because of the two or three Saturdays that were trading each month these periods are correspondingly lengthened. In the first half of the month the mean return is 0.01142% per day while in the second half it is an insignifiant 0.00048% per day.

Table 7: Turn-of-the-Month Data, 1949-1988

Trading Day	Sample Size	Mean Return, %	t-Statistic	Trading Day	Sample Size	Mean Return, %	t-Statistic
-5	471	.0899*	2.75	9	471	.1065*	2.46
-4	471	.1041*	2.65	10	471	.0620	1.58
-3	471	.1733**	3.82	11	471	.0395	1.05
-2	471	.1334**	3.18	12	471	-.0196	-0.50
-1	471	.2255***	5.36	13	471	.0115	0.24
1	471	.0980*	2.43	14	471	-.0042	-0.10
2	471	.1006*	2.47	15	471	-.0306	-0.54
3	471	.0307	0.72	16	471	.0716	1.35
4	471	.0592	1.15	17	471	-.0498	-1.20
5	471	.0358	0.81	18	429	-.0207	-0.49
6	471	-.0005	-0.01	19	350	.0162	0.36
7	471	.0357	0.09	20	229	-.0286	-0.48
8	471	-.0585	-1.34	21	118	-.0476	-0.46
				22	39	.0562	0.45

	trading days	
1st Half	22-7	.01142
2nd Half	8-21	.00048

Source: Yamaichi Research Institute reported in Ziemba (1989a).

Figure 8: Turn-of-the-Month Data, 1949-1988

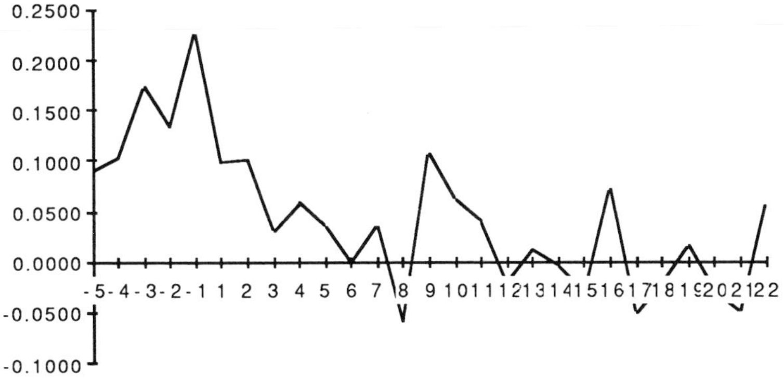

The turn of the month effect with high returns on days -5 to +2 seems to still be there but the SIMEX and Osaka 50 futures markets totally anticipate the effect. On the SIMEX, days -8 to -5 have all the gains of about 2.8% per month on average. This is a huge average gain in only four days. This is the whole turn of the month effect with the rest of the period about even. Although lower than in the futures markets, the spot market also has large gains on days -8 to -5. But the spot gains in the -5 to +2 period are still abnormally high. On the Osaka 50 futures market the anticipation seems to be on days -7, -6 and -5 with a total gain of about 1%. Both markets lose back much of the gain on -4 and -3. The effect in the spot market is similar to that mentioned above for the ND. The SIMEX seems to lead the Osaka 50 futures and the spot ND in this effect. Table 8 and Figure 9 describe the results. Since there is only one or two turn of the years this data is lumped in with that for the other months. These were calculated separately, but this does not seem to change the results much.

Table 8: The Turn of the Month Effect on the ND

	ND Spot on TSE				ND Futures on SIMEX			
Day	Sample Size	Mean Return	t-Statistic	% Positive	Sample Size	Mean Return	t-Statistic	% Positive
-7	24	0.432*	2.17	66.7	22	0.668*	2.18	68.2
-6	24	-0.095	-0.40	62.5	21	-0.061	-0.19	57.1
-5	24	0.333*	1.99	62.5	22	0.625*	1.96	54.5
-4	24	0.347*	2.00	62.5	23	-0.356	-1.02	47.8
-3	24	-0.100	-0.40	54.2	18	0.445	0.15	61.1
-2	24	0.315	1.10	70.8	20	0.349	0.84	65.0
-1	24	0.161	0.79	50.0	18	-0.448	-0.90	33.3
1	24	0.142	0.69	66.7	19	0.256	0.76	57.9
2	24	0.689	0.31	54.2	21	0.314	1.32	61.9
3	24	0.160	0.55	41.7	24	0.355	0.99	54.2
4	25	0.261	1.61	68.0	21	0.103	0.45	57.1
5	25	0.112	0.69	60.0	24	0.244	1.15	54.2
6	25	-0.869	-0.64	40.0	20	-0.106	-0.51	55.0
7	25	0.963	0.46	56.0	23	-0.438	-0.14	56.5
8	25	-0.046	-0.02	56.0	25	0.252	0.97	60.0
9	25	0.534*	2.50	76.0	25	0.297	1.40	76.0
10	25	0.227	1.09	64.0	24	0.358	1.75	66.7
11	25	-0.097	-0.47	56.0	25	0.158	0.07	68.0
12	25	-0.341	-1.93	40.0	25	-0.383*	-2.12	40.0
13	25	-0.019	-0.10	48.0	24	0.043	0.17	41.7
14	24	0.154	0.79	58.3	22	0.933	0.35	68.2
15	24	-0.601	-0.92	54.1	23	-0.923	-0.72	60.9
16	24	0.446	1.04	62.5	21	0.012	0.07	61.9
17	24	0.022	0.92	62.5	24	1.472	1.32	66.7

Figure 9: The Turn of the Month Effect on the ND

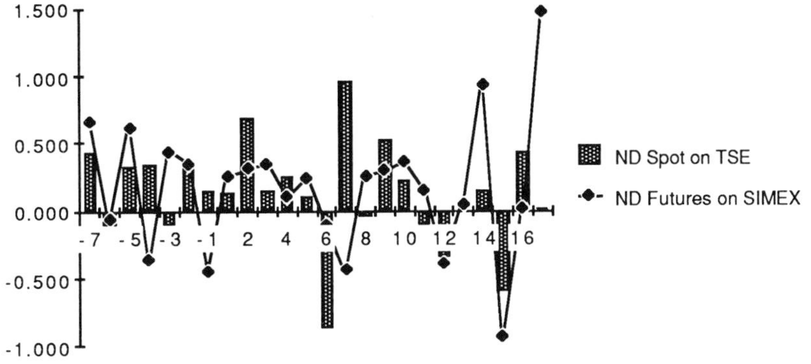

Table 9: The Turn of the Month Effect on the Osaka 50

	Osaka 50 Spot on TSE				Osaka 50 Futures on OSE			
Day	Sample Size	Mean Return	t-Statistic	% Positive	Sample Size	Mean Return	t-Statistic	% Positive
-7	15	0.391	1.41	66.7	15	0.270	1.26	60.0
-6	15	-0.185	-0.53	66.7	15	-0.082	-0.21	60.0
-5	15	0.380	1.44	66.7	15	0.702	1.41	53.3
-4	15	0.263	1.19	66.7	15	-0.548	-1.45	46.7
-3	15	-0.217	-0.78	46.7	15	-0.253	-0.82	40.0
-2	15	0.330	0.95	80.0	15	0.131	0.27	66.7
-1	15	0.110	0.45	53.3	15	0.054	0.19	53.3
1	15	-0.029	-0.12	66.7	15	-0.062	-0.16	53.3
2	15	0.197	0.85	60.0	15	0.121	0.40	46.7
3	15	0.083	0.19	26.7	15	0.120	0.24	33.3
4	15	-0.030	-0.19	60.0	15	0.086	0.29	46.7
5	15	0.100	0.51	66.7	15	0.049	0.19	60.0
6	15	-0.225	-1.21	26.7	15	-0.305	-1.27	33.3
7	15	0.058	0.18	53.3	15	0.117	0.28	53.3
8	15	-0.115	-0.41	53.3	15	-0.037	-0.20	40.0
9	16	0.517	1.86	75.0	16	0.361	1.62	68.8
10	16	0.493	1.75	81.3	16	0.446	1.86	75.0
11	16	0.118	0.94	62.5	16	0.028	0.18	50.0
12	16	-0.306*	-2.16	43.8	16	-0.259	-1.33	43.8
13	16	0.011	0.07	43.8	16	-0.015	-0.07	31.3
14	16	-0.108	-0.43	43.8	16	-0.274	-1.11	50.0
15	15	-0.940	-0.91	60.0	14	0.007	0.02	57.1
16	15	0.606	0.93	60.0	15	-0.068	-0.24	60.0
17	15	-0.083	-0.27	53.3	15	-0.255	-0.69	46.7

Figure 10: The Turn of the Month Effect on the Osaka 50

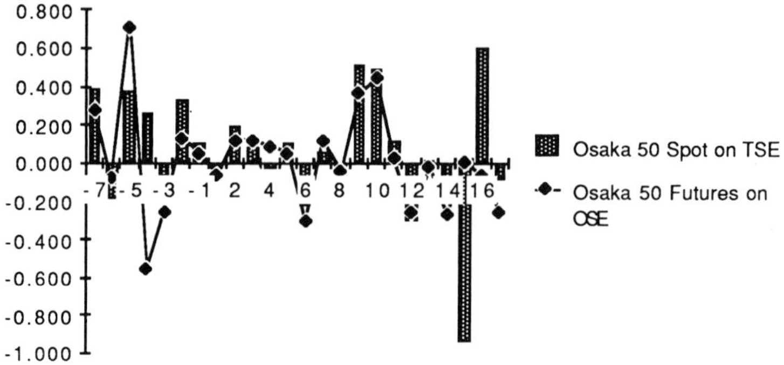

5. FIRST HALF OF THE MONTH

The effect that most or all of the gains on the TSE occur on trading days -5 to +7 seems to be working according to the script in the spot market. It is as well in the Osaka 50 futures market. The SIMEX futures though seems to at least partially smooth out the returns. This first half has higher returns by a 50% margin but it does not have *all* the gains. The following strategy would have been profitable during the sample period: buy the SIMEX on the close of -9, sell on the open of -5; on the Osaka 50, buy on the close of -8 and sell on the open of -5.

Table 10: Test of the hypothesis that first half of month has all the returns.

half	N	Mean %	Std Dev	Std Error
1	292	.15	1.023	0.0598
2	265	.008	1.355	0.0942

The F test with 264 and 291 degrees of freedom indicates that with F=2.25 the variances are equal at the 0.1% level. The t test with equal variances then indicates that the first half of the month has all the gains with 19.24% confidence using a pooled variance with 555 degrees of freedom.

Table 11: The First Half of the Month Effect on the ND

	ND Spot on TSE				ND Futures on SIMEX			
Day	Sample Size	Mean Return %	t-Statistic	% Positive	Sample Size	Mean Return	t-Statistic	% Positive
All	557	0.082	1.50	56.5	508	0.098	1.00	56.9
1st Half	292	0.150*	2.51	57.1	253	0.119	1.29	54.9
2nd Half	265	0.008	0.08	55.8	255	0.077	0.45	58.8

Figure 11: The First Half of the Month Effect on the ND

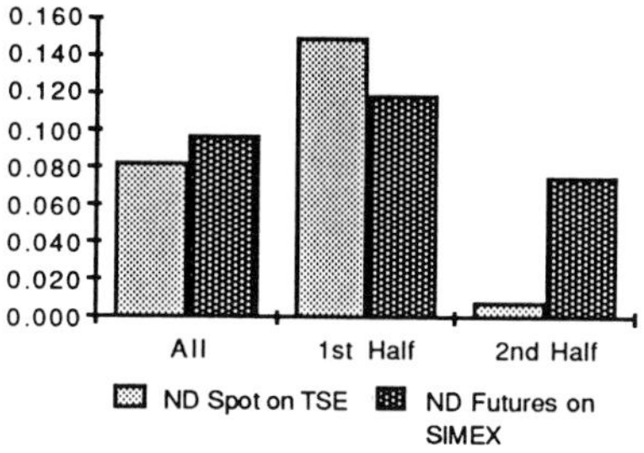

Figure 12: The First Half of the Month Effect on the Osaka 50

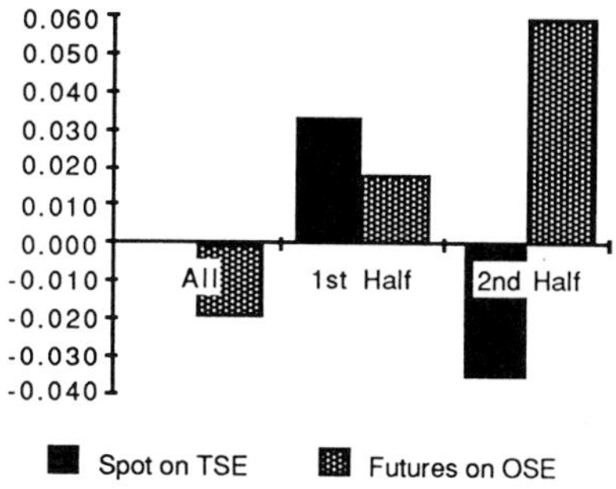

Table 12: The First Half of the Month Effect on the Osaka 50

	Spot on TSE				Futures on OSE			
Day	Sample Size	Mean Return	t-Statistic	% Positive	Sample Size	Mean Return	t-Statistic	% Positive
All	553	-0.000	-0.00	52.1	352	-0.020	-0.30	49.4
1st Half	180	0.034	0.37	52.8	180	0.018	0.17	48.9
2nd Half	173	-0.036	-0.25	51.4	172	0.060	-0.71	50.0

6. The Monthly Effect

Because of its length of about 30 days one would expect the futures markets to closely mirror the spot markets over a monthly period. Research on the spot market in Japan appears in Hawawani (1988b), the data of Horimoto (1988) reported in Ziemba (1989a) along with additional data reported there. These results are summarized in Table 13.

Table 13: Monthly Effects on the Tokyo Stock Exchange

Average Monthly Return Over	Hawawani (1988) 373-566 stocks Jan 1955-Dec 1985 Equally Weighted: Sample Size	Mean Monthly Return	t statistic	Horimoto (1988) All TSE 1st Section, 1965-87 Equally Weighted: Mean Monthly Return	Ziemba (1989a) ND 225 1949-88 Price Weighted: Sample Size	Mean Daily Return	t statistic
All months	372	1.60%*	6.40	1.76	11529	0.0482***	5.56
all but January	341	1.24%***	4.75	1.42	na	na	na
January	31	5.58%***	13.17	5.44	885	0.1816***	5.80
February	31	1.00	1.85	1.71	905	0.0549	1.87
March	31	2.90%**	3.77	2.88	986	0.0457	1.50
April	31	0.51	0.57	0.82	947	0.0623*	2.10
May	31	0.18	0.20	1.29	956	0.0074	0.27
June	31	2.51%***	4.59	2.83	1011	0.0641*	2.39
July	31	0.65	0.75	1.12	1043	0.0083	0.27
August	31	0.92	0.85	1.16	1038	0.0790**	2.96
September	31	0.13	0.17	0.28	931	0.0059	-0.22
October	31	0.52	0.48	0.17	998	0.0088	0.24
November	31	1.81	1.76	1.11	910	0.0371	1.27
December	31	2.48%**	3.02	2.27	919	0.0470	1.37

January, March, June and December have had the highest mean returns in that order in both Hawawani's and Horimoto's samples. Also September and October had the lowest returns. Ziemba's longer data set shows similar very high returns in January, and the low September and October returns. But there are differences in the other months from the Hawawani and Horimoto samples. The sample sizes for Horimoto's data are unavailable.

There is only one January in the Osaka 50 data and two in the SIMEX data but the daily data used do give us some results that are significant at the 5% level. Tables 14 and 15 and Figures 13 and 14 describe the results.

Table 14: The Monthly Effect on the ND Spot and the SIMEX

	ND Spot on TSE				*ND Futures on SIMEX*			
Month	Sample Size	Mean Return	t-Statistic	% Positive	Sample Size	Mean Return	t-Statistic	% Positive
all days	532	0.094	1.00	56.8	557	0.082	1.50	56.6
Jan	39	0.380*	1.97	61.5	42	0.396*	2.24	69.0
Feb	40	0.226*	2.06	62.5	43	0.232*	2.26	65.1
Mar	44	0.205	1.79	68.2	48	0.164	1.53	64.6
Apr	41	0.254	1.34	63.4	46	0.272	1.87	60.9
May	37	0.204	0.90	59.5	43	0.154	1.02	55.8
Jun	46	-0.003	-0.02	60.9	48	-0.032	-0.29	54.2
Jul	48	-0.002	-0.01	50.0	49	0.064	0.40	57.1
Aug	45	0.128	0.87	46.7	49	0.066	0.65	53.1
Sep	57	-0.079	-0.47	54.4	54	-0.027	-0.20	57.4
Oct	47	-0.242	-0.26	51.0	49	-0.283	-0.64	44.9
Nov	43	0.204	0.85	58.1	42	0.134	0.65	57.1
Dec	45	0.014	0.08	48.9	44	-0.066	-0.52	40.9

Figure 13: The Monthly Effect on the ND Spot and the SIMEX

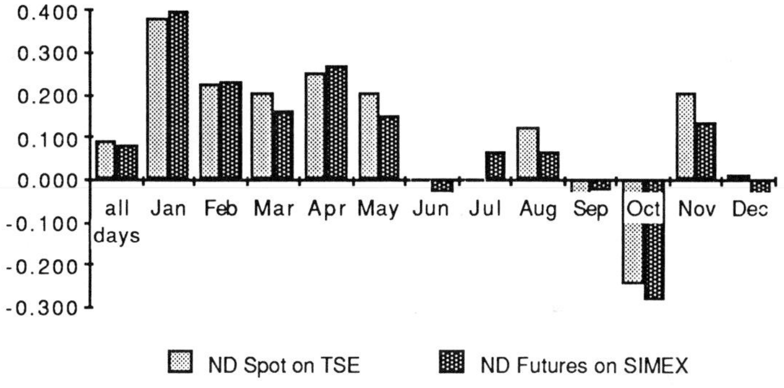

Table 15: The Monthly Effect on the Osaka 50

	ND Spot on TSE				*Osaka 50 Spot on TSE*			
Month	Sample Size	Mean Return	t-Statistic	% Positive	Sample Size	Mean Return	t-Statistic	% Positive
all days	353	0.033	0.45	56.4	353	-0.000	-0.00	52.1
Jan	21	0.465	1.42	66.7	21	0.410	1.07	57.1
Feb	20	0.284**	3.21	72.7	20	0.254*	2.40	63.6
Mar	24	0.167	1.20	58.3	24	0.124	0.77	45.8
Apr	23	0.204	1.87	65.2	23	0.159	1.09	69.6
May	21	-0.014	-0.09	52.4	21	-0.219	-1.22	38.1
Jun	40	-0.086	-0.69	52.5	40	-0.084	-0.59	52.5
Jul	49	0.064	0.40	57.1	49	0.026	0.14	61.2
Aug	49	0.066	0.65	53.1	49	0.055	0.46	53.1
Sep	36	0.020	0.15	61.1	36	0.044	0.26	50.0
Oct	25	-0.351	-0.43	56.0	25	-0.399	-0.45	48.0
Nov	21	-0.118	-0.31	47.6	21	-0.137	-0.33	38.1
Dec	22	-0.226	-1.08	36.4	22	-0.256	-1.00	36.4

Osaka 50 Futures on OSE

Month	Sample Size	Mean Return	t-Statistic	% Positive
all days	353	-0.020	-0.28	49.4
Jan	21	0.358	0.95	52.4
Feb	20	0.244*	2.68	68.2
Mar	24	0.162	1.04	50.0
Apr	23	0.170	1.14	65.2
May	21	-0.280	-1.50	42.9
Jun	40	0.076	-0.65	47.5
Jul	49	-0.081	-0.47	51.0
Aug	49	0.097	0.86	46.9
Sep	36	0.008	0.05	55.6
Oct	25	-0.494	-0.84	33.3
Nov	21	-0.121	-0.27	42.9
Dec	22	-0.256	-0.92	36.4

Figure 14: The Monthly Effect on the Osaka 50

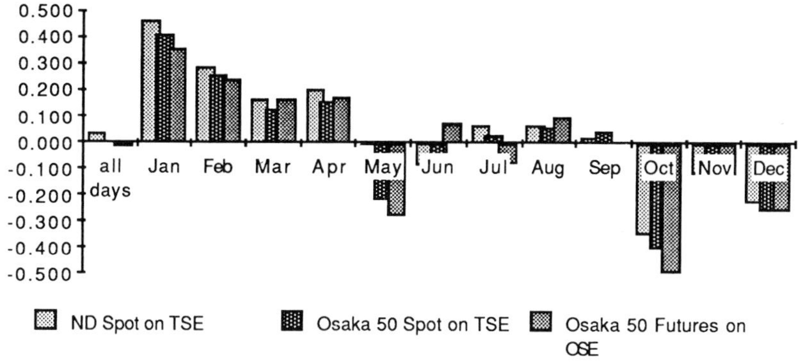

7. TURN OF THE YEAR - JANUARY EFFECT

The turn of the year effect based on the ND for 1949-88 is very strong. Days -7 to +14 all have positive returns that average 0.142% per day for a cumulative return of about 3% in this twenty-one day period. There is only one turn of the year in the Osaka 50 data and only two in the SIMEX data. In the spot data for the thirty-nine years from 1949 to 1988 trading days -8 to +14 all have positive returns. Four of these days have gains in excess of 0.4% and seven others have gains of more than 0.2%. See Table 16 and Figure 15.

For the 1987 and 1988 turn of the years there are modest gains but nothing like the long historical record. In addition many of the days have negative returns. The +2 and +3 days had a total return of about 9% on the Osaka 50. Volatility was very high. The Osaka 50 futures and spot prices are very consistent. All in all the Turn of the Year effect did not seem as strong as usual in 1987 and 1988. Perhaps the October 1987 crash's effect on 1987 was a contributing factor to this.

Table 16: Rates of Return for the Thirty-Nine Turn of the Years, ND, 1949-1988 and for the one turn of the year in the Osaka 50 Futures data set and the two turns of the year in the SIMEX data set

Trading Day	ND Spot Mean Return, %	t-Statistic	Osaka 50 Futures	SIMEX Futures	ND Spot SIMEX data	ND Spot Osaka data	Osaka 50 Spot
-15	0.0292	0.24	-0.411	0.110	-0.424	-0.273	-0.411
-14	-0.0603	-0.38	1.305	0.705	1.330	1.727	1.516
-13	-0.2631	-1.29	-1.265	-0.236	-0.646	-1.053	-1.535
-12	0.2210	0.72	0.083	0.279	0.028	-0.476	-0.680
-11	-0.1036	-0.90	0.413	0.117	-0.284	-0.347	-0.259
-10	0.0202	0.09	-0.165	-0.059	0.324	-0.120	-0.176
-9	-0.1197	-0.54	0.577	1.176	-0.049	0.352	0.855
-8	0.0347	0.17	0.000	-0.575	-0.488	-0.318	-0.449
-7	0.1413	0.76	0.328	0.553	0.835	0.569	0.868
-6	0.1738	1.31	-0.449	-0.510	-0.746	-0.940	-1.018
-5	0.1303	1.08	-0.164	-0.266	-0.149	-0.207	-0.184
-4	0.4683***	4.48	-0.534	0.063	-0.081	-0.663	-0.327
-3	0.4413*	2.49	-2.188	0.000	-1.277	-1.874	-2.412
-2	0.0613	0.39	-3.757	-5.795	-1.204	-2.656	-3.239
-1	0.2457*	2.01	-0.263	-0.550	-0.246	0.142	0.917
1	0.0369	0.22	-1.671	1.653	-0.486	-1.609	-2.329
2	0.1539	0.91	2.683	2.463	1.153	1.689	1.553
3	0.3812	1.92	6.272	-0.138	2.567	5.633	6.657
4	0.246	1.46	-0.656	0.202	-0.165	0.007	-0.312
5	0.4067*	2.74	0.248	-1.223	0.261	0.353	-0.184
6	0.0856	0.68	-1.482	-0.473	-1.019	-1.286	-1.389
7	0.2546	1.51	-0.084	-0.420	-0.232	0.207	0.335
8	0.0985	0.74	-1.212	2.119	-0.015	-1.326	-1.494
9	0.4007*	2.91	1.185	0.766	1.597	1.248	1.302
10	0.2736*	2.50	1.589	0.186	0.780	1.356	1.443
11	0.2243*	1.95	-0.865	-0.235	0.047	-0.053	-0.144
12	0.0375	0.32	-0.332	-0.456	0.432	-0.240	-0.119
13	0.1101	0.98	-0.917	na	-0.416	-0.582	-0.357
14	0.2180*	2.04	0.883	1.007	0.563	0.732	0.285
15	-0.0334	-0.14	0.542	0.658	0.757	1.087	1.157

Figure 15: Rates of Return for the Thirty-Nine Turn-of-the Years, ND, 1949-88

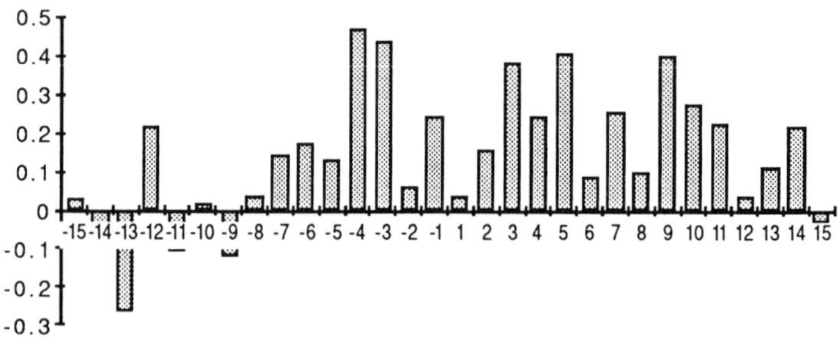

REFERENCES

Ariel, Robert A. (1987) A Monthly Effect in Stock Returns, *Journal of Financial Economics, 18:* 1-14.

Ariel, Robert A. (1988) High Stock Returns before Holidays, working paper, Baruch College.

Bailey, Warren (1989) The Market for Japanese Stock Index Futures: Some Preliminary Evidence, *Journal of Futures Markets,* forthcoming.

Brenner, Menachem, Marti G. Subrahmanyam, and Jun Uno (1987) Arbitrage Opportunities in the Nikkei Spot and Futures Markets, working paper, Graduate School of Business, New York University, November.

Brenner, Menachem, Marti G. Subrahmanyam, and Jun Uno (1988) Arbitrage in the Japanese Stock Index Futures Markets, working paper, Graduate School of Business, New York University.

Cornell, Bradford (1985) The Weekly Pattern in Stock Returns: Cash versus Futures: A Note, *The Journal of Finance, XL:* 583-588.

Dimson, E., ed. (1988) *Stock Market Regularities,* Cambridge University Press.

Elton, Edwin J. and Martin J. Gruber (1988) Multi-Index Risk Model, *Japan and the World Economy 1,* 44.

Elton, Edwin J. and Martin J. Gruber, eds. (1989) *Japanese Capital Markets,* Ballinger, forthcoming.

Hamao, Yasushi (1988) An Empirical Examination of the Arbitrage Pricing Theory Using Japanese Data, *Japan and the World Economy 1,*:45-61.

Hamao, Yasushi (1989) Fifteen-year Performance of Japanese Capital Markets, *Journal of Portfolio Management,* Winter: 21-26.

Hawawini, Gabriel (1988a) Market Efficiency and Equity Pricing: International Evidence and Implications for Global Industry, working paper, INSEAD, Fontainbleau, March.

Hawawini, Gabriel (1988b) Stock Market Anomalies and the Pricing of Equity on the Tokyo Stock Exchange, working paper, INSEAD, Fontainbleau, France, May.

Hiraki, Takato, Raj Aggarwal and Ramesh P. Rao (1988) Stock Market Anomalies and Investors Behavior in Japan, Working Paper, International University of Japan.

Horimoto, Saburo (1988) Private correspondence using raw results from forthcoming paper.

Ikeda, M. (1985) The Day of the Week Effects and Monthly Effects in the Tokyo Stock Exchange, Working Paper, University of Tokyo

Ikeda, M. (1988) Day of the Week Effects and the Mixture of Normal Distributions Hypothesis, *Japan Financial Review, Vol 8:* 27-53.

Jacobs, Bruce I. and Kenneth N. Levy (1988) Disentangling Equity Return Regularities: New Insights and Investment Opportunities, *Financial Analysts Journal,* May-June, pp 18-43.

Jaffe, J. and R. Westerfield (1985a) The Weekend Effect in Common Stock Returns: The International Evidence, *Journal of Finance* 40, 433-454.

Jaffe, J. and R. Westerfield (1985b) Patterns in Japanese Common Stock Returns: Day of the Week and Turn of the Year Effects, *Journal of Financial and Quantitative Analysis* 20, 243-260.

Kato, Kiyoshi (1988a) Weekly Patterns in Japanese Stock Returns, Working Paper, Nanzan University, Nagoya, Japan, April.

Kato, Kiyoshi (1988b) A Further Investigation of Anomalies on the Tokyo Stock Exchange, Working Paper, Nanzan University, Nagoya, Japan, August.

Kato, Kiyoshi and Yoshii Iihara (1988) Valuation of Japanese Warrants and Convertibles, Working Paper, Nanzan University

Kato, Kiyoshi and James S. Schallheim (1985) Seasonal and Size Anomalies in the Japanese Stock Market, *Journal of Financial and Quantitative Analysis*, 20, 2, 243-272.

Kato, Kiyoshi, S. L. Schwartz and William T. Ziemba (1989) Day of the Week Effects in Japanese Stocks, in Edwin J. Elton and Martin J. Gruber, eds, *Japanese Capital Markets*, Ballinger, forthcoming..

Komatsu, Asaji and William T. Ziemba (1989) Some Tests of Plausible Causes for Anomalous Behavior in Japanese Security Markets, working paper, Yamaichi Research Institute.

Kunimura, Michio (1984) The Information Content of Forecasts by Corporate Officials and by Financial Analysts in the Japanese Capital Market, Working Paper No. 84-3 U.S.-Japan Management Studies Center, University of Pennsylvania.

Lakonishok, Josef and Seymour Smidt (1989) Are Seasonal Anomalies Real? A Ninety-Year Perspective, *Review of Financial Studies,* forthcoming.

Lau, S., S. Quay and C. Ramsey (1974) The Tokyo Stock Exchange and the Capital Asset Pricing Model, *Journal of Finance* 28 (May), 507-514.

Nakamura, Takeo and Nobaru Terada (1984) The Size Effect and Seasonality in Japanese Stock Returns, unpublished manuscript, Institute for Quantitative Research in Finance.

Pettway, R. and T. Tapley (1984) The Tokyo Stock Exchange: An Analysis of Stock Market Prices, *Keio Business Review*, 75-93.

Pieptea, Dan R. and Eliezer Prisman (1988) The Monday Effect and Speculative Opportunities in the Stock-Index Futures Market, mimeo, University of Texas, Dallas.

Ritter, Jay and Navin Chopra (1989) Portfolio Rebalancing and the Turn of the Year Effect, *Journal of Finance, 44:* 149-166..

Roehl, Tom (1985) Data Sources for Research in Japanese Finance, *Journal of Financial and Quantitative Analysis* 20, 2.

Rubinstein, Mark (1982) Derivative Assets Analysis, *Journal of Economic Perspectives Vol 1:* 73-93.

Schoenfeld, Steven A. (1988) The Coming Explosion of the Japanese Futures Markets, *Intermarket,* September 22-26.

Sick, Gordon and William T. Ziemba (1989) The Turn of the Year Effect in U.S. Futures Markets,1982-1989, Working Paper, University of British Columbia.

Suzuki, Yoshio (1988) *The Japanese Financial System,* Oxford, England, Oxford University Press.

Ziemba, William T. (1990) *Strategies for Making and Keeping Excess Profits in the Stock Market,* New York, William Morrow.

Ziemba, William T. with S. L. Schwartz (1990) *Investing in Japan,* forthcoming.

Ziemba, William T. (1989a) Japanese Security Market Regularities: Monthly, Turn of the Month and Year, Holiday and Golden Week Effects, Yamaichi Research Institute, Tokyo.

Ziemba, William T. (1989b) The Chicken or the Egg: Land and Stock Prices in Japan, Yamaichi Research Institute, Tokyo.

Zweig, Martin (1986) *Winning on Wall Street,* New York, Warner Books.

Japanese Financial Market Research
W.T. Ziemba, W. Bailey and Y. Hamao (Editors)

STOCK INDEX FUTURES ARBITRAGE IN THE JAPANESE MARKETS *

Menachem BRENNER

New York University, New York, NY 10006, USA
Hebrew University, Jerusalem, Israel

Marti G. SUBRAHMANYAM

New York University, New York, NY 10006, USA

Jun UNO

Nihon Keizai Shimbun Inc., Tokyo 100-66, Japan

Received August 1988, final version received January 1989

This study examines the behavior of the prices of the first two futures contracts on Japanese stock price indices to be traded, the Nikkei Stock Average (NSA) contract on the Singapore International Monetary Exchange (SIMEX), and the Osaka Stock Futures 50 (OSF50) contract on the Osaka Securities Exchange (OSE). We find significant departures between the actual prices of the contracts and their 'fair' prices in the early months of trading from June 1987 to June 1988. The NSA contract was dominated by discounts of the actual prices in relation to the 'fair' price while the OSF50 contract was characterized by both premiums and discounts during this period. This suggests the viability of 'cross-spreading' strategies which were analyzed and found to be profitable during much of the period under study.

Keywords: Stock index futures, index arbitrage, program trading, fair pricing, cost of carry, Japanese financial markets, cross spreading, transactions costs, trading restrictions, mispricing, market inefficiency, implied interest rate.

1. Introduction

Futures contracts on stock indices have been an important innovation in world financial markets in the past few years. Stock index futures contracts are currently being traded in several countries including the United States, the United Kingdom, Japan, Australia, New Zealand, Hong Kong, Singapore and the Scandinavian countries. They are soon to be traded in France, Switzerland

* We thank S. Sundaresan, W. Ziemba and an anonymous referee for helpful comments. We are grateful to Nihon Keizai Shimbun Inc. for providing us with the data for the study.

and many other countries in Europe. In terms of value, the volume of trading in these contracts before the October 1987 crash often rivalled the volume of trading in the underlying stocks. Although the volume of trading has declined in many markets since the crash, stock index futures remain an important traded instrument in many financial markets.

Futures contracts on Japanese stock indices were introduced more recently than on U.S. and U.K. stock indices. The first index futures contract, the Nikkei Stock Average (NSA) contract started trading on the Singapore International Monetary Exchange (SIMEX) in September 1986. The next contract, the Osaka Stock Futures 50 (OSF50) was introduced on the Osaka Securities Exchange in June 1987. Although the volume of trading in these contracts has been fairly modest in relation to the underlying cash markets, there are indications that the volume of trading has been increasing. Also, two new stock index futures contracts based on the NSA and the Tokyo Stock Price Index (TOPIX) have been introduced more recently, on the Osaka Securities Exchange (OSE) and the Tokyo Stock Exchange (TSE) respectively. Given the size and importance of Japanese financial markets, the behavior of Japanese stock index futures markets is of interest to financial economists and practitioners alike.

The purpose of the present study is to examine the behavior of the prices of the two existing futures contracts on Japanese stock price indices, the NSA and the OSF50. We analyze the evidence on the prices of the futures contracts, both in relation to the respective underlying indices and in relation to each other, in the early months of trading, to see if there were significant deviations from 'fair' pricing. An important feature of the analysis is the incorporation of the effects of transactions costs and the settlement procedures of the two contracts. Transactions costs and trading restrictions are more important in Japanese financial markets than their U.S. or U.K. counterparts. We take into account the effects of these costs for various trading strategies and also discuss the impact of the trading restrictions on the pricing of the future contracts.

In section 2, we outline briefly the basic principles of stock index futures pricing in the presence of transactions costs. In section 3, we describe the main features of the two index futures contracts we study, the NSA and the OSF50, and the transactions costs of trading in them. In section 4, we present the statistical evidence on the pricing of the two contracts in relation to their underlying indices in the early months of trading. Section 5 deals with the relationship between the two indices and the opportunities for cross-spreading between the two contracts. In the final section, we present our conclusions.

2. The fair pricing of stock index futures contracts

Stock index futures contracts can be replicated by positions in the underlying index (i.e. the basket of stocks making up the index) and the riskless asset.

The 'fair' price of the index futures contract can be computed from the price of the 'replicating' portfolio. In particular, the 'fair' price of the futures contract can be shown to be equal to the price of the underlying spot index plus the 'cost of carry' for the spot between the current date and the expiration data of the futures contract.

In general, for all futures contracts, carrying costs for the underlying asset consists of interest costs and storage costs, less the 'convenience yield' from holding the spot asset. For stock index futures, storage costs for the underlying asset are zero and the 'convenience yield' is represented by the dividend payment on the underlying stocks. Hence, the 'cost of carry' is the difference between the interest costs paid and the dividends received by holding the spot asset rather than the futures contract.

In the absence of transactions costs and restrictions on short sales, the arbitrage-free or 'fair price' of a forward contract (or a futures contract, in the absence of interest rate uncertainty) can be written as [1]

$$FP_t = S_t \exp[r\tau] - DIV_t, \tag{1}$$

where

t is the current date,
T is the expiration date of the futures contract,
S is the price of the spot asset,
r is the riskless annual interest rate at time t,
$\tau = (T-t)/365$ is the fraction of the year represented by the time interval between t and T.
D_{t+j} is the dividend paid on the spot asset on date $t+j$, and,

$$DIV_t = \sum_{j=1}^{j=(T-t)} D_{t+j} \exp[r(T-(t+j))/365]$$

is the future value at T of the dividends between t and T on the spot asset.

Transactions costs create a band around the 'fair' price given by eq. (1), within which arbitrage is not profitable. Suppose c_t^+ represents the transactions costs expressed as a percentage of the spot price, in present value terms at time t, involved in buying the spot and selling the futures contract and reversing the position on the expiration date T. Similarly, let c_t^- represent the yen amount of the transactions costs, in present value terms at time t, of selling the spot and buying the futures contract and reversing the position on the expiration date T. These transactions costs imply that only if the futures price exceeds the 'fair' price given in eq. (1) by more than is implied by the percentage c_t^+ does it become profitable to execute a buy spot–sell futures transaction. Similarly, only if the futures price is below the spot price by more

[1] See, for example, MacKinlay and Ramaswamy (1988) for details.

than implied by the percentage c_t^-, does the buy futures–sell spot arbitrage become viable. Hence, there is, a band whose upper bound is F_t^+ and whose lower bound is F_t^-, given by eqs. (2a) and (2b) below, within which there are no arbitrage opportunities: [2]

$$FT_t^+ = \{S_t(1 + c_t^+)\}\exp[r\tau] - DIV_t, \tag{2a}$$

$$FP_t^- = \{S_t(1 - c_t^-)\}\exp[r\tau] - DIV_t. \tag{2b}$$

In the above discussion, it was implicitly assumed that either there are no taxes, or, profits and losses in spot and futures transactions are taxed at the same tax rate, as they are for institutions that are most likely to engage in arbitrage activities. [3] It is also assumed that the established positions are held to the expiration date of the futures contract. [4]

3. The Japanese stock index contracts and transactions costs

The two stock index futures markets we study here are those for the NSA and OSF50 contracts. Both contracts are based on stock price indices computed from the prices of leading stocks listed on the First Section of the leading stock exchanges, the TSE in the case of the NSA and the OSE in the case of the OSF50. [5] The NSA is an arithmetic price average computed by adding the prices of the 225 component stocks adjusted for par value differences and dividing by a divisor that changes over time to adjust for stock splits, rights issues, etc. The OSF50 is also an arithmetic price average, but of 50 stocks. This index was designed to be highly correlated with the NSA. Currently, both indices are calculated and announced at one-minute intervals during trading hours.

The futures contract on the NSA started trading on September 3, 1986 on the SIMEX. The main features of the contract are set out in table 1. Certain aspects of the NSA contract are worth emphasizing in the context of stock

[2] In addition to the incremental transactions costs of selling short due to the cost of borrowing stock, there are, for many investors, restrictions on selling stocks short. In the presence of such restrictions, the traders who may be able to actually execute the buy futures–sell stock strategy are those who already hold the stocks in their portfolio, such as banks, insurance companies and mutual funds. To the extent that these financial institutions have higher transactions costs than broker-dealers, as in Japan, the lower bound of the transactions costs band may be pushed down.

[3] For individual investors, the capital gains tax rate in Japan was zero during the period under study. For financial institutions and brokers, who are the most likely arbitrageurs, the tax rate on income and capital gains is identical.

[4] In some cases, it may be profitable to 'unwind' the position early or 'roll' it over into the next contract. As pointed out by Merrick (1987) and Brennan and Schwartz (1988), the option to 'unwind' may make it profitable to execute an arbitrage trade *within* the transactions costs bounds. Since these opportunities are rare in our sample, as we shall see, we choose to ignore this option. It should be pointed out that our analysis of arbitrage opportunities is, therefore, conservative, since the profits may be higher than computed in our analysis.

[5] For the OSF50, the spot index based on closing prices both on the OSE and the TSE are considered in our empirical analysis.

Table 1
Features of the NSA (SIMEX) and OSF50 (OSE) stock index futures contracts.

	NSA	OSF50
1. Underlying asset	Nikkei Stock Average of 225 stocks	Package portfolio of 50 stocks
2. Contract size	Nikkei Stock Average multiplied by 500	One trading unit of package portfolio multiplied by 1,000
3. Contract months	March, June, September, December (five contract months open at a time)	March, June, September, December (five contract months open at a time)
4. Expiration day	Third Wednesday of contract month	15th day of contract month
5. Last trading day	Third Wednesday of contract month	Sixth business day prior to the 15th of contract month
6. Trading hours	8 a.m. – 2.15 p.m. Singapore time (9 a.m. – 3.15 p.m. Tokyo time) on trading days	9 a.m. – 11 a.m. 1 p.m. – 3 p.m. Tokyo time on trading days [b]
	8 a.m. – 10.15 a.m. Singapore time (9 a.m. – 11.15 a.m. Tokyo time) on half trading days	9 a.m. – 11 a.m. Tokyo time on half trading days
7. Method of trading	Open outcry (individual auctions)	Computerized (competitive bids and offers)
8. Tick size	¥ 5 × 500 = ¥ 2,500	¥ 0.5 × 50,000 = ¥ 25,000
9. Settlement on last trading day	Cash settlement	Physical delivery
10. Price limits	No [a]	Yes

[a] After October 1987, price limits were introduced for the NSA contract by the SIMEX authorities.
[b] Before September 1988.

index futures contracts in general, and the OSF50 contract in particular. First, the NSA contract, like most stock index futures contracts, is settled by payment or receipt of the cash difference based on the closing price of the NSA, for all contracts open on the last trading day of the delivery month. Second, the NSA contract trades continuously throughout the trading day, even though the underlying stocks do not trade between 11 a.m. and 1 p.m. Tokyo time (10 a.m. and 12 noon Singapore time). Third, as in the case of the major stock index futures contracts in the U.S., such as the Standard and Poor's 500 (SPX) contract trading on the Chicago Mercantile Exchange, the settlement price of this contract is determined 15 minutes after the close of trading in the underlying stocks. [6]

The OSF50 contract was introduced on June 9, 1987 for trading on the OSE. The important features of the contract are listed in table 1. The main characteristics that distinguish this contract from the NSA contract on SIMEX are settlement procedures and trading hours. Unlike most stock index futures contracts, and the NSA contract, in particular, the OSF50 contract is settled by physical delivery of the underlying securities, for all contracts open on the last trading day of the delivery month. [7] In contrast to the NSA contract traded on the SIMEX, the trading hours for the OSF50 contract coincide with those of the Japanese exchanges trading the underlying stocks (9 a.m. to 11 a.m. and 1 p.m. to 3 pm., Monday to Friday and 9 a.m. to 11 a.m. on trading Saturdays) during the period of this study.

The trading volume on both contracts picked up in the first year since the initiation of the two contracts. However, it should be pointed out that, like most other stock index futures contracts, trading volumes declined somewhat in the NSA contract in the aftermath of the October 1987 crash. In contrast, trading volumes in the OSF50 market continued to grow. However, after the introduction of two new stock index futures contracts in late 1988, the NSA contract on the OSE and the TOPIX contract on the TSE, the trading volume on the OSF50 contract became practically nil. fig. 1 and 2 provide charts of the trading volumes in the OSF50 and NSA contracts since the inception of the OSF50 contract in June 1987 until June 1988.

There are six types of transactions costs involved in stock index arbitrage:

1. brokerage commissions charged for buying and selling stocks in the underlying index,
2. commissions charged for selling and buying back the futures contract,
3. securities transfer taxes paid when the stocks are sold,
4. 'market impact' costs involved in buying and selling the stocks in the underlying stocks,
5. 'market impact' costs involved in selling and buying back the futures contract, and,
6. cost of 'borrowing' the underlying stocks when the stocks in the spot index are sold short.

[6] In the case of the NSA, since the settlement price is computed 15 minutes after the close of trading in the underlying stocks on the TSE, the data are not exactly synchronized. However, when time-stamped data using the closing spot prices on the TSE and synchronous futures prices on the SIMEX were examined in a prior study, the deviation from 'fair price' was practically the same as for the data based on closing and settlement prices. See Brenner, Subrahmanyam and Uno (1989) for details.

[7] The reason for this feature is that when this contract was introduced, the Japanese legal system did not permit cash-settled futures contracts.

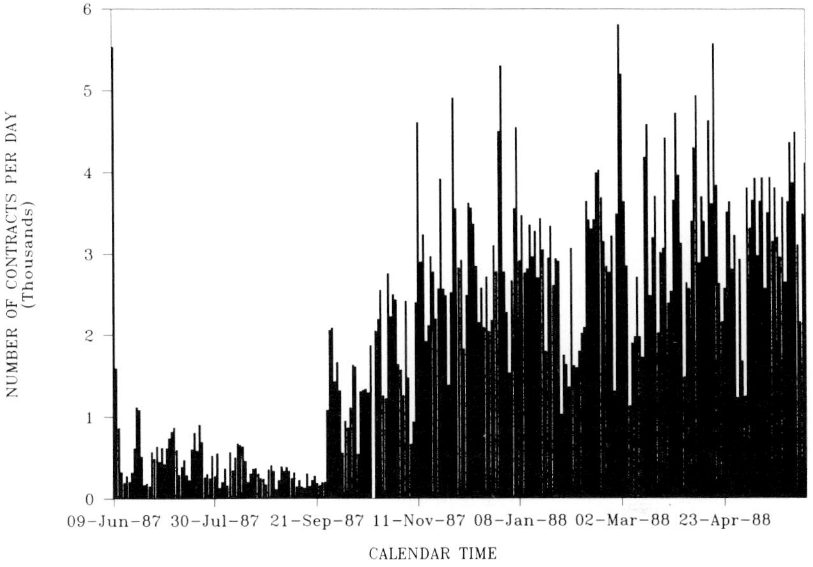

Fig. 1. Trading volume, OSF50 futures contract.

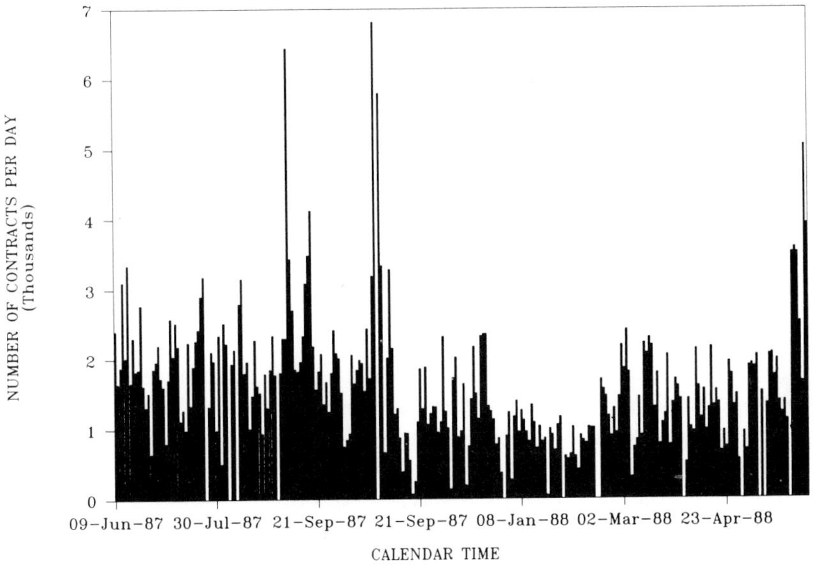

Fig. 2. Trading volume, NSA futures contract.

Table 2
Transactions costs for arbitrage/spreading strategies.

Trading strategy	Trader trans.	Costs(%)
Arbitrage [a]		
1. Buy spot–Sell futures (OSF50) deliver OSF50	Broker	0.7472/0.5597 [c]
2. Buy spot–Sell futures (NSA) Sell spot–Settle NSA	Broker	1.01
3. Buy spot–Sell futures (OSF50) Deliver OSF50	Investor	2.5820/2.3945 [c]
4. Buy spot–Sell futures (NSA) Sell spot–Settle NSA	Investor	2.77
Spreading [b]		
5. Buy NSA futures–Sell OSF50 futures Settle NSA futures–Deliver OSF50	Broker	0.9372/0.7497 [c]
6. Buy NSA futures–Sell OSF50 futures Sell NSA futures–Buy OSF50 futures	Broker	1.0434/0.6684 [c]
7. Buy NSA futures–Sell OSF50 futures Settle NSA futures–Deliver OSF50	Investor	2.7720/2.5845 [c]
8. Buy NSA Futures–Sell OSF50 futures Sell NSA Futures–Buy OSF50 futures	Investor	1.2040/0.8290 [c]

[a] Sell spot–Buy futures costs 0.1% more due to the additional cost of borrowing stock.
[b] Buy OSF50 futures–Sell NSA futures involves the same transactions costs.
[c] The first and second figures represent the transactions costs before and after September 25, 1987, respectively, when the securities transfer tax/commission structures was reduced.

Items 1 and 2 are the direct transactions costs of dealing in the underlying stocks and in the futures contracts and do not need any further explanation. Item 3 is a tax charged in Japan when stocks are sold. The 'market impact' costs, items 4 and 5, arise due to the fact that a sizeable transaction cannot be undertaken in the stock and futures markets without changing the previous market price. The 'market impact' would, at a minimum, be the current bid–ask spread in the respective markets, which may widen for a large transaction. The last item is the fee charged by another investor to 'lend' the short-seller the underlying stocks that he does not own, since they have to be in the possession of the latter when the transaction is initiated.

There are several alternative arbitrage strategies involving the two futures contracts and the underlying spot indices. Some of these involve stock index arbitrage in the two futures markets and others involve 'cross-spreading' between the two markets. In each case, the transactions costs depend on whether the arbitrageur is a broker-dealer or institutional investor. Table 2 presents the details of the transactions costs for the various types of arbitrage transactions. An example of how these numbers were derived is given below for Case 5:

Transaction:	Buy NSA futures–Sell OSF50 futures Cash settle NSA futures–Deliver OSF50	
Trader:	Broker	
Costs:	*Transaction*	*Costs*
	Buy NSA futures	
	–Futures commission s	0.02%
	–Market impact	0.15%
	SEll OSF50 futures	
	–Futures commissions	0.0017%
	–Stock exchange fee	0.2%
	–Market impact	0.15%
	Buy OSF50 stocks	
	–Stock commissions	0.01%
	–Market impact	0.2%
	Deliver OSF50 stocks	
	–Stock commissions	0.0055%
	–Securities transfer tax	0.18%
	Settle NSA contract	
	–Futures commissions	0.02%
	Total	0.9372%

4. Deviations from 'fair pricing': Empirical observations

In order to compute the deviations of the actual futures prices from the 'fair price' given in eqs. (1), (2a) and (2b), we need the following data:

1. the closing values of the two stock price indices,
2. the settlement prices of the two stock index futures contracts,
3. the riskless interest rate between each date and the expiration date of the respective contract,
4. the dividend stream on the two indices.

Items 1 and 2 have been discussed in section 3. Item 3, the riskless interest rate used in our study is the three-month Gensaki rate (a 'repo' rate) that is commonly used as the short-term Japanese interest rate analogous to the Treasury bill rate in the U.S. and the U.K. [8] As has been noted by Brenner, Subrahmanyam and Uno (1989), item 4, the dividend payments of Japanese companies tend to be more clustered than their U.S. counterparts. Most

[8] Since there is no available interest rate whose maturity matches the maturity of the futures contract on each trading day, the riskless interest rate could be approximated by interpolating between the one-month and the three-month Gensaki rates. However, this adjustment made a trivial difference to the calculations.

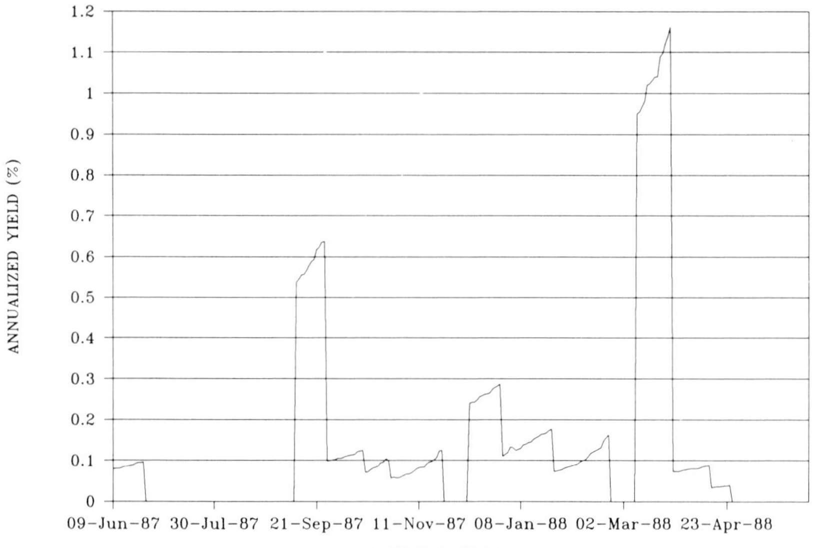

Fig. 3. Daily dividend yield of OSF50, nearest futures contract.

Japanese companies pay dividends twice a year (occasionally once a year) with the payments being concentrated at the end of March and September, each year. Also, the actual dividend payments are announced after the ex-dividend dates. However, since the dividend payments on each stock are fairly stable, the dividend stream for a portfolio of stocks is quite predictable. The actual dividend yield for the OSF50 and NSA, respectively, are shown in figs. 3 and 4. Note that, although the dividend yields are small relative to other countries, the dividend streams on the two Japanese spot indices are very similar.

This study covers the period June 1987 to June 1988, during which four active contracts, September 1987, December 1987, March 1988 and June 1988 contracts were traded on the NSA and OSF50 futures markets. Table 3 presents the summary statistics of the percentage change in price on a daily basis for each contract period and for the whole sample for the two spot indices and for the two futures contracts. [9] Since the closing value of the OSF50 spot index based on Osaka prices may be somewhat different from that in Tokyo, the larger and deeper market, which may be used for arbitrage purposes, the relevant statistics for the OSF50 spot index in both markets are furnished. Note that the behavior of the two spot indices is quite similar. In terms of the summary statistics, the data for the OSF50 in the two spot markets are close, though not identical. Comparing the NSA and the OSF50

[9] In order to ensure that all the data refer to daily changes in price, data from Mondays and days after other holidays were dropped from the calculations.

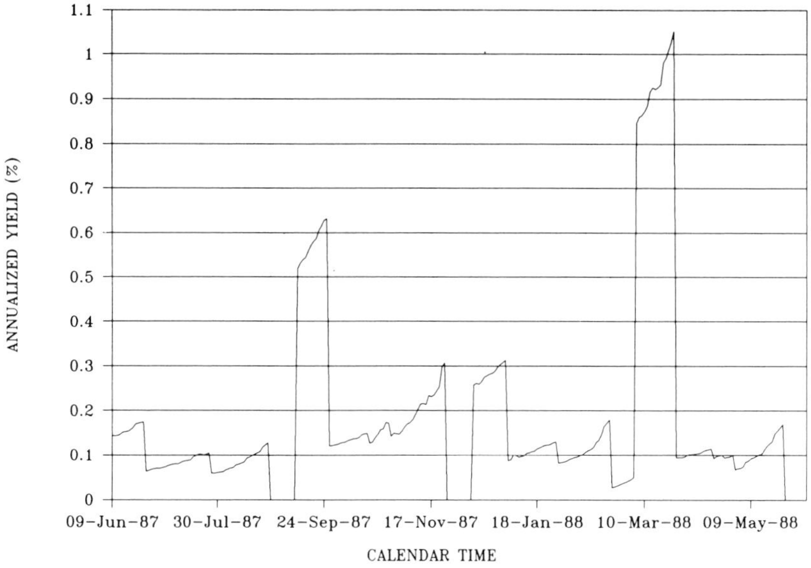

Fig. 4. Daily dividend yield of NSA, nearest futures contract.

spot indices, the means are different from each other but the standard deviations are quite similar. However, there are even larger differences between the statistics for the two futures contracts and between the futures contracts and their respective spot indices. These differences are suggestive of the possibility of arbitrage opportunities in these markets, which we now discuss.

We first examine the opportunities for stock index arbitrage in the OSF50 and NSA markets. Tables 4 and 6 refer to the OSF50 contract, while tables 5 and 7 deal with the NSA contract. These tables provide evidence on the deviations from the 'fair price' of the two stock index futures contracts as defined in eqs. (1), (2a) and (2b). Specifically, the deviation from the 'fair price' or mispricing is given by

$$M_t = (F_t - FP_t)/FP_t, \tag{3}$$

where FP_t is defined by eq. (1), when transactions costs are ignored. When transactions costs are taken into account, the deviation from the 'fair price' is defined as

$$M_t = \begin{cases} (F_t - FP_t^+)/FP_t^+ & \text{if} \quad F_t > FP_t^+, \\ 0 & \text{if} \quad F_t^+ \geq F_t \geq FP_t^-, \\ (F_t - FP_t^-)/FP_t^- & \text{if} \quad F_t < FP_t^-. \end{cases} \tag{4}$$

Table 3
Percentage price changes of OSF50 and NSA indices and their futures contracts: Summary statistics.

Contract		OSF50 index		OSF50 futures	NSA225 index	NSA225 futures	Number of obs.
		Tokyo	Osaka				
Sep. 87	Mean	0.063	0.071	−0.094	0.109	0.025	55
	Max	3.957	3.959	2.814	3.935	4.445	
	Min	−2.646	−2.921	−3.352	−1.796	−3.112	
	Stdv	1.158	1.127	1.016	0.997	1.206	
Dec. 87	Mean	0.071	0.063	0.037	0.056	0.238	48
	Max	4.656	4.634	6.661	4.185	6.145	
	Min	−5.431	−5.218	−5.805	−4.93	−7.227	
	Stdv	1.862	1.791	2.188	1.613	2.501	
Mar. 88	Mean	0.276	0.258	0.26	0.283	0.309	45
	Max	6.661	7.035	6.272	5.632	5.287	
	Min	−1.535	−1.332	−1.265	−1.326	−1.656	
	Stdv	1.195	1.214	1.173	1.042	1.049	
Jun. 88	Mean	0.083	0.046	0.078	0.136	0.166	47
	Max	1.967	1.893	1.836	1.414	2.038	
	Min	−1.687	−1.647	−2.657	−1.42	−1.903	
	Stdv	0.814	0.764	0.83	0.634	0.819	
Total	Mean	0.119	0.106	0.061	0.143	0.177	195
	Max	6.661	7.035	6.661	5.632	6.145	
	Min	−5.431	−5.218	−5.805	−4.93	−7.227	
	Stdv	1.315	1.279	1.403	1.129	1.542	
Oct. 20.87	Change	−15.521	−14.113	−3.072	−14.901	−27.806	

The evidence on the mispricing in the OSF50 contract in the absence of transactions costs is presented in table 4 and graphically represented in fig. 5. Since transactions in the spot market may be conducted in either Osaka or Tokyo, the deviations from 'fair price' are calculated with data from both the OSE and the TSE. Though the differences between the deviations in the two cases are statistically significant, they are too small to affect the results differentially.[10] Out of 272 observations, there were about 30% more positive than negative deviations – 154 versus 118 in the case of the TSE data and 152 versus 120 for the OSE data. The September and June contracts had more positive deviations while the December and March contracts had somewhat more negative deviations.[11] Turning to the size of the deviations, the mean of

[10] The mean difference was 0.048 percent and statistically significant at the 5% level.

[11] We also partitioned the data for the December 1987 contract into two subperiods, before and after September 25, 1987, when the transactions costs structure in the Japanese market was changed. When the data for the December contract are broken down in this manner, the first sub-period of the second contract had a preponderance of positive deviations, similar to the first contract.

Table 4
Summary statistics of premiums and discounts (OSF50 cash index vs OSF50 futures).

Contract	number positive	Number negative	Mean positive %	Mean negative %	Mean absolute %	Mean M^2 (%)SQD.	Number of obs.
SEP. 87 [a]	40	32	1.83	−0.66	1.31	2.63	72
SEP. 87 [b]	40	32	1.74	−0.65	1.26	2.43	72
DEC. 87 [a]	30	37	0.94	−0.92	0.93	1.20	67
DEC. 87 [b]	31	36	0.92	−1.00	0.96	1.32	67
MAR. 88 [a]	30	35	0.68	−0.96	0.83	0.86	65
MAR. 88 [b]	29	36	0.64	−0.97	0.82	0.86	65
JUN. 88 [a]	54	14	0.67	−0.19	0.58	0.50	68
JUN. 88 [b]	52	16	0.66	−0.26	0.57	0.47	68
TOTAL [a]	154	118	1.03	−0.77	0.92	1.32	272
TOTAL [b]	152	120	0.99	−0.80	0.91	1.29	272

[a] Cash index calculated based on closing prices on the Tokyo Stock Exchange.
[b] Cash index calculated based on closing prices on the Osaka Securities Exchange.

the positive deviations was much larger in absolute magnitude (0.99%) than that of the negative deviations (−0.80%), for the sample as a whole (using the OSE prices). A closer examination reveals that the mean of the positive deviations was roughly three times as large as the mean of the negative deviations for the September and June contracts. For the December contract, the absolute magnitudes of the means of the positive and negative deviations

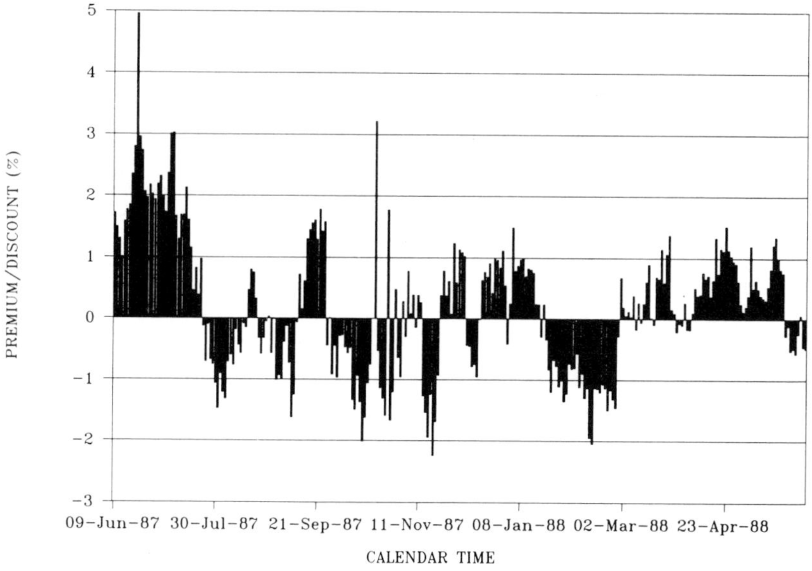

Fig. 5. Premiums & discounts, OSF50 futures vs. cash index.

Table 5
Summary statistics of premiums and discounts (NSA cash index vs NSA futures).

Contract	Number positive	Number negative	Mean positive %	Mean negative %	Mean absolute %	Mean M^2 (%)SQD	Number of obs.
Sep. 87	18	52	0.76	−1.73	1.48	3.16	70
Dec. 87	8	58	0.41	−2.16	1.94	7.84	66
Mar. 88	4	58	0.20	−0.99	0.94	1.22	62
Jun. 88	21	43	0.17	−0.61	0.47	0.40	64
Total	51	211	0.42	−1.41	1.22	3.21	262

were approximately equal, while the March contract showed a smaller positive deviation. Further, the mean absolute deviation declined steadily from 1.31 percent for the September contract to 0.58 percent for the June contract. [12]

The pattern of the deviations for the NSA contract during the same period in the absence of transactions costs is shown in table 5 and fig. 6. Unlike the OSF50 contract, the NSA contract was dominated by negative deviations for all four expiration dates. The importance of the negative deviations was accentuated by their large size compared with the positive deviations, for all four contracts. The mean of the negative deviations was more than three times as large as the mean of the positive deviations. [13] Overall, the deviations for the NSA contract were larger, and significantly so, than for the OSF50 contract. For the sample as a whole, the mean absolute deviation is 1.22 percent for the NSA contract versus 0.92 percent for the OSF50 contract. [14] Qualitatively, the results for the NSA contract are similar to those in the previous study by Brenner, Subrahmanyam and Uno (1989), that examined the first year of the SIMEX (the December 1986 to September 1987 contracts) and found that large and negative deviations dominated the NSA market. It

[12] For the December contract, we excluded the data for October 20, since the stock market and OSF50 futures market stopped trading due to the triggering of price limits. The large positive deviation observed on that day in closing prices is due to the fact that the futures market stopped at a 3 percent limit down while the stock market stopped at roughly 15 percent down on the index. (Price limits on the TSE differ from stock to stock based on the price of the stock.) Since the NSA futures on the SIMEX had no price limits at that time, the futures declined to a much lower level, and therefore, the SIMEX contract shows a large negative deviation for this day.

[13] Since the week after October 19 was very volatile and many stocks in Japan stopped trading on several occasions due to price limits, arbitrage activity became very risky. This may explain the large deviations during this period. When the seven trading days after October 19 are excluded from the sample, the mean negative deviation for the December 1987 contract declined substantially from −2.16 percent to −1.54 percent and the mean absolute deviations declined from 1.94 percent to 1.38 percent. Our general conclusions remain unaffected, however. The mean negative deviation, for the sample as a whole, is still about three times as large as the mean positive deviation – −1.23 percent versus 0.42 percent.

[14] The mean difference between the absolute deviations was 0.298 percent, while the standard error was 0.0858 percent.

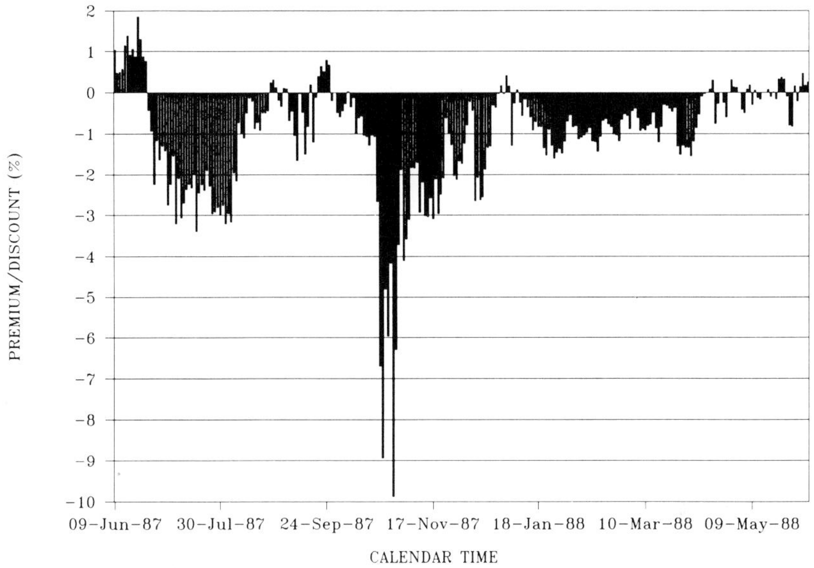

Fig. 6. Premiums & discounts, NSA futures vs. cash index.

should be noted that, similar to the OSF50 market, the deviations declined in magnitude in the NSA market over time. The mean absolute deviation fell from 1.48 percent to 0.47 percent, during the period under study. However, this is in contrast to the first year of the NSA contract, when no such trend was noticeable.

Tables 6 and 7 present the data on mispricing after adjusting for realistic transactions costs (see table 2) for brokers – 0.75% before September 25 and 0.5% after September 25 for the OSF50 contract and 1% for the NSA contract. The deviations, after taking transactions costs into account, are plotted in figs. 7 and 8. The results indicate that a majority of the deviations documented in tables 4 and 5 were large enough to compensate for transactions costs. In the case of the OSF50 contract, 106 out of 154 positive deviations and 70 out of 118 negative deviations were outside the transactions costs bounds. In the case of the NSA contract, only 6 out of the 51 positive observations fell outside the transactions costs bounds, against 110 out of the 211 negative deviations.

An interesting feature of the mispricing series, observed also in the U.S., was the persistence of the deviations, both positive and negative. [15] This path-dependence showed up in the autocorrelation coefficients, given in table 8. The first-order coefficients were very high, between 0.64 and 0.89, and

[15] See MacKinlay and Ramaswamy (1988).

Table 6
Summary statistics of premiums and discounts with transactions costs [a] (OSF50 cash index vs futures).

Contract	Number positive	Number negative	Mean positive %	Mean negative %	Mean absolute %	Mean M^2 (%)SQD.	Number of obs
Sep. 87 [b]	34	14	1.33	−0.29	0.69	1.16	48
Sep. 87 [c]	34	12	1.23	−0.35	0.64	1.04	46
Dec. 87 [b]	19	26	0.68	−0.68	0.46	0.45	45
Dec. 87 [c]	18	26	0.74	−0.76	0.49	0.53	44
Mar. 88 [b]	19	30	0.43	−0.55	0.38	0.27	49
Mar. 88 [c]	19	30	0.36	−0.60	0.38	0.27	49
Jun. 88 [b]	34	0	0.43	–	0.21	0.12	34
Jun. 88 [c]	32	2	0.41	−0.04	0.19	0.11	34
Total [b]	106	70	0.76	−0.55	0.44	0.51	176
Total [c]	103	70	0.73	−0.60	0.43	0.50	173

[a] Transactions costs before and after September 25, 1987 are 0.75% and 0.5%, respectively.
[b] Cash index calculated based on closing prices on the Tokyo Stock Exchange.
[c] Cash index calculated based on closing prices on the Osaka Securities Exchange.

Table 7
Summary statistics of premiums and discounts with transaction cost [a] (NSA cash index vs NSA futures).

Contract	Number positive	Number negative	Mean positive %	Mean negative %	Mean absolute %	Mean M^2 (%)SQD.	Number of obs.
Sep. 87	6	35	0.30	−1.30	0.68	1.07	41
Dec. 87	0	41	–	−1.87	1.16	4.80	41
Mar. 88	0	26	–	−0.47	0.20	0.19	26
Jun. 88	0	8	–	−0.34	0.04	0.02	8
Total	6	110	0.30	−1.25	0.53	1.55	116

[a] Transactions costs are 1%.

decline slowly.[16] One possible explanation for this persistence is the price discovery role of the stock index futures market, in spite of the lack of arbitrage activity. In other words, even though the price of the futures contract may have deviated from its ‘fair price’, information affecting the spot market was speedily incorporated in the futures price. However, transactions costs and other trading restrictions caused the deviation to be preserved on a day-to-day basis. In other words, new information affected both the spot and futures prices, but did not necessarily change the relationship to one another.

[16] All the correlation coefficients are positive and statistically significant at the 1 percent level.

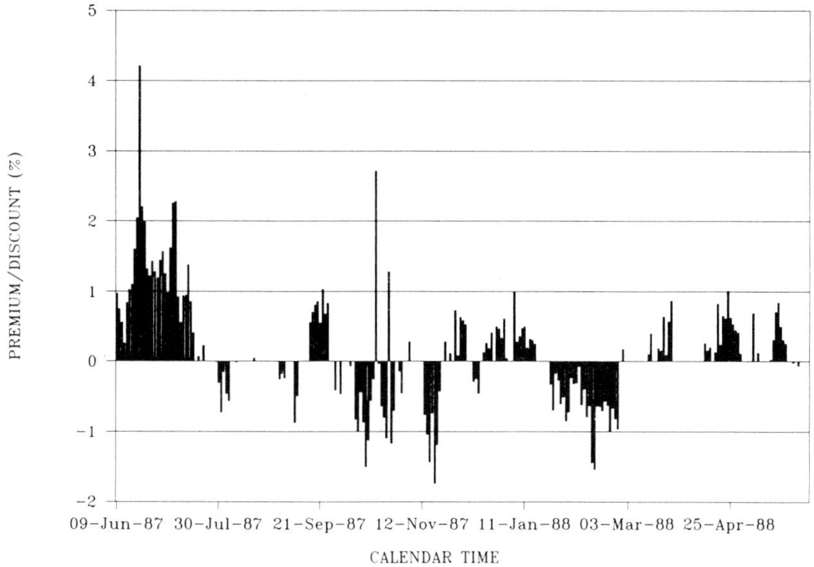

Fig. 7. Premiums & discounts with transactions costs, OSF50 futures vs. cash index.

The data on mispricing can be looked at in a different manner. Rather than measuring the mispricing as a deviation from the 'fair' price, the interest rate implied by the market prices of the spot and futures contract can be computed

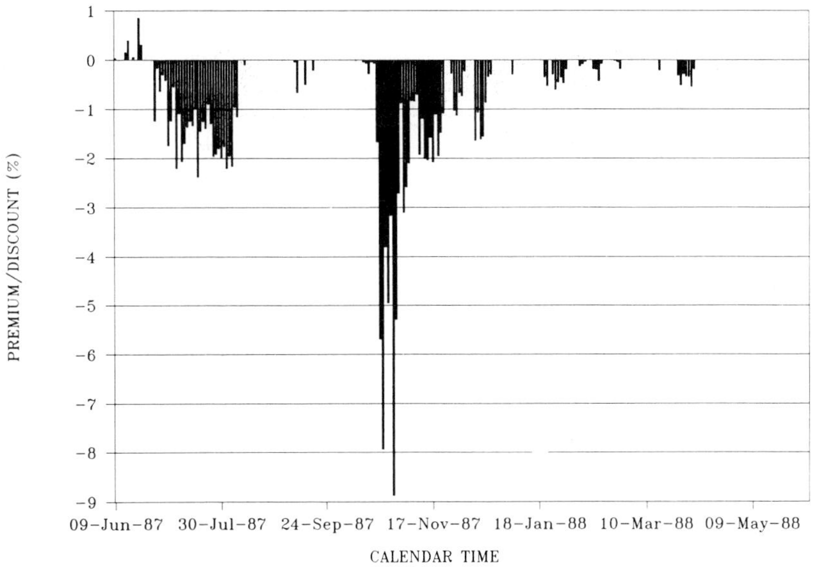

Fig. 8. Premiums & discounts with transactions costs, NSA futures vs. cash index.

Table 8
Autocorrelation coefficients (to lag 4) of premiums and discounts.

Contract		OSF50			NSA		
		Auto-corr. coeff	Std. err.	No. of obs.	Auto-corr. coeff	Std. err.	No. of obs.
Sep. 87	Lag 1	0.897	0.117	70	0.887	0.117	70
	2	0.816	0.116		0.848	0.116	
	3	0.752	0.115		0.782	0.115	
	4	0.732	0.114		0.705	0.114	
Dec. 87	Lag 1	0.640	0.119	66	0.762	0.119	66
	2	0.571	0.118		0.653	0.118	
	3	0.487	0.118		0.565	0.118	
	4	0.363	0.117		0.594	0.117	
Mar. 88	Lag 1	0.861	0.124	62	0.746	0.124	62
	2	0.742	0.123		0.579	0.123	
	3	0.679	0.122		0.459	0.122	
	4	0.623	0.121		0.274	0.121	
Jun. 88	Lag 1	0.679	0.122	64	0.756	0.122	64
	2	0.470	0.121		0.557	0.121	
	3	0.326	0.120		0.461	0.120	
	4	0.191	0.119		0.351	0.191	

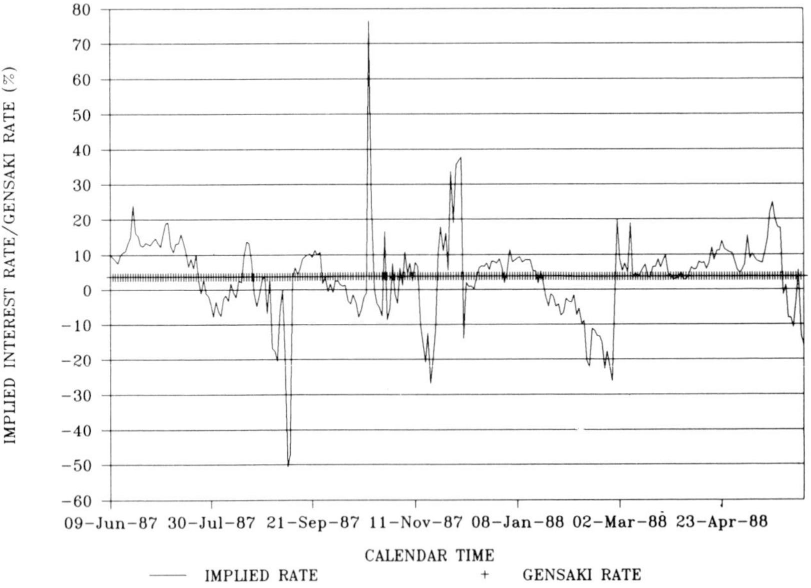

Fig. 9. Implied interest rate, OSF50 futures vs. cash index.

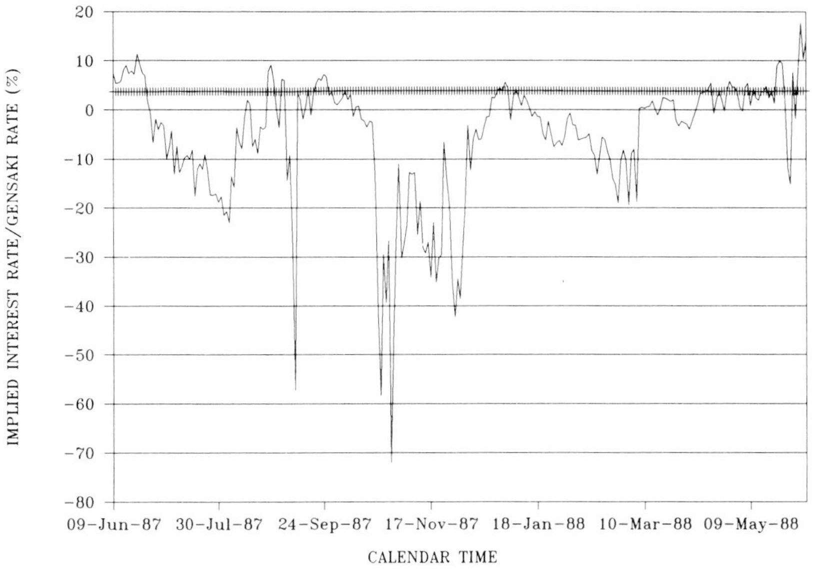

Fig. 10. Implied interest rate, NSA futures vs. cash index.

and compared with the market interest rate. Taking into account the effect of transactions costs, the implied interest rate can be defined as follows:

$$R_t = \begin{cases} \dfrac{1}{\tau}\left[\ln\{F_t/(S_t(1+c_t^+) - PV(DIV_t))\}\right] & \text{if} \quad F_t > FP_t^+ , \\ r_t & \text{if} \quad FP_t \geq F_t \geq FP_t^- , \\ \dfrac{1}{\tau}\left[\ln\{F_t/(S_t(1-c_t^-) - PV(DIV_t))\}\right] & \text{if} \quad F_t < FP_t^- . \end{cases}$$

where $PV(DIV_t)$ = Present Value of DIV_t. The implied interest rates on the stock index arbitrage in the two markets are plotted in figs. 9 and 10,

Table 9

Summary statistics of the excess implied interest rate in the OŞF50 arbitrage.

Contract	Mean positive %	Standard deviation %	Mean negative %	Standard deviation %	Max %	Min %	Number of obs.
Sep. 87	8.50	3.77	−10.53	12.74	20.47	−54.29	72
Dec. 87	9.89	9.92	−8.63	7.41	33.76	−30.72	67
Mar. 88	4.32	3.53	−11.09	8.14	16.24	−29.90	65
Jun. 88	5.49	4.65	−5.62	7.15	21.10	−19.87	68
Total	6.96	5.70	−9.44	9.15	33.76	−54.29	272

Table 10
Summary statistics of the excess implied interest rate in the NSA arbitrage.

Contract	Mean positive %	Standard deviation %	Mean negative %	Standard deviation %	Max %	Min %	Number of obs.
Sep. 87	3.70	1.56	−14.11	9.51	7.63	−60.97	70
Dec. 87	1.90	1.21	−20.84	17.58	3.37	−76.00	66
Mar. 88	0.83	0.62	−9.06	5.50	1.71	−23.34	62
Jun. 88	3.62	3.80	−3.59	3.73	13.95	−18.99	64
Total	3.16	2.54	−12.34	10.79	13.95	−76.00	262

respectively. The summary statistics of the excess of the implied interest rates over the Gensaki rate are presented in tables 9 and 10.

Several general conclusions can be drawn from the analysis of the data for the two contracts. First, there were large deviations from the 'fair price' in the case of both the OSF50 and NSA stock index futures markets. Many of these deviations were large enough to compensate for realistic estimates of costs for traders with the lowest transactions costs. Second, positive deviations dominated the sample both in terms of magnitude as well as frequency in the case of the OSF50 contract. In contrast, negative deviations were much more frequent, accounting for virtually all the mispricing, in the NSA market. This difference is puzzling and calls for an examination of 'cross-spreading' strategies, which we now turn to.

5. Cross-spreading and inter-market profit opportunities

The summary statistics furnished in table 3 and the differences in the pattern of the deviations from 'fair price' for the two contracts discussed in section 4 suggest that the two futures contracts and/or the two spot indices were imperfectly related to each other. The question is how closely did the price changes in the two spot indices and the respective futures contracts move together. If the returns on the two spot indices were imperfectly related to each other, then no conclusion can be drawn about the possibilities for inter-market profit opportunities without making adjustments for risk, as with any two risky assets. However, if the returns on the two spot indices were highly correlated and the returns on the respective futures contracts were not, this *may* indicate inter-market profit opportunities. In order to check which of these two alternatives is more descriptive of the data, it is necessary to examine the correlation matrix between the daily percentage changes in price.

Table 11 provides the coefficients of correlation coefficient between the daily percentage change in price for the two spot indices and the respective futures contracts. For the OSF50 contract, there are two different underlying spot series, based on the Tokyo and Osaka prices, respectively. Several points

Table 11
Correlation matrix of the percentage daily price change of the indices and the futures contracts.

	NSA index	OSF50 index Osaka	OSF50 index Tokyo	OSF50 futures	NSA futures	No. of obs.
NSA index	1					195
OSF50 index Osaka	0.9579 [a]	1				195
OSF50 index Tokyo	0.9677 [a]	0.9851 [a]	1			195
OSF50 futures	0.8795 [a]	0.8926 [a]	0.8994 [a]	1		195
NSA futures	0.8503 [a]	0.8461 [a]	0.8588 [a]	0.8859 [a]	1	195

[a] 1-tailed significant at the 0.001 level.

are worth noting from the tables. The correlation coefficient between the daily changes in the OSF50 spot indices based on TSE and OSE closing prices was very high – around 0.99 for the overall sample and for the individual contracts. For all practical purposes, we could ignore the differences between the indices based on two different sets of market prices. The correlation coefficient between daily changes in the NSA and the OSF50 was somewhat lower, but still quite high, around 0.96 in the whole sample. However, the correlation coefficient between changes in the two futures contracts was not as high, around 0.88. This statistic tells us only part of the story. A more revealing statistic is the coefficient of correlation between the deviations in the two markets. Table 12 shows that this correlation was as low as 0.3 and at most 0.5, in each contract period. This suggests that a 'cross-spreading' strategy in the two futures contracts may have been profitable.

The close correlation between the two spot indices and the imperfect correlation between the two futures contracts suggests that there *may* have been inter-market profit opportunities. In other words, there was an alternative to index arbitrage involving the spot and the corresponding futures contract. For example, rather than buying the futures contract and selling the corresponding spot contract, it may have been more profitable to buy the futures contract on one index and sell the futures contract on the other, i.e.,

Table 12
Correlation coefficients of premiums and discounts for the NSA and OSF50 contracts.

Contract	Corr. coeff.	No. of obs.
(A) Sep. 1987 contract	0.2963 [a]	70
(B) Dec. 1987 contract	0.4138 [a]	66
(C) Mar. 1988 contract	0.5091 [b]	62
(D) Jun. 1988 contract	0.3876 [b]	64

[a] 1-tailed significant at the 0.01 level.
[b] 1-tailed significant at the 0.001 level.

the latter futures contract may have been a better substitute for the underlying spot of the former.

There are two alternative rules for setting up a 'cross-spread', one based on the relative deviations from 'fair pricing' and the other on the ratio of the prices of the two futures contracts. We first discuss the strategy based on the relative deviations from 'fair pricing'. A reasonable rule for creating a spread between the two contracts is: when one contract has a positive mispricing deviation and the other a negative one, buy the contract with a negative deviation and sell the one with a positive deviation. A less obvious variant of this strategy would arise when both contracts have deviations with the same sign. For instance, when both contracts have positive deviations, buy the contract with the smaller deviation and sell the one with the larger deviation. Similarly, when both contracts have negative deviations, buy the contract whose underpricing is larger and sell the other. In all cases, the positions are 'unwound' either on the expiration date of the contracts or on the last trading day. We now discuss the results of these two cases of the spreading strategy.

Since there is no net investment in a futures spreading strategy, a rate of return on the strategy cannot be computed. Therefore, we simply compute the yen amount that a spreader would make every time he buys or sells an OSF50 contract against the matching number of NSA contracts. This profit is specified in index points of the OSF50 contract. Figs. 11 through 14 show the size and distribution of the yen realized profits and losses in terms of points of the OSF50 index. For the case where the position is carried to expiration, the

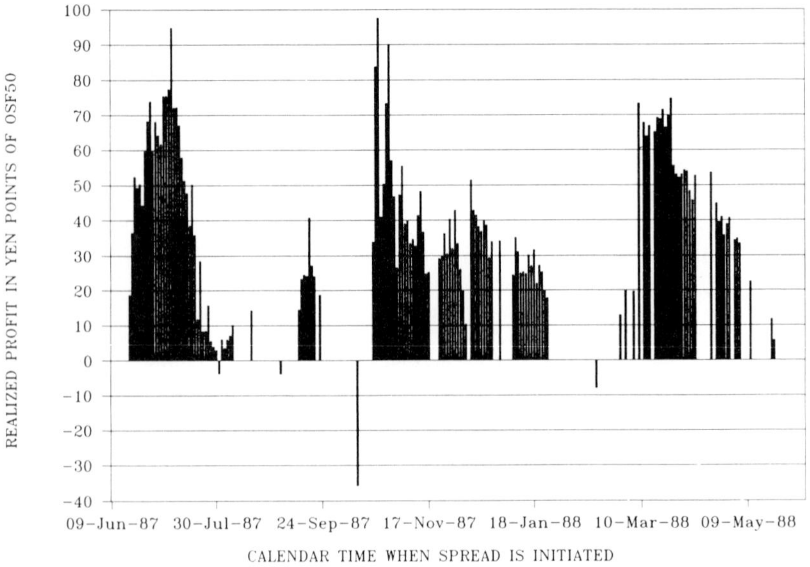

Fig. 11. Realized profit at expiration, futures mispricing cross-spreading.

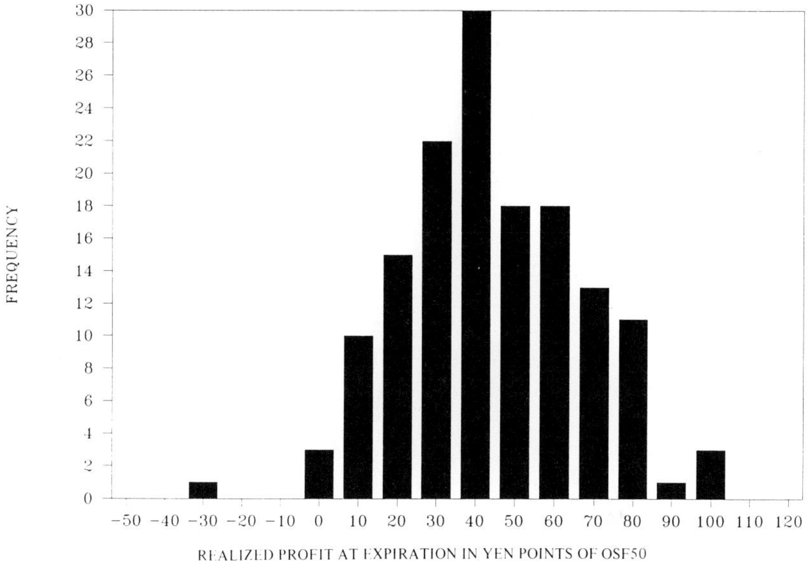

Fig. 12. Distribution of profit at expiration, futures mispricing cross-spreading.

strategy could have been implemented on 141 days out of the 262 days in our sample, of which 140 days would be profitable (See table 13). For the case where the position is reversed on the last trading day, a strategy involving

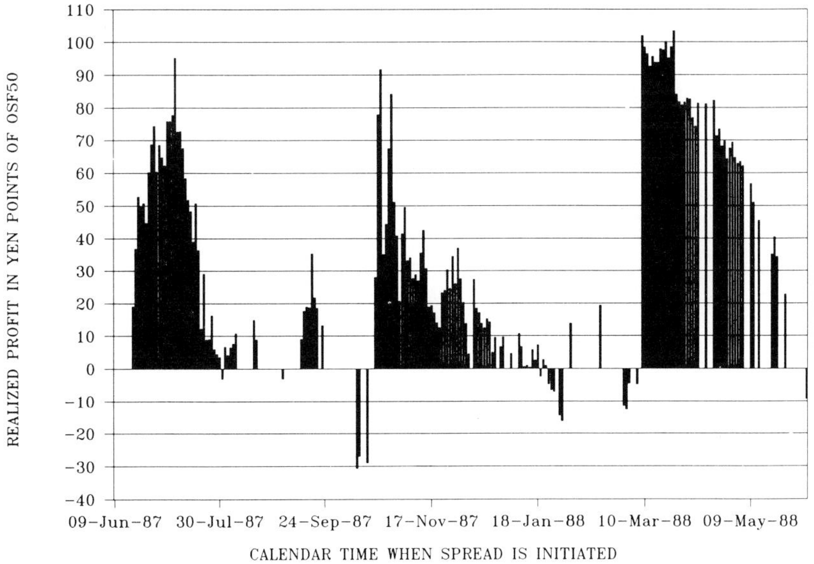

Fig. 13. Realized profit on the last trading day, futures mispricing cross-spreading.

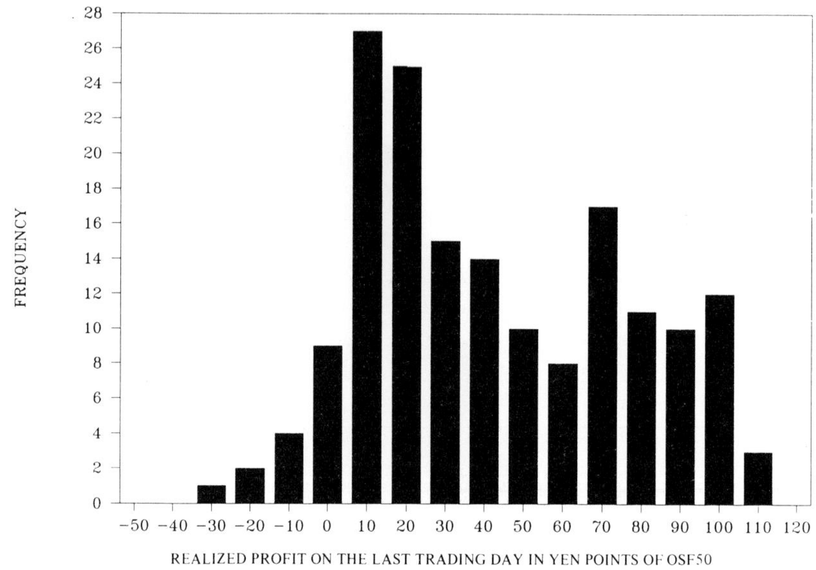

Fig. 14. Distribution of profit on the last trading day, futures mispricing cross spreading.

Table 13
Frequency distribution of realized profit in yen points per OSF50 contract.

Yen per OSF50 contract	Number of observations [futures mispricing spreading]		Number of observations [futures ratio spreading]	
	Expiration	Last trading day	Expiration	Last trading day
−60				3
−50				4
−40				3
−30	1	1	3	1
−20		2	2	
−10		4	5	2
0	3	9	2	5
10	10	27		1
20	15	25	7	10
30	22	15		5
40	30	14	5	8
50	18	10	8	6
60	18	8	7	4
70	13	17	6	8
80	11	11	7	7
90	1	10	1	1
100	3	12	3	2
110	0	3		
Total no. of obs	262	262	262	262
No. of positions	145	168	56	70
Profit positions	141	152	44	52
Loss positions	4	16	12	18
Mean yen profit	41.11	37.51	37.07	22.26
Std. dev. yen profit	23.12	33.41	35.96	42.46

lower transaction costs but higher risks, the strategy could be implemented more frequently but with somewhat greater potential for losses. There are 159 days when the strategy could have been implemented out of which 152 days are profitable. The mean profit for the first case is 41 yen, and for the second case, it is 37.5 yen, per OSF50 contract. To get an idea of the actual profits per contract, these figures should be multiplied by twice the tick size or 50,000 (See table 2.)

We now turn to the alternative spreading rule based on the relationship between the ratio of the two futures contracts and the historic ratio of their respective spot indices. This rule would suggest buying the NSA and selling the OSF50 contract when the ratio of the futures prices is below the historic ratio and the opposite when the ratio is greater. In both cases, the positions are reversed at expiration on the last trading day.

This strategy usually assumes that the ratio of the two indices does not change much over time. However, to reduce the risk due to a sizeable change in the ratio of the two indices, a conservative trading rule was devised. First, the ratio of the two indices is based on daily values for a three-month period and is updated daily by adding the latest day's observation and dropping the first day's observation. Second, the strategy is implemented only when the ratio of the two futures prices is outside a band consisting of one standard deviation of the historical ratio plus transactions costs on each side of the historical mean ratio. This is a conservative strategy since it is triggered only when the differences are outside a very wide band, thus minimizing the

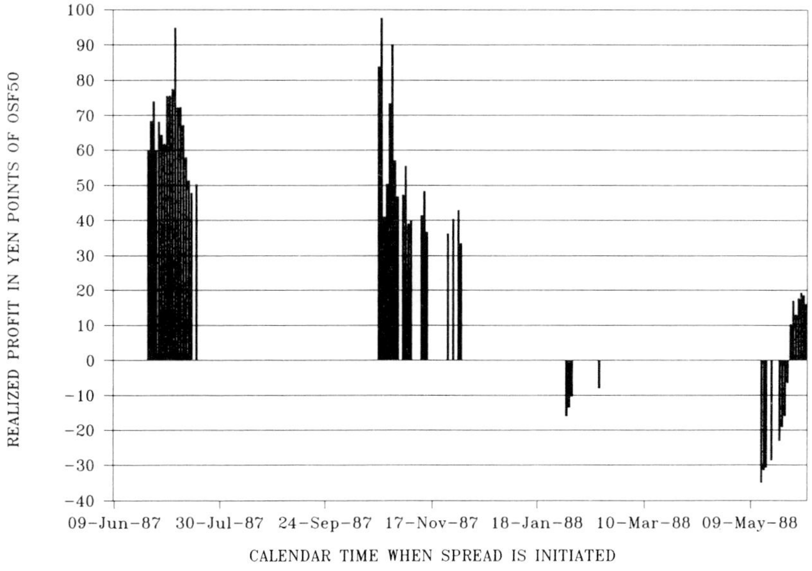

Fig. 15. Realized profit at expiration, futures ratio cross-spreading.

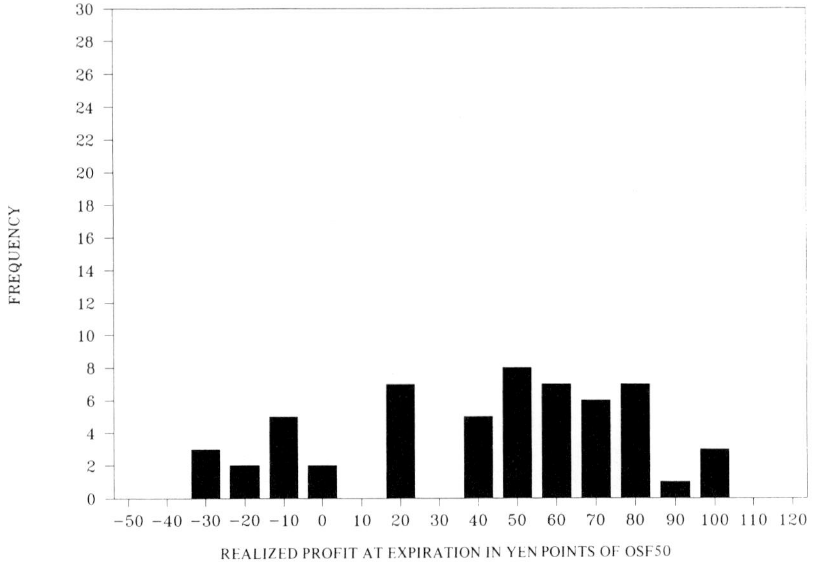

Fig. 16. Distribution of profit at expiration, futures ratio cross-spreading.

expected number of profitable trades and reducing the risk from these trades as well. When held to expiration, this strategy triggered a spread position on only 56 out of 262 days resulting in 44 profitable positions, with a mean of 37

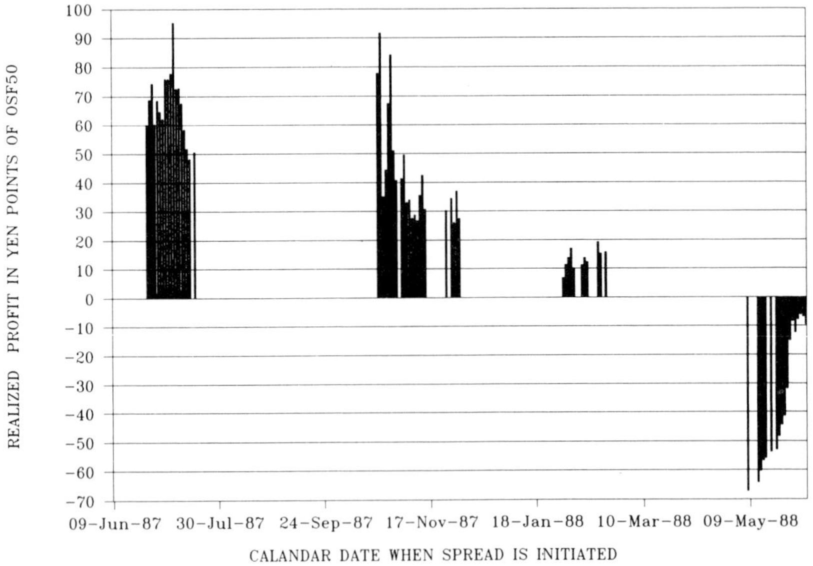

Fig. 17. Realized profit on the last trading day, futures ratio cross-spreading.

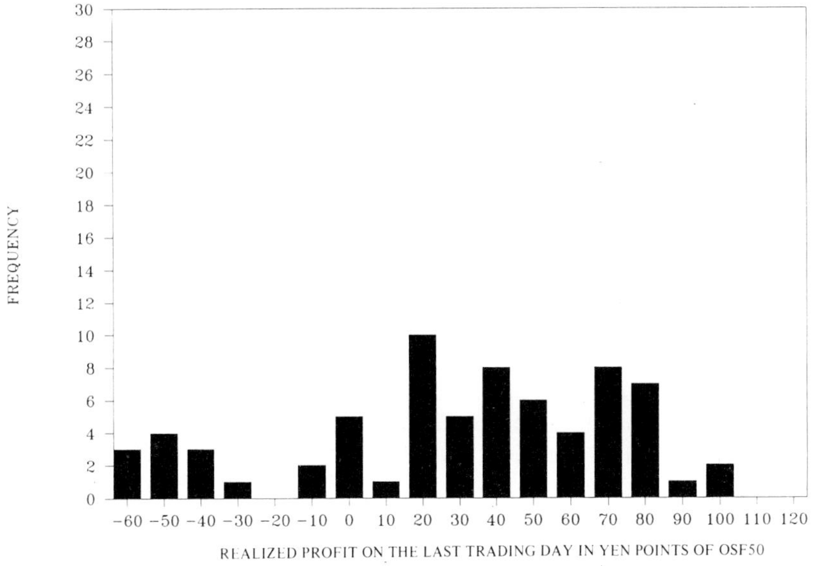

Fig. 18. Distribution of profit on the last trading day, futures ratio cross-spreading.

yen. (See table 13). Again, to measure the actual profits, these numbers should be multiplied by 50,000. A look at figs. 15 through 18 reveals that the distribution of the yen profits are strongly skewed with few large negative observations. However, it is clear that the spreading strategy based on the relative mispricing dominates the strategy based on the historical ratio.

6. Conclusions

The persistent underpricing of stock index futures contracts in relation to their 'fair' price in the early years of trading has been documented in many markets, in particular in the United States. The first year of trading in the NSA contract on the SIMEX exhibited a similar pattern. However, the size of these negative deviations showed a downward trend in the second year. In contrast to stock index futures contracts, in general, and the NSA contract, in particular, positive deviations were more frequent in the OSF50 contract on the OSE. Here too, the magnitude of the deviations has declined since the inception of the contract.

There are two major reasons for the deviations from 'fair price' in these two index futures markets – transactions costs and restrictions on trading. While these two sources of deviations are common to many markets, they are particularly important in the Japanese markets. Transactions costs are much larger in the Japanese stock markets than the U.S. or U.K. markets. Also, restrictions on trading, particularly relating to selling stocks short are important impediments to the arbitrage process in the Japanese market. Trading restrictions are compounded by the cost and difficulty involved in borrowing stock for short sales. Other restrictions include restrictions placed on U.S. and Japanese financial institutions on participating in the Japanese stock index futures markets in the early period of trading. The decrease in the size of the absolute deviations is indirect evidence that the transactions costs and restrictions are less inhibiting than they were in the early months of trading in the NSA contract.

An interesting phenomenon that is specific to the Japanese markets is the low correlation between the deviations in the two futures markets. This relationship suggests a spreading strategy that would usually be initiated by selling OSF50 futures and buying NSA futures. If held to expiration such a strategy produced substantial profits over and above transactions costs. It should be emphasized, however, that this strategy is not riskless, although, in our sample, the risk seems to be very small. In general, this strategy depends on the magnitude of the deviations and the correlation of these deviations. It should be emphasized that these opportunities may diminish as the markets get more liquid and more integrated due to arbitrage activity by Japanese and non-Japanese institutions.

References

Billingsley, R.S. and D.M. Chance, 1988, The pricing and performance of stock index futures spreads, Journal of Futures Markets 8, June, 303–318.

Brennan, M.J. and E.S. Schwartz, 1988, Arbitrage in stock index futures, Working paper, (Graduate School of Management, UCLA, Los Angeles, CA).

Brenner, M., M.G. Subrahmanyam and J. Uno, 1989, The behavior of prices in the Nikkei spot and futures markets, Journal of Financial Economics, forthcoming.

Figlewski, S., 1984, Explaining the early discounts on stock index futures: The case for disequilibrium, Financial Analysts Journal 40, July-Aug., 43–47.

Kobashi, Y., 1987, Profits through spreading, Working paper (Institutional Research and Advisory Department, The Nomura Securities Co., Ltd., Tokyo) June 1987.

MacKinlay, A. and K. Ramaswamy, 1988, Index futures arbitrage and the behavior of stock index futures prices, Review of Financial Studies 1, 137–158.

Merrick, J., 1987, Early unwindings and rollovers of stock index futures arbitrage programs: Analysis and implications for predicting expiration day effects, Working paper (New York University, New York).

Japanese Financial Market Research
W.T. Ziemba, W. Bailey and Y. Hamao (Editors)
1991 Elsevier Science Publishers B.V.

Arbitrage Opportunities in the Japanese Stock and Futures Markets

Menachem Brenner, Marti G. Subrahmanyam and Jun Uno

In their first two years, Japanese stock index futures contracts exhibited persistent departures from "fair" price, offering potentially profitable arbitrage opportunities. As the markets have matured and new contracts have been introduced, however, deviations from fair pricing have declined substantially. For the three active contracts based on Japanese stock indexes—the Nikkei Stock Average contracts traded on the Singapore International Monetary Exchange and the Osaka Securities Exchange and the Tokyo Stock Price Index contract traded on the Tokyo Stock Exchange—deviations are currently within the bounds implied by transaction costs.

Past deviations from fair price can be explained by relatively high transaction costs and by trading restrictions such as restraints on short selling and arbitrage activity by Japanese securities firms. Since late 1988, however, transaction costs have declined substantially and trading restrictions have been eased. The evidence in the Japanese markets lends support to the view that trading restrictions have an adverse impact on financial market efficiency.

STOCK INDEX FUTURES contracts, introduced in U.S. markets only in 1982, have become a significant factor in the U.S. investment arena, despite a decline in trading volume since the 1987 market crash. They are also becoming a major factor in exchanges outside the U.S.—in the United Kingdom, Australia, New Zealand, Hong Kong, Singapore, France, Sweden and, especially, Japan.

The Singapore International Monetary Exchange (SIMEX) introduced the first futures contract on a Japanese stock index—the Nikkei Stock Average (NSA)—on September 3, 1986. The first stock index futures contract traded in Japan, the Osaka Stock Futures 50 (OSF 50), started trading on the Osaka Securities Exchange (OSE) on June 9, 1987. Prior studies have documented the behavior of these two contracts and presented evidence of arbitrage and "cross-spreading" profits in their markets.[1] But the Japanese futures markets have witnessed major changes since September 1988, the end of the period covered by these studies.

On September 3, 1988, two new Japanese futures contracts started trading—an OSE-listed contract on the NSA, and a new contract based on the Tokyo Stock Price Index (TOPIX) and listed on the Tokyo Stock Exchange (TSE). Both have enjoyed good trading volume, while the OSF 50 has, for all practical purposes, "died." Furthermore, transaction costs have declined, and some trading restrictions have been eased since late 1988.

This article updates and summarizes the evidence of the behavior of Japanese stock index futures contracts in relation to their underlying indexes. In particular, we analyze the recent

Menachem Brenner is Professor of Finance at the Leonard N. Stern School of Business, New York University, and at Hebrew University, Jerusalem. Marti Subrahmanyam is Research Professor of Finance and Economics at the Stern School of Business, New York University. Jun Uno is with Nihon Keizai Shimbun Inc., New York and Tokyo.

1. Footnotes appear at end of article.

data to determine whether persistent departures from "fair" prices continue and, if so, whether they provide arbitrage opportunities after taking into account transaction costs and trading restrictions. We begin with an explanation of the "fair" pricing model for stock index futures contracts.

Pricing of Stock Index Contracts

A stock index futures contract can be priced by using the "replication principle." According to this, the "fair" price of a contract is related to the price of a portfolio that replicates its future payoffs.

The replicating portfolio of a stock index futures contract combines a position in a "basket" of stocks with a riskless asset. The fair price for an index futures contract equals the price of this basket (i.e., the underlying stock index) plus its "cost of carry." The cost of carry consists of the interest costs incurred by buying and holding the basket of stocks at the riskless interest rate, less the dividends received from the stocks in the index.

In the absence of transaction costs and restrictions on short sales, the fair price of a stock index futures contract can be written as:

$$FP_t = S_t \exp(r\tau) - D_t, \tag{1}$$

where

FP_t = the fair price of the stock index futures contract at the present time, t,
D_t = the compounded value of dividends received from time t to the expiration of the futures contract,
S_t = the spot index value at time t,
r = the riskless interest rate over the period from time t to the expiration date and
τ = the fraction of the year between t and the expiration date.

Transaction costs create a band around this fair price, within which arbitrage is not profitable.

Let c_t^+ represent the transaction costs (as a percentage of the spot index value at time t) incurred by buying the index and selling the futures contract at time t, then reversing these positions at the expiration date. Let c_t^- represent the percentage transaction costs incurred by selling the index and buying the futures contract, then reversing the positions at expiration. These transaction costs imply that it becomes profitable to execute a buy spot–sell futures transaction only if the actual futures price exceeds the fair value given in Equation (1) by more than the percentage c_t^+. And only if the futures price is *below* the spot price by more than the percentage c_t^- does the buy futures–sell spot arbitrage become viable. Transaction costs thus create a band with an upper bound of F_t^+ and a lower bound of F_t^-, within which there are no arbitrage opportunities.[2] These bounds are given by:

$$\begin{aligned} FP_t^+ &= [S_t(1 + c_t^+)] \exp[r\tau] - D_t, \\ FP_t^- &= [S_t(1 - c_t^-)] \exp[r\tau] - D_t. \end{aligned} \tag{2}$$

We have assumed that there are no taxes, or that profits and losses in the spot and futures transactions are taxed at the same tax rate (which is the case for those institutions most likely to engage in arbitrage activities).[3] Furthermore, the positions put on are assumed to be held to the expiration date of the futures contract.[4]

Data and Method

We examined the behavior of four Japanese stock index futures contracts—the NSA futures traded on the SIMEX (NSA-SIMEX); the OSF 50 futures traded on the OSE; the NSA futures traded on the OSE (NSA-OSE); and the TOPIX futures traded on the TSE. All these contracts are based on stock market indexes computed from the prices of common stocks listed on the First Section of the leading Japanese stock exchanges, the TSE in the case of the NSA and TOPIX and the OSE in the case of the OSF 50.

Table I lists the main features of the four futures contracts and their underlying indexes. The NSA is an arithmetic price average computed by adding the prices of the 225 component stocks and dividing by a divisor that changes over time to adjust for stock splits, rights issues, etc. The OSF 50 is also an arithmetic price average, but it includes only 50 of the NSA stocks. The TOPIX is a value-weighted index of *all* the common stocks listed on the First Section of the TSE (currently about 1150). All three stock indexes are announced at one-minute intervals during trading hours.

As is the case for the major stock index futures contracts in the U.S., such as the S&P 500 contract traded on the Chicago Mercantile Exchange, the settlement prices of the Japanese contracts are determined 15 minutes after the close of trading in the underlying stocks. Rather than the open outcry system used in the Chicago futures exchanges, however, the futures contracts in Japan are traded in computer-assisted auctions. The NSA-SIMEX contract, however, uses the open outcry system.

The NSA-SIMEX contract also trades continuously throughout the trading day, even though the underlying stocks do not trade in Osaka and Tokyo between 11 a.m. and 1 p.m. Tokyo time (10 a.m. and 12 noon Singapore time). The NSA-OSE contract, as well as the OSF 50 and TOPIX contracts, do not trade between 11 a.m. and 1 p.m. Tokyo time.

The OSF 50 contract is distinguished from the other contracts by its settlement procedure. Unlike most stock index futures contracts, the OSF 50 can be settled by physical delivery of the underlying securities, for all contracts open on the last trading day of the delivery month.[5]

Trading volume in the TOPIX and NSA-OSE contracts has been large from the outset, averaging about 20,000 contacts a day. The NSA-SIMEX contract trades about 4000 a day. In contrast, the OSF 50 contract, formerly quite active, has been "dead" since the introduction of the TOPIX and the NSA-OSE contracts, with only one or two contracts being traded each day. We thus omitted this contract from further study.

Transaction Costs

Transaction costs in the Japanese securities markets are nontrivial, hence play an important role in explaining the deviations of observed futures prices from "fair" prices. Arbitrage activity in the stock and futures markets involves the following costs:

(1) brokerage commissions charged for buying and selling stocks in the underlying index;
(2) the securities transfer tax paid when stocks are sold;
(3) the "market impact" costs involved in buying and selling the stocks in the underlying index;
(4) the commissions charged for selling and buying the futures contract;
(5) the "market impact" costs involved in selling and buying back the futures contract; and
(6) the cost of "borrowing" the underlying stocks when the stocks in the spot index are sold short.

Table II Transaction Costs for Stock Index Arbitrage in the Japanese Financial Markets, September 1986–September 1989*

	Brokers		*Investors*	
	Dec. 1986	*April 1989*	*Dec. 1986*	*April 1989*
Stocks				
Brokerage Commissions	0.01%	0.01%	0.14%	0.12%
Security Transfer Tax	0.18%	0.12%	0.55%	0.30%
Market Impact	0.40%	0.20%	0.40%	0.20%
Cost of Borrowing Stock for Short Sales	0.10%	0.10%	0.10%	0.10%
Futures				
Brokerage Commissions	0.04%	0.04%	0.04%	0.04%
Exchange Tax	–	–	–	–
Market Impact	0.30%	0.06%	0.30%	0.06%
Total Costs	1.03%	0.53%	1.53%	0.82%

* The transaction cost estimates refer to typical figures for the NSA-SIMEX in December 1986 and for the NSA-OSE in April 1989.

The brokerage commissions in the stock and futures markets, Items (1) and (4), do not require further explanation. The securities transfer tax, Item (2), is a common feature outside the United States. The market impact costs, Items (3) and (5), arise because a sizable transaction cannot be undertaken in the stock or futures market without changing prevailing market prices. For an arbitrageur who has to buy and sell simultaneously, the market impact will at a minimum reflect current bid-ask spreads in the respective markets; these will tend to be wider, the larger the transaction.[6] Item (6) covers the fee charged by another investor to "lend" the short-seller the underlying stock he does not own; the short-seller must be in possession of the stock when the transaction is initiated.

In the case of arbitrage strategies, whether these involve stock index arbitrage in the two futures markets or "cross-spreading" between the two markets, the transaction costs depend on whether the arbitrageur is a broker-dealer or an institutional investor. We concentrated on stock index arbitrage involving each futures contract and the stocks in the underlying index.

Table II details the transaction costs for stock index arbitrage in the futures markets that are currently active and the respective underlying stocks. Total transaction costs have declined somewhat since late 1988, and this decline is reflected in the pricing of the futures contracts.

Table I Main Features of Japanese Stock Index Futures Contracts

	TOPIX	*NSA-SIMEX*	*NSA-OSE*	*OSF 50*
1. Underlying Asset	Tokyo Stock Price Index of all common stocks (currently about 1150) on the First Section of the Tokyo Stock Exchange	Nikkei Stock Average of 225 stocks on the First Section of the Tokyo Stock Exchange	Same as NSA-SIMEX	Osaka Stock Futures 50 Package Portfolio of 50 stocks on the First Section of the Osaka Securities Exchange
2. Contract Size	TOPIX multiplied by 10,000	NSA multiplied by 500	NSA multiplied by 1000	OSF 50 multiplied by 50,000
3. Contract Months	March, June, September, December (five contract months open at a time)	March, June, September, December and spot (five contract months open at a time)	Same as TOPIX	Same as TOPIX
4. Last Day of Trading	The business day prior to the second Friday (or the preceding Thursday if the second Friday is a holiday)	The third Wednesday of the contract month (or the preceding business day if the third Wednesday is a holiday)	Same as TOPIX	Six business days prior to the settlement day
5. Settlement Date	The third business day following the second Friday (or the preceding Thursday if the second Friday is a holiday)	The next business day after the last day of trading	Same as TOPIX	Fifteenth of contract month (or the next business day if the fifteenth is a holiday)
6. Trading Hours	9:00 a.m.–11:15 a.m. 1:00 a.m.—3:15 p.m. (3:00 p.m. on last trading day) (only morning session on half-days)	8:00 a.m.–2:15 p.m. Singapore time (9:00 a.m.–3:15 p.m. Tokyo time) 8:00 a.m.–10:15 a.m. Singapore time on half-days (9:00 a.m.–11:15 a.m. Tokyo time)	Same as TOPIX	Same as TOPIX

7. Method of Trading	Computer-assisted auction	Open outcry	Computer-assisted auction	Computer-assisted auction
8. Tick Size	Y1 × 10,000 = Y10,000	Y5 × 500 = Y 2,500	Y10 × 1,000 = Y10,000	Y0.5 × 50,000 = Y25,000
9. Settlement Procedure	Cash settlement	Cash settlement	Cash settlement	Cash settlement or physical delivery
10. Price Limits	Approximately 3 per cent of the previous settlement price	10 per cent of the previous settlement price (or an expanded limit of 15%)	Same as TOPIX	Same as TOPIX
11. Margin	9 per cent of transaction value (Y 6 million minimum) as initial margin (3% as cash deposit); maintenance margin of 6% of transaction value	Y 1 million as initial margin; Y 850,000 as maintenance margin; Y 150,000 as spread initial margin; Y 75,000 as spread maintenance margin	Same as TOPIX	Same as TOPIX
12. Exchange Tax	None (to be decided)	None	None (to be decided)	0.0125 per cent of contract value
13. Commission	*Amount in Y Million* — *Commission* <Y 100 — 0.04% Y 100–Y 300 — 0.03% + Y10,000 Y 300–Y 500 — 0.07% + Y40,000 Y 500–Y1,000 — 0.01% + Y90,000 > Y1,000 — 0.05% + Y140,000	*No. of Contracts* — *Commission Per Contract* <10 — Y 3,750 11–50 — Y 2,500 51–150 — Y 1,000 >150 — Y 700	Same as TOPIX	Approximately 0.5 to 0.9 per cent of transaction value

Table III Percentage Price Changes of Japanese Stock Indexes and Index Futures

Contract		Spot Index		Futures			Number of Obs.
		NSA	*TOPIX*	*NSA-OSE*	*TOPIX*	*NSA-SIMEX*	
Dec. 1988	Avg.	0.116	0.117	0.096	0.101	0.097	64
	Max.	1.156	1.672	1.902	1.667	1.901	
	Min.	−1.295	−1.311	−0.951	−1.209	−0.967	
	Std.	0.557	0.579	0.443	0.513	0.459	
Mar. 1989	Avg.	0.130	0.113	0.119	0.096	0.086	61
	Max.	1.552	1.474	1.560	1.579	1.854	
	Min.	−0.971	−0.881	−0.910	−1.482	−0.902	
	Std.	0.493	0.504	0.441	0.566	0.441	
June 1989	Avg.	0.113	0.060	0.085	0.039	0.066	62
	Max.	2.520	2.459	1.126	1.392	1.140	
	Min.	−1.144	−1.097	−0.984	−1.416	−1.146	
	Std.	0.615	0.612	0.520	0.619	0.546	
Sept. 1989	Avg.	0.009	0.040	−0.001	0.041	0.014	66
	Max.	1.307	1.471	1.210	1.472	1.133	
	Min.	−1.467	−1.321	−1.331	−1.600	−1.388	
	Std.	0.511	0.497	0.497	0.596	0.514	
Total	Avg.	0.091	0.082	0.074	0.069	0.066	253
	Max.	2.520	2.459	1.902	1.667	1.901	
	Min.	−1.467	−1.321	−1.331	−1.600	−1.388	
	Std.	0.548	0.551	0.479	0.575	0.492	

Measuring Deviations from Fair Price

Deviations of actual futures prices from "fair" prices can be measured in two different ways. The mispricing can be expressed as a percentage deviation, given by:

$$M_t = (F_t - FP_t)/FP_t, \tag{3}$$

where M_t is the mispricing, expressed as the difference between the actual futures price, F_t, and the fair futures price, FP_t, as a percentage of the fair price.

To take transaction costs into account, we measured the mispricing in relation to the band created by transaction costs, given by Equation (2). If the fair futures price is 100 and transaction costs are about 1 per cent on either side, then the band is 99 to 101. If the actual futures price happened to be 103, the mispricing would amount to 1.98 per cent [(103 − 101)/101]—a premium. If the actual futures price were 98, the mispricing would be −1.01 per cent [(98 − 99)/99]—a discount.

Alternatively, the deviation of actual from fair prices can be measured in terms of the interest rate implied by the arbitrage. This is computed from the actual spot and futures prices, as follows:

$$R_t = 1/\tau[\ln \{F_t/[S_t - PV(D_t)]\}], \tag{4}$$

where $PV(D_t)$ is the present value at time t of the dividends paid between t and the expiration date.

If the implied interest rate is higher than the riskless interest rate ($R_t > r_t$), borrowing at the market interest rate and lending at the implied interest rate of the futures contract provides riskless profits without any investment. In other words, it would be profitable to buy the spot index and sell the futures contract, locking in an implied interest rate that exceeds the market interest rate. If the implied rate is less than the riskless rate ($R_t < r_t$), the implied rate of the futures contract is cheaper than the market rate. In this case, it would be profitable to buy the futures contract and sell the stocks in the index short, effectively borrowing at below-market interest rates. This measure is also computed after taking transaction costs into account.[7]

We used both measures to gauge the extent of mispricing in Japanese futures contracts. In making the computations, we used the following data: (1) the closing values of the NSA and TOPIX stock indexes; (2) the settlement prices for the NSA-SIMEX, NSA-OSE and TOPIX futures contracts; (3) the actual dividend streams on the stocks in the NSA and TOPIX indexes between the current date t and the expiration

Table IV Premiums and Discounts on Japanese Stock Index Futures Contracts, September 1988–August 1989

Contract	*Number Positive*	*Number Negative*	*Mean Positive (%)*	*Mean Negative (%)*	*Mean Absolute (%)*	*Mean Sqd. (%)*	*Number of Obs.*
Dec. 1988							
NSA-OSE	36	29	0.46	−0.41	0.44	0.27	65
TOPIX	39	26	0.43	−0.42	0.42	0.27	65
NSA-SIMEX	35	29	0.34	−0.52	0.42	0.27	64
Mar. 1989							
NSA-OSE	54	7	0.70	−0.24	0.65	0.56	61
TOPIX	59	2	0.95	−0.19	0.92	1.05	61
NSA-SIMEX	52	6	0.73	−0.17	0.67	0.58	58
June 1989							
NSA-OSE	36	26	0.60	−0.20	0.43	0.40	62
TOPIX	31	31	0.76	−0.26	0.51	0.53	62
NSA-SIMEX	32	26	0.54	−0.24	0.40	0.34	58
Sept. 1989							
NSA-OSE	37	29	0.38	−0.37	0.27	0.18	66
TOPIX	36	30	0.35	−0.40	0.27	0.20	66
NSA-SIMEX	35	29	0.35	−0.44	0.27	0.20	64
Total							
NSA-OSE	163	91	0.55	−0.33	0.43	0.35	254
TOPIX	165	89	0.66	−0.35	0.50	0.50	254
NSA-SIMEX	154	90	0.52	−0.39	0.42	0.34	244

date of the futures contract; and (4) the three-month Gensaki rate (a "repo" rate), used as the short-term riskless interest rate.[8]

Results

Table III presents summary statistics of the percentage price changes in the three active Japanese stock index contracts—the NSA-SIMEX, NSA-OSE and TOPIX contracts—and their underlying indexes from September 1988 to August 1989.

Note the volatilities of the price changes in the futures contracts relative to those of the underlying indexes. The volatilities of the NSA futures contracts, on both the SIMEX and the OSE, are lower than the volatility of the underlying index (on a daily basis for the whole period, 0.492 and 0.479 per cent, respectively,

Figure A Premiums and Discounts on NSA-OSE Futures

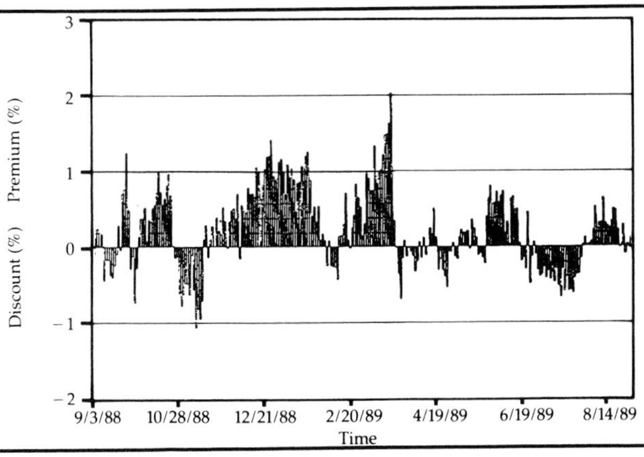

Figure B Premiums and Discounts on TOPIX Futures

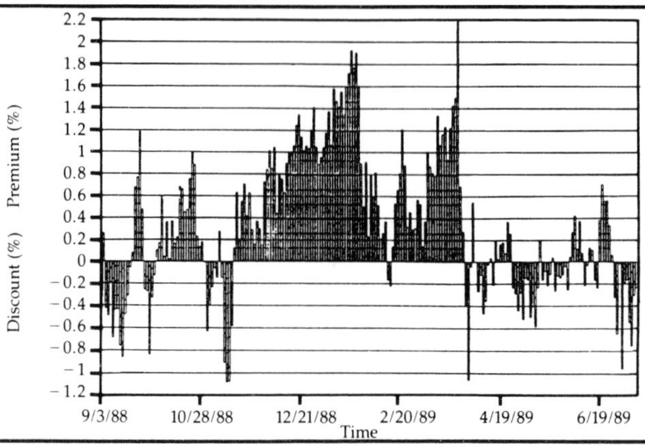

for the SIMEX and OSE contracts, compared with 0.548 per cent for the underlying index).[9] This behavior differs markedly from that of the major stock index futures contracts in the U.S., which are invariably more volatile than their underlying stock indexes.[10]

Table IV summarizes the mispricing in the Japanese contracts, as measured by the premiums and discounts for the four expiration dates during the study period—December 1988, March 1989, June 1989 and September 1989. Figures A and B illustrate the premiums and discounts on the NSA-OSE and TOPIX contracts since their inception in September 1988. Figure C provides similar information for the NSA-SIMEX contract over the period September 1988 to September 1989. Figures D, E and F show how the premiums and discounts change when transaction costs equal to 0.5 per cent of the level of the spot index are taken into account.

Several interesting observations emerge from these tables and figures. All three futures contracts exhibit remarkable similarity over time. In particular, the two NSA contracts—the NSA-OSE and the NSA-SIMEX—have a virtually identical pattern of premiums and discounts over time. All three contracts exhibit a secular decline in the size of the premiums and discounts, especially since April 1989.

In number and size, positive deviations (pre-

Figure C Premiums and Discounts on NSA-SIMEX Futures

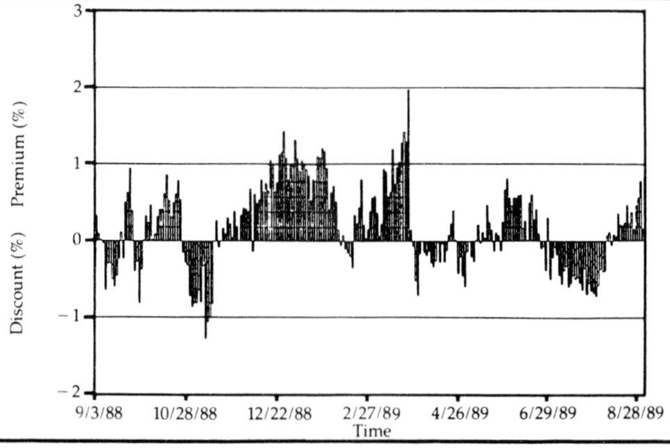

Figure D Premiums and Discounts on NSA-OSE Futures with 0.5% Transaction Costs

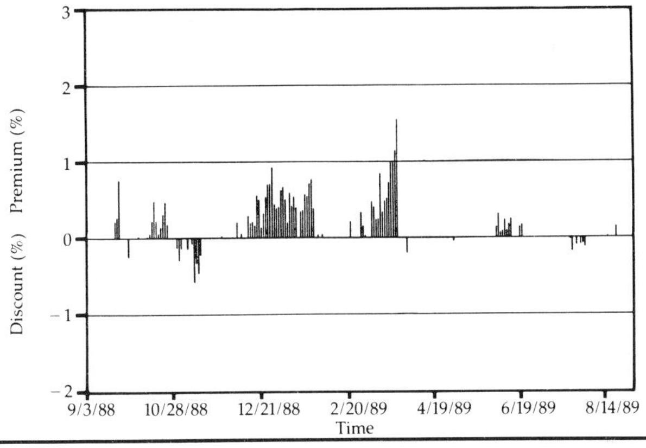

miums) are about 180 per cent of negative deviations. The NSA-OSE average premium, for example, is 0.55 per cent, while the average discount is −0.33 per cent. The mean absolute deviation is about 0.43 per cent for the two NSA contracts and about 0.50 per cent for the TOPIX contract (which is based on a broader index).

The deviations shrink in size after the March 1989 expiration. For the two NSA contracts, the mean absolute deviation for the September 1989 contract was 0.27 per cent, compared with an average of about 0.50 per cent for the previous three contracts. After taking into account a realistic transaction cost estimate of 0.5 per cent, we find that deviations in the post-March 1989 period disappear almost entirely (see Figures D, E and F). Several large deviations in February and March 1989 could be explained by changes in the institutional setting of the Japanese markets.

Some Exogenous Events

These observations can be related to some major events that affected the Japanese stock index futures markets in general and index arbitrage activity in particular during the study period. In early December 1988, arbitrage activity by the major Japanese securities firms de-

Figure E Premiums and Discounts on TOPIX Futures with 0.5% Transaction Costs

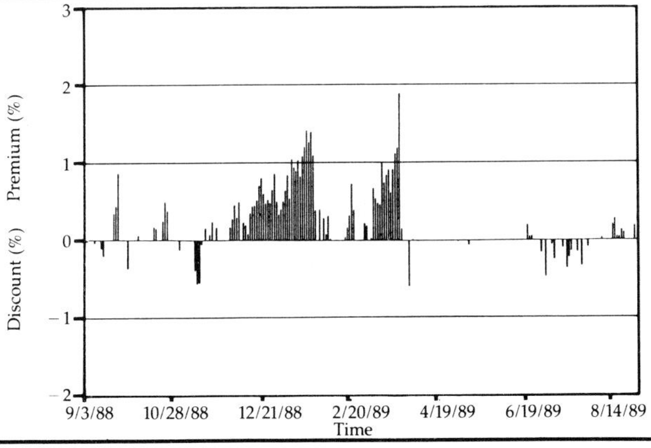

Figure F Premiums and Discounts on NSA-SIMEX Futures with 0.5% Transaction Costs

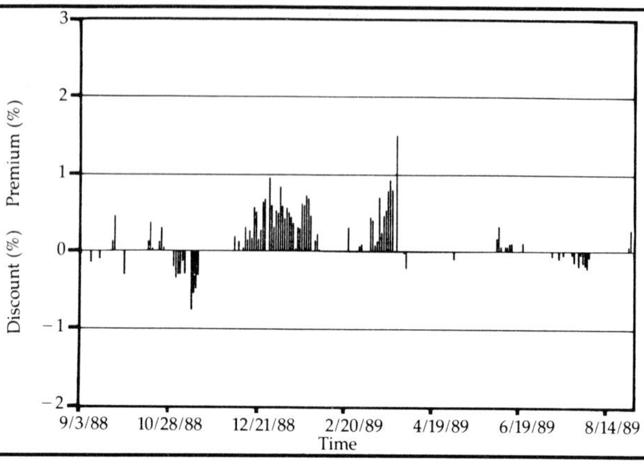

clined, mainly because of an investigation by the Japanese Ministry of Finance (MOF) and the securities firms' fear of violating insider trading rules. At the same time, Japanese institutional investors were holding back because of high commission costs. Most of the index arbitrage activity was thus being carried out by foreign investment banks and securities firms.

The low level of arbitrage activity continued until the March 1989 expiration, with many institutions simply rolling over existing positions. In January 1989, however, the Japanese securities industry submitted a reform plan for arbitrage trading to the MOF. The plan called for easing the rules on arbitrage trading by securities firms (e.g., short-selling constraints, trading at new prices and trading in stocks that are being underwritten), in exchange for ending arbitrage activity 30 minutes before the close of the underlying stock markets. This plan was accepted, and arbitrage activity received another boost in April 1989, when the securities transfer tax was reduced and restraints on arbitrage activity were relaxed.

Figures G, H and I illustrate deviations from fair price as measured by the implied interest rate. These show a similar pattern—smaller deviations from the Gensaki rate (the riskless

Figure G Implied Interest Rate, NSA-OSE Futures

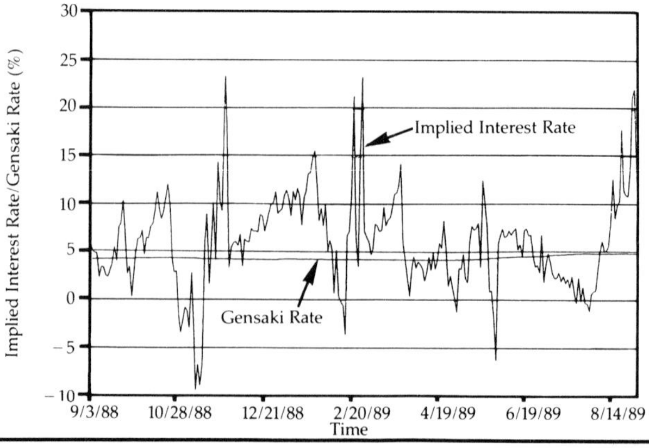

Figure H Implied Interest Rate, TOPIX Futures

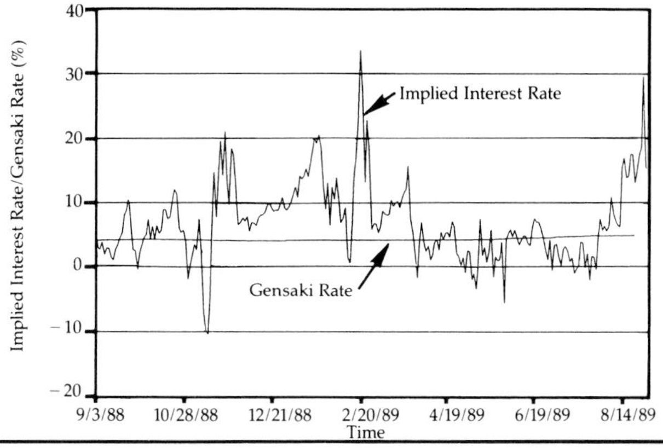

interest rate), explained mostly by changes in regulation and reduced transaction costs. These changes have contributed to increased arbitrage activity and, as a consequence, a reduction in the size of the premiums and discounts on Japanese futures contracts.

Contrast with Earlier Period

These recent results, including the relatively large deviations in the March contract, contrast sharply with the experience in the first two years of trading in Japanese futures contracts.[11] From September 1986 to September 1988, the NSA-SIMEX contract was dominated by large negative deviations. The mean negative deviation in the first nine months of trading, September 1986 to June 1987, was about −1.4 per cent, compared with −0.39 per cent during the September 1988 to September 1989 period. Even after taking into account transaction costs of 1 per cent, we still find a mean deviation for 1986–88 of −1.2 per cent.

The OSF 50 contract, introduced in June 1987 and active until September 1988, exhibited large deviations that were more positive than negative. The mean deviation during the period was 0.99 per cent, compared with a mean deviation of 0.55 per cent for the NSA-OSE contract in the

Figure I Implied Interest Rates, NSA-SIMEX Futures

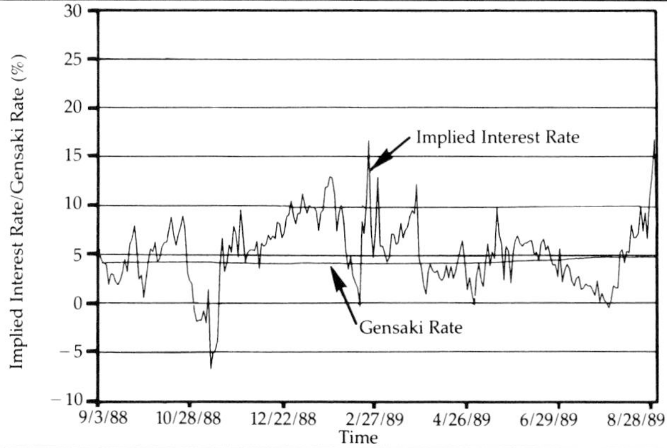

September 1988 to September 1989 period. Many of the OSF 50's deviations did not disappear, even after reasonable transaction costs were taken into account.

The preponderance of positive deviations in the OSF 50 contract and negative deviations in the NSA-SIMEX contract formed the basis of the cross-spreading profits documented in earlier research. It should be noted, however, that a downward trend in the size of these deviations, evident in early 1988, increased after the introduction of the two new futures contracts in September 1988.

In their first two years, then, Japanese futures contracts exhibited persistent departures from their fair prices. As the markets matured, these deviations, which are indicative of arbitrage opportunities, declined substantially. For the three currently active contracts based on Japanese stock indexes—the NSA contracts on the SIMEX and the OSE and the TOPIX contract on the TSE—the deviations are currently within the bounds implied by transaction costs. ■

Footnotes

1. M. Brenner, M. G. Subrahmanyam and J. Uno, "The Behavior of Prices in the Nikkei Spot and Futures Markets," *Journal of Financial Economics*, August 1989, and M. Brenner, M. G. Subrahmanyam and J. Uno, "Stock Index Futures Arbitrage in the Japanese Markets," *Japan and the World Economy*, June 1989. The first study relates to arbitrage opportunities in the NSA-SIMEX contract. The second examines the profitability of "cross-spreading" strategies—i.e., strategies involving positions in both the NSA-SIMEX and OSF 50 contracts.
2. In addition to the incremental transaction costs of selling short due to the cost of borrowing stock, there are for many investors restrictions on selling stocks short. In the presence of such restrictions, the traders who may be able to execute the buy futures–sell stock strategy are those who already hold the stocks in their portfolio, such as banks, insurance companies and mutual funds. To the extent that these financial institutions have higher transaction costs than broker-dealers (as in Japan), the lower bound of the transaction cost band may be pushed down. However, there is an offsetting effect to the extent that they save on one item of transaction costs—the cost of selling short.
3. For individual investors, the capital gains tax rate in Japan is practically zero. For financial institutions and brokers, who are the most likely arbitrageurs, the tax rates on income and capital gains are identical.
4. In some cases, it may be profitable to "unwind" the position early, or roll it over into the next contract. The option to unwind may make it profitable to execute an arbitrage trade even within the transaction-cost bounds. (See J. Merrick, "Early Unwindings and Rollovers of Stock Index Futures Arbitrage Programs" (Working paper, New York University, 1987) and M. J. Brennan and E. S. Schwartz, "Arbitrage in Stock Index Futures," *Journal of Business*, 1989.) Our analysis of arbitrage opportunities is therefore conservative, since the profits may be higher than we compute when the option to unwind is taken into account.
5. The reason for this feature is that when this contract was introduced, the Japanese legal system did not permit cash-settled futures contracts.
6. For a trader with an existing long position, the market impact for stocks would be, on average, only half the bid-ask spread. Hence the estimates here are on the conservative side.
7. See Brenner, Subrahmanyam and Uno, "The Behavior of Prices," *op. cit.*, for details.
8. As discussed in previous studies, the differences between using the three-month rate and the interpolated rate for the actual maturity behavior between the current date and the expiration date are trivial.
9. The behavior of the TOPIX contract did not show any clear-cut pattern.
10. See, for example, A. MacKinlay and K. Ramaswamy, "Index Futures Arbitrage and the Behavior of Stock Index Futures Prices," *Review of Financial Studies*, Summer 1988.
11. See footnote 1.

Japanese Financial Market Research
W.T. Ziemba, W. Bailey and Y. Hamao (Editors)

An Introduction to Japanese Stock Index Options

Warren Bailey and William T. Ziemba [1]

Johnson Graduate School of Management, Cornell University, Ithaca, NY 14853, U.S.A.

Faculty of Commerce, University of British Columbia, Vancouver, BC, Canada V6T 1W5

Abstract

We survey emerging markets for option and warrant contracts based on Japanese stock indexes. Existing organized and over-the-counter markets are described and the use of a simple option pricing model to estimate Japanese index option prices is demonstrated. We discuss a number of factors which may necessitate the use of more complex option pricing models to value Japanese index option products and design risk management strategies which employ them.

1. Introduction

From humble beginnings in little noticed over-the-counter markets, option and warrant trading has grown enormously in size and importance in the last twenty years. The risk management potential these securities offer has drawn great attention from markets increasingly characterized by large professional investors and institutions. There has been a corresponding increase in applied and academic research on the subject of options markets. The models of Black and Scholes (1973), Merton (1973), and Cox, Ross, and Rubinstein (1979), for example, are widely used both to value option contracts and to design risk management strategies involving options.

Japanese securities markets were slow in developing derivative instruments such as futures and options based on stock market indices or on the value of individual stocks. The futures markets are now in full bloom and expanding rapidly. There are three index futures contracts currently traded in Japan, one in Singapore, and two in

[1]This research was partially supported by the Social Sciences and Humanities Research Council of Canada and the Centre for International Business Research at the University of British Columbia.

the U.S.A. These contracts have large trading units, hence the vast bulk of trading is institutional. Option contracts have begun trading within the last two years. They provide additional investment, hedging, and risk management opportunities, as well as the possibility of more trading by individuals since the contract sizes are typically smaller than the corresponding futures contracts.

Three index options contracts began trading in 1989. The options are based on the TOPIX, the Nikkei 225, and a new twenty-five share index designed to track both the TOPIX and the Nikkei but with a tilt towards the future growth of the economy. Options on this new twenty five share index are traded on the Nagoya Stock Exchange. Japanese index warrants began trading on North American stock exchanges in 1989 while three U.S. options markets initiated Japanese index option trading in 1990.

As in more mature markets, Japanese index option markets offer both put and call options. Call options permit the owner to purchase shares at a prespecified price during the life of the option contract while put options offer the right to sell shares at a prespecified price. Index options have traded in the U.S.A. for close to a decade and are among the most popular securities, as measured by trading volume. The Standard and Poor's 100 Index options traded on the Chicago Board Options Exchange, for example, is typically the most heavily traded of all U.S. listed option contracts.

The size, volatility, and growth of the Japanese equity market and the success of U.S. index options bode well for the Japanese index option markets. The investment community is confronted with such problems as understanding the new Japanese markets, applying well-known option models to Japanese index option valuation and hedging problems, and considering the relevance of recent advances in our understanding of options for these markets. We offer a brief introduction to each of these topics in this paper. Section 2 discusses the existing markets for Japanese index option products. Section 3 discusses and applies the Black and Scholes model to the Nikkei 225 options market. Section 4 introduces several advanced issues in option pricing and discusses their relevance for Japanese index options markets. Section 5 is a summary and conclusion.

2. Details of Japanese Index Option Contracts

In this section, we list and briefly describe the Japanese stock index options and warrants which are currently available.

2.1 Over-The-Counter Options

The first options on Japanese indices were sold not on organized exchanges but in an informal over-the-counter market run largely by large U.S. investment banking and brokerage firms. Trading activity commenced in 1988. Subsidiaries of the big four Japanese brokerage firms are also marketing such puts and calls, mainly in Europe.

A typical offering is a European style put on the Nikkei 225 with a three year expiry. The buyers are usually investors who believe the Japanese market is likely to crash or portfolio managers who use them essentially as portfolio insurance. In 1988 and 1989, sellers were typically Japanese companies who were bullish on the Tokyo market. They were happy to pocket the money from selling such options, believing it likely that the Nikkei index would be higher, not lower, in three years and that the options would expire worthless. However, recent large declines in the Japanese market have resulted in losses for unhedged put option writers. Since the options are European, only the value at the end of three years matters; transitory downturns in the index do not affect the terminal payoff.

Not all the options sold have long expirations. The big four Japanese firms have been selling American style options over horizons as short as a month, and with strike prices that put the options only slightly out-of-the-money. At times, it appears that the options have been sold for rather large premiums. This implies that the Japanese market is perceived to be very risky or, alternatively, that there remain considerable economic rents to be earned by the sopisticated players making markets in these options.

2.2 Nikkei 225 Put and Call Warrants

The concept of long maturity options on Japanese stock indexes has been extended to organized securities markets. Nikkei put warrants began to trade on the Toronto Stock Exchange in February 1989. The BT Bank of Canada, a subsidiary of Banker's Trust of New York, pioneered the listing of such options. American style Nikkei put warrants have also been listed on the American Stock Exchange by Salomon Inc., Banker's Trust of New York, the Kingdom of Denmark, and Paine Weber while the Trilon Group, SEK, and the BT Bank of Canada have listed additional issues on the Toronto exchange. Similar issues have been proposed for European securities exchanges. Nikkei call warrants created by Salomon and Paine Weber began trading in 1990. Nikkei warrant products have, at times, been the most heavily traded securities listed on the American Stock Exchange. [2]

These options offer the advantage of a liquid, competitive marketplace, unlike similar over-the-counter options. The warrants are small enough to appeal to a variety of investors. For example, the Banker's Trust put listed on the American Stock Exchange typically trades in lots of one hundred and each index point is worth one-half yen. Therefore, a difference of one index point between the Nikkei index level and the strike price is worth 50 yen per lot of one hundred warrants.

Given that the options trade in North America, there is exchange rate risk in that transactions are in U.S. or Canadian dollars but the underlying asset is denominated in yen. Furthermore, some of the contracts have an element of exchange rate risk built into the exercise price. Consider, for example, the BT Nikkei Put Warrant II issued on June 15th 1989 and expiring on June 15th 1992. If the option is exercised at expiration, it is settled in cash. Thus, the owner gains by the difference between the Canadian dollar exercise price and the Canadian dollar value of the Nikkei index.

[2]See Ziemba and Schwartz (1991) for details.

However, the Canadian dollar value of the Nikkei index is computed using the exchange rate prevailing on June 15th 1989. Thus, the option holder may gain or lose due not only to moves in the Nikkei index but due to changes in the exchange rate as well.

Given both OTC and listed long-maturity put markets, an interesting complex of broadly similar Nikkei puts trades in London, Toronto, and New York. The degree to which prices have been consistent and arbitrage-free across markets represents an interesting issue for both academics and investors. Shaw, Thorp, and Ziemba (1990) describe the markets and present empirical evidence.

2.3 Nikkei 225 Options

The Osaka Securities Exchange (OSE) introduced American style put and call options on the price-weighted Nikkei 225 index on June 12, 1989. American style options offer the flexibility of exercise at any time during the option life, as opposed to European style options which can be exercised only at the time they expire. [3] The Nikkei 225 options expire on the tenth day of the expiration month. There are four contract months and five different strike prices available in a given month, with strike prices differing by 500 yen. Each option is worth 1000 times its price quoted in index points. On June 12, 1989, for example, the Nikkei index closed at 33,398.01 and a July call with an exercise price of 33,000 sold for 895. The option's actual purchase price was 895 times 1000, or 895,000 yen. If exercised immediately, the owner would have received 1000 times the difference between the Nikkei index and the strike price, $(33,398.01 - 33,000) \times 1000$ or 398,010 yen. The option sells at a premium to its immediate exercise value because it is worth more than its immediate exercise payoff.

As is typical of options trading in all markets, most of the volume has concentrated in short maturity options with strike prices near the current value of the Nikkei index. See Baring Securities (1990) for a discussion. As has been the case for futures contracts, Nikkei 225 options trading has now expanded overseas. On September 25th 1990, the Chicago Mercantile Exchange (CME) inaugurated index option trading based on the Nikkei 225.

2.4 TOPIX Options

The Tokyo Securities Exchange (TSE) launched its options on the TOPIX index on October 20th 1989. The value of the contract is 10,000 yen per index point, yielding exercise prices of about twenty million yen given current levels of the index. American style options with expirations of one, two, three, and four months are available. Each month has five strike prices, staggered in fifty yen increments about the current level of the index. These options offer the opportunity to trade on an index which represents a broader selection of TSE listed shares than the Nikkei 225, since the TOPIX includes all of the approximately 1200 companies listed on the

[3] Strictly speaking, the Nikkei options can be exercised only once a week, rather than at any time as is the case for true American options. The difference in value is likely to be insignificant. See Geske and Johnson (1984).

first section of the Tokyo exchange. Although the price-weighted Nikkei 225 includes the largest companies, the value-weighted TOPIX has a larger total capitalization. In an effort to compete with the inauguration of Nikkei 225 option trading by their cross-town rival CME, the Chicago Board of Trade (CBT) has recently listed TOPIX futures and option products.

2.5 Nagoya's Option 25 Contract

Starting in October 1989, the Nagoya Stock Exchange has offered both European puts and calls based on the value of a price-weighted index of twenty five large capitalization shares which are listed on the first sections of the Tokyo, Osaka, and Nagoya exchanges. The component shares are diversified over many industrial classifications but have a tilt towards industries which are likely to experience growth and increasing importance in the future. The index consists of shares from twenty industrial sectors and includes such companies as Toray Industries, Kajima, Matsushita Electric, Toyota Motor, and NTT. Each company has a total market value of at least 200 billion yen, at least 300 million outstanding shares, and trading volume of at least 300 million shares in 1988 and one billion shares over the three year period from 1986 to 1988.

In computing the index, the prices of the twenty five stocks are normalized to have an initial value of fifty yen per share on January 4th 1988. The index at any time is computed as follows:

$$I_t = 1000 \times \frac{\sum_{i=1}^{25} \frac{P_{i,t}}{b_i}}{A \sum_{i=1}^{25} \frac{P_{i,0}}{b_i}} \tag{1}$$

where $P_{i,0}$ is the price of the ith stock on January 4th, 1988, $P_{i,t}$ is the price of the ith stock at time t, b_i is the divisor which normalizes $P_{i,0}$ to 50 yen, and A is a factor to adjust for rights offerings. The value of A was set to unity on January 4th, 1988.

The index, known as the Option 25, has been found to be slightly more volatile than the Nikkei 225 and TOPIX indices. For example, daily returns in the year 1988 had a standard deviation of 13.74% for the TOPIX, 12.68% for the Nikkei 225, and 16.88% for the Option 25. Given that the Option 25 is very highly correlated with the TOPIX and the Nikkei, its higher volatility implies that it has a higher beta with respect to the other indices and tends to move more severely than the TOPIX or the Nikkei 225.

2.6 Japan Index Options

On September 27th 1990, the American Stock Exchange (AMEX) began trading cash-settled European options on the Japan Index. This index of 210 stocks was designed by the AMEX to correspond closely to the Nikkei 225 and is reported to have a correlation of 99% with changes in the Nikkei. The fifteen excluded stocks are thinly traded shares so that the 210 index is easier to trade and more difficult to manipulate. Furthermore, the index is scaled so that its value at any point in time equals approximately $\frac{1}{100}$th of the value of the Nikkei 225. In addition to the usual range of short maturity options, maturities of two or more years (in six month intervals) can also be traded.

An interesting feature of the Japan Index option contract is that it is free of yen/dollar exchange rate risk. Suppose, for example, that the yen prices of the 210 component shares imply a value of 240 for the Japan Index and an investor is considering exercising a call option with a strike price of 235. The payoff to exercise would be \$500, that is, the difference between the index value and the strike price multiplied by \$100. Thus, Japan Index options will be particularly useful in managing Japanese equity portfolios which have already been hedged against yen/dollar exchange rate risk with forwards, futures, or yen denominated borrowing. [4]

3. Valuation of Index Options

3.1 The Black and Scholes Model

Many models for the valuation of option contracts have appeared in the last thirty years but the models derived by Black and Scholes (1973), Merton (1973), and Cox, Ross, and Rubinstein (1979) have gained the widest acceptance in the investments industry because of their usefulness and the relative ease with which they can be implemented. The Black and Scholes model is based on the assumption that a stock's price follows a diffusion process akin to the Brownian motion concept of physics. A second important aspect of the model is based in economics: in an arbitrage free asset market, securities with identical characteristics sell for identical prices.

The basic formula for the value of a call option in the Black and Scholes environment is:

$$C = SN\{d_1\} - Xe^{-r\tau}N\{d_2\} \tag{2}$$

where the current value of the underlying asset is represented by S, X is the option strike price, r is the riskless interest rate, and τ is the time, in years, until the option expires. The function $N\{\cdot\}$ is the standard cumulative normal distribution while its arguments are defined as follows:

$$d_1 = \frac{\ln \frac{S}{Xe^{-r\tau}}}{\sigma\sqrt{\tau}} + \frac{1}{2}\sigma\sqrt{\tau} \tag{3}$$

$$d_2 = d_1 - \sigma\sqrt{\tau}. \tag{4}$$

The parameter σ is the annualized standard deviation of log differences in S, that is, the rate of return on S. An analogous formula is available for put options:

$$P = Xe^{-r\tau}N\{-d_2\} - SN\{-d_1\}. \tag{5}$$

[4]See Bailey, Ng, and Stulz (1990) for discussion and evidence on hedging the yen/dollar exchange rate exposure of Japanese equity portfolios.

These formulas were derived in a no arbitrage economy: if a portfolio of the underlying asset and riskless debt can mimic the payoff on the option perfectly, then the value of the option must equal the value of the portfolio. By knowing the portfolio of stocks and riskless debt which exactly mimics the value of an option, we know the value of the option must equal the known value of the mimicing portfolio.

Given that the underlying asset in this case, the Nikkei 225 basket of stocks, pays a dividend, the model is adjusted following Jarrow and Rudd (1983). The Nikkei basket pays a dividend of δ per year. [5] If received in perpetuity, the value of the dividend stream is $\frac{\delta}{r}$. If received only for the life, τ, of the option contract, the value is $\frac{\delta}{r}(1-e^{-r\tau})$. Therefore, we replace S in equations 2, 3, and 5 with $S-\frac{\delta}{r}(1-e^{-r\tau})$. The intuition behind the adjustment is that the present value of the cost of purchasing the Nikkei 225 and holding it for the life of an option contract is the value of the Nikkei 225 minus the value of the dividends received. It is this net cost of buying and holding the Nikkei basket which, in turn, helps us determine the cost of the portfolio which mimics the value of an option and, thus, the value of the option.

Empirical evidence on these type of models is encouraging. It appears that the Black and Scholes model (and its variations) offer reasonably accurate prices: prices computed with the formula are usually close to prices generated by the market. See Rubinstein (1985) and Geske and Trautmann (1986) for a summary of evidence.

3.2 Implementing the Model

Much of the data needed to apply the Black and Scholes model to the pricing of Nikkei 225 options is readily available. The level of the Nikkei 225 index is available from numerous sources while the option strike price and time to expiration are known. The Black and Scholes model requires an estimate of the riskless interest rate spanning the same maturity as the option's expiration. Unlike the U.S. or Canada, a variety of maturities of heavily-traded government securities is not available in Japan. However, yields on short maturity Gensaki (repo) contracts or three month Euroyen deposits can be used. Given that dividends on the stocks underlying the index are very predictable, we use published figures for an estimate of δ. Strictly speaking, there is some risk that estimated dividends will not equal actual dividends, though the amount of dividends involved with Japanese stocks is so small (less than $\frac{1}{2}$% per year on average) as to render this problem trivial.

The only value which is difficult to estimate is the volatility parameter, σ. One approach is to obtain an historical series of returns on the Nikkei index, compute their standard deviation, and annualize appropriately. [6] This approach requires some judgement, since there are a variety of return intervals (daily, weekly, monthly) and

[5] δ equals about 150 yen for the time period we study. Merton (1973) presents a model with a dividend *yield* but we prefer, in the case of the Nikkei 225, to work with the dividend *amount* since it has been more stable and predictable.

[6] For example, if we compute the standard deviation of weekly Nikkei returns, we recognize that a week represents $\frac{1}{52}$nd of a year and multiply the standard deviation by $\sqrt{52}$ to obtain the estimate of σ to input to the Black and Scholes formula.

time periods (six months, one year, five years) over which the standard deviation can be computed. Furthermore, historical standard deviation estimates do not necessarily represent an estimate of the expected future volatility of the index, which is what the Black and Scholes formula requires. Typically, the historical standard deviation will be updated by the investor to reflect current and expected market conditions.

Another approach to estimating the volatility is the implied standard deviation. In this approach, we estimate σ for a given day using the option values for the previous day. Given yesterday's price for a particular option, we substitute all the information needed by the Black and Scholes formula, except for σ. We then subsitute various estimated values of σ into the Black and Scholes formula until we find the value which equates the Black and Scholes estimated price to the actual price observed in the newspaper. The advantage of this approach is that is provides an up-to-date estimate based on the most recent market prices which, presumably, are formed by expert investors with a good sense for what the volatility is. On the other hand, this method assumes the Black and Scholes formula is correct and tends to adapt to the model's errors. Therefore, we cannot use the implied standard deviation to test the Black and Scholes model, though we can use it for the day-to-day purpose of estimating reasonable prices for options.

Once the parameters of the model have been obtained, computations are straightforward. The normal distribution function, $N\{\cdot\}$, can be approximated with a simple polynomial so that all calculcations can be performed with a spread sheet program or even with pencil and paper. [7]

3.3 Application to the Osaka Nikkei 225 options

In this section, we perform a brief test of the ability of the Black and Scholes model to match actual market prices of Nikkei 225 puts and calls. We use closing quotes for all puts and calls traded from the inception of the market on June 12th 1989 to October 5th 1989. To estimate the riskless interest rate, we use the three month Euroyen ask rate. [8] Weekly returns on the Nikkei 225 index from June 12th 1988 through June 11th 1989 were used to compute an estimate of the volatility parameter, σ, of 10.34%. The test consists of computing a Black and Scholes price for each actual closing price in the sample, then seeing how close the model prices come to the actual prices.

Table 1 presents the results. Across all call options, the average pricing error is about 16 yen and the average absolute pricing error is about 60 yen. Given an average call price of about 500 yen, this implies average errors of about 3% and average absolute errors of about 11%. Across all put options, the average pricing error is about 31 yen and the average absolute pricing error is about 69 yen. Given an average put price of about 360 yen, this implies average errors of about 9% and

[7] Jarrow and Rudd (1983) provide the formula for a polynomial to approximate the normal distribution function. Many finance texts include tables which estimate the function.

[8] We repeated the tests using three month Gensaki rates and obtained virtually identical results.

average absolute errors of about 20%. The table also indicates that errors tend to increase with deeper in-the-money, longer lived, or lightly traded options. This is broadly consistent with the evidence from U.S. options markets. The degree to which these errors are deemed large or small depends on the level of transactions costs, taxes, and other imperfections in the market.

Table 1. Mean and Standard Deviation of Difference Between Nikkei 225 Option Price and Black Scholes Estimated Price[a]

	Calls			Puts		
	N^b	Difference	Absolute Value	N	Difference	Absolute Value
All	512	15.8	60.1	498	31.3	69.1
		(87.9)	(66.0)		(87.7)	(62.3)
$S-X<-500^b$	153	23.8	44.6	105	31.6	88.7
		(75.8)	(65.6)		(115.4)	(79.9)
$-500<S-X<500$	229	19.6	59.5	220	27.0	78.5
		(86.3)	(55.4)		(93.5)	(57.3)
$S-X>500$	130	-0.3	79.4	173	36.5	45.2
		(101.6)	(63.0)		(54.5)	(47.5)
$\tau<\frac{1}{12}^c$	380	9.5	49.1	387	22.2	59.2
		(71.7)	(53.0)		(77.2)	(54.3)
$\frac{1}{12}<\tau<\frac{2}{12}$	124	22.2	83.9	99	50.8	93.1
		(111.9)	(77.0)		(104.3)	(68.8)
$\tau>\frac{1}{12}$	8	213.3	213.3	12	162.9	190.7
		(133.7)	(133.7)		(126.1)	(71.9)
volume< 1000	229	25.6	76.5	242	56.3	82.5
		(107.6)	(79.8)		(95.6)	(74.0)
$1000<volume<5000$	96	32.6	53.4	88	14.0	50.7
		(67.8)	(52.7)		(68.3)	(47.6)
$5000<volume<10000$	79	-0.4	34.4	85	17.3	51.3
		(49.2)	(34.9)		(66.4)	(45.4)
10000 <volume	108	-8.2	50.1	83	-8.9	67.7
		(71.8)	(51.8)		(78.9)	(40.9)

Standard deviation of difference is reported in parentheses beneath each mean difference. [a] Time period is 12th June 1989 through 5th October 1989. Volatility parameter, σ, is estimated at 10.34%. Three month Euroyen ask is used to proxy for the riskless interest rate. Following Jarrow and Rudd (1983), dividend flow of 150 yen per year is discounted from the index price. Errors are reported in index points, each of which is worth 1000 yen. Closing option prices and all other data are supplied by the Yamaichi Research Institute. Average option price in the sample is 512.9 for calls and 362.7 for puts.

[b] S-X is the difference between the Nikkei index and the option exercise price.

[c] τ is time, in years, until option expires.

4. Beyond the Black and Scholes Model

There are several factors which the Black and Scholes model does not account for that are included in more complex models. We briefly survey the relevant literature and discuss the potential importance of each factor for Japanese stock index options.

4.1 Early Exercise of American-Style Options

Most of the options on Japanese indexes are of the American type which can be exercised at any time during its life. The Black and Scholes model does not include the American feature, so in effect we assume that the American feature has no value when we use the Black and Scholes model on American style options. In some cases the American feature is worthless. Merton (1973) proves that an American call will never be exercised early if the dividend yield on the underlying asset is less than the riskless interest rate. The intuition is that one can earn the rate of interest on the exercise price so why give up the exercise price to receive a stock paying a lower yield. However, this argument never holds for American puts: regardless of the size, if any, of the underlying asset dividend yield, there is always a possibility that it will be optimal to exercise an American put early. Therefore, the American feature has positive value and must be considered as part of the value of the put.

Cox, Ross, and Rubinstein (1979) and Geske and Johnson (1984) discuss techniques for computing the value of the American put. Unlike the European put, there is no simple formula for the American put so that values must be computed with numerical techniques or approximations. To determine whether the American feature is a significant part of the value of Nikkei 225 puts, we repeat the empirical tests of Section 3 using an American, instead of European, put model. Results are presented in Table 2 and should be compared to the European put pricing results in Table 1. In most cases, there is little difference between the average errors and average absolute errors of the two models, suggesting that the American feature is of little incremental value. Interestingly, the biggest differences occur for long maturity puts, where the American model gives an average reduction of about 41 yen for the error and 24 yen for the absolute error. This suggests, quite reasonably, that the American feature is important only for longer-maturity puts.

Table 2. Mean (Standard Deviation) of Difference Between Nikkei 225 Put Price and American Put Model Estimated Price[a]

	N^b	Difference	Absolute Value
All	498	26.2	71.2
		(108.9)	(86.4)
$S - X < -500^b$	105	-2.8	82.1
		(112.8)	(77.1)
$-500 < S - X < 500$	220	21.5	77.2
		(91.7)	(53.6)
$S - X > 500$	173	49.6	57.0
		(121.4)	(118.1)
$\tau < \frac{1}{12}^c$	387	21.5	63.4
		(106.8)	(88.6)
$\frac{1}{12} < \tau < \frac{2}{12}$	99	33.1	90.4
		(109.5)	(69.7)
$\tau > \frac{1}{12}$	12	121.5	167.8
		(131.6)	(52.1)

[a] Time period is 12th June 1989 through 5th October 1989. Standard deviation, σ, is estimated at 10.34%. Three month Euroyen ask is used to proxy for the riskless interest rate. The model used is the binomial model of Cox, Ross, and Rubinstein (1979) implemented with 180 steps per year and a dividend of 150 yen per year. Errors are reported in index points, each of which is worth 1000 yen. Closing option prices and all other data are supplied by the Yamaichi Research Institute. Average put price in the sample is 362.7.

[b] S-X is the difference between the Nikkei 225 index and the option exercise price.

[c] τ is time, in years, until put expires.

4.2 Stochastic Interest Rates

The Black and Scholes model assumes that the riskless interest rate, r, is nonstochastic over the life of the option. There is much theoretical work to suggest that the relaxation of this assumption can yield substantially different option prices. Merton (1973) presents a variation on the Black and Scholes model in which the price of a zero coupon bond (with the same maturity as the option's expiration) is stochastic. The size of the zero coupon bond's volatility and the covariance between changes in the bond price and changes in the stock price can have a significant effect on the option value. Ramaswamy and Sundaresan (1985) adapt the stochastic interest rate model of Cox, Ingersoll, and Ross (1985) to the Black and Scholes environment and find substantially different option values.

There is also a small body of empirical evidence to suggest that the nonstochastic interest rate assumption of Black and Scholes may fit reality poorly. Dietrich-Campbell and Schwartz (1986) and Bailey (1987) present empirical evidence indicating that models which include a stochastic interest rate predict actual option prices (in certain markets) better than the Black and Scholes model.

Given the weight of theoretical and empirical evidence, it may be useful to see if stochastic interest rates have an effect on the pricing of Japanese index contingent claims. Bailey (1989) applied the Ramaswamy and Sundaresan (1985) model to the valuation of Nikkei 225 and Osaka Stock 50 futures contracts. The results indicate that the volatility of Japanese interest rates is so low that there is no incremental impact for futures pricing.

The data used to implement the Black and Scholes model suggests a similar effect. We estimated σ using weekly Nikkei 225 returns from the period June 12th 1988 to June 11th 1989 to yield 10.36%. We also have three month Euroyen ask and Gensaki yields for that period. We convert these yields into three month zero coupon bond prices using the discounting formula, $e^{-0.25 \times yield}$, then convert the prices into return series comparable to the Nikkei return series. The bond returns based on the Euroyen yield have a standard devation of only 0.18% while those based on Gensaki yields have a miniscule standard devation of 0.06%. The correlations between Nikkei and bond returns are marginally significant, 0.391 for Euroyen and 0.239 for Gensaki. The small size of these standard deviations, plus the small implied covariance of stock and bond (the product of the correlation and the two standard deviations) suggest that stochastic interest rates are not likely to be a significant issue, at least for shorter maturity Japanese index option products.

4.3 Dividend Yield on the Underlying Basket of Stocks

In implementing the Black and Scholes model for the Osaka Nikkei 225 options, we have assumed that the underlying basket of shares pays a known dividend of 150 yen per year and that this dividend is distributed equally and smoothly across the calendar year. Based on the theory and evidence which exists in the literature, there are two potential reasons to object to this procedure.

First, Geske (1978) presents a model in which a stochastic dividend yield leads to option prices different from Black and Scholes model suggests. Thus, the degree to which future dividends differ from the historical pattern can alter the option's value. Second, Brenner, Subrahmanyam, and Uno (1989) report that the dividend yield on the Nikkei 225 is not smooth (as our modified Black and Scholes model requires) but is rather lumpy due to the clustering of dividend payment dates by the underlying 225 companies in March and September. This implies that there may be certain short maturity call options (those whose life spans March or September) which should be exercised early. However, the low level of Japanese index dividends, less than $\frac{1}{2}$%, suggests that any such issues will be of little importance. The impact of dividend payments on Japanese index option pricing is clearly a subject for future research.

4.4 Stochastic Variance for the Stock Index

The Black and Scholes model assumes that the volatility parameter, σ, is a constant. However, many authors present models which show that option values given a stochastic variance are substantially different from Black and Scholes or Merton constant-variance prices. See Hull and White (1987), Johnson and Shanno (1987), Scott (1987), Wiggins (1987), and Bailey and Stulz (1989). Furthermore, much evidence exists that asset return volatilities tend to vary through time.

Figure 1 plots the month-by-month standard deviations of daily Nikkei 225 returns. [9] It is apparant that the volatility is not constant, varies considerably, and may follow a mean-reverting process. Chan and Karolyi (1991) show that Nikkei returns are well fit by a GARCH model which includes a time varying volatility. This evidence suggests that stochastic variance models may more accurately value Japanese stock index option products.

Figure 1

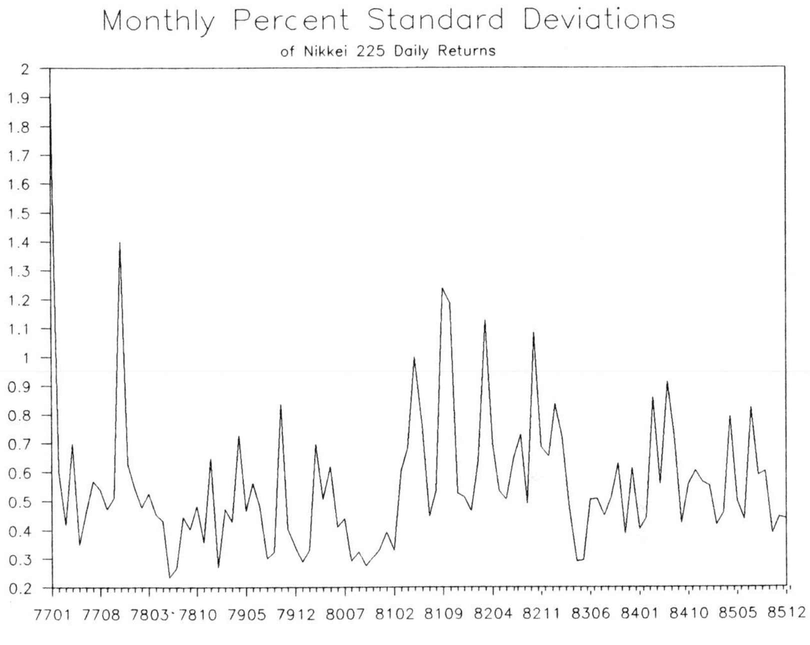

4.5 General Equilibrium Considerations

An additional issue is the potential interaction between stock index levels and interest rates. The stock index is, roughly speaking, a measure of aggregate wealth in the economy. General equilibrium relations link the joint distribution of the stock in-

[9]Standard deviations are computed using the method of French, Schwert, and Stambaugh (1987).

dex, stock index variance, the interest rate, and other factors. These interactions may affect stock index option values in more complex ways than the simple correlations of the Merton (1973) and Ramaswamy and Sundaresan (1985) models.

Bailey and Stulz (1989) derive a general equilibrium index option pricing model and show that it can yield prices which differ substantially from those of non general equilibrium models. The divergences are strongest for cases where the volatility is high, suggesting that there may be little effect in the generally low volatility Japanese markets. However, recent episodes in Japanese markets suggest that the general equilibrium linkages between stock index returns and interest rates may, at times, be significant. The large decline in Japanese stock prices in early 1990 concurs with large increases in Japanese interest rates. [10] Thus, the potential connection between interest rates and stock prices may be significant for Japanese index option pricing.

4.6 Long maturity put and call warrants

The same models, computational techniques, and parameter estimation methods we use for short maturity index options also apply to the longer maturity put and call warrants which have been listed on North American stock exchanges recently. However, the two or three year maturity of these options will magnify the issues and problems we have listed above. The effects of the American early exercise feature and the volatilities of dividends, interest rates, and the volatility parameter are accentuated for the put and call warrants, due to their longer life. Addtionally, there is the an element of exchange rate risk, due to pre-specified exchange rates associated with some contracts.

5. Summary and Conclusion

We have offered a brief introduction to the markets for Japanese stock index options and applied the well-known Black and Scholes formula to the Nikkei 225 options market. We have also identified an interesting agenda of topics for future research into the pricing of Japanese stock index option products. To conclude, we need only note that these contracts, though new, are bound to become very important. A great deal of academic and applied research is justified.

References

[1] Bailey, Warren, 1987, "An Empirical Investigation of the Market for Comex Gold Futures Options," *Journal of Finance* 42 (December), 1187-94.

[2] Bailey, Warren, 1989, "The Market for Japanese Index Futures: Some Preliminary Evidence," *Journal of Futures Markets* 4 (August), 283-96.

[3] Bailey, Warren, Ng, Edward, and Stulz, Rene, 1990, "Optimal Hedging of Stock Portfolios Against Foreign Exchange Risk: The Case of the Nikkei 225," Ohio State University working paper (November).

[10] See Ziemba and Schwartz (1991) for evidence.

[4] Bailey, Warren, and Stulz, Rene, 1989, "The Pricing of Stock Index Options in a General Equilibrium Model," *Journal of Financial and Quantitative Analysis* 24 (March), 1-12.

[5] Baring Securities, 1990, "Japanese Index Futures and Options," *Japanese Futures and Options Research* (February), Baring Securities, London.

[6] Black, Fischer, and Scholes, Myron, 1973, "The Pricing of Options and Corporate Liabilities," *Journal of Political Economy* 81 (May/June), 637-54.

[7] Brenner, M., Subrahmanyam, M. G., and Uno, J., 1989, "Stock Index Futures Arbitrage in the Japanese Markets," *Japan and the World Economy* 1 (July), 303-30.

[8] Chan, K. C., and Karolyi, G. Andrew, 1991, "The Volatility of the Japanese Stock Market: Evidence from 1977 to 1990," this volume.

[9] Cox, J. C., Ingersoll, J. E., and Ross, S. A., 1985, "A Theory of the Term Structure of Interest Rates," *Econometrica* 53 (March), 385-407.

[10] Cox, J. C., Ross, S. A., and Rubinstein, M., 1979, "Option Pricing: A Simplified Approach," *Journal of Financial Economics* 7 (October), 229-63.

[11] Dietrich-Campbell, Bruce, and Schwartz, Eduardo S., 1986, "Valuing Debt Options: Empirical Evidence," *Journal of Financial Economics* 16 (July), 321-43.

[12] French, Kenneth, Schwert, G. William, and Stambaugh, Robert, 1987, "Expected Stock Returns and Volatility," *Journal of Financial Economics* 19 (September), 3-30.

[13] Geske, Robert, 1978, "The Pricing of Options with Stochastic Dividend Yield," *Journal of Finance* 33 (May), 617-25.

[14] Geske, Robert, and Johnson, Herb, 1984, "The American Put Valued Analytically," *Journal of Finance* 39 (December), 1511-24.

[15] Geske, Robert, and Trautmann, Siegfried, 1986, "Option Valuation: Theory and Empirical Evidence," in *Capital Market Equilibria*, Bamberg, G., and Spremann, K., eds., Springer- Verlag, Berlin, 79-133.

[16] Hull, John, and White, Alan, 1987, "The Pricing of Options on Assets with Stochastic Volatilities," *Journal of Finance* 42 (June), 281-301.

[17] Jarrow, Robert A., and Rudd, Andrew, 1983, *Option Pricing*, Dow Jones Irwin, Homewood, Illinois.

[18] Johnson, Herb, and Shanno, David, 1987, "Option Pricing When the Variance is Changing," *Journal of Financial and Quantitative Analysis* 22 (June), 143-53.

[19] Merton, Robert, 1973, "The Theory of Rational Option Pricing," *Bell Journal of Economics and Management Science* 4 (Spring), 141-83.

[20] Ramaswamy, Krishna, and Sundaresan, Mahavedan, 1985, "The Valuation of Options on Futures Contracts," *Journal of Finance* 40 (December), 1319-40.

[21] Rubinstein, Mark, 1985, "Non-Parametric Tests of Alternative Option Pricing Models Using All Reported Trades and Quotes on the 30 Most Active CBOE Option Classes From August 23, 1976 Through Through August 31st, 1978," *Journal of Finance* 40 (June), 455-80.

[22] Scott, Louis, 1987, "Option Pricing When the Variance Changes Randomly: Theory, Estimation, and Application," *Journal of Financial and Quantitative Analysis* 22 (December), 419-38.

[23] Shaw, G., Thorp, E.O., and Ziemba, W.T., 1990, "Convergence to Efficiency of the Nikkei Put Warrant Market of 1990," University of British Columbia working paper (November).

[24] Subrahmanyam, M., Uno, T., and Saito, K., 1989, "The Stock Index Options Market in Japan: The Early Experience," *Japanese Security Analysts Journal* (September).

[25] Wiggins, James, 1987, "Stochastic Volatility Option Valuation: Theory and Empirical Estimates," *Journal of Financial Economics* 19 (December), 351-72.

[26] Ziemba, William T., and Schwartz, Sandra L., 1991, *Investing in Japan*, Probus Publishing, Chicago.

Japanese Financial Market Research
W.T. Ziemba, W. Bailey and Y. Hamao (Editors)

Valuing Bonds with Detachable Warrants

Peter Carr[1], Cornell University, Ithaca, NY, USA 14853

Abstract

This paper presents analytical valuation formulas for bonds with detachable warrants on Japanese equities. The bonds bear default risk on both coupons and principal. The warrants also bear default risk, and are American-style, with a positive early exercise premium due to the existence of stock dividends.

1. INTRODUCTION

Since the first[2] Euro-bond with detachable Japanese equity warrants was issued in 1982, the market for these instruments have flourished. While the market grew steadily from 1982 to 1985, the combination of a surging Japanese equity market, low Japanese interest rates, and financial market deregulation[3] in 1986 prompted an explosion in popularity. From 1987-89, Japanese companies issued $115 billion of Euro-bonds with warrants attached, bringing the total outstanding to $140 billion.

The Euro-bonds usually mature in four to five years, and the detachable warrants give the right during the Euro-bond's life to buy new shares for slightly more than the share price just after issuance. In return for this right, the coupon rate on the Euro-bond is much lower (eg. 400-450 basis points in March 1989) than for straight Euro-dollar corporate bonds. Although the detachable warrant's strike price and underlying stock are denominated in yen, the Euro-bond is typically denominated in US dollars. The strike price per share and the number of shares controlled by each warrant are chosen so that the yen received from warrant exercise at expiration covers the dollar payout to bondholders (assuming a constant exchange rate).

A Euro-bond issued in July of 1988 by Nippon Steel is a good example of a typical "cum-warrant" bond. The issue amount is $600 million with each bond having a $5,000 face value and one warrant attached. The warrant is detachable and gives the right to purchase 980 shares of Nippon Steel at 687 yen per share at any time over the four year life of the bond. The strike price per share was chosen to be 2.5% above the share closing price of 670 yen per share on the setting date. The number of shares per warrant was chosen so that Nippon Steel's yen inflow from exercise of the warrant at expiration (980 shares x 687 yen per share) covers the dollar outflow required to retire the bond ($5,000), using the spot exchange rate on the setting date (134.70 yen per dollar). In return for attaching a warrant to each bond, the bond's coupon rate is only 3.25% per year.

[1]I would like to thank Warren Bailey, Ann Calkins, Terry Liow, Francis Longstaff, Ramesh Menon, Ming Wong, and Bill Ziemba for their help. Any errors are mine alone.

[2]A 1981 amendment to the Commercial Code allowed the issuance of Euro-bonds with warrants. The first Euro-bond with warrants on Japanese equity was issued in December 1981, but the warrants were non-detachable. In January 1982, Mitsubishi Kasei (4010) became the first Japanese company to issue a Euro-bond with detachable warrants.

[3]In 1986, The Ministry of Finance abolished restrictions on Japanese investment in the London market.

The warrant described above is attached to a U.S. dollar denominated bond. Warrants on Japanese equity have also been attached to bonds denominated in other foreign currencies. However, the U.S. dollar denominated market is the largest with over 400 issues, of which 200 trade actively (at the end of September 1988). The Swiss Franc market is the second largest with over 170 issues of which about 70 trade actively. Denominations in this market are generally smaller in size than the U.S. dollar market. The other markets are significantly smaller than the U.S. dollar and Swiss Franc denominated markets. There are about 30 issues denominated in Deutschmarks, and a few others denominated in ECU's, Dutch Gilders, Sterling, and Yen.

The four big Japanese security houses (Nomura, Daiwa, Nikko, and Yamaichi) organize almost all of the issues in the primary market (97% in 1989). Issuers typically swap their proceeds into yen immediately after issuance. The secondary market for Euro-warrants is strictly over-the-counter, dominated by foreign brokerage houses such as Baring Securities and Morgan Stanley. Since 1987, Japanese investors comprised about 70 per cent of the end investors. While London has been the traditional marketplace for these issues, the market is slowly drifting to Tokyo, largely due to efforts by the Ministry of Finance.

The popularity of Euro-bonds with detachable warrants from 1987-89 was prompted by favorable market conditions for both issuers and investors. Issuers paid coupons of less than 4%. After swapping their exposure into yen (whose interest rate was then as much as 5% below dollar rates), their cost of capital was either zero or negative. Furthermore, exercise of the warrants financed retirement of the debt, so that the only cost of the debt issue to shareholders in this event was dilution. Investors held a safe debt instrument coupled with warrants whose value soared as the Japanese equity market surged.

In 1990, these market conditions reversed, dramatically slowing down new issuance. The drop in the Tokyo stockmarket (38% as of September 1990) and the rise in Japanese interest rates to dollar levels has dramatically increased issuers' capital costs. Furthermore, the Japanese government is discouraging new issuance due to its recent concern about the warrrants' dilution effect on stock prices. For many firms, there is a high probability[4] that existing warrants will expire worthless, requiring issuers to refinance their debt at high rates. This prospect has made potential issuers wary of these instruments, and has soured investor demand for them.

In their seminal papers, Black-Scholes[2] and Merton[14] recognized that their option pricing approach could be applied in developing a unified theory of corporate liabilities. Merton[15] priced corporate discount bonds in the presence of default risk. Ingersoll[11] and Brennan and Schwartz[3] extended Merton's analysis to convertible bonds. In particular, under certain assumptions, Ingersoll proved that a non-callable coupon-bearing convertible bond has the same value as an ordinary bond with the same coupons, principal and maturity, plus an attached stock purchase warrant. This warrant has an identical maturity, is exchangeable for as many shares as is the convertible, and has a gross exercise payment equal to the face value of the bond.

Ingersoll states that the bond-warrant combination can differ in value from the con-

[4]About $125 billion of the $140 billion worth of outstanding bonds with detachable warrants were out-of-the-money as of September 1990

vertible bond only when early exercise of the warrant or conversion of the bond may be optimal. He shows that a convertible bond will never be converted prior to maturity under the three assumptions of perfect markets, constant conversion terms, and no dividends. Maintaining these three assumptions, it follows that a bond with European warrants attached may be priced as a convertible bond using the methods given in Ingersoll[11] and Brennan and Schwartz[3],[4].

The purpose of this paper is to price Euro-dollar bonds with Japanese equity warrants attached. Since the attached warrants are American-style and the underlying stock receives dividends, the value of the cum-warrant bond reflects an early exercise premium. The paper provides analytic expressions for the Euro-dollar bond and for this early exercise premium. However, the premium is expressed in terms of a quantity which must be determined numerically[5].

To lend some reality to the analysis, the bond is allowed to bear coupons. To simplify matters, the coupon payout to bondholders and the dividend payout to shareholders are both assumed to be continuous. While bond and equity payouts are discrete in reality, the effect of assuming continuous payout over long horizons is negligible. The coupon payout to bondholders is assumed to be constant over time while the dividend payout to shareholders is assumed to increase with the share price. Again, while dividend payouts tend to be sticky over short horizons in reality, the effect of this dividend assumption over long horizons is probably minimal.

To model the default risk of debt, the firm is allowed to go bankrupt either at the debt's maturity date or beforehand. The model posits that bankruptcy occurs at maturity if the market value of the firm's assets is below the debt's face value. Bankruptcy occurs prior to maturity if the firm is unable to meet its coupon payout. Since the coupon payout is continuous, the firm can always sell off assets as long as its assets have positive value. Thus, bankruptcy occurs prior to maturity when the firm's assets become worthless.

In technical terms, bankruptcy is possible when the stochastic process for the firm's asset value can reach zero in finite time. Financial considerations also require that the origin be an absorbing boundary. For the familiar geometric Brownian motion, the origin is absorbing, but not attainable. Consequently, a Feller process is employed instead. This process has linear drift and instantaneous variance proportional to the firm's value. The parameters describing the drift and diffusion coefficients are chosen so that the origin is both attainable and absorbing.

The paper presents formulas for the value of a bond with warrants attached. The model can be used to determine the coupon rate on new issues and to identify mispriced issues in the secondary market. The model can also be used by issuers and arbitrageurs to hedge the risks associated with long and short positions in these securities.

The remainder of the paper is organized as follows. Section 2 sets up notation and delineates the model. For simplicity, the model ignores exchange rate issues and assumes that the bond is denominated in yen. Section 3 studies the pricing of bonds with warrants attached under the usual assumption that the warrants are European-style. Section 4 then relaxes this assumption and determines the value of the early exercise premium.

[5]The analytic American option pricing formulas of Roll[17] and Geske and Johnson[9] are also expressed in terms of a numerically determined quantity.

The final section summarizes and provides directions for future research. An appendix provides a proof of a mathematical result used in the paper.

2. THE MODEL

The following assumption is maintained in this section and the next only:

A1) European Warrants

The warrants outstanding are European-style.

In contrast, the remaining assumptions hold throughout the paper:

A2) Frictionless Markets

There are no taxes, transactions costs, or other market frictions.

A3) Capital Structure

The firm's capital structure contains bonds and stocks only. The bonds consist of straight debt with warrants attached.

Further assumptions apply to these components of the capital structure:

A3i) Straight Debt

The firm has a single debt issue outstanding, which matures at date T. Bondholders receive coupons continuously at rate c so long as the value of the firm's assets, V_t, is positive. Letting F denote the bond's total face value, the bondholders also receive $\min(V_T, F)$ *at the maturity date T.*

In reality, several issuers have multiple debt issues with detachable warrants (eg. Nippon Steel and Yamaichi). The warrants differ in strike price and maturity. Assumption **A3i)** is made for simplicity. The payoff of the debt at maturity reflects the standard assumption that debtholders liquidate the firm at maturity if its assets do not have sufficient value to cover the principle. If the firm has gone bankrupt prior to maturity, the debtholders receive nothing at expiration.

A3ii) Warrants

There is a single warrant issue, which has a total strike price of K yen and matures with the bond at date T.

Exercise of the warrants augments the value of the firm's assets by K yen and requires the firm to issue new shares to the former warrantholders. Enough new shares are issued so that the former warrantholders own $100 \cdot \alpha$ percent of all the firm's shares. The warrants will only be exercised if the exercise benefit exceeds the exercise cost K. After the value of the firm's assets V_T is augmented by the strike price, the total equity value is $\max[0, V_T + K - F]$. Since the former warrantholders own $100 \cdot \alpha$ percent of this new firm value, their exercise benefit is $\max[0, \alpha(V_T - F + K)]$. Requiring this exercise benefit to exceed the exercise cost K implies that:

$$\alpha V_T > \alpha F + (1 - \alpha)K \equiv X \tag{1}$$

If the warrants are exercised rationally, the warrantholders receive the excess of the exercise benefit over the cost i.e. $\alpha V_T - X$. Conversely, if the warrants expire rationally unexercised, they are worthless. Thus, the terminal value of the warrants is $\max[0, \alpha V_T - X]$.

A3iii) Equity

The stockholders receive dividends continuously[6] *at rate* $a \cdot V_t$. *If the warrants are not exercised at expiration, the shareholders also get* $\max[0, V_T - F]$ *at* T. *If the warrants are (rationally) exercised, they get the smaller amount* $(1-\alpha)(V_T + K - F)$ *instead.*

The bond value B_t has three sources of value, namely, principal P_t, coupons C_t, and European warrants W_t^e:

$$B_t \equiv P_t + C_t + W_t^e \tag{2}$$

In order to price these claims, the following three assumptions are appended:

A4) Continuous Trading

Investors can trade in the firm's assets and liabilities continuously.

A5) Constant Interest Rate

The riskless rate of interest is a positive constant r.

A6) Firm Value Dynamics

The value of the firm's assets V_t *obeys the following diffusion process:*

$$dV_t = \mu(V_t, t)dt + \sigma(V_t, t)dZ_t, t \in [0, T]. \tag{3}$$

The growth rate $\mu(V_t, t)$ *and the instantaneous volatility* $\sigma(V_t, t)$ *are both assumed to be bounded. The Wiener process* $\{W_t; t \in [0, T]\}$ *is defined on the probability space* $(\Omega, \mathcal{F}, Q)$.

Under these assumptions, the preclusion of arbitrage opportunities implies the existence of a probability measure $\tilde{Q}$, equivalent to Q, validating risk-neutral pricing (see Harrison and Pliska[10]). Let $\tilde{E}_v$ denote expectations under this measure given that the initial firm value is V_0. Then the claims comprising the bond value have the following representation.

$$P_0 = e^{-rT} \tilde{E}_v \min(V_T, F) \tag{4}$$

$$C_0 = \tilde{E}_v \int_0^T ce^{-rt} 1_{\{V_t > 0\}} dt \tag{5}$$

$$W_0^e = e^{-rT} \tilde{E}_v \max(0, \alpha V_T - X), \text{ where } X \equiv \alpha F + (1-\alpha)K. \tag{6}$$

To value these claims, one final assumption is added:

A7) Feller Process

The value of the firm's assets obeys a Feller process:

$$dV_t = [(\mu - a)V_t - c]dt + \sigma\sqrt{V_t} dZ_t, \tag{7}$$

where μ, a, c, *and* σ *are constants*[7], *with* $a, c, \sigma > 0$.

Since $c > 0$, Feller (1951) has shown that this process is absorbed at the origin. Note that under the "risk-neutral" probability measure $\tilde{Q}$, one can define a Wiener process $\tilde{Z}_t$ such that the following equation holds:

---

[6] It is possible to model the stockholders' dividend as $c_t^s + a_t^s \cdot V_t$, where c_t^s and a_t^s are non-negative functions of time. In this case, the bondholders' coupon payments would be modeled as $c_t^b + a_t^b \cdot V_t$, where $c_t^b \equiv c - c_t^s$ and $a_t^b \equiv a - a_t^s$.

[7] For what follows, the expected rate of return in the firm's assets μ can be an unknown bounded function of V and t.

$$dV_t = [(r-a)V_t - c]dt + \sigma\sqrt{V_t}d\tilde{Z}_t. \tag{8}$$

This equation is the starting point for the analysis in the next section.

3. EUROPEAN WARRANTS

This section is concerned with pricing bonds with detachable European warrants. The bond value B_0 has three components, the first of which is the principal P_0. From (4):

$$\begin{aligned} P_0 &= e^{-rT}\tilde{E}_v \min(V_T, F) \\ &= \int_0^F e^{-rT} V_T f(V_T, T; V_0, 0) dV_T + Fe^{-rT}\int_F^\infty f(V_T, T; V_0, 0) dV_T, \end{aligned} \tag{9}$$

where $f(V_T, T; V_0, 0)$ is the transition density of the risk-neutral Feller process (8), which is given in the Appendix. In words, the bond's principal is the present value of the partial mean of the terminal firm value, V_T, summed with the product of the default-free price, Fe^{-rT}, and the complementary distribution function of V_T.

Cox and Ross[6] determine the partial mean as:

$$\begin{aligned} M(F,T) &\equiv \int_0^F e^{-rT} V_T f(V_T, T; V_0, 0) dV_T \\ &= V_0 e^{-aT}\sum_{n=0}^{\infty}\frac{(n+1)e^{-\lambda_T/2}(\lambda_T/2)^{n+2c/\sigma^2}\Gamma(k_T F, n+2)}{\Gamma(n+2+2c/\sigma^2)}, \end{aligned} \tag{10}$$

where $\lambda_T \equiv 2k_T V_0 e^{(r-a)T}$, $k_T \equiv \frac{2(r-a)}{\sigma^2(e^{(r-a)T}-1)}$, and where $\Gamma(k_T F; n+2)$ is the gamma distribution function evaluated at $k_T F$ with parameter $n+2$:

$$\Gamma(z;\alpha) \equiv \frac{1}{\Gamma(\alpha)}\int_0^z e^{-x}x^{\alpha-1}dx, \tag{11}$$

with $\Gamma(\alpha)$ as the gamma function $\Gamma(\alpha) \equiv \int_0^\infty e^{-x}x^{\alpha-1}dx$.

It is shown in the Appendix that the complementary distribution function of the random variable V_T can be transformed into the non-central chi-squared distribution function:

$$\int_F^\infty f(V_T, T; V_0, 0)dV_T = \chi^2(\lambda_T; 2(1+2c/\sigma^2), 2k_T F), \tag{12}$$

where $\chi^2(\lambda_T; \nu, 2k_T F)$ is the non-central chi-square distribution function (see Johnson and Kotz[13], p. 133) evaluated at λ_T with $2(1+2c/\sigma^2)$ degrees of freedom and non-centrality parameter $2k_T F$. If $Z_1, \ldots, Z_n$ are independent standard normal random variables and $\delta_1, ..., \delta_n$ are constants, then the sum $\sum_{j=1}^{\nu}(Z_i+\delta_i)$ has a non-central chi-square distribution with ν degrees of freedom and non-centrality parameter $\sum_{j=1}^{\nu}\delta_i^2$. The right side of (12) is the probability that this sum is less than the number $\lambda_T \equiv 2k_T V_0 e^{(r-a)T}$, when the sum has $2(1+2c/\sigma^2)$ degrees of freedom and its non-centrality parameter is $2k_T F$. This is also the probability that the firm is solvent at expiration, under the process (8).

The non-central chi-square distribution has widespread application, including coverage problems in ballistics and estimating the power of the chi-square test. Algorithms for exact valuation and analytic approximation formulas for the distribution function are given in Schroder[19] and Sankaran[18] respectively.

Putting these results together gives the valuation formula for the principal component of the bond's value:

$$P_0 = V_0 e^{-aT} M(F,T) + F e^{-rT} \chi^2(\lambda_T; 2(1+2c/\sigma^2), 2k_T F), \tag{13}$$

where $k_T \equiv \frac{2(r-a)}{\sigma^2(e^{(r-a)T}-1)}$ and $\lambda_T \equiv 2k_T V_0 e^{(r-a)T}$.

The second component of bond value is the coupon stream c received so long as firm value is positive, i.e., from (5):

$$\begin{aligned} C_0 &= \tilde{E}_v \int_0^T c e^{-rt} 1_{\{V_t>0\}} dt \\ &= c \int_0^T e^{-rt} \tilde{Q}(\{\omega : V_t(\omega) > 0\}) dt, \end{aligned} \tag{14}$$

where $\tilde{Q}$ is the equivalent martingale measure. Feller[7] gives the probability that the process (8) has not been absorbed by date t so that:

$$C_0 = c \int_0^T e^{-rt} \Gamma(\lambda_t; 1 + 2c/\sigma^2) dt. \tag{15}$$

The final component of bond value is the European warrant. From (6):

$$W_0^e = e^{-rT} \tilde{E}_v \max(0, \alpha V_T - X), \tag{16}$$

where $X \equiv \alpha F + (1-\alpha)K$. Using the transition probability density function:

$$W_0^e = \alpha \int_X^\infty e^{-rT} V_T f(V_T, T; V_0, 0) dV_T - X e^{-rT} \int_X^\infty f(V_T, T; V_0, 0) dV_T. \tag{17}$$

From (10) and (12):

$$W_0^e = \alpha V_0 e^{-aT}[1 - M(X,T)] - X e^{-rT} \chi^2(\lambda_T; 2(1+2c/\sigma^2), 2k_T X). \tag{18}$$

Note that this equation is roughly similar to the Black-Scholes formula.

Summing the three components of bond value together gives the following valuation result:

$$\begin{aligned} B_0(c) &= P_0 + C_0 + W_0^e \\ &= V_0 e^{-aT} M(F,T) + F e^{-rT} \chi^2(\lambda_T; 2(1+2c/\sigma^2), 2k_T F) \\ &\quad + c \int_0^T e^{-rt} \Gamma(\lambda_t; 1 + 2c/\sigma^2) dt \\ &\quad + \alpha V_0 e^{-aT}[1 - M(X,T)] - X e^{-rT} \chi^2(\lambda_T; 2(1+2c/\sigma^2), 2k_T X), \end{aligned} \tag{19}$$

where $k_T \equiv \frac{2(r-a)}{\sigma^2(e^{(r-a)T}-1)}$, $\lambda_T \equiv 2k_T V_0 e^{(r-a)T}$, and $X \equiv \alpha F + (1-\alpha)K$.

Bonds are usually issued at par. To determine the coupon rate which prices the bond at par, set the initial bond value equal to its face value ($B_0(c) = F$) and solve for c

using a numerical search routine. Since the bond price is increasing in the coupon rate $(\frac{\partial B_0(c)}{\partial c} > 0)$ and warrant value is strictly positive, the inclusion of warrants lowers the coupon rate required to price bonds at par. To value the equity, one need merely subtract

Merton[15] proves that the Modigliani-Miller[16] Theorem holds in this framework. Consequently, the equity is valued by subtracting the initial bond price from the initial firm value:

$$S_0 = V_0 - B_0. \tag{20}$$

4. AMERICAN WARRANTS

The warrants are now assumed to be American rather than European. Since the stockholders receive proportional dividends, the ability to exercise early has positive value. This section determines the magnitude of this early exercise premium, using results in Carr, Jarrow, and Myneni[5] and Jamshidian[12]. For simplicity, it is assumed that if the warrants are exercised, they are exercised as a block and that the exercise proceeds are paid out as a special dividend. Upon exercise, the former warrant-holders own $100 \cdot \alpha$ percent of the firm's shares, so they receive $100 \cdot \alpha$ percent of this special dividend, as before.

From previous work on American option valuation, there exists an optimal exercise boundary B_t^*, independent of V_t, above which it is optimal to exercise early, i.e., letting W_t^a denote the American warrant value:

$$\begin{aligned} &\text{if } V_t \geq B_t^*, \quad \text{then} \quad W_t^a = \max[0, \alpha[V_t - P_t - C_t] - (1-\alpha)K] \\ &\text{if } V_t < B_t^*, \quad \text{then} \quad W_t^a > \max[0, \alpha[V_t - P_t - C_t] - (1-\alpha)K]. \end{aligned} \tag{21}$$

Since the American warrant value is given by (21) if the firm value starts at or above the optimal exercise boundary, assume henceforth that the warrant is initially alive on the valuation date 0, i.e., $V_0 < B_0^*$.

The intrinsic value of the warrant is:

$$\begin{aligned} I(V,t) &\equiv \max[0, \alpha[V - P(V,t) - C(V,t)] - (1-\alpha)K] \\ &= \max[0, \alpha V - X(V,t)], \end{aligned} \tag{22}$$

where $X(V,t) \equiv \alpha[P(V,t) + C(V,t)] + (1-\alpha)K$. Thus, the warrant may be viewed as being written on $100 \cdot \alpha$ percent of the firm's assets, with exercise price X depending on the firm value V and time t. Define B_t^x as the value of the firm solving:

$$\alpha B_t^x = X(B_t^x, t) \text{ or } \alpha[B_t^x - P(B_t^x, t) - C(B_t^x, t)] = (1-\alpha)K. \tag{23}$$

When $V_t > B_t^x$, exercise of the warrants has positive value and the warrants are in-the-money. Since the warrant holder is never forced to exercise:

$$B_t^* \geq B_t^x, t \in [0, T]. \tag{24}$$

As time evolves, the straight debt value, $P(V,t) + C(V,t)$, increases, *ceteris paribus*, so that B_t^x must increase to maintain equality in (23). As time evolves, the gap between B_t^* and B_t^x narrows. At expiration, equation (23) is:

$$\alpha B_T^x = \alpha \min(B_T^x, F) + (1 - \alpha)K. \tag{25}$$

If $B_T^x < F$, a contradiction arises so:

$$B_T^x = F + \frac{1-\alpha}{\alpha} K. \tag{26}$$

Applying the results of Van Moerbeke[20] shows that $B_T^* = B_T^x$, if $a \geq r$. However, if $0 < a < r$, then $B_T^* = \frac{r}{a} B_T^x > B_T^x$, reflecting the decreased value of early exercise.

While alive, the warrant value satisfies the fundamental partial differential equation:

$$\mathcal{L}W^a(V,t) \equiv \frac{\partial W^a}{\partial t} + \frac{\sigma^2 V}{2} \frac{\partial^2 W^a}{\partial V^2} + [(r-a)V - c]\frac{\partial W^a}{\partial V} - rW^a = 0 \tag{27}$$

To gain an understanding of this equation, define the discounted process $Y(V,t) \equiv e^{-rt}W^a(V,t)$. Recall the "risk-neutral" process (8):

$$dV_t = [(r-a)V_t - c]dt + \sigma\sqrt{V_t}d\tilde{Z}_t. \tag{28}$$

From Itô's lemma:

$$dY_t = e^{-rt}\mathcal{L}W^a(V,t)dt + \frac{\partial W^a}{\partial V}\sigma\sqrt{V_t}d\tilde{Z}_t. \tag{29}$$

Thus, the fundamental partial differential equation (27) asserts that a necessary condition for the preclusion of arbitrage opportunities is that the discounted warrant process Y_t is a (local) martingale.

In the exercise region, (29) still obtains. However, the drift need not vanish since the warrant, if it exists, should be exercised, not held. In the exercise region, $V_t > B_t^* > B_t^x$ from (24). Consequently:

$$W_t^a = \alpha[V - P(V,t) - C(V,t)] - (1-\alpha)K \text{ from (21).} \tag{30}$$

In the exercise region, the warrant price is the sum of the values of two claims. The value of the first claim is $100 \cdot \alpha$ percent of the firm's assets net of the straight debt obligation. The second claim is a short position in a bond paying interest continuously so that its value is constant over time at $(1-\alpha)K$.

Since $\mathcal{L}$ is a linear operator

$$\begin{aligned} \mathcal{L}W_t^a &= \alpha[\mathcal{L}V - \mathcal{L}P(V,t) - \mathcal{L}C(V,t)] - (1-\alpha)\mathcal{L}K \\ &= \alpha[-aV - c - 0 - (-c) - (1-\alpha)rK \\ &= \alpha aV - (1-\alpha)rK \end{aligned} \tag{31}$$

from Merton[15].

Thus on the whole region, the warrant value $W^a(V,t)$ satisfies:

$$\mathcal{L}W_t^a = 1_{\{V_t > B_t^*\}}[\alpha a V_t - (1-\alpha)rK] \tag{32}$$

subject to the following boundary conditions:

$$W^a(V,t) = \max[0, \alpha \max[0, V_T - F] - (1-\alpha)K] \tag{33}$$
$$W^a(B_t^*,t) = \alpha B_t^* - X(B_t^*,t) \tag{34}$$
$$\frac{\partial W^a(B_t^*,t)}{\partial V} = \alpha - \frac{\partial X(B_t^*,t)}{\partial V} \tag{35}$$
$$\lim_{V\downarrow 0} W(V,t) = 0. \tag{36}$$

The first boundary condition reflects the fact that the American warrant is European at expiration. The next two boundary conditions reflect the result that along the optimal exercise boundary, the warrant value and its derivative are continuous. The final condition serves to uniquely determine the warrant value $W^a(V,t)$ and the optimal exercise boundary B_t^*.

Using the Feynman-Kac Theorem (see Friedman[8]):

$$W^a(V,t) = e^{-r(T-t)}\tilde{E}\max[\alpha V - X] + \tilde{E}\int_t^T e^{-r(u-t)}1_{\{V_u > B_u^*\}}[\alpha a V_u - (1-\alpha)rK]du.$$

The first term is the value of the European warrant. Therefore:

$$W_0^a = W_0^e + \pi_0, \tag{37}$$

where π_0 is the early exercise premium given by:

$$\pi_0 \equiv \alpha a V_0 \int_0^T e^{-at}[1 - M(B_t^*,t)]dt - (1-\alpha)rK\int_0^T e^{-rt}\chi^2(\lambda_t; 2(1+2c/\sigma^2), 2k_t B_t^*)dt,$$

and where $k_t \equiv \frac{2(r-a)}{\sigma^2(e^{(r-a)t}-1)}$, $\lambda_t \equiv 2k_t V_0 e^{(r-a)t}$.

The early exercise premium is non-negative. It has the same value as a claim which pays $\alpha a V_t - (1-\alpha)rK$ continuously whenever the value of the firm V_t exceeds the optimal exercise boundary B_t^*. The value of this boundary can be determined implicitly from the value matching condition (34):

$$W^a(B_t^*,t) = \alpha B_t^* - X(B_t^*,t), \tag{38}$$

or from the high contact condition (35):

$$\frac{\partial W^a(B_t^*,t)}{\partial V} = \alpha - \frac{\partial X(B_t^*,t)}{\partial V}. \tag{39}$$

Either integral equation can be solved numerically.

5. SUMMARY AND FUTURE RESEARCH

This paper valued bonds with detachable warrants. The bonds bear default risk on both coupons and principal. The warrants are American with a positive early exercise premium due to the existence of stock dividends. A major avenue for future research would incorporate exchange rate risk into the bond's price while retaining the risk of default. A second avenue for future research would allow for stochastic interest rates while retaining the American feature of the warrants. A third research direction involves the imposition of an exogenous stochastic process on stock prices rather than firm values. In such a model, the effect of future warrant exercise on current stock prices should be explicitly taken into account.

APPENDIX

Theorem 1 *Let $f(V_T, T; V_0, 0)$ denote the transition density of the Feller process $dV_t = [(r-a)V_t - c]dt + \sigma\sqrt{V_t}d\tilde{Z}_t$. Let $\chi^2(x; \nu, \lambda)$ denote the non-central chi-square distribution function with ν degrees of freedom and noncentrality parameter λ. Then:*

$$\int_F^\infty f(V_T, T; V_0, 0)dV_T = \chi^2(\lambda_T\ ; 2(1 + 2c/\sigma^2), 2k_T F), \tag{40}$$

where $k_T \equiv \frac{2(r-a)}{\sigma^2(e^{(r-a)T}-1)}$ and $\lambda_T \equiv 2k_T V_0 e^{(r-a)T}$.

Proof

Let:

$$I \equiv \int_F^\infty f(V_T, T; V_0, 0)dV_T, \tag{41}$$

where from Cox and Ross ([6], p. 161, equation 35):

$$\begin{aligned} f(V_T, T; V_0, 0) &= \left(\frac{2(r-a)}{\sigma^2(e^{(r-a)T}-1)}\right)\left(\frac{V_0 e^{(r-a)T}}{V_T}\right)^{(1+2c/\sigma^2)/2} \\ &\cdot \exp\left[-\frac{2(r-a)(V_0 e^{(r-a)T} + V_T)}{\sigma^2(e^{(r-a)T}-1)}\right] \\ &\cdot I_{1+2c/\sigma^2}\left[\frac{4(r-a)\sqrt{V_T V_0 e^{(r-a)T}}}{\sigma^2(e^{(r-a)T}-1)}\right], \end{aligned} \tag{42}$$

and where $I_q(z) \equiv \left(\frac{z}{2}\right)^q \sum_{j=0}^\infty \frac{(z^2/4)^j}{j!\Gamma(q+j+1)}$ is the modified Bessel function of the first kind of order q (see Abramowitz and Stegun ([1], p. 375, equation 9.6.10).

Performing the change of variables:

$$x \equiv 2k_T V_T \text{ where } k_T \equiv \frac{2(r-a)}{\sigma^2(e^{(r-a)T}-1)} \tag{43}$$

in (41) yields:

$$\begin{aligned} I &= \int_{2k_T F}^\infty \frac{1}{2}\left(\frac{2k_T V_0 e^{(r-a)T}}{x}\right)^{(1+2c/\sigma^2)/2} \\ &\cdot \exp[-(2k_T V_0 e^{(r-a)T} + x)/2] I_{1+2c/\sigma^2}(\sqrt{2k_T V_0 e^{(r-a)T} x})dx. \end{aligned} \tag{44}$$

Letting:

$$\lambda_T \equiv 2k_T V_0 e^{(r-a)T} \text{ and } \nu \equiv 2(1 + 2c/\sigma^2) \tag{45}$$

simplifies the result to:

$$I = \int_{2k_T F}^{\infty} \frac{1}{2}\left(\frac{\lambda_T}{x}\right)^{\nu/4} I_{\nu/2}(\sqrt{\lambda_T x}) \exp[-(\lambda_T + x)/2]dx. \tag{46}$$

From Johnson and Kotz[13], the integrand is recognized as the probability density function $p(\lambda_T; \nu+2, x)$ of a non-central chi-squared random variable, with $\nu + 2$ degrees of freedom and non-centrality parameter x. Schroder, ([19], p. 213), proves that:

$$\int_{2k_T F}^{\infty} p(\lambda_T; \nu+2, x)dx = \chi^2(\lambda_T; \nu, 2k_T F), \tag{47}$$

where $\chi^2(\lambda_T\ ; \nu, 2k_T F)$ is the non-central chi-squared distribution function:

$$\begin{aligned} \chi^2(\lambda_T\ ; \nu, 2k_T F) &\equiv \int_0^{\lambda_T} p(w; \nu, 2k_T F)dw \\ &= \int_0^{\lambda_T} \frac{1}{2}\left(\frac{w}{2k_T F}\right)^{(\nu-2)/4} I_{\frac{\nu-2}{2}}(\sqrt{2k_T F w}) \exp\left[-\frac{2k_T F + w}{2}\right] dw. \end{aligned}$$

Q.E.D.

References

[1] Abramowitz, M. and I. Stegun, 1965, "Handbook of Mathematical Functions," Dover Publications, Inc., New York.

[2] Black, F. and M. Scholes, 1973, "The Pricing of Options and Corporate Liabilities," *Journal of Political Economy*, **83**, 637–654.

[3] Brennan, M. and E. Schwartz, 1977, "Convertible Bonds: Valuation and Optimal Strategies for Call and Conversion," *Journal of Finance*, **32**, 1699–1715.

[4] Brennan, M. and E. Schwartz, 1980, "Analyzing Convertible Bonds," *Journal of Financial and Quantitative Analysis*, **15**, 907–915.

[5] Carr, P., R. Jarrow, and R. Myneni, 1990, "Alternative Characterizations of American Put Options," Cornell Working Paper.

[6] Cox, J. and S. Ross, 1976, "The Valuation of Options for Alternative Stochastic Processes," *Journal of Financial Economics*, **3**, 145–166.

[7] Feller, W., 1951, "Two Singular Diffusion Problems," *Annals of Mathematics*, **54**, 173–182.

[8] Friedman, A., 1975, Stochastic Differential Equations and Applications, Vol. 1, Academic Press, San Diego, CA.

[9] Geske, R. and H. Johnson, 1984, "The American Put Option Valued Analytically," *Journal of Finance*, **39**, 1511–1524.

[10] Harrison, J. and S. Pliska, 1981, "Martingales and Stochastic Integrals in the Theory of Continuous Trading," *Stochastic Processes and Their Applications*, **11**, 215–260.

[11] Ingersoll, J., 1977, "A Contingent-Claims Valuation of Convertible Securities," *Journal of Financial Economics*, **4**, 289–322.

[12] Jamshidian, F., 1990, "Formulas for American Options," Merrill Lynch Working Paper.

[13] Johnson, W. and S. Kotz, 1970, Distributions in Statistics: Continuous Univariate Distributions 2, Boston: Houghton Mifflin Company.

[14] Merton, R.C., 1973, "Theory of Rational Option Pricing," *Bell Journal of Economics and Management Science*, **4**, 141–183.

[15] Merton, R.C., 1974, "On the Pricing of Corporate Debt: The Risk Structure of Interest Rates," *Journal of Finance*, **29**, 449–470.

[16] Modigliani F. and M. Miller, 1958, "The Cost of Capital, Corporation Finance, and the Theory of Investment," *American Economic Review*, 261–297.

[17] Roll, R., 1977, "An Analytic Valuation Formula for Unprotected American Call Options on Dividend-Paying Stocks," *Journal of Financial Economics*, **5**, 251–258.

[18] Sankaran, M., 1963, "Approximations to the Non-Central Chi-Square Distribution," *Biometrika*, **50**, 199–204.

[19] Schroder, M., 1989, "Computing the Constant Elasticity of Variance Option Pricing Formula," *Journal of Finance*, **44**, 211–219.

[20] Van Moerbeke, P., 1976, "On Optimal Stopping and Free Boundary Problems," *Archive for Rational Mechanics and Analysis*, **60**, 101–148.

PART V:
INTEGRATION OF CAPITAL MARKETS

Japanese Financial Market Research
W.T. Ziemba, W. Bailey and Y. Hamao (Editors)

The Effect of the 1987 Stock Crash on International Financial Integration

Yasushi Hamao, Columbia University
Ronald W. Masulis, Vanderbilt University
Victor Ng, University of Michigan[1]

ABSTRACT

This paper examines daily open-to-close returns from three major stock markets over the past five years including the October 1987 Stock Market Crash. We find some evidence that volatility spillover effects emanating from Japan have been gathering strength over time, especially after the 1987 Crash. This may be attributed to a growing awareness of domestic investors about the economic interdependence of international financial markets.

1. Introduction

The October 19, 1987 stock market Crash is noteworthy not only for the severity of its impact on the U.S. market, but also for the pervasiveness of its impact throughout the world's stock markets. Prior to the Crash, the correlation in returns across international stock markets in high-frequency data was found to be weak and difficult to detect above the normal noise associated with domestic trading. However, around the time of the Crash a strong correlation was exhibited across markets. This strong interdependence among financial markets could have fundamentally altered investor perceptions concerning the importance of foreign financial news, thereby permanently increasing the correlation in stock returns and volatility across markets.

Numerous studies have examined various aspects of the 1987 Crash.[2] Roll (1988) offers a comprehensive analysis of the international transmission of the 1987 Crash across all major world stock markets. King-Wadhwani (1990) examine an eight month period surrounding the 1987 Crash and document a "contagion" effect where a "mistake" in one market such as the Crash is transmitted to other markets. They also show increased correlation between markets just after the Crash. Neumark-Tinsley-Tosini (1988) study U.S.

---

[1] We thank participants of the conference "Statistical Models for Financial Volatility" at the University of California, San Diego for their useful comments.

[2] See Roll (1989) for an extensive review of this literature.

stocks that are dually listed in Tokyo or London. Previous overnight price change in Tokyo or London is used to predict New York price movements. They find significantly increased predictability after the Crash for a one month period. Both von Furstenberg-Jeon (1989) and Rogers (1990) hypothesize that a structural shift in relations among international stock returns occurs following the Crash.

Several recent papers have explored possible spillover effects across international financial markets. Ito-Roley (1987) investigate the effect of actual news announcements on the volatility of yen/dollar exchange rate in various geographic segments of the market around the clock. They find that the U.S. money supply announcement surprises have the most consistent effects on exchange rate volatility. Bailey (1990) examines the effect of U.S. money supply announcements on Pacific Rim stock indexes and reports that a number of these stock markets exhibit price reactions similar to reactions observed in New York. He finds that the differential sensitivity of this news across these markets can be partially explained by the degree of international capital flow restrictions that exist in these capital markets.

Engle-Ito-Lin (1990) examine intra-day foreign exchange rates in New York and Tokyo and find volatility spillover effects using a GARCH model. Ng-Chang-Chou (1991) present evidence on the extent of transmission of price volatility from the U.S. stock market to various Pacific Rim stock markets and the importance of government regulation of capital flows. Hamao-Masulis-Ng (1990) explore price change and volatility spillovers across Tokyo, London, and New York stock markets using a GARCH-M model. They report that over the pre-Crash period the transmission process of volatility across these markets differs in its impacts on domestic stock exchanges; while the Japanese market appears most sensitive to foreign volatility shocks, other markets, particularly the U.S. market is relatively insensitive to foreign (especially Japanese) volatility surprises.

Over the last two years, the international stock markets have exhibited several interesting phenomena, including the "mini-crash of October 1989, the sustained period of stock price rises in Japan followed by the recent severe price drops and high volatility observed in the Tokyo Stock Exchange. These events have further increased interest in comovements of prices across international stock markets, as is illustrated by the following quotes in the business press:

> "On January 12, a 666-point plunge in Tokyo's key Nikkei average kicked off a 71-point sell-off in the Dow-Jones industrials. A few weeks later, a 600-point plunge in Japan sent the Dow tumbling 60 points in the first half-hour of trading. They used to say that when the U.S. sneezes, the rest of the world catches pneumonia. No more. Japan's awesome financial and economic muscle has reached the point where its *kushami*, or "sneezes," can make Wall Street sick." ("When Japan Gets the Jitters, the Rest of the World Trembles," *Business Week*, February 12, 1990).

> "Many of the people who thought Japan's stock market was stupendously overpriced worried that the bubble's inevitable burst would set of a chain reaction of stock market plunges around the globe. So far, there is no sign of that doomsday link. While the Tokyo stock market is down 14.37% this year, stock market elsewhere in the world haven't fallen as steeply and don't seem to be following the Nippon lead." ("So Far, Tokyo Isn't Dragging Rest of World Markets Down," *Wall Street Journal*, February 27, 1990).

These two contradictory perspectives highlight the current controversy concerning the strength of international financial integration and its impacts on the relations among major stock markets.

This paper studies the price processes and the relations of the world's largest stock exchanges over the last five years. The purpose of this study is to explore whether there are significant shifts in the stock return generating processes and the importance of volatility spillovers from foreign markets preceding and following the October 1987 Stock Market Crash. We use a modification of the GARCH return generating process for measuring structural shifts in this process at and around the 1987 Crash. The normalized residuals from some of our models exhibit high kurtosis compared to a normal distribution. Leptokurtosis generally causes the estimated standard errors to be unreliable which invalidates conventional statistical inference using t-tests. Therefore, we also use robust standard error based on the quasi maximum likelihood approach developed by Wooldridge (1988, 1990) and Bollerslev-Wooldridge (1990) to compute t-values.

The paper is organized as follows. Section 2 describes the stock price data and is followed by Section 3 which reviews the basic ARCH framework and the particular modifications that we employ. Section 4 presents initial estimates of the GARCH model and then presents estimates of volatility spillover effects in intraday returns among the three international stock markets using a GARCH-M framework. Section 5 presents estimates of the structural changes in spillover effects at and around the 1987 Crash. Evidence of non-Crash related time trends in these spillover effects is presented in Section 6. Section 7 concludes the paper.

2. Data

Our database covers the five year period, April 1, 1985 to February 28, 1990 and encompasses daily open and closing prices of major market indices on the Tokyo, London and New York stock exchanges.[3] For the Tokyo Stock Exchange, we use the Nikkei 225 Stock Index, which is a price-weighted average stock price index. Opening price data were recorded at 9:15 am until December 18, 1987 and at 9:01 am thereafter, while closing prices are recorded at 3:00 pm Tokyo time. The price data were obtained from Nihon Keizai Shimbun Sha. There are several peculiarities about the Tokyo market. First, no trading

[3] These indices do not include dividend reinvestment which causes a small negative bias in the size of these recorded returns.

takes place between 11:00 am and 1:00 pm local time. Second, there was Saturday morning trading three times (or later twice) a month through January 1989. Third, there are price limits on individual stocks though they only apply for extremely large price changes.

In the London stock market, we use the Financial Times-Stock Exchange 100 Share (FTSE) Index which is a value weighted index. The opening price data were recorded at 9:00 am, while the official closing price was at 3:30 pm London time. While the actual close of the London market is at 5:00 pm, to minimize the overlap in trading periods with New York to one hour, we use the earlier official close used for U.K. tax purposes. The data source was the London International Stock Exchange and the London *Financial Times*.[4]

In the New York stock market, we use the Standard & Poor's 500 Composite Index. The S&P 500 is an equity value weighted arithmetic index. The primary data source was S&P's monthly "500 Information Bulletin." The opening stock price was measured at 10:01 am until September 30, 1985 and at 9:31 am thereafter and the close is at 4:00 pm EST.

Figure 1 shows trading hours of the three exchanges in Eastern Standard Time.

Figure 1

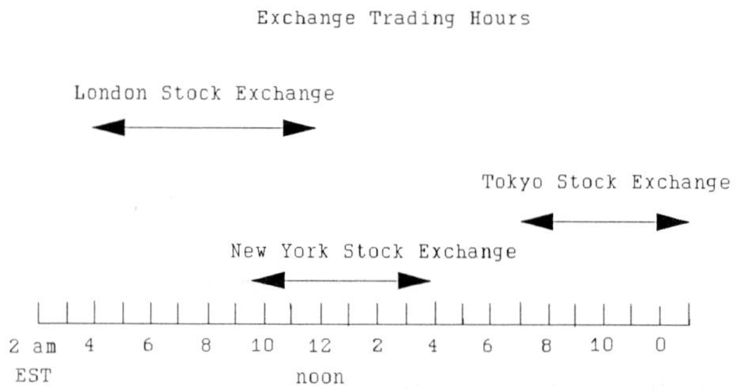

From these daily opening and closing prices, we compute daily open-to-close returns for our three stock indices. By studying open-to-close returns, we

---

[4] Unfortunately, on October 16, 1987 the United Kingdom experienced a severe hurricane which caused the London market to remain closed for the day.

can focus our analysis on periods when trading is actively taking place (which is when most information appears to be released to the market) and which has the advantage of representing periods of non-contemporaneous trading on our three stock exchanges.[5] While London stock market prices are based on the average of the bid and ask quotes which must be available from 9:00 am to 5:00 pm local time, in New York and Tokyo only transaction prices are used and markets can frequently experience delayed openings of individual stocks. When delays of the open occur, the Nikkei 225 and the S&P 500 indices use the prior day's closing price as a substitute for the unavailable opening price. This procedure introduces some artificial effects (*e.g.*, serial correlation) in the open-to-close and close-to-open returns of the New York and Tokyo stock indices.[6]

Figure 2 depicts the difference between daily high and low prices divided by the average of high and low of the day for the period surrounding the 1987 Crash. It is clear from the figure that volatility rises at the time of the Crash and persists for a prolonged period thereafter for all of the three markets.

Figure 2

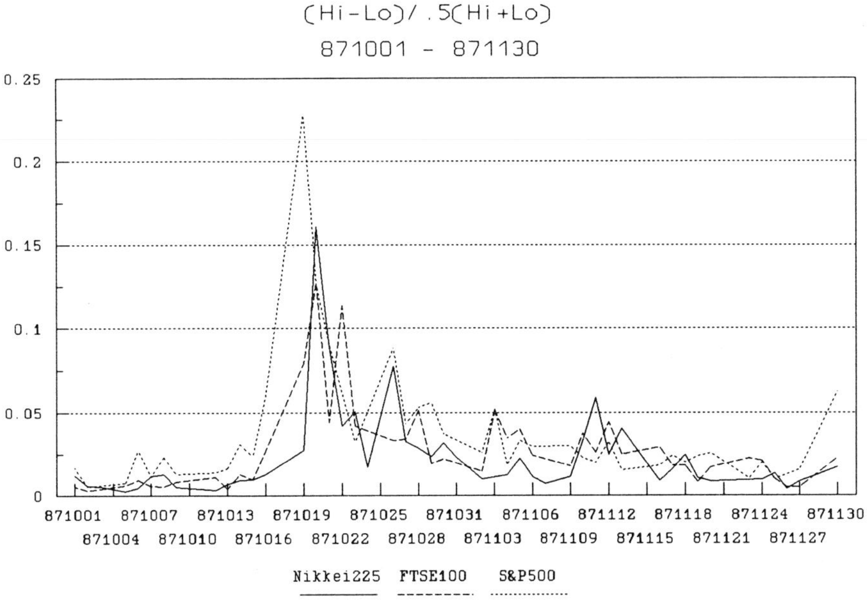

[5] The one exception to this statement is the last hour of trading on the London Stock Exchange represents the first hour of trading in New York.

[6] This is not a serious problem for the Nikkei prior to December 18, 1987 since we are using prices fifteen minutes after the market opens.

3. Application of the ARCH Framework to Intraday Stock Returns

To evaluate the interrelations of price movements among major international stock markets, we utilize variants of the autoregressive conditional heteroskedasticity (ARCH) model developed by Engle (1982) and extended by Bollerslev (1986, 1987), and Engle-Lilien-Robins (1987).[7] In this framework, the conditional variance, h, is assumed to be a linear function of past squared errors as well as possible exogenous variables. This feature captures the observed serial correlation of second moments that stock returns typically manifest and is consistent with the leptokurtic frequency distributions that stock return time series exhibit.

We begin by specifying a GARCH-M model with weekend/holiday dummy variables in both the conditional mean and variance equations to capture not only the negative Monday effect in mean returns but also Monday's higher volatility as found in Gibbons-Hess (1981) and Keim-Stambaugh (1984). Following earlier studies that document serial correlations in daily returns, we adjust the conditional mean return for a first order moving average process in an effort to insure the serial independence of the conditional error.[8] The resulting GARCH(1,1)-M model is specified below:

$$R_t = \alpha + \beta h_t + \delta W_t + \gamma \epsilon_{t-1} + \epsilon_t \tag{1}$$
$$h_t = a_t + b h_{t-1} + c \epsilon_{t-1}^2 + d W_t \quad ,$$

where $a > 0$, b, $c \geq 0$, h_t is conditional variance of the error term ϵ_t, and W_t is a weekend/holiday dummy variable which equals one on a day following a weekend or holidays and zero otherwise.

4. Spillover Effects Under a GARCH Model

The results of estimating this GARCH model for our three stock exchanges using daily open-to-close returns for the full sample period are presented in Table 1. The formulation assumes that there are no structural shifts or nonstationarities across the estimation period and in particular that the return generating process is not altered around the October 1987 Crash. In all three markets, the GARCH parameters (b and c) are highly significant and these two parameter estimates sum to values between .9 and .92. On the other hand, the GARCH-M parameter estimate (β) is insignificant, or if marginally significant, it can take on either a positive or negative sign. The diagnostic statistics for skewness and serial correlations of residuals and residuals squared all appear to indicate that the model is successful in characterizing the returns data in these markets. On the other hand, the

---

[7] For a survey of the literature on applications of ARCH in finance, see Bollerslev-Chou-Kroner (1990).

[8] This specification is based on the earlier results of Hamao-Masulis-Ng (1990).

coefficients of kurtosis display somewhat high values relative to a normal distribution, indicating that conventional t-values used to evaluate parameter estimates may be misstated. In order to cope with this problem, we present robust t-statistics in the third column for each market.

The significance of the conditional variance parameter estimate in the mean equation is a controversial issue as the contradictory evidence and conclusions of Akgiray (1989) and French-Schwert-Stambaugh (1987) indicate. We present new evidence on this issue by estimating this parameter in our model and find that the GARCH model is a more persuasive characterization of our data than the GARCH-M model. We also find that the weekend/holiday dummy variable in the mean equation has a negative parameter value in all these markets, though it is not statistically significant for the U.S. market. On the other hand, the weekend/holiday variable in the conditional variance equation has a significant negative parameter value in the U.S., and an insignificant value in other two markets.

We next modify model (1) to include a volatility spillover effect from both foreign markets trading while the domestic market was closed. The expanded model is specified below:

$$R_t = \alpha + \beta h_t + \delta W_t + \gamma \epsilon_{t-1} + \epsilon_t$$

(2)

$$h_t = a_t + bh_{t-1} + c\epsilon^2_{t-1} + dW_t + fX_{1t} + pX_{2t} \quad ,$$

where X_{it} is the most recent residual squared estimated from model (1) in foreign market i. X_{it} can be interpreted as the most recent volatility "surprise" realized in the foreign market while the domestic market is closed. Throughout the analysis, whenever the foreign market is closed for a holiday while the domestic market is open, we use the prior day's squared residual in the foreign market to estimate the spillover effect.

Table 2 shows the results of applying model (2) to intraday returns on the three exchanges over the full sample period. This model implicitly assumes that there is no structural change over the sample period including the period subsequent to the October 1987 Crash. Consistent with the results of Hamao-Masulis-Ng (1990), significant spillover effects from both foreign markets onto each of the three domestic markets are observed. It is also interesting to observe the substantial drop in the persistence parameters in the conditional variance, especially for the U.S. market. Further, much of the leptokurtosis evident in Table 1 is eliminated by allowing cross market spillover effects. The Ljung-Box statistics also indicate no significant serial correlation in residuals or squared residuals of the model for any the three markets.

Figure 3 visualizes the extent of volatility spillover effects around the Crash. The figure presents the natural logs of the conditional variances (h_t) estimated from model (1). A jump in the U.S. conditional variance is followed by an even larger reaction in the Japanese market and an increase in the U.K. market as well. The persistence of the increased level of volatility in the three international markets after the Crash is also clearly depicted.

Figure 3

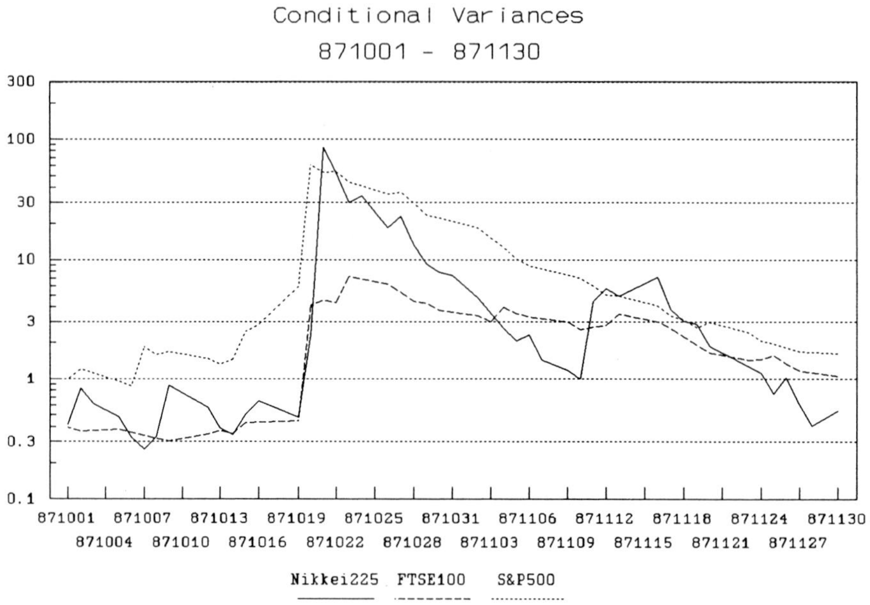

5. Estimates of Structural Changes in Spillover Effects

The model we use to estimate potential shifts in these spillover relations involves two step functions representing the Crash (the month of October 1987) and post Crash (from November 1987 to February 1990) subperiods, which allow for shifts in the impacts of the foreign volatility surprises. This expanded model is described below:

$$R_t = \alpha + \beta h_t + \delta W_t + \gamma \epsilon_{t-1} + \epsilon_t$$

(3)

$$h_t = a_t + bh_{t-1} + c\epsilon^2_{t-1} + dW_t + (f + gD_t + kA_t)X_{1t} + (p + qD_t + rA_t)X_{2t} \quad ,$$

where D_t equals one if t is in October 1987 (during the Crash month) and zero otherwise, and A_t equals one if t is in the post-Crash period (November 1987-February 1990) and zero otherwise. Modifying the model as described in (3) enables us to examine not only the significance of volatility spillover effects, but also the extent of discrete shifts in the levels of these effects across the three subperiods. As such, this evidence can be interpreted as a robustness test of the stationary model described by (2).

The results of estimating model (3) are presented in Table 3. Overall, the diagnostic statistics do not indicate model misspecification. The Ljung-Box statistics are not significant and importantly the measures of kurtosis do not appear to be particularly leptokurtic relative to a normal distribution. This suggests that the conventional t-statistics are likely to be valid, especially once it is recognized that the sample period was chosen precisely because a large set of abnormal price changes were known to occur.

The spillover effect from the U.S. market to Japan is significant before the Crash, but does not change significantly during the Crash month or thereafter. This pattern can also be discerned from Figure 4, which shows the response of the Japanese market to U.S. price volatility shocks. This figure is obtained by recursively solving the variance equation in model (3). The impulse response to foreign market i is given by coefficients on X_{it}, X_{it-1}, ..., holding the effect of the other foreign market (X_{j}. terms) constant.

Figure 4

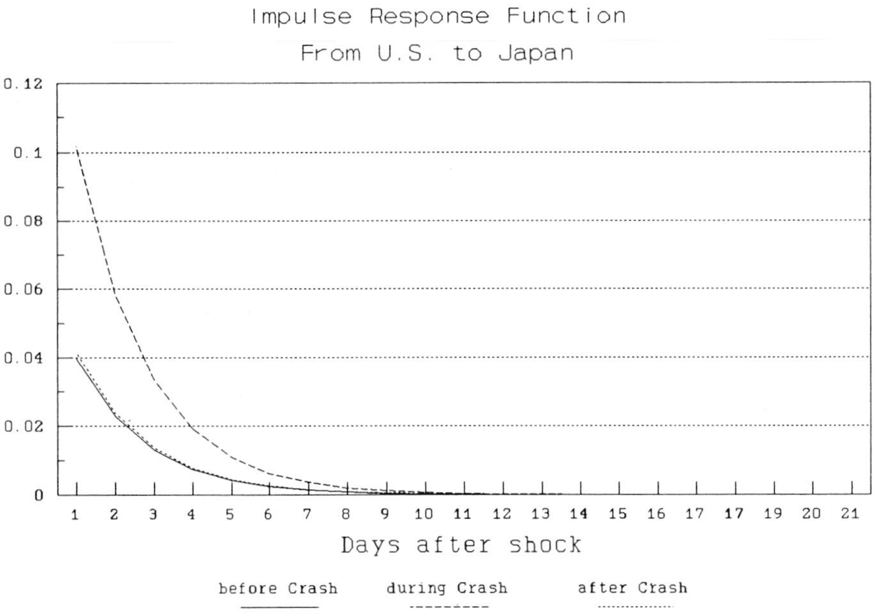

The volatility spillover effect from the U.K. onto the Japanese market is significant before October 1987, exhibits no significant change in October 1987, and shows a decrease in spillover level after the Crash. The post-Crash level, defined by the sum of parameters f and k is 0.032. This is approximately one-third the pre-Crash level, 0.090.[9]

Looking at the volatility spillover experienced in the U.K. market, we find that the Japanese market's influence is significant before October 1987, but there is no evidence of a significant change during the Crash month or afterwards. On the other hand, we find that the U.S. market's influence on U.K. price volatility to be insignificant before, during, and after the Crash month. This may be due to the fact that U.S. market movements occur further back in time or that their influence is felt indirectly through its effect on the Japanese market which in turn spills over on the U.K. market.[10]

Turning to volatility spillovers experienced in the U.S. market, we find that the volatility spillover effect from the U.K. onto the U.S. market to be significant before October 1987, and increases during October 1987.[11] However, after the Crash, the spillover effect diminishes and falls below its pre-Crash level. In contrast, the Japanese market has an insignificant influence before and in the month of October 1987, but then acquires a significant positive effect thereafter. Figure 5 depicts the impulse response function of the U.S. market to Japanese price volatility surprises. The figure suggests an increase in the Japanese market's influence after the Crash.

---

[9] It is noteworthy that the b and c parameter estimates in the conditional variance equation shown in Table 3 which allow for structural shift in the Crash month and beyond, are very similar in magnitude to the corresponding parameter estimates in Table 4 of Hamao-Masulis-Ng (1990) which specifies a stationary GARCH model using only pre-Crash data. This similarity and the insignificance of nearly all the parameters associated with the step functions indicate that the GARCH model does not appear to experience significant structural shifts after the Crash with the possible exception of the U.S. market.

[10] This may be further caused by the overlap in London and New York trading periods.

[11] The strength of this spillover effect may be exaggerated by the partially overlapping trading period in London and New York. It is also noteworthy that the volatility persistence in the U.S. market strengthens noticeably once we allow a shift in the GARCH process after the Crash.

Figure 5

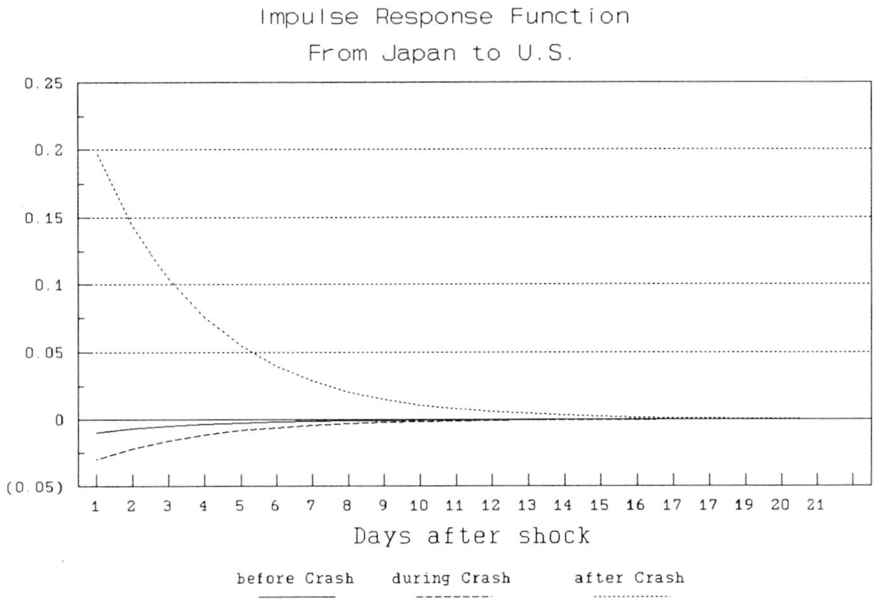

The above results are consistent with our earlier study which document a pronounced asymmetry in the transmission of volatility between Japan and the U.S. However, the current analysis which utilizes more recent data suggest a potentially important shift in these relationships subsequent to the 1987 Crash. We find that while the volatility spillover effect from the U.S. to Japan is consistently significant before, during and after the Crash, the volatility spillover effect from Japan to the U.S., though insignificant before and during the Crash period, increases to a possibly significant positive level in the post-Crash period.[12]

6. Time-Varying Spillover Effects

The previous section documents that the volatility spillover effect exhibits significant shifts around the 1987 Crash. This leads us to question whether the volatility spillover effects actually exhibit a general time trend instead of a structural shift. In order to investigate this issue, we further modify our basic GARCH model to allow for a non-stochastic time trend in the volatility spillover variable which may be linear or non-linear as well as the step functions for the Crash and post-Crash periods as specified below:

---

[12] This conclusion depends on whether or not one judges that the model residuals are significantly leptokurtic which would necessitate the use of robust standard errors.

$$
\begin{aligned}
R_t &= \alpha + \beta h_t + \delta W_t + \gamma\epsilon_{t-1} + \epsilon_t \\
h_t &= a_t + bh_{t-1} + c\epsilon^2_{t-1} + dW_t + [f(t^m) + gD_t + kA_t]X_{1t} \\
&\quad + [p(t^s) + qD_t + rA_t]X_{2t} \quad ,
\end{aligned}
\tag{4}
$$

where parameters m and s signify trends in spillover effects and

$m, s = 0$	stationary spillover effect;
$m, s < -1$	spillover effect decreasing at an increasing rate;
$-1 < m, s < 0$	spillover effect decreasing at a decreasing rate;
$0 < m, s < 1$	spillover effect increasing at a decreasing rate; and
$1 < m, s$	spillover effect increasing at an increasing rate.

This formulation also allows us to examine whether the spillover effect exhibits a discrete jump after the Crash. The results of estimating the GARCH model as specified above are presented in Table 4. As in Table 3, the coefficients of kurtosis for the model residuals are not particularly high, indicating that the use of conventional t-statistics may be justified.[13] The spillover effect from the U.S. market to Japan exhibits some upward trend which drops after the Crash. The spillover effect from the U.K. market to Japan exhibits a relatively large positive effect with an insignificant trend, but after October 1987 this effect declines. When we examine the U.K. market, we find no significant spillover effects from either the Japanese or U.S. markets. Turning to the U.S. market, we find no evidence of any trend in the spillover effect from the Japanese market, although there is evidence of a jump up in its level after the 1987 Crash. In looking at volatility spillovers from the U.K. market, we find a positive effect on the U.S. market during the Crash month, but not before or after. The coefficients for dummy variables for during and after the Crash (g, k, q, and r) show qualitatively similar patterns as Table 3.

While in most cases volatility spillover effects increase during the Crash period and then decline afterwards, the spillover effects from the Japanese market appear to be an exception. The spillover effects from the Japanese market to the U.S. market steadily increase over time, and experience a further jump in magnitude after the Crash period. One might attribute this change following the Crash to the increased awareness by U.S. investors of the importance of the Japanese economy to global economic conditions.

7. Conclusions

This study analyzes daily open-to-close returns from three major stock markets over the past five years, a period that includes the celebrated October 1987 Stock Market Crash. We find that the international transmission of volatility does not occur evenly around the world; instead,

---

[13] This is especially true when we take into account the fact that the sample period was explicitly chosen to include a period of abnormally large price changes.

there are spillover effects of disproportionate size from one market to the next. We also find that the volatility spillover effects have been relatively stable over our five year period even when we separate the Crash and post-Crash periods. The one major exception to this statement is that there is some weak evidence that volatility spillover effects emanating from Japan have been gathering strength over time, and these changes appear to be more pronounced following the 1987 Crash. This latter evidence is weakly supportive of the proposition that domestic investors have become more aware of the growing economic interdependence of international financial markets and the importance of Japanese financial developments for non-Japanese markets, since the 1987 Crash.

Table 1. GARCH Estimation of Open-Close Returns: Sample period April 1, 1985 - February 28, 1990

$$R_t = \alpha + \beta h_t + \delta W_t + \gamma \epsilon_{t-1} + \epsilon_t$$

$$h_t = a_t + b h_{t-1} + c \epsilon^2_{t-1} + d W_t \quad ,$$

where h_t represents the conditional variance of R_t, the stock index return and W_t represents a dummy variable which takes a value of one on days following weekends and holidays and zero otherwise.

	Japan Nikkei 225:			U.K. FTSE 100:			U.S. S&P 500:		
Number of Obs.:	1330			1242			1243		
	coeff.	t-stat.	robust t-stat.	coeff.	t-stat.	robust t-stat.	coeff.	t-stat.	robust t-stat.
α	.047	1.68	1.98	.144	3.38	2.12	.122	2.41	3.10
β	.074	1.36	1.66	-.176	-2.14	-1.26	-.007	-.16	-.22
γ	.108	3.10	3.23	-.049	-1.55	-1.63	.012	.32	.40
δ	-.080	-2.34	-1.30	-.133	-2.80	-2.79	-.077	-1.34	-1.22
a	.074	6.22	3.15	.037	3.57	1.30	.115	9.87	1.59
b	.522	17.70	3.51	.833	40.54	6.79	.792	46.07	6.24
c	.381	24.51	1.64	.068	5.83	1.34	.134	21.06	.98
d	.038	1.56	.61	.038	1.51	.19	-.127	-2.93	-.67
LR(6) for Ho: constant mean and variance:		743.81			251.30			545.47	
Coefficient of skewness for normalized residuals:		-1.04			-1.25			-1.16	
Coefficient of kurtosis for normalized residuals:		10.60			14.01			11.36	
Ljung-Box(12) for normalized residuals:		9.13			18.10			4.49	
Ljung-Box(12) for normalized squared residuals:		5.37			7.43			4.14	

Table 2. Volatility Spillover Effects Estimated from a GARCH-M model

$$R_t = \alpha + \beta h_t + \delta W_t + \gamma \epsilon_{t-1} + \epsilon_t$$

$$h_t = a_t + bh_{t-1} + c\epsilon^2_{t-1} + dW_t + fX_{1t} + pX_{2t},$$

where h_t represents the conditional variance of R_t, the stock index return, W_t represents a dummy variable which takes a value of one on days following weekends and holidays and zero otherwise, and X_{it} is the most recent residual squared from model (1) for each foreign market.

	From U.K.(f) and U.S.(p) to Japan:			From U.S.(f) and Japan (p) to U.K.:			From Japan (f) and U.K.(p) to U.S.:		
Number of obs.:	1330			1242			1243		
	coeff.	t-stat.	robust t-stat.	coeff.	t-stat.	robust t-stat.	coeff.	t-stat.	robust t-stat.
α	.056	2.03	2.28	.089	2.41	1.93	.136	2.62	2.47
β	.028	.62	.63	-.084	-1.16	-.81	-.038	-.79	-.72
γ	.103	3.06	3.31	-.040	-1.36	-1.37	.029	.84	.98
δ	-.094	-2.23	-2.13	-.133	-3.02	-2.85	-.061	-.98	-.96
a	.046	3.65	2.06	.044	3.69	1.51	.179	5.33	2.30
b	.522	12.23	8.46	.847	33.20	5.31	.587	11.66	4.14
c	.265	7.49	5.52	.031	2.46	1.62	.068	4.23	1.52
d	.066	2.32	1.24	-.042	-1.03	-.77	-.014	-.29	-.08
f	.062	3.28	2.26	.007	6.73	.19	.122	4.20	1.93
p	.044	5.55	1.99	.016	3.09	1.32	.231	8.19	1.26
LR(8) for Ho: constant mean and variance:		869.72			336.16			584.26	
Coefficient of skewness for normalized residuals:		-.41			-.70			-.70	
Coefficient of kurtosis for normalized residuals:		5.20			7.33			7.63	
Ljung-Box(12) for normalized residuals:		8.83			18.02			3.72	
Ljung-Box(12) for normalized squared residuals:		11.94			4.67			12.91	

Table 3. Volatility Spillover Effects Estimated from a GARCH(1,1)-M Model with Crash and Post Crash Dummies

$$R_t = \alpha + \beta h_t + \delta W_t + \gamma \epsilon_{t-1} + \epsilon_t$$

$$h_t = a_t + bh_{t-1} + c\epsilon^2_{t-1} + dW_t + (f + gD_t + kA_t)X_{1t} + (p + qD_t + rA_t)X_{2t} \quad ,$$

where D = 1 if t is in October 1987 (during the Crash month), and 0 otherwise, and A = 1 if t is in the after-Crash period (November 1987 - February 1990), and 0 otherwise.

	From U.K.(f, g, k) and U.S.(p, q, r) to Japan:			From U.S.(f, g, k) and Japan (p, q, r) to U.K.:			From Japan (f, g, k) and U.K.(p, q, r) to U.S.:		
Number of obs.:	1330			1242			1243		
	coeff.	t-stat.	robust t-stat.	coeff.	t-stat.	robust t-stat.	coeff.	t-stat.	robust t-stat.
α	.038	1.30	1.27	.080	1.95	2.17	.117	2.63	3.43
β	.088	1.53	1.33	-.062	-.74	-.82	-.015	-.36	-.61
γ	.105	3.09	3.40	-.035	-1.19	-1.21	.027	.81	.93
δ	-.087	-2.06	-2.03	-.134	-3.03	-2.91	-.052	-.84	-.84
a	.030	2.60	1.49	.047	3.48	2.02	.113	3.77	2.13
b	.572	15.07	9.45	.832	24.25	17.81	.724	14.70	11.33
c	.254	7.70	5.48	.027	2.06	1.16	.048	2.53	2.27
d	.054	1.90	1.10	-.028	-.65	-.43	.072	1.25	.53
f	.090	3.44	2.08	.005	.85	.60	-.009	-.67	-.70
g	-.443	-.83	-1.57	-.002	-.23	-.003	-.020	-.11	-.04
k	-.058	-2.18	-1.18	.008	1.00	.69	.208	5.10	1.41
p	.039	3.69	1.41	.021	2.72	1.66	.092	2.18	1.97
q	.061	.82	.51	.025	.58	.01	1.444	2.33	.79
r	.001	.12	.06	-.014	-1.47	-.69	-.040	-1.05	-.43
LR(12) for Ho: constant mean and variance:	877.06			342.18			655.99		
Coefficient of skewness for normalized residuals:	-.41			-.67			-.52		
Coefficient of kurtosis for normalized residuals:	5.17			6.96			6.33		
Ljung-Box(12) for normalized residuals:	9.22			18.18			4.92		
Ljung-Box(12) for normalized squared residuals:	9.72			4.04			7.94		

Table 4. Time-Varying Volatility Spillover Effects Estimated from a GARCH(1,1)-M Model

$$R_t = \alpha + \beta h_t + \delta W_t + \gamma \epsilon_{t-1} + \epsilon_t$$

$$h_t = a_t + bh_{t-1} + c\epsilon^2_{t-1} + dW_t + [f(t^m) + gD_t + kA_t]X_{1t} + [p(t^s) + qD_t + rA_t]X_{2t} \quad ,$$

where D = 1 if t is in October 1987 (during the Crash month), and 0 otherwise, and A = 1 if t is in the after-Crash period (November 1987 - February 1990), and 0 otherwise. Parameters m and s represent trends in spillover effects and

$m, s = 0$	stationary spillover effect;
$m, s < -1$	spillover effect decreasing at an increasing rate;
$-1 < m, s < 0$	spillover effect decreasing at an decreasing rate;
$0 < m, s < 1$	spillover effect increasing at a decreasing rate; and
$1 < m, s$	spillover effect increasing at an increasing rate.

	From U.K.(f, g, k, m) and U.S. (p, q, r, s) to Japan:			From U.S.(f, g, k, m) and Japan (p, q, r, s) to U.K.:			From Japan (f, g, k, m) and U.K. (p, q, r, s) to U.S.:		
Number of obs.:	1330			1242			1243		
	coeff.	t-stat.	robust t-stat.	coeff.	t-stat.	robust t-stat.	coeff.	t-stat.	robust t-stat.
α	.042	1.46	1.49	.084	2.10	2.31	.120	2.88	3.66
β	.076	1.31	1.23	-.067	-.81	-.88	-.017	-.40	-.71
γ	.105	3.16	3.36	-.037	-1.25	-1.27	.023	.71	.81
δ	-.085	-2.00	-2.03	-.137	-3.10	-2.98	-.051	-.85	-.83
a	.029	2.52	1.61	.047	3.61	1.97	.101	3.70	2.05
b	.582	15.53	9.64	.835	25.57	17.39	.728	15.94	11.55
c	.244	7.93	5.15	.029	2.21	1.25	.042	2.53	2.07
d	.043	1.62	.92	-.032	-.73	-.52	.095	1.72	.72
f	.141	1.54	.24	.030	.17	.15	-.041	-.51	-.33
g	-.510	-1.06	-1.59	-.003	-.29	-.004	-.002	-.02	-.01
k	-.053	-1.82	-.45	.010	.96	.71	.204	5.41	1.37
m	-.075	-.66	-.10	-.226	-.23	-.19	-.258	-.48	-.39
p	.000	.42	.23	.000	.25	.18	.008	.36	.19
q	.063	.86	.50	.024	.51	.01	1.496	2.33	.82
r	-.037	-1.78	-.70	-.036	-1.82	-1.55	-.089	-1.40	-.49
s	.902	2.48	1.40	.894	1.48	1.01	.399	.86	.49

Table 4 [continued]

	From U.K. (f, g, k, m) and U.S. (p, q, r, s) to Japan:	From U.S. (f, g, k, m) and Japan (p, q, r, s) to U.K.:	From Japan (f, g, k, m) and U.K. (p, q, r, s) to U.S.:
Coefficient of skewness for normalized residuals:	-.40	-.63	-.53
Coefficient of kurtosis for normalized residuals:	5.06	6.63	6.30
Ljung-Box(12) for normalized residuals:	8.68	18.28	5.02
Ljung-Box (12) for normalized squared residuals:	8.45	3.91	7.49

References

Akgiray, Vedat, 1989, "Conditional Heteroscedasticity in Time Series of Stock Returns: Evidence and Forecasts," *Journal of Business*, 62: 55-80.

Bailey, Warren, 1990, "U.S. Money Supply Announcements and Pacific Rim Stock Markets: Evidence and Implications," *Journal of International Money and Finance*, 9: 344-356.

Bollerslev, Tim, 1986, "Generalized Autoregressive Conditional Heteroskedasticity," *Journal of Econometrics*, 31: 307-327.

Bollerslev, Tim, 1987, "A Conditional Heteroskedastic Time Series Model for Speculative Prices and Rates of Return," *Review of Economics and Statistics*, 69: 542-547.

Bollerslev, Tim, Ray Y. Chou, and Kenneth Kroner, 1990, "ARCH Modeling in Finance: A Selective Review of the Theory and Empirical Evidence with Suggestions for Future Research," Working Paper, Northwestern University.

Bollerslev, Tim, and Jeffrey M. Wooldridge, 1990, "Quasi Maximum Likelihood Estimation of Dynamic Models With Time Varying Covariances," Working Paper, MIT.

Engle, Robert F., 1982, "Autoregressive Conditional Heteroskedasticity with Estimates of the Variance of United Kingdom Inflation," *Econometrica*, 50: 987-1007.

Engle, Robert F., Takatoshi Ito, and Wen-Ling Lin, 1990, "Meteor Showers or Heat Waves?: Heteroskedastic Intra-Daily Volatility in the Foreign Exchange Market," *Econometrica*, 58: 525-542.

Engle, Robert, David Lilien, and Russell Robins, 1987, "Estimating Time Varying Risk Premia in the Term Structure: The ARCH-M Model," *Econometrica*, 55: 391-407.

von Furstenberg, George M, and Bang Nam Jeon, 1989, "International Stock Price Movements: Links and Messages," *Brookings Papers on Economic Activity*, I: 125-179.

French, Kenneth R., G. William Schwert, and Robert F. Stambaugh, 1987, "Expected Stock Returns and Volatility," *Journal of Financial Economics*, 19: 3-29.

Gibbons, Michael R. and Patrick Hess, 1981, "Day of the Week Effects and Asset Returns," *Journal of Business*, 54: 579-596.

Hamao, Yasushi, Ronald W. Masulis, and Victor Ng, 1990, "Correlations in Price Changes and Volatility Across International Stock Markets," *Review of Financial Studies*, 3: 281-307.

Ito, Takatoshi, and Vance Roley, 1987, "News from the U.S. and Japan: Which Moves The Yen/Dollar Exchange Rate?" *Journal of Monetary Economics*, 19: 255-277, reprinted in this volume.

Keim, Donald and Robert Stambaugh, 1984, "A Further Investigation of the Weekend Effect in Stock Returns," *Journal of Finance*, 39: 819-837.

King, Mervyn and Sushil Wadhwani, 1990, "Transmission of Volatility Between Stock Markets," *Review of Financial Studies*, 3: 5-33.

Neumark, David, P.A. Tinsley, and Susan Tosini, 1988, "After-Hours Stock Prices and Post-Crash Hangovers," Working Paper, Federal Reserve Board, Washington, D.C.

Ng, Victor K., Rosita P. Chang, and Ray Y. Chou, 1991, "An Examination of the Behavior of the Pacific Basin Stock Market Volatility," in *Pacific Basin Capital Markets Research*, Vol. 2, Amsterdam: North-Holland, forthcoming.

Rogers, John H., 1990, "International Stock Price Movements, the Crash, and the Mini-Crash: The Case of Emerging Markets," Working Paper, Pennsylvania State University.

Roll, Richard W., 1988, "The International Crash of October 1987," in Robert W. Kamphius, Roger C. Kormendi, and J.W. Henry Watson, (eds.) *Black Monday and the Future of Financial Markets*, Homewood, IL: Irwin.

Roll, Richard W., 1989,"Price Volatility, International Market Links and Their Implication for Regulatory Policies," *Journal of Financial Services Research*, 3: 27-60.

Wooldridge, Jeffrey M., 1988, "Specification Testing and Quasi Maximum Likelihood Estimation," Working Paper, MIT.

Wooldridge, Jeffrey M., 1990, "A Unified Approach to Robust Regression-Based Specification Tests," *Econometric Theory*, 6: 17-43.

Japanese Financial Market Research
W.T. Ziemba, W. Bailey and Y. Hamao (Editors)
1991 Elsevier Science Publishers B.V.

Private Information, Trading Volume, and Stock-Return Variances

Michael J. Barclay
University of Rochester

Robert H. Litzenberger
Wharton School
University of Pennsylvania

Jerold B. Warner
University of Rochester

New evidence is provided on the determinants of stock-return variances. First, when the Tokyo Stock Exchange is open on Saturday, the weekend variance increases; weekly variance is unaffected, however, despite an increase in weekly volume. Second, the listing of U.S. stocks in Tokyo substantially increases the number of trading hours, but Tokyo volume is negligible for these U.S. stocks and their 24-hour variance is unaffected. The overall results are consistent with the predictions of private-information-based rational trading models, but inconsistent with both the irrational trading noise and public-information hypotheses.

Support for this research was provided by the Managerial Economics Research Center at the University of Rochester (Barclay and Warner). The authors thank Fischer Black, Harry DeAngelo, Eugene Fama, Kenneth French, Michael Gibbons, Ronen Israel, Craig MacKinlay, Wayne Mikkelson, John Long, Bill Schwert, Jay Shanken, Ross Watts, Mark Weinstein, Jerold Zimmerman, seminar participants at the University of Chicago, Harvard Business School, the University of Michigan, Ohio State University, the University of Rochester, Stanford University, and the Wharton School of the University of Pennsylvania, and an anonymous referee for helpful comments. We are especially grateful to Tomio Arai of Nomura Securities, Inc., for helpful discussions and for providing some of the data. Address reprint requests to Michael J. Barclay, Assistant Professor of Business Administration, University of Rochester, Rochester, NY 14627.

Return variances for common stocks are higher during trading than nontrading hours [Fama (1965), Granger and Morgenstern (1970), Oldfield and Rogalski (1980), Christie (1981)]. The higher return variances are not fully explained by more public information released during trading hours [French and Roll (1986)]. This article provides new evidence on the determinants of stock-return variance, and in particular on the relation between variance, private information, and trading volume.

The Tokyo Stock Exchange is the world's largest exchange,[1] and has two institutional features that provide an almost ideal experiment for our study. First, until recently, the Tokyo Stock Exchange was open for half a normal trading day approximately three Saturdays per month, and closed on other Saturdays. By examining the variance of stock returns over weekends with and without Saturday trading, we can analyze the effects of trading on stock-return variance, holding constant the normal flow of public information. This Tokyo weekend analysis is similar to French and Roll (1986), who examine how the variance of New York Stock Exchange (NYSE) returns was affected when the NYSE closed on 24 Wednesdays in 1968 to clear a paperwork backlog. The present study, however, examines Tokyo trading volume as well as return variances, and it is based on a much longer time series of data. The volume data allow us to study the separate effects of trading volume and trading hours on stock-return variance.

A second feature of the Tokyo Stock Exchange is that trading takes place when the U.S. exchanges are closed, and vice versa.[2] Thus, U.S. stocks traded on the Tokyo exchange or Japanese stocks traded on U.S. exchanges have increased trading hours. The volume of a stock traded on a foreign exchange is light, however, in relation to its volume traded in the domestic market. Internationally listed firms, therefore, permit study of the effects of increasing the number of available trading hours, holding constant total trading volume.

When the Tokyo Stock Exchange is open on Saturday, the weekend (i.e., Friday close to Monday close) variance of Japanese stock returns is roughly twice as large as when the exchange is closed on Saturday. The weekly variance does not increase, however, even though Saturday trading increases weekly share volume. The increase in variance over weekends with Saturday trading appears to be offset by lower variance on surrounding days.

---

[1] The total market value of equities listed on the Tokyo Stock Exchange in December 1987 was $2515 billion, 13 percent larger than on the New York Stock Exchange. See Nomura Research Institute (1988, p. 21).

[2] On weekdays, the Tokyo Stock Exchange is open from 9 to 11 A.M. and from 1 to 3 P.M. local time. Since Tokyo is 14 hours ahead of New York, this corresponds to 7 to 9 P.M. and 11 P.M. to 1 A.M. Eastern Standard Time. Saturday trading hours on the Tokyo Stock Exchange were from 9 to 11 A.M. local time.

The higher weekend but unchanged weekly variance is consistent with the analysis of Kyle (1985), who provides a structural link between the volume of trading and stock-return variance. Kyle models the trading strategy of uninformed liquidity traders and traders with private information, and shows that variance is caused by private information revealed through trades. An alternative explanation for the higher weekend variance is that traders overreact to each other's trades. Although this irrational trading noise hypothesis is loosely specified, several versions are inconsistent with the data. For example, if irrational trading noise is related to either hours or volume of trading, then weeks with Saturday trading should have higher weekly variance. We also reject the view that the higher variance during exchange trading hours is due to increased public-information releases.

Secondary listing on a foreign stock exchange does not affect the pattern or increase the level of stock-return variance. Moreover, U.S. firms traded on the Tokyo exchange do not have a higher weekend variance when the Tokyo exchange is open on Saturday. Both pieces of evidence suggest that there is no causal relation between trading hours and stock-return variance as would be expected if irrational noise is related to the number of hours of trading. A significant volume of trading is required for private information to be incorporated into stock prices. This is consistent with the analysis of Admati and Pfleiderer (1988), who conclude that it is optimal for traders with private information (and a low intraday rate of information decay) to execute their trades during periods when uninformed liquidity traders are normally most active.

In Section 1, the article's testable propositions are discussed. The results are presented in Section 2, and the conclusions in Section 3.

1. Theory and Empirical Implications

In this section, the role of private information in generating variance is discussed first. The theoretical work of Kyle (1985) and Admati and Pfleiderer (1988) provides a useful framework for developing our predictions. These predictions of the private-information hypothesis are then contrasted with the predictions of the irrational trading noise and public-information hypotheses.

1.1 Private information and stock-return variances: background

The recent work of Kyle and Admati and Pfleiderer provides a structural link between private information, trading volume, and stock-return variances. Kyle models a market with three types of traders:

informed investors who trade strategically to maximize the profits from their private information, random liquidity traders whose buy and sell orders arrive randomly and exogenously through time, and a specialist who has no private information, but learns from price and volume changes. In this model, private information is incorporated into prices over time at a constant rate per trading hour, with the price at the end of the relevant trading interval reflecting all private information. The variance of returns over the entire trading interval reflects only the arrival of new information. Within the trading interval, the variance is affected by the volume of trade by random liquidity traders because specialists cannot distinguish between informed and liquidity trades. Thus, trading noise (i.e., variance in excess of that generated in a fully revealing rational expectations model) arises endogenously in this model because price movements and associated volumes are noisy signals for the information of informed traders. This trading noise is rational, however, since the price established by the specialist is an unbiased estimate of the true price conditional on his information set, and the trading noise does not result in pricing errors that are systematically reversed. The variance generated in this model is associated with trading volume, and trading hours per se do not cause variance.

In related work, Admati and Pfleiderer (1988) extend Kyle's analysis to include a fourth class of traders called discretionary liquidity traders. Discretionary liquidity traders have no private information. Unlike the random liquidity traders, these traders have some discretion over the timing of their trades. Admati and Pfleiderer show that, in general, trades of both discretionary liquidity traders and informed traders will cluster, with each group preferring to trade when the market is thick. This clustering of trades causes variance to be highest when trading is most active. Only random liquidity traders and informed traders for whom the intraday rate of decay for private information is high will trade during inactive periods when markets are thin. As in Kyle's model, returns are serially uncorrelated (conditional on the uninformed traders' information set), and trading hours per se do not cause variance.

1.2 Saturday trading: testable propositions

Although neither Kyle nor Admati and Pfleiderer explicitly examine the impact of increased trading hours, their analyses provide useful intuition. Specifically, Kyle's model suggests that opening the Tokyo exchange on Saturday should not change the variance of weekly returns as long as the total amount of new public and private information is unaltered. Within the week, however, a change in the pattern of daily variances would be expected, reflecting the effects of the new trading hours on the arrival of traders. If the normal volume of liquidity trading on Saturdays is substantial, informed traders will shift some of their trades from the surrounding days to Saturday. If some discretionary liquidity traders (as in the Admati and Pfleiderer model) also move their trades to Saturday, the shift of informed trades will be reinforced. This shift of informed trades will cause the return variance to be larger during weekends when the exchange is open on Saturday because of the additional private information revealed through trading during this interval. Assuming that the arrival of private informtion to informed investors is unaffected by Saturday trading, variance will be lower on surrounding days because of the reduction in the amount of information revealed through informed trades.

Our tests also provide information on the nature of traders' private information. The variances examined in this article are for a market index, a variety of industry indexes, and individual Japanese stocks that are also listed on the NYSE. If the private information revealed through trading is predominantly firm-specific, significant increases in the weekend return variances for individual stocks are expected when there is Saturday trading. Since firm-specific information is effectively diversified away in large portfolios, however, no change in the variance of the industry indexes or the market index is expected. On the other hand, if private information contains firm-specific, industry, and marketwide components, then the weekend return variances will also increase for the industry and market indexes.

Saturday trading and irrational trading noise. In contrast to analyses in which variance is caused by private information, the possibility that variance is caused by the overreaction of traders to each other's trades has been raised by a number of authors [e.g., Shiller (1981, 1986), Black (1986), French and Roll (1986), and Summers (1986)]. Although the specific model underlying irrational trading noise is often imprecise, Tokyo Saturday trading provides information about several plausible versions.

Permanent trading noise. French and Roll (1986, p. 14) assume that any permanent irrational trading noise is related to the number of trading hours. Unlike the private-information view, their characterization of irrational trading noise predicts a positive relation between the weekly variance and the amount of trading time in a week. For Japanese stocks, weeks with Tokyo Saturday trading should have higher variance than weeks with no Saturday trading. Moreover, if irrational trading noise is related only to the amount of trading time, variances on days surrounding weekends should not be affected by whether or not there is Saturday trading. An alternative characterization of permanent irrational trading noise is that it is positively related to trading volume. Under this view, if the additional weekend volume caused by Saturday trading also increases the weekly volume for weeks with Saturday trading, then an increase in weekly return variance is predicted.

Temporary trading noise. If irrational trading noise is temporary and if the increased variance generated by Saturday trading is attributable to pricing errors that are reversed in the following week, the covariance between the Saturday return and the return early in the following week will be negative. We investigate several aspects of this issue, although a detailed model of how trading noise affects the autocorrelation structure of returns is beyond the scope of this paper.

Saturday trading and public information. Our tests also provide insights into whether the higher variance during trading hours is caused by public-information releases. Saturday is not a normal business day in Japan. Although many Japanese companies are open on some Saturdays, the Saturdays that nonfinancial firms are open appear to be independent of the Saturdays the exchange is open.[3] In addition, Japanese corporations infrequently release information on a Saturday. This reduces the likelihood that any discretionary public-information releases will occur or be timed to whether the exchange is open or closed on Saturday.[4] Thus, if variance is caused primarily by public information, there should be no difference between the weekend return variance with and without Saturday trading.

1.3 The effect of listing on a foreign exchange

Trading in Tokyo takes place when U.S. exchanges are closed, and vice versa. Thus, U.S. stocks traded on the Tokyo Stock Exchange and Japanese stocks traded in the United States have increased trading hours. These extended trading hours provide the basis for several additional tests.

If a stock is traded in more than one market, liquidity traders will concentrate their activity in the market with the lowest transaction costs. For stocks that are internationally listed, transaction costs are likely to be lower on the domestic than on the foreign exchange.[5]

---

[3] Some financial institutions, including banks and foreign exchange traders, are open on the same Saturdays as the exchange. In addition, the financial wire service is operating whenever the exchange is open.

[4] This summary is based on informal interviews with individuals at Japanese banks, brokerage firms, and the Tokyo Stock Exchange.

[5] For example, in a speech delivered to the Brookings Institute, Mr. Kurokawa, Chairman of Nomura Securities International, stated: "Although stocks of 93 foreign companies are listed on the [Tokyo

Since discretionary liquidity traders in rational trading models prefer to cluster their trades, most liquidity trading would be expected to occur on the lower-cost domestic market. Since informed traders attempt to conceal their identity by trading when liquidity trading is normally high, informed traders having a sufficiently low intraday decay rate for private information will also concentrate their trades in the domestic market. Thus, the Admati and Pfleiderer model suggests that volume will be lower in the foreign than in the domestic market, and that international listing of a common stock will have little effect on either the level or the pattern of the stock-return variance. With few informed traders active in the foreign market, the extended trading hours will have little effect on return variance.

Secondary listing on a foreign exchange and permanent irrational trading noise. If irrational trading noise is permanent and positively related to the number of trading hours, a stock's overnight return variance will increase when the firm is listed internationally. Similarly, U.S. stocks traded in Tokyo will have higher weekend return variances when the exchange is open on Saturday. If irrational trading noise is positively related to volume, however, and secondary listing does not increase total trading volume, return variance will be unchanged. Under these conditions, the predictions of the volume-related irrational trading noise hypothesis and the private-information hypothesis are the same.

2. Empirical Results

2.1 General characteristics of returns on the Tokyo Stock Exchange Composite Index

Table 1 shows the pattern of daily trading volume on the Tokyo Stock Exchange and the pattern of daily return variance for the Tokyo Composite Index.[6] The variance of the return on the Tokyo Composite Index is no higher over a typical weekend than over a single trading day, even though the weekend is two or three times as long.[7] The

Stock Exchange], their trading volume in Tokyo is not very heavy. The reason for this is that large institutional investors tend to trade foreign stocks in each mother country, where there is greater liquidity. A major portion of the orders from non-residents is directed to each stock's home market." See Kurokawa (1988).

[6] The Tokyo Stock Exchange Composite Index (TOPIX) is a value-weighted portfolio of all stocks listed on the first section of the exchange. The first section includes most active issues traded in Japan (1055 issues in 1986). The index is not adjusted for dividend payments. See the Tokyo Stock Exchange (1987). Our sources for the Tokyo return data are the Nikkei Telecom data retrieval service and Nomura Securities.

[7] The Monday return variance is calculated using two-day returns (measured from Saturday close to Monday close) for weekends when the exchange is open on Saturday and three-day returns (measured from Friday close to Monday close) when the exchange is closed on Saturday.

Table 1
Variance of returns and trading volume for the Tokyo Stock Exchange Composite Index by day of week, January 1, 1973, to January 31, 1989

Day of week	Ratio of return variance to average weekday return variance	Ratio of trading volume to average weekday trading volume
Monday	0.96	0.77
Tuesday	0.91	0.91
Wednesday	1.04	1.05
Thursday	0.99	1.00
Friday	1.01	1.04
Saturday	0.63	0.60
One-day holiday	1.30	0.86
Year-end six-day holiday	1.34	0.51

Monday's return is based on Saturday close to Monday close for weeks when the exchange was open on Saturday and Friday close to Monday close for other weeks. Weekday (Tuesday through Friday) returns are 24-hour close-to-close returns. The average weekday return variance is 4.70×10^{-5}. The average weekday volume is 441,946,000 shares.

variance of returns is also lower over holidays when the Tokyo exchange is closed than when it is open. For example, the variance of two-day returns including a one-day holiday is only 30 percent higher than the variance over a normal trading day, and the variance of seven-day returns including a six-day year-end holiday is only 34 percent higher than the variance over a normal trading day. This evidence of higher stock-return variance during Tokyo exchange trading hours than during nontrading hours is similar to the relation between variance and exchange trading hours found in previous studies of U.S. markets.

From January 1973 through January 1989, the Tokyo Stock Exchange was open for half a normal trading day on 585 Saturdays and closed on 254. From Table 1, both the average volume and the return variance are lower on trading Saturdays than on any of the five weekdays. However, the return variance as a fraction of the normal weekday return variance, 0.63, and the trading volume as a fraction of the normal weekday trading volume, 0.60, are both similar to the relative number of trading hours, 0.50. Thus, although Saturday is not a normal business day, neither the trading volume nor the return variance is lower per hour of trading on Saturday than during the rest of the week. This suggests that the release of public information is not the primary determinant of stock-return variances.

2.2 Saturday trading on the Tokyo Stock Exchange

Methodology. Our tests compare the volume and variance for intervals (e.g., Friday close to Monday close) with Saturday trading to the volume and variance over the same intervals without Saturday trading. As discussed in the Appendix, estimation procedures that give equal

Table 2
Ratio of return variances and trading volumes for the Tokyo Stock Exchange Composite Index for periods near Saturdays when the exchange is open in relation to periods near Saturdays when the exchange is closed, January 1, 1973, to January 31, 1989

	Ratio of variances	Ratio of volumes
Periods including Saturdays		
Friday to Monday	2.12* (0.001)	1.92‡ (0.001)
Friday to Tuesday	1.21 (0.156)	1.46‡ (0.001)
Friday to Wednesday	0.91 (0.622)	1.32‡ (0.001)
Wednesday to Wednesday	0.87 (0.744)	1.21‡ (0.002)
Periods preceding Saturdays		
Wednesday to Friday	1.25 (0.826)	1.04 (0.284)
Periods following Saturdays		
Monday to Wednesday	0.72† (0.094)	1.06 (0.181)

p values are in parentheses. For periods including Saturdays, the variance ratio *p* value is the fraction of the empirical bootstrap distribution that is less than 1.0; for periods excluding Saturdays, the variance ratio *p* value is the fraction of the empirical bootstrap distribution that exceeds 1.0. For the volume ratios, the *p* values are the tail probabilities of the normal distribution for a two-tailed difference of means test. All returns are calculated with closing prices.

Number of observations: 585 Saturdays with trading and 254 Saturdays with no trading.

* One-tailed test significantly greater than 1.0 at .01 level using a bootstrap algorithm.

† One-tailed test significantly less than 1.0 at .1 level using a bootstrap algorithm.

‡ One-tailed test significantly greater than 1.0 at .01 level using difference of means *t*-test.

weight to each observation yield severely downward-biased estimates of the volume and variance ratios. This bias arises because the relative frequency of nontrading Saturdays doubled after August 1986,[8] and annual trading volume and return variance increased dramatically at that time. Our estimation procedures weight the observations to provide unbiased estimates of the volume and variance ratios. These procedures are described in the Appendix.

Effects of Saturday trading on trading volume. Table 2 shows trading volume for weeks with and without Saturday trading.[9] The average combined Saturday and Monday volume when there is Saturday trading exceeds the average Monday volume when there is no Saturday trading by 92 percent. The *t*-statistic for the difference is

[8] The Tokyo Stock Exchange was closed on the third Saturday of the month from January 1973 to July 1983, on the second Saturday of the month from August 1983 to July 1986, and on the second and third Saturdays of the month from August 1986 through January 1989. The exchange is now closed on all Saturdays.

[9] Data for 1987 exclude October to insulate the results from any undue influence of the global market crash. The conclusions are not sensitive to this deletion.

11.32. The average weekly volume (measured Wednesday close to Wednesday close) centered on a trading Saturday is 21 percent higher than the average weekly volume centered on a nontrading Saturday, and the difference is statistically significant at the .01 level using a one-tailed test ($t = 2.84$). The higher weekly volume appears largely attributable to the higher weekend volume. Although the average trading volume over our sample period is from 2 to 6 percent higher for each weekday near a Saturday when the exchange is open, the differences are not statistically significant.

Effects of Saturday trading on return variance. From Table 2, the weekend return variance for the Tokyo Composite Index, measured from Friday close to Monday close, is 112 percent higher for weekends with Saturday trading than for weekends without Saturday trading. Using a bootstrap algorithm,[10] the variance ratio of 2.12 is statistically significantly greater than 1.0 at the .01 level. This evidence is inconsistent with the hypothesis that the higher variance during trading hours is caused by a greater flow of public information, since the likelihood of a public-information release on a Saturday when the exchange is open does not differ from the corresponding likelihood on a Saturday when the exchange is closed. Our conclusion about the significance of the increase in the weekend variance does not appear to be sensitive to the bootstrap test procedure. To examine the robustness of the results, we use a squared ranks test for equal variances to calculate significance levels for all variance ratios in Table 2.[11] The qualitative results are unchanged.

Despite the increased weekend variance, it does not appear that the weekly return variance on the Tokyo Stock Exchange Composite Index is higher for weeks with Saturday trading than for weeks without Saturday trading. The ratio of weekly return variances (measured Wednesday close to Wednesday close) for weeks with and without Saturday trading is 0.87, which is not statistically different from 1.0 at the .1 level using the bootstrap test.[12]

Our finding that the increased weekly volume and number of trading hours do not increase the weekly return variance helps distinguish between competing explanations for why variance occurs. The finding is consistent with rational trading models such as Kyle's. These models predict that the weekly variance will be unaffected if there is no change in the arrival of private information. Our results do not support

[10] The algorithm for calculating bootstrap p values is provided in the Appendix.

[11] The squared ranks test is described in the Appendix.

[12] Fractiles for the empirical distribution of the bootstrap weekly variance ratios are 0.01 (0.59), 0.05 (0.69), 0.1 (0.73), 0.9 (1.14), 0.95 (1.22), 0.99 (1.33).

the hypothesis that irrational trading noise is permanent and proportional to either hours of trading or trading volume. If irrational trading noise is proportional to trading volume, the weekly volume and variance ratios should be equal. Using a bootstrap procedure, we reject this hypothesis at the .02 level.

The evidence also does not support the view that the higher weekend variance is generated by temporary pricing errors that are reversed in the following week. For weeks with Saturday trading, the correlation between the Friday close to Saturday close return and the Saturday close to Wednesday close return on the Tokyo Composite Index is .01, and is not significantly different from zero.[13] Stock indexes typically exhibit positive serial correlation caused by the nonsynchronous trading of the stocks in the index. As discussed below, we have return data for eight Japanese stocks. The average correlation between the Friday close to Saturday close return and the Saturday close to Wednesday close return is −.08 (three of the correlation coefficients are significant at the .05 level).

There is some evidence that the dissipation of the variance generated during Saturday trading is explained by reduced variance for the weekdays immediately following Saturdays when the exchange is open. From Monday close to Wednesday close, the ratio of the variance with Saturday trading to the variance without Saturday trading is only 0.72, with a bootstrap p value of .09. Individually, the Tuesday and Wednesday variance ratios are 0.80 and 0.70.[14] A lower return variance but unchanged volume on individual weekdays following Saturday trading is inconsistent with the hypothesis that irrational trading noise is related to volume. Rather, the variance ratios suggest that privately informed traders accelerate some of their trades from Tuesday and Wednesday to the preceding Saturday when there is Saturday trading. The variance ratio for the preceding Wednesday through Friday is 1.25 (with a p value of 0.83) and suggests that informed traders do not postpone their trades from Thursday or Friday until Saturday.

Results for industry indexes and individual stocks. In addition to daily return data for the Tokyo Stock Exchange Composite Index, our tests use daily return data from July 1982 through January 1989 for 28 Japanese industry indexes and eight Japanese stocks that are also listed on the NYSE. This period includes 219 Saturdays when the Tokyo exchange was open and 119 Saturdays when it was closed.

[13] The correlation is similar if the return from Saturday close to the following Friday is substituted for the Saturday close to Wednesday close return.

[14] Consistent with the conclusion that variance is lower following Saturday trading, Puffer (1989) finds that the variance ratio for the period from Monday open to Monday close is 0.72 for the Nikkei index from 1985 to 1989.

Table 3
Ratio of variances for 28 industrial group indexes and 8 individual stocks for periods including Saturdays when the Tokyo Stock Exchange is open and periods including Saturdays when the exchange is closed. All returns are calculated with closing prices, July 1, 1982, to January 31, 1989

	Friday to Monday	Friday to Tuesday	Friday to Wednesday	Wednesday to Wednesday
	Panel A: 28 Industrial groups			
Average	2.18	1.49	1.30	1.17
Marine	2.88†	1.25	1.62*	1.03
Mining	2.38†	2.19†	1.45*	1.79†
Construction	2.33†	1.97†	1.22	0.81
Foods	2.44†	1.53	1.40	1.32
Fiber/textiles	2.28†	1.52*	1.14	1.09
Pulp/paper	2.41†	1.20	1.07	1.40
Chemicals	2.21†	1.31	1.32	1.26
Oil/coal	2.11†	1.78†	1.66*	1.77†
Gum	2.64†	2.08†	1.77*	0.97
Glass/cement	2.07†	1.46*	1.14	0.98
Steel	2.74†	1.66*	0.98	0.98
Nonsteel	2.66†	1.53*	1.57*	1.29
Metal	1.96†	2.51†	1.90†	1.22
General machinery	1.76†	1.45*	1.28	1.08
Electrical	1.79*	1.38	1.25	0.90
Shipbuilding/automobile	2.56†	1.53*	1.44*	1.23
Precision instruments	1.93†	1.46*	1.24	0.94
Other manufacturing	1.94†	1.41	1.47*	1.12
Trade/retail	2.37†	1.72*	1.37	1.05
Financial	1.70	0.96	1.84	0.59
Real estate	2.05†	1.58*	1.25	1.39
Transportation: Land	2.05†	1.02	0.84	0.91
Sea	2.14†	1.49*	1.40	1.46*
Air	1.53	0.89	0.66	0.75
Warehouses	1.64*	1.31	1.69*	1.93†
Communication	1.82*	0.86	1.03	0.85
Utilities	2.61†	1.06	0.97	1.49*
Leisure	2.03†	1.57†	1.55†	1.23
	Panel B: 8 Individual stocks			
Average	1.80	1.38	1.17	0.99
Hitachi	2.01†	1.27	1.19	1.08
Matsushita	1.73*	1.37	1.31	0.95
Sony	1.46	1.23	0.83	0.77
Honda	1.32	1.27	1.12	0.93
TDK	1.91*	1.52*	1.28	1.11
Pioneer	1.88†	1.43*	1.26	1.20
Kubota	1.99†	1.63*	1.40	1.00
Kyocera	1.92†	1.30	0.98	0.88

Number of observations: 219 Saturdays with trading, 119 Saturdays with no trading.

* One-tailed test significant at .05 level using a bootstrap algorithm.

† One-tailed test significant at .01 level using a bootstrap algorithm.

From Table 3, the average weekend return variance with Saturday trading is 118 percent higher for the 28 industry indexes and 80 percent higher for the eight Japanese stocks than the weekend return variance with no Saturday trading. The weekend return variance is greater when there is Saturday trading for all 28 industry indexes and for all eight of the internationally traded Japanese stocks. The ratios for these industry indexes and the individual stocks are strikingly similar to the results for the composite index, suggesting that private information revealed through trading has marketwide, industry, and firm-specific components.

2.3 Internationally listed firms

Under the private-information hypothesis, the addition of exchange trading hours when liquidity traders are normally inactive should have little impact on the rate of dissemination of private information. Informed traders having a sufficiently low intraday rate of decay in the value of their private information will postpone their trades to periods when liquidity traders are more active. Thus, the listing of an NYSE stock on the Tokyo exchange accompanied by inactive trading on the Tokyo exchange should not significantly affect the stock's overnight variance. An alternative to the private-information hypothesis is that irrational trading noise causes variance and is related to the number of hours of trading. In this view, a stock's overnight return variance should rise when a firm is listed internationally. If irrational trading noise is positively related to volume, however, and secondary exchange volume is negligible, there will be no change in the overnight return variance.

Tests using a matched sample. The ratios of trading day (open to close) to 24-hour (close-to-close) NYSE return variance are examined for 21 stocks with a primary listing on the NYSE and a secondary listing on the Tokyo Stock Exchange and compared with the ratios for a matched sample of firms that are not listed internationally.[15] The matched sample is chosen on the basis of both industry and size.[16] Although many of the 21 internationally listed U.S. firms have large international operations, the trading volume in Tokyo is small in relation to the NYSE volume. The average trading volume per issue of non-Japanese stocks listed on the Tokyo Stock Exchange increased dramatically between 1980 and 1986, from approximately 150 shares per day to about 30,000. Even in the latter period, however, Table 4 indicates that the Tokyo volume is less than 10 percent of the average NYSE volume for U.S. stocks having secondary listings on the Tokyo exchange.

---

[15] The matched sample is constructed from firms not traded in either Tokyo or London. The sample of internationally listed U.S. firms includes all U.S. firms that were listed on both the NYSE and the Tokyo Stock Exchange for at least 40 trading days between 1980 and 1986.

[16] For each of the 21 internationally listed U.S. firms, we choose the firm in the same Value Line industry classification with the closest match in line of business and market value. The results are similar using matched pairs that have the closest market value within two- or four-digit SIC categories.

Table 4
Trading volume of internationally listed stocks on the foreign market as a percentage of their domestic trading volume, 1982–1986

Year	Average volume of U.S. stocks on the Tokyo Stock Exchange as a percentage of their volume on the NYSE,[1] %	Average volume of Japanese stocks on the NYSE as a percentage of their volume on the Tokyo Stock Exchange, %
1982	0.17	4.01
1983	0.59	5.14
1984	0.53	6.67
1985	9.36	9.48
1986	7.83	2.74

Source: *Manual of Securities Statistics*, Nomura Research Institute, Tokyo, Japan.
[1] Volume of U.S. stocks on the Tokyo Stock Exchange is estimated as the average share volume of all non-Japanese stocks on the Tokyo exchange.

From Table 5, the average ratio of within-day (open-to-close) to 24-hour (close-to-close) return variance for the internationally traded U.S. stocks is 0.83, which is almost identical to the corresponding average ratio for the matched non-internationally-traded stocks, 0.82. Further, results for individual firms indicate that international listing does not result in a greater fraction of a firm's total variance occurring overnight during the period of foreign trading hours. For each internationally traded firm and its match, we examine the ratio of the trading day to 24-hour variance. The statistical significance of the difference is assessed using an asymptotic test statistic based on a general convergence result for the distribution of a function of random variables.[17] Only one of the 21 internationally traded stocks has a trading day to 24-hour variance ratio significantly different from that of its matched pair at the .05 level. These results are consistent with the private-information hypothesis and the hypothesis that irrational trading noise is permanent and related to trading volume, but inconsistent with the hypothesis that trading noise is directly related to trading hours.[18]

The absolute level of both the 24-hour return variance and the within-day return variance is lower for the internationally traded stocks than for their matched pairs. This is likely to occur because the inter-

[17] Let σ_1^2 be the sample variance of the open-to-close returns and σ_2^2 be the sample variance of the close-to-close returns for the internationally traded firm and let σ_3^2 and σ_4^2 be the corresponding sample return variances for the matched firm. Finally, let $R_1 = \sigma_1^2/\sigma_2^2$ and let $R_2 = \sigma_3^2/\sigma_4^2$. Then $T^{1/2}(R_1 - R_2)$ is asymptotically normally distributed with mean 0 and variance $\alpha'\Sigma\alpha$ where T is the number of observations per firm, Σ is the 4×4 covariance matrix for the squared returns, and $\alpha' = [1/\sigma_2^2, -\sigma_1^2/(\sigma_2^2)^2, -1/\sigma_4^2, \sigma_3^2/(\sigma_4^2)^2]$. For the general convergence result, see Dhrymes (1974, pp. 112–113). The number of observations per firm ranges from 40 to 1366.

[18] Foreign stocks on the Tokyo Stock Exchange currently trade four hours per day, the same as Japanese stocks. Prior to January 4, 1986, however, foreign stocks traded only one hour per day (one-half hour on Saturdays). All of our results are unaffected when the pre- and post-January 1986 periods are examined separately.

Table 5
Variance of returns on the New York Stock Exchange for stocks that are also traded on the Tokyo Stock Exchange, January 1, 1980, to December 31, 1986

	Open-to-close return variance (×10,000)	Close-to-close return variance (×10,000)	Ratio of variances
Stocks of 21 U.S. firms also traded in Tokyo			
Mean	2.334	2.883	.833
Median	2.121	2.565	.839
Matched sample of 21 stocks not internationally traded			
Mean	3.659	5.351	.819
Median	2.426	3.240	.834
Stocks of 7 Japanese firms also traded in New York			
Mean	1.294	5.058	.261
Median	1.117	4.520	.245

nationally listed firms tend to be the largest firms in their industry, making them difficult to match by size. Nevertheless, there is no evidence that international listing increases the overall variance.

Table 5 also indicates that on average the trading day return variance on the New York Stock Exchange for Japanese stocks is only about one-fourth of the average 24-hour return variance.[19] This contrasts sharply with U.S. stocks listed on the NYSE, for which on average approximately 80 percent of the 24-hour variance occurs during the trading day. Although this is consistent with the view that significant trading volume is necessary for stock prices to reflect private information, it is also consistent with the hypothesis that variance is mainly generated by increased public-information releases during trading hours on the primary exchange.

Variance changes following Tokyo listing. Sixteen of the 21 internationally listed U.S. stocks used in the matched pair tests were first listed on the Tokyo Stock Exchange between 1980 and 1986. In Table 6, we examine the ratio of trading day to 24-hour variance for these 16 NYSE firms before and after they were listed on the Tokyo exchange. The average of the 16 variance ratios before Tokyo listing is 0.852, lower than the corresponding average ratio after Tokyo listing of 0.856. No firm has a statistically significantly lower trading day to 24-hour variance ratio following Tokyo listing.

There is also no evidence that the 24-hour variances increase following Tokyo listing. The mean and median of the 16 individual 24-hour return variance estimates are lower after Tokyo listing than before. The result that 24-hour variances do not rise after international listing

[19] We had too few New York prices to calculate meaningful statistics for Kubota Corp. Thus, when we are using New York data, we present results for only seven Japanese stocks.

Table 6
Variance of returns on the New York Stock Exchange before and after listing on the Tokyo Stock Exchange for 16 U.S. firms listed on the Tokyo Stock Exchange between January 1, 1980, and December 31, 1986

	Open-to-close return variance (×10,000)	Close-to-close return variance (×10,000)	Ratio of variances
Panel A: Stocks of 16 U.S. firms newly listed in Tokyo			
Before Tokyo listing			
Mean	2.481	2.871	.852
Median	2.398	2.836	.840
After Tokyo listing			
Mean	1.925	2.302	.856
Median	1.855	2.206	.858
Panel B: Matched sample of 16 stocks not internationally traded			
Before Tokyo listing for matched pair			
Mean	3.602	4.514	.832
Median	2.630	3.513	.843
After Tokyo listing for matched pair			
Mean	3.929	5.661	.803
Median	2.143	3.130	.826

is unchanged after controlling for general marketwide changes in the level of return variances. As Table 6 indicates, for the 16 matched pair firms over the same period, the mean of the point estimates of the 24-hour return variances increases slightly although the median falls slightly. These results on overnight and 24-hour variance changes following Tokyo listing again indicate that stock-return variance is more closely related to the level of normal trading volume than to the number of hours a stock is traded on world markets.

Weekend variances for internationally listed firms. Since trading on a foreign exchange is light in relation to domestic volume, if trading volume (rather than simply more trading hours) is necessary for private information to be revealed through trading, Tokyo Saturday trading should have a different effect for U.S. companies than for Japanese firms. Our earlier tests for the effects of Saturday trading are repeated for the 17 U.S. firms traded in Tokyo with sufficient available data.[20] As Table 7 indicates, the average New York Friday close to Monday open variance ratio with and without Saturday trading is only 1.15 (median = 1.09). Of the 17 stocks, 11 have ratios in excess of 1.0, but only two of these are statistically significant. Similar results are obtained using Tokyo Friday close to Monday close prices. The

[20] All U.S. firms were included in this analysis if they were listed on both the NYSE and the Tokyo Stock Exchange for at least 10 weeks with Saturday trading in Tokyo and at least 10 weeks with no Saturday trading in Tokyo between 1980 and 1988. Four firms included in the matched pairs test did not meet this criterion and thus were not included in this analysis.

Table 7
Average ratios of return variances with and without Saturday trading for 17 U.S. firms that are also traded on the Tokyo Stock Exchange and 7 Japanese firms that are also traded on the New York Stock Exchange, January 1, 1980, to December 31, 1986

Period	Japanese stocks also traded on NYSE	U.S. stocks also traded on Tokyo Stock Exchange
Friday close to Monday open using New York prices	1.93	1.15
Friday close to Monday close using Tokyo prices	1.47	1.14

unchanged weekend variance for the Tokyo-listed U.S. stocks when there is Tokyo Saturday trading again indicates that longer trading hours do not themselves increase variance.[21]

3. Conclusions

We have provided new evidence on the determinants of stock-return variances. The results are generally consistent with the rational trading models of Kyle (1985) and Admati and Pfleiderer (1988), in which private information revealed through trading causes variance. The results do not support the irrational trading noise hypothesis, which is based on the notion that variance is the result of traders' overreaction to each other's trades. We also reject the view that higher variance during exchange trading hours is due to increased public-information releases.

Saturday trading. When the Tokyo exchange is open on Saturday, the weekend variance is 112 percent higher than when the exchange is closed. While weekly volume also increases, the weekly variance is unaffected. The unchanged weekly variance does not support the hypothesis that variance is generated by irrational trading noise that is permanent and directly related to either trading hours, trading volume, or both.

The dissipation of the higher weekend variance is not caused by temporary pricing errors that are reversed in the following week. Rather, the evidence suggests that the dissipation of the variance generated during Saturday trading is explained by reduced variance for the weekdays immediately following Saturday trading. Since vol-

[21] For Japanese companies listed on the NYSE, Tokyo Saturday trading is also associated with statistically significant additional variance on the NYSE in the following week, although the impact on 24-hour variance is small. The average open-to-close return variance ratio for Monday following Saturdays with Tokyo trading in relation to Mondays without Saturday Tokyo trading is 1.52, and the average volume ratio is 1.25. Similar results apply to Tuesday. This suggests that New York traders react to the additional private information revealed through price changes during Tokyo Saturday trading.

ume is no lower on weekdays following Saturdays with trading, lower variance on these days cannot be explained by a reduction in irrational trading noise that is related to volume. If variance is related to private information, however, then lower variance on weekdays following Saturday trading is expected if privately informed traders accelerate some of their trades to Saturday.

International listing. Secondary listing of U.S. stocks on the Tokyo exchange does not increase the overall level of variance or affect its overnight pattern, despite a substantial increase in trading hours. This result applies in both time-series and matched pair tests, and is inconsistent with the hypothesis that there is a causal relationship between trading hours and variance. Similarly, the higher weekend variance associated with Saturday trading does not occur for U.S. firms listed in Tokyo. Since the volume of foreign trading is light, this evidence suggests that substantial normal trading volume is required to affect return variance.

Appendix

This appendix describes the volume ratio and variance ratio tests reported in the article. Two important features of the data are reflected in our tests. First, the frequency of trading and nontrading Saturdays changed over time. The Tokyo Stock Exchange was closed one Saturday per month from January 1973 through July 1986, and two Saturdays per month from August 1986 through January 1989. Second, the levels of volume and variance were much higher in the latter period. In 1986, 1987,[22] and 1988, the average daily share volume on the Tokyo Stock Exchange was, respectively, 2.4, 3.2, and 3.5 times the average daily volume from 1973 through 1985. The average daily volume in these three years ranked third, second, and first, respectively, out of the 16 years from 1973 through 1988. The daily return variance on the Tokyo Composite Index in 1986, 1987, and 1988 was, respectively, 2.5, 4.1, and 1.7 times the daily return variance from 1973 through 1985, and the variance during these three years ranked third, first, and fifth, respectively, out of the 16 years from 1973 to 1988.

The combined effect of the higher frequency of nontrading Saturdays and higher levels of volume and variance after August 1986 is to bias downward any estimate of the volume and variance ratios that gives equal weight to all observations. To illustrate this bias, consider

[22] Data for 1987 used in the article exclude the month of October to insulate the results from any undue influence of the global market crash.

the following numerical example. Suppose there are data for eight weeks, comprising two subperiods of four weeks each. Suppose also that trading volume (and return variance) is unaffected by whether or not there is Saturday trading, but both the number of nontrading Saturdays and the total level of trading volume are higher in the second subperiod. Specifically, suppose the first subperiod has three weeks with Saturday trading, each with a trading volume of 1.0, and one week with no Saturday trading, also with a volume of 1.0; and suppose the second subperiod has two weeks with Saturday trading, each with a trading volume of 2.0, and two weeks with no Saturday trading, also each with a trading volume of 2.0. In this example, the true ratio of volumes for weeks with and without Saturday trading is always 1.0. However, the estimated ratio of volumes is only 0.84 if each observation is given equal weight.[23]

Weighting procedures

Throughout the article, we report volume and variance ratios that are weighted to provide unbiased estimates.[24] The procedure is as follows. First, the data are partitioned into two subperiods, pre-August 1986 when the exchange was closed one Saturday per month, and post-August 1986 when the exchange was closed two Saturdays per month. The observations in the numerator of the variance or volume ratio are then weighted to yield the same relative weighted frequency of trading and nontrading Saturdays in each subperiod. The observations in the denominator each receive equal weight.

The weights are calculated as follows. Let $N_{1,t}$ be the number of Saturdays with trading in the first subperiod, let $N_{1,n}$ be the number of Saturdays without trading in the first subperiod, and let $N_{2,t}$ and $N_{2,n}$ be the number of Saturdays with and without trading, respectively, in the second subperiod. Then for each of the weeks with Saturday trading (in the numerator of the volume or variance ratio) the observation is weighted by

$$W_1 = (N_{1,n}/N_{1,t})/[(N_{1,n} + N_{2,n})/(N_{1,t} + N_{2,t})] \qquad \text{(A1)}$$

[23] Partitioning the sample into subperiods yields unbiased estimates of the ratios in each subperiod, but this procedure is inefficient. Discarding a number of observations to leave the same relative frequency of trading and nontrading Saturdays in every subperiod also yields unbiased estimates, but it is again inefficient.

[24] As a check, we compared the article's results using these weighting procedures to those using unweighted procedures. The biases using unweighted procedures are in the predicted direction and, in several cases, sufficiently severe to result in false inferences. For example, weekly volume ratios with and without Saturday trading are greater than 1.0 using unweighted data in each of the subperiods, but less than 1.0 using unweighted data for the entire period. With our weighting procedure, however, the estimated weekly volume ratio is statistically significantly greater than 1.0 for the overall period.

if it is in the first subperiod, or by

$$W_2 = (N_{2,n}/N_{2,t})/[(N_{1,n} + N_{2,n})/(N_{1,t} + N_{2,t})] \qquad \text{(A2)}$$

if it is in the second subperiod.

In the numerical example above, the weights are $\frac{5}{9}$ for each week with Saturday trading in the first subperiod, and $\frac{5}{3}$ for each week with Saturday trading in the second subperiod. These weights yield a volume ratio of 1.0 in the numerical example.

Statistical tests

It is straightforward to assess the statistical significance of volume ratios based on weighted data. A t-statistic from a difference of (weighted) means test is used.

Under the null hypothesis, variance ratios based on unweighted data are distributed F if the underlying returns are normally distributed. The F-test, however, is highly sensitive to departures from normality. In addition, with our weighting of the observations used to calculate the variances, the variance ratio is no longer distributed F. Consequently, we use a bootstrap procedure to assess the statistical significance of the variance ratios. The estimation and interpretation of the bootstrap p values follow Efron (1982, chap. 5, especially pp. 31–33).

The bootstrap p values are estimated with the following algorithm. Using the notation above, sample with replacement $N_{1,t}$ times from the set of first-period returns with Saturday trading, $N_{2,t}$ times from the set of second-period returns with Saturday trading, and calculate the sample variance using the weights W_1 and W_2 given above. Next, sample with replacement $N_{1,n}$ times from the set of first-period returns without Saturday trading, $N_{2,n}$ times from the set of second-period returns without Saturday trading, and calculate the (unweighted) sample variance. Then calculate the variance ratio. Finally, repeat this procedure 10,000 times to estimate the empirical distribution of the variance ratio. The fraction of these variance ratios that exceed (are less than) 1.0 is the bootstrap probability that the population variance ratio exceeds (is less than) 1.0.

As an alternative to the bootstrap procedures, we use a standard nonparametric test for equal variances, the squared rank test [see Conover (1980, pp. 239–248) for a detailed discussion]. To use this test, $N_{1,t} - N_{1,n}N_{2,t}/N_{2,n}$ observations are discarded at random from the set of first-period weeks with Saturday trading. All of the returns (for weeks with and without Saturday trading) are then converted into deviations from their respective means and squared. The squared deviations are ranked (for the combined sample) and the test statistic is the sum of the squared ranks of the returns in weeks with Saturday trading.

Although discarding some of the observations is inefficient, this procedure yields the same relative frequency of trading and nontrading Saturdays in the two subperiods. Thus, the standard squared ranks test will be unbiased (given the higher variance and frequency of nontrading weeks after August 1986). The squared ranks test thus provides a check that the bootstrap results are not induced by our weighting scheme.

References

Admati, A. R., and P. Pfleiderer, 1988, "A Theory of Intraday Trading Patterns: Volume and Price Variability," *Review of Financial Studies,* 1, 3–40.

Black, F., 1986, "Noise," *Journal of Finance,* 41, 529–543.

Christie, A. A., 1981, "On the Efficient Estimation and Intra-Week Behavior of Common Stock Variances," working paper, University of Rochester.

Conover, W. J., 1980, *Practical Nonparametric Statistics* (2d ed.), Wiley, New York.

Dhrymes, P. J., 1974, *Econometrics: Statistical Foundations and Applications,* Springer, New York.

Efron, B., 1982, *The Jacknife, the Bootstrap and Other Resampling Plans,* Society for Industrial and Applied Mathematics, Philadelphia.

Fama, E. F., 1965, "The Behavior of Stock Market Prices," *Journal of Business,* 38, 34–105.

French, K. R., and R. Roll, 1986, "Stock Return Variances: The Arrival of Information and the Reaction of Traders," *Journal of Financial Economics,* 17, 5–26.

Granger, C. W., and O. Morgenstern, 1970, *Predictability of Stock Market Prices,* Heath-Lexington, Lexington, Mass.

Kurokawa, M., 1988, "On the Stock Market Collapse: A View from Tokyo," Speech to the Brookings Institute, March 8, 1988.

Kyle, A. S., 1985, "Continuous Auctions and Insider Trading," *Econometrica,* 53, 1315–1335.

Nomura Research Institute, 1988, *Nomura Fact Book,* Tokyo.

Oldfield, G. S., and R. J. Rogalski, 1980, "A Theory of Common Stock Returns over Trading and Non-trading Periods," *Journal of Finance,* 35, 729–751.

Puffer, M. K., 1989, "The Interaction of World Markets and the Distribution of Trading and Non-trading Returns," working paper, University of Rochester.

Shiller, R. J., 1981, "Do Stock Prices Move Too Much to Be Justified by Subsequent Changes in Dividends?," *American Economic Review,* 71, 421–436.

Shiller, R. J., 1986, "Comments on Merton and Kleidon," *Journal of Business,* 59 Supplement, s317–s322.

Summers, L. H., 1986, "Does the Stock Market Rationally Reflect Fundamental Values?," *Journal of Finance,* 41, 591–601.

Tokyo Stock Exchange, 1987, *Tokyo Stock Exchange Fact Book 1987,* Tokyo.

PART VI:
BOND AND FIXED INCOME MARKETS

Japanese Financial Market Research
W.T. Ziemba, W. Bailey and Y. Hamao (Editors)
1991 Elsevier Science Publishers B.V.

Interpreting Changes in the Volatility of Yields on Japanese Long-term Bonds

KENNETH J. SINGLETON*

This paper investigates empirically the relations between changes in volatilities of holding period returns on JGBs and changes in U.S. interest rates and the yen/dollar exchange rate. Weekly and quarterly holding period returns are constructed for the period March 1986 through May 1988. Then quadratic and Fourier series approximations to the conditional variances of these yields are estimated. Significant variation in the conditional variances of holding period returns is documented. These results are interpreted in the light of the changing patterns of trading volumes and capital flows between the U.S. and Japan in the 1980s.

I. Introduction

The liberalization of financial markets in Japan during the past decade has contributed to a much broader participation by domestic and overseas investors in Japanese long-term government bond (JGB) markets. The associated increases in trading volumes and international capital flows have, in turn, increased the influence of global economic developments on the time-series properties of yields in these markets. In this paper, I investigate empirically the relative contributions of various domestic and foreign financial variables to the temporal changes in the levels and volatilities of Japanese long-term bond yields. Particular attention is given to the correlations between changes in the volatility of bond yields in Japan and shifts in the term structure of U.S. Treasury bond yields and the yen/dollar exchange rate.

The linkages between interest rates in Japanese, European, and U.S. bond markets have been studied recently by the Bank of Japan (1986, 1988), Bomhoff and Schotman (1987), and Kool and Tatom (1988). Bank of Japan (1986, 1988) and Kool and Tatom

* Professor, Graduate School of Business, Stanford University, U.S.A.

This paper was written while the author was a visiting scholar at the Institute for Monetary and Economic Studies, the Bank of Japan. The author has benefited from helpful discussions with the members of the Institute and personnel at the Industrial Bank of Japan, Nomura Research Institute, Yamaichi Securities, and Morgan Stanley, Japan. The author is also very grateful to Mari Yamada of Morgan Stanley, Japan and Takuma Amano and Kozo Ono of Yamaichi Securities for providing data, and to Yuka Kai, Miki Seno, and Motoko Akiyama of the Bank of Japan for assistance with data collection and presentation; and Kobi Boudoukh for research assistance.

(1988) estimated best linear predictors of bond yields based on contemporaneous and lagged values of Japanese interest rates and other domestic and foreign macroeconomic variables. Bomhoff and Schotman (1987) study a version of an ARCH-M model (Engle, Lilian and Robbins 1987) of Japanese bond yields.

The analysis of Japanese bond markets in this paper differs in several important respects from these previous studies. First, this study focuses primarily on changes in volatility instead of the conditional mean of returns. Volatility in holding period returns is measured as the variance of the holding period return conditional on a set of economic variables known at the date the investment is undertaken. Thus, the perspective is that of a forward looking investor using current and lagged information to forecast the future. Both domestic and international sources of conditional volatility are examined, including past changes in Japanese and U.S. short- and long-term rates and changes in the yen/dollar exchange rate.

The first step in calculating an estimate of volatility is the estimation of the best predictor of a holding period return conditioned on these variables. In order that a wide variety of possible representations of this best forecast can be accommodated, it is modeled using a Fourier series approximation (Gallant 1982; Pagan and Hong 1988) to a general functional form. This representation permits nonlinear conditional mean functions. In particular, it accommodates the ARCH-M like relations studied by Bomhoff and Shotman (1987), without restricting *a priori* the conditional mean of excess returns to be proportional to the conditional variance. Next, the prediction error implied by this best forecast is calculated. Finally, the conditional variance of the holding period return is modeled as the best forecast of the square of this forecast error, with forecasts being based on a Fourier functional form. The conditioning information is lagged squared forecast errors and the macroeconomic information used to forecast the levels of returns.

The measurement of returns and the sampling interval of the data is also notably different from previous studies. Previous investigations of long-term Japanese bond returns have typically focused on post-1978, monthly data on yields-to-maturity. In contrast, I study weekly data on holding period returns over a sample period beginning in 1986. Holding period returns are the *ex post* investment yields obtained in the bond markets and, therefore, the risk characteristics of these yields are more relevant for portfolio decisions than is the volatility of yields to maturity. Two different holding period returns are examined: the return on the bond with maturity closest to ten years and the return on the current "benchmark" ten year bond. The institutional considerations outlined subsequently suggest that the volatilities of these two return series may be quite different. The returns are calculated for both one week and three-month holding periods.

The sample period is restricted to the relatively short 1986–88 period in an attempt to control for some of the fundamental changes that occurred in Japanese financial markets over the past decade. There were several developments in 1984 and 1985 in particular that lead to significant changes in the trading patterns of Japanese investors in both domestic and foreign bond markets. I argue subsequently that these changes may explain the recent increases in the correlations between returns on JGBs and changes in foreign interest rates and exchange rates documented, for instance by the Bank of Japan (1988). In the variance decompositions associated with the monthly vector autoregressions fit by the Bank of Japan (1988) for the sample period January 1978 through March 1983, over half of the variation in the Japanese long-term yield-to-maturity was due to its own past history. In contrast, for the sample period April 1983 through June 1988, this percentage declined to 22 percent, with about 86 percent of the variation in JGB yields being attributable to variation in the U.S. long-term rate and the exchange rate. This paper explores the linkages between the volatility of holding period returns and foreign financial variables over the recent period of increased integration and capital flows.

The focus will be primarily on the yields on long-term bonds. One reason for this focus is that the long-term market is more developed, less regulated, and has a much larger trading volume by both domestic and foreign investors than the short-term bond markets in Japan (see Section II). In addition, the economic reasons for the sympathetic movements in short- and long-term rates that underlie the expectations-based theories of the term structure commonly applied to the U.S. government bond markets are much weaker (and in some cases virtually absent) in Japan. Thus, while changes in short-term yields may be correlated with the temporal behavior of yields in long-term markets, a preliminary exploration of the volatility of bond yields without the imposition of the structure of specific term structure models seems warranted.[1]

The remainder of this paper is organized as follows. In Section II changes in the regulations affecting trading in Japanese bond markets are related to recent trading patterns by Japanese investors in both the domestic and foreign bond markets. The high turnover ratios of domestic and foreign bond holdings documented in this section suggest that many investors have very short investment horizons. These patterns are used to motivate the choice of conditioning variables underlying the specification of the conditional variance of holding period returns on bonds. The econometric model of conditional means and variances is set forth in more detail in Section III. The empirical results are presented in Section IV, and concluding remarks are presented in Section V.

II. Historical Background

Though the liberalization of domestic bond markets in Japan has narrowed substantially the organizational differences between markets in Japan, the U.S., and Europe,

[1] Dunn and Singleton (1986) and Singleton (1988) derive term structure models relating the volatilities of short- and long-term yields under the assumption that marginal rates of substitution of consumption and real bond yields are jointly log-normally distributed. The validity of the assumptions about trading opportunities underlying these derivations seems questionable for Japan.

significant differences in legal restrictions on trading and in trading practices by large institutional investors across countries remain. In this section I discuss some implications of these differences, as well as several recent regulatory changes, for modeling changes in interest rates on Japanese government bonds.[2]

Prior to 1974, there was a small stock of outstanding government debt and a correspondingly low transactions volume in the secondary markets for government debt. Furthermore, only ten year bonds were issued and these bonds were priced by a syndicate in consultation with the Bank of Japan. Bonds were typically bought by an underwriting syndicate of financial institutions at prices above the prices of securities in the secondary market. There was an (implicit) understanding that the Bank of Japan would purchase these bonds after a period of one year and in practice such purchases were frequently consummated (Takagi 1988). Banks were not allowed to resell these bonds in the secondary market.[3]

The slowdown in economic growth after 1974 resulted in large issues of government bonds to finance the growing budget deficits. As a consequence of the substantial increase in government bonds held by banks, the Bank of Japan suspended its guarantee to repurchase these securities. This, in turn, contributed to a significant deterioration in the liquidity of the investment portfolios of the members of the syndicate. Consequently, in April 1977, financial institutions were allowed to sell government bonds in the secondary market after a minimum holding period of one year. The secondary sales of bonds by banks after holding securities for 100 days were authorized during 1981. And over-the-counter sales of newly issued bonds were permitted starting in October 1983. The last two changes also apply to the sale of intermediate term government bonds (maturities of 2, 3, and 4 years), which were issued for the first time between 1978 and 1980.

In June, 1984 bank dealing in bonds was authorized. Initially, 34 banks were allowed to trade as dealers in bonds, and dealing was restricted to bonds with less than two years remaining to maturity. Bank dealings in bonds were completely liberalized in June 1985. At this time banks were also allowed to use the interdealer brokerage services provided by the Nihon Sogo Shoken.[4] Throughout this period the composition of the bonds being traded was evolving and the number of days following the subscription of a bank to a bond issue that had to elapse before secondary trading could begin changed several times. Currently, secondary trading for the dealing account can begin immediately after

[2] Excellent descriptions of the evolution of financial markets during the past fifteen years can be found in Suzuki (1987), Bank of Japan (1986), and Takagi (1988).

[3] Secondary trading in government bonds on organized securities exchanges commenced in October 1966. There were no restrictions subsequently on trading by individuals and life insurance companies of the small amount of government bonds held by these agents (Kuroda 1982).

[4] The Nihon Sogo Shoken is a "broker's broker" that processes anonymously trades for dealers. All of the dealers trading with the Nihon Sogo Shoken (142 securities companies and 184 banks as of April 1989) can see a list of up-to-the-second quotes (bids and asks).

(starting on the day of) each issue; and for the investment account after ten days following the issue date.

With the admission of banks as dealers in 1985 came a substantial increase in volume in the over-the-counter markets for long-term government bonds; see the graph of over-the-counter (OTC) turnover of interest bearing JGBs displayed in Figure 1. Since the middle of 1985, the monthly turnover of JGBs in the OTC market has exceeded the outstanding balance of JGBs in all but four months. Accompanying the increased volume was a notable decline in transactions costs, as measured by the bid-ask spread, in the OTC markets for bonds (Takagi 1987). The spreads are now comparable or smaller than those on the corresponding government bonds in the U.S. (Bank of Japan 1986).

Most of the trading in the OTC market for government bonds has been between dealers. As recently as 1983, transactions by securities companies and banks through their dealing accounts represented only 30% of secondary market transactions. By 1985, this percentage had increased to 70% (Bank of Japan 1988). The total transactions volume of securities companies and banks in their portfolio and dealing accounts represents about 90% of all secondary market transactions. In other words, the secondary market is effectively an inter-dealer market for these financial institutions.

Furthermore, a striking feature of the Japanese bond market is that most of this turnover has been concentrated in a single "benchmark" issue. Figure 1 grossly understates the turnover ratio for the benchmark, since the benchmark issue has the largest trading volume among long-term bonds and at the same time is a small percentage of the outstanding stock of JGBs. Indeed, the percentage of the total trading volume through the broker's broker market accounted for by the benchmark issue 105 ranged between 90% and 95% in late 1988. Furthermore, the daily volume during October, 1988 was typically between ¥1 and ¥2 trillion and the outstanding stock of the benchmark was about ¥1. 5 trillion, so the stock often turned over more than once per trading day.

Because of the high "liquidity" in this market relative to the OTC markets for other intermediate and long-term government bonds, the benchmark issue trades at a substantial premium relative to non-benchmark issues. The spread has been 5 or 6 times larger than the typical spread in the U.S. between "on" and "off the run" government bonds (e.g., Sargen, Schoenholtz, Blitz and Elhabashi 1986). During the sample period for this study, March 1986–May 1988, three different bond issues served as the benchmark issue (see Section III for details). When a benchmark issue looses its status as the benchmark bond, then the volume of trade declines substantially as does the premium reflected in the price. Concurrently, the price of the new benchmark bond adjusts to reflect the increased liquidity associated with the increase in its trading volume. Typically, the transition period lasts for about a month, during which time price volatility appears to increase with the uncertainty regarding which of the candidate issues will become the next benchmark (Sargen, et. al. 1986).

There is an institutional feature of the Japanese financial markets that seems to

Figure 1. Turnover and Stock of JGB

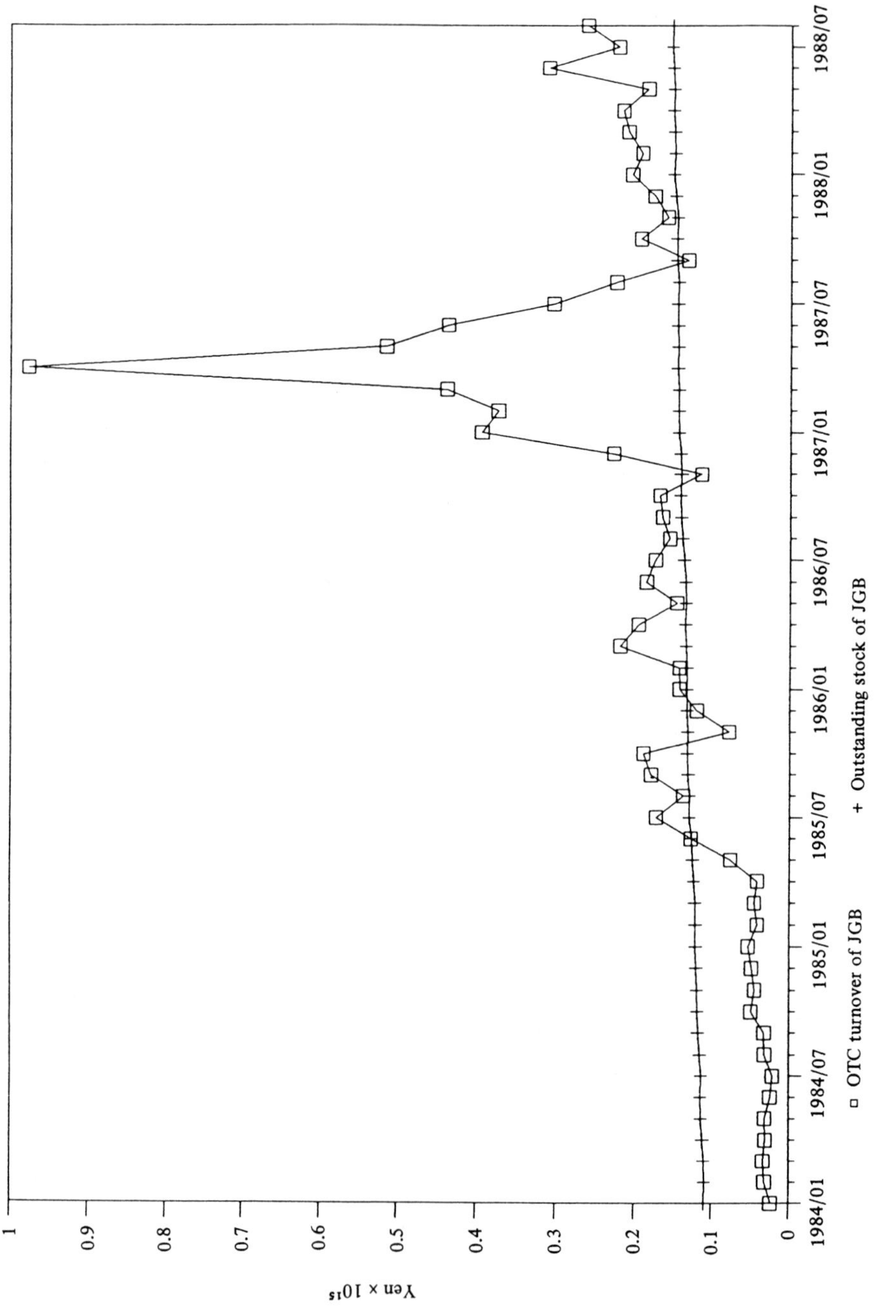

reinforce the presence of this benchmark phenomenon. Specifically, the payment by insurance companies of dividends to policy holders from capital gains is limited under current law. And until recently only coupon income could be used for dividends. These regulations encourage a buy-and-hold strategy on the part of insurance companies for bonds with relatively high coupon yields. Thus, bonds that are being traded at a discount relative to otherwise comparable bonds are bought by insurance companies and some pension fund managers. This behavior may be contributing to the low volume in non-benchmark issues.

While institutional investors pursued a buy-and-hold investment strategy for portions of their fixed income portfolios, other portions of their portfolios experienced relatively high turnover ratios. In particular, starting in the early 1980s insurance companies had high turnover ratios on their total bond portfolios compared to many other institutional investors, as well as relatively large investments in foreign bonds (Bank of Japan 1982). The investment patterns by insurance companies in Japanese government bonds during the period 1984–88 are displayed in Figure 2. Notice that there has been an upward trend in both buy and sell transactions by insurance companies since mid-1985.

Interestingly, there were corresponding increases in the turnover ratios for foreign investors in Japan and Japanese investors in foreign countries. Regarding the former, the Bank of Japan (1986) estimated that from 1981 to 1984 the number of turnovers per year in the total government bond portfolios of overseas investors in Japan increased from 2 to 6. Overall, however, the dollar value of the investments in Japanese bonds by overseas investors was on average less than 25% of the value of the investments in foreign bonds by Japanese investors between 1986 and 1988.[5]

The buy and sell transactions in foreign bonds by Japanese investors, on monthly basis, are displayed in Figure 3. What is perhaps most striking about Figure 3, is the close relation between buy and sell transactions. The net acquisitions of bonds were small indicating that most of the trading was associated with rapid turnover of bonds. Furthermore most of the trading activity was concentrated in the U.S. markets. In 1985, about 85% of the turnover of foreign bond holdings by Japanese investors was trading activity in the U.S., while 51.4% of the total portfolio of bonds was comprised of U.S. securities. In contrast, in June 1988, about 35% of the stock of foreign bond holdings by Japanese was U.S. bonds, yet over 90% of the turnover of their portfolios was attributable to trading in the U.S. bond markets. Evidently, while the international bond portfolios of the Japanese have become more diversified, the concentration of trading activity has increased.

These changes in trading patterns both by Japanese investors in the U.S. and overseas investors in Japan occurred around the times of the development of the benchmark

[5] For the period 1986–88, the volume of investments by overseas investors in the Japanese market was typically less than $50 billion.

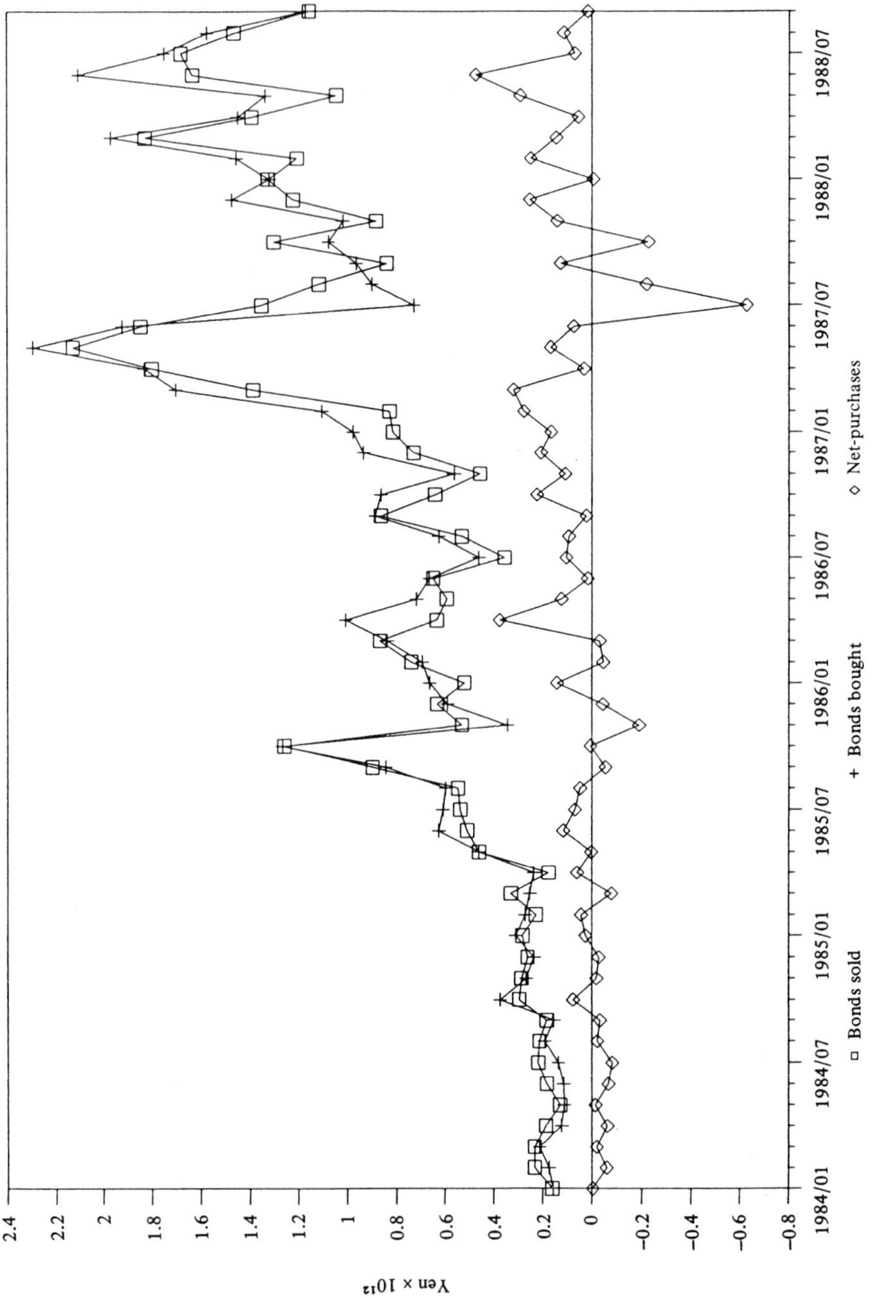

Figure 2. Sales and Purchases of JGB by Japanese Insurance Companies

Figure 3. Sales and Purchases of Foreign Bonds by Japanese Investors

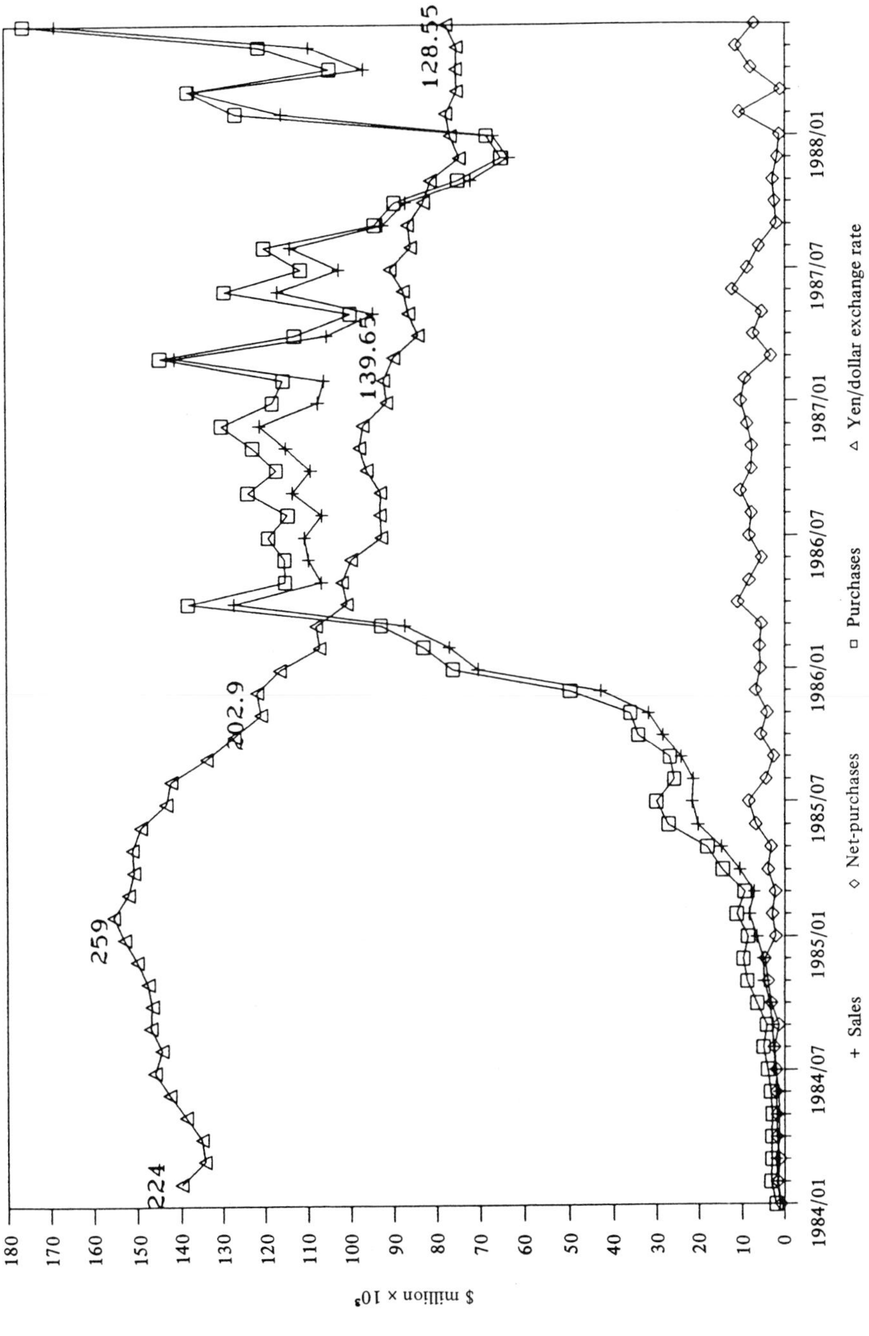

phenomenon in the Japanese ten-year bond market, the initiation of trading of futures on bonds in Tokyo (October 1985), and the elimination of the withholding tax on foreign investors imposed by the U.S. Treasury. They are suggestive of substantial increases in the degree of international integraиon of bond markets and an increased importance of capital flows in the determination of bond yields in Japan. The trading patterns of Japanese investors further suggest that U.S. interest rate movements, in particular, may have had significant effects on the volatility of bond yields in Japan. It is for this reason that shifts in the U.S. term structure of government bonds enter prominently in the empirical analysis of Section IV.

Though the presumption of this analysis is that the levels and volatilities in yields on short- and long-term bonds are inter-related, a specific model of the term structure linking the temporal behavior of short- and long-terms bonds is not imposed on the data. Instead, the econometric relations set forth in Section III are chosen in order to provide a flexible descriptive representation of the distribution of bond yields. Perhaps the primary reason for not conducting the empirical analysis in the context of a formal model of the term structure is that the market structures that underlie many expectations based theories of the term structure were not in place in Japan during the sample period. Specifically, short sales of bonds were tightly restricted in the spot market and there was not an active organized market for borrowing securities.[6] Furthermore, the futures markets, which have existed only since October 1985, were available only for ten and twenty year bonds. Thirdly, as noted above, there was relatively little liquidity in the intermediate-term bond markets. Therefore, the arbitrage trading that links the long and short ends of the yield curve in expectations theories was relatively costly in Japan.

III. Representations of Volatility in Holding Period Yields

Numerous approaches to modeling the conditional variances of asset returns have recently been proposed in the literature. Perhaps the most widely studied specification is the ARCH model originally proposed by Engle (1982), and subsequently applied by Engle, Lilian and Robbins (1987) to the U.S. market and Bomhoff and Schotman (1987) to the U.S. and Japanese bond markets. In these applications, the expected excess holding period returns on long-term bonds are interpreted as risk premia and are assumed to be proportional to the conditional covariance matrix of the vector of returns studied (the ARCH-M model).

Though convenient to implement, the ARCH model of conditional volatility has several limitations as a model of the conditional variances of bond yields. First, the assumed proportionality of risk premia to the conditional covariance matrix of returns is

[6] In June 1989 borrowing-lending markets, similar to the U.S. repurchase markets, were authorized by the Ministry of Finance. As of August 1980, these markets were being shunned by dealers and volume was low. Fees were also sufficiently high to make borrowing not economical.

an implication only of very special models of asset price determination (Glosten, Jagannathan and Runkle 1989). Most dynamic models do not imply a simple linear relation among these moments. Second, the conditional distributions of disturbances in ARCH specifications are typically assumed to be normal. However, there is growing evidence that many asset returns are not well described by a conditional normal distribution. For instance, Gallant, Hseih and Tauchen (1987) show in the context of a semi-nonparametric specification of the distribution of daily exchange rate changes that exchange rates are not adequately described by an ARCH model with conditional normal or conditional t distributions. Furthermore, the findings in Pagan and Hong (1988) suggest that the conditional variance of excess U.S. Treasury bill yields is not a symmetric function of past yield differentials or forecast errors as is assumed in most ARCH specifications.[7] They reject the ARCH model for U.S. Treasury bill returns.

In the light of these findings, a nonparametric specification of the conditional means and variances of the holding period returns on JGBs is adopted. Specifically, I follow Pagan and Ullah (1988) and Pagan and Hong (1988) and adopt Fourier series approximations. The construction of the estimates for the conditional variances proceeds as follows. Let H_t^i denote the i-week holding period return from date $t-i$ to date t on a bond with a maturity of n weeks, $i \leq n$. Let x_t denote a vector of variables that is in investors' information set at date t and which generates the conditioning information set for expectations. Though this information set is dated at t, the vector x_t will in general include lagged values of various financial variables. The expected holding period return from t to $t+i$ conditioned on x_t is approximated by fitting a truncated Fourier series representation as in Gallant (1982):

$$E[H_{t+i}^i \mid x_t] = \beta_o + \beta_1' x_t + \beta_2' [x_t x_t'] + \sum_{j=1}^{m} [\sigma_j' \cos(jx_t) + \phi_j' \sin(jx_t)] \tag{1}$$

where $[x_t x_t']$ denotes the vector of distinct elements of the cross-product matrix $x_t x_t'$, $\cos(jx_t)$ denotes the vector of cosine transformations of the elements of jx_t, etc. This approximation extends the commonly used autoregressive representation of expectations by including quadratic and trigonometric terms.

Fourier expansions approximate arbitrarily closely continuous functions on the interval $[0,2\pi]$ as m becomes large.[8] In applying the Fourier methods, the data is scaled so that the sample lies within the interval $(0,2\pi)$. Among the potential problems with using such an approximation—and indeed most nonparametric methods—is that the conditioning information and the variable being forecasted may exhibit growth over time. And growing series will not satisfy the assumption that the transformed series, constructed using a

[7] Nelson (1987) has proposed one possible modification to the standard ARCH model that allows for asymmetric responses of conditional variances to changes in the conditioning variables.

[8] General Fourier series approximations involve sine and cosine functions of linear combinations of the elements of x. In order to keep the size of the parameter space relative to the sample size from becoming large, I consider only sine and cosine functions of the individual elements of x.

fixed transformation function, stay within the approximation interval (here $[0,2\pi]$). The potential importance of this observation for this study is discussed after describing the data used in the analysis.

Having approximated the conditional mean, the forecast errors $\varepsilon_{t+i}=H^i_{t+i}-E[H^i_{t+i}|x_t]$ are formed and then the conditional variance is modeled as

$$\sigma^2_{Ht}(i) = E[\varepsilon^2_{t+i} \mid x_t] = \alpha_0+\alpha_1'x_t+\alpha_2'[x_tx_t'] + \sum_{j=1}^{m} [\Psi_j' \cos(jx_t) + \theta_j' \sin(jx_t)]. \qquad (2)$$

Unlike ARCH representation of conditional variances, lagged values of ε^2_{t+i} do not enter explicitly in x_t in this formulation. However, the ARCH model with a linear conditional mean implies a representation of $\sigma^2_{Ht}(i)$ which can be approximated very closely by (2) with a sufficiently long history of the levels and squared values of H^i_t in x_t. At the same time, (2) is more flexible than ARCH models because of the inclusion of trigonometric terms.

If the slope coefficients in (2) are not all zero, then the disturbance term in (1) is conditionally heteroskedastic. The forecast error $(\varepsilon^2_{t+i}-\sigma^2_{Ht}(i))$ may also be heteroskedastic, so heteroskedastic-consistent standard errors (Hansen 1982) are presented for the parameter estimates. The estimate of the parameter vector $\alpha'=[\alpha_0, \alpha_1, \alpha_2, \Psi'_1, \theta'_1, \ldots, \Psi'_m, \theta'_m]$ for (2) is calculated using a two-step estimation procedure: first the parameter vector $\beta'=[\beta_0, \beta_1, \beta_2, \sigma'_1, \phi'_1, \ldots, \sigma'_m, \phi'_m]$ for (1) is estimated and then the squared values of the estimated residuals are taken to be the dependent variable when fitting the variance equation (2). Notice, however, that the standard errors from the second stage do not need to be adjusted for the use of the first stage estimator of β. This follows from the observation that, under the null hypothesis $E[\varepsilon_{t+i}\partial\varepsilon_{t+i}/\partial\beta]=E[\varepsilon_{t+i}h(x_t)]=0$; see Newey (1984).

Two values of i are considered:1 and 13. The first value corresponds to the case of weekly holding period returns on ten-year bonds, while the second case corresponds to 13 week (quarterly) holding period returns. When $i=1$, the disturbance ε_{t+1} is serially uncorrelated by construction as long as x_t includes a sufficiently long history of H^1_t.[9] In the case of $i=13$, the forecast error ε_{t+13} follows an MA(12) process (again assuming that the history of holding period returns is included in x_t). Therefore, the standard errors of the estimated parameters in both (1) and (2) are also adjusted for the serial correlation of the disturbances.[10]

[9] The projection error $(\varepsilon^2_{t+1}-\sigma^2_{Ht}(1))$ may be serially correlated since the past history of the squared forecast errors is not included in x_t. Standard errors and test statistics were calculated both under the assumption that $(\varepsilon^2_{t+1}-\sigma^2_{Ht}(1))$ is serially uncorrelated and under the assumption this error follows an MA(6) process. The results were qualitatively similar with the tests of exclusion restrictions providing more evidence against the null hypotheses under the MA(6) assumption. The results assuming no serial correlation are presented for the case $i=1$.

[10] The MA(12) error in (1) with $i=13$ can in principle be accommodated using the estimator of the standard error discussed by Hansen (1982) and Hansen and Singleton (1982). In practice, however, this approach lead to a non-positive definite parameter covariance matrix and, therefore, the Newey-West procedure with twelve lags was also applied for this equation.

Turning next to the selection of the data for the empirical analysis, there are several choices for the returns on long-term JGBs. Typically, in studying the term structure, holding period returns on a sequence of bonds with a common fixed maturity are examined. A potential drawback of examining such a series for Japan is that many of the bonds considered will not be benchmark bonds at the time the holding periods are calculated. And, as noted in Section II, there will be relatively small trading volumes in non-benchmark bonds. A series of holding period returns on the actively traded benchmark securities can be constructed. Since a given bond issue remains the benchmark bond for several months, the constant maturity assumption underlying term structure analyses will be violated more severely for this series. Nevertheless, since the benchmark is the most actively traded security, it may more rapidly and accurately reflect domestic and international developments which affect economic activity in Japan. Results for holding period returns on both the benchmark and constant maturity bond series will be examined.

Holding period returns were calculated for the benchmark series from a series of daily observations on closing prices on the Tokyo Stock Exchange (TSE). A comparable series was not available for the constant maturity series. Instead, I constructed a weekly over-the-counter (OTC) series of yields-to-maturity on the bonds with maturities closest to ten years. Then approximate weekly holding period returns on this constant maturity series of bonds were calculated as follows. As in Shiller (1979), Singleton (1980), and Shiller, Campbell and Schoenholtz (1983), the i-week holding period return, H_t^i, on a bond with maturity "in" weeks was approximated by

$$H_{t+i}^i = [R_t^{in} - \bar{\gamma}R_{t+i}^{i(n-1)}]/(1-\bar{\gamma}), \tag{3}$$

where $\bar{\gamma}=(\gamma-\gamma^n)/(1-\gamma^n)$ and γ was set equal to $1/(1+R^*)$ with R^* being the average yield-to-maturity of the bond over the sample period.

In order to assess the potential magnitudes of the approximation errors from using (3) instead of the exact holding period returns, the weekly holding period returns ($i=1$) were calculated for the benchmark series using the price data (exact returns) and the associated yields-to-maturity (equation (3)). The results are displayed in Figure 4. The two series track each other quite closely, suggesting that the approximation errors are in practice small. The approximation errors are likely to be smaller for the constant maturity series, since fixed values of γ and n were used in (3) even though a benchmark bond may have remained the benchmark for nearly a year.

The first part of Table 1 displays the issue numbers and the periods during which each issue served as the benchmark for the sample period March 14, 1986 through May 20, 1988. The second part of this table displays the corresponding information for the bond with maturity closest to ten years (the most recently issued ten-year JGB). The constant maturity yields are end of week values. Since the bond markets in Japan were open on some Saturdays, the end of the week could be at the close of the market on

Figure 4. Seven Day Return – Returns from Yields and Prices

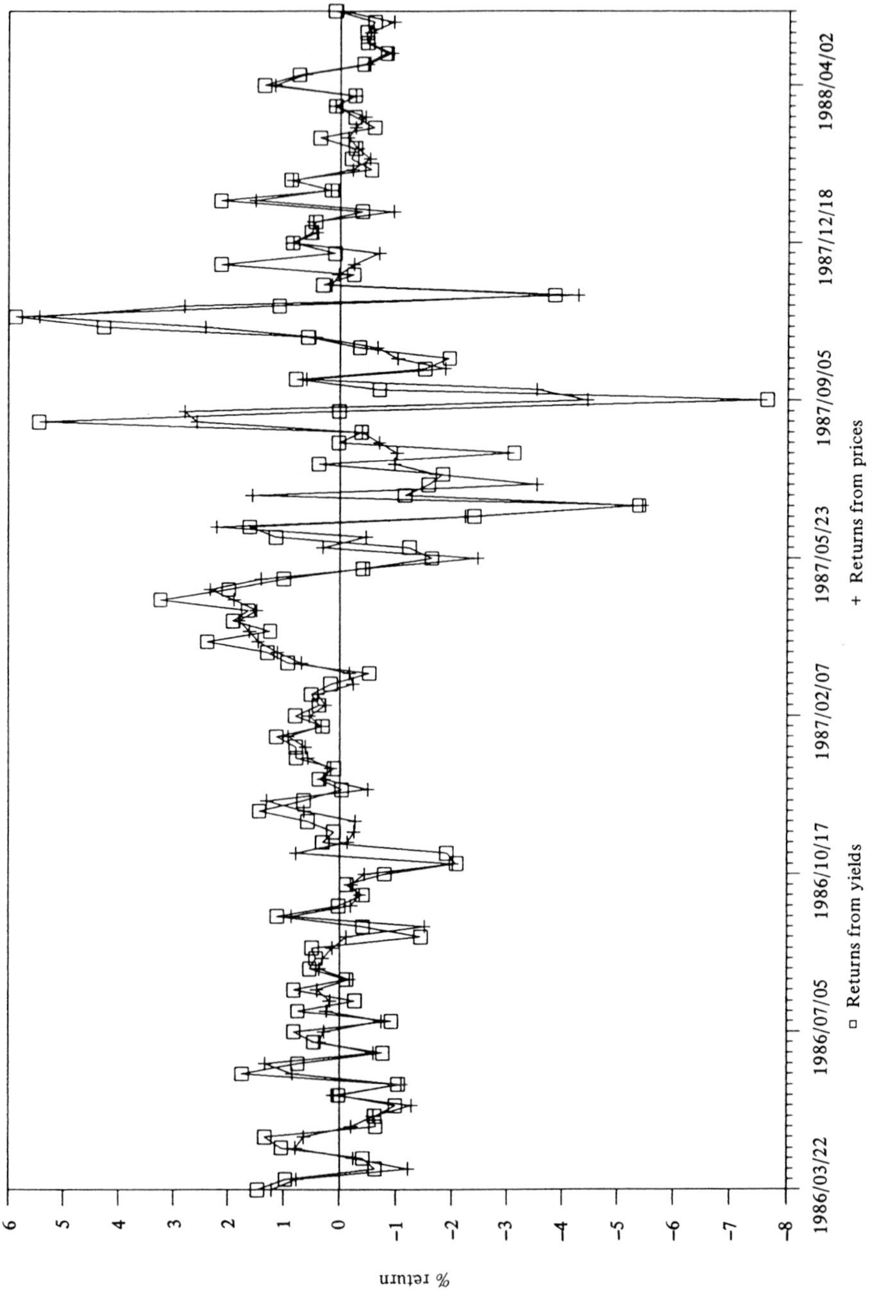

Table 1. Composition of JGB Series

Benchmark Series

March 14, 1986 – October 25, 1986	Issue 78
November 1, 1986 – November 28, 1987	Issue 89
December 5, 1987 – May 20, 1988	Issue 105

Fixed Maturity Series

March 14, 1986 – May 9, 1986	Issue 80
May 17, 1986 – August 15, 1986	Issue 89
August 23, 1986 – November 29, 1986	Issue 90
December 6, 1986 – December 27, 1986	Issue 92
January 9, 1986 – March 7, 1987	Issue 93
March 13, 1987 – May 2, 1987	Issue 97
May 8, 1987 – May 30, 1987	Issue 99
June 6, 1987 – August 7, 1987	Issue 100
August 14, 1987 – September 5, 1987	Issue 102
September 11, 1987 – October 9, 1987	Issue 103
October 16, 1987 – November 28, 1987	Issue 104
December 5, 1987 – January 30, 1988	Issue 105
February 6, 1988 – February 27, 1988	Issue 106
March 5, 1988 – April 8, 1988	Issue 108
April 15, 1988 – May 20, 1988	Issue 109

Table 2. Descriptive Statistics for Weekly Yields
March 14, 1986 – May 20, 1988

Series	Mean	S.D.	Autocorrelations						γ
			1	2	3	4	5	6	
OTC	.00094	.00012	.938	.844	.765	.693	.610	.515	
OTF	.00100	.00011	.925	.845	.766	.684	.584	.479	
HOTC	.00119	.01658	.287	–.117	–.065	.089	.105	.061	.997
HOTF	.00107	.01652	.051	–.003	.020	.120	.043	.080	.997
HTSE	.00109	.01460	.201	–.059	.066	.020	.019	–.068	
HTSEW	.00022	.01463	.205	–.055	.061	.019	.023	–.065	

Friday or Saturday. Comparisons of weekly holding period returns on the benchmark bonds calculated using TSE data and either end of week or Friday closing prices suggest that the time series properties of these two return series were very similar. That is, the small amount of additional variation in maturity induced by occasional Saturday trading had small effects on the yields constructed. Subsequent results for the benchmark series are based on closing prices for Friday, while the constant maturity results are based on the end of week yields.[11]

Descriptive statistics for the various series are presented in Table 2. The weekly OTC yields-to-maturity on the benchmark series are denoted OTC, while the yields-to-maturity on the constant maturity OTC series is denoted OTF. Comparing the statistics for OTC with those for OTF, one sees that the average return on OTC was smaller than the average return on OTF. This difference is the manifestation of the liquidity premium associated with the relatively low volume of trade in OTF. The autocorrelations of the series are comparable.

The remaining rows in Table 2 display descriptive statistics for the holding period returns. When $i=1$, the implied values of $\bar{\gamma}$ for the OTC and OTF series is .997. Therefore, construction of the approximate holding period returns using (3) amounts to taking a quasi-difference of the yields with a filter that has a root very close to the unit circle. As a consequence, the approximate holding period returns, HOTC and HOTF, exhibit substantially less autocorrelation than the underlying yields-to-maturity. Indeed, in the case of HOTF, the autocorrelations are all near zero which suggests that the conditional distributions of HOTC and HOTF may be very different. The last two rows display statistics for the weekly holding periods constructed from daily TSE benchmark prices with (HTSE) and without (HTSEW) including the coupon payments. The standard deviations and autocorrelations of these series are comparable to those of HOTC as might be expected from the patterns in Figure 4.

A notable feature of Figure 4 is the substantial increase in the volatilities of the benchmark holding period returns during 1987. The increased volatility between January and April of 1987 may have been attributable to the substantial increase in the trading volume in the benchmark JGB (Figure 1). Concurrent with this high trading volume, there was a substantial decline in the yield on the benchmark series to the point where the benchmark yield was approximately equal to the Bank of Japan's discount rate.

The largest swings in returns were after this period of high turnover in JGB markets, however. There was a substantial appreciation of the yen against the dollar between August and December 1987. The yen/dollar exchange rate reached 152 in late August and then fell to 122 by late December. During most of this period Japanese investors were net sellers of foreign (and in particular U.S.) bonds, and the turnover of foreign

[11] Of course, for some weeks there were holidays on Friday or Saturday in which case the yield was calculated at the close of the day closest to the end of the week.

bonds fell substantially (Figure 3). Moreover in September the long-term JGB yields rose above 6% (they were 4.11% in June 1987), while long- and short-term U.S. Treasury bond yields rose sharply through the third quarter of 1987 and then fell equally sharply at the end of 1987. Thus, the relatively large fluctuations in holding period yields during the second half of 1987 coincided with changes in exchange rates and yield differentials between Japan and the U.S., and associated international capital flows.[12]

Therefore, the following variables are included in the conditioning information set used to estimate the conditional variances. First, two yields from the U.S. Treasury bond market were included: the yield on three-month Treasury bills and the constant maturity yield on ten-year Treasury bonds. Both series were constructed from the daily series compiled by the Federal Reserve. Also, the yen/dollar exchange rate as recorded in the Tokyo foreign exchange market was included. All of these series were recorded at the close of trading on the day before the yields in the Japanese bond market were recorded to assure that they were known to market participants at the time OTC and TSE prices were sampled.

Finally, the yield on a yen-denominated short-term bond is included. In selecting this yield, consideration was given to the fact that the short-term government bond markets were not as well developed in Japan as in some other countries. The treasury bill market is in its infancy. Issues of short-term government debt have been infrequent and the stock of outstanding bills at any one time is small compared to, say, the U.S. Treasury bill market. In addition, income from government bills in Japan is subject to a withholding tax for residents and nonresidents.[13] In contrast, there are active secondary markets for large denomination Euroyen deposits. The yields on these deposits are studied in Section IV.

IV. Empirical Results

Before estimating the mean and variance relations (1) and (2), the data were transformed to induce stationarity. The autocorrelations of the holding period returns displayed in Table 2 suggest that these returns are stationary. The U.S. Treasury bill data was transformed by time differencing the three-month Treasury bill yield (DTB3) and taking the contemporaneous difference between the yield on the ten-year bond and the three-month yield (SPD). The latter spread variable is a measure of the shape of the term structure of Treasury bonds. Finally, the yen/dollar exchange rate (DY$) and the yield on one-week Euroyen deposits were first-differenced (DEURO). These transformed series

[12] The financial market uncertainty during this period was compounded by the stock market crash in October 1987.

[13] Because of the lack of depth in the Japanese government bill market, open market operations in the conventional sense of this term is not a primary tool of monetary policy in Japan. The Bank of Japan trades in security markets, but primarily in the commercial bill market (Suzuki 1987).

were assumed to be free of significant trends over the sample period.

The sample period examined was March 14, 1986 through May 20, 1988. The choice of the beginning date reflects the large increase in trading volume in foreign markets by Japanese investors up through the early part of 1986 (see Figure 3). In addition, the beginning date is after the initiation of trading in long-term bond futures in October 1985 and the notable intervention by the Bank of Japan in domestic financial markets in late 1985.

Initially, only the linear and quadratic terms were included in (1) and (2); the sine and cosine terms were omitted. Since the transformation of the data to a range of $[0,2\pi]$ amounts to a simple rescaling of the regressors, the test results for this quadratic approximation are identical to those that would be obtained from estimating a quadratic representation of the untransformed data. Thus, the results from these regressions permit a preliminary assessment of the gains in fit from including quadratic terms in the commonly studied linear forecasting models for holding period yields.

The results for weekly holding period returns on the benchmark (HTSE) series are displayed in Table 3. Column one displays the results for the mean equation (1) and column two displays the estimates for the conditional variance (2). The variables H2, EURO2, DY\$2, DTB2, and SPD2 represent the squared values of HTSE, DEURO, DY\$, DTB, and SPD, respectively. The subscripts indicate the number of time periods the variable is lagged in the regression (e.g., $HTSE_1$ is HTSE lagged one week). The numbers in parentheses are the estimated values of the asymptotic standard errors for the parameters and marginal significance levels for the chi-square tests of exclusion restrictions. A "*" (**) adjacent to a standard error of an estimate indicates the null hypothesis that the coefficient is zero is rejected at the 5% (1%) significance level.

There was clearly significant variation in the conditional mean of HTSE during this sample period. Furthermore, the results suggest that the inclusion of quadratic terms increases significantly the explanatory power of the regression: the estimated coefficients on $H2_2$ and $DTB2_2$ are significant at the 1% level based on the asymptotic standard errors. Chi-square statistics for the joint hypothesis that the linear and quadratic terms for each of the variables all have zero coefficients are presented at the bottom of Table 3. The subscripts E, Y, T, and S indicate DEURO, DY\$, DTB, and SPD, respectively. The joint hypothesis for DTB is rejected at conventional significance levels.

There is also evidence of substantial time variation in the conditional variance of the holding period return on the benchmark series. The estimates displayed in the second column of Table 3 suggest that changes in the U.S. Treasury bill rate, the Euroyen deposit rate, and long-short U.S. Treasury yield spread predicted changes in $\sigma^2_{Ht}(1)$. Thus variables which, according to conventional significance levels, do not predict changes in the conditional mean may impact significantly on the conditional variance. Compare, for example, the results in the first and second columns of Table 3 for SPD and DEURO. In this sense, the sources of risk underlying trading in long-term bonds may not be reliably

Table 3. Estimates of Quadratic Regressions for Benchmark Weekly Holding Period Returns
March 14, 1986 – May 20, 1988

	HTSE	ϵ_t^2
$HTSE_1$	−.5243 (.398)	−.6337 (.624)
$HTSE_2$	1.651 (.288)**	.1786 (.407)
$HTSE_3$	.2014 (.082)	−.0034 (.142)
$HTSE_4$	.1761 (.075)*	−.0403 (.092)
$H2_1$	.1444 (.088)	.1281 (.136)
$H2_2$	−.3204 (.057)**	.0295 (.095)
$DEURO_1$	−.2998 (.366)	−.0322 (.493)
$DEURO_2$	.1066 (.273)	.8829 (.431)
$DEURO_3$	.0326 (.094)	−.1397 (.139)
$EURO2_1$	.0543 (.049)	−.0354 (.066)
$EURO2_2$	−.0137 (.058)	−.1804 (.082)
$DY\$_1$	−.1384 (.332)	−.4551 (.376)
$DY\$_2$	.0498 (.347)	−.6429 (.479)
$DY\$_3$	.0871 (.075)	.0513 (.091)
$DY\$2_1$	.0090 (.048)	.0705 (.050)
$DY\$2_2$	.0086 (.050)	.1033 (.069)
DTB_1	−1.534 (.314)**	.2166 (.948)
DTB_2	−.4085 (.539)	1.537 (.776)*
DTB_3	.0312 (.146)	.6475 (.217)*
$DTB2_1$	.1888 (.044)**	−.0210 (.060)
$DTB2_2$	.0414 (.057)	−.1789 (.083)
SPD_1	.3830 (.418)	.5793 (.483)
SPD_2	−.4519 (.485)	.1050 (.638)
SPD_3	−.0075 (.192)	.0393 (.296)
$SPD2_1$	−.0396 (.061)	−.1198 (.075)
$SPD2_2$	.0458 (.070)	.0202 (.089)
R^2	.482	.322
χ_E^2 (5)	6.888 (.229)	15.65 (.008)
χ_Y^2 (5)	2.644 (.755)	5.606 (.346)
χ_T^2 (5)	64.14 (.000)	15.58 (.008)
χ_S^2 (5)	1.820 (.873)	11.90 (.036)

Note: * (**) indicates the null hypothesis that the coefficient is zero is rejected at 5% (1%) significance level.

identified from analyses of correlations between the level of HTSE and other macroeconomic variables.

A potentially important caveat regarding interpretations of estimates of conditional volatility based on the projection equation (2) is that they will in general be sensitive to the specification of the conditional mean (1), since the *a priori* specification of the conditional mean identifies the conditional variance. If, for instance, the conditional mean is a nonlinear, nonquadratic function of the conditioning information, then fitting a quadratic function for the mean may lead to an overestimate of the degree of variation in the conditional variance. On the other hand, even if (1) is correctly specified, quadratic versions of (2) may underestimate the degree of conditional variation in returns if the conditional variance is a nonquadratic function of the conditioning information.

To explore the robustness of the findings in Table 3 to alternative functional forms for the conditional moments, a Fourier series approximation including sine and cosine terms was estimated. Specifically, m was set to 3 in (1) and (2) for $HTSE_1$ and $DY\$_1$, while m was set to 2 for DTB_1; only trigonometric functions of the first lag of these variables were added.[14] Chi-square statistics for various exclusion restrictions on these regressors are presented in Table 4. Each column represents a different specification of the conditioning information. Runs with trigonometric terms for all of the variables were not attempted, because of the large number of regressors relative to the sample size for such models. Additionally, DEURO and SPD, as well as their squared values, were omitted from all of the regressions. A larger percentage of the variation in HTSE is explained by all of the approximations in Table 4 compared to the quadratic approximation underlying Table 3. And the coefficients of determination for the ε_t^2 equations are correspondingly smaller in Table 4 relative to Table 3. Fourier terms enter significantly in all of the projection equations.

A more direct comparison of the conditional variances implied by the quadratic and Fourier approximations is provided by Figures 5 and 6 which display the actual squared residuals and their respective fitted values from the quadratic model (Model 3) and the Fourier model in the first column of Table 4 (Model 4.1). Overall, the patterns of squared residuals, $\hat{\varepsilon}_t^2$, are similar across the two approximations. The relatively smaller values of $\hat{\varepsilon}_t^2$ during 1987 and 1988 in Figure 6 compared to Figure 5 are a consequence of the additional predictive power of the Fourier terms for the conditional mean of HTSE. Similarly, the estimated conditional variances displayed in Figures 5 and 6 follow qualitatively similar time paths.[15] Together, Figures 5 and 6 suggest that the inclusion of Fourier terms in the approximation does not alter the qualitative features of the estimated conditional variances.

Interestingly, the largest conditional variances in Figure 6 occur around April 1987

[14] Attempts to estimate the models with $m=3$ for DTB often failed because of multicollinearity in the series.

[15] The conditional variance equation (2) does not constrain the estimated conditional variances to be positive and a few of the point estimates did take on small negative values in the sample.

Table 4. Chi-square Statistics for Fourier Series Approximation Benchmark Series
March 14, 1986 – May 20, 1988

		HTSE	
$\chi^2_{HF}(6)$	33.96 (.000)	.....	11.60 (.071)
$\chi^2_{Y}(5)$	21.29 (.000)	30.59 (.000)	6.842 (.232)
$\chi^2_{YF}(6)$	56.78 (.000)	33.22 (.000)	.....
$\chi^2_{T}(5)$	59.98 (.000)	54.68 (.000)	17.02 (.004)
$\chi^2_{TF}(4)$	.....	6.531 (.163)	1.973 (.741)
R^2	.619	.524	.535
		Squared residual	
$\chi^2_{HF}(6)$	17.07 (.009)	.....	11.06 (.087)
$\chi^2_{Y}(4)$	18.17 (.003)	5.457 (.363)	7.357 (.195)
$\chi^2_{YF}(6)$	16.29 (.012)	9.154 (.165)	.....
$\chi^2_{T}(4)$	14.59 (.012)	11.80 (.038)	7.295 (.200)
$\chi^2_{TF}(4)$	.....	7.090 (.131)	9.444 (.051)
R^2	.314	.295	.285

HF = Fourier terms for HTSE
Y = Linear and quadratic terms for DY$
YF = Fourier terms for DY$
T = Linear and quadratic terms for DTB
TF = Fourier terms for DTB
Marginal significance levels of the test statistics are given in parentheses.

when there was a large increase in the trading volume in government bonds. More precisely, volatility rose along with volume, fell near the peak of the high turnover ratios at the end of April 1987, and then conditional volatility increased as volume fell to more normal levels. Moreover, this period is also characterized by the largest deviations between the actual and fitted values of $\hat{\varepsilon}_t^2$. That is, the conditional variances, as measured by (2), understated by substantial margins the actual squared forecast errors for returns.

Other periods of relatively large conditional variances for the holding period returns were July-August 1987 and December 1987 (especially for the quadratic approximation). As noted previously, the yen/dollar exchange rate peaked in late August 1987 and fell substantially until December 1987. Furthermore, July 1987 was the beginning of a significant decline in the trading of foreign bonds by Japanese investors. This decline continued until November 1987 and then the trading of foreign bonds by Japanese increased substantially (Figure 3). These observations are consistent with the view that

Figure 5. Squared Deviation and their Fitted Values: Model 3

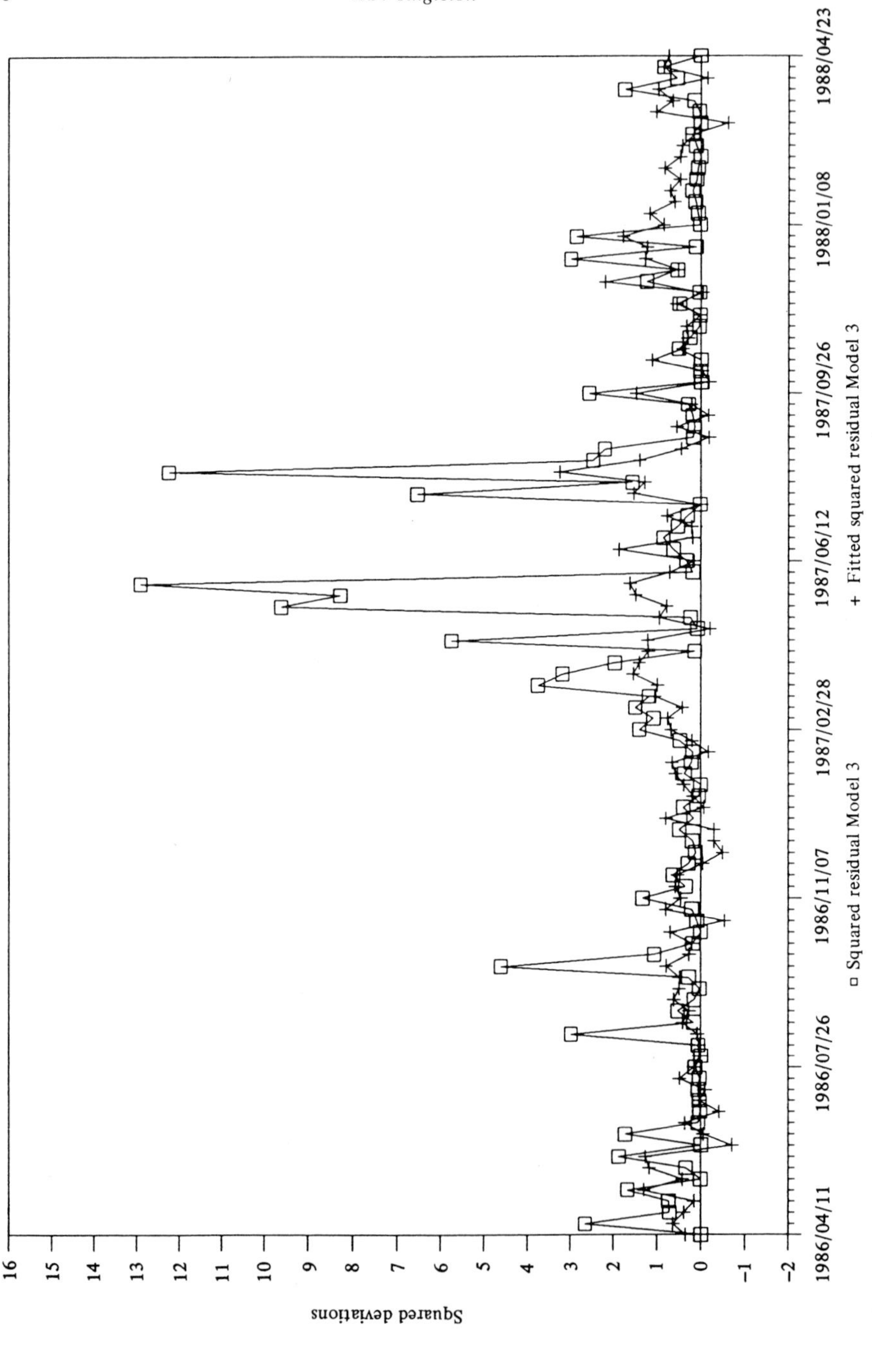

Figure 6. Squared Deviation and their Fitted Values: Model 4.1

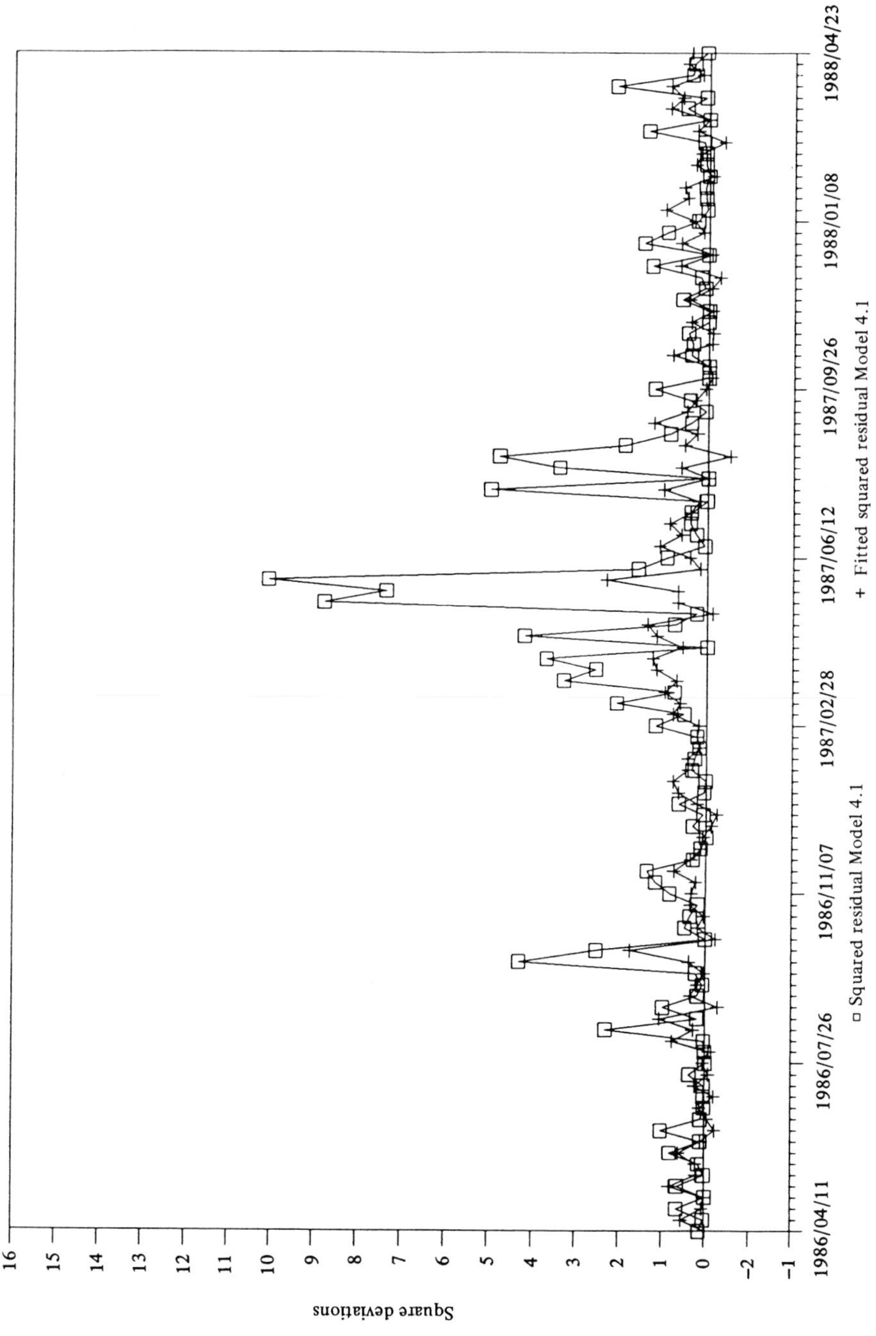

exchange rate changes and capital flows to and from Japan were associated with increased *ex ante* volatility in the Japanese bond markets. The regression results in Tables 3 and 4 suggest in addition that changes in short-term interest rates in the U.S. were highly correlated with these capital flows and volatility changes.

Estimates of the quadratic approximations to the conditional moments for quarterly (13 week) returns are displayed in Table 5. The explanatory variables were lagged at least 13 periods to account for the 13 week forecast horizon associated with the expectations in (1) and (2). Also, the weekly Euroyen deposit rate was replaced with the 13 week deposit rate in order to match the length of the holding period for the benchmark JGB. For this longer forecast horizon, all of the conditioning variables enter the mean approximation significantly at conventional significance levels except for the Euroyen deposit rate. These findings are consistent with previous monthly studies in which exchange rates and U.S. interest rates were statistically significant explanators of yields on benchmark JGBs.

The results for the estimated conditional variances (last column of Table 5) are similar to those obtained for weekly holding period returns. The Euroyen deposit rate and the U.S. Treasury yield spread are again significant explanators of the squared forecast errors, while the coefficients on changes in the three-month U.S. Treasury bill yield are somewhat less significant as a group in the 13 week forecast equation. The diminished role for DTB relative to SPD in the conditional variance equations for 13 week holding periods may reflect different investment considerations over 13 versus 1 week holding periods.

For comparison, the estimates of the quadratic approximations to the moments of the constant maturity, holding period returns are displayed in Table 6. The holding period return (HOTF) was calculated using the OTC data and the approximation (3), and squared values of HOTF are denoted by HF2. As with HTSE, there is significant variation in the conditional mean of HOTF, and this variation is associated primarily with past changes in HOTF and the U.S. Treasury bill yield.

While the test results for the estimated conditional means of HTSE and HOTF are similar, the results for the (quadratic approximate) conditional variances are notably different.[16] The relatively small marginal significance level for the block of coefficients on SPD suggest that volatility of the constant maturity, holding period yields does change sympathetically with the shape of the term structure of interest rates in the U.S. But none of the other financial variables seem to have significant explanatory power for the conditional variance of HOTF. This result is consistent with the observations in Section II about the institutional buy-and-hold strategies for off-the-run bonds and the absence of

[16] This finding appears to be inconsistent with the ARCH in mean specification of expected returns adopted by Bomhoff and Schotman (1987) for the Japanese bond market. It is interesting to note that, using very different data and a different sample period, they found that the ARCH effect on the conditional mean was insignificant. For an ARCH in mean model this implies that the risk premium on the bond is constant, but the evidence for reported here for constant maturity bond series does not support this conclusion.

Table 5. Estimates of Quadratic Regressions for Benchmark Quarterly Holding Period Returns
March 14, 1986 – May 20, 1988

	HTSE	ϵ_t^2
$HTSE_{13}$	.6799 (.343)*	–.6254 (.426)
$HTSE_{14}$	.3326 (.349)	.1599 (.480)
$HTSE_{15}$	.1267 (.204)	.0729 (.304)
$HTSE_{16}$	–.7161 (.219)**	–.1822 (.345)
$H2_{13}$	–.0380 (.051)	.1240 (.082)
$H2_{14}$	–.1015 (.034)**	–.0225 (.086)
$DEURO_{13}$	–.2731 (.284)	.7423 (.312)*
$DEURO_{14}$	–.0178 (.289)	.0479 (.346)
$DEURO_{15}$	–.1238 (.113)	.2197 (.141)
$EURO2_{13}$	.0278 (.042)	–.1133 (.060)
$EURO2_{14}$	–.5045 (.041)	–.0317 (.053)
$DY\$_{13}$	.0750 (.357)	.1157 (.317)
$DY\$_{14}$	.7761 (.423)	.0462 (.543)
$DY\$_{15}$	.1259 (.149)	.0459 (.226)
$DY\$2_{13}$	.0075 (.045)	–.1019 (.035)
$DY\$2_{14}$	–.0834 (.054)	–.0345 (.068)
DTB_{13}	.2399 (.293)	.5017 (.296)
DTB_{14}	.9531 (.538)	.4744 (.425)
DTB_{15}	.5354 (.140)**	–.2949 (.190)
$DTB2_{13}$	.0419 (.066)	–.0994 (.048)*
$DTB2_{14}$	–.0414 (.088)	–.0969 (.067)
SPD_{13}	–.9756 (.515)	–2.021 (.701)**
SPD_{14}	–.4714 (.508)	.4785 (.712)
SPD_{15}	–.0708 (.195)	.5664 (.230)*
$SPD2_{13}$	.1648 (.072)*	.2647 (.093)**
$SPD2_{14}$	.0827 (.086)	–.1447 (.104)
R^2	.623	.364
$\chi_E^2(5)$	2.332 (.801)	11.75 (.038)
$\chi_Y^2(5)$	15.17 (.009)	5.846 (.321)
$\chi_T^2(5)$	29.57 (.000)	8.185 (.146)
$\chi_S^2(5)$	32.65 (.000)	22.05 (.000)

Note: * (**) indicates the null hypothesis that the coefficient is zero is rejected at 5% (1%) significance level.

Table 6. Estimates of Quadratic Regressions for Constant Maturity Weekly Holding Period Returns
March 14, 1986 – May 20, 1988

	HOTF	ϵ_t^2	HOTF-EURO
$HOTF_1$	.2980 (.256)	−.0480 (.178)	.2929 (.256)
$HOTF_2$	.8436 (.303)**	.2162 (.234)	.8388 (.303)**
$HOTF_3$	.0599 (.090)	−.0626 (.048)	.0585 (.090)
$HOTF_4$	.2206 (.117)	.0774 (.090)	.2201 (.118)
$HF2_1$	−.0848 (.039)**	−.0020 (.027)	−.0840 (.039)**
$HF2_2$	−.1507 (.050)**	−.0213 (.040)	−.1502 (.050)**
$DEURO_1$	−.7164 (.426)	−.0544 (.194)	−.7178 (.426)
$DEURO_2$	.0704 (.426)	.3288 (.256)	.0686 (.332)
$DEURO_3$	−.1974 (.119)	.0043 (.087)	−.2001 (.119)
$EURO2_1$	.8312 (.062)	.0029 (.030)	.0823 (.062)
$EURO2_2$	−.0519 (.067)	−.0596 (.045)	−.0524 (.067)
$DY\$_1$	−.2163 (.271)	−.0560 (.117)	−.2162 (.272)
$DY\$_2$	.2255 (.300)	−.1060 (.142)	.2242 (.300)
$DY\$_3$	−.0011 (.083)	−.0538 (.057)	−.0008 (.083)
$DY\$2_1$	.0077 (.044)	−.0484 (.022)	.0075 (.044)
$DY\$2_2$	−.0204 (.044)	.0108 (.020)	−.0203 (.044)
DTB_1	−1.390 (.258)**	.0411 (.158)	−1.395 (.258)**
DTB_2	−.6909 (.338)*	.1998 (.234)	−.6943 (.229)**
DTB_3	.1961 (.177)	.0704 (.137)	.1964 (.177)
$DTB2_1$	.1852 (.050)**	−.0438 (.040)	.1859 (.050)**
$DTB2_2$	.0789 (.045)	−.0167 (.027)	.0792 (.045)
SPD_1	−.0641 (.512)	.1716 (.223)	−.0641 (.513)
SPD_2	.0204 (.729)	.8994 (.741)	.0234 (.730)
SPD_3	−.3767 (.320)	−.4159 (.324)	−.3765 (.320)
$SPD2_1$	.0837 (.090)	−.0970 (.041)*	.0838 (.090)
$SPD2_2$	−.0129 (.090)	.0016 (.051)	−.0133 (.090)
R^2	.343	.266	.343
$\chi_E^2(5)$	5.420 (.367)	4.307 (.506)	5.561 (.351)
$\chi_Y^2(5)$	5.587 (.348)	3.347 (.647)	5.585 (.349)
$\chi_T^2(5)$	35.68 (.000)	8.871 (.114)	35.90 (.000)
$\chi_S^2(5)$	7.475 (.188)	10.39 (.065)	7.473 (.188)

Note: * (**) indicates the null hypothesis that the coefficient is zero is rejected at 5% (1%) significance level.

large trading volumes for these securities. Evidently, neither the level or volatility of the constant-maturity yields are as forecastable from near-term changes in exchange rates or short-term bond yields as the benchmark yields.

Though the focus of this analysis is not on the term structure of interest rates in Japan, some insights into the validity of the expectations theories of the term structure can be gained by examining the corresponding results for the excess holding period returns on long-term bonds. The expected difference between the (constant maturity) holding period return H_t^1 and the Euroyen one-week deposit rate $EURO_t$ is often interpreted as the risk premium from holding long-term bonds. Evidence of time variation in this difference is inconsistent with some expectations theories of the term structure of interest rates.

To test whether there was significant time variation in the risk premium, the excess returns (H_t^1–$EURO_t$) for HOTF was regressed on the same information used for the quadratic approximations.[17] The results are reported in the third column of Table 6. The point estimates indicate that there is significant time variation in the *ex ante* risk premium. Equally interesting is the close similarity between the parameter estimates in the first and third columns within Table 6. This similarity suggests that there is relatively little variation in EURO compared to variation in HOTF. Put differently, the comovements between expected holding period returns and the Euroyen rate are much too weak to be consistent with at least simple versions of the expectations theory of the term structure. This finding is perhaps not unexpected for the reasons set forth in Sections II and III.

V. Concluding Remarks

This paper has investigated the time series properties of the conditional variances of holding period returns on Japanese government bonds using weekly data on 1 and 13 week holding period returns for the period March 1986 through May 1988. The findings suggest that the conditional mean of the weekly holding period returns on the benchmark bond series is strongly correlated with changes in the three-month U.S. Treasury bill rate. The conditional variances of the holding period returns were also correlated significantly with changes in Euroyen and U.S. Treasury bill rates and the U.S. Treasury bond long-short yields spread. While the Fourier terms in the approximations to the conditional variances often entered significantly as groups, the qualitative patterns of the implied fitted conditional variances were similar to the fitted variances obtained using quadratic approximations.

The large increase in the turnover of foreign bonds by Japanese investors beginning

[17] By the law of iterated projections, the projection of (H_t^1–$EURO_t$) onto a set of regressors x_{t-1} gives the same results as projecting the *ex ante* risk premium onto x_t.

in early 1986 and the concentration of trading by Japanese investors, outside of Japan, in U.S. bond markets suggests a possible explanation for the significant correlations between yields changes in the U.S. and Japan. Namely, to the extent that the large turnover ratios in their portfolios of U.S. bonds are associated with trading in the U.S. Treasury bill markets, the significant correlations may reflect portfolio reallocations between long-term JGBs and Treasury bills over short investment horizons. Over a 13 week investment horizon, the conditional mean of the holding period returns were also significantly correlated with yen/dollar exchange rate changes and the U.S. Treasury long-short spread. Interestingly, for the sample period examined, the largest values of the estimated conditional variances occurred during 1987 and about the same time as substantial changes in trading volumes in Japanese and U.S. government bond markets by Japanese investors.

Overall, the results for the benchmark series suggest that there is a significant predictable component to the variation in the holding period returns. Since it is the conditional variances and covariances of returns which underlie optimal dynamic portfolio decisions, these findings also suggest the statistical representations of conditional second moments examined here may be useful for formulating optimal hedging strategies for bond portfolios that include JGBs.

More generally, the results from this study, together with previous results by the Bank of Japan (1986, 1988), highlight the increased influence of foreign economic developments on the time series properties of JGB yields that has occurred along with the deregulation of financial markets during the 1980s in Japan. As the process of deregulation continues in Japan and Europe, the influence of external factors on volatility is likely to remain significant and may well increase in importance.

The corresponding results for the holding period returns on the relatively thinly traded constant maturity bond series were very different. Only the U.S. long-short yield spread entered the conditional variance equation significantly at the ten percent significance level. This result may be attributable to the institutional influences which seem to underlie the relatively low trading volume in non-benchmark JGBs. As trading activity increases and the costs of shorting on and off-the-run securities decline, the constant maturity yield series should become increasingly correlated with external and internal economic developments. At that time, the observations regarding hedging the risk of fluctuations in benchmark yields may apply with equal force to the risk of changes in yields on non-benchmark securities.

REFERENCES

Bank of Japan, "Recent Portfolio Management of Institutional Investors", Special Paper No. 97, Research and Statistics Department, 1982.

———, "Structural Changes in the Secondary Market for Bonds and the Recent Trends in Yields on Long-Term Bonds", Special Paper No. 132, Research and Statistics Department, 1986.

———, "Recent Developments in the Long-term Bond Market", Special Paper No. 170, Research and Statistics Department, 1988.

Bomhoff, Eduard J., and Peter C. Shotman, "The Term Structure in the United States, Japan and West Germany", manuscript, Erasmus University, Netherlands, 1987.

Dunn, Kenneth, and Kenneth J. Singleton, "Modeling the Term Structure of Interest Rates under Nonseparable Utility and Durability of Goods", *Journal of Financial Economics*, 1986.

Engle, Robert, "Autoregressive Conditional Heteroskedasticity with Estimates of the Variances of U.K. Inflation", *Econometrica*, 1982.

———, D. Lillien, and R. Robins, "Estimating Time Varying Risk Premia in the Term Structure: The ARCH-M Model", *Econometrica* 55, 1987, pp. 391–407.

Gallant, A. Ronald, "Unbiased Determination of Production Technologies", *Journal of Econometrics* 20, 1982, pp. 285–323.

———, David Hseih, and George Tauchen, "On Fitting Recalcitrant Series: The Pound/Dollar Exchange Rate", manuscript 1988.

Glosten, Larry, Ravi Jagannathan, and David Runkle, "A Relationship between the Expected Value and the Volatililty of the Nominal Excess Return on Stocks", manuscript, Northwestern Uiversity, April 1989.

Hansen, Lars, "Large Sample Properties of Generalized Method of Moments Estimators", *Econometrica* 50, 1982, pp.1029-1054.

———, and Kenneth Singleton, "Generalized Instrumental Variables Estimation of Nonlinear Rational Expectations Models", *Econometrica* 50, 1982, pp.1269-1286.

Kool, Clemens, and John Tatom, "International Linkages in the Term Structure of Interest Rates", *Review* 70, Federal Reserve Bank of St. Louis, 1988, pp. 30–43.

Kuroda, Akio, *Nihon no Kinri Kozo* (in Japanese), Toyo Keizai Shimposha, 1982.

Newey, Whitney, "A Method of Moments Interpretation of Sequential Estimators", *Economics Letters* 14, 1984, pp. 201–206.

Pagan, Adrian, and Y. Hong, "Non-parametric Estimation of the Risk Premium", manuscript, University of Rochester, 1988.

———, and A. Ullah, "The Econometric Analysis of Models with Risk Terms", *Journal of Applied Econometrics*, 1988.

Sargen, Nicholas, Kermit Schoenholtz, Steven Blitz, and Sahar Elhabashi, "Trading Patterns in the Japanese Government Bond Market", Salomon Brothers Research Department, 1986.

Shiller, Robert, "The Volatility of Long-term Interest Rates and Expectations Models of the Term Structure", *Journal of Political Economy* 87, 1979, pp. 1190–1219.

———, John Campbell, and Kermit Schoenholtz, "Forward Rates and Future Policy: Interpreting the Term Structure of Interest Rates", *Brookings Papers on Economic Activity*, 1983, pp. 173–217.

Singleton, Kenneth J., "Expectations Models of the Term Structure and Implied Variance Bounds", *Journal of Political Economy* 88, 1980, pp. 1159–1176.

———, "Specification and Estimation of Intertemporal Asset Pricing Models", in B. Friedman and F. Hahn, eds., *Handbook of Monetary Economics*, North Holland, 1988.

Suzuki, Yoshio, *The Japanese Financial System*, Oxford University Press, 1987.

Takagi, Shinji, "Transactions Costs and the Term Structure of Interest Rates in the OTC Bond Market in Japan", *Journal of Money, Credit and Banking* 19, 1987, pp. 515–527.

———, "Recent Developments in Japan's Bond and Money Markets", *Journal of Japanese and International Economics* 2, 1988, pp. 63–91.

Japanese Financial Market Research
W.T. Ziemba, W. Bailey and Y. Hamao (Editors)

The Structural Behavior of the Japanese Gensaki Rate

Kwok-Wai Leung[a], Anthony Sanders[b] and Haluk Unal[a]

[a] College of Business and Management, University of Maryland, College Park, MD 20742

[b] Academic Faculty of Finance, Ohio State University, Columbus, OH 43210

Abstract

This paper empirically examines variation in the time series behavior of the three-month Gensaki rate, a principal indicator of the time value of money in Japan, for the period from February 1980 through September 1989. Employing the mean-reverting model and the switching regression method, we find no evidence of mean reversion for the entire sample period, but significant mean reversion in two of the subperiods. Furthermore, we find evidence of dramatic declines in the volatility of the Gensaki rate over the sample period. Shifts in estimated mean reversion and volatility appear to be related to the liberalization of Japan's capital markets.

1. INTRODUCTION

In the past decade there have been a number of changes in the Japanese financial market. In particular, there has been dramatic deregulation and liberalization of the Japanese financial environment which has changed Japan from a tightly controlled market to a more competitive one. This paper examines the structural behavior of the Japanese short-term interest rate (Gensaki rate - a three year bond with a repurchase provision) during this decade of financial deregulation and liberalization. By examining the behavior of the Gensaki rate, we are able to document changes in the Japanese financial market that may impact on the selection of models used to price interest-contingent claims (e.g., bonds and mortgages).

The behavior of the Gensaki rate over the period February 1980 to September 1989 is examined in the paper. Following the methodology of Sanders and Unal [1], we examine the intertemporal characteristics of the Gensaki rate and estimate the parameters in a mean-reverting process (Vasicek's elastic random walk model [2]), assuming that the Gensaki rate is stochastic and mean-reverting. To identify the interest rate regimes over which the parameter estimates are stable, Goldfeld and Quandt's ([3],[4],[5]) switching regression method (GQSRM) is used. This method allows the mean-reverting model applicable to the Gensaki rate to switch parameters over the sample period in an unrestricted way.

The empirical findings demonstrate the nonstationarity of the parameter estimates over the sample period. For the period from February 1980 through September 1989, five interest rate regimes (four structural switches) are estimated. These switches correspond to deregulatory events in the secondary bond market, securities sector and interdealer market. We find no evidence of mean reversion for the entire sample period, but significant mean reversion in two of the regimes. Furthermore, we find evidence of dramatic changes in the volatility of the Gensaki rate over the sample period with volatility declining over the course of the decade.

The paper is presented as follows. Section 2 specifies the mean-reverting model and the switching regression method. Section 3 presents the results and discusses their implications. Concluding remarks are in the Section 4. A summary of chronological events is listed in the Appendix to facilitate future research concerning Japanese financial market.

2. METHODOLOGY

Following Vasicek [2], the short-term rate of interest, r, is presumed to be driven by the following mean-reverting process

$$dr = \kappa(\mu - r)\,dt + \sigma dz \quad , \tag{1}$$

where κ is the speed-of-adjustment coefficient, μ is the steady-state mean, σ is the standard deviation of the short-term rate, and dz is a Gauss-Wiener process. A discrete-time analogue to equation (1) is

$$\Delta r_t = \kappa(\mu - r_{t-1}) + e_t \quad , \tag{2}$$

which can be rewritten as

$$\Delta r_t = \kappa\mu - \kappa r_{t-1} + e_t \quad . \tag{3}$$

In order to examine the temporal variability in the parameters of Equation (3) without imposing a set of prior beliefs as to when the regime changes occurred, we employ the Goldfeld and Quandt ([3],[4],[5]) switching regression method (GQSRM). This technique provides a flexible way to identify changes in the model parameters over a number of regimes.

Equation (3) can be rewritten as a multi-regime mean-reverting model as follows:

$$\Delta \tilde{r}_t = \beta_{0j}\beta_{1j} + \beta_{1j}\tilde{r}_{t-1} + \tilde{e}_{tj} \quad , \quad j = 1, \ldots, k, \ldots, p \ . \tag{4}$$

where j is the regime index, β_0 estimates μ and β_1 estimates κ. The transition between regimes is governed by an extraneous classifying variable Z_t with unknown cutoff values, Z_j^*. The classifying variable is assumed to be time. In order to transform Equation (4) into a single regression model, the GQSRM uses a series of transitional dummy variables, D_{tj}. The p-1 sets of variables D_{tj} are approximated as

$$D_{tj} = \int_{-\infty}^{Z_t} \frac{1}{\sqrt{2\pi}\,\sigma_j^*} \exp^{-\frac{1}{2}\left(\frac{\xi - Z_j^*}{\sigma_j^*}\right)^2} d\xi \quad , \tag{5}$$

where j goes from 1 to p-1. In Equation (5), Z_j^* represents the unknown switch dates. The value of σ_j^* gives information about the smoothness of the structural change. The smaller σ_j^* is, the more sudden the transition between the regimes. If σ_j^* is significantly different from zero, the hypothesis that the structural change is abrupt in the vicinity of Z_j^* should be rejected.

In (4), the equation representing the k-th regime is then multiplied by

$$v_{tk} = \prod_{j=0}^{k-1} D_{tj} \prod_{j=k}^{p} (1 - D_{tj}) \quad , \tag{6}$$

where D_{t0} and D_{tp} are defined to be 1 and 0 respectively. The resulting equations for p regimes are added together to obtain the composite equation that is estimated:

$$\sum_{k=1}^{p} \Delta \tilde{r}_t v_{tk} = \sum_{k=1}^{p} [(\beta_{0k}\beta_{1k} + \beta_{1k}\tilde{r}_{t-1} + \tilde{e}_{tk})(v_{tk})] \quad . \tag{7}$$

The likelihood function for the p-regime mean-reverting process is obtained assuming that $\Sigma \Delta r_t v_{tk}$ to be normally distributed with mean

$$\mu_t = \sum_{k=1}^{p} [(\beta_{0k}\beta_{1k} + \beta_{1k}\tilde{r}_{t-1})(v_{tk})]$$

and variance

$$\sigma_t^2 = \sum_{k=1}^{p} \left[(\sigma_{ek}^2)\ (v_{tk}^2) \right] \quad .$$

The likelihood function then becomes

$$\ln L = -\frac{T}{2} \ln 2\pi - \frac{1}{2} \sum_{t=1}^{T} \ln \sigma_t^2 - \frac{1}{2} \sum_{t=1}^{T} \frac{\left[\sum_{k=1}^{p} e_{tk} v_{tk} \right]^2}{\sigma_t^2} \quad . \tag{8}$$

Maximizing (8) with respect to the unknown parameters gives maximum-likelihood estimates of the parameters of the regression relation given in (7), the switch points Z_t^*, and the parameters σ_j^* which provides information about the smoothness of the structural changes.

3. EMPIRICAL RESULTS

Panel A of Table 1 summarizes the switching regression tests of the number of regimes in effect during the 1980-1989 period. Panel B reports likely regime-switch dates and measures of the gradualness of each switch. Four switches are estimated dated April 1981, April 1983, August 1985 and January 1987. Standard errors of the switch points are not statistically different from zero, indicating that switches were abrupt in nature.

The first switch (April 1981) corresponds to a month when a series of deregulatory events took place. First, the Ministry of Finance relaxed its restrictions on secondary sales of government bonds by banks. Second, the minimum holding period of the subscribing banks before they were allowed to sell government bonds in the secondary market was reduced from 1 year to approximately 100 days. Finally, the city banks were authorized to invest in the Gensaki market for the first time; furthermore, they were permitted to simultaneous borrow in the bill-discount market and invest in the call market. This date was identified to be of importance by Takagi [6] as well.

The second switch (April 1983) occurs in the month when the over-the-counter sales of newly issued long-term (10 year) bonds by banks were authorized. Variable interest rate 15 year bonds were allowed to be issued also. Once again, this date was identified as being important by Takagi [6].

The third switch (August 1985) coincides again with a couple of deregulatory events. Bank dealings in bonds were deregulated and they are allowed to use interdealer brokerage services. The minimum holding period of government bonds after subscription was further reduced to 40 days. New secured and unsecured short term instruments were introduced in the bill-discounting market and the call market. A bond futures market was also established around this time.

Table 1
Results of Goldfeld-Quandt Tests Identifying the Number of Switches, Most Likely Switch Dates, and Gradualness of Switches in the Mean-Reverting Interest-Rate Process

Panel A: Likelihood-Ratio Test Results

Regime[a]	$-2Ln(L^*/L)$[b]
R_1 vs R_2	125.77**
R_2 vs R_3	24.99**
R_3 vs R_4	31.34**
R_4 vs R_5	27.32**
R_5 vs R_6	14.87

Panel B: Switch Dates and Gradualness[c]

	Switch Point (Z_j^*)	Implied Switch Date	Gradualness Parameter (σ_j^*)
First Switch	16	1981/4	0.67
	(0.67)		(1.05)
Second Switch	40	1983/4	0.10
	(0.59)		(0.71)
Third Switch	68	1985/8	0.12
	(1.03)		(0.60)
Fourth Switch	85	1987/1	0.34
	(1.75)		(0.97)

a R_j represents the hypothesis that the mean-reverting interest-rate process switches exactly j-1 times during the 1980/2 to 1989/9 period.
b The test statistic is $-2Ln(L^*/L)$ where L^* and L are restricted and unrestricted maximum likelihood values. Critical value for 5 d.f. at 1-percent significance is 15.09.
c Asymptotic standard errors are in parentheses.
** Significant at the 1-percent level.

Finally, we observe a structural change in the Gensaki rate following the fourth switch in January 1987. This change coincides with the establishment of the Tokyo offshore market. This allowed Japanese institutions to have special accounts free from domestic regulation.

It is important to note that there were a substantial number of other changes in the Japanese financial system during the 1980s (see the appendix).

We do not imply that these other changes were unimportant. In fact, the changing structure of the Gensaki rate over the decade reflects the cumulative effect of many of the regulatory changes as well as other economic events (e.g., changes in the U.S. financial markets).

Table 2 reports the estimates of the mean-reverting process. During the sample period, the speed-of-adjustment, κ, gradually rose and reached its peak in period 1983/04 to 1985/07, then declined afterward and became negative after 1986.

Table 2
Maximum-Likelihood Estimates of Regime Parameters for the Mean-Reverting Interest-Rate Process

$$\Delta r_t = \kappa(\mu - r_{t-1}) + e_t \quad (2)$$

Regime	μ	κ	σ_e	N
A. Full Period				
1980/2 - 1989/9	5.44**	0.03	0.48	117
	(1.49)	(0.02)		
B. Estimated Sub-Periods				
1980/2 - 1981/3	9.65**	0.17	1.24	15
	(1.98)	(0.20)		
1981/4 - 1983/3	6.83**	0.29	0.28	24
	(0.20)	(0.18)		
1983/4 - 1985/7	6.35**	0.50**	0.09	28
	(0.03)	(0.16)		
1985/8 - 1986/12	2.31	0.04	0.42	17
	(7.45)	(0.10)		
1987/1 - 1989/9	3.83**	-0.19**	0.12	33
	(0.14)	(0.07)		

Gensaki interest rate is used in the estimation of model parameters. μ, κ, and σ_e are estimates of the steady-state mean, the speed-of-adjustment coefficient, and the standard deviation of the interest rate process. N is the number of observations in each regimes. Asymptotic standard errors are in parentheses.

The speed of adjustment estimate is statistically significant in only two of the five regimes (1983/04-1985/07 and 1987/01-1989/09). When κ is not statistically different from zero, the mean-reverting model is reduced to a simple random walk time series model. In other words, the interest rate patterns in periods 1980/02-1981/03, 1981/04-1983/03, and 1985/08-1986/12 follow a random walk. During the subperiod 1983/04-1985/08, a series of easing of restrictions contribute to the expansion of secondary trading market and the reduction of transaction costs. The term structure of interest rates might also be affected and speed up the interest rate adjustment.

It is interesting to note that Japan experienced a negative κ after 1986. While a positive κ implies that the interest rate would adjust in a direction such that it converges back to the long term steady mean, a negative κ indicates the divergence of short term interest rate from the mean. When the interest rate is above (below) the mean, it would adjust upward (downward) instead. Therefore, basically Japan has switched from stabilizing interest rates to destabilizing interest rates after 1986. If we pool the data and estimate the parameters in the mean-reverting model for the whole sample period, it is found that the interest rates behave as random walk. This evidence provides support to the view that pooling time series data sometimes would average the periodic effects and mask our interpretation.

Table 3 tests for coefficient equality constraints across the five regimes to identify whether and how the parameter varies. Dummy-variable tests, which stack observations for two regimes, with D=0 across the first set of observations and D=1 for observations in the second group, are conducted. This produces the following model in which significant κ' would provide evidence of speed of adjustment difference between the focal groups:

$$\Delta\tilde{r}_t = a + \kappa\tilde{r}_{t-1} + a'D + \kappa' D\tilde{r}_{t-1} + \tilde{w}_t \quad . \tag{9}$$

Although the coefficient shows an upward and then downward pattern, no significant parameter shift is found between successive regimes. This implies the transition of the speed-of-adjustment is quite smooth from one regime to the other. However, the change of speed-of-adjustment across the regimes still can be shown when we compare the parameter estimates between periods 1983/04-1985/07 and 1987/01-1989/09, and between periods 1981/04-1983/03 and 1987/01-1989/09.

Table 4 shows the significance of shifts in the variance of the Gensaki rate. From the values and related F-statistics we observe that the interest rate variance changes significantly across regimes. The variance at the end of 80's is substantially smaller than in the early 80's. The substantial decrease in the level of uncertainty in the Gensaki rate over the sample period appears to correspond to the liberalization of Japanese financial market. However, other economics forces cannot be ruled out in explaining these structural shifts.

Table 3
Significance Tests for Changes in Speed of Adjustment (κ) between Regimes

$$\Delta \tilde{r}_t = a + \kappa \tilde{r}_{t-1} + a'D + \kappa' D \tilde{r}_{t-1} + \tilde{w}_t \quad . \tag{9}$$

Regime	κ'
(1980/2 - 1981/3) vs (1981/4 - 1983/3)[a]	-0.12 (-0.24)
(1981/4 - 1983/3) vs (1983/4 - 1985/7)[b]	-0.21 (0.52)
(1983/4 - 1985/7) vs (1985/8 - 1986/12)[c]	0.46 (0.92)
(1985/8 - 1986/12) vs (1987/1 - 1989/9)[d]	0.23 (1.47)
(1981/4 - 1983/3) vs (1987/1 - 1989/9)[e]	0.36* (2.08)
(1983/4 - 1985/7) vs (1987/1 - 1989/9)[f]	0.56* (3.21)

[a] For 1980/2-1981/3 observations D = 0, 1981/4-1983/3 observations D = 1.
[b] For 1981/4-1983/3 observations D = 0, 1983/4-1985/7 observations D = 1.
[c] For 1983/4-1985/7 observations D = 0, 1985/8-1986/12 observations D = 1.
[d] For 1985/8-1986/12 observations D = 0, 1987/1-1989/9 observations D = 1.
[e] For 1981/4-1983/3 observations D = 0, 1987/1-1989/9 observations D = 1.
[f] For 1983/4-1985/7 observations D = 0, 1987/1-1989/9 observations D = 1.
* Significant at the 5-percent. The t-statistics are in parentheses.

4. CONCLUSION

In this paper, we examine the structural behavior of the Japanese Gensaki rate from 1980 to 1989. Using Goldfeld and Quandt's switching regression methodology, we find evidence of five distinct regimes. There is no evidence of mean reversion in the Gensaki rate over the sample period, but there is evidence of mean reversion in two of the subperiods. The volatility of the Gensaki rate changed dramatically over the sample period. The changes in the regimes correspond to changes in the regulatory atmosphere in Japan, although there are other important economic events that could lead to changes in volatility that we do not consider.

Table 4
Estimates of Shifts in the Variance of the
Mean-Reverting Process Across Regimes[a]

Regime	Variance	F
1980/2 - 1981/3	1.54	
		19.25[b]**
1981/4 - 1983/3	0.08	
		10.00[c]**
1983/4 - 1985/7	0.008	
		22.50[d]**
1985/8 - 1986/12	0.18	
		12.86[e]**
1987/1 - 1989/9	0.014	

a Var (Group A)/Var (Group B) ~ F (v_1,v_2) for each case.
Group A represents the group with the larger variance and Group B the smaller variance.
b Var (Group A)/Var (Group B) ~ F (15, 24)
Group A refers to 1980/2 - 1981/3, Group B refers to 1981/4 - 1983/3.
c Var (Group A)/Var (Group B) ~ F (24, 28)
Group A refers to 1981/4 - 1983/3, Group B refers to 1983/4 - 1985/7.
d Var (Group A)/Var (Group B) ~ F (17, 28)
Group A refers to 1985/8 - 1986/12, Group B refers to 1983/4 -1985/7.
e Var (Group A)/Var (Group B) ~ F (17, 33)
Group A refers to 1985/8 - 1986/12, Group B refers to 1987/1 -1989/9.
** Significant at the 1- percent level.

Although this paper documents the existence of five interest rate regimes and documents the deregulatory actions that correspond to the changes in regimes, we have no formal model of why the Gensaki rate changes. Future research should include a comparison of Japanese and U.S. financial markets to determine the interactions between these markets.

6. REFERENCES

1 Sanders, A. B., and H. Unal. "On the Intertemporal Behavior of the Short-Term Rate of Interest." *Journal of Financial and Quantitative Analysis,* 23 (Dec. 1988), 417-423.

2 Vasicek, O. A. "An Equilibrium Characterization of the Term Structure." *Journal of Financial Economics,* 5 (Nov. 1977), 177-188.

3 Goldfeld, S. M., and R. E. Quandt. *Nonlinear Methods in Econometrics.* Amsterdam: North-Holland Publishing Co. (1972).

4 Goldfeld, S. M., and R. E. Quandt. "The Estimation of Structural Shifts by Switching Regressions." *Annals of Economic and Social Measurement,* 2 (Oct. 1973), 475-485.

5 Goldfeld, S. M., and R. E. Quandt. "Techniques for Estimating Switching Regressions." In *Studies in Nonlinear Estimation,* Goldfeld and Quandt, eds. Cambridge,MA: Ballinger (1976).

6 Takagi, S. "Transactions Costs and the Term Structure of Interest Rates in the OTC Bond Market in Japan." *Journal of Money, Credit, and Banking,* 19 (Nov. 1987), 515-527.

7 Takagi, S. "Recent Developments in Japan's Bond and Money Markets." *Journal of the Japanese and International Economies,* 2 (Mar. 1988), 63-91.

8 Singleton, K. J. "Interpreting Changes in the Volatility of Yields on Japanese Long-term Bonds." *Unpublished paper, Stanford University,* (Aug. 1989).

7. APPENDIX

Brief Chronological Summary of Events Most Likely Affecting Interest Rates in Japan 1980-1987[1]

Apr. 1980	The ceiling for CD's raised to 50% of net worth.
Apr. 1980	The ceiling on Gensaki borrowing by city banks raised to 150 billion Yen (the stepwise easing completed).
May 1980	Secondary sales of bonds by banks authorized following the commencement of trading in organized securities exchange (i.e., about 7-9 months after the subscription).
June 1980	4 year bonds issued at market rates.
Nov. 1980	Simultaneous borrowing in the call market and investing in the bill-discount market authorized for regional and trust banks.
Nov. 1980	The four largest securities companies authorized for the first time since 1965, to borrow in the call market up to 10 billion Yen.

[1] The list is basically adapted from the appendix of Takagi [7]. Other sources are Takagi [6] and Singleton [8].

Dec. 1980	Implementation of the new Foreign Exchange Loan removed virtually all restrictions on cross-border capital flows.
Apr. 1981	Secondary sales of bonds by banks authorized following the first business day in the fourth month after subscription (i.e., about 100 days).
Apr. 1981	Simultaneous borrowing in the bill-discount market and investing in the call market authorized for city banks.
Apr. 1981	City banks authorized to invest in the Gensaki market for the first time.
Dec. 1981	Borrowing in the call market authorized for eight additional securities companies up to 5 billion Yen each.
Dec. 1981	The ceiling on borrowing in the call market by the four largest securities companies raised to 30 billion Yen.
Jan. 1982	Two additional securities companies permitted to borrow in the call market.
Apr. 1982	Money brokers authorized to deal in the bill-discount market.
Feb. 1983	The ceiling for CD's raised to 75% of net worth.
Feb. 1983	15 year bonds with variable interest rates issued.
Apr. 1983	Over-the-counter sales of the newly issued long-term (10 year) bonds by banks authorized.
Sept 1983	20-year bonds with fixed interest rates issued.
Oct. 1983	Over-the-Counter sales of the newly issued medium-term (2 to 5 year) bonds by banks authorized.
Jan. 1984	The minimum denomination for CD's reduced to 300 million Yen.
June 1984	Bank dealing in bonds with remaining maturity of less than 2 years authorized.
Mar. 1985	Simultaneous borrowing and investing in the bill-discount market authorized.
Mar. 1985	Money Market Certificates (MMCs) with maturities of 1 to 6 months and the minimum denomination of 50 million Yen introduced.
Apr. 1985	The ceiling for CD's raised to 100% of net worth; the minimum denomination reduced to 100 million Yen; and the minimum maturity reduced to 1 month.
May 1985	Securities companies authorized to lend in the interbank market.
June 1985	Banks allowed to use interdealer brokerage services provided by the Nition Sogo Shoken.
June 1985	Bank dealing in bonds completely liberalized.
June 1985	Secondary sales of bonds by bank authorized following the first business day in the second calendar month after subscription (i.e., about 40 days) for the dealing account only.

June 1985	New 5 and 6-month instruments introduced in the bill-discount market.
June 1985	Yen denominated bankers' acceptance (BA) market established with the minimum denomination of 100 million Yen and maturities of 1 to 6 months.
June 1985	Securities companies authorized to deal in secondary bank CD's.
July 1985	Unsecured call loans authorized.
Aug. 1985	New 2- and 3- week instruments (secured) introduced in the call market.
Sept 1985	New 2- and 3- week instruments (unsecured) introduced in the call market.
Oct. 1985	A bond futures market established.
Oct. 1985	The ceiling for CD's raised to 150% of net worth.
Dec. 1985	Mutual savings and loans banks authorized to raise funds in the bill-discount market.
Feb. 1986	6 month bonds issued at market rates with the minimum denomination of 100 million Yen.
Apr. 1986	Secondary sales of bonds by banks authorized following the first business day in the first calendar month after subscription (i.e.; about 10 days) for the dealing account; following the first business day in the second calendar month after subscription (i.e., about 40 days) for the investment account.
Apr. 1986	The ceiling for CD's raised to 200% of net worth.
Apr. 1986	The maximum maturity of CD's and MMC's increased to 12 months.
Apr. 1986	Securities companies authorized to deal in Yen BA's.
Sept 1986	The minimum denomination of MMC's reduced to 30 million Yen.
Sept 1986	The ceiling for CD's raised to 250% of net worth.
Dec. 1986	Tokyo offshore market was established. This allowed Japanese institutions to have special accounts free from domestic regulation.
Apr. 1987	The minimum denomination of MMC's reduced to 20 million Yen; the maximum maturity of MMC's increased to 2 years.
Apr. 1987	The ceiling for CD's raised to 300% of net worth; the ceiling for foreign banks abolished.
Oct. 1987	The minimum denomination of MMC's reduced to 10 million.
Oct. 1987	The ceiling for CD's abolished for all banks.

The authors would like to thank Warren Bailey, Coleman Kendall, and Rene Stulz for their helpful comments.

PART VII:
FINANCING OF JAPANESE CORPORATIONS

Japanese Financial Market Research
W.T. Ziemba, W. Bailey and Y. Hamao (Editors)

THE COST OF CAPITAL FOR INDUSTRIAL FIRMS IN THE U.S. AND JAPAN*

James E. Hodder

Industrial Engineering and Engineering Management Department,
Stanford University, Stanford, California

Abstract

This paper examines the debate regarding cost of capital differences between the U.S. and Japan. It is argued that the "Pecking Order Theory" of capital structure implies a firm's cost of capital depends on its investment budget, which can vary across time. From this perspective, cost of capital estimates which average across firms and time can be very misleading. The current paper also argues that lender monitoring in Japan may have flattened the cost of capital function faced by industrial firms. While this effect may not be advantageous for all firms, it does appear beneficial for rapidly growing firms.

1. INTRODUCTION

During the last few years, several studies have focused on the possibility of corporate cost of capital differences between the U.S. and Japan. Much of the discussion of this issue was triggered by a study conducted for the Semiconductor Industry Association (SIA) and completed in June 1980. That study as well as one by Hatsopoulos (1983) argued that Japanese firms enjoyed a large cost of capital advantage over their U.S. competitors. Given the major trade imbalances between the two countries, such findings had potential government policy implications. Indeed, these two studies were used to support arguments that the U.S. government should take steps to neutralize the Japanese advantage through trade sanctions, changes in the U.S. tax laws, and pressure on the Japanese government to eliminate financial subsidies.

These early studies received quite a bit of popular attention; however, they contained technical errors which severely damaged their credibility among financial economists.[1] Subsequent papers by Ando and Auerbach (1988a) and Baldwin (1986) generally found no substantial cost of capital differences between the U.S. and Japan.[2] Both papers can be viewed as responses

---

*An earlier version of this paper was entitled, "Capital Structure and Cost of Capital in the U.S. and Japan." Research on this topic was begun while the author was a Visiting Scholar at Osaka University and supported by a fellowship from the Japan Society for Promotion of Science. Support was also received from the Center for Teaching and Research in Integrated Manufacturing Systems (Stanford University).

to the SIA and Hatsopoulos studies and are considerably more credible. There is also a 1984 volume edited by Holland which provides cost of capital and rate of return estimates for the U.S. and Japan. Since the chapters in that book are by different authors using somewhat different techniques, the estimates are not completely comparable. However, they tend to indicate a relatively modest advantage for Japanese firms (roughly 1.5-2 percent on a before-tax basis and less than 1 percent after tax).

Up to this point, the more credible papers seem to indicate no major difference in overall capital costs for U.S. and Japanese firms. However, a subsequent analysis by Ando and Auerbach (1988b) found a relatively large cost of capital advantage for Japanese firms--a finding which contradicts results in their earlier paper. This later paper uses essentially the same methodology as Ando and Auerbach (1988a) but with a much larger sample of firms. Consequently, its results appear more convincing and alter the balance of evidence in favor of a cost of capital difference.[3]

A major cost of capital differential between the U.S. and Japan would seem to require a substantial segmentation between the two capital markets. In most papers, the segmentation assumption is implicit. However, Flaherty and Itami (1984) explicitly base their argument for a cost of capital differential on the relative isolation of Japanese financial markets coupled with Japan's higher saving rate. They feel this combination resulted in a greater aggregate supply of funds relative to demand in Japan compared with the United States, leading to a lower cost of capital for Japanese firms.

The current relevance of such an isolation argument is open to question considering the rapid deregulation of Japanese financial markets and the massive outflow of funds from Japan during the last few years. If Japanese financial markets are now substantially integrated with capital markets in the rest of the world, the continued existence of a cost of capital differential must rest on a more subtle segmentation argument. Even for the past, there is evidence which suggests that despite their apparent isolation the cost of funds in Japanese financial markets was similar on a risk-adjusted basis to that in U.S. markets.

In particular, Baldwin (1986) estimated the expected return and its standard deviation for weighted portfolios of stocks and bonds in each country over the 1960-1980 period. The estimations were performed on an inflation-adjusted basis using annual return data from Ibbotson, Carr, and Robinson (1982). The resulting "efficient frontier" for the U.S. was very similar to that for Japan, indicating that investors and firms faced similar risk-return tradeoffs in each country's financial markets. That is, the cost of funds varied with risk but on a risk-adjusted basis was quite similar--as Baldwin reports, "for all risk levels, the difference is never greater than 1 percent."[4]

Baldwin's result is appealing since it seems to confirm the notion that arbitrage will keep risk-return tradeoffs the same across internationally integrated markets. However, the result is surprising given the heavy regulation of Japanese markets during this period. One possible explanation is the existence of sufficient "leakage" around the regulations to keep the U.S. and Japanese financial markets fairly closely linked. On the other hand, the risk-return tradeoffs in the two countries may not have been that closely linked through time but simply turned out to be similar on average over the 20 year period.[5] In either case, there appears to have been no consistent advantage for Japanese firms regarding their risk-adjusted cost of funds from the capital markets during the 1960-1980 period.

Other evidence against the notion of a Japanese cost of capital advantage includes the aggressive overseas borrowing by Japanese firms during the last few years. This behavior seems to indicate that Japanese firms find the cost of funds lower outside of Japan, which certainly contradicts the notion of a Japanese advantage. Another trend in recent years is the declining importance of debt in the capital structures of Japanese firms. High debt to equity ratios have been interpreted as a source of Japanese advantage in some of the studies mentioned above. However, the debt to equity ratios of most major Japanese firms have declined quite substantially since the mid-1970s. In many cases, these firms have actually lowered their total borrowing despite alleged pressure from the Japanese banks to maintain their outstanding loan positions. This gives the appearance that such firms are "throwing away" part of their cost of capital advantage and again suggests that they do not perceive the same advantage as some U.S. observers.

The major purpose of the current paper is to suggest a different perspective on the cost of capital issue, which allows us to reconcile the apparently conflicting evidence mentioned above. For example, the results in the two Ando and Auerbach papers are not inherently inconsistent with each other or with the cost of funds in financial markets being similar across the two countries. More importantly, this paper argues that all the above studies have failed to focus on what is probably the key issue regarding cost of capital differences between the U.S. and Japan.

The next section of this paper starts to provide the basis for these assertions by examining implications of several recent papers on capital structure and equity issue costs. Section 3 extends this discussion to an analysis of comparative cost of capital estimates. The significance of lender monitoring in the capital acquisition process is addressed in Section 4. Ownership patterns and equity issue practices are discussed in Section 5. Finally, Section 6 describes implications of this analysis for the question of whether or not Japanese firms have enjoyed a cost of capital advantage.

2. THE ROLE OF EQUITY ISSUE COSTS

The basic approach taken in the above studies is to view a firm's cost of capital as a weighted average of its debt and equity costs, which in turn represent the expected returns required by its lenders and shareholders. The Ando and Auerbach papers as well as McCauley and Zimmer (1989) plus the chapters in Holland (1984) were based on reported earnings coupled with the premise that a firm's average earnings over a substantial time period must be sufficient to support the expected returns desired by its security holders.[6] The other papers used various estimates of security market returns as their starting point. The individual studies then made a variety of adjustments for differences in taxation, inflation, and accounting practices between the U.S. and Japan.

Capital structure generally entered the cost of capital estimates in these papers through the possibility that tax deductibility for interest payments may have provided an advantage to more highly levered corporations. This aspect receives varying emphasis in the different studies. For example, it is extremely important in SIA (1980) and Hatsopoulos (1983). In contrast, Baldwin (1986) argues that any such advantage for Japanese firms was very minor--perhaps (if it existed) lowering their weighted average cost of capital by one percentage point.

Baldwin's view was based on a modified version of a Miller (1977) equilibrium such as suggested by DeAngelo and Masulis (1980) or Barnea, Haugen, and Senbet (1981a). In such a modified Miller equilibrium, the personal tax treatment of interest income substantially (but not completely) offsets the corporate tax advantage for borrowing and highly levered firms have only a rather modest cost of capital advantage.

In all these cost of capital comparisons, capital structure was viewed as basically a static phenomenon where the tax advantage (possible small) of borrowing was traded off against agency or financial distress costs which increased with the relative use of debt.[7] Under this "traditional" approach, an optimal capital structure minimizes the firm's cost of capital; however, that optimum is not viewed as a function of the firm's demand for external funds.

In his presidential address to the American Finance Association, Myers (1984) argued for a quite different perspective which he called the "Pecking Order Theory" of capital structure. He suggested that capital structure is more of a dynamic phenomenon driven by a firm's need for external funds and their relative cost. According to this theory, firms prefer to finance investment projects with internal funds (retained earnings and depreciation). When external funds are needed, additional borrowing is preferred to new equity issues as long as the default premium in interest rates on added debt is not too great.

This relative aversion towards equity issues is attributed to an asymmetric information problem which makes it relatively expensive to acquire funds via a stock issue. The theoretical motivation for Myers' argument was largely based on Myers and Majluf (1984); however, subsequent papers by Miller and Rock (1985) as well as John and Williams (1985) contain closely related models where equity issues may be an adverse signal regarding the firm's future prospects. In these models, management has superior information and may issue new shares to strengthen the firm's financial position in anticipation of unfavorable events. An alternative interpretation is simply that managers will view selling equity as unattractive when they feel shares are underpriced and vice versa when they feel shares are overpriced. Thus, an equity issue suggests that management may feel the firm's shares are overpriced and consequently represents a potentially negative signal.

On the other hand, an equity issue may be needed to obtain funds for desirable new projects. However, these models imply that potential purchasers have difficulty identifying the true motivation for stock issues and will seek to protect themselves against the possibility that management is issuing shares when it has unfavorable information. As a consequence, these models suggest that shares which are actually issued to finance desirable new investment projects will tend to be undervalued relative to their price if purchasers had the same information as management.

From an empirical perspective, this implicit cost for an equity issue appears to be quite substantial relative to the size of the issue. Asquith and Mullins (1986) provide estimates which suggest that the average cost is roughly 30 percent. Related estimates from Masulis and Korwar (1986) as well as from Mikkelson and Partch (1986) imply a somewhat smaller average cost--around 23 percent. However, all these estimates are strikingly consistent in their support for the view that equity issues are a relatively expensive mechanism for funding corporate investment projects.

Although Myers (1984) doesn't explore the issue, the Pecking Order Theory of capital structure has important implications for a firm's cost of capital. Consider an unlevered firm and assume, for simplicity, that equity issue costs (explicit plus implicit) are a constant fraction of the issue size. Let k be the generic representation for a firm's cost of capital, with k^d denoting that cost when the firm can finance all its investments internally. The notation k^u will be used to designate the cost of capital including equity issue costs. As indicated in Figure 1, the unlevered firm's cost of capital for a given period takes an upward jump when its total investment budget for that period surpasses the level, denoted by Q*(t), that can be supported by internally generated funds. In light of the empirical estimates mentioned above, the size of this jump for an all-equity firm is far from trivial, being apparently on the order of 25 to 30 percent.

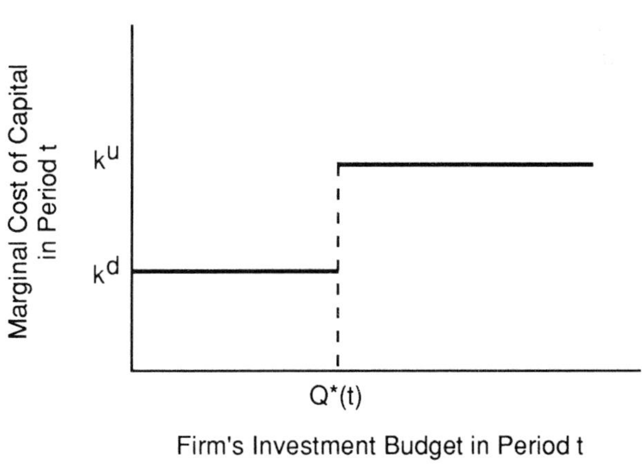

Figure 1. Cost of capital function for an all-equity firm which issues additional shares to finance investment budgets exceeding Q*(t)

It is important to emphasize that the cost of capital depicted in Figure 1 is for only a single period. Frequently a firm's cost of capital is treated as a constant which can be employed as a discount rate for evaluating multiperiod projects in a Net Present Value analysis. In the type of situation suggested by Figure 1, the firm's cost of capital could vary dramatically from period to period depending on whether its investment budget was above or below Q*(t). Under such circumstances, the use of a single-valued discount rate is quite inappropriate.

An all-equity firm could seek to smooth the discontinuity in its cost of capital function by borrowing rather than issuing equity to finance an investment budget exceeding Q*(t). In fact, the Pecking Order Theory suggests that such a firm would borrow rather than issue equity as long as the cost of borrowing is less than the cost of newly issued equity funds. This sort of strategy is depicted in Figure 2, with the firm issuing additional debt but not equity for investment budgets between Q*(t) and QE(t). In this range, the increasing cost of capital reflects an assumption of either agency or financial distress costs which are an increasing function of borrowing levels. At QE(t), it becomes cost effective to issue additional equity.

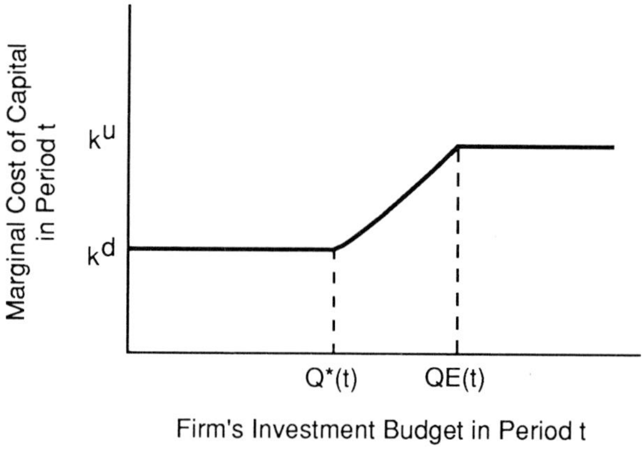

Figure 2. Cost of capital function with borrowing used to smooth the jump from k^d to k^u

Instead of (or in conjunction with) borrowing to avoid incurring equity issue costs, the firm could defer investment projects to lower its investment budget at time t. Presumably this strategy implies additional costs since it causes the firm to undertake investments at apparently suboptimal times. Thus, it might result in an implicit cost of capital function (including costs for project deferral) similar to Figure 2. A potentially more efficient strategy would be to carry forward "excess" funds from periods of financial slack (investment budget below Q*) using marketable securities or other investments designed to payoff in tight-budget periods.

Clearly, this approach is not much help for firms with investment budgets consistently above their Q*(t) values.

The above discussion of Figures 1 and 2 was couched in terms of a firm which, at least initially, was unlevered. Essentially the same arguments apply to levered firms with the marginal cost of capital representing a weighted average of debt and equity costs. However, for a levered firm, Q*(t) exceeds the amount of internally generated funds by the additional debt those funds will support at the firm's target debt to equity ratio. If the value of agency and financial distress costs are viewed as an increasing function of leverage, a flat cost of capital function to the left of Q*(t) implies that the firm is maintaining a constant debt to equity ratio in that region. This suggests that internally generated funds in excess of what is need to maintain that ratio are paid out as dividends. Alternatively, the firm might seek to carry such excess funds forward by purchasing marketable securities and/or allowing its debt to equity ratio to decline. There could well be costs associated with such strategies (e.g., for deviating from an optimal capital structure); and once again, such strategies are only open to firms which are not consistently above their Q*(t) values.

Attempts to avoid the large equity issue costs described above can lead to complex capital budgeting problems reminiscent of the literature on "capital rationing".[8] In effect, the Pecking Order Theory of capital structure resuscitates the notion of an increasing cost of capital function and, consequently, the issue of capital rationing. These concepts have been out-of-vogue and largely rejected by finance theorists for over a decade. Indeed, virtually all finance textbooks assume that a firm's cost of capital is not a function of the quantity demanded. When capital rationing is discussed, it is frequently treated as an internal budgeting problem between profit centers or as a proxy for some nonmonetary constraint on the firm's ability to grow--e.g. a labor or capacity shortage.[9] Consequently, it is not surprising that the studies comparing U.S. and Japanese costs of capital did not focus on the implications of an increasing cost of capital function at the firm level.

Baldwin (1986) recognizes the possibility of a large implicit cost for equity issues but does not pursue the question of whether this phenomenon could cause a significant cost of capital difference between the U.S. and Japan. In a different context, Hodder (1988) argues that the Pecking Order Theory seems to fit the Japanese capital structure evidence very well; however, that paper does not address the resulting cost of capital implications. This oversight is unfortunate, since as discussed in subsequent sections the implications of this theory coupled with the differing structure of financial institutions in the U.S. and Japan provide important insights into possible cost of capital differences.

3. COMPARATIVE COST OF CAPITAL ESTIMATES

It is hypothetically possible to discuss a multiperiod "cost of capital" which represents an average over time of the one-period costs for a particular firm. In the current framework, such an intertemporal average would depend heavily on the fraction of periods in which that firm's investment budget exceeds Q*(t). In the simplified context of Figure 1, $k = pk^u + (1-p)k^d$ where p denotes the fraction of periods (within the relevant time horizon) in which the investment budget exceeds Q*(t). In the context of Figure 2, k would depend on not only how frequently the firm exceeded Q*(t) but also the size of this excess (which determines how the excess is financed). Note also that Q*(t) is both firm-specific and variable across periods as a function of (e.g.) net cash flows generated by prior investments.

It is also possible to consider averaging across firms as well as over time to obtain an industry-wide or an economy-wide cost of capital. Again, our current framework suggests that such averages will depend heavily on whether firms are exceeding their respective Q*(t) values and how frequently. This is in addition to the usual considerations that the cost of capital differs with risk and may also be a function of capital structure for tax reasons. Indeed, two sets of firms with identical cost of capital functions could have dramatically different average capital costs due simply to differing growth patterns.

In light of the above discussion, it is rather unclear what aggregate cost of capital estimates from studies such as those in Holland (1984) or the Ando and Auerbach papers are actually measuring. To get a clearer (but still hazy) picture, it is useful to examine some characteristics of those studies. Our discussion will focus on the two Ando and Auerbach papers since that comparison is the most illuminating. Ando and Auerbach (1988a) provided cost of capital estimates for a loosely matched sample of 19 U.S. and 21 Japanese firms. These are essentially all large "blue chip" firms and collectively represent several nonfinancial industries in each country. The reported average market value (including debt and equity) for the U.S. sample was slightly over $15 billion with the average for the Japanese sample slightly above ¥800 billion.

The cost of capital estimate for each firm was based on a multiperiod average of reported earnings plus net interest payments as a percentage of firm value. Firm value for each year was estimated as the market value of equity plus the book value of financial liabilities (debt), excluding Accounts Payable as well as "Pension Reserves" (unfunded pension liabilities on the balance sheets of most Japanese firms). There were several adjustments to earnings for inflation as well as accounting differences across the two countries. Although these adjustments are a bit rough, they are not unreasonable.

If the book and market values of financial liabilities are similar for a given year, then the ratio of adjusted earnings before interest and taxes (EBIT) to firm value should be a reasonable estimate of real before-tax earnings as a percentage of firm value for that year.[10] The stream of such percentages for each firm was averaged over the 1966-1981 period to obtain an estimate of that firm's before-tax cost of capital. It is this last step, interpreting the average real earnings percentage as a cost of capital estimate, which is the most problematic.

A similar procedure was used to obtain streams of after-tax earnings plus interest payments adjusted for taxes. For each firm in the sample, its stream was then averaged to obtain an after-tax cost of capital estimate. Both before and after-tax estimates were compared across firms of differing nationality but (roughly) within the same industry. There is evidence of a lower cost of capital for Japanese firms, but the difference is not great. Averaging across the U.S. firms, the before-tax and after-tax estimates are 10.5 percent and 5.0 percent respectively. The comparable estimates for the Japanese sample are 8.2 percent before-tax and 3.8 percent after-tax.

Ando and Auerbach also briefly examine average returns (dividends plus capital gains) to equity over the 1971-1981 period for their two samples of firms. The results indicate substantially higher returns on average for the Japanese sample, which tends to counter the above evidence based on adjusted earnings. As a consequence, they observe that "there do not seem to be any grounds to conclude that the cost of capital in Japan was significantly lower than in the United States for the period covered."[11]

Ando and Auerbach's second study employs the same basic methodology for adjusting reported earnings; however, a much larger sample of 1095 U.S. and 1287 Japanese firms is utilized. The second study also covers a slightly different period, from 1967-1983 for the Japanese firms and 1967-1984 for the U.S. sample. Again, these are nonfinancial firms listed on major stock exchanges. In fact, the Japanese companies comprise nearly all the non-financial firms listed on the Tokyo Stock Exchange.

Relative to their previous study, the estimated average cost of capital for the U.S. sample is now a somewhat higher 12.3 percent before tax and 5.6 percent on an after-tax basis. Furthermore, the difference appears to be due almost entirely to the different sample of firms rather than the somewhat different time period. Using yearly figures reported in the 1988b paper, we can readily recalculate average cost of capital estimates for the 1967-1981 period (which almost matches the 1966-1981 period of their earlier study). The before and after-tax estimates change only slightly to 12.4 and 5.5 percent respectively.

In contrast with the increased cost of capital estimates for U.S. firms, the estimates for Japanese firms are now lower than the previous study. The 1988b study estimates the cost of capital for the sample of Japanese firms at 6.5 percent before tax and 2.5 percent on an after-tax basis. Again, recalculating these estimates for the 1967-1981 period yields very similar results (6.4 percent before tax and 2.4 percent after tax). Thus for both the U.S. and Japanese estimates, it seems clear that the differing results between the two studies are primarily due to the much larger samples of firms in the 1988b study.

The estimated gap between U.S. and Japanese costs of capital in the 1988b study is almost 6 percent on a before-tax basis, which is large enough to attract the attention of government policy makers. Roughly speaking, the U.S. cost of capital appears 2 percent higher than in their previous study while the Japanese cost estimate is about 2 percent lower. It is natural to infer that the larger sample of the second study resulted in a better estimate of the true costs in the two countries. Indeed, Ando and Auerbach appear to accept that view. However, the interpretation is less clear when we consider the problems of averaging across time and firms, which individually face period-specific and increasing cost of capital functions.

Since average firm size in the 1988b sample is apparently much smaller, it is not surprising to see an increase in the cost of capital estimate for the U.S. firms. Such an increase could easily be the result of higher systematic risk and/or more rapid average growth rates with an increasing cost of capital function. Similar arguments would suggest that the cost of capital estimate for Japan should also have increased. Instead it declined, which seems surprising. This result will have an interesting interpretation later on, but first let us examine a different perspective on relative U.S. and Japanese costs of capital.

Suppose that U.S. and Japanese financial markets are sufficiently integrated so that expected returns in the two markets are approximately equal for traded securities of equivalent risk. This assumption is more plausible with today's relatively open Japanese financial markets; however, Baldwin's estimates suggest that this situation prevailed (at least on average) over the 1960-1980 period. Also assume (for the moment) that equity issue costs as well as the agency and financial distress costs for increased borrowing are similar across the two countries. With the exception of potentially different $Q^*(t)$ values, these assumptions imply that the cost of capital function depicted in Figure 2 would be similar for firms with the same risk class and capital structure from either country.

With this idealized set of assumptions, there are reasons to believe that during the 1960s and early 1970s the average cost of capital for a typical Japanese firm should have exceeded that of a U.S. counterpart with the same risk class and desired capital structure. First of all, Japanese firms were growing more rapidly on average during that period -- which implies a greater tendency for exceeding their $Q^*(t)$ values. Secondly, the profitability of the average Japanese firm was apparently lower than its U.S. counterpart. This implies generally lower Japanese $Q^*(t)$ values and an even greater tendency to exceed those values. Particularly in light of the problems with averaging discussed above, we should not put too much emphasis on such aggregate characterizations. However, the presumption is clearly not for a lower average Japanese cost of capital. Admittedly, we are imposing an idealized set of assumptions; however once again, the empirical evidence for Japan seems to run counter to what we would have anticipated.

There is certainly an appearance that something different is going on in Japan as compared with the United States. The next section suggests that the primary difference is the much larger degree of monitoring and control exercised by Japanese financial intermediaries. There are doubtless other factors involved in explaining the apparent cost of capital differences between the U.S. and Japan. However, the role of financial intermediaries has received virtually no attention and yet seems to explain the differences quite well.

4. THE ROLE OF LENDER MONITORING

Suppose that firms desiring to invest more than Q*(t) could finance such investments entirely by borrowing and thus avoid equity issue costs. Previously, it was suggested that such borrowing would result in increasing agency or financial distress costs and an upward sloping cost of capital function such as that between Q*(t) and QE(t) in Figure 2. However, suppose that lenders could effectively monitor firm behavior and also possessed sufficient intervention mechanisms to protect their position against adverse management actions. If such monitoring and intervention capabilities were available, lenders should be able to dramatically reduce or even eliminate the agency costs attributed to highly levered capital structures.

There remains the possibility of bankruptcy or financial distress costs. The probability of incurring such costs is traditionally viewed as an increasing function of the firm's leverage. However, as pointed out by Haugen and Senbet (1978) such costs could be avoided if firms can be readily reorganized to avoid a threatened bankruptcy. The essence of their argument is that in an efficient capital market, shareholders should be able to purchase lenders' claims (or vice versa) and reorganize the firm in order to avoid dead-weight losses associated with bankruptcy or financial distress.[12]

If such monitoring, intervention, and reorganization capabilities were costless, high degrees of leverage should not result in increased premiums to compensate for agency or financial distress costs. Under these circumstances, a firm would have little reason to sell additional equity but could simply use increased borrowing positions to fund investment projects in excess of Q*(t). Even if lender monitoring (etc.) were not costless, it might still be less costly than equity issues for a rapidly growing firm. The presumption here is that the costs of such lender services would be born (directly or indirectly) by the borrowing firm.

For simplicity, the terminology "lender monitoring" will be used to refer to the collection of lender services which includes monitoring, intervention, and reorganization with "monitoring costs" referring to the overall expected cost associated with such services. Figure 3 illustrates the possibility of lender monitoring with the monitoring cost represented as an increasing percentage of the firm's investment budget. QE(t) and QEM(t) indicate the equity issue points for non-monitored firms and monitored firms respectively.

The particular structure of monitoring costs in Figure 3 is only intended as an illustration. Nevertheless, it seems plausible that monitoring costs are an increasing function of the extent to which the firm exceeds Q*(t) in a given period as well as its initial leverage. This could result, for example, from the greater probability of incurring some intervention or reorganization costs when lending to more highly levered firms. This would imply an upward sloping k^m function as well as one which shifted upward with initial leverage. As depicted in Figure 3, it would become cost effective for monitored firms to issue equity if their investment budget were sufficiently large.

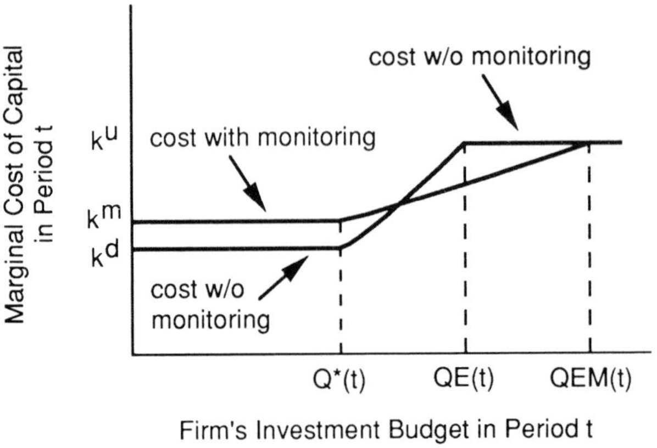

Figure 3. Cost of capital function with and without lender monitoring

Figure 3 suggests that lender monitoring would only be attractive to some firms. It would not be attractive for firms which expected to be able to finance their growth from internal sources, plus perhaps a moderate use of debt. On the other hand, it is probably not feasible to rapidly switch back-and-forth between monitored and non-monitored borrowing commitments. Indeed, efficient and effective monitoring relationships appear to be inherently long term. Consequently, the choice of lender monitoring is probably a multiperiod commitment which can only be undone after the firm returns to a relatively modest degree of leverage. Thus, a lender-borrower relationship with intensive monitoring would presumably be most attractive for firms which expect several years of more rapid growth than their internally generated funds will be able to support.

A lender monitoring situation which allows greater leverage can have very substantial implications for the firm's ability to grow. For example, a firm whose retained earnings were growing 6 percent annually could only fund a 6 percent growth rate for total assets without either increasing its leverage or selling additional equity. In contrast, a firm with the same retained earnings growth whose debt to total asset position was allowed to grow from .30 to .80 over a 20 year period could sustain annual asset growth of almost 13 percent.

To a very substantial degree the sort of lender monitoring situation described above has characterized the Japanese "main bank" lending system.[13] Under that system, most large industrial firms had a main bank which acted as monitor and, in some cases, quasi-guarantor on its loans. At least in the past, the power of the main bank was awesome. For example, Pascale and Rohlen (1983) provide a vivid discussion of Sumitomo Bank's 1974 intervention to rescue Toyo Kogyo (Mazda) from financial collapse. In addition to sending some of its own executives to run Toyo Kogyo,

Sumitomo Bank prevailed on over 70 other lenders to maintain their lending positions with the automaker. It also announced that any additional loans would be provided by Sumitomo Trust (a member of the Sumitomo group) and arranged for a subsequent major equity infusion from Ford Motor Company.

Although this is a dramatic example of intervention by a Japanese main bank, it is by no means an isolated case. It has not been at all uncommon for a main bank to replace executives of a troubled borrower with bank personnel as well as exercising considerable influence over the business strategy and capital spending of such a firm. Furthermore, this type of intervention has frequently occurred well before the client firm was on the brink of financial collapse.

The influence of the main bank appears to be an increasing function of the level of borrowing by the client firm. For cash-rich firms, the main bank's influence and access to confidential information appear to be minimal. In contrast, with heavy borrowers there is extensive monitoring through both formal and informal contacts at a variety of levels within the firm. In such situations, the main bank has timely access to a substantial range of confidential information on the borrower's current performance and future plans. The main bank can be viewed as a financial advisor whose influence grows dramatically with the borrower's need for bank support. In extreme situations such as with Toyo Kogyo, the main bank effectively takes over control of the troubled firm or directs its liquidation.

In liquidation situations, the main bank has traditionally absorbed losses for other lenders, effectively providing a (sometimes partial) guarantee on those loans. There are variations and numerous subtleties with this process; however, there have been cases where main banks took large losses which they were not legally obliged to absorb. A dramatic example was the Ataka bankruptcy in 1977, where the firm's two main banks took almost all the losses and wrote off over 150 billion yen. At the time, Andreas Prindle was General Manager of Morgan Guaranty's Tokyo office. He discusses the situation in a 1981 book and states that Ataka's foreign creditors lost nothing, although their loans were basically unsecured.

The main bank's power is derived from several reinforcing sources. It acts as not only advisor but de facto syndicator on client borrowing from other sources. It also typically acts as trustee for client bond issues; and until recently, virtually all corporate bond issues in Japan were mortgage bonds. Also, the majority of borrowing by Japanese manufacturers has traditionally been short-term bank loans which needed to be frequently rolled over (with main bank concurrence). In addition, Japanese banks have had strong legal powers to seize collateral and other assets of a borrower without an actual default if there is the threat of insolvency.

It is also important to recognize that for roughly the last forty years, a very small group of 8 to 10 banks have largely controlled private lending to major Japanese corporations. For example, Hodder and Tschoegl (1985) estimate that 90 percent or more of private lending to large industrial firms was from 25 to 30 Japanese banks and insurance companies. These same institutions then owned over a third of the publicly traded shares in Japan and roughly two-thirds of domestic corporate bond issues (excluding electric power companies). Within this somewhat larger group, 8 to 10 banks have been the key institutions whose lead has been followed by the other lenders. Although competition between these banks has sometimes been rather fierce, they also appear to have cooperated very closely when it comes to monitoring and controlling lending risks with heavy borrowers.

Thus, there are substantial indications that the main bank system in Japan may have been very effective at providing lender monitoring and control mechanisms to reduce or avoid agency risks with heavy borrowers. In addition, it appears that main banks have been able to quickly and smoothly reorganize even large firms, such as Toyo Kogyo, to also avoid bankruptcy or financial distress costs. Thus, we seem to have exactly the kind of lender monitoring situation which would result in a relatively flat cost of capital function such as illustrated in Figure 3.

There are situations where U.S. firms have been subject to intensive lender monitoring which is somewhat analogous to the main bank lending system. Examples include leveraged buyouts (LBOs), loans associated with venture capital financing, and "workout" situations of financially distressed firms. However, the aggregate significance of these special cases for funding practices by U.S. firms is relatively minor. Indeed, such situations would have virtually no effect in studies, such as those by Ando and Auerbach, where the sample of U.S. firms only included ones listed on the New York or American Stock Exchanges. Consequently, a cost of capital function similar to that in Figure 2 appears to have been substantially more likely for a major U.S. firm than for its Japanese competitors.

5. OWNERSHIP PATTERNS AND EQUITY ISSUE PRACTICES

As indicated in Tables 1 and 2, equity issues have represented a rather minor source of industrial funds in both the U.S. and Japan over the period covered by the Ando and Auerbach papers. This is clearly consistent with a Pecking Order Theory of capital structure. We can also see that Japanese firms have been substantially more dependent on external funds but have made much less use of market debt instruments such as bonds and commercial paper, which tend to dilute the control of a main bank. All these characteristics are quite consistent with Japanese firms financing investment budgets beyond their respective $Q^*(t)$ values primarily via increased leverage subject to lender monitoring.

Although equity issues have not been a popular funding source in either country, we should explore the possibility that reducing the implicit cost of an equity issue could also flatten the cost of capital function. To the extent that asymmetric information induces a large implicit issue cost for additional equity to fund desirable investment projects, this cost should disappear if management and potential share purchasers have the same information about the firm's prospects. The existence of such a cost suggests either credibility problems or deterrents to a firm revealing more information about its future prospects. For example, publicly revealed information might be damaging to the firm's competitive position in its product or input markets.

Table 1
Net Sources of Industrial Funds in Japan (percentage)

Year	Equity Issues	Corporate Bonds	Loans from Private Financial Institutions	Borrowing From Gov't Institutions	Internal Funds (Depreciation and Retained Earnings)
1967	2.5	2.1	43.0	4.6	47.9
1968	3.1	1.0	38.1	5.0	52.7
1969	3.8	1.5	41.7	4.4	48.7
1970	3.9	1.4	40.4	4.0	50.3
1971	2.9	2.2	48.9	4.0	41.9
1972	3.3	1.0	50.5	3.3	41.8
1973	3.2	2.1	48.9	4.8	40.9
1974	3.4	1.9	46.9	6.7	41.0
1975	4.0	4.1	45.4	7.2	39.3
1976	2.6	2.0	43.6	6.2	45.6
1977	3.3	2.1	34.5	6.0	54.2
1978	3.1	2.0	28.2	5.3	61.3
1979	3.5	2.3	28.5	6.8	58.9
1980	3.3	1.3	34.8	5.7	54.8
1981	4.4	2.2	35.4	6.6	51.4
1982	4.2	1.3	36.5	4.8	53.3
1983	2.7	0.6	36.3	3.0	57.4
Avg.	3.4	1.8	40.1	5.2	49.5

Source: The Bank of Japan, *Economic Statistics Annual*.

Under such circumstances, there might be an advantage for closely held firms where the shareholders are effectively insiders with approximately the same information as management.[14] In this context, there are characteristics of share ownership in Japan which suggest a potentially lower problem with asymmetric information on equity issues. Roughly two-thirds of listed shares in Japan are held by banks, insurance companies, and non-financial business corporations. To a large extent, the latter category involves firms in related business groups (keiretsu) as well as other customers and suppliers. Thus, the majority of a firm's shares are apt to be held by either its lenders or related business. These are frequently referred to in Japan as a firm's "stable shareholders". Their positions are typically very long term and often used to cement a business relationship.

Although these "quasi-inside" investors may not have quite the same information as a firm's management, the nature of their business relationship suggests they are not an attractive target for exploitation via an overvalued equity issue. Furthermore, the fractional holdings of these groups have been steadily growing since the early 1950s while those of individuals, security companies, and investment trusts (similar to mutual funds) have generally been declining.[15] A plausible interpretation of this

Table 2
Net Sources of Funds for U.S. Nonfinancial Corporations (percentage*)

Year	Equity Issues	Corporate Bonds	Industrial Revenue Bonds	Commercial Paper and Acceptances	Loans from Private Financial Institutions	Internal Funds (Depreciation and Retained Earnings)
1967	2.6	16.2		1.7	11.9	67.4
1968	-0.2	13.8		1.7	18.2	66.3
1969	3.4	11.9		2.7	20.6	61.3
1970	5.8	20.2		2.6	11.4	59.8
1971	9.6	15.8	0.1	-0.5	13.0	61.9
1972	7.6	8.5	0.3	0.5	23.5	59.4
1973	4.8	5.6	1.1	1.2	31.5	55.7
1974	2.6	12.6	1.0	3.5	24.3	54.9
1975	6.6	18.1	1.7	-1.8	-4.3	79.5
1976	5.6	12.1	1.3	1.4	8.5	71.0
1977	1.2	10.0	2.9	1.0	16.5	68.5
1978	~0	8.2	3.0	1.5	18.0	68.6
1979	-2.8	6.2	3.6	3.6	20.8	68.2
1980	4.6	9.4	3.9	1.7	12.9	67.0
1981	-3.6	6.8	4.2	5.2	15.6	71.5
1982	3.6	5.9	4.8	-1.7	13.3	73.8
1983	7.8	4.4	2.6	-0.3	8.4	77.2
Avg.	3.5	10.9	1.8	1.4	15.5	66.6

*Rows do not add to 100% because of excluding loans from the U.S. Government. Such loans averaged 0.3% of the annual totals during this period.

Source: Board of Governors of the Federal Reserve System, *Flow of Funds Accounts*.

phenomenon is that quasi-insiders have consistently been the marginal purchasers of additional shares because of a lower concern about being exploited and/or better information about firm prospects.

This does not rule out the possibility that some equity issues in Japan are related to adverse information. However, it suggests that quasi-insiders may have sufficiently accurate information to identify the true motives for a share issue. Under such circumstances, the implicit cost for an equity issue to fund desirable investment projects may be much less in Japan than in U.S. security markets.

A related phenomenon has been the recent extensive use of convertible bonds by Japanese firms. For example, during the 1978-1984 period convertible issues totaled approximately 1.5 times the value of public equity offerings. The conversion price on these bonds was generally set at only a slight premium above the current market price; and they have been widely viewed as largely an equity issue mechanism. The significant aspect of convertibles for our discussion is that they implicitly contain a put option which, at least partially, protects the purchaser against potential asymmetric information problems. Consequently, we should expect a lower implicit cost of equity issue via this mechanism.[16]

Certainly the financial practices we have been describing are quite different from the situation for most U.S. firms. By comparison, U.S. convertible debt issues during the 1981-1986 period were only 25 percent as large as common stock issues.[17] Also, U.S. households control over 60 percent of corporate equities while U.S. commercial banks are largely precluded from owning shares. Indeed, the Federal Reserve's "Flow of Funds Accounts" indicates that households (including personal trusts and non-profit institutions) plus pension and mutual funds held almost 90 percent of U.S. equities at the end of 1986. While all of these holdings may not qualify as "arms length," the overall structure is dramatically different from Japan.

Thus, there are reasons to believe that equity ownership practices in Japan as well as the apparent propensity for using convertible bonds to issue equity may also have helped to flatten the cost of capital function for major Japanese firms. This effect may have been relatively minor due to the small fraction of funds coming from equity issues in Japan. However, it reinforces the effect of lender monitoring practices in Japan and strengthens the notion that a cost of capital function similar to that in Figure 2 is much more likely for a U.S. firm than for its Japanese counterpart.

6. IS THE COST OF CAPITAL LOWER IN JAPAN?

The above arguments suggest that Japanese firms may have faced a flatter cost of capital function; however, that does not necessarily mean a uniformly lower function than faced by U.S. firms. In Figure 3, for example, the cost with monitoring is not consistently below that without monitoring. Furthermore, it seems likely that the cost function with monitoring shifts upward with increasing firm leverage. Presumably, firms would seek to choose the more advantageous function; however as mentioned earlier, their ability to switch between functions is apt to be limited. Thus, Japanese firms which enjoyed an advantage from monitoring during their rapid growth in the past may have been relatively disadvantaged while growing more slowly in recent years. This would be quite consistent with recent general trends toward dramatically reduced leverage and lessened main bank dependence by Japanese firms.

There are also problems regarding the measurement of monitoring costs. Presumably, these costs were ultimately born by the borrowers; however, it appears that the compensation mechanisms frequently had the effect of reducing the borrower's reported profits rather than increasing its interest payments. For example, the widespread Japanese use of compensating balances had this effect. The main bank relationship should be viewed as including a package of services with compensation derived from a variety of sources including fees for collections and payments clearing, foreign exchange transactions, etc. The overall effect is an understatement of the borrower's reported earnings relative to an environment characterized by more arms-length financial relationships.

This suggests that cost of capital estimates based on reported Japanese earnings plus interest payments may be understated, which could explain the seemingly anomalous drop in the estimate for Japanese firms between the two Ando and Auerbach studies. The Japanese firms in the 1988b study were substantially more levered on average as well as smaller. Consequently, it is likely that they were more heavily monitored. If the added monitoring costs had the effect of reducing earnings instead of increasing interest payments, this could easily have caused the 1.7 percent drop in the estimated before-tax cost of capital. In this regard, it is interesting to note that the U.S. estimate rose by 1.8 percent--almost exactly equal to the Japanese decline.

It is also interesting to note that the average yield differential between the Moody's indices for Baa and AAA industrial bonds in the U.S. has been on the order of 1.5 percent in recent years. This suggests that comparable monitoring costs would be warranted in order to reduce the lending risk from the equivalent of a Baa bond to that for a AAA issue. The implication is that the apparent difference in cost of capital estimates between the two Ando and Auerbach studies may be largely due to hidden monitoring costs. It is also worth emphasizing that hidden monitoring costs have a double impact -- they are effectively being subtracted when they should be added to earnings for a cost of capital estimate. Consequently, hidden monitoring costs of 1.5 to 2 percent would cause an apparent 3 to 4 percent cost of capital differential. While this evidence is far from conclusive, it suggests that we should be concerned about the possibility of hidden monitoring costs.

Given the measurement problems in the studies cited above, it remains unclear whether there has been a substantial difference in the cost of funds across U.S. and Japanese financial markets. Nevertheless, the availability of lender monitoring could still have been quite advantageous for rapidly growing Japanese firms. This would be true even if the average cost of capital were actually higher in Japan than in the United States, as is suggested by Japanese firms borrowing overseas. The extent of an advantage due to lender monitoring remains open to question since monitoring costs are not easily measured. However, the existence of widespread monitoring in Japan seems clear; and there is a presumption that Japanese firms entered main bank relationships because it was advantageous. Symmetrically, many Japanese firms are now weakening their main bank ties presumably because those relationships are costly and are now less advantageous.

In many ways, this paper raises more questions than it answers. However, it attempts to shift the focus of the U.S.-Japan cost of capital debate towards a more appropriate target. That is, the extent to which lender monitoring can flatten the cost of capital function facing a particular firm. It appears that this phenomenon can explain many of the apparent anomalies in comparative cost of capital estimates without recourse to arguments about "unfair" government subsidies. There is nevertheless an implication that the form of financial intermediation can be an important determinate of corporate growth. Consequently, closer examination of this phenomenon could yield policy recommendations of particular significance for governments seeking to promote industrial growth, such as those in newly industrializing countries.

FOOTNOTES

1. Baldwin (1986) describes major criticisms of the SIA and Hatsopoulos studies. There is a 1986 paper by Hatsopoulos and Brooks which employs a methodology similar to Hatsopoulos (1983) and again finds that Japanese firms enjoy a large cost of capital advantage. That paper corrects the most glaring fault in Hatsopoulos (1983); however, it still contains some dubious estimation procedures which make its results questionable.

2. These papers were written considerably before their publication dates and were presented at conferences in 1985 and 1984, respectively.

3. Recent papers by Bernheim and Shoven (1987) as well as McCauley and Zimmer (1989) also suggest a substantial cost of capital advantage for Japanese firms. Although it contains additional adjustments, the McCauley and Zimmer paper employs an approach which is similar to that of Ando and Auerbach. In contrast, Bernheim and Shoven examine tax-adjusted riskless rates. Consequently, their paper represents more of a statement about capital market integration than about risk-adjusted capital costs at the firm level.

4. Baldwin (1986), page 193.

5. This notion is supported by evidence in the appendix to Ando and Auerbach (1988b) which indicates the Japanese efficient frontier had a much steeper slope and deviated substantially from that for the U.S. during both the 1955-1986 and 1967-1983 periods.

6. These studies also briefly examined measures based on security market returns; however, market-based measures were not their primary emphasis.

7. Barnea, Haugen, and Senbet (1981b) contains a good survey of this approach to capital structure determination with a particular emphasis on the agency cost issue.

8. See, for example, Weingartner (1963) as well as the critical review in Weingartner (1977).

9. See for example Brealey and Myers (1988) or Levy and Sarnat (1986).

10. The assumption of similar market and book values of financial liabilities is probably more accurate for Japan where an extremely large fraction of debt tends to be short term.

11. Ando and Auerbach (1988a), page 46.

12. A part of this argument is the notion that any loss of tax shields can be largely eliminated through carrybacks, carryforwards, or a leasing strategy which effectively results in the sale of excess tax shields.

13. See Hodder and Tschoegl (1985) or Sheard (1989) for a more extensive description of the main bank system as well as related aspects of Japanese financing practices.

14. Funding the growth of a closely held firm may force its shareholders to have less diversified investment portfolios than they would have otherwise desired. This suggests that such shareholders might require a return premium to compensate for their reduced diversification. Consequently, whether being closely held represents a cost of capital advantage may partially depend on the aggregate wealth of the firm's shareholders.

15. In recent years, foreign corporations have also become major net purchasers of Japanese equities, although their fractional holdings are still rather small. For example, their shareholdings tripled from 1980-1984 and accounted for almost 25 percent of the total increase in listed Japanese shares. Since at least some of these corporations are off-shore subsidiaries of Japanese firms (particularly the insurance companies), it is unclear what fraction of these holdings should also be viewed as controlled by quasi-insiders. On the other hand, excluding foreign shareholders from the total, Japanese banks plus insurance companies and nonfinancial business corporations acquired over 87 percent of the remaining increase in listed shares over the 1980-1984 period.

16. There is some empirical support for this argument with regard to U.S. firms. For example, Eckbo (1986) contains results which indicate an implicit issue cost for convertibles of 9.6 percent, which is substantially lower than the figures cited earlier for common stock issues. This is similar to results in Mikkelson and Partch (1986) which indicate an implicit issue cost of 8.8 percent for convertibles.

17. Based on data from various issues of *Investment Dealers' Digest*.

REFERENCES

Ando, A. and A.J. Auerbach (1988a), "The corporate cost of capital in Japan and the United States: a comparison," in *Government policy towards industry in the United States and Japan*, J.B. Shoven, ed., Cambridge University Press, New York, pp. 21-49.

Ando, A. and A.J. Auerbach (1988b), "The Cost of Capital in the United States and Japan: A Comparison," *Journal of the Japanese and International Economies*, Vol. 2, pp. 134-158.

Asquith, P. and D.W. Mullins, Jr. (1986), "Equity Issues and Offering Dilution," *Journal of Financial Economics*, Vol. 15 (1/2), January/February, pp. 61-89.

Bank of Japan, *Economic Statistics Annual*, various issues.

Barnea, A., R.A. Haugen, and L.W. Senbet (1981a), "An Equilibrium Analysis of Debt Financing Under Costly Tax Arbitrage and Agency Problems," *Journal of Finance*, Vol. 36 (3), June, pp. 569-581.

Barnea, A., R.A. Haugen, and L.W. Senbet (1981b), "Market Imperfections, Agency Problems, and Capital Structure: A Review," *Financial Management*, Vol. 10 (3), Summer, pp. 7-22.

Baldwin, C.Y. (1986), "The Capital Factor: Competing for Capital in a Global Environment," in *Competition in Global Industries*, M.E. Porter, ed., Harvard Business School Press, Boston, MA, pp. 185-223.

Bernheim, B.D. and J.B. Shoven (1987), "Taxation and the Cost of Capital: An International Comparison," in *The Consumption Tax: A Better Alternative?*, C.E. Walker and M.A. Bloomfield, eds., Ballinger, Cambridge, MA, pp. 61-85.

Board of Governors of the Federal Reserve System, *Flow of Funds Accounts*, various issues.

Brealey, R. and S.C. Myers (1988), *Principles of Corporate Finance*, Third Edition, McGraw-Hill, New York.

DeAngelo, H. and R.W. Masulis (1980), "Optimal Capital Structure Under Corporate and Personal Taxation," *Journal of Financial Economics*, Vol. 8 (1), March, pp. 3-29.

Eckbo, B.E. (1986), "Valuation Effects of Corporate Debt Offerings," *Journal of Financial Economics*, Vol. 15 (1/2), January/February, pp. 119-151.

Flaherty, M.T. and H. Itami (1984), "Finance," in *Competitive Edge*, D.I. Okimoto, et al., eds., Stanford University Press, Stanford, CA.

Hatsopoulos, G.N. (1983), "High Cost of Capital: Handicap of American Industry," Study sponsored by the American Business Conference and Thermo Electron Corporation, April.

Hatsopoulos, G.N. and S.H. Brooks (1986), "The Gap in the Cost of Capital: Causes, Effects, and Remedies," in *Technology and Economic Policy*, R. Landau and D. Jorgenson, eds., Ballinger Pub. Co., Cambridge, MA, pp. 221-280.

Haugen, R.A. and L.W. Senbet (1978), "The Insignificance of Bankruptcy Costs to the Theory of Optimal Capital Structure," *Journal of Finance*, Vol. 33 (2), May, pp. 383-393.

Hodder, J.E. (1988) "Corporate capital structure in the United States and Japan: financial intermediation and implications of financial deregulation," in *Government policy towards industry in the United States and Japan*, J.B. Shoven, ed., Cambridge University Press, New York, pp. 241-263.

Hodder, J.E. and A.E. Tschoegl (1985), "Some Aspects of Japanese Corporate Finance," *Journal of Financial and Quantitative Analysis*, Vol. 20 (2), June, pp. 173-191.

Holland, D.M., ed. (1984), *Measuring Profitability and Capital Costs*, Lexington Books, Lexington Books, MA.

Ibbotson, R.G., R.C. Carr, and A.W. Robinson (1982), "International Equity and Bond Returns," *Financial Analysts Journal*, Vol. 38 (4), July-August, pp. 61-83.

Investment Dealers' Digest, statistics taken from Vol. 52 (2), pg. 30, January 13, 1986; and Vol. 53 (2), pp. 36-38, January 12, 1987.

John, K. and J. Williams (1985), "Dividends, Dilution, and Taxes: A Signalling Equilibrium," *Journal of Finance*, Vol. 40 (4), September, pp. 1053-1070.

Levy, H. and M. Sarnat (1986), *Capital Investment and Financial Decisions*, Third Edition, Prentice-Hall International, London.

Masulis, R.W. and A.N. Korwar (1986), "Seasoned Equity Offerings: An Empirical Investigation," *Journal of Financial Economics*, Vol. 15 (1/2), January/February, pp. 91-118.

McCauley, R.N. and S.A. Zimmer (1989), "Explaining International Differences in the Cost of Capital," *Federal Reserve Bank of New York Quarterly Review*, Vol. 13 (2), Summer, pp. 7-28.

Mikkelson, W.H. and M.M. Partch (1986), "Valuation Effects of Security Offerings and the Issuance Process," *Journal of Financial Economics*, Vol. 15 (1/2), January/February, pp. 31-60.

Miller, M.H. (1977), "Debt and Taxes," *Journal of Finance*, Vol. 32 (2), May, pp. 261-275.

Miller, M.H. and K. Rock (1985), "Dividend Policy under Asymmetric Information," *Journal of Finance*, Vol. 40 (4), September, pp. 1031-1051.

Myers, S.C. (1984), "The Capital Structure Puzzle," *Journal of Finance*, Vol. 39 (3), July, pp. 575-592.

Myers, S.C. and N.S. Majluf (1984), "Corporate Financing and Investment Decisions When Firms Have Information that Investors Do Not Have," *Journal of Financial Economics*, Vol. 13 (2), June, pp. 187-221.

Pascale, R.T., and T.P. Rohlen (1983), "The Mazda Turnaround," *Journal of Japanese Studies*, Vol. 9 (2), pp. 219-263.

Prindle, A.R. (1981), *Japanese Finance: A Guide to Banking in Japan*, John Wiley & Sons, New York.

Semiconductor Industry Association (1980), "U.S. and Japanese Semiconductor Industries: A Financial Comparison," Report prepared by Chase Financial Policy, June.

Sheard, P. (1989), "The Main Bank System and Corporate Monitoring and Control in Japan," *Journal of Economic Behavior and Organization*, Vol. 11, pp. 399-422.

Tokyo Stock Exchange, *Tokyo Stock Exchange Fact Book*, various issues.

Weingartner, H.M. (1963), *Mathematical Programming and the Analysis of Capital Budgeting Problems*, Prentice Hall, Englewood Cliffs, NJ.

Weingartner, H.M. (1977), "Capital Rationing: n Authors in Search of a Plot," *Journal of Finance*, Vol. 32 (5), December, pp. 1403-1432.

Japanese Financial Market Research
W.T. Ziemba, W. Bailey and Y. Hamao (Editors)

JAPANESE MERGERS AND DIRECT INVESTMENT IN THE U.S.

Richard H. Pettway

Department of Finance, 239 Middlebush Hall, University of Missouri, Columbia, Missouri 65211, U.S.A.

Abstract

This paper is a study of Japanese mergers and direct investment levels in the U.S. After a discussion of the nature of corporate mergers in Japan, Japanese merger research is summarized. Then these results are extended to suggest the potential characteristics of Japanese acquisitions of U.S. firms. Finally, these suggestions are compared to the recent levels of Japanese mergers and direct investments in the U.S.

1. THE NATURE OF CORPORATE MERGERS IN JAPAN

In order to understand Japanese mergers, it is necessary to understand the nature of Japanese business practices in general of which M & As are a part. Japanese business is a series of related and interrelated activities, a system often called "corporate collectivism." Few firms operate totally independently. Reciprocal stock ownership or cross-holdings of shares is very common and the system is often called *Mochiai*.[1] Many companies persuade banks, securities firms, and customers to buy and hold company shares to form and solidify a business relationship. Shimizu (1980), for example, reports that of 894 firms surveyed, 90% owned shares of other firms in the same affiliated group. Graven (1989) reports in a recent survey by the Nihon Keizai Shimbun that more than 60% of publicly traded Japanese companies think it desirable to have 60% to 70% of outstanding shares held by stable shareholders. "The big reason: By not having to bend to uppity shareholders, Japanese executives say they have more time to concentrate on business goals rather than wasting time plotting takeover defense strategies."

Japanese combinations such as: Mitsubishi, Mitsui, Sumitomo, and other groups are what Franko (1983) calls a *keiretsu*. Within a *keiretsu* there are wholly-owned subsidiaries as well as various degrees of mutual stock ownership. Three types of ownership relationships exist among nonsubsidiary group members. First is what Ballon-Tomita-Usami (1976), BTU, call *oya-ko*, or a parent-child relationship of affiliated companies, where more than 50% of the shares of the "child" are owned by the "parent." *Kanren gaisha*, or related companies, have 20% to 50% of the shares of one firm are owned by the other. Third are companies owned as investments by other firms with which they are not related or affiliated. In this last case, ownership is less than 20% shares outstanding.

Japanese mergers occur in a different environment from American mergers. Japan's traditional corporate paternalism, illustrated by lifetime employment, restricted labor mobility, a seniority-based wage system, and company unions has been a major protection for an enterprise's autonomy. Sato-Hoshino (1984) argue that "both management and labor believe that the company belongs to them, not to the shareholders." Moreover, BTU finds that the acquiring firm rarely takes the initiative in mergers. Often, the acquired firm will seek business or financial assistance from the acquiring company. Thus, a third party often is required to approach the acquiring firm. Under such conditions, the Japanese selling firm may not be able to command as large a price as its U.S. counterpart. Additionally, if the selling firm is financially weaker than the buying firm, there may be more abnormal returns to the acquiring firm in Japan than in the U.S.

There are major differences in managerial objectives in the two countries. A questionnaire survey by Kagono *et al.* (1984) of 291 Japanese industrial firms listed on the Tokyo Stock Exchange and 227 U.S. firms listed in the Fortune top 1,000 industrial firms found that the management objective of the two groups are very different. Shimizu (1980) queried the managers of 894 Japanese firms and found no firm that said increasing its share price was the company's most important objective and only 0.2% said that it was the second most important. Aoki (1984b) reported that protecting their access to future loanable funds is often said to be more important to Japanese firms than stockholders' wealth maximization. For these reasons, the typical motivation for mergers in Japan may be different from that in the U.S.

There have been few empirical studies of Japanese mergers. Suto (1981) analyzed the effects of Japanese mergers around the effective date using monthly data over a long test period and found that mergers had little impact upon shareholders' wealth. Hoshino (1982, 1983, 1984) studied the accounting performance and other financial characteristics of Japanese firms that merged compared to nonmerged firms. Generally, Hoshino found an adverse effect in accounting and financial ratios from merger as the group of companies that merged had poorer financial ratio performance than nonmerged firms. Pettway and Yamada (1986) studied the impacts of Japanese mergers upon stockholders' wealth from 1977 through 1984 and found that the market for Japanese mergers was competitive and the acquiring firms shareholders' had positive, but insignificant gains from mergers. On the other hand, the acquired firms' shareholders had significantly positive returns, but they were smaller than returns for U.S. selling firms. Pettway, Sicherman and Yamada (1989) stated that Japanese managers face less monitoring activities and have less employment risk because of corporate collectivism and lifetime employment and an under-utilized managerial labor market; thus, there is a higher potential for agency costs. Their analysis of a decade of Japanese mergers, revealed that the impacts on stockholders' wealth are consistent with shareholder wealth maximization objectives. Thus, they concluded that the requirements of a higher level of monitoring activities as well as a competitive managerial labor market with *ex post* settling up, were not necessary to assure that Japanese managers operate in a way that was consistent with the interest of stockholders. Pettway, Sicherman and Yamada (1990) found that the impact of relative size of the acquired to acquiring firm upon shareholders' wealth from Japanese mergers is significant. When the acquiring firm is much larger than the selling firm, it gained significant abnormal returns. Further a study of the changes in systematic and unsystematic risk of the acquiring firm before and after the merger revealed that there was no evidence of a dramatic risk change from merger during the decade from 1977 trough 1986. Finally, a study of the impacts of a significant change in the Japanese Commercial Code that reduced the impact of corporate collectivism and increased the role of independent stockholders in Japanese corporations, showed that the Code change resulted in a significant change in abnormal returns from mergers. It was found that the market for corporate control became more competitive after the change in the Code in October 1982.

2. JAPANESE MERGERS IN JAPAN AND INFERENCES AS TO JAPANESE DIRECT INVESTMENT IN THE U.S.

2.1. The Size of the Merger Market in Japan is Small.

The number of Tokyo Stock Exchange, TSE, listed buyers is much smaller than in the U.S. In the decade from 1977 through 1986 there were 201 mergers between listed nonfinancial firms.[2] In the U.S., the merger market is much larger. Japanese managers prefer to establish their own new company *de novo* rather than purchase an existing firm. This activity supports the expansion of existing management and avoids many personnel problems associated with combining of different firms in a merger. For example, one of the largest mergers in the history of Japan occurred between the Dai-Ichi and Kangyo banks. Over the past ten years there have been rotations of "D" men and "K" men in upper management. Brauchli and Sesit (1989) recently describe the events of this merger as what **not** to do in a merger. It simply has presented too many personnel problems and insufficient leadership to overcome the problems. Mr. Kuniji Miyazaki, president of Dai-Ichi Kangyo Bank was quoted as saying "For a merger like ours to really work, it takes about 30 years in Japan. But the times we're living in doesn't permit us 30 years. We can be patient for 10 years, but not longer."[3] Perhaps these views are well known and that is why Japanese mergers have been so few.

Since the merger market is small in Japan, the inference is that Japanese mergers and acquisitions will be smaller than their direct start ups of new firms in the U.S. We can see this in the case of the establishment of automobile assembly plants in the U.S. by Nissan, Honda, and Mazda. They did not acquire American firms, but started their own subsidiaries. This is completely consistent with the desire to establish a *de novo* firm using parts of their existing management team rather than buying another firm's management team.

In Japan, the vast majority of the mergers are friendly and all are for exchange of shares, not cash purchases or buyouts. There are extremely few "hostile" takeovers and there is strong resentment against such activity by either Japanese firms or foreign firms. In fact, some of this resentment was used effectively against T. Boone Pickens in the case of his 1989 and 1990 attempts to become a board member of Koito Manufacturing of which he owned 26% of the shares outstanding. Meanwhile, Toyota had 3 seats and owned only 19% of the shares. After investing about $770 million in Koito, T. Boone was still not allowed a seat on the board. He appears too much like an American raider, for the Japanese management. In fact, a corporate raider is called *nottoriya* in Japanese which has a very bad connotation as it literally means a hijacker. Perhaps time will change attitudes. But the facts remain, the Japanese prefer and often require friendly purchases or consolidations. It has often been said that the Japanese will add a sweetener to a pending merger deal just to make sure that the selling firm views their intention as friendly.

2.2. The abnormal gains to shareholders of acquiring firms in Japan are similar to the returns for U.S. acquiring firms.

Even though there are many different characteristics between the management of Japanese and U.S. firms, the results of mergers by Japanese firms are approximately the same as for U.S. firms that merge.[4] Since the prices of selling firms are bid up to their economic value, there are not significant wealth impacts for buying firms associated with mergers in either Japan or in the U.S. Thus, the Japanese merger market is found to be just as competitive as is the U.S. merger market. It does not appear that Japanese acquiring firms when buying other Japanese firms are paying too high a price for the firms that they acquire.

Based upon this finding, the Japanese will be hard negotiators and will try not to overpay for the U.S. firms they acquire. Yet, with a lower cost of capital until 1990, for a Japanese firm, due to lower cost of debt and higher leverage, it is possible that Japanese firms would be able to pay a larger price in dollars for a company with known earnings than would a U.S. firm that has a higher cost of capital.[5] The Japanese firm would be using a lower discount rate than would a U.S. firm who wanted to bid on the same firm. Thus, it may appear to U.S. firms and investors that the Japanese are paying too high a price for U.S. firms.

2.3. In Japan, the purchase of relatively small firms have higher wealth effects than buying larger firms.

Japanese buying firms prefer to purchase relatively smaller firms than relatively larger firms since they generally generate more wealth than the purchase of larger firms.[6] This may be due to the personnel problems created when larger firms are merged. The larger firm has created its own identity and it is very hard to change.

Applying this to U.S. firms attractive to Japanese buyers, it appears that the Japanese may continue to prefer to purchase small firms relative to their size.

Japanese managers would give first preference to starting their own subsidiary rather than purchasing an existing firm via merger. But if a merger were contemplated, the preference would be to purchase an existing firm that is relatively small in size compared to the acquiring firm, rather than to purchase a relatively larger firm. On the other hand, there are some very large mergers of American firms by Japanese companies.

As an example of this interest in smaller firms, Carlson (1989) states that "the Japanese companies bankroll many small U.S. companies with promising products or ideas, frequently putting their money behind projects that commercial banks won't touch." Venture Economics, Inc. reports that Japanese corporations invested $214 million in the first half of 1989 in minority positions in U.S. companies which was an increase of 61% over a similar period in 1987. Many of these minority investments have been made by Japanese *sogo-shosha* or trading companies. Mr. Klasuser, advisor to the president of Mitsui, U.S.A., states that his company has 75 U.S. subsidiaries in which it holds 35% interest or more and the trading company hopes to double the number of its U.S. affiliates in 1990. He adds "unlike corporations in this country, trading companies aren't so much interested in a high return on investment as they are on increasing trade flows. To the extent they can do this, they're quite content to get a return on investments of 1% to 2%." This movement is reminiscent of an earlier era when many of the electronic firms in California's Silicon Valley were financed with trading-company venture capital. The Japanese are very interested in buying portions of small U.S. businesses and often this investment really is beneficial as it is supplementary to bank lending that would not be available for such an investment.

On the other hand, there have been extensive acquisitions of U.S. financial institutions by Japanese banks and these mergers appear to be at odds with the suggestions concerning *de novo* and relative small firm preferences. For example, 1984, Mitsubishi Bank purchased the Bank of California for $282 million, Sanwa bank purchased Continental Illinois Leasing, and Fuji bank purchased Walter E. Heller & Company for $425 million. Recently, Sumitomo bank make a $500 million investment in Goldman Sach, and Sanwa bank bought Lloyds Bank of California and merged it with Golden State Sanwa's Bank to form California's seventh largest bank. In late 1988, the Bank of Tokyo purchased Union Bank of Los Angeles for $750 million. On the 29th of August 1989, it was announced that Mitsui Bank and Taiyo Kobe Bank would merge on April 1, 1990. In September of 1989, Daiwa purchased the 15 U.S. offices of Lloyds Bank for about $200 million. Also in September of 1989, Dai-ichi Kangyo, the world's largest bank, purchased 4.9% equity shares of Manufacturer's Hanover for $120 million and purchased controlling interest (approximately 60%) in Manny Hanny's CIT Group for $1.28 billion. This purchase of CIT was the largest U.S. investment in history by a Japanese bank. Dai-ichi is a massive bank as it has $400 billion in assets (almost double Citicorp's size).

Thus, the comments about size and the desire to establish a *de novo* subsidiary applies more to the nonfinancial sector. In fact, the financial sector acquisitions fall under different rules where large size and market presence are important positive elements for Japanese banks to consider in their acquisition policies. These exceptions may be due to the large costs and time required to form a new firm in the financial sector. Further, *de novo* entrance in banking is restricted. Thus, the financial sector operates under different conditions that require a modification of general merger and acquisition policies.

2.4. Many Japanese mergers occur among firms in the same keiretsu.

Many Japanese firms band together in groups called *keiretsu* that are united with reciprocal or cross-holdings of stock ownership.[7] It is from these mutual holdings of stock that the term "corporate collectivism" comes. This means that member firms in the *keiretsu* band together for their mutual protection and improvement. In such cases, the role of the independent investors to monitor the activities of management is much less than in a U.S. firm. It is this corporate collectivism that has caused T. Boone Pickens trouble in Koito Manufacturing which is part of the Toyota *keiretsu* or group.

Japanese managers prefer to have a friendly group of shareholders and related companies with which to work. They will bring these views with them to the U.S. and Europe and try to locate in regions where there are already Japanese firms. Further, they will encourage the Japanese firms in their *keiretsu* to also come and operate in the same location. This is already clearly the case for Japanese auto assembly plants located in the U.S. Honda, Nissan, and Mazda have each tried to bring their suppliers and *keiretsu* members to the U.S. with them so that they can perform business in a similar fashion to that in Japanese assembly plants. Many Japanese firms prefer to do banking business with the same banks that they used in Japan that were a member of their *keiretsu*. Thus, the desire for familiar business partners will have two effects. First, it will mean an increased infusion of direct investment into the U.S. from Japan as more and more companies are lured here. On the other hand, U.S. banks and financial institutions will be required to offer very attractive priced products as the competition with Japanese financial firms will be very intense.

3. ACQUISITIONS AND DIRECT INVESTMENT IN THE U.S.

After describing the way Japanese firms merge in Japan and making inferences as to how they will acquire U.S. firms, we look at the data on foreign direct investment in the U.S. first from all sources and then specifically from Japan.

The most recent data from Howenstine (1989) of U.S. direct investment by foreign investors reveals that there was a 10.5% increase in the nonbank U.S. assets held by foreign investors from 1986 though 1987. See Table 1. In 1987, the level of foreign owned nonbank total assets was $926 billion. Over half of the foreign ownership of these assets were from European countries and 40.6% from the EC (European Community) specifically. Looking at the individual countries among Canada, U.K., Netherlands, Japan and FRG, Japan leads with the largest percentage of ownership at 21.1% of the total nonbank assets held by foreigners. Japanese investment in 1987 increased dramatically from the 1986 level of $98.1 billion to $195.7 billion. In 1986

Table 1

Direct Investment in U.S. by Foreign Investors Nonbank Total Assets, Total Sales, Employment, and Land held in U.S. by Foreign Investors

Country	1986 Assets (Mil. $)	1986 Sales (Mil. $)	1986 Emplmt (Thous)	1986 Land (Th Acres)	1987 Assets (Mil. $)	1987 Sales (Mil. $)	1987 Emplmt (Thous)	1987 Land (Th Acres)	% Change Assets %	% Change Sales %	% Change Emplmt %	% Change Land (Th Acres)
Total	838,039	672,004	2,938	13,991	926,042	731,392	3,160	13,829	10.5%	8.8%	7.5%	-1.2%
Europe	437,324	346,741	1,783	8,976	467,607	387,010	1,904	8,658	6.9%	11.6%	6.9%	-3.5%
% of T	52.2%	51.6%	60.7%	64.2%	50.5%	52.9%	60.2%	62.6%				
European Comm. (EC)	343,927	287,703	1,480	7,311	376,065	324,942	1,593	7,004	9.3%	12.9%	7.6%	-4.2%
% of T	41.0%	42.8%	50.4%	52.3%	40.6%	44.4%	50.4%	50.6%				
Canada	130,373	83,590	609	2,817	140,822	89,303	591	2,090	8.0%	6.8%	-3.1%	-25.8%
% of T	15.6%	12.4%	20.7%	20.1%	15.2%	12.2%	18.7%	15.1%				
Rank	2	3	2	2	3	3	2	2				
U.K.	137,378	115,342	623	3,435	156,223	130,450	630	3,442	13.7%	13.1%	1.2%	0.2%
% of T	16.4%	17.2%	21.1%	24.6%	16.9%	17.8%	19.9%	24.9%				
Rank	1	2	1	1	2	2	1	1				
Netherlands	67,676	44,805	242	439	69,958	52,057	270	316	3.4%	16.2%	11.2%	-28.0%
% of T	8.1%	6.7%	8.3%	3.1%	7.6%	7.1%	8.5%	2.3%				
Rank	4	5	4	4	4	5	5	4				
Japan	98,098	166,575	221	116	195,773	182,327	285	104	99.6%	9.5%	28.9%	-10.3%
% of T	11.7%	24.8%	7.5%	0.8%	21.1%	24.9%	9.0%	0.8%				
Rank	3	1	5	5	1	1	4	5				
Federal Rep. Germany	50,186	62,811	312	667	58,540	72,173	363	561	5.6%	5.6%	8.1%	-14.9%
% of T	6.0%	9.3%	10.6%	4.8%	6.3%	9.9%	11.5%	4.1%				
Rank	5	4	3	3	5	4	3	3				

Source: Howenstine, N.G. "U.S. Affiliates of Foreign Companies: 1987 Benchmark Survey Results," Survey of Current Business (July 1989).

Japan ranked third, behind U.K. and Canada. However, in 1987 Japan increased its direct investment by almost $100 billion in U.S. assets which moved it ahead of both U.K. and Canada.

The data in Table 2 illustrate that acquisitions of U.S. companies from 1980-1989 have been rising substantially since 1985. There were 515 purchases of U.S. firms by foreign firms in 1988 having a total value of $61.7 billion. In 1989, there were 521 deals worth $52.7 billion. For each year since 1980, the U.S. has invested much less in foreign countries than have foreign countries invested in the U.S. The net capital inflow for acquisitions is not new, but the size of the net inflow over outflow was in excess of $54.5 billion in 1988 and $38.3 billion in 1989.

In Table 3 are listed the twenty largest Japanese acquisitions in the U.S. through the end of 1990. Until the recent huge purchases of CBS Records and Columbia Pictures by Sony and of MCA by Matsushita, most of the large mergers were in the financial sector. In fact, most of the acquiring Japanese firms are found in the financial sector consisting of banks and insurance companies. Only two Japanese manufacturing firms other than the electronic firms of Sony and Matsushita have made large acquisitions in the U.S. namely, Dainippon Ink & Chemicals and Nippon Kokan.

The data in Table 4 show that foreign firms from the United Kingdom were most active in the acquisitions market in 1989 as they acquired 158 firms with a total value of $23.8 billion of U.S. companies. Canada and Japan were almost tied for second in terms of the number of acquisitions. The vast majority in terms of the dollar value of the mergers by foreign companies have been made in the printing and publishing industry followed by industrial and commercial machinery, computer equipment industry.

Looking at Japanese acquisitions specifically, the data in Table 5 reveal that there was a substantial increase in the number of Japanese acquisitions of U.S. companies from 1982-1989. The acquisitions rose substantially in 1988 when there were 48 deals with a combined value of $12 billion, and 81 deals worth $9.4 billion in 1989.

Going back to Table 1 which refers to total investment to date for various countries in the U.S., it is clear in terms of sales created from investment, that the European Countries had 52.9% of the total sales by foreign firms and 44.4% from the EC controlled firms. In terms of individual countries, Japan ranked 1st with 24.9% of all U.S. sales owned by foreign firms. In terms of employment, U.K. firms rank 1st in both 1986 and 1987 for individual countries. Japan ranks 4th in total employees with 9% of the total employment of all foreign firms in 1987. The Japanese rank 5th in terms of individual countries in terms of acres of land owned, far behind the investments by firms from U.K. and Canada.

Japanese have substantially increased their acquisitions of U.S. firms and their combined total of assets acquired and sales produced lead all other individual countries in 1987. They are behind the combination of countries in the EC. Further, Japan lags behind in terms of employment and land held. Thus, it appears that the Japanese have invested in ventures that are capital intensive with high levels of assets and high value of sales, but low number of employees and low amount of land utilized.

Since employment is a critical variable that reduces the threat of foreign direct investment in a political sense, the data in Table 6 are focussed directly upon the issue of employment by nonbank U.S. affiliates. The total employees of all foreign

Table 2

Foreign Acquisitions of U.S. Companies
1980 - 1989

	Foreign-U.S.		U.S.-Foreign	
	No. of Deals	Value $ mil	No. of Deals	Value $ mil
1980	167	6,773.7	116	1,093.0
1981	286	15,350.1	94	603.3
1982	227	5,401.1	137	925.2
1983	116	2,185.4	149	1,411.3
1984	190	8,409.8	154	2,197.8
1985	214	19,230.9	199	1,181.5
1986	364	25,262.7	174	2,422.1
1987	377	44,822.2	198	7,161.1
1988	515	61,688.4	180	7,203.1
1989	521	52,719.3	243	14,438.5

Source: Mergers & Acquisitions, various issues.

Table 3
Twenty Largest Japanese Acquisitions in the U.S.

Buyer	Target	Value ($ Billions)	Year	Industry
Matsushita Electric	MCA, Inc.	$6.6	1990	Entertainment
Sony Corp.	Columbia Pictures	5.0	1989	Entertainment
Bridgestone	Firestone Tire	2.65	1988	Tires
Seibu Salson	Inter Continental Hotel	2.27	1988	Hotels
Sony Corp.	CBS Records	2.0	1988	Records and tapes
Aoki Corp.	Westin Hotel & Resorts	1.53	1987	Hotels
Dai-Ichi Kangyo	CIT Group	1.28	1989	Finance
Nippon Mining	Gould Inc.	1.05	1988	Manufacturing
Mitsubishi Corp.	Aristech	.859	1990	Chemical
Mitsubishi Estate Corp.	Rockefeller Group	.846	1989	Real Estate
Bank of Tokyo	Union Bank Calif.	.75	1988	Banking

Table 3 Continued

Buyer	Target	Value ($ Billions)	Year	Industry
Fujisawa Pharma-ceutical	Lyphomed Inc.	.67	1989	Pharmaceutical
Nippon Life Insurance	Shearson Lehman Hutton (13%)	.538	1987	Investment banking
Dainippon Ink & Chemicals	Reichhold Chemicals	.520	1987	Printing inks
Dainippon Ink & Chemicals	Graphic Arts Group of Sun Chemical	.5	1986	Printing inks
Sumitomo Bank	Goldman, Sachs (12.5%)	.5	1986	Investment banking
Fuji Bank	Commercial financial business of Walter E. Heller, Int'l.	.425	1984	Finance
Yasuda Mutual Life	Paine Webber Group (18%)	.3	1987	Investment banking
Nippon Kokan	National Steel (50%)	.292	1984	Primary steel
Mitsubishi Bank	BanCal Tri-State	.282	1984	Banking

Sources: AP Wire Services (11/27/90), Wall Street Journal (11/27/90), and Mergers & Acquisitions, Data Base

Table 4
Countries Most Active in U.S. Acquisitions 1989

Countries	Transactions	Value ($ Millions)
United Kingdom	158	23,764.6
Japan	81	9,424.9
Canada	76	2,800.5
West Germany	28	2,021.7
Switzerland	25	2,237.0

Source: Mergers & Acquisitions, May/June 1990.

Table 5
Japanese Acquisitions of U.S. Companies
1982 - 1989

Year	No. of Deals	Value ($ Billions)
1982	5	$ .05
1983	5	.05
1984	12	1.2
1985	12	0.2
1986	27	2.0
1987	30	1.5
1988	48	12.0
1989	81	9.4

Source: Mergers & Acquisitions, Data Base

Table 6

Regional Employment by Nonbank U.S. Affiliates, by States, 1986-1987
(Thousands of employees)

	1986					1987				
Regions and States	All	Canada	UK	FRG	J	All	Canada	UK	FRG	J
Total	2,937.9	609.2	622.9	312.4	220.8	3,159.7	590.5	630.1	363.3	284.6
						7.5%	-3.1%	1.2%	16.3%	28.9%
New England	178.6					200.7				
Percent change						12.4%				
Massachusetts	74.4	17.5	19.8	8.4	3.5	90.8	17.7	22.0	10.4	7.8
Percent change						22.0%	1.1%	11.1%	23.8%	122.9%
Mideast	667.1					735.2				
Percent change						10.2%				
New York	268.2	41.5	66.4	20.7	17.9	300.1	39.0	66.2	39.4	35.5
Percent change						11.9%	-6.0%	-0.3%	90.3%	98.3%
Great Lakes	487.6					512.0				
Percent change						5.0%				
Illinois	153.7	27.7	39.1	14.9	15.6	166.1	25.3	40.1	16.9	20.4
Percent change						8.1%	-8.7%	2.6%	13.4%	30.8%
Plains	132.6					139.6				
Percent change						5.3%				
Missouri	47.9	14.5	8.6	4.6	1.1	48.5	15.1	9.0	4.1	1.4
Percent change						1.3%	4.1%	4.7%	-10.9%	27.3%
Southeast	739.1					788.9				
Percent change						6.7%				
Florida	104.6	26.3	22.1	8.3	3.3	116.8	27.1	24.9	6.0	5.4
Percent change						11.7%	3.0%	12.7%	-27.7%	63.6%
Georgia	107.7	21.3	24.2	9.3	8.1	117.7	22.4	24.7	10.1	10.2
Percent change						9.3%	5.2%	2.1%	8.6%	25.9%
North Carolina	123.3	26.8	29.3	21.2	3.6	132.9	29.2	27.9	25.8	4.1
Percent change						7.8%	9.0%	-4.8%	21.7%	13.9%

Table 6 continued

Regional Employment by Nonbank U.S. Affiliates, by States, 1986-1987
(Thousands of employees)

Regions and States	1986 All	1986 Canada	1986 UK	1986 FRG	1986 J	1987 All	1987 Canada	1987 UK	1987 FRG	1987 J
Tennessee	77.4	18.1	14.0	5.9	8.1	80.7	16.1	15.4	6.6	7.9
Percent change						4.3%	-11.0%	10.0%	11.9%	-2.5%
<u>Southwest</u>	286.6					290.5				
Percent change						1.4%				
Texas	214.7	43.0	43.0	23.9	7.4	207.6	30.1	36.5	27.8	8.6
Percent change						-3.3%	-30.0%	-15.1%	16.3%	16.2%
<u>Rocky Mountains</u>	54.9					53.1				
Percent change						-3.3%				
Colorado	32.8	7.5	11.6	1.9	1.2	29.5	6.3	9.3	1.4	1.3
Percent change						-10.1%	-16.0%	-19.8%	-26.3%	8.3%
<u>Far West</u>	350.6					393.8				
Percent change						12.3%				
California	289.2	34.8	53.5	24.1	61.0	324.2	32.5	12.6	25.7	2.6
Percent change						12.1%	-6.6%	-76.4%	6.6%	-95.7%
<u>Other</u>										
Hawaii	18.4	0.7	1.3	0.0	10.9	22.4	0.7	0.4	0.1	No Data
Percent change						21.7%	0.0%	-69.2%	0.0%	0

Source: Howenstine, N.G. "U.S. Affiliates of Foreign Companies: 1987 Benchmark Survey Results," <u>Survey of Current Business</u> (July 1989), pp. 116-139.

corporations rose to 3.2 million in 1987 which was an increase of 7.5% over the levels in 1986. The Southeast as a region had the most employees followed by the Mideast and Great Lakes regions. The foreign employment was lowest in the Rocky Mountain region.

Japanese firms have not been large employers as they ranked well below the number of employees of other countries in 1987. Even firms from the Netherlands employed more individuals than did Japanese firms, but the Japanese employment did increase 28.9% in 1987 which was the largest increase among Canada, U.K., FRG, and the Netherlands. The regional employment patterns of Japanese firms generally parallel the patterns of other foreign investors. Japanese employment is concentrated primarily in California, New York, Illinois, Hawaii, and Georgia.

4. SUMMARY AND CONCLUSIONS

This paper presents a discussion of the nature of corporate mergers in Japan containing a review of mergers studies. Then these results are extended to suggest the potential characteristics of Japanese acquisitions of U.S. firms. Finally, these suggestions are compared to the recent levels of Japanese direct investment in the U.S.

Some of the findings and suggestions are as follow: Since the size of the merger market in Japan is small, the acquisitions of existing American firms will be small as well. The Japanese prefer to start a new business rather than acquire one. Since studies have found that the abnormal gains to shareholders of acquiring firms in Japan are similar to the returns for U.S. firms that acquire U.S. firms, the Japanese will try not to overpay for U.S. firms they acquire. In Japan, the purchases of relatively small firms have higher wealth effect than buying larger firms; thus the Japanese would prefer to acquire relatively smaller firms. This suggestion does not apply to acquisitions in the financial and entertainment sectors. Many Japanese mergers occur among firms in the same *keiretsu*. Since Japanese firms prefer to have a friendly group of shareholders and related companies with which to work, they will try to locate in regions that have existing Japanese firms and will try to bring other *keiretsu* members to their location.

Reviewing the data on direct investment in the U.S., it is clear that firms from Europe and the European Community, EC, have the largest percentage of ownership of the total nonbank assets held by foreigners. The levels of investment from Japanese firms is rising and over the past decade most of the mergers were in the U.S. financial sector. Recent very large acquisitions by Sony and Matsushita have shown that Japanese nonfinancial firms are very active in the U.S. merger market as well. From the most recent data available (i.e., end of 1987), it is clear that Japanese firms have purchased U.S. firms so that their combined total of assets acquired and sales produced lead all other individual countries, but are behind the combination of countries in the EC. On the other hand, Japanese firms lag behind in terms of employment and land held by foreign firms. It appears that the Japanese have invested in ventures that are capital intensive with high levels of assets and high value of sales, but low number of employees and low amount of land utilized.

FOOTNOTES

1. See McDonald (1989) for a discussion of the *Mochiai* effect.

2. This data is taken from Pettway, Sicherman and Yamada (1989).

3. This material is taken from Brauchli and Sesit (1989).

4. Pettway and Yamada (1986) find positive significant two-day announcement effects for 31 mergers, where the acquired and acquiring firm were not in the same group of companies. The over-all effect from 30 days before the announcement through 30 days after the effective date of the merger the CAR values were also positive but insignificant.

5. It has often been suggested that this lower cost of capital for Japanese firms is due to their higher use of financial leverage but there is a debate as to whether the leverage ratios are higher in Japan than in the U.S. See Aoki (1984a) for a discussion of the necessary balance sheet adjustments to reflect the true values of the debt ratios of Japanese firms and a comparison between adjusted ratios for Japanese and U.S. firms. Even after adjustments, Aoki finds that debt ratios in Japan tend to be larger than U.S. firms. When the market value of equity is used, Kester (1986) finds that Japanese manufacturing firms are similar to U.S. manufacturing firms in terms of their book-value debt to market-value equity ratios. Further, these higher debt ratios in book-value terms appear to have been an historical phenomenon as equity sales increased in the late 1980s so that by the end of the decade the book-value ratios of Japanese manufacturing firms were very similar to corresponding U.S. firms. See the article by James E. Hodder in this volume for a further discussion of this issue.

6. See Pettway and Yamada (1986) and Pettway, Sicherman and Yamada (1990).

7. *Keiretsu* firms may be divided into two different types. The financial *keiretsu* are best known and are groups of firms organized around a large bank. The six largest of this type are Mitsui, Mitsubishi, Sumitomo, Fuyo, Sanwa, and Dai-Ichi groups. A second type is called industrial *keiretsu* or enterprise groups organized around an independent firm, often a manufacturer, but sometimes a retailer or a railroad company. For example, Sony Corporation; Daiei, Inc.; and Tokyu Corporation are of this type. The different types of *keiretsu* may overlap. For example, Toyota Motor Corporation has organized it subcontractors into an enterprise group of hundreds of affiliated companies. Yet, Toyota Motor is part of the Mitsui financial *keiretsu*. Further, some of these industrial groups span more than one financial *keiretsu*. Hitachi industrial group is part of both the Fuyo and Sanwa financial *keiretsu*. For a good current discussion of these groups see "The Disputed Powers of Keiretsu" (1990).

REFERENCES

Aoki, M., 1984a, "Aspects of the Japanese Firm, in M. Aoki, Editor, The Economic Analysis of the Japanese Firm. (Amsterdam: North-Holland), 3-43.

Aoki, M., 1984b, "Shareholders' Non-Unanimity on Investment Financing: Banks vs. Individual Investors," in M. Aoki, Editor, The Economic Analysis of the Japanese Firm. (Amsterdam: North-Holland), 193-224.

Ballon, R. J., Tomita, I., and Usami, H., 1976, Financial Reporting in Japan. (Tokyo: Kodansha International Ltd.).

Brauchli, M. W. and Sesit, M. R., 1989, "Sleeping Giant: Dai-Ichi Kangyo Bank, The World's Largest, Now Pushes Profits," Wall Street Journal, (September 27).

Carlson, E., 1989, "Japanese Bankroll Small U.S. Firms," Wall Street Journal (November 2, 1989 pp. B1 - B2).

Franko, L. G., 1983, The Threat of Japanese Multinationals, (New York: John Wiley & Sons).

Graven, K., 1989, "In Corporate Japan, Cross Shareholding Remains a Useful Defense Mechanism," Wall Street Journal, (November 17).

Hoshino, Y., 1983, Corporate Mergers in Japan (Tokyo: Toyo University, Research Paper No. 1).

----------., 1982, "The Performance of Corporate Mergers in Japan," Journal of Business Finance and Accounting, Vol. 9, 153-165.

-----------., 1984, General Comparison of Financial Characteristics between Merging and Nonmerging Firms in Japan, (Nagoya, Japan: Nagoya Economic Study Paper #61).

Howenstine, N. G., 1989, "U.S. Affiliates of Foreign Companies: 1987 Benchmark Survey Results," Survey of Current Business (July).

Kagono, T., Nonaka, I., Sakakibara, K. and Okumura, A., 1984, "Mechanistic vs. Organic Management Systems: A Comparative Study of Adaptive Patterns of American and Japanese Firms," in K. Sato and Y. Hoshino, Editors, The Anatomy of Japanese Business, (Armonk, NY: M. E. Sharpe, Inc.), 27-69.

Kester, W. C., 1986, "Capital and Ownership Structure: A Comparison of United States and Japanese Manufacturing Corporations," Financial Management (Spring), 17-24.

McDonald, J., 1989, "The Mochiai effect: Japanese corporate cross-holdings," Journal of Portfolio Management (Fall), 90-94.

Pettway, R. H., Yamada, T., 1986, "Mergers in Japan and Their Impacts Upon Stockholders' Wealth," Financial Management Vol. 15, No. 4 (Winter), 43-52.

Pettway, R. H., Sicherman, N. W., and Yamada, T., 1989, "The Market for Corporate Control, the Level of Agency Costs, and Corporate Collectivism in Japanese Mergers," Chapter 14 in Japanese Financial Markets Edited by W. J. Elton and M. J. Gruber (New York: Ballinger Publishing Company), 337-355.

Pettway, R. H., Sicherman, N. W., and Yamada, T., 1990, "Japanese Mergers: Relative Size, Corporate Collectivism, and Shareholders' Wealth," in Research on Pacific-Basin Capital Markets Volume I. Edited by S. G. Rhee and R. P. Chang (Amsterdam: North-Holland), 181-202.

Sato, K. and Hoshino, Y., 1984, The Anatomy of Japanese Business. (Armonk, NY: M. E. Sharpe, Inc.).

Sesit, Michael R., 1989, "Japanese Acquirers in U.S. Look Poised to Pass British, if 1989 is Indication," Wall Street Journal (January 17), A12.

Shimizu, R., 1980, The Growth of Firms in Japan (Tokyo: Keio Tsushin).

Suto, M., 1981, "The Effect of Mergers on Stockholders," Keisoku-shitsu Technical Paper, No. 53. (February), 1-53, written in Japanese.

"The Disputed Powers of Keiretsu, 1990, "Japan Economic Survey (July) 6-11. This is a publication of the Japan Economic Institute, 1000 Connecticut Ave., N.W., Washington, DC 20036.

BIOGRAPHIES OF THE EDITORS

Warren Bailey is an Assistant Professor of Finance at the Johnson Graduate School of Management of Cornell University. He received his A.B. in Economics from Cornell University, M.B.A. in Finance from McGill University and Ph.D. in Finance from the University of California, Los Angeles. Prior to joining Cornell, he was a faculty member at Ohio State University. He has published articles on options, futures, monetary economics, international finance and international securities markets in such journals as *the Journal of Finance, Journal of Economic Dynamics and Control, Journal of Money, Credit and Banking, Journal of Financial and Quantitative Analysis, Journal of International Money and Finance, Journal of Portfolio Management, Journal of Futures Markets, Journal of Portfolio Management* and the *Canadian Journal of Economics* He is a regular speaker at academic and professional conferences throughout North America and Asia. He has conducted applied research for financial institutions and securities exchanges and is an Associate Editor of the journal *Management Science.*

Yasushi Hamao is Assistant Professor of Finance at the Graduate School of Business, Columbia University. His research is supported in part by the Mitsubishi Trust and Banking Corporation Professorship at Columbia University. Previously, he was on the faculty at the University of California, San Diego. A native of Japan, Professor Hamao received his B.A. from the University of Tokyo, and a Ph.D. from Yale University. He is actively involved in research in international finance, especially on Japanese financial markets. His articles have appeared in such journals as *Japan and the World Economy, Journal of Business, Journal of Finance, Journal of Portfolio Management,* and the *Review of Financial Studies.* Professor Hamao is a 1991-1992 recipient of the Batterymarch Fellowship awarded by Batterymarch Financial Management. He is also Vice President of International Operations at Roll and Ross Asset Management Corporation and a consultant to several financial institutions.

William T. Ziemba is the Alumni Professor of Management Science at the University of British Columbia, Vancouver, BC, Canada During 1988/89 he was the Yamaichi Visiting Professor of Finance at the University of Tsukuba, Japan, and consultant to the Yamaichi Research Institute. He is currently a consultant on international portfolio strategy to the Gordon Capital Corporation, Toronto, Edward O. Thorp and Associates, Newport Beach California, and the Frank Russell Company, Tacoma, Washington. He received a B.S. in Chemical Engineering from the University of Massachusetts and an MBA and a Ph.D. in Management Science from the University of California, Berkeley. His current research focuses on portfolio management and investments, particularly the study of anomalous behavior, dynamic asset allocation, stochastic optimization, security and sports betting market efficiency studies and Japanese financial markets. He is the departmental editor for finance of the journal Management Science and has published about eighty research papers and seventeen books. He has a triology of books on investing in Japan forthcoming from Probus and is writing a textbook on *Japanese Financial Markets* for Prentice Hall. His articles have appeared in journals such as the *American Economic Review, The Bell Journal of Economics, The Journal of Business, Journal of Finance, Economic Perspectives, Interfaces, Japan and the World Economy, Journal of Financial and Quantitative Analysis, Management Science, Operations Research, Mathematical Programming and The Mathematics of Operations Research.*